launchpadworks.com

At Macmillan Education, we are committed to providing online resources that meet the needs of instructors and students in powerful yet simple ways. LaunchPad, our course space, offers our trusted content and student-friendly approach, organized for easy assignability in a simple user interface.

- **Interactive e-Book:** The e-book for *Ways of the World* comes with powerful study tools, multimedia content, and easy customization for instructors. Students can search, highlight, and bookmark, making it easier to study.

- **LearningCurve:** Game-like adaptive quizzing motivates students to engage with their course, and reporting tools help teachers identify the needs of their students.

- **Easy to Start:** Pre-built, curated units are easy to assign or adapt with additional material, such as readings, videos, quizzes, discussion groups, and more.

LaunchPad also provides access to a gradebook that offers a window into students' performance — either individually or as a whole. Use LaunchPad on its own or integrate it with your school's learning management system so your class is always on the same page.

To learn more about LaunchPad for *Ways of the World* or to request access, go to **launchpadworks.com**. If your book came packaged with an access card to LaunchPad, follow the card's login instructions.

Ways of the World

A Brief Global History
with Sources

VOLUME 2: SINCE THE
FIFTEENTH CENTURY

Ways of the World
A Brief Global History
with Sources

ROBERT W. STRAYER
The College of Brockport: State University of New York

ERIC W. NELSON
Missouri State University

THIRD EDITION

Bedford/St.Martin's
A Macmillan Education Imprint

Boston • New York

For Evelyn Rhiannon with Love

For Bedford/St. Martin's

Vice President, Editorial, Macmillan Higher Education Humanities: Edwin Hill
Publisher for History: Michael Rosenberg
Director of Development for History: Jane Knetzger
Senior Developmental Editor: Leah R. Strauss
Senior Production Editor: Christina M. Horn
Senior Production Supervisor: Dennis J. Conroy
Executive Marketing Manager: Sandra McGuire
Media Editor: Jennifer Jovin
Associate Editor: Tess Fletcher

Production Assistant: Erica Zhang
Copy Editor: Jennifer Brett Greenstein
Indexer: Leoni Z. McVey
Cartography: Mapping Specialists, Ltd.
Photo Researcher: Bruce Carson
Director of Rights and Permissions: Hilary Newman
Senior Art Director: Anna Palchik
Text Design: Joyce Weston
Cover Design: William Boardman
Composition: Jouve
Printing and Binding: RR Donnelley and Sons

Manufactured in the United States of America.

0   9   8
f   e   d

For information, write: Bedford/St. Martin's, 75 Arlington Street, Boston, MA 02116
(617-399-4000)

ISBN 978-1-4576-9991-7 (Combined Edition)
ISBN 978-1-319-01841-2 (Volume 1)
ISBN 978-1-319-01844-3 (Loose-leaf Edition, Volume 1)
ISBN 978-1-319-01842-9 (Volume 2)
ISBN 978-1-319-01845-0 (Loose-leaf Edition, Volume 2)

Acknowledgments

Preface

Why This Book This Way

Publishing this third edition of *Ways of the World* feels to me, its original author, a little like sending a child off to college or into the world. This familiar but changed and enhanced book is, I hope, more mature than it was at its birth in the first edition or in its growing-up years in the second. Much of this maturing of *Ways of the World* derives from its recent acquisition of a coauthor, Eric Nelson, a professor of history at Missouri State University, where he teaches world history and early modern European history. With a D.Phil. from the University of Oxford, Eric has written several books about sectarian conflict and religious peacemaking in early modern France. And he is known as an enormously popular and skilled teacher, winning numerous awards, including the CASE/Carnegie Endowment for the Advancement of Teaching Professor of the Year in Missouri Award for 2012. Furthermore, he has become a national leader in online course design and pedagogy. More personally, Eric has been a delight to work with as we have collaborated in every dimension of preparing *Ways of the World* for its third edition. So henceforth and with great pleasure, the authorial "I" becomes a "we."

Over the years following its initial appearance in 2008, *Ways of the World* has changed, or "grown up," in other ways as well. Most substantially, since 2010 it has become not simply a textbook but also a "docutext" or sourcebook, containing chapter-based sets of written and visual primary sources. Reflected in the subtitle of the book, *A Brief Global History with Sources*, this addition has provided a "laboratory" experience located within the textbook, enabling students to engage directly with the evidence of documents and images—in short to "do history" even as they are reading history. Following the narrative portion of each chapter is a set of primary sources, either documentary or visual. Each collection is organized around a particular theme, issue, or question that derives from the chapter narrative. As the title of these features suggests, they enable students to **"work with evidence"** and thus begin to understand the craft of historians as well as their conclusions. They include brief headnotes that provide context for the sources, and they are accompanied by a series of probing Doing History questions appropriate for in-class discussion and writing assignments.

Furthermore, the organization of the narrative has been tightened and its content enhanced by integrating both the gender and the environmental material more fully. Coverage of particular areas of the world, such as Southeast Asia, Latin America, and Pacific Oceania, has been strengthened. And the book has more often highlighted individual people and particular events, which sometimes get lost in the broad sweep of world history. Finally, *Ways of the World* has acquired a very substantial electronic and online presence with a considerable array of pedagogical and learning aids.

Despite these changes, *Ways of the World* is also recognizably the same book that it was in earlier versions—it has the same narrative brevity, the same big picture focus, the same thematic and comparative structure, the same clear and accessible writing, and the same musing or reflective tone. All of this has attracted for *Ways of the World* a remarkable, and somewhat surprising, audience. Even before this third edition appeared, the book had been adopted by world history instructors at over 600 colleges and universities, and more than 275,000 students have used the book.

Tools for the Digital Age

Because the teaching of history is changing rapidly, we are pleased to offer online novel interactive complements to the new edition of *Ways of the World* via Bedford's learning platform, known as **LaunchPad**. Available for packaging with the book, LaunchPad's course space and interactive e-book are ready to use as is, or can be edited and customized with your own material and assigned right away. Developed with extensive feedback from history instructors and students, LaunchPad includes the complete narrative e-book, as well as abundant primary documents, assignments, and activities. Key learning outcomes are addressed via formative and summative assessment, short-answer and essay questions, multiple-choice quizzing, and **LearningCurve**, an adaptive learning tool designed to get students to read before they come to class. With LearningCurve, students move through the narrative text at their own pace and accumulate points as they go, in a game-like fashion. Feedback for incorrect responses explains why the answer is incorrect and directs students back to the text to review before they attempt to answer the question again. The end result is a better understanding of the key elements of the text.

In addition to LearningCurve, we are delighted to offer 23 new online **primary source projects called Thinking through Sources**, one for each chapter of the book. These features, available only in LaunchPad, extend and substantially amplify the Working with Evidence source projects provided in the print book and also available in LaunchPad. They explore in greater depth a central theme from each chapter, and they integrate both documentary and visual sources. Most importantly, these LaunchPad features are uniquely surrounded by a distinctive and sophisticated pedagogy of self-grading exercises. Featuring immediate substantive feedback for each rejoinder, these exercises help students learn even when they select the wrong answer. More broadly, such exercises guide students in assessing their understanding of the sources, in organizing those sources for use in an essay, and in drawing useful conclusions from them. In this interactive learning environment, students will enhance their ability to build arguments and to practice histori-cal reasoning. Thus this LaunchPad pedagogy does for skill development what LearningCurve does for content mastery and reading comprehension.

More specifically, a short **quiz after each source** offers students the oppor-tunity to check their understanding of materials that often derive from quite distant times and places. Some questions focus on audience, purpose, point of view, limi-tations, or context, while others challenge students to draw conclusions about the source or to compare one source with another. Immediate substantive feedback for each rejoinder and the opportunity to try again create an active learning environ-ment where students are rewarded for reaching the correct answer through their own process of exploration.

Two activities at the end of each Thinking through Sources exercise ask stu-dents to make supportable inferences and draw appropriate conclusions from sources with reference to a **Guiding Question**. In the **Organize the Evidence activity**, students identify which sources provide evidence for a topic that would potentially compose part of an answer to the guiding question. In the **Draw Conclusions from the Evidence activity**, students assess whether a specific piece of evidence drawn from the sources supports or challenges a conclusion related to the guiding question. Collectively these assignments create an active learning environment where reading with a purpose is reinforced by immediate feedback and support. The guiding question provides a foundation for in-class activities or a summative writing assignment.

These guiding questions challenge students to assess what the sources collec-tively reveal, drawing on documents and images alike. The Thinking through Sources feature linked to Chapter 5, for instance, presents a range of sources deal-ing with expressions of patriarchy in the Mediterranean, Indian, and Chinese civi-lizations. Its guiding question asks students to compare them, while its Organize the Evidence activity invites students to identify in turn those sources that shed light on marriage, the confinement of women, the authority of men, and opposi-tion to patriarchal norms. The feature related to Chapter 21 offers both written and visual sources probing the nature of the Stalinist phenomenon with a guiding ques-tion that asks students to identify various postures—both positive and critical—toward it. The Draw Conclusions from the Evidence activity attached to this feature challenges students to identify whether specific pieces of evidence drawn from the sources support particular conclusions: that some individuals found oppor-tunities for personal advancement in Stalin's Soviet Union; that socialist ideals and values were betrayed during his rule; and that the Soviet Union accomplished some of the fundamental goals of Stalinism.

In a further set of features available only in LaunchPad, the text's narrative is enhanced through **Author Preview Videos (with Bob Strayer)**, which imagina-tively introduce each chapter, and **Another Voice Podcasts (with Eric Nelson)**, which enrich the treatment of particular issues and sometimes gently argue with the narrative text. Both the videos and the podcasts make extensive use of visuals.

LaunchPad also provides a simple, user-friendly platform for individual instructors to add their own voice, materials, and assignments to the text, guiding their students' learning outside of the traditional classroom setting.

Available with training and support, LaunchPad can help take history teaching and learning into a new era. To learn more about the benefits of Learning-Curve and LaunchPad and the different versions to package with LaunchPad, visit **macmillanhighered.com/strayersources/catalog** and see the Versions and Supplements section on page xix.

What Else Is New in the Third Edition?

In addition to the new online Thinking through Sources exercises and Eric Nelson's Another Voice Podcasts described above, further substantive changes to this third edition include the following:

- A much-enhanced treatment of **environmental issues** in world history throughout the book, including a more thorough account of environmentalism and climate change during the past century.
- A more frequent and thorough **inclusion of Pacific Oceania** within the narrative, especially in Chapter 6, where it takes its rightful place as a distinctive cultural region alongside other such regions in Africa and the Americas.
- A new feature called **Zooming In** calls attention twice in each chapter to particular people, places, and events, situating them in a larger global context. It incorporates many of the biographical "portraits" from the second edition, while adding many new examples as well. These include the remarkable archeological sites of Göbekli Tepe and Caral, the Buddhist "university" of Nalanda, an account of the camel, tales of the Islamic folk character Mullah Nasruddin, the Ottoman devshirme, the Russian Decembrists, the Cuban Revolution, the civil war in Mozambique, and many more.
- The **map program** in the book has been revised and strengthened.
- The **source-based features** in the print book (Working with Evidence) include a number of new entries such as Australian Dreamtime stories in Chapter 1 and conflicting views of Islam and women's dress in Chapter 22. An entirely new feature in Chapter 3 probes outsiders' accounts of Persia and Egypt, the Germanic peoples of Central Europe, and the Xiongnu living to the north of China. And in Chapter 17, students will now encounter a variety of socialist voices from an industrializing Europe.

Promoting Active Learning

As all instructors know, students can often "do the assignment" or read the required chapter and yet have little understanding of it when they come to class. The problem, frequently, is passive studying—a quick once-over, perhaps some highlighting

of the text—but little sustained involvement with the material. A central pedagogical problem in all teaching is how to encourage more active, engaged styles of
learning. We want to enable students to manipulate the information of the book,
using its ideas and data to answer questions, to make comparisons, to draw conclusions, to criticize assumptions, and to infer implications that are not explicitly disclosed in the text itself.

Ways of the World seeks to promote active learning in various ways. Most obviously, the source-based features in the book itself (Working with Evidence) and
those housed separately on LaunchPad (Thinking through Sources) invite students
to engage actively with documents and images alike, assisted by abundant questions to guide that engagement. The wrap-around pedagogy that accompanies
the Thinking through Sources activities virtually ensures active learning, if it is
required by instructors. So do the LearningCurve quizzes that help students actively
rehearse what they have read and foster a deeper understanding and retention of
the material.

Another active learning element involves motivation. A **contemporary vignette**
opens each chapter with a story that links the past and the present to show the
continuing resonance of history in the lives of contemporary people. Chapter 6,
for example, begins by describing the inauguration in 2010 of Bolivian president
Evo Morales at an impressive ceremony at Tiwanaku, the center of an ancient
Andean empire, and emphasizing the continuing importance of this ancient civilization in Bolivian culture. At the end of each chapter, a short **Reflections** section
raises provocative, sometimes quasi-philosophical, questions about the craft of the
historian and the unfolding of the human story. We hope these brief essays provide
an incentive for our students' own pondering and grist for the mill of vigorous class
discussions.

A further technique for encouraging active learning lies in the provision of
frequent contextual markers. Student readers need to know where they are going
and where they have been. Thus part-opening **Big Picture essays** preview what
follows in the subsequent chapters. A **chapter outline** opens each chapter, while
A Map of Time provides a chronological overview of major events and processes. In addition, a **Seeking the Main Point** question helps students focus on
the main theme of the chapter. Each chapter also has at least one **Summing Up
So Far** question that invites students to reflect on what they have learned to that
point in the chapter. **Snapshot boxes** present succinct glimpses of particular themes,
regions, or time periods, adding some trees to the forest of world history. A **list of
terms** at the end of each chapter invites students to check their grasp of the material. As usual with books published by Bedford/St. Martin's, a **rich illustration
program** enhances the narrative.

Active learning means approaching the text with something to look for, rather
than simply dutifully completing the assignment. *Ways of the World* provides such
cues in abundance. A series of **questions in the margins**, labeled "change,"
"comparison," or "connection," allows students to read the adjacent material with

a clear purpose in mind. **Big Picture Questions** at the end of each chapter deal with matters not directly addressed in the text. Instead, they provide opportunities for integration, comparison, analysis, and sometimes speculation.

What's in a Title?

The title of a book should evoke something of its character and outlook. The main title *Ways of the World* is intended to suggest at least three dimensions of the text.

The first is **diversity** or **variation**, for the "ways of the world," or the ways of being human in the world, have been many and constantly changing. This book seeks to embrace the global experience of humankind in its vast diversity, while noticing the changing location of particular centers of innovation and wider influence.

Second, the title *Ways of the World* invokes major **panoramas**, **patterns**, or **pathways** in world history, as opposed to highly detailed narratives. Many world history instructors have found that students often feel overwhelmed by the sheer quantity of information that a course in global history can require of them. In the narrative sections of this book, the larger patterns or the "big pictures" of world history appear in the foreground on center stage, while the still-plentiful details, data, and facts occupy the background, serving in supporting roles.

A third implication of the book's title lies in a certain **reflective** or **musing quality** of *Ways of the World*, which appears especially in the Big Picture essays that introduce each part of the book and in a Reflections section at the end of each chapter. These features of the book offer many opportunities for pondering larger questions. The Reflections section in Chapter 4, for example, explores how historians and religious believers sometimes rub each other the wrong way, while that of Chapter 12 probes the role of chance and coincidence in world history. The Chapter 21 Reflections asks whether historians should make judgments about the societies they study and whether it is possible to avoid doing so. The Big Picture introductions to Parts Three and Six raise questions about periodization, while that of Part Five explores how historians might avoid Eurocentrism when considering an era when Europe was increasingly central in world history. None of these issues can be easily or permanently resolved, but the opportunity to contemplate them is among the great gifts that the study of history offers us.

The Dilemma of World History: Inclusivity and Coherence

The great virtue of world history lies in its inclusivity, for its subject matter is the human species itself. No one is excluded, and all may find a place within the grand narrative of the human journey. But that virtue is also the source of world history's greatest difficulty — telling a coherent story. How can we meaningfully present the planet's many and distinct peoples and their intersections with one another in the confines of a single book or a single term? What prevents that telling from bogging down in the endless detail of various civilizations or cultures, from losing the forest for the trees, from implying that history is just "one damned thing after another"?

Less Can Be More

From the beginning, *Ways of the World* set out to cope with this fundamental conundrum of world history — the tension between inclusion and coherence — in several ways. The first is the relative brevity of the narrative. This means leaving some things out or treating them more succinctly than some instructors might expect. But it also means that the textbook need not overwhelm students or dominate the course. It allows for more creativity from instructors in constructing their own world history courses, giving them the opportunity to mix and match text, sources, and other materials in distinctive ways. Coherence is facilitated as well by a themes and cases approach to world history. Most chapters are organized in terms of broad themes that are illustrated with a limited number of specific examples.

The Centrality of Context: Change, Comparison, Connection

A further aid to achieving coherence amid the fragmenting possibilities of inclusion lies in maintaining the centrality of context, for in world history nothing stands alone. Those of us who practice world history as teachers or textbook authors are seldom specialists in the particulars of what we study and teach. Rather, we are "specialists of the whole," seeking to find the richest, most suggestive, and most meaningful contexts in which to embed those particulars. Our task, fundamentally, is to teach contextual thinking.

To aid in this task, *Ways of the World* repeatedly highlights three such contexts, what I call the "**three Cs**" of world history: **change/continuity**, **comparison**, and **connection**. The first "C" emphasizes large-scale **change**, both within and especially across major regions of the world. Examples include the peopling of the planet, the breakthrough to agriculture, the emergence of "civilization," the rise of universal religions, the changing shape of the Islamic world, the linking of Eastern and Western hemispheres in the wake of Columbus's voyages, the Industrial Revolution, the rise and fall of world communism, and the acceleration of globalization during the twentieth century. The flip side of change, of course, is continuity, implying a focus on what persists over long periods of time. And so *Ways of the World* seeks to juxtapose these contrasting elements of human experience. While civilizations have changed dramatically over time, some of their essential features — cities, states, patriarchy, and class inequality, for example — have long endured.

The second "C" involves frequent **comparison**, a technique of integration through juxtaposition, bringing several regions or cultures into our field of vision at the same time. It encourages reflection both on the common elements of the human experience and on its many variations. Such comparisons are pervasive throughout the book, informing both the chapter narratives and many of the docutext features. *Ways of the World* explicitly examines the difference, for example, between the Agricultural Revolution in the Eastern and Western hemispheres; between the beginnings of Buddhism and the early history of Christianity and Islam; between patriarchy in Athens and in Sparta; between European and Asian empires of the early modern era; between the Chinese and the Japanese response to European intrusion; between the Russian and Chinese revolutions; and many more. Many of the primary source features are also broadly comparative or cross-cultural. For example, a document-based feature in Chapter 11 explores perceptions of the Mongols from the perspective of Persians, Russians, Europeans, and the Mongols themselves. Likewise, an image-based feature in Chapter 15 uses art and architecture to examine various expressions of Christianity in Reformation Europe, colonial Bolivia, seventeenth-century China, and Mughal India.

The final "C" emphasizes **connection**, networks of communication and exchange that increasingly shaped the character of the societies that participated in them. For world historians, cross-cultural interaction becomes one of the major motors of historical transformation. Such connections are addressed in nearly every chapter and in many docutext features. Examples include the clash of the ancient Greeks and the Persians; the long-distance commercial networks that linked the Afro-Eurasian world; the numerous cross-cultural encounters spawned by the spread of Islam; the trans-hemispheric Columbian exchange of the early modern era; and the growth of a genuinely global economy.

Organizing World History: Time, Place, and Theme

All historical writing occurs at the intersection of time, place, and theme. **Time** is the matrix in which history takes shape, allowing us to chart the changes and the continuities of human experience. **Place** recognizes variation and distinctiveness among societies and cultures as well as the importance of the environmental setting in which history unfolds. **Theme** reflects the need to write or teach about one thing at a time—the creation of empires, gender identity, the development of religious traditions, or cross-cultural trade, for example—even while exploring the linkages among them. Organizing a world history textbook involves balancing these three principles of organization in a flexible format that can accommodate a variety of teaching approaches and curricular strategies. In doing so, we have also drawn on our own sense of "what works" in the classroom and on best practice in the field.

This book addresses the question of time or chronology by dividing world history into six major periods. Each of these six "parts" begins with a **Big Picture essay** that introduces the general patterns of a particular period and raises questions about the problems historians face in periodizing the human past.

Part One (to 500 B.C.E.) deals in two chapters with beginnings—of human migration and social construction from the Paleolithic era through the Agricultural Revolution and the development of the First Civilizations. These chapters pursue such important themes on a global scale, illustrating them with regional examples treated comparatively.

Part Two examines the millennium of second-wave civilizations (500 B.C.E.– 500 C.E.) and employs the thematic principle in exploring the major civilizations of Eurasia (Chinese, Indian, Persian, and Mediterranean), with separate chapters focusing on their empires (Chapter 3), their religious and cultural traditions (Chapter 4), and their social organization (Chapter 5). These Afro-Eurasian chapters are followed by a single chapter (Chapter 6) that examines regionally the second-wave era in sub-Saharan Africa, the Americas, and Pacific Oceania.

Part Three, embracing the thousand years between 500 and 1500 C.E., reflects a mix of theme and place. Chapter 7 focuses topically on commercial networks across the world, while Chapters 8, 9, and 10 deal regionally with the Chinese, Islamic, and Christian worlds respectively. Chapter 11 treats pastoral societies as a broad theme and the Mongols as the most dramatic illustration of their impact on the larger stage of world history. Chapter 12, which bridges the two volumes of the book, presents an around-the-world tour in the fifteenth century, which serves both to conclude Volume 1 and to open Volume 2.

Part Four considers the early modern era (1450–1750) and treats each of its three chapters thematically. Chapter 13 compares European and Asian empires; Chapter 14 lays out the major patterns of global commerce and their consequences; and Chapter 15 focuses on cultural patterns, including the globalization of Christianity and the rise of modern science.

Part Five takes up the era of maximum European influence in the world, from 1750 to 1914. It charts the emergence of distinctively modern societies, devoting separate chapters to the Atlantic revolutions (Chapter 16) and the Industrial Revolution (Chapter 17). Chapters 18 and 19 focus on the growing impact of those European societies on the rest of humankind—first on the world of formal colonies and then on the still-independent states of China, the Ottoman Empire, and Japan.

Part Six, which looks at the most recent century (1914–2015), is perhaps the most problematic for world historians, given the abundance of data and the absence of time to sort out what is fundamental and what is peripheral. Its four chapters explore themes of global significance. Chapter 20 focuses on the descent of Europe into war, depression, and the Holocaust, and the global outcomes of this collapse. Chapter 21 examines global communism—its birth in revolution, its efforts to create socialist societies, its role in the cold war, and its abandonment by the end of the twentieth century. Chapter 22 turns the spotlight on the African, Asian, and Latin American majority of the world's inhabitants, describing their exit from formal colonial rule and their emergence on the world stage as the developing countries. Chapter 23 concludes this account of the human journey by assessing the economic, environmental, and cultural dimensions of what we know as globalization.

"It Takes a Village"

In any enterprise of significance, "it takes a village," as they say. Bringing *Ways of the World* to life in this new edition, it seems, has occupied the energies of several villages. Among the privileges and delights of writing and revising this book has been the opportunity to interact with our fellow villagers.

We are grateful to the community of fellow historians who contributed their expertise to this revision. Carter Findley, Humanities Distinguished Professor at Ohio State University, carefully read the sections of the book dealing with the Islamic world, offering us very useful guidance. Gregory Cushman from the University of Kansas provided us with an extraordinarily detailed analysis of places where our coverage of environmental issues might be strengthened. He also gave us a similarly comprehensive review of our Latin American and Pacific Oceania material. We also extend a special thanks to Stanley Burstein, emeritus at California State University–Los Angeles, who has been a wonderfully helpful mentor on all matters ancient, and to Edward Gutting and Suzanne Sturn for original translations of particular documents. We are grateful for their contributions.

The largest of these communities consists of the many people who read earlier editions and made suggestions for improvement. We offer our thanks to the following reviewers: Maria S. Arbelaez, University of Nebraska–Omaha; Veronica L. Bale, Mira Costa College; Christopher Bellitto, Kean University; Monica Bord-Lamberty, Northwood High School; Ralph Croizier, University of Victoria; Edward Dandrow, University of Central Florida; Peter L. de Rosa, Bridgewater State University; Amy Forss, Metropolitan Community College; Denis Gainty, Georgia State University; Steven A. Glazer, Graceland University; Sue Gronewald, Kean University; Andrew Hamilton, Viterbo University; J. Laurence Hare, University of Arkansas; Michael Hinckley, Northern Kentucky University; Bram Hubbell, Friends Seminary; Ronald Huch, Eastern Kentucky University; Elizabeth Hyde, Kean University; Mark Lentz, University of Louisiana–Lafayette; Kate McGrath, Central Connecticut State University; C. Brid Nicholson, Kean University; Donna Patch, Westside High School; Jonathan T. Reynolds, Northern Kentucky University; James Sabathne, Hononegah High School; Christopher Sleeper, Mira Costa College; Ira Spar, Ramapo College and Metropolitan Museum of Art; Kristen Strobel, Lexington High School; Michael Vann, Sacramento State University; Peter Winn, Tufts University; and Judith Zinsser, Miami University of Ohio.

We extend our thanks to the contributors to the supplements: Lisa Tran, California State University–Fullerton; Michael Vann, Sacramento State University; and John Reisbord. We would also like to offer a special thanks to Mike Fisher and Eric Taylor for their time and expertise producing the Another Voice Podcasts.

The Bedford village has been a second community sustaining this enterprise and the one most directly responsible for the book's third edition. It would be difficult for any author to imagine a more supportive and professional publishing team. Our chief point of contact with the Bedford village has been Leah Strauss, our development editor. She has coordinated the immensely complex task of assembling a new edition of the book and has done so with great professional care, with timely responses to our many queries, and with sensitivity to the needs and feelings of authors, even when she found it necessary to decline our suggestions.

Others on the team have also exhibited that lovely combination of personal kindness and professional competence that is so characteristic of the Bedford way. Editorial director Edwin Hill and publisher Michael Rosenberg have kept an eye on the project amid many duties. Jane Knetzger, director of development, provided overall guidance as well as the necessary resources. Christina Horn, our production editor, managed the process of turning a manuscript into a published book and did so with both grace and efficiency. Operating behind the scenes in the Bedford village, a series of highly competent and always supportive people have shepherded this revised edition along its way. Photo researcher Bruce Carson identified and acquired the many images that grace this new edition of *Ways of the World* and did so with a keen eye and courtesy. Copy editor Jennifer Brett Greenstein polished the prose and sorted out our many inconsistent usages with a seasoned and perceptive eye. Sandra McGuire has overseen the marketing process, while Bedford's sales representatives have reintroduced the book to the academic world. Jen Jovin supervised the development of ancillary materials to support the book, and William Boardman ably coordinated research for the lovely covers that mark *Ways of the World*. Eve Lehman conducted the always-difficult negotiations surrounding permissions with more equanimity than we could have imagined. And our editorial assistant Tess Fletcher handled the thousand and one details of this process so well that we were hardly aware that they were being handled.

Yet another "village" that contributed much to *Ways of the World* is the group of distinguished scholars and teachers who worked with Robert Strayer on an earlier world history text, *The Making of the Modern World*, published by St. Martin's Press (1988, 1995). They include Sandria Freitag, Edwin Hirschmann, Donald Holsinger, James Horn, Robert Marks, Joe Moore, Lynn Parsons, and Robert Smith. That collective effort resembled participation in an extended seminar, from which I benefited immensely. Their ideas and insights have shaped my own understanding of world history in many ways and greatly enriched *Ways of the World*.

A final and much smaller community sustained this project and its authors. It is that most intimate of villages that we know as a marriage. Sharing that village with me (Robert Strayer) is my wife, Suzanne Sturn. It is her work to bring ideas and people to life onstage, even as I try to do so between these covers. She knows how I feel about her love and support, and no one else needs to. And across the street, I (Eric Nelson) would also like to thank two new residents of this village: my wife, Alice Victoria, and our little girl, Evelyn Rhiannon, to whom this new edition is dedicated. Without their patience and support, I could not have become part of such an interesting journey.

To all of our fellow villagers, we offer deep thanks for an immensely rewarding experience. We are grateful beyond measure.

Robert Strayer, La Selva Beach, California, Summer 2015
Eric Nelson, Springfield, Missouri, Summer 2015

Versions and Supplements

Adopters of *Ways of the World* and their students have access to abundant print and digital resources and tools, including documents, assessment and presentation materials, the acclaimed Bedford Series in History and Culture volumes, and much more. The LaunchPad course space provides access to the narrative with all assignment and assessment opportunities at the ready. See below for more information, visit the book's catalog site at **macmillanhighered.com/strayersources /catalog**, or contact your local Bedford/St. Martin's sales representative.

Get the Right Version for Your Class

To accommodate different course lengths and course budgets, *Ways of the World* is available in several different formats, including 3-hole-punched loose-leaf Budget Books versions and low-priced PDF e-books. And for the best value of all, package a new print book with LaunchPad at no additional charge to get the best each format offers—a print version for easy portability and reading with a LaunchPad interactive e-book and course space with loads of additional assignment and assessment options.

- **Combined Volume** (Chapters 1–23): available in paperback and e-book formats and in LaunchPad
- **Volume 1, Through the Fifteenth Century** (Chapters 1–12): available in paperback, loose-leaf, and e-book formats and in LaunchPad
- **Volume 2, Since the Fifteenth Century** (Chapters 12–23): available in paperback, loose-leaf, and e-book formats and in LaunchPad

As noted below, any of these volumes can be packaged with additional titles for a discount. To get ISBNs for discount packages, see the online catalog at **macmillanhighered.com/strayersources/catalog** or contact your Bedford/St. Martin's representative.

LaunchPad Assign LaunchPad—an Assessment-Ready Interactive E-book and Course Space

Available for discount purchase on its own or for packaging with new books at no additional charge, LaunchPad is a breakthrough solution for today's courses. Intuitive and easy to use for students and instructors alike, LaunchPad is ready to use as is and can be edited, customized with your own material, and assigned in seconds. *LaunchPad for Ways of the World* provides Bedford/St. Martin's high-quality content all in one place, including the full interactive e-book plus LearningCurve formative quizzing; guided reading activities designed to help students read actively for key concepts; additional primary sources, with auto-graded source-based questions to build skill development; images; videos; chapter summative quizzes; and more.

Through a wealth of formative and summative assessments, including the adaptive learning program of LearningCurve (see the full description below), students gain confidence and get into their reading before class. In addition to Learning-Curve, we are delighted to offer new online primary source projects called Thinking through Sources, one for each chapter of *Ways of the World*. These features, available only in LaunchPad, explore in greater depth a central theme from each chapter and, most importantly, are uniquely surrounded by a distinctive and sophisticated pedagogy of self-grading exercises. Featuring immediate substantive feedback for each rejoinder, these exercises help students learn even when they select the wrong answer. These exercises guide students in assessing their understanding of the sources, in organizing those sources for use in an essay, and in drawing useful conclusions from them. In this interactive learning environment, students will enhance their ability to build arguments and to practice historical reasoning. Thus this LaunchPad pedagogy does for skill development what LearningCurve does for content mastery and reading comprehension.

LaunchPad easily integrates with course management systems, and with fast ways to build assignments, rearrange chapters, and add new pages, sections, or links, it lets teachers build the courses they want to teach and hold students accountable. For more information, visit **launchpadworks.com**, or to arrange a demo, contact us at **history@macmillanhighered.com**.

LearningCurve Assign LearningCurve So Your Students Come to Class Prepared

Students using LaunchPad receive access to LearningCurve for *Ways of the World*. Assigning LearningCurve in place of reading quizzes is easy for instructors, and the reporting features help instructors track overall class trends and spot topics that are giving students trouble so they can adjust their lectures and class activities. This online learning tool is popular with students because it was designed to help them rehearse content at their own pace in a nonthreatening, game-like environment. The feedback for wrong answers provides instructional coaching and sends students back to the book for review. Students answer as many questions as necessary to reach a target score, with repeated chances to revisit material they haven't mastered. When LearningCurve is assigned, students come to class better prepared.

Take Advantage of Instructor Resources

Bedford/St. Martin's has developed a rich array of teaching resources for this book and for this course. They range from lecture and presentation materials and assessment tools to course management options. Most can be found in LaunchPad or can be downloaded or ordered at **macmillanhighered.com/strayersources/catalog**.

Bedford Coursepack for Blackboard, Canvas, D2L, or Moodle. We can help you integrate our rich content into your course management system. Registered instructors can download coursepacks that include our popular free resources and book-specific content for *Ways of the World*. Visit **macmillanhighered.com/cms** to find your version or download your coursepack.

Instructor's Resource Manual. The instructor's manual offers both experienced and first-time instructors tools presenting textbook material in engaging ways. It includes content learning objectives, annotated chapter outlines, and strategies for teaching with the textbook, plus suggestions on how to get the most out of LearningCurve and a survival guide for first-time teaching assistants.

Guide to Changing Editions. Designed to facilitate an instructor's transition from the previous edition of *Ways of the World* to this new edition, this guide presents an overview of major changes as well as of changes in each chapter.

Online Test Bank. The test bank includes a mix of fresh, carefully crafted multiple-choice, matching, short-answer, and essay questions for each chapter. All questions appear in Microsoft Word format and in easy-to-use test bank software that allows instructors to add, edit, re-sequence, and print questions and answers. Instructors can also export questions into a variety of course management systems.

The Bedford Lecture Kit: **Lecture Outlines, Maps, and Images.** Be effective and save time with *The Bedford Lecture Kit*. These presentation materials are downloadable individually from the Instructor Resources tab at **macmillanhighered .com/strayersources/catalog**. They include fully customizable multimedia presentations built around chapter outlines that are embedded with maps, figures, and images from the textbook and are supplemented by more detailed instructor notes on key points and concepts.

Package and Save Your Students Money

For information on free packages and discounts up to 50%, visit **macmillanhighered .com/strayersources/catalog**, or contact your local Bedford/St. Martin's sales representative. The products that follow all qualify for discount packaging.

The Bedford Series in History and Culture. More than 100 titles in this highly praised series combine first-rate scholarship, historical narrative, and important primary documents for undergraduate courses. Each book is brief, inexpensive, and focused on a specific topic or period. For a complete list of titles, visit **bedford stmartins.com/history/series**.

Rand McNally Atlas of World History. This collection of almost 70 full-color maps illustrates the eras and civilizations in world history from the emergence of human societies to the present.

The Bedford Glossary for World History. This handy supplement for the survey course gives students historically contextualized definitions for hundreds of terms— from *abolitionism* to *Zoroastrianism*—that they will encounter in lectures, reading, and exams.

World History Matters: A Student Guide to World History Online. Based on the popular "World History Matters" Web site produced by the Center for History and New Media, this unique resource, edited by Kristin Lehner (The Johns Hopkins University), Kelly Schrum (George Mason University), and T. Mills Kelly (George Mason University), combines reviews of 150 of the most useful and reliable world history Web sites with an introduction that guides students in locating, evaluating, and correctly citing online sources.

Trade Books. Titles published by sister companies Hill and Wang; Farrar, Straus and Giroux; Henry Holt and Company; St. Martin's Press; Picador; and Palgrave Macmillan are available at a 50% discount when packaged with Bedford/St. Martin's textbooks. For more information, visit **macmillanhighered.com/tradeup**.

A Pocket Guide to Writing in History. This portable and affordable reference tool by Mary Lynn Rampolla provides reading, writing, and research advice useful to students in all history courses. Concise yet comprehensive advice on approaching typical history assignments, developing critical reading skills, writing effective history papers, conducting research, using and documenting sources, and avoiding plagiarism—enhanced with practical tips and examples throughout—has made this slim reference a best seller.

A Student's Guide to History. This complete guide to success in any history course provides the practical help students need to be successful. In addition to introducing students to the nature of the discipline, author Jules Benjamin teaches a wide range of skills from preparing for exams to approaching common writing assignments, and explains the research and documentation process with plentiful examples.

Brief Contents

Contents

photo: French painting, 19th century/Monastery of La Rabida, Huelva, Andalusia, Spain/ Bridgeman Images

---

photo: Illustration from the
Padshahnama, ca. 1630–1640
(bodycolour with gold on paper)/
Royal Collection Trust © Her
Majesty Queen Elizabeth II,
2014/Bridgeman Images

photos: Slave Merchant in
Gorée Island, Senegal, from
Encyclopédie des Voyages,
engraved by L. F. Labrousse,
1796/Bibliothèque des Arts
Décoratifs, Paris, France/
Archives Charmet/Bridgeman
Images; National Palace, Mexico
City, Mexico/The Art Archive
at Art Resource, NY

photo: Musée de la Ville de Paris, Musée Carnavalet, Paris, France/© RMN–Grand Palais/ Art Resource, NY

17 Revolutions of Industrialization, 1750–1914 737

photo: Vivian's copper foundry,
Swansea, Wales, engraving by
Durand-Brager/Bibliothèque des
Arts décoratifs, Paris, France/
Gianni Dagli Orti/The Art Archive
at Art Resource, NY

18 Colonial Encounters in Asia, Africa, and Oceania, 1750–1950   787

photo: © Topham/The Image Works

PART SIX   The Most Recent Century, 1914–2015   872

photo: The Chinese Cake, from *Le Petit Journal*, 1898, lithograph by Henri Meyer (1844–1899)/Private Collection/Roger-Viollet, Paris, France/Bridgeman Images

22 The End of Empire: The Global South on the Global Stage, 1914–present

photo: Image created by Reto Stockli, Nazmi El Saleous, and Marit Jentoft-Nilsen, NASA GSFC

Maps

Big Picture Maps

Chapter Maps

Features

Zooming In

Snapshot

Thinking through Sources

Primary Source Exercises Available Only in LaunchPad

For more information, visit **macmillanhighered.com/strayersources/catalog** or contact your Bedford/St. Martin's representative.

Working with Evidence

At the end of each chapter of *Ways of the World* is a set of primary sources called **Working with Evidence** that represent the kind of evidence that historians use in drawing their conclusions about the past. In addition, there are primary source activities surrounded by a distinctive and sophisticated pedagogy of self-grading exercises called **Thinking through Sources** available only in LaunchPad, the interactive course space for this book. (For more information about LaunchPad, visit **launchpadworks.com**, or to arrange a demo, contact us at **history@macmillan .com**.) Some of the primary sources are written—inscriptions, letters, diaries, law codes, official records, sacred texts, and much more. Others are visual—paintings, sculptures, engravings, photographs, posters, cartoons, buildings, and artifacts. Collectively they provide an opportunity for you to practice the work of historians in a kind of guided "history laboratory." In working with this evidence, you are "doing history," much as students conducting lab experiments in chemistry or biology courses are "doing science."

Since each feature explores a theme of the chapter, the chapter narrative itself provides a broad context for analyzing these sources. Furthermore, brief introductions to each feature and to each document or image offer more specific context or background information, while questions provide specific elements to look for as you examine each source. Other more integrative questions offer a focus for using those sources together to probe larger historical issues. What follows are a few more specific suggestions for assessing these raw materials of history.

Working with Written Sources

Written sources or documents are the most common type of primary source that historians use. Analysis of documents usually begins with the basics:

- Who wrote the document?
- When and where was it written?
- What type of document is it (for example, a letter to a friend, a political decree, an exposition of a religious teaching)?

Sometimes the document itself will provide answers to these questions. On other occasions, you may need to rely on the introductions.

Once these basics have been established, a historian is then likely to consider several further questions, which situate the document in its particular historical context:

- Why was the document written, for what audience, and under what circumstances?

- What point of view does it reflect? What other views or opinions is the document arguing against?

Inspiration and intention are crucial factors that shape the form and content of a source. For instance, one might examine a document differently depending on whether it was composed for a private or a public readership, or whether it was intended to be read by a small elite or a wider audience.

Still another level of analysis seeks to elicit useful information from the document.

- What material in the document is believable, and what is not?
- What might historians learn from this document?
- What can the document tell us about the individual who produced it and the society from which he or she came?

In all of this, historical imagination is essential. Informed by knowledge of the context and the content of the document, your imagination will help you read it through the eyes of its author and its audience. You should ask yourself: how might this document have been understood at the time it was written? But in using your imagination, you must take care not to read into the documents your own assumptions and understandings. It is a delicate balance, a kind of dance that historians constantly undertake. Even documents that contain material that historians find unbelievable can be useful, for we seek not only to know what actually happened in the past but also to grasp the world as the people who lived that past understood it. And so historians sometimes speak about reading documents "against the grain," looking for meanings that the author might not have intended to convey.

While each source must be read and understood individually, historians typically draw their strongest conclusions when they analyze a number of such sources together. The document features in *Ways of the World* are designed to explore sets of primary sources that address a central theme of the chapter by drawing on several related texts. In the documents for Chapter 11, for example, you can reflect on the Mongol Empire by reading several accounts written by Mongols themselves and several others composed by Russian or Persian victims of Mongol aggression. And in Chapter 22, you will encounter a debate among Muslims about the relationship between their faith and the modern world, with positions ranging from those that advocate the removal of Islam from public life to those that seek to embed Islamic law in the social and cultural fabric of their countries.

Working with Visual Sources

Visual sources derive from the material culture of the past—religious icons or paintings that add to our understanding of belief systems, a family portrait that provides insight into presentations of self in a particular time and place, a building or sculpture that reveals how power and authority were displayed in a specific empire. These kinds of evidence represent another category of primary source material that historians can use to re-create and understand the past. But such visual sources can be even more difficult to interpret than written documents. The ideas that animated the creators of particular images or artifacts are often not obvious. Nor are the meanings they conveyed to those who viewed or used them. The lovely images from the Indus River valley civilization contained in the visual sources feature for Chapter 2, for example, remain enigmatic although still engaging to twenty-first-century viewers.

Despite the difficulties of interpretation, visual sources can provide insights not offered by written documents. Various images of the Buddha shown in Chapter 4 effectively illustrate how the faith that he initiated changed as it spread beyond India to other parts of Asia. And the posters from Mao Zedong's China in Chapter 21 convey an immediate emotional sense about the meanings attached to communism at the time, at least to its supporters. Indeed, for preliterate societies, such as those described in Chapter 1, archeological and artistic evidence is almost all that remains of their history.

To use visual sources, we must try as best we can to see these pieces of evidence through the eyes of the societies that produced them and to decode the symbols and other features that imbue them with meaning. Thus context is, if anything, even more crucial for analyzing visual evidence than it is for documents. Understanding scenes from the life of Muhammad, featured in Chapter 9, depends heavily on some knowledge of Islamic history and culture. And the images in Chapter 16, illustrating various perceptions of the French Revolution, require some grasp of the unfolding of that enormous upheaval.

A set of basic questions, similar to those you would ask about a written document, provides a starting point for analyzing visual sources:

- When and where was the image or artifact created?
- Who made the image or artifact? Who paid for or commissioned it? For what audience(s) was it intended?
- Where was the image or artifact originally displayed or used?

Having established this basic information about the image or artifact, you may simply want to describe it, as if to someone who had never seen it before.

- If the source is an image, who or what is depicted? What activities are shown? How might you describe the positioning of figures, their clothing, hairstyles, and other visual cues?
- If the source is an object or building, how would you describe its major features?

Finally, you will want to take a stab at more interpretive issues, making use of what you know about the context in which the visual source was created.

- What likely purpose or function did the image or artifact serve?
- What message(s) does it seek to convey?

- How could it be interpreted differently depending on who viewed or used it?
- What are the meanings of any symbols or other abstract features in the visual source?
- What can the image or artifact tell us about the society that produced it and the time period in which it was created?

Beyond analyzing particular images or objects, you will be invited to draw conclusions from sets of related visual sources that address a central theme in the chapter. What can you learn, for example, about the life of Chinese elites from the visual sources in Chapter 8? And what do the images in the Working with Evidence feature of Chapter 15 disclose about the reception of Christianity in various cultural settings?

Primary sources—documentary and visual alike—are the foundation for all historical accounts. To read only secondary sources, such as textbooks or articles, is to miss much of the flavor and texture of history as it was actually experienced by people in the past. But immersing yourself in the documents and visual sources presented here allows you to catch a glimpse of the messiness, the ambiguity, the heartaches, and the achievements of history as it was lived.

Using these sources effectively, however, is no easy task. In fact, the work of historians might well be compared with that of Sisyphus, the ancient Greek king who, having offended the gods, was condemned to eternally roll a large rock up a mountain, only to have it ceaselessly fall back down. Like Sisyphus, historians work at a mission that can never be completely successful—to recapture the past before it is lost forever in the mists of time and fading memory. The evidence available is always partial and fragmentary. Historians and students of history alike are limited and fallible, for we operate often at a great distance—in both time and culture—from those we are studying. And we rarely agree on important matters, divided as we are by sex, nationality, religion, race, and values, all of which shape our understandings of the past.

Despite these challenges, scholars and students alike have long found their revisiting of the past a compelling project—intensely interesting, personally meaningful, and even fun—particularly when working with "primary" or "original" sources, which are the building blocks of all historical accounts. Such sources are windows into the lives of our ancestors, though these windows are often smudged and foggy. We hope that working with the evidence contained in these sources will enrich your own life as you listen in on multiple conversations from the past, eavesdropping, as it were, on our ancestors.

Prologue

Considering World History

Not long ago—in the mid-twentieth century, for example—virtually all college-level history courses were organized in terms of particular civilizations or nations. In the United States, it was Western Civilization or some version of American History that served to introduce students to the study of the past. Since then, however, a set of profound changes has pushed the historical profession in a different direction.

The world wars of the twentieth century, revealing as they did the horrendous consequences of unchecked nationalism, persuaded some historians that a broader view of the past might contribute to notions of global citizenship. Economic and cultural globalization has highlighted both the interdependence of the world's peoples and their very unequal positions within the global network. Moreover, we are aware as never before that our problems—whether they involve economic well-being, global warming, disease, or terrorism—respect no national boundaries. To many thoughtful people, a global present seemed to call for a global past.

Change
What historical circumstances help explain a growing interest in world history in recent decades?

Furthermore, as colonial empires shrank and new nations asserted themselves on the world stage, these peoples also insisted that their histories be accorded equivalent treatment with those of Europe and North America. An explosion of new knowledge about the histories of Asia, Africa, and pre-Columbian America erupted from the research of scholars around the world. All of this has generated a "world history movement," reflected in college and high school curricula, in numerous conferences and specialized studies, and in a proliferation of textbooks, of which this is one.

This world history movement has attempted to create a global understanding of the human past that highlights broad patterns cutting across particular civilizations and countries, while acknowledging in an inclusive fashion the distinctive histories of its many peoples. This is, to put it mildly, a tall order. How is it possible to encompass within a single book or course the separate stories of the world's various peoples? Surely it must be something more than just recounting the history of one civilization or culture after another. How can we distill a common history of humankind as a whole from the distinct trajectories of particular peoples? Because no world history book or course can cover everything, what criteria should we use for deciding what to include and what to leave out? Such questions have ensured no end of controversy among students, teachers, and scholars of world history, making it one of the most exciting fields of historical inquiry.

Despite much debate and argument, one thing is reasonably clear: in world history, nothing stands alone. Every event, every historical figure, every culture, society, or civilization gains significance from its inclusion in some larger context. In this respect, history books in general, and world history textbooks in particular, share something in common with those Russian nested dolls in which a series of carved figures fit inside one another. In much the same fashion, all historical accounts take place within some larger context, as stories within stories unfold. Individual biographies and histories of local communities, particularly modern ones, occur within the context of one nation or another. Nations often find a place in some more encompassing civilization, such as the Islamic world or the West, or in a regional or continental context such as Southeast Asia, Latin America, or Africa. And those civilizational or regional histories in turn take on richer meaning when they are understood within the even broader story of world history, which embraces humankind as a whole.

Description

What potential misunderstandings of the past do the "three Cs" address?

Most world historians would probably agree on three important contexts that define their field of study: change, comparison, and connection, the "three Cs" of world history. Each of them confronts a particular problem in our understanding of the past.

Context in World History: Change

The first context for the study of world history is **change** over time. The last five centuries of the human journey, which constitute the subject matter of this book, need to be understood in the context of human history as a whole. That history occupied roughly the last 250,000 years, conventionally divided into three major phases, based on the kind of technology that was most widely practiced. The enormously long Paleolithic age, with its gathering and hunting way of life, accounts for 95 percent or more of the time that humans have occupied the planet. People utilizing a stone-age Paleolithic technology initially settled every major landmass on the earth and constructed the first human societies. Then beginning with the first Agricultural Revolution, about 12,000 years ago, the domestication of plants and animals increasingly became the primary means of sustaining human life and societies. In giving rise to agricultural villages and chiefdoms, to pastoral communities depending on their herds of animals, and to state- and city-based civilizations, this agrarian way of life changed virtually everything and fundamentally reshaped human societies and their relationship to the natural order. Finally, in the centuries after 1500 two major changes ushered in a new phase of the human story. One was the new network of relationships between the Eastern and Western hemispheres following the voyages of Columbus. And the second, beginning around 1750, involved a quite sudden spurt in the rate of technological change, which we know as the Industrial Revolution. These enormous processes once again reshaped virtually every aspect of human life and gave rise to new kinds of societies that we call "modern." Volume 2 of *Ways of the World* turns the spotlight of history on this distinctive chapter of the global past.

Within these past five centuries, many questions about change arise. What lay behind the emergence of a new balance of global power after 1500, one that featured the growing prominence of Europeans on the world stage? What global changes did the Atlantic slave trade generate? Why did the ancient civilizations of Russia and China explode in revolution during the twentieth century? How might we explain the emergence of Islamic radicalism as well as global environmentalism during the final third of that century?

A focus on change provides an antidote to a persistent tendency of human thinking that historians call "essentialism." A more common term is "stereotyping." It refers to our inclination to define particular groups of people with an unchanging or essential set of characteristics. Women are nurturing; peasants are conservative; Americans are aggressive; Hindus are religious. Serious students of history soon become aware that every significant category of people contains endless divisions and conflicts and that those human communities are constantly in flux. Peasants may often accept the status quo, except of course when they rebel, as they frequently have. Americans have experienced periods of official isolationism and withdrawal from the world as well as times of aggressive engagement with it. Things change.

But some things persist, even if they also change. We should not allow an emphasis on change to blind us to the continuities of human experience. A recognizably Chinese state has operated for more than 2,000 years. Slavery and patriarchy persisted as human institutions for thousands of years until they were challenged in recent centuries, and in various forms they exist still. Sharp class inequalities have been prominent in human affairs since the first civilizations over 5,000 years ago. The teachings of Buddhism, Christianity, and Islam have endured for centuries, though with endless variations and transformations.

Context in World History: Comparison

A second major context that operates constantly in world history is **comparison**, efforts to identify similarities and differences in the experience of the world's peoples. In what respects did European empires in the Americas differ from the Ottoman Empire in the Middle East or the Russian Empire across northern Asia or Chinese expansion into Central Asia? Why did the Scientific and Industrial Revolutions and a modern way of life evolve first in Western Europe rather than somewhere else? What distinguished the French, Haitian, Russian, and Chinese revolutions? How might we compare the modern transformation of capitalist, communist, and colonial societies? Did feminist movements in the developing countries resemble those of the industrial West? Describing and, if possible, explaining such similarities and differences are among the major tasks of world history.

Comparison has proven an effective tool in countering Eurocentrism, the notion that Europeans or people of European descent have long been the primary movers and shakers of the historical process. That notion arose in recent centuries when Europeans were in fact the major source of innovation in the world and did in fact exercise something close to world domination. But this temporary preeminence decisively shaped the way Europeans thought and wrote about their own histories and those of other people. In their own eyes, Europeans alone were progressive people, thanks to a cultural or racial superiority. Everyone else was to some degree stagnant, backward, savage, or barbarian. The unusual power of Europeans allowed them for a time to act on those beliefs and to convey such ways of thinking to much of the world. But comparative world history sets European achievements in a global and historical context, helping us to sort out what was distinctive about the development of Europe and what similarities it bore to other major regions of the world. Puncturing the pretensions of Eurocentrism has been high on the agenda of world history.

Context in World History: Connection

A third context that informs world history involves the **connections** among different and often distant peoples. World history is less about what happened within particular civilizations or cultures than about the processes and outcomes of their interactions or encounters with one another. Focusing on these connections— whether those of conflict or more peaceful exchange—represents an effort to counteract a habit of thinking about particular peoples, states, or cultures as self-contained or isolated communities. Despite the historical emergence of many separate and distinct societies, none of them developed alone. Each was embedded in a network of relationships with both near and more distant peoples.

The growing depth and significance of such cross-cultural relationships, known now as globalization, has been a distinguishing feature of the modern era. The voyages of Columbus brought the peoples of the Eastern and Western hemispheres into sustained contact for the first time with enormous global consequences. Several centuries later, Europeans took advantage of their industrial power to bring much of the world temporarily under their control. The technologies of the twentieth century have intertwined the economies, societies, and cultures of the world's peoples more tightly than ever before. During these past five centuries, the encounter with strangers, or at least with their ideas and practices, was everywhere among the most powerful motors of change in human societies.

Changes, comparisons, and connections—all of them operating on a global scale—represent three contexts or frameworks that can help us bring some coherence to the multiple and complex stories of modern world history. They will recur repeatedly in the pages that follow.

A final observation about this account of world history: *Ways of the World*, like all other world history textbooks, is radically unbalanced in terms of coverage. Volume 1 of this book, for example, takes on the whole of human history up to about 1500, most of it focused on the era of agricultural civilizations beginning some 5,000 years ago. By contrast, this volume focuses on only the past five centuries, and in fact the last century alone occupies four entire chapters. This imbalance owes something to the relative scarcity of information about earlier periods of our history. But it also reflects a certain "present mindedness," for we look to history, always, to make sense of our current needs and circumstances. And in doing so, we often assume that more recent events have a greater significance for our own lives in the here and now than those that occurred in more distant times. Whether you agree with this assumption or not, you will have occasion to ponder it as you consider the many and various "ways of the world" that have emerged in recent centuries and as you contemplate their relevance for your own journey.

Second Thoughts

What's the Significance?

world history movement, xliii

the three Cs, xliv

essentialism, xlv

Eurocentrism, xlv

globalization, xlvi

Big Picture Questions

1. Why and how did the world history movement emerge to challenge Eurocentrism in history?
2. What examples of change, comparison, and connection in world history would you like to explore further as your course unfolds?
3. In what larger contexts might you place your own life history?

Next Steps: For Further Study

David Christian, *This Fleeting World: A Short History of Humanity* (2008). A big picture overview of the human experience in less than 100 pages by a leading world historian.

Ross E. Dunn, ed., *The New World History: A Teacher's Companion* (2000). A collection of articles dealing with the teaching of world history.

Patrick Manning, *Navigating World History: Historians Create a Global Past* (2003). An up-to-date overview of the growth of world history, the field's achievements, and the debates within it.

J. R. McNeill and William H. McNeill, *The Human Web: A Bird's-Eye View of World History* (2003). An approach to world history that emphasizes the changing webs of connection among human communities.

Heidi Roupp, ed., *Teaching World History in the Twenty-First Century: A Resource Book* (2010). A practical resource book for the teaching of world history.

"World History Matters," http://worldhistorymatters.org/. A point of entry to many world history Web sites, featuring numerous images and essays.

Ways of the World

A Brief Global History
with Sources

French painting, 19th century/Monastery of La Rabida, Huelva, Andalusia, Spain/Bridgeman Images

The Worlds of the Fifteenth Century

"Columbus was a perpetrator of genocide . . . , a slave trader, a thief, a pirate, and most certainly not a hero. To celebrate Columbus is to congratulate the process and history of the invasion."[1] This was the view of Winona LaDuke, president of the Indigenous Women's Network, on the occasion in 1992 of the 500th anniversary of Columbus's arrival in the Americas. Much of the commentary surrounding the event echoed the same themes, citing the history of death, slavery, racism, and exploitation that followed in the wake of Columbus's first voyage to what was for him an altogether New World. A century earlier, in 1892, the tone of celebration had been very different. A presidential proclamation cited Columbus as a brave "pioneer of progress and enlightenment" and instructed Americans to "express honor to the discoverer and their appreciation of the great achievements of four completed centuries of American life." The century that followed witnessed the erosion of Western dominance in the world and the discrediting of racism and imperialism and, with it, the reputation of Columbus.

This sharp reversal of opinion about Columbus provides a reminder that the past is as unpredictable as the future. Few Americans in 1892 could have guessed that their daring hero could emerge so tarnished only a century later. And few people living in 1492 could have imagined the enormous global processes set in motion by the voyage of Columbus's three small ships—the Atlantic slave trade, the decimation of the native peoples of the Americas, the massive growth of world population, the Industrial Revolution, and the growing prominence of Europeans on the world stage. None of these developments were even remotely foreseeable in 1492.

The Meeting of Two Worlds   This nineteenth-century painting shows Columbus on his first voyage to the New World. He is reassuring his anxious sailors by pointing to the first sight of land. In light of its long-range consequences, this voyage represents a major turning point in world history.

Thus, in historical hindsight, that voyage of Columbus was arguably the single most important event of the fifteenth century. But it was not the only significant marker of that century. A Central Asian Turkic warrior named Timur launched the last major pastoral invasion of adjacent civilizations. Russia emerged from two centuries of Mongol rule to begin a huge empire-building project across northern Asia. A new European civilization was taking shape in the Renaissance. In 1405, an enormous Chinese fleet, dwarfing that of Columbus, set out across the entire Indian Ocean basin, only to voluntarily withdraw twenty-eight years later. The Islamic Ottoman Empire put a final end to Christian Byzantium with the conquest of Constantinople in 1453, even as Spanish Christians completed the "reconquest" of the Iberian Peninsula from the Muslims in 1492. And in the Americas, the Aztec and Inca empires gave a final and spectacular expression to Mesoamerican and Andean civilizations before they were both swallowed up in the burst of European imperialism that followed the arrival of Columbus.

Because the fifteenth century was a hinge of major historical change on many fronts, it provides an occasion for a bird's-eye view of the world through a kind of global tour. This excursion around the world will serve to briefly review the human saga thus far and to establish a baseline from which the enormous transformations of the centuries that followed might be measured. How, then, might we describe the world, and the worlds, of the fifteenth century?

SEEKING THE MAIN POINT

What predictions about the future might a global traveler in the fifteenth century have reasonably made?

The Shapes of Human Communities

One way to describe the world of the fifteenth century is to identify the various types of societies that it contained. Bands of hunters and gatherers, villages of agricultural peoples, newly emerging chiefdoms or small states, pastoral communities, established civilizations and empires—all of these social or political forms would have been apparent to a widely traveled visitor in the fifteenth century. Representing alternative ways of organizing human life, all of them were long established by the fifteenth century, but the balance among these distinctive kinds of societies in 1500 was quite different than it had been a thousand years earlier.

Paleolithic Persistence: Australia and North America

Despite millennia of agricultural advance, substantial areas of the world still hosted gathering and hunting societies, known to historians as Paleolithic (Old Stone Age) peoples. All of Australia, much of Siberia, the arctic coastlands, and parts of Africa and the Americas fell into this category. These peoples were not simply relics of a bygone age. They too had changed over time, though more slowly than their agricultural counterparts, and they too interacted with their neighbors. In short, they had a history, although most history books largely ignore them after the age of agri-

A MAP OF TIME

1345–1521	Aztec Empire in Mesoamerica
1368–1644	Ming dynasty in China
1370–1405	Conquests of Timur
15th century	Spread of Islam in Southeast Asia Civil war among Japanese warlords Rise of Hindu state of Vijayanagara in southern India European Renaissance Flourishing of African states of Ethiopia, Kongo, Benin, Zimbabwe
1405–1433	Chinese maritime voyages
1415	Beginning of Portuguese exploration of West African coast
1438–1533	Inca Empire along the Andes
1453	Ottoman seizure of Constantinople
1464–1591	Songhay Empire in West Africa
1492	Christian reconquest of Spain from Muslims completed; Columbus's first transatlantic voyage
1497–1520s	Portuguese entry into the Indian Ocean world
1501	Founding of Safavid Empire in Persia
1526	Founding of Mughal Empire in India

culture arrived. Nonetheless, this most ancient way of life still had a sizable and variable presence in the world of the fifteenth century.

Consider, for example, Australia. That continent's many separate groups, some 250 of them, still practiced a gathering and hunting way of life in the fifteenth century, a pattern that continued well after Europeans arrived in the late eighteenth century. Over many thousands of years, these people had assimilated various material items or cultural practices from outsiders—outrigger canoes, fishhooks, complex netting techniques, artistic styles, rituals, and mythological ideas—but despite the presence of farmers in nearby New Guinea, no agricultural practices penetrated the Australian mainland. Was it because large areas of Australia were unsuited for the kind of agriculture practiced in New Guinea? Or did the peoples of Australia, enjoying an environment of sufficient resources, simply see no need to change their way of life?

Despite the absence of agriculture, Australia's peoples had mastered and manipulated their environment, in part through the practice of "firestick farming," a pattern of deliberately set fires, which they described as "cleaning up the country."

■ **Comparison**

In what ways did the gathering and hunting people of Australia differ from those of the northwest coast of North America?

These controlled burns served to clear the underbrush, thus making hunting easier and encouraging the growth of certain plant and animal species. In addition, native Australians exchanged goods among themselves over distances of hundreds of miles, created elaborate mythologies and ritual practices, and developed sophisticated traditions of sculpture and rock painting. They accomplished all of this on the basis of an economy and technology rooted in the distant Paleolithic past.

A very different kind of gathering and hunting society flourished in the fifteenth century along the northwest coast of North America among the Chinookan, Tulalip, Skagit, and other peoples. With some 300 edible animal species and an abundance of salmon and other fish, this extraordinarily bounteous environment provided the foundation for what scholars sometimes call "complex" or "affluent" gathering and hunting cultures. What distinguished the northwest coast peoples from those of Australia were permanent village settlements with large and sturdy houses, considerable economic specialization, ranked societies that sometimes included slavery, chiefdoms dominated by powerful clan leaders or "big men," and extensive storage of food.

Although these and other gathering and hunting peoples persisted still in the fifteenth century, both their numbers and the area they inhabited had contracted greatly as the Agricultural Revolution unfolded across the planet. That relentless advance of the farming frontier continued in the centuries ahead as the Russian, Chinese, and European empires encompassed the lands of the remaining Paleolithic peoples. By the early twenty-first century, what was once the only human way of life had been reduced to minuscule pockets of people whose cultures seemed doomed to a final extinction.

Agricultural Village Societies: The Igbo and the Iroquois

Far more numerous than gatherers and hunters were those many peoples who, though fully agricultural, had avoided incorporation into larger empires or civilizations and had not developed their own city- or state-based societies. Living usually in small village-based communities and organized in terms of kinship relations, such people predominated during the fifteenth century in much of North America; in most of the tropical lowlands of South America and the Caribbean; in parts of the Amazon River basin, Southeast Asia, and Africa south of the equator; and throughout Pacific Oceania. Historians have largely relegated such societies to the periphery of world history, viewing them as marginal to the cities, states, and large-scale civilizations that predominate in most accounts of the global past. Viewed from within their own circles, though, these societies were at the center of things, each with its own history of migration, cultural transformation, social conflict, incorporation of new people, political rise and fall, and interaction with strangers. In short, they too changed as their histories took shape.

East of the Niger River in the heavily forested region of West Africa lay the lands of the Igbo (EE-boh) peoples. By the fifteenth century, their neighbors, the

■ **Change**
What kinds of changes were transforming the societies of the West African Igbo and the North American Iroquois as the fifteenth century unfolded?

Yoruba and Bini, had begun to develop small states and urban centers. But the Igbo, whose dense population and extensive trading networks might well have given rise to states, declined to follow suit. The deliberate Igbo preference was to reject the kingship and state-building efforts of their neighbors. They boasted on occasion that "the Igbo have no kings." Instead, they relied on other institutions to maintain social cohesion beyond the level of the village: title societies in which wealthy men received a series of prestigious ranks, women's associations, hereditary ritual experts serving as mediators, and a balance of power among kinship groups. It was a "stateless society," famously described in Chinua Achebe's *Things Fall Apart*, the most widely read novel to emerge from twentieth-century Africa.

But the Igbo peoples and their neighbors did not live in isolated, self-contained societies. They traded actively among themselves and with more distant peoples, such as the large African kingdom of Songhay (sahn-GEYE) far to the north. Cotton cloth, fish, copper and iron goods, decorative objects, and more drew neighboring peoples into networks of exchange. Common artistic traditions reflected a measure of cultural unity in a politically fragmented region, and all of these peoples seem to have changed from a matrilineal to a patrilineal system of tracing their descent. Little of this registered in the larger civilizations of the Afro-Eurasian world, but to the peoples of the West African forest during the fifteenth century, these processes were central to their history and their daily lives. Soon, however, all of them would be caught up in the transatlantic slave trade and would be changed substantially in the process.

Across the Atlantic in what is now central New York State, other agricultural village societies were also in the process of substantial change during the several centuries preceding their incorporation into European trading networks and empires. The Iroquois-speaking peoples of that region had only recently become fully agricultural, adopting maize- and bean-farming techniques that had originated centuries earlier in Mesoamerica. As this productive agriculture took hold by 1300 or so, the population grew, the size of settlements increased, and distinct peoples emerged. Frequent warfare also erupted among them. Some scholars have speculated that as agriculture, largely seen as women's work, became the primary economic activity, "warfare replaced successful food getting as the avenue to male prestige."[2]

Whatever caused it, this increased level of conflict among Iroquois peoples triggered a remarkable political innovation around the fifteenth century: a loose alliance or confederation among five Iroquois-speaking peoples—the Mohawk, Oneida, Onondaga, Cayuga, and Seneca. Based on an agreement known as the Great Law of Peace (see Map 12.5, page 523), the Five Nations, as they called themselves, agreed to settle their differences peacefully through a confederation council of clan leaders, some fifty of them altogether, who had the authority to adjudicate disputes and set reparation payments. Operating by consensus, the Iroquois League of Five

Igbo Art
Widely known for their masks, used in a variety of ritual and ceremonial occasions, the Igbo were also among the first to produce bronze castings using the "lost wax" method. This exquisite bronze pendant in the form of a human head derives from the Igbo Ukwu archeological site in eastern Nigeria and dates to the ninth century C.E. (The British Museum, London, UK/ Werner Forman/Art Resource, NY)

Nations effectively suppressed the blood feuds and tribal conflicts that had only recently been so widespread. It also coordinated their peoples' relationship with outsiders, including the Europeans, who arrived in growing numbers in the centuries after 1500.

The Iroquois League gave expression to values of limited government, social equality, and personal freedom, concepts that some European colonists found highly attractive. One British colonial administrator declared in 1749 that the Iroquois had "such absolute Notions of Liberty that they allow no Kind of Superiority of one over another, and banish all Servitude from their Territories."[3] Such equality extended to gender relationships, for among the Iroquois, descent was matrilineal (reckoned through the woman's line), married couples lived with the wife's family, and women controlled agriculture and property. While men were hunters, warriors, and the primary political officeholders, women selected and could depose those leaders.

Wherever they lived in 1500, over the next several centuries independent agricultural peoples such as the Iroquois and Igbo were increasingly encompassed in expanding economic networks and conquest empires based in Western Europe, Russia, China, or India. In this respect, they replicated the experience of many other village-based farming communities that had much earlier found themselves forcibly included in the powerful embrace of Egyptian, Mesopotamian, Roman, Indian, Chinese, and other civilizations.

Pastoral Peoples: Central Asia and West Africa

Pastoral peoples had long impinged more directly and dramatically on civilizations than did hunting and gathering or agricultural village societies. The Mongol incursion, along with the enormous empire to which it gave rise, was one in a long series of challenges from the steppes, but it was not quite the last. As the Mongol Empire disintegrated, a brief attempt to restore it occurred in the late fourteenth and early fifteenth centuries under the leadership of a Turkic warrior named Timur, born in what is now Uzbekistan and known in the West as Tamerlane (see Map 12.1, page 506).

■ Significance
What role did Central Asian and West African pastoralists play in their respective regions?

With a ferocity that matched or exceeded that of his model, Chinggis Khan, Timur's army of pastoralists brought immense devastation yet again to Russia, Persia, and India. Timur himself died in 1405, while preparing for an invasion of China. Conflicts among his successors prevented any lasting empire, although his descendants retained control of the area between Persia and Afghanistan for the rest of the fifteenth century. That state hosted a sophisticated elite culture, combining Turkic and Persian elements, particularly at its splendid capital of Samarkand, as its rulers patronized artists, poets, traders, and craftsmen. Timur's conquest proved to be the last great military success of pastoral peoples from Central Asia. In the centuries that followed, their homelands were swallowed up in the expanding Russian and Chinese empires, as the balance of power between steppe pastoralists of inner Eurasia and the civilizations of outer Eurasia turned decisively in favor of the latter.

In Africa, pastoral peoples stayed independent of established empires several centuries longer than those of Inner Asia, for not until the late nineteenth century were they incorporated into European colonial states. The experience of the Fulbe, West Africa's largest pastoral society, provides an example of an African herding people with a highly significant role in the fifteenth century and beyond. From their homeland in the western fringe of the Sahara along the upper Senegal River, the Fulbe had migrated gradually eastward in the centuries after 1000 c.e. (see Map 12.3, page 514). Unlike the pastoral peoples of Inner Asia, they generally lived in small communities among agricultural peoples and paid various grazing fees and taxes for the privilege of pasturing their cattle. Relations with their farming hosts often were tense because the Fulbe resented their subordination to agricultural peoples, whose way of life they despised. That sense of cultural superiority became even more pronounced as the Fulbe, in the course of their eastward movement, slowly adopted Islam. Some of them in fact dropped out of a pastoral life and settled in towns, where they became highly respected religious leaders. In the eighteenth and nineteenth centuries, the Fulbe were at the center of a wave of religiously based uprisings, or jihads, which greatly expanded the practice of Islam and gave rise to a series of new states, ruled by the Fulbe themselves.

Civilizations of the Fifteenth Century: Comparing China and Europe

Beyond the foraging, farming, and pastoral societies of the fifteenth-century world were its civilizations, those city-centered and state-based societies that were far larger and more densely populated, more powerful and innovative, and much more unequal in terms of class and gender than other forms of human community. Since the First Civilizations had emerged between 3500 and 1000 b.c.e., both the geographic space they encompassed and the number of people they embraced had grown substantially. By the fifteenth century, a considerable majority of the world's population lived within one or another of these civilizations, although most of these people no doubt identified more with local communities than with a larger civilization. What might an imaginary global traveler notice about the world's major civilizations in the fifteenth century?

Ming Dynasty China

Such a traveler might well begin his or her journey in China, heir to a long tradition of effective governance, Confucian and Daoist philosophy, a major Buddhist presence, sophisticated artistic achievements, and a highly productive economy. That civilization, however, had been greatly disrupted by a century of Mongol rule, and its population had been sharply reduced by the plague. During the Ming dynasty (1368–1644), however, China recovered (see Map 12.1). The early decades of that dynasty witnessed an effort to eliminate all signs of foreign rule, discouraging the use of Mongol names and dress, while promoting Confucian learning and orthodox

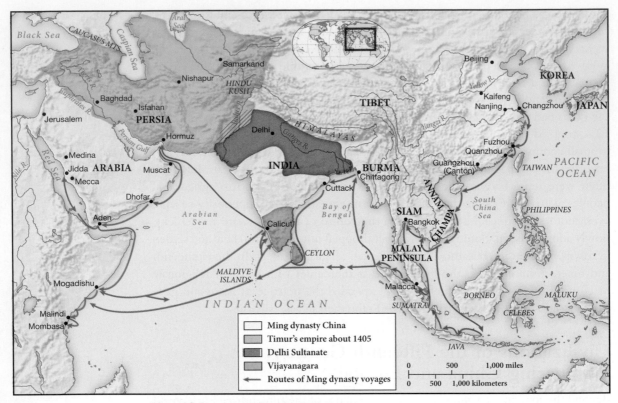

Map 12.1   Asia in the Fifteenth Century

The fifteenth century in Asia witnessed the massive Ming dynasty voyages into the Indian Ocean, the last major eruption of pastoral power in Timur's empire, and the flourishing of the maritime city of Malacca.

gender roles, based on earlier models from the Han, Tang, and Song dynasties. Emperor Yongle (YAHNG-leh) (r. 1402–1422) sponsored an enormous *Encyclopedia* of some 11,000 volumes. With contributions from more than 2,000 scholars, this work sought to summarize or compile all previous writing on history, geography, philosophy, ethics, government, and more. Yongle also relocated the capital to Beijing, ordered the building of a magnificent imperial residence known as the Forbidden City, and constructed the Temple of Heaven, where subsequent rulers performed Confucian-based rituals to ensure the well-being of Chinese society. Two empresses wrote instructions for female behavior, emphasizing traditional expectations after the disruptions of the previous century. Culturally speaking, China was looking to its past.

■ **Description**

How would you define the major achievements of Ming dynasty China?

Politically, the Ming dynasty reestablished the civil service examination system that had been neglected under Mongol rule and went on to create a highly centralized government. Power was concentrated in the hands of the emperor himself, while a cadre of eunuchs (castrated men) personally loyal to the emperor exercised great authority, much to the dismay of the official bureaucrats. The state acted vigorously to repair the damage of the Mongol years by restoring millions of acres to cultivation; rebuilding canals, reservoirs, and irrigation works; and planting, according to some estimates, a billion trees in an effort to reforest China. As a result, the economy rebounded, both international and domestic trade flourished, and the population grew. During the fifteenth century, China had recovered and was perhaps the best governed and most prosperous of the world's major civilizations.

China also undertook the largest and most impressive maritime expeditions the world had ever seen. Since the eleventh century, Chinese sailors and traders had been a major presence in the South China Sea and in Southeast Asian port cities, with much of this activity in private hands. But now, after decades of preparation, an enormous fleet, commissioned by Emperor Yongle himself, was launched in 1405, followed over the next twenty-eight years by six more such expeditions. On board more than 300 ships of the first voyage was a crew of some 27,000, including 180 physicians, hundreds of government officials, 5 astrologers, 7 high-ranking or grand eunuchs, carpenters, tailors, accountants, merchants, translators, cooks, and thousands of soldiers and sailors. Visiting many ports in Southeast Asia, Indonesia, India, Arabia, and East Africa, these fleets, captained by the Muslim eunuch Zheng He (JUHNG-huh), sought to enroll distant peoples and states in the Chinese tribute system (see Map 12.1). Dozens of rulers accompanied the fleets back to China, where they presented tribute, performed the required rituals of submission, and received in return abundant gifts, titles, and trading opportunities. Chinese officials were amused by some of the exotic products to be found abroad— ostriches, zebras, and giraffes, for example. Officially described as "bringing order to the world," Zheng He's expeditions served to establish Chinese power and prestige in the Indian Ocean and to exert Chinese control over foreign trade in the region. The Chinese, however, did not seek to conquer new territories, establish Chinese settlements, or spread their culture, though they did intervene in a number of local disputes. (See Zooming In: Zheng He, page 508.)

Temple of Heaven

Set in a forest of more than 650 acres, the Temple of Heaven was constructed in the early fifteenth century. In Chinese thinking, it was the primary place where Heaven and Earth met. From his residence in the Forbidden City, the Chinese emperor led a procession of thousands twice a year to this sacred site, where he offered sacrifices, implored the gods for a good harvest, and performed the rituals that maintained the cosmic balance. (Imaginechina for AP Images)

Zheng He,
China's Non-Chinese Admiral

At the helm of China's massive maritime expeditions in the early fifteenth century was a most unusual person named Zheng He.[4] Born in 1371 in the frontier region of Yunnan in southwestern China, his family roots were in Central Asia in what is now Uzbekistan. Both his father and grandfather were devout Muslims who had made the pilgrimage to Mecca. The family had also achieved local prominence as high officials serving the Mongol rulers of China for a century. Zheng He would surely have continued in this tradition had not a major turning point in China's history decisively altered the trajectory of his life.

Zheng He's birth, as it happened, coincided with the end of Mongol rule. His own father was killed resist-ing the forces of the new Ming dynasty that ousted the Mongols from Yunnan in 1382. Eleven-year-old Zheng He was taken prisoner along with hundreds of Mongols and their Muslim supporters. But young Zheng He lost more than his freedom; he also lost his male sex organs as he underwent castration, becoming a eunuch. The practice had a long history in China as well as in Chris-

Among the acquisitions of Zheng He's expeditions, none excited more interest in the Chinese court than an African giraffe.

tian and Islamic civilizations. During the 276 years of the Ming dynasty (1368–1644), some 1 mil-lion eunuchs served the Chinese emperor and members of the elite. A small number became powerful officials, especially at the central imperial court, where their utter dependence upon and loyalty to the emperor gained them the enduring hostility of the scholar-bureaucrats of China's civil service. Strangely enough, substantial numbers of Chinese men voluntarily became eunuchs, trading their manhood for the possibility of achieving power, prestige, and wealth.

After his castration, pure chance shaped Zheng He's life as he was assigned to Zhu Di, the fourth son of the reigning emperor, who was then establishing himself in the northern Chinese region around Beijing. Zheng He soon won the confidence of his master, and eventually the almost seven-foot-tall eunuch proved himself an effective military leader in various skirmishes against the Mongols

photo: *Tribute Giraffe with Attendant*, 1414, China, Ming Dynasty (1368–1644), Yongle Period (1403–1424), ink and color on silk/Gift of John T. Dorrance, 1977 (1977-42-1)/The Philadelphia Museum of Art/Art Resource, NY

The most surprising feature of these voyages was how abruptly and deliberately they were ended. After 1433, Chinese authorities simply stopped such expeditions and allowed this enormous and expensive fleet to deteriorate in port. "In less than a hundred years," wrote a recent historian of these voyages, "the greatest navy the world had ever known had ordered itself into extinction."[5] Part of the reason involved the death of the emperor Yongle, who had been the chief patron of the enterprise. Many high-ranking officials had long seen the expeditions as a waste of resources because China, they believed, was the self-sufficient "middle kingdom,"

and in the civil war that brought Zhu Di to power as the emperor Yongle in 1402. With his master as emperor, Zheng He served first as Grand Director of Palace Servants. Now he could don the prestigious red robe, rather than the blue one assigned to lower-ranking eunuchs. But soon Zheng He found himself with a far more ambitious assignment—commander of China's huge oceangoing fleet.

The seven voyages that Zheng He led between 1405 and 1433 have defined his role in Chinese and world history. But they also revealed something of the man himself. Clearly, he was not an explorer in the mold of Columbus, for he sailed in well-traveled waters and usually knew where he was going. While his journeys were largely peaceful, with no effort to establish colonies or control trade, on several occasions Zheng He used force to suppress piracy or to punish those who resisted Chinese overtures. Once he personally led 2,000 Chinese soldiers against a hostile ruler in the interior of Ceylon. He also had a keen eye for the kind of exotica that the imperial court found fascinating, returning to China with ostriches, zebras, lions, elephants, and a giraffe.

The voyages also disclose Zheng He's changing religious commitments. Born and raised a Muslim, he had not lived in a primarily Islamic setting since his capture at the age of eleven. Thus it is hardly surprising that he adopted the more eclectic posture toward religion common in China. During his third voyage in Ceylon, he erected a trilingual tablet recording lavish gifts and praise to the Buddha, to Allah, and to a local form of the Hindu deity Vishnu. He also apparently expressed some interest in a famous relic said to be a tooth of the Buddha. And Zheng He credited the success of his journeys to the Daoist goddess Tianfei, protector of sailors and seafarers.

To Zheng He, the voyages surely represented the essential meaning of his own life. In an inscription erected just prior to his last voyage, Zheng He summarized his achievements: "When we arrived at the foreign countries, barbarian kings who resisted transformation [by Chinese civilization] and were not respectful we captured alive, and bandit soldiers who looted and plundered recklessly we exterminated. Because of this, the sea routes became pure and peaceful and the foreign peoples could rely upon them and pursue their occupations in safety." But after his death, Zheng He vanished from the historical record, even as his country largely withdrew from the sea, and most Chinese forgot about the unusual man who had led those remarkable voyages. In the early twenty-first century, however, Zheng He has been resurrected as a potent symbol of China's growing global position and of its peaceful intentions. In such ways, the past is appropriated, and sometimes distorted, as it proves useful in the present.

Questions: How might you describe the arc of Zheng He's life? What were its major turning points? How did Zheng He's castration shape his life?

requiring little from the outside world. In their eyes, the real danger to China came from the north, where barbarians constantly threatened. Finally, they viewed the voyages as the project of the court eunuchs, whom these officials despised. Even as these voices of Chinese officialdom prevailed, private Chinese merchants and craftsmen continued to settle and trade in Japan, the Philippines, Taiwan, and Southeast Asia, but they did so without the support of their government. The Chinese state quite deliberately turned its back on what was surely within its reach—a large-scale maritime empire in the Indian Ocean basin.

European Comparisons: State Building and Cultural Renewal

At the other end of the Eurasian continent, similar processes of demographic recovery, political consolidation, cultural flowering, and overseas expansion were under way. Western Europe, having escaped Mongol conquest but devastated by the plague, began to regrow its population during the second half of the fifteenth century. As in China, the infrastructure of civilization proved a durable foundation for demographic and economic revival.

■ **Comparison**

What political and cultural differences stand out in the histories of fifteenth-century China and Western Europe? What similarities are apparent?

Politically too Europe joined China in continuing earlier patterns of state building. In China, however, this meant a unitary and centralized government that encompassed almost the whole of its civilization, while in Europe a decidedly fragmented system of many separate, independent, and highly competitive states made for a sharply divided Western civilization (see Map 12.2). Many of these states—Spain, Portugal, France, England, the city-states of Italy (Milan, Venice, and Florence), various German principalities—learned to tax their citizens more efficiently, to create more effective administrative structures, and to raise standing armies. A small Russian state centered on the city of Moscow also emerged in the fifteenth century as Mongol rule faded away. Much of this state building was driven by the needs of war, a frequent occurrence in such a fragmented and competitive political environment. England and France, for example, fought intermittently for more than a century in the Hundred Years' War (1337–1453) over rival claims to territory in France. Nothing remotely similar disturbed the internal life of Ming dynasty China.

A renewed cultural blossoming, known in European history as the Renaissance, likewise paralleled the revival of all things Confucian in Ming dynasty China. In Europe, however, that blossoming celebrated and reclaimed a classical Greco-Roman tradition that earlier had been lost or obscured. Beginning in the vibrant commercial cities of Italy between roughly 1350 and 1500, the Renaissance reflected the belief of the wealthy male elite that they were living in a wholly new era, far removed from the confined religious world of feudal Europe. Educated citizens of these cities sought inspiration in the art and literature of ancient Greece and Rome; they were "returning to the sources," as they put it. Their purpose was not so much to reconcile these works with the ideas of Christianity, as the twelfth- and thirteenth-century university scholars had done, but to use them as a cultural standard to imitate and then to surpass. The elite patronized great Renaissance artists such as Leonardo da Vinci, Michelangelo, and Raphael, whose paintings and sculptures were far more naturalistic, particularly in portraying the human body, than those of their medieval counterparts. Some of these artists looked to the Islamic world for standards of excellence, sophistication, and abundance. (See Working with Evidence: Islam and Renaissance Europe, page 536.)

Although religious themes remained prominent, Renaissance artists now included portraits and busts of well-known contemporary figures, scenes from ancient

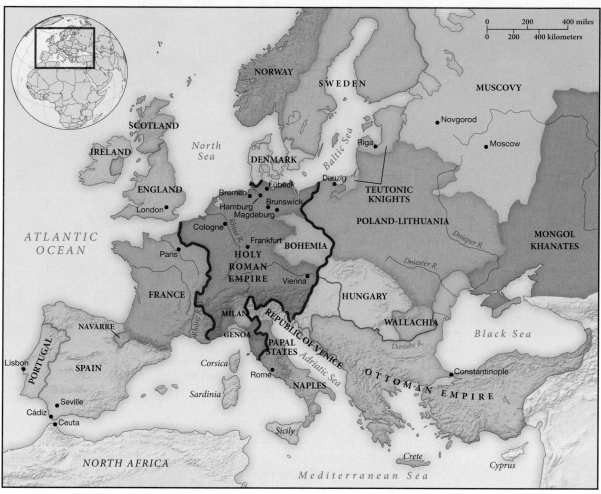

Map 12.2   Europe in 1500

By the end of the fifteenth century, Christian Europe had assumed its early modern political shape as a system of competing states threatened by an expanding Muslim Ottoman Empire.

mythology, and depictions of Islamic splendor. In the work of scholars, known as humanists, reflections on secular topics such as grammar, history, politics, poetry, rhetoric, and ethics complemented more religious matters. For example, Niccolò Machiavelli's (1469–1527) famous work *The Prince* was a prescription for political success based on the way politics actually operated in a highly competitive Italy of rival city-states rather than on idealistic and religiously based principles. To the question of whether a prince should be feared or loved, Machiavelli replied:

> One ought to be both feared and loved, but as it is difficult for the two to go together, it is much safer to be feared than loved. . . . For it may be said of men in general that they are ungrateful, voluble, dissemblers, anxious to avoid danger,

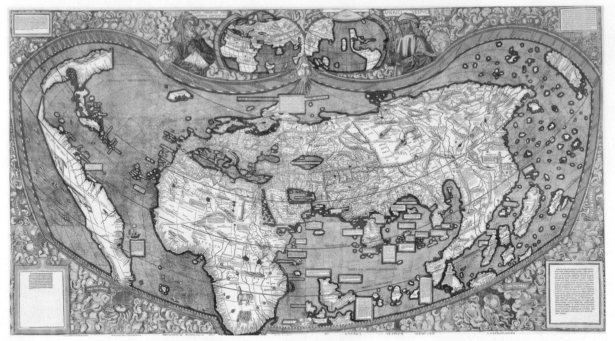

The Waldseemüller Map of 1507
Just fifteen years after Columbus landed in the Western Hemisphere, this map, which was created by the German cartographer Martin Waldseemüller, reflected a dawning European awareness of the planet's global dimensions and the location of the world's major landmasses. (bpk, Berlin/Staatsbibliothek zu Berlin, Stiftung Preussischer Kulturbesitz/Photo: Ruth Schacht/Art Resource, NY)

and covetous of gain. . . . Fear is maintained by dread of punishment which never fails. . . . In the actions of men, and especially of princes, from which there is no appeal, the end justifies the means.[6]

While the great majority of Renaissance writers and artists were men, among the remarkable exceptions to that rule was Christine de Pizan (1363–1430), the daughter of a Venetian official, who lived mostly in Paris. Her writings pushed against the misogyny of so many European thinkers of the time. In her *City of Ladies*, she mobilized numerous women from history, Christian and pagan alike, to demonstrate that women too could be active members of society and deserved an education equal to that of men. Aiding in the construction of this allegorical city is Lady Reason, who offers to assist Christine in dispelling her poor opinion of her own sex. "No matter which way I looked at it," she wrote, "I could find no evidence from my own experience to bear out such a negative view of female nature and habits. Even so . . . I could scarcely find a moral work by any author which didn't devote some chapter or paragraph to attacking the female sex."[7]

Heavily influenced by classical models, Renaissance figures were more interested in capturing the unique qualities of particular individuals and in describing the world as it was than in portraying or exploring eternal religious truths. In its focus on the affairs of this world, Renaissance culture reflected the urban bustle and commercial preoccupations of Italian cities. Its secular elements challenged the other-worldliness of Christian culture, and its individualism signaled the dawning of a more capitalist economy of private entrepreneurs. A new Europe was in the making, one more different from its own recent past than Ming dynasty China was from its pre-Mongol glory.

European Comparisons: Maritime Voyaging

A global traveler during the fifteenth century might be surprised to find that Europeans, like the Chinese, were also launching outward-bound maritime expeditions. Initiated in 1415 by the small country of Portugal, those voyages sailed ever farther down the west coast of Africa, supported by the state and blessed by the pope (see Map 12.3). As the century ended, two expeditions marked major breakthroughs, although few suspected it at the time. In 1492, Christopher Columbus, funded by Spain, Portugal's neighbor and rival, made his way west across the Atlantic hoping to arrive in the East and, in one of history's most consequential mistakes, ran into the Americas. Five years later, in 1497, Vasco da Gama launched a voyage that took him around the tip of South Africa, along the East African coast, and, with the help of a Muslim pilot, across the Indian Ocean to Calicut in southern India.

The differences between the Chinese and European oceangoing ventures were striking, most notably perhaps in terms of size. Columbus captained three ships and a crew of about 90, while da Gama had four ships, manned by perhaps 170 sailors. These were minuscule fleets compared to Zheng He's hundreds of ships and a crew in the many thousands. "All the ships of Columbus and da Gama combined," according to a recent account, "could have been stored on a single deck of a single vessel in the fleet that set sail under Zheng He."[8]

Motivation as well as size differentiated the two ventures. Europeans were seeking the wealth of Africa and Asia—gold, spices, silk, and more. They also were in search of Christian converts and of possible Christian allies with whom to continue their long crusading struggle against threatening Muslim powers. China, by contrast, faced no equivalent power, needed no military allies in the Indian Ocean basin, and required little that these regions produced. Nor did China possess an impulse to convert foreigners to its culture or religion, as the Europeans surely did. Furthermore, the confident and overwhelmingly powerful Chinese fleet sought neither conquests nor colonies, while the Europeans soon tried to monopolize by force the commerce of the Indian Ocean and violently carved out huge empires in the Americas.

The most striking difference in these two cases lay in the sharp contrast between China's decisive ending of its voyages and the continuing, indeed escalating, European effort, which soon brought the world's oceans and growing numbers of the world's people under its control. This is why Zheng He's voyages were so long neglected in China's historical memory. They led nowhere, whereas the initial

■ **Comparison**

In what ways did European maritime voyaging in the fifteenth century differ from that of China? What accounts for these differences?

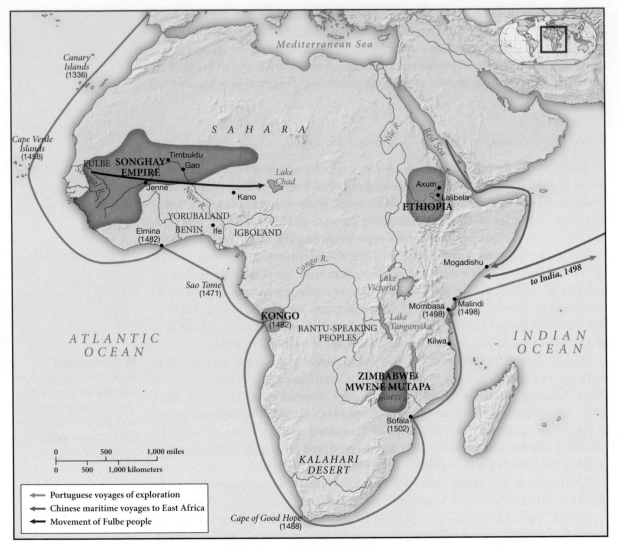

Map 12.3   Africa in the Fifteenth Century

By the fifteenth century, Africa was a virtual museum of political and cultural diversity, encompassing large empires, such as Songhay; smaller kingdoms, such as Kongo; city-states among the Yoruba, Hausa, and Swahili peoples; village-based societies without states at all, as among the Igbo; and pastoral peoples, such as the Fulbe. Both European and Chinese maritime expeditions touched on Africa during that century, even as Islam continued to find acceptance in the northern half of the continent.

European expeditions, so much smaller and less promising, were but the first steps on a journey to world power. But why did the Europeans continue a process that the Chinese had deliberately abandoned?

In the first place, Europe had no unified political authority with the power to order an end to its maritime outreach. Its system of competing states, so unlike

China's single unified empire, ensured that once begun, rivalry alone would drive the Europeans to the ends of the earth. Beyond this, much of Europe's elite had an interest in overseas expansion. Its budding merchant communities saw opportunity for profit; its competing monarchs eyed the revenue from taxing overseas trade or from seizing overseas resources; the Church foresaw the possibility of widespread conversion; impoverished nobles might imagine fame and fortune abroad. In China, by contrast, support for Zheng He's voyages was very shallow in official circles, and when the emperor Yongle passed from the scene, those opposed to the voyages prevailed within the politics of the court.

Finally, the Chinese were very much aware of their own antiquity, believed strongly in the absolute superiority of their culture, and felt with good reason that, should they desire something from abroad, others would bring it to them. Europeans too believed themselves unique, particularly in religious terms as the possessors of Christianity, the "one true religion." In material terms, though, they were seeking out the greater riches of the East, and they were highly conscious that Muslim power blocked easy access to these treasures and posed a military and religious threat to Europe itself. All of this propelled continuing European expansion in the centuries that followed.

The Chinese withdrawal from the Indian Ocean actually facilitated the European entry. It cleared the way for the Portuguese to penetrate the region, where they faced only the eventual naval power of the Ottomans. Had Vasco da Gama encountered Zheng He's massive fleet as his four small ships sailed into Asian waters in 1498, world history may well have taken quite a different turn. As it was, however, China's abandonment of oceanic voyaging and Europe's embrace of the seas marked different responses to a common problem that both civilizations shared—growing populations and land shortage. In the centuries that followed, China's rice-based agriculture was able to expand production internally by more intensive use of the land, while the country's territorial expansion was inland toward Central Asia. By contrast, Europe's agriculture, based on wheat and livestock, expanded primarily by acquiring new lands in overseas possessions, which were gained as a consequence of a commitment to oceanic expansion.

Civilizations of the Fifteenth Century: The Islamic World

Beyond the domains of Chinese and European civilization, our fifteenth-century global traveler would surely have been impressed with the transformations of the Islamic world. Stretching across much of Afro-Eurasia, the enormous realm of Islam experienced a set of remarkable changes during the fifteenth and early sixteenth centuries, as well as the continuation of earlier patterns. The most notable change lay in the political realm, for an Islamic civilization that had been severely fragmented since at least 900 now crystallized into four major states or empires (see Map 12.4). At the same time, a long-term process of conversion to Islam continued the cultural transformation of Afro-Eurasian societies both within and beyond these new states.

In the Islamic Heartland: The Ottoman and Safavid Empires

■ Comparison
What differences can you identify among the four major empires in the Islamic world of the fifteenth and sixteenth centuries?

The most impressive and enduring of the new Islamic states was the Ottoman Empire, which lasted in one form or another from the fourteenth to the early twentieth century. It was the creation of one of the many Turkic warrior groups that had migrated into Anatolia, slowly and sporadically, in the several centuries following 1000 C.E. By the mid-fifteenth century, these Ottoman Turks had already carved out a state that encompassed much of the Anatolian peninsula and had pushed deep into southeastern Europe (the Balkans), acquiring in the process a substantial Christian population. During the sixteenth century, the Ottoman Empire extended its control to much of the Middle East, coastal North Africa, the lands surrounding the Black Sea, and even farther into Eastern Europe.

The Ottoman Empire was a state of enormous significance in the world of the fifteenth century and beyond. In its huge territory, long duration, incorporation of many diverse peoples, and economic and cultural sophistication, it was one of the great empires of world history. In the fifteenth century, only Ming dynasty China and the Incas matched it in terms of wealth, power, and splendor. The empire represented the emergence of the Turks as the dominant people of the Islamic world, ruling now over many Arabs, who had initiated this new faith more than 800 years before. In adding "caliph" (successor to the Prophet) to their other titles, Ottoman sultans claimed the legacy of the earlier Abbasid Empire. They sought to bring a renewed unity to the Islamic world, while also serving as protector of the faith, the "strong sword of Islam."

The Ottoman Empire also represented a new phase in the long encounter between Christendom and the world of Islam. In the Crusades, Europeans had taken the aggressive initiative in that encounter, but the rise of the Ottoman Empire reversed their roles. The seizure of Constantinople in 1453 marked the final demise of Christian Byzantium and allowed Ottoman rulers to see themselves as successors to the Roman Empire. (See Zooming In: 1453 in Constantinople, page 518.) It also opened the way to further expansion in heartland Europe, and in 1529 a rapidly expanding Ottoman Empire laid siege to Vienna in the heart of Central Europe. The political and military expansion of Islam, at the expense of Christendom, seemed clearly under way. Many Europeans spoke fearfully of the "terror of the Turk."

In the neighboring Persian lands to the east of the Ottoman Empire, another Islamic state was also taking shape in the late fifteenth and early sixteenth centuries—the Safavid (SAH-fah-vihd) Empire. Its leadership was also Turkic, but in this case it had emerged from a Sufi religious order founded several centuries earlier by Safi al-Din (1252–1334). The long-term significance of the Safavid Empire, which was established in the decade following 1500, was its decision to forcibly

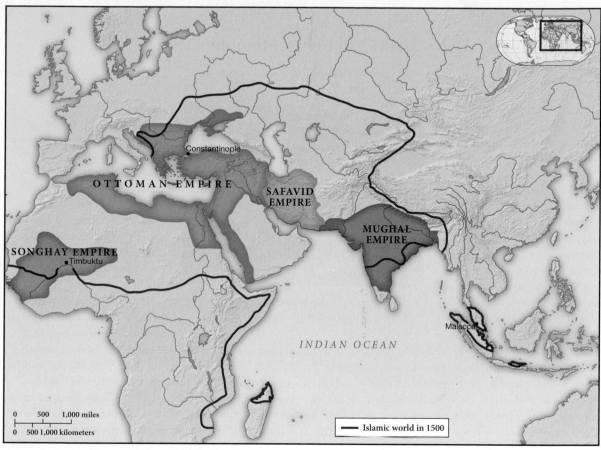

Map 12.4   Empires of the Islamic World

The most prominent political features of the vast Islamic world in the fifteenth and sixteenth centuries were four large states: the Songhay, Ottoman, Safavid, and Mughal empires.

impose a Shia version of Islam as the official religion of the state. Over time, this form of Islam gained popular support and came to define the unique identity of Persian (Iranian) culture.

This Shia empire also introduced a sharp divide into the political and religious life of heartland Islam, for almost all of Persia's neighbors practiced a Sunni form of the faith. For a century (1534–1639), periodic military conflict erupted between the Ottoman and Safavid empires, reflecting both territorial rivalry and sharp religious differences. In 1514, the Ottoman sultan wrote to the Safavid ruler in the most bitter of terms:

You have denied the sanctity of divine law . . . you have deserted the path of salvation and the sacred commandments . . . you have opened to Muslims the gates of tyranny and oppression . . . you have raised the standard of irreligion

1453 in Constantinople

On May 29, 1453, forces of the Muslim Ottoman sultan Mehmed II seized control of the great Christian city of Constantinople, an event that marked the final end of the Roman/ Byzantine Empire and the ascendency of the Ottoman Empire. In retrospect, this event acquired a certain air of inevitability about it, for the Byzantine Empire had been retreating for almost two centuries before the steady advance of the Ottomans. By 1453, that once-great empire, heir to all things Roman, had shrunk to little more than the city itself, with only some 50,000 inhabitants and 8,000 active defenders compared to a vast Ottoman army of 60,000 soldiers. And little was left of the fabled wealth of the city. But what later observers see as inevitable generally occurs only with great human effort and amid vast uncertainty about the outcome. So it was in Constantinople in 1453.

Constantine XI, the last Byzantine emperor, was well aware of the odds he faced. Yet his great city, protected by water on two sides and a great wall on a third, had repeatedly withstood many attacks and sieges. Furthermore, until the very end, he had hoped for assistance

Ottoman Turks storm the walls of Constantinople in 1453.

from Western Christians, even promising union with the Roman Church to obtain it. But no such help arrived, at least not in sufficient quantities to make a difference, though rumors of a fleet from Venice persisted. The internal problems of the Western powers as well as the long-standing hostility between Eastern Orthodoxy and Roman Catholicism ensured that Constantinople would meet its end alone.

On the Ottoman side, enormous effort was expended with no assurance of success. In 1451, a new sultan came to the throne of the Ottoman Empire, Mehmed II, only nineteen years old and widely regarded as not very promising. Furthermore, some among the court officials had reservations about an attack on Constantinople. But the young sultan seemed determined to gain the honor promised in Islamic prophesies going back to Muhammad himself to the one who conquered the city. Doing so could also rid him of a potential rival to the Ottoman throne, who had taken refuge in Constantinople.

photo: © ullstein bild/The Image Works

and heresy. . . . [Therefore] the *ulama* and our doctors have pronounced a sentence of death against you, perjurer and blasphemer.[9]

This Sunni/Shia hostility has continued to divide the Islamic world into the twenty-first century.

On the Frontiers of Islam: The Songhay and Mughal Empires

While the Ottoman and Safavid empires brought both a new political unity and a sharp division to the heartland of Islam, two other states performed a similar role on the expanding African and Asian frontiers of the faith. In the West African savan-

And so preparations began for an assault on the once-great city. The Ottomans assembled a huge fleet, gathered men and materials, and constructed a fortress to control access to Constantinople by water. In late 1452, Mehmed secured the services of a Hungarian master cannon builder named Orban, who constructed a number of huge cannons, one of which could hurl a 600-pound stone ball over a mile. These weapons subsequently had a devastating effect on the walls surrounding Constantinople. Interestingly enough, Orban had first offered his services to the Byzantine emperor, who simply could not afford to pay for this very expensive project.

In early April of 1453, the siege began, and it lasted for fifty-seven days. As required by Islamic law, Mehmed offered three times to spare the emperor and his people if they surrendered. Constantine apparently considered the offer seriously, but he finally refused, declaring, "We have all decided to die with our own free will." After weeks of furious bombardment, an ominous silence descended on May 28. Mehmed had declared a day of rest and prayer before the final assault the next day. That evening, the Byzantine emperor ordered a procession of icons and relics about the city and then entered the ancient Christian church of Hagia Sophia, seeking forgiveness for his sins and receiving Holy Communion.

And then, early the next day, the final assault began as Ottoman forces breached the walls of Constantinople and took the city. The Christians bravely defended their city, and Constantine discarded his royal regalia and died fighting like a common soldier. A later legend suggested that angels turned Constantine into marble and buried him in a nearby cave from which he would eventually reappear to retake the city for Christendom.

Islamic law required that soldiers be permitted three days of plundering the spoils, but Mehmed was reluctant, eager to spare the city he longed for as his capital. So he limited plundering to one day. Even so, the aftermath was terrible. According to a Christian eyewitness, "The enraged Turkish soldiers . . . gave no quarter. When they had massacred and there was no longer any resistance, they were intent on pillage and roamed through the town stealing, disrobing, pillaging, killing, raping, taking captive men, women, children, monks, priests."[10] When Mehmed himself entered the city, praying at the Christian altar of Hagia Sophia, he reportedly wept at seeing the destruction that had occurred.

Constantinople was now a Muslim city, capital of the Ottoman Empire, and Hagia Sophia became a mosque. A momentous change had occurred in the relationship between the world of Islam and that of Christendom.

Questions: What factors contributed to Mehmed's victory? Under what circumstances might a different outcome have been possible?

nas, the Songhay Empire rose in the second half of the fifteenth century. It was the most recent and the largest in a series of impressive states that operated at a crucial intersection of the trans-Saharan trade routes and that derived much of their revenue from taxing that commerce. Islam was a growing faith in Songhay but was limited largely to urban elites. This cultural divide within Songhay largely accounts for the religious behavior of its fifteenth-century monarch Sonni Ali (r. 1465–1492), who gave alms and fasted during Ramadan in proper Islamic style but also enjoyed a reputation as a magician and possessed a charm thought to render his soldiers invisible to their enemies. Nonetheless, Songhay had become a major center of Islamic learning and commerce by the early sixteenth century. A North African traveler known as Leo Africanus remarked on the city of Timbuktu:

Ottoman Janissaries
Originating in the fourteenth century, the Janissaries became the elite infantry force of the Ottoman Empire. Complete with uniforms, cash salaries, and marching music, they were the first standing army in the region since the days of the Roman Empire. When gunpowder technology became available, Janissary forces soon were armed with muskets, grenades, and handheld cannons. This Turkish miniature painting dates from the sixteenth century. (Turkish miniature, Topkapi Palace Library, Istanbul, Turkey/Album/Art Resource, NY)

Here are great numbers of [Muslim] religious teachers, judges, scholars, and other learned persons who are bountifully maintained at the king's expense. Here too are brought various manuscripts or written books from Barbary [North Africa] which are sold for more money than any other merchandise. . . . Here are very rich merchants and to here journey continually large numbers of negroes who purchase here cloth from Barbary and Europe. . . . It is a wonder to see the quality of merchandise that is daily brought here and how costly and sumptuous everything is.[11]

See Working with Evidence, Source 7.3, page 318, for more from Leo Africanus about West Africa in the early sixteenth century. Sonni Ali's successor made the pilgrimage to Mecca and asked to be given the title "Caliph of the Land of the Blacks." Songhay then represented a substantial Islamic state on the African frontier of a still-expanding Muslim world. (See the photo on page 305 for manuscripts long preserved in Timbuktu.)

The Mughal (MOO-guhl) Empire in India bore similarities to Songhay, for both governed largely non-Muslim populations. Much as the Ottoman Empire initiated a new phase in the interaction of Islam and Christendom, so too did the Mughal Empire continue an ongoing encounter between Islamic and Hindu civilizations. Established in the early sixteenth century, the Mughal Empire was the creation of yet another Islamized Turkic group, which invaded India in 1526. Over the next century, the Mughals (a Persian term for Mongols) established unified control over most of the Indian peninsula, giving it a rare period of political unity and laying the foundation for subsequent British colonial rule. During its first 150 years, the Mughal Empire, a land of great wealth and imperial splendor, undertook a remarkable effort to blend many Hindu groups and a variety of Muslims into an effective partnership. The inclusive policies of the early Mughal emperors showed that Muslim rulers could accommodate their overwhelmingly Hindu subjects in somewhat the same fashion as Ottoman authorities provided religious autonomy for their Christian minority. In southernmost India, however, the distinctly Hindu kingdom of Vijayanagara flourished in the fifteenth century, even as it borrowed architectural styles from the Muslim states of northern India and sometimes employed Muslim mercenaries in its military forces.

Together these four Muslim empires—Ottoman, Safavid, Songhay, and Mughal—brought to the Islamic world a greater measure of political coherence, military power, economic prosperity, and cultural brilliance than it had known since the early centuries of Islam. This new energy, sometimes called a "second flowering of Islam," impelled the continuing spread of the faith to yet new regions. The most prominent of these was oceanic Southeast Asia, which for centuries had been intimately bound up in the world of Indian Ocean commerce, while borrowing elements of both Hindu and Buddhist traditions. By the fifteenth century, that trading network was largely in Muslim hands, and the demand for Southeast Asian spices was mounting as the Eurasian world recovered from the devastation of Mongol conquest and the plague. Growing numbers of Muslim traders, many of them from India, settled in Java and Sumatra, bringing their faith with them. Eager to attract those traders to their port cities, a number of Hindu or Buddhist rulers along the Malay Peninsula and in Indonesia converted to Islam, while transforming themselves into Muslim sultans and imposing Islamic law. Thus, unlike in the Middle East and India, where Islam was established in the wake of Arab or Turkic conquest, in Southeast Asia, as in West Africa, it was introduced by traveling merchants and solidified through the activities of Sufi holy men.

The rise of Malacca, strategically located on the waterway between Sumatra and Malaya, was a sign of the times (see Map 12.1, page 506). During the fifteenth century, it was transformed from a small fishing village to a major Muslim port city. A Portuguese visitor in 1512 observed that Malacca had "no equal in the world. . . . Commerce between different nations for a thousand leagues on every hand must come to Malacca."[12] That city also became a springboard for the spread of Islam throughout the region. In the eclectic style of Southeast Asian religious history, the Islam of Malacca demonstrated much blending with local and Hindu/Buddhist traditions, while the city itself, like many port towns, had a reputation for "rough behavior." An Arab Muslim pilot in the 1480s commented critically: "They have no culture at all. . . . You do not know whether they are Muslim or not."[13] Nonetheless, Malacca, like Timbuktu on the West African frontier of an expanding Islamic world, became a center for Islamic learning, and students from elsewhere in Southeast Asia were studying there in the fifteenth century. As the more central regions of Islam were consolidating politically, the frontier of the faith continued to move steadily outward.

SUMMING UP SO FAR

In what ways did the civilizations of China, Europe, and the Islamic world in the fifteenth century seem to be moving in the same direction, and in what respects were they diverging from one another?

Civilizations of the Fifteenth Century: The Americas

Across the Atlantic, centers of civilization had long flourished in Mesoamerica and in the Andes. The fifteenth century witnessed new, larger, and more politically unified expressions of those civilizations, embodied in the Aztec and Inca empires. Both were the work of previously marginal peoples who had forcibly taken over and absorbed older cultures, giving them new energy, and both were decimated in the sixteenth century at the hands of Spanish conquistadores and their diseases. To conclude this global tour of world civilizations, we will send our intrepid traveler to the Western Hemisphere for a brief look at these American civilizations (see Map 12.5).

The Aztec Empire

■ **Comparison**

What distinguished the Aztec and Inca empires from each other?

The empire known to history as the Aztec state was largely the work of the Mexica (meh-SHEEH-kah) people, a semi-nomadic group from northern Mexico who had migrated southward and by 1325 had established themselves on a small island in Lake Texcoco. Over the next century, the Mexica developed their military capacity, served as mercenaries for more powerful people, negotiated elite marriage alliances with them, and built up their own capital city of Tenochtitlán. In 1428, a Triple Alliance between the Mexica and two other nearby city-states launched a highly aggressive program of military conquest, which in less than 100 years brought more of Mesoamerica within a single political framework than ever before. Aztec authorities, eager to shed their rather undistinguished past, now claimed descent from earlier Mesoamerican peoples such as the Toltecs and Teotihuacán.

With a core population recently estimated at 5 to 6 million people, the Aztec Empire was a loosely structured and unstable conquest state that witnessed frequent rebellions by its subject peoples. Conquered peoples and cities were required to provide labor for Aztec projects and to regularly deliver to their Aztec rulers

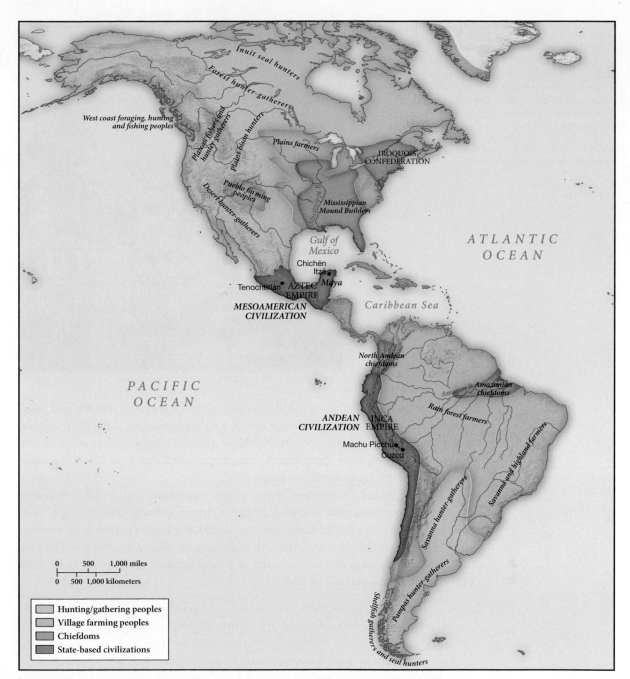

Map 12.5   The Americas in the Fifteenth Century

The Americas before Columbus represented a world almost completely separate from Afro-Eurasia. It featured similar kinds of societies, though with a different balance among them, but it largely lacked the pastoral economies that were so important in the Eastern Hemisphere.

Aztec Women
Within the home, Aztec women cooked, cleaned, spun and wove cloth, raised their children, and undertook ritual activities. Outside the home, they served as officials in palaces, priestesses in temples, traders in markets, teachers in schools, and members of craft workers' organizations. This domestic image comes from the sixteenth-century Florentine Codex, which was compiled by the Spanish but illustrated by Aztec artists. (Facsimile from Book IV of Florentine Codex, *General History of Things in New Spain*, 16th century, Mexico/Museo del Templo Mayor, Mexico City, Mexico/De Agostino Picture Library/Bridgeman Images)

impressive quantities of textiles and clothing, military supplies, jewelry and other luxuries, various foodstuffs, animal products, building materials, rubber balls, paper, and more. The process was overseen by local imperial tribute collectors, who sent the required goods on to Tenochtitlán, a metropolis of 150,000 to 200,000 people, where they were meticulously recorded.

That city featured numerous canals, dikes, causeways, and bridges. A central walled area of palaces and temples included a pyramid almost 200 feet high. Surrounding the city were "floating gardens," artificial islands created from swamplands that supported a highly productive agriculture. Vast marketplaces reflected the commercialization of the economy. A young Spanish soldier who beheld the city in 1519 described his reaction:

> Gazing on such wonderful sights, we did not know what to say, or whether what appeared before us was real, for on one side, on the land there were great cities, and in the lake ever so many more, and the lake was crowded with canoes, and in the causeway were many bridges at intervals, and in front of us stood the great city of Mexico.[14]

Beyond tribute from conquered peoples, ordinary trade, both local and long-distance, permeated Aztec domains. The extent of empire and rapid population growth stimulated the development of markets and the production of craft goods, particularly in the fifteenth century. Virtually every settlement, from the capital city to the smallest village, had a marketplace that hummed with activity during weekly market days. The largest was that of Tlatelolco, near the capital city, which stunned the Spanish with its huge size, its good order, and the immense range of goods available. Hernán Cortés, the Spanish conquistador who defeated the Aztecs, wrote that "every kind of merchandise such as can be met with in every land is for sale there, whether of food and victuals, or ornaments of gold and silver, or lead, brass, copper, tin, precious stones, bones, shells, snails and feathers."[15] Professional merchants, known as *pochteca*, were legally commoners, but their wealth, often exceeding that of the nobility, allowed them to rise in society and become "magnates of the land."

Among the "goods" that the pochteca obtained were slaves, many of whom were destined for sacrifice in the bloody rituals so central to Aztec religious life. Long a part of Mesoamerican and many other world cultures, human sacrifice assumed an unusually prominent role in Aztec public life and thought during the fifteenth century. Tlacaelel (1398–1480), who was for more than half a century a prominent official of the Aztec Empire, is often credited with crystallizing the ideology of state that gave human sacrifice such great importance.

In that cyclical understanding of the world, the sun, central to all life and identified with the Aztec patron deity Huitzilopochtli (wee-tsee-loh-pockt-lee), tended to lose its energy in a constant battle against encroaching darkness. Thus the Aztec world hovered always on the edge of catastrophe. To replenish its energy and thus postpone the descent into endless darkness, the sun required the life-giving force found in human blood. Because the gods had shed their blood ages ago in creating humankind, it was wholly proper for people to offer their own blood to nourish the gods in the present. The high calling of the Aztec state was to supply this blood, largely through its wars of expansion and from prisoners of war, who were destined for sacrifice. The victims were "those who have died for the god." The growth of the Aztec Empire therefore became the means for maintaining cosmic order and avoiding utter catastrophe. This ideology also shaped the techniques of Aztec warfare, which put a premium on capturing prisoners rather than on killing the enemy. As the empire grew, priests and rulers became mutually dependent, and "human sacrifices were carried out in the service of politics."[16] Massive sacrificial rituals, together with a display of great wealth, served to impress enemies, allies, and subjects alike with the immense power of the Aztecs and their gods.

Alongside these sacrificial rituals was a philosophical and poetic tradition of great beauty, much of which mused on the fragility and brevity of human life. Such an outlook characterized the work of Nezahualcoyotl (1402–1472), a poet and king of the city-state of Texcoco, which was part of the Aztec Empire:

> Truly do we live on Earth?
> Not forever on earth; only a little while here.
> Although it be jade, it will be broken.
> Although it be gold, it is crushed.
> Although it be a quetzal feather, it is torn asunder.
> Not forever on earth; only a little while here.[17]

■ **Description**
How did Aztec religious thinking support the empire?

The Inca Empire

While the Mexica were constructing an empire in Mesoamerica, a relatively small community of Quechua-speaking people, known to us as the Incas, was building the Western Hemisphere's largest imperial state along the entire spine of the Andes Mountains. Much as the Aztecs drew on the traditions of the Toltecs and Teoti-huacán, the Incas incorporated the lands and cultures of earlier Andean civiliza-tions: the Chavín, Moche, Wari, and Tiwanaku. The Inca Empire, however, was much larger than the Aztec state; it stretched some 2,500 miles along the Andes and contained perhaps 10 million subjects. Although the Aztec Empire controlled only part of the Mesoamerican cultural region, the Inca state encompassed practically the whole of Andean civilization during its short life in the fifteenth and early sixteenth centuries. In the speed of its creation and the extent of its territory, the Inca Empire bears some similarity to that of the Mongols.

Both the Aztec and Inca empires represent rags-to-riches stories in which quite modest and remotely located people very quickly created by military conquest the largest states ever witnessed in their respective regions, but the empires themselves were quite different. In the Aztec realm, the Mexica rulers largely left their con-quered people alone, if the required tribute was forthcoming. No elaborate admin-istrative system arose to integrate the conquered territories or to assimilate their people to Aztec culture.

■ **Description**
In what ways did Inca authorities seek to integrate their vast domains?

The Incas, on the other hand, erected a rather more bureaucratic empire. At the top reigned the emperor, an absolute ruler regarded as divine, a descendant of the creator god Viracocha and the son of the sun god Inti. Each of the some eighty provinces in the empire had an Inca governor. In theory, the state owned all land and resources, though in practice state lands, known as "lands of the sun," existed alongside properties owned by temples, elites, and traditional communities. At least in the central regions of the empire, subjects were grouped into hierarchical units of 10, 50, 100, 500, 1,000, 5,000, and 10,000 people, each headed by local officials, who were appointed and supervised by an Inca governor or the emperor. A sepa-rate set of "inspectors" provided the imperial center with an independent check on provincial officials. Births, deaths, marriages, and other population data were care-fully recorded on *quipus*, the knotted cords that served as an accounting device. A resettlement program moved one-quarter or more of the population to new loca-tions, in part to disperse conquered and no doubt resentful people and sometimes to reward loyal followers with promising opportunities. Efforts at cultural integra-tion required the leaders of conquered peoples to learn Quechua. Their sons were removed to the capital of Cuzco for instruction in Inca culture and language. Even now, millions of people from Ecuador to Chile still speak Quechua, and it is the official second language of Peru after Spanish.

But the sheer human variety of the Incas' enormous empire required great flex-ibility. In some places Inca rulers encountered bitter resistance; in others local elites were willing to accommodate Incas and thus benefit from their inclusion in the

Machu Picchu
Machu Picchu, high in the Andes Mountains, was constructed by the Incas in the fifteenth century on a spot long held sacred by local people. Its 200 buildings stand at some 8,000 feet above sea level, making it a "city in the sky." It was probably a royal retreat or religious center, rather than serving administrative, commercial, or military purposes. The outside world became aware of Machu Picchu only in 1911, when it was discovered by a Yale University archeologist. (fStop/Superstock)

empire. Where centralized political systems already existed, Inca overlords could delegate control to native authorities. Elsewhere they had to construct an administrative system from scratch. Everywhere they sought to incorporate local people into the lower levels of the administrative hierarchy. While the Incas required their subject peoples to acknowledge major Inca deities, these peoples were then largely free to carry on their own religious traditions. The Inca Empire was a fluid system that varied greatly from place to place and over time. It depended as much on the posture of conquered peoples as on the demands and desires of Inca authorities.

Like the Aztec Empire, the Inca state represented an especially dense and extended network of economic relationships within the "American web," but these relationships took shape in quite a different fashion. Inca demands on their conquered people were expressed, not so much in terms of tribute, but as labor service, known as *mita*, which was required periodically of every household. What people produced at home usually stayed at home, but almost everyone also had to work for the state. Some labored on large state farms or on "sun farms," which supported temples and religious institutions; others herded, mined, served in the military, or toiled on state-directed construction projects.

Those with particular skills were put to work manufacturing textiles, metal goods, ceramics, and stonework. The most well-known of these specialists were the "chosen women," who were removed from their homes as young girls, trained in Inca ideology, and set to producing corn beer and cloth at state centers. Later they were given as wives to men of distinction or sent to serve as priestesses in various temples, where they were known as "wives of the Sun." In return for such labor services, Inca ideology, expressed in terms of family relationships, required the state to arrange elaborate feasts at which large quantities of food and drink were consumed and to provide food and other necessities when disaster struck. Thus the authority of the state penetrated and directed Inca society and economy far more than did that of the Aztecs. (See Working with Evidence, Source 13.4, page 596, for an early Spanish account of Inca governing practices.)

If the Inca and Aztec civilizations differed sharply in their political and economic arrangements, they resembled each other more closely in their gender systems. Both societies practiced what scholars call "gender parallelism," in which "women and men operate in two separate but equivalent spheres, each gender enjoying autonomy in its own sphere."[18]

In both Mesoamerican and Andean societies, such systems had emerged long before their incorporation into the Aztec and Inca empires. In the Andes, men reckoned their descent from their fathers and women from their mothers, while Mesoamericans had long viewed children as belonging equally to their mothers and fathers. Parallel religious cults for women and men likewise flourished in both societies. Inca men venerated the sun, while women worshipped the moon, with matching religious officials. In Aztec temples, both male and female priests presided over rituals dedicated to deities of both sexes. Particularly among the Incas, parallel hierarchies of male and female political officials governed the empire, while in Aztec society, women officials exercised local authority under a title that meant "female person in charge of people." Social roles were clearly defined and different for men and women, but the domestic concerns of women — childbirth, cooking, weaving, cleaning — were not regarded as inferior to the activities of men. Among the Aztecs, for example, sweeping was a powerful and sacred act with symbolic significance as "an act of purification and a preventative against evil elements penetrating the center of the Aztec universe, the home."[19] In the Andes, men broke the ground, women sowed, and both took part in the harvest.

This was gender complementarity, not gender equality. Men occupied the top positions in both political and religious life, and male infidelity was treated more lightly than was women's unfaithfulness. As the Inca and Aztec empires expanded, military life, limited to men, grew in prestige, perhaps skewing an earlier gender parallelism. The Incas in particular imposed a more rigidly patriarchal order on their subject peoples. In other ways, the new Aztec and Inca rulers adapted to the gender systems of the people they had conquered. Among the Aztecs, the tools of women's work, the broom and the weaving spindle, were ritualized as weapons; sweeping the home was believed to assist men at war; and childbirth was regarded by women as "our kind of war."[20] Inca rulers replicated the gender parallelism of their subjects at a higher level, as the *sapay Inca* (the Inca ruler) and the *coya* (his female consort) governed jointly, claiming descent respectively from the sun and the moon.

Webs of Connection

Few people in the fifteenth century lived in entirely separate and self-contained communities. Almost all were caught up, to one degree or another, in various and overlapping webs of influence, communication, and exchange.[21] Perhaps most obvious were the webs of empire, large-scale political systems that brought together a variety of culturally different people. Christians and Muslims encountered each other directly in the Ottoman Empire, as did Hindus and Muslims in the Mughal Empire. And no empire tried more diligently to integrate its diverse peoples than the fifteenth-century Incas.

Religion too linked far-flung peoples, and divided them as well. Christianity provided a common religious culture for peoples from England to Russia, although the great divide between Roman Catholicism and Eastern Orthodoxy endured, and in the sixteenth century the Protestant Reformation would shatter permanently the Christian unity of the Latin West. Although Buddhism had largely vanished from its South Asian homeland, it remained a link among China, Korea, Tibet, Japan, and parts of Southeast Asia, even as it splintered into a variety of sects and practices. More than either of these, Islam actively brought together its many peoples. In the hajj, the pilgrimage to Mecca, Africans, Arabs, Persians, Turks, Indians, and many others joined as one people as they rehearsed together the events that gave birth to their common faith. And yet divisions and conflicts persisted within the vast realm of Islam, as the violent hostility between the Sunni Ottoman Empire and the Shia Safavid Empire so vividly illustrates.

Long-established patterns of trade among peoples occupying different environments and producing different goods were certainly much in evidence during the fifteenth century, as they had been for millennia. Hunting societies of Siberia funneled furs and other products of the forest into the Silk Road trading network traversing the civilizations of Eurasia. In the fifteenth century, some of the agricultural peoples in southern Nigeria were receiving horses brought overland from the drier regions of Africa to the north, where those animals flourished better. The Mississippi River in North America and the Orinoco and Amazon rivers in South America facilitated a canoe-borne commerce along those waterways. Coastal shipping in large seagoing canoes operated in the Caribbean and along the Pacific coast between Mexico and Peru. In Pacific Polynesia, the great voyaging networks across vast oceanic distances that had flourished especially since 1000 were in decline by 1500 or earlier, leading to the abandonment of a number of islands. Ecological devastation perhaps played a role, and some scholars believe that a cooling and fluctuating climate change known as the Little Ice Age created less favorable conditions

■ **Connection**
In what different ways did the peoples of the fifteenth century interact with one another?

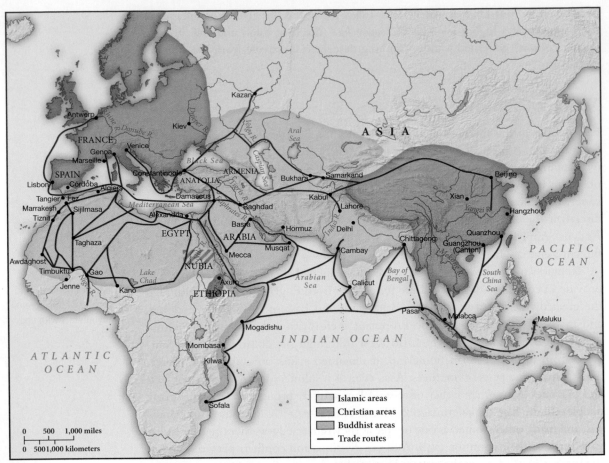

Map 12.6   Religion and Commerce in the Afro-Eurasian World

By the fifteenth century, the many distinct peoples and societies of the Eastern Hemisphere were linked to one another by ties of religion and commerce. Of course, most people were not directly involved in long-distance trade, and many people in areas shown as Buddhist or Islamic on the map practiced other religions. While much of India, for example, was ruled by Muslims, the majority of its people followed some form of Hinduism. And although Islam had spread to West Africa, that religion had not penetrated much beyond the urban centers of the region.

for inter-island exchange. The great long-distance trading patterns of the Afro-Eurasian world, in operation for a thousand years or more, continued in the fifteenth century, although the balance among them was changing (see Map 12.6). The Silk Road overland network, which had flourished under Mongol control in the thirteenth and fourteenth centuries, contracted in the fifteenth century as the Mongol Empire broke up and the devastation of the plague reduced demand for its products. The rise of the Ottoman Empire also blocked direct commercial contact between Europe and China, but oceanic trade from Japan, Korea, and China through the islands of Southeast Asia and across the Indian Ocean picked up considerably. Larger ships made it possible to trade in bulk goods such as grain as well as luxury products, while more sophisticated partnerships and credit mechanisms greased the wheels of commerce. A common Islamic culture over much of this vast region likewise smoothed the passage of goods among very different peoples, as it also did for the trans-Saharan trade.

A Preview of Coming Attractions: Looking Ahead to the Modern Era, 1500–2015

While ties of empire, culture, commerce, and disease surely linked many of the peoples in the world of the fifteenth century, none of those connections operated on a genuinely global scale. Although the densest webs of connection had been woven within the Afro-Eurasian zone of interaction, this huge region had no sustained ties with the Americas, and neither of them had sustained contact with the peoples of Pacific Oceania. That situation was about to change as Europeans in the sixteenth century and beyond forged a set of genuinely global relationships that generated sustained interaction among all of these regions. That huge process and the many outcomes that flowed from it marked the beginning of what world historians commonly call the modern age—the more than five centuries that followed the voyages of Columbus starting in 1492.

Over those five centuries, the previously separate worlds of Afro-Eurasia, the Americas, and Pacific Oceania became inextricably linked, with enormous consequences for everyone involved. Global empires, a global economy, global cultural exchanges, global migrations, global disease, global wars, and global environmental changes have made the past 500 years a unique phase in the human journey. Those webs of communication and exchange—the first defining feature of the modern era—have progressively deepened, so much so that by the end of the twentieth century few if any people lived beyond the cultural influences, economic ties, or political relationships of a globalized world.

Several centuries after the Columbian voyages, and clearly connected to them, a second distinctive feature of the modern era took shape: the emergence of a radically new kind of human society, first in Europe during the nineteenth century and then in various forms elsewhere in the world. The core feature of such societies was industrialization, with its sustained growth of technological innovation and its massive consumption of energy and raw materials. The human ability to create wealth made an enormous leap forward in a very short period of time, at least by world history standards. Accompanying this economic or industrial revolution was an equally distinctive and unprecedented jump in human numbers, a phenomenon that has affected not only human beings but also many other living species and the earth itself. (See Snapshot, page 532.)

Moreover, these modern societies were far more urbanized and much more commercialized than ever before, as more and more people began to work for wages, to produce for the market, and to buy the requirements of daily life rather

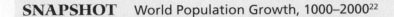

SNAPSHOT   World Population Growth, 1000–2000[22]

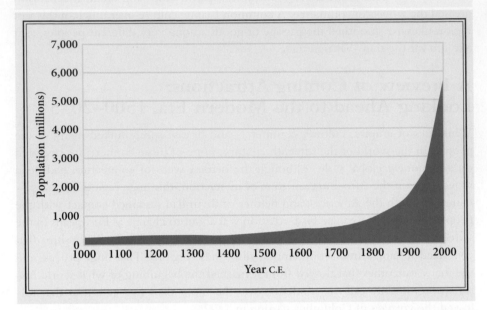

than growing or making those products for their own use. These societies gave prominence and power to holders of urban wealth—merchants, bankers, industrialists, educated professionals—at the expense of rural landowning elites, while simultaneously generating a substantial factory working class and diminishing the role of peasants and handicraft artisans.

Modern societies were generally governed by states that were more powerful and intrusive than earlier states and empires had been, and they offered more of their people an opportunity to play an active role in public and political life. Literacy in modern societies was far more widespread than ever before, while new national identities became increasingly prominent, competing with more local loyalties and with those of empire. To the mix of established religious ideas and folk traditions were now added the challenging outlook and values of modern science, with its secular emphasis on the ability of human rationality to know and manipulate the world. Modernity has usually meant a self-conscious awareness of living and thinking in new ways that deliberately departed from tradition.

This revolution of modernity, comparable in its pervasive consequences only to the Agricultural Revolution of some 10,000 years ago, introduced new divisions and new conflicts into the experience of humankind. The ancient tensions between rich and poor within particular societies were now paralleled by new economic inequalities among entire regions and civilizations and a much-altered global balance of power. The first societies to experience the modern transformation—those in Western Europe and North America—became both a threat and a source of envy to much of the rest of the world. As modern societies emerged and spread, they were enormously destructive of older patterns of human life, even as they gave rise to many new ways of living. Sorting out what was gained and what was lost during the modern transformation has been a persistent and highly controversial thread of human thought over the past several centuries.

A third defining feature of the last 500 years was the growing prominence of European peoples on the global stage. In ancient times, the European world, focused in the Mediterranean basin of Greek culture and the Roman Empire, was but one of several second-wave civilizations in the Eastern Hemisphere. After 500 C.E., Western Europe was something of a backwater, compared to the more prosperous and powerful civilizations of China and the Islamic world.

In the centuries following 1500, however, this western peninsula of the Eurasian continent became the most innovative, most prosperous, most powerful, most expansive, and most imitated part of the world. European empires spanned the globe. European peoples created new societies all across the Americas and as far away as South Africa, Australia, and New Zealand. Their languages were spoken and their Christian religion was widely practiced throughout the Americas and in parts of Asia and Africa. Their businessmen bought, sold, and produced goods around the world. It was among Europeans that the Scientific and Industrial Revolutions first took shape, with enormously powerful intellectual and economic consequences for the entire planet. The quintessentially modern ideas of liberalism, nationalism, feminism, and socialism all bore the imprint of their European origin. By the beginning of the twentieth century, Europeans or peoples of European descent exercised unprecedented influence and control over the earth's many other peoples, a wholly novel experience in human history.

For the rest of the world, growing European dominance posed a common challenge. Despite their many differences, the peoples of Asia, Africa, the Middle East, the Americas, and Pacific Oceania all found themselves confronted by powerful and intrusive Europeans. The impact of this intrusion and how various peoples responded to it—resistance, submission, acceptance, imitation, adaptation—represent critically important threads in the world history of the past five centuries.

REFLECTIONS

What If? Chance and Contingency in World History

Seeking meaning in the stories they tell, historians are inclined to look for deeply rooted or underlying causes for the events they recount. And yet, is it possible that, at least on occasion, historical change derives less from profound and long-term sources than from coincidence, chance, or the decisions of a few that might well have gone another way?

Consider, for example, the problem of explaining the rise of Europe to a position of global power in the modern era. What if the Great Khan Ogodei had not died in 1241, requiring the Mongol forces then poised for an assault on Germany to return to Mongolia? It is surely possible that Central and Western Europe might have been overrun by Mongol armies as so many other civilizations had been, a prospect that could have drastically altered the trajectory of European history. Or what if the Chinese had decided in 1433 to continue their huge maritime expeditions, creating an empire in the Indian Ocean basin and perhaps moving on to "discover" the Americas and Europe? Such a scenario suggests a wholly different future for world history than the one that in fact occurred. Or what if the forces of the Ottoman Empire had taken the besieged city of Vienna in 1529? Might they then have incorporated even larger parts of Europe into their expanding domain, requiring a halt to Europe's overseas empire-building enterprise?

None of this necessarily means that the rise of Europe was merely a fluke or an accident of history, but it does raise the issue of "contingency," the role of unforeseen or small events in the unfolding of the human story. An occasional "what if" approach to history reminds us that alternative possibilities existed in the past and that the only certainty about the future is that we will be surprised.

Second Thoughts

What's the Significance?

Paleolithic persistence, 500–2

Igbo, 502–3

Iroquois, 503–4

Timur, 504

Fulbe, 505

Ming dynasty China, 505–9

Zheng He, 507–9

European Renaissance, 510–13

Ottoman Empire, 516

seizure of Constantinople in 1453, 516, 518–19

Safavid Empire, 516–18

Songhay Empire, 518–20

Timbuktu, 519–20

Mughal Empire, 521

Malacca, 521–22

Aztec Empire, 522–25

Inca Empire, 526–29

Big Picture Questions

1. Assume for the moment that the Chinese had not ended their maritime voyages in 1433. How might the subsequent development of world history have been different? What value is there in asking this kind of "what if" or counterfactual question?

2. How does this chapter distinguish among the various kinds of societies contained in the world of the fifteenth century? What other ways of categorizing the world's peoples might work as well or better?

3. What common patterns might you notice across the world of the fifteenth century? And what variations in the historical trajectories of various regions can you identify?

4. **Looking Back:** What would surprise a knowledgeable observer from 500 or 1000 C.E., were he or she to make a global tour in the fifteenth century? What features of that earlier world might still be recognizable?

Next Steps: For Further Study

Terence N. D'Altroy, *The Incas* (2002). A history of the Inca Empire that draws on recent archeological and historical research.

Edward L. Dreyer, *Zheng He: China and the Oceans in the Early Ming Dynasty* (2006). The most recent scholarly account of the Ming dynasty voyages.

Halil Inalcik and Donald Quataert, *An Economic and Social History of the Ottoman Empire, 1300–1914* (1994). A classic study of the Ottoman Empire.

Robin Kirkpatrick, *The European Renaissance, 1400–1600* (2002). A beautifully illustrated history of Renaissance culture as well as the social and economic life of the period.

Charles C. Mann, *1491: New Revelations of the Americas before Columbus* (2005). A review of Western Hemisphere societies and academic debates about their pre-Columbian history.

J. R. McNeill and William H. McNeill, *The Human Web* (2003). A succinct account of the evolving webs or relationships among human societies in world history.

Michael Smith, *The Aztecs* (2003). A history of the Aztec Empire, with an emphasis on the lives of ordinary people.

"Italian Renaissance," http://www.history.com/topics/italian-renaissance. A History channel presentation of the European Renaissance, with a number of brief videos.

"Ming Dynasty," http://www.metmuseum.org/toah/hd/ming/hd_ming.htm. A sample of Chinese art from the Ming dynasty from the collection of the Metropolitan Museum of Art.

Islam and Renaissance Europe

The Renaissance era in Europe, roughly 1400 to 1600, represented the crystallization of a new civilization at the western end of Eurasia. In cultural terms, its writers and artists sought to link themselves to the legacy of the pre-Christian Greeks and Romans. But if Europeans were reaching back to their classical past, they were also reaching out—westward to the wholly new world of the Americas, southward to Africa, and eastward to Asia generally and the Islamic world in particular. The European Renaissance, in short, was shaped not only from within but also by its encounters with a wider world.

Interaction with the world of Islam was, of course, nothing new. Centuries of Muslim rule in Spain, the Crusades, and the expansion of the Ottoman Empire were markers in the long relationship of conflict, cooperation, and mutual influence between Christendom and the realm of Islam. Politically, that relationship was changing in the fifteenth century. The Christian reconquest of Spain from Muslim rule was completed by 1492. At the other end of the Mediterranean Sea, the Turkish Ottoman Empire was expanding into the previously Christian regions of the Balkans (southeastern Europe), seizing the ancient capital of the Byzantine Empire, Constantinople, in 1453, while becoming a major player in European international politics. Despite such conflicts, commerce flourished across political and religious divides. European bulk goods such as wool, timber, and glassware, along with silver and gold, were exchanged for high-value luxury goods from the Islamic world or funneled through it from farther east. These included spices, silks, carpets, tapestries, brocades, art objects, precious stones, gold, dyes, and pigments. In 1384, a Christian pilgrim from the Italian city of Florence wrote: "Really all of Christendom could be supplied for a year with the merchandise of Damascus."[23] And a fifteenth-century Italian nobleman said of Venice: "It seems as if all the world flocks here, and that human beings have concentrated there all their force for trading."[24]

The acquisition of such Eastern goods was important for elite Europeans as they sought to delineate and measure their emerging civilization. As that civilization began to take shape in the centuries after 1100 or so, it had drawn extensively on Arab or Muslim learning—in medicine, astronomy, philosophy, architecture, mathematics, business practices, and more. As early as the twelfth century, a Spanish priest and Latin translator of Arab texts wrote, "It befits us to imitate the Arabs, for they are as it were our teachers and the pio-neers." During the Renaissance centuries as well, according to a recent account, "Europe began to define itself by purchasing and emulating the opulence and cultured sophistication of the cities, merchants, scholars, and empires of the Ottomans, Persians, and the Egyptian Mamluks." That engagement with the Islamic world found various expressions in Renaissance art, as the images that follow illustrate.

The year 1453 marked a watershed in the long relationship between Christendom and the Islamic world, for it was in that year that the Ottoman sultan Mehmed II decisively conquered the great Christian city of Constan-tinople, bringing the thousand-year history of Byzantium to an inglorious end. To many Europeans, that event was a catastrophe and Mehmed was the "terror of the world." On hearing the news, one Italian bishop, later to become the pope, foresaw a dismal future for both the Church and West-ern civilization: "Who can doubt that the Turks will vent their wrath upon the churches of God? . . . This will be a second death to Homer and a second destruction of Plato." Others, however, saw opportunity. Less than a year after that event, the northern Italian city of Venice signed a peace treaty with the Ottoman sultan, declaring, "It is our intention to live in peace and friendship with the Turkish emperor." Some even expressed admiration for the con-quering Muslim ruler. George of Trebizond, a Greek-speaking Renaissance scholar, described Mehmed as "a wise king and one who philosophizes about the greatest matters."

For his part, Mehmed admired both classical and contemporary European culture, even as his armies threatened European powers. This cosmopolitan emperor employed Italian scholars to read to him from ancient Greek and Roman literature, stocked his library with Western texts, and decorated the walls of his palace with Renaissance-style frescoes. Seeing himself as heir to Roman imperial authority, he now added "Caesar" to his other titles. Although Islam generally prohibited the depiction of human figures, Mehmed's long interest in caricatures and busts and his desire to celebrate his many conquests led him to commission numerous medals by European artists, bearing his image. In 1480, he also had his portrait painted by the leading artist of Ven-ice, Gentile Bellini, who had been sent to the Ottoman court as a cultural ambassador of his city.

Source 12.1 shows Bellini's portrait of the emperor sitting under a marble arch, a symbol of triumph that evokes his dramatic conquest of Constanti-nople. The three golden crowns on the upper left and right likely represent the lands recently acquired for the Ottoman Empire, and the inscription at the bottom describes Mehmed as "Conqueror of the World." Not long after the painting was made, Mehmed died, and shortly thereafter his son and succes-sor sold it to Venetian merchants to help finance a large mosque complex. Thus the portrait returned to Venice.

National Gallery, London, UK/Bridgeman Images

Source 12.1 Gentile Bellini, Portrait of Mehmed II

- What overall impression of the sultan does this portrait convey?

- Why might this Muslim ruler want his portrait painted by a Christian artist from Venice?

- Why might Bellini and the city government of Venice be willing—even eager—to undertake the assignment, less than thirty years after the Muslim conquest of Constantinople?

■ The candelabra decorating the arch were a common feature in Venetian church architecture. Why might the sultan have agreed to this element of Christian symbolism in his portrait?

■ What does the episode surrounding this portrait indicate about the relationship of Venice and the Ottoman Empire in the wake of the conquest of Constantinople?

Venice had long been the primary point of commercial contact between Europe and the East and the source of the much-desired luxury goods that its merchants obtained from Alexandria in Egypt. At that time, Muslim Egypt was ruled by the Mamluks, a warrior caste of slave origins, who had checked the westward advance of the Mongols in 1260 and had driven the last of the European Crusaders out of the Middle East in 1291. Venetian traders, however, were more interested in commerce than in religion and by the fifteenth century enjoyed a highly profitable relationship with the Mamluk rulers of Egypt and Syria, despite the periodic opposition of the pope and threats of excommunication. Thus it is not surprising that the Renaissance artists of Venice were prominent among those who reflected the influence of the Islamic world in their work. By the late fifteenth century, something of a fad for oriental themes surfaced in Venetian pictorial art.

Source 12.2, painted by an anonymous Venetian artist in 1511, expresses this intense interest in the Islamic world. The setting is Damascus in Syria, then ruled by the Egyptian Mamluk regime. The local Mamluk governor of the city, seated on a low platform with an elaborate headdress, is receiving an ambassador from Venice, shown in a red robe and standing in front of the governor. Behind him in black robes are other members of the Venetian delegation, while in the foreground various members of Damascus society—both officials and merchants—are distinguished from one another by variations in their turbans. Behind the wall lies the city of Damascus with its famous Umayyad mosque, formerly a Roman temple to Jupiter and later a Christian church, together with its three minarets. The city's lush gardens and its homes with wooden balconies and rooftop terraces complete the picture of urban Islam.

■ What impressions of the city and its relationship with Venice does the artist seek to convey?

■ How are the various social groups of Damascus distinguished from one another in this painting? What does the very precise visual description of these differences suggest about Venetian understanding of urban Mamluk society?

■ What does the total absence of women suggest about their role in the public life of Damascus?

Louvre, Paris, France/Bridgeman Images

Source 12.2 The Venetian Ambassador Visits Damascus

■ How would you know that this is a Muslim city? What role, if any, does religion play in this depiction of the relationship between Christian Venice and Islamic Damascus?

Beyond political and commercial relationships, Europeans had long engaged with the Islamic world intellectually as well. Source 12.3 illustrates that engagement in a work by Girolamo da Cremona, a fifteenth-century Italian painter known for his "illuminations" of early printed books. Created in 1483 (only some forty years after the invention of the printing press in Europe), it served as the frontispiece for one of the first printed versions of Aristotle's writings, translated into Latin, along with commentaries by the twelfth-century Muslim scholar Ibn Rushd, better known in the West as Averroes.

Aristotle, of course, was the great Greek philosopher of the fourth century B.C.E. whose writings presented a systematic and rational view of the world, while commenting on practically every branch of knowledge. The legacy of Greek thought in general and Aristotle in particular passed into both the Christian and Islamic worlds. Ibn Rushd (1126–1198), who wrote voluminous commentaries on Aristotle's works and much else as well, lived in Muslim Spain, where he argued for the compatibility of Aristotelian philosophy and the religious perspectives of Islam. While that outlook faced growing

Source 12.3 Aristotle and Averroes

opposition in the Islamic world, Aristotle's writings found more fertile ground among European scholars in the new universities of the twelfth and thirteenth centuries, where they became the foundation of university curricula and nourished the growth of "natural philosophy." In large measure it was through translations of Ibn Rushd's Arabic commentaries on Aristotle that Europeans regained access to the thinking of that ancient philosopher. A long line of European scholars defined themselves as "Averroists."

The painting in Source 12.3 is presented as a parchment leaf, torn to disclose two worlds behind Aristotle's text. At the top in a rural setting, Aristotle, dressed in a blue robe, is speaking to Ibn Rushd, clad in a yellow robe with a round white turban. The bottom of the painting depicts the world of classical Greek mythology. The painted jewels, gems, and pearls testify to the great value placed on such illuminated and printed texts.

- What might the possession of such a book say about the social status, tastes, and outlook of its owner?

- What overall impression of Renaissance thinking about the classical world and the world of Islam does this painting convey?

- Notice the gestures of the two men at the top as well as the pen in Ibn Rushd's hand and the book at his feet. How might you describe the relationship between them?

- What made it possible for at least some European Christians of the Renaissance era to embrace both the pagan Aristotle and the Islamic Ibn Rushd?

Despite the fluid relationship of Renaissance Europe with the world of Islam, the Ottoman Empire, apparently expanding inexorably, was a growing threat to Christian Europe, and Islam was a false religion to many Christians. Those themes too found expression in the art of the Renaissance. Source 12.4 provides an example. Painted during the first decade of the sixteenth century by the Venetian artist Vittore Carpaccio, it reflects the popular "orientalist" style with its elaborate and exotic depiction of Eastern settings, buildings, and costumes. This particular painting was part of a series illustrating the life of Saint George, a legendary soldier-saint who rescued a Libyan princess, slew the dragon about to devour her, and by his courageous example converted a large number of pagans to Christianity. Earlier paintings in this series portrayed the killing of the dragon, while this one shows the conversion of the infidels to the "true faith."

The setting for Source 12.4 is Muslim-ruled Jerusalem, where the action focuses on Saint George, on the right, baptizing a bareheaded Muslim ruler and a woman (perhaps his wife). Several others await their turns below the steps, while a group of Mamluk musicians play in honor of the occasion.

By Vittore Carpaccio (ca. 1460–1523), 1501–1507/Scuola di San Giorgio degli Schiavoni, Venice, Italy/Giraudon/Bridgeman Images

Source 12.4 Saint George Baptizes the Pagans of Jerusalem

■ What posture toward the Islamic world does this painting represent? Does it convey resistance to Ottoman expansion, or does it hold out the hope for the peaceful conversion of that powerful empire?

■ What is the significance of the large Ottoman turban at the foot of the steps?

■ Why might the legend of Saint George provide a potent symbol for European interaction with the Islamic world in the circumstances of the early sixteenth century?

■ Compare this urban scene with that of Source 12.2. What common features do you notice? Apart from any religious meanings, what do these paintings suggest about Venetian interests in the Islamic world?

An even more vitriolic anti-Muslim sensibility had long circulated in Europe, based on the fear of Islamic power, the distortions growing out of the Crusades, and the perception of religious heresy. In the early fourteenth century, the Italian poet Dante, author of *The Divine Comedy*, placed Muhammad in the eighth circle of Hell, where the "sowers of discord" were punished and mutilated. To many Christians, Muhammad was a "false prophet," sometimes portrayed as drunk. Protestants such as Martin Luther on occasion equated their great enemy, the pope, with the Muslim "Turk," both of them leading people away from authentic religion.

The most infamous Renaissance example of hostility to Islam as a religion is displayed in Source 12.5, a fresco by the Italian artist Giovanni da Modena, painted on a church wall in the northern Italian city of Bologna in 1415. It was a small part of a much larger depiction of Hell, featuring a gigantic image of Satan devouring and excreting the damned, while many others endured horrific punishments. Among them was Muhammad—naked, bound to a rock, and tortured by a winged demon with long horns. It reflected common understandings of Muhammad as a religious heretic, a false prophet, and even the anti-Christ and therefore "hell-bound."

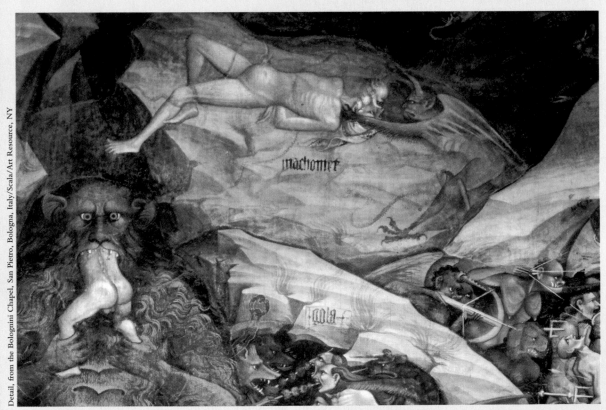

Detail, from the Bolognini Chapel, San Pietro, Bologna, Italy/Scala/Art Resource, NY

Source 12.5 Giovanni da Modena, Muhammad in Hell

- How does this fresco depict Hell? What does the larger context of the fresco as a whole suggest about Modena's view of Muhammad?

- How does this image differ from that of Source 12.4, particularly in its posture toward Islam?

- Italian Muslims have long objected to this image, noting that Islam portrays Jesus in a very positive light. In 2002 a radical group linked to al-Qaeda plotted unsuccessfully to blow up the church that housed this image in order to destroy the offending portrayal of their prophet. What particular objections do you imagine motivated Muslim opposition to this element of the fresco?

DOING HISTORY

Islam and Renaissance Europe

1. **Making comparisons:** What range of postures toward the Islamic world do these images convey? How might you account for the differences among them?

2. **Imagining reactions:** How might the artists who created the first four images respond to Source 12.5?

3. **Examining the content of visual sources:** While all of these images deal with the Islamic world, with what different aspects of that world are they concerned?

4. **Considering art and society:** In what ways were these images shaped by the concrete political, economic, and cultural conditions of Renaissance Europe? What role did the Islamic world play in the emerging identity of European civilization?

P A R T   F O U R

THE EARLY MODERN WORLD

1450–1750

Contents

DEBATING THE CHARACTER OF AN ERA

For the sake of clarity and coherence, historians often characterize a particular period of time in a brief phrase—the age of First Civilizations, the age of empires, the era of revolutions, and so on. Though useful and even necessary, such capsule descriptions leave a lot out and vastly oversimplify what actually happened. Historical reality is always more messy, more complicated, and more uncertain than any shorthand label can convey. Such is surely the case when we examine the three centuries spanning the years from roughly 1450 to 1750.

An Early Modern Era?

Those three centuries, which are addressed in Chapters 13 through 15, are conventionally labeled as "the early modern era." In using this term, historians are suggesting that during these three centuries we can find some initial signs or markers of the modern world, such as those described at the end of Chapter 12: the beginnings of genuine globalization, elements of distinctly modern societies, and a growing European presence in world affairs.

The most obvious expression of globalization, of course, lay in the oceanic journeys of European explorers and the European conquest and colonial settlement of the Americas. The Atlantic slave trade linked Africa permanently to the Western Hemisphere, while the global silver trade allowed Europeans to use New World precious metals to buy their way into ancient Asian trade routes. The massive transfer of plants, animals, diseases, and people, known to historians as the Columbian exchange, created wholly new networks of interaction across both the Atlantic and Pacific oceans, with enormous global implications. Missionaries carried Christianity far beyond Europe, allowing it to become a genuinely world religion, with a presence in the Americas, China, Japan, the Philippines, and south-central Africa. Other threads in the emerging global web were also woven as Russians marched across Siberia to the Pacific, as China expanded deep into Inner Asia, and as the Ottoman Empire encompassed much of the Middle East, North Africa, and southeastern Europe (see Chapter 13).

Scattered signs of what later generations thought of as "modernity" appeared in various places around the world. The most obviously modern cultural development took place in Europe, where the Scientific Revolution transformed, at least for a few people, their view of the world, their approach to knowledge, and their understanding of traditional Christianity. Demographically, China,

Japan, India, and Europe experienced the beginnings of modern population growth as Eurasia recovered from the Black Death and Mongol wars and as the foods of the Americas—corn and potatoes, for example—provided nutrition to support larger numbers. World population more than doubled between 1400 and 1800 (from about 374 million to 968 million), even as the globalization of disease produced a demographic catastrophe in the Americas and the slave trade limited African population growth. More highly commercialized economies centered in large cities developed in various parts of Eurasia and the Americas. By the early eighteenth century, for example, Japan was one of the most urbanized societies in the world, with Edo (Tokyo) housing more than a million inhabitants and ranking as the world's largest city. In China, Southeast Asia, India, and across the Atlantic basin, more and more people found themselves, sometimes willingly and at other times involuntarily, producing for distant markets rather than for the use of their local communities.

Stronger and more cohesive states represented yet another global pattern as they incorporated various local societies into larger units while actively promoting trade, manufacturing, and a common culture within their borders. France, the Dutch Republic, Russia, Morocco, the Mughal Empire, Vietnam, Burma, Siam, and Japan all represent this kind of state.[1] Their military power likewise soared as the "gunpowder revolution" kicked in around the world. Thus large-scale empires proliferated across Asia and the Middle East, while various European powers carved out new domains in the Americas. Within these empires, human pressures on the land intensified as forests were felled, marshes drained, and the hunting grounds of foragers and the grazing lands of pastoralists were confiscated for farming or ranching.

A Late Agrarian Era?

All of these developments give some validity to the notion of an early modern era. But this is far from the whole story, and it may be misleading if it suggests that European world domination and more fully modern societies were a sure thing, an inevitable outgrowth of early modern developments. In fact, that future was far from clear in 1750.

Although Europeans ruled the Americas and controlled the world's sea routes, their political and military power in mainland Asia and Africa was very limited. Eighteenth-century China and Japan strictly controlled the European missionaries and merchants who operated in their societies, and African authorities frequently set the terms under which the slave trade was conducted. Islam, not Christianity, was the most rapidly spreading faith in much of Asia and Africa, and in 1750 Europe, India, and China were roughly comparable in their manufacturing output. In short, it was not obvious that Europeans would soon dominate the planet. Moreover, populations and economies had surged at various points in the past, only to fall back again in a cyclical pattern. Nothing guaranteed that the early modern surge would be any more lasting than the others.

Nor was there much to suggest that anything approaching modern industrial society was on the horizon. Animal and human muscles, wind, and water still provided almost all of the energy that powered human economies. Handicraft techniques of manufacturing had nowhere been displaced by factory-based production or steam power. Long-established elites, not middle-class upstarts, everywhere provided leadership and enjoyed the greatest privileges, while rural peasants, not urban workers, represented the primary social group in the lower classes. Kings and nobles, not parliaments and parties, governed. Female subordination was assumed to be natural almost everywhere. While the texture of patriarchy varied among cultures and fluctuated over time, nowhere had ideas of gender equality taken root. Modern society, with its promise of liberation from ancient inequalities and from mass poverty, hardly seemed around the corner.

Most of the world's peoples, in fact, continued to live in long-established ways, and their societies operated according to traditional principles. Kings ruled most of Europe, and male landowning aristocrats remained at the top of the social hierarchy. Another change in ruling dynasties occurred in China, while that huge country affirmed Confucian values and a social structure that privileged landowning and office-holding elites, all of them men. Most Indians practiced some form of Hinduism and owed their most fundamental loyalty to local castes, even as South Asia continued its centuries-long incorporation into the Islamic world. The realm of Islam maintained its central role in the Eastern Hemisphere as the Ottoman Empire revived the political fortunes of Islam, and the religion sustained its long-term expansion into Africa and Southeast Asia.

In short, for the majority of humankind, the three centuries between 1450 and 1750 marked less an entry into the modern era than the continuing development of older agrarian societies. It was as much a late agrarian era as an early modern age. Persistent patterns rooted in the past characterized that period, along with new departures and sprouts of modernity. And change was not always in the direction of what we now regard as "modern." In European, Islamic, and Chinese societies alike, some people urged a return to earlier ways of living and thinking rather than embracing what was new and untried. Although Europeans were increasingly prominent on the world stage, they certainly did not hold all the leading roles in the global drama of these three centuries.

From this mixture of what was new and what was old during the early modern era, the three chapters that follow highlight the changes. Chapter 13 turns the spotlight on the new empires of those three centuries—European, Middle Eastern, and Asian. New global patterns of long-distance trade in spices, sugar, silver, fur, and slaves represent the themes of Chapter 14. New cultural trends—both within the major religious traditions of the world and in the emergence of modern science—come together in Chapter 15. With the benefit of hindsight, we may see many of these developments as harbingers of a modern world to come, but from the viewpoint of 1700 or so, the future was open and uncertain, as it almost always is.

MAPPING PART FOUR

North American
fur trade
Chapter 14

Britain's thirteen
colonies
Chapters 13, 15

Spain's American
Empire
Chapters 13, 15

Slave trade
Chapter 14

Potosí silver mines
Chapter 14

Brazil / Portuguese
Empire
Chapters 14, 15

Islamic penetration of Europe
Chapter 13

Protestant Reformation
Chapter 15

Ottoman Empire
Chapter 13

Russian Empire / fur trade
Chapter 14

Scientific Revolution
Chapter 15

Mughal Empire
Chapter 13

Tokugawa
shogunate
Chapter 13

Chinese imperial expansion
Chapter 13

Spanish Philippines
Chapter 14

Wahhabi Islam
Chapter 15

Kongo
Chapter 14

British East India
Company
Chapter 14

Dutch East India
Company
Chapter 14

Dutch colonial
settlement
Chapter 14

Illustration from the *Padshahnama*, ca. 1630–1640 (bodycolour with gold on paper)/Royal Collection Trust © Her Majesty Queen Elizabeth II, 2014/Bridgeman Images

CHAPTER 13

Political Transformations

Empires and Encounters
1450–1750

"What he [Vladimir Putin] wants to do, you can just see the lust in his eyes, he wants to re-create the Russian empire, and this move on Crimea is his first step." So said U.S. senator Bill Nelson in March of 2014, referring to the Russian president's actions in seizing Crimea and in pressuring Ukraine to remain within a Russian sphere of influence. In reflecting on this very current political situation, the senator, and many others as well, invoked the Russian Empire, which had taken shape during the early modern era. In the same vein, commentators on the economic and political resurgence of twenty-first-century Turkey often refer to it as an effort "to rebuild the Ottoman Empire," likewise a creation of the early modern era.[1] In such ways, the memories of these earlier empires continue to shape understanding of current events and perhaps to inspire actions in the present as well.

As these comments imply, empire building has been largely discredited during the twentieth and twenty-first centuries, and "imperialist" has become a term of insult rather than a source of pride. How very different were the three centuries (1450–1750) of the early modern era, when empire building was a global process! In the Americas, the Aztec and Inca empires flourished before they were incorporated into the rival empires of the Spanish, Portuguese, British, French, and Dutch, constructed all across the Western Hemisphere. Within those imperial systems, vast transformations took place: old societies were destroyed, and new societies arose as Native Americans, Europeans, and Africans came into sustained contact with one another for the first time in world history.

The Mughal Empire Among the most magnificent of the early modern empires was that of the Mughals in India. In this painting by an unknown Mughal artist, the seventeenth-century emperor Shah Jahan is holding a *durbar*, or ceremonial assembly, in the audience hall of his palace. The material splendor of the setting shows the immense wealth of the court, while the halo around Shah Jahan's head indicates the special spiritual grace or enlightenment associated with emperors.

It was a revolutionary encounter with implications that extended far beyond the Americas themselves.

But European empires in the Americas were not alone on the imperial stage of the early modern era. Across the immense expanse of Siberia, the Russians constructed what was then the world's largest territorial empire, making Russia an Asian as well as a European power. Qing (chihng) dynasty China penetrated deep into Inner Asia, doubling the size of the country while incorporating millions of non-Chinese people who practiced Islam, Buddhism, or animistic religions. On the South Asian peninsula, the Islamic Mughal Empire brought Hindus and Muslims into a closer relationship than ever before, sometimes quite peacefully and at other times with great conflict. In the Middle East, the Turkish Ottoman Empire reestablished something of the earlier political unity of heartland Islam and posed a serious military and religious threat to European Christendom.

SEEKING THE MAIN POINT

In what ways did European empires in the Americas resemble their Russian, Chinese, Mughal, and Ottoman counterparts, and in what respects were they different? Do you find the similarities or the differences more striking?

Thus the early modern era was an age of empire. Within their borders, those empires mixed and mingled diverse peoples in a wide variety of ways. Those relationships represented a new stage in the globalization process and new arenas of cross-cultural encounter. The transformations they set in motion echo still in the twenty-first century.

European Empires in the Americas

Among the early modern empires, those of Western Europe were distinctive because the conquered territories lay an ocean away from the imperial heartland, rather than adjacent to it. Following the breakthrough voyages of Columbus, the Spanish focused their empire-building efforts in the Caribbean and then, in the early sixteenth century, turned to the mainland, with stunning conquests of the powerful but fragile Aztec and Inca empires. Meanwhile, the Portuguese established themselves along the coast of present-day Brazil. In the early seventeenth century, the British, French, and Dutch launched colonial settlements along the eastern coast of North America. From these beginnings, Europeans extended their empires to encompass most of the Americas, at least nominally, by the mid-eighteenth century (see Map 13.1). It was a remarkable achievement. What had made it possible?

The European Advantage

■ Connection
What enabled Europeans to carve out huge empires an ocean away from their homelands?

Geography provides a starting point for explaining Europe's American empires. Countries on the Atlantic rim of Europe (Portugal, Spain, Britain, and France) were simply closer to the Americas than were any potential Asian competitors. Furthermore, the fixed winds of the Atlantic blew steadily in the same direction. Once these air currents were understood and mastered, they provided a far different maritime environment than the alternating monsoon winds of the Indian Ocean, in

A MAP OF TIME

1453	Ottoman conquest of Constantinople
1464–1591	Songhay Empire in West Africa
1480	Russia emerges from Mongol rule
1494	Treaty of Tordesillas divides the Americas between Spain and Portugal
1501	Safavid Empire established in Persia/Iran
1519–1521	Spanish conquest of Aztec Empire
1526	Mughal Empire established in India
1529	Ottoman siege of Vienna
1530s	First Portuguese plantations in Brazil
1532–1540	Spanish conquest of Inca Empire
1550	Russian expansion across Siberia begins
1565	Spanish takeover of Philippines begins
1607	Jamestown, Virginia: first permanent English settlement in Americas
1608	French colony established in Quebec
1680–1760	Chinese expansion into Inner Asia
1683	Second Ottoman siege of Vienna
After 1707	Fragmentation of Mughal Empire

which Asian powers had long operated. European innovations in mapmaking, navigation, sailing techniques, and ship design—building on earlier models from the Mediterranean, Indian Ocean, and Chinese regions—likewise enabled Europeans to penetrate the Atlantic Ocean. The enormously rich markets of the Indian Ocean world provided little incentive for its Chinese, Indian, or Muslim participants to venture much beyond their own waters.

Europeans, however, were powerfully motivated to do so. After 1200 or so, European elites were increasingly aware of their region's marginal position in the rich world of Eurasian commerce and were determined to gain access to that world. Once the Americas were discovered, windfalls of natural resources, including highly productive agricultural lands, drove further expansion, ultimately underpinning the long-term growth of the European economy into the nineteenth and twentieth centuries. Beyond these economic or ecological stimuli, rulers were driven by the enduring rivalries of competing states. The growing and relatively independent merchant class in a rapidly commercializing Europe sought direct access to Asian wealth

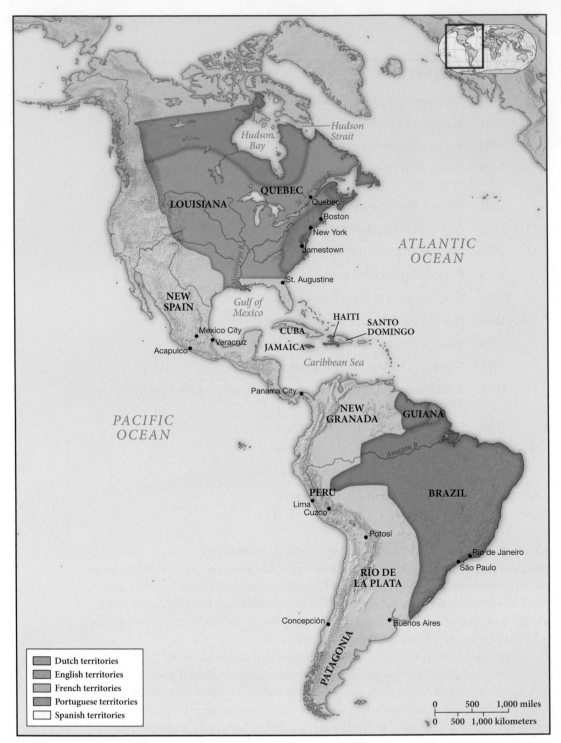

Map 13.1 European Colonial Empires in the Americas

By the beginning of the eighteenth century, European powers had laid claim to most of the Western Hemisphere. Their wars and rivalries during that century led to an expansion of Spanish and English claims, at the expense of the French.

to avoid the reliance on Muslim intermediaries that they found so distasteful. Impoverished nobles and commoners alike found opportunity for gaining wealth and status in the colonies. Missionaries and others were inspired by crusading zeal to enlarge the realm of Christendom. Persecuted minorities were in search of a new start in life. All of these compelling motives drove the relentlessly expanding imperial frontier in the Americas. Summarizing their intentions, one Spanish conquistador declared: "We came here to serve God and the King, and also to get rich."[2]

In carving out these empires, often against great odds and with great difficulty, Europeans nonetheless bore certain advantages, despite their distance from home. Their states and trading companies enabled the effective mobilization of both human and material resources. Their seafaring technology, built on Chinese and Islamic precedents, allowed them to cross the Atlantic with growing ease, transporting people and supplies across great distances. Their ironworking technology, gunpowder weapons, and horses initially had no parallel in the Americas, although many peoples subsequently acquired them.

Divisions within and between local societies provided allies for the determined European invaders. Various subject peoples of the Aztec Empire, for example, resented Mexica domination and willingly joined Hernán Cortés in the Spanish assault on that empire. In the final attack on the Aztec capital of Tenochtitlán, Cortés's forces contained fewer than 1,000 Spaniards and many times that number of Tlaxcalans, former subjects of the Aztecs. After their defeat, tens of thousands of Aztecs themselves joined Cortés as he carved out a Spanish Mesoamerican empire far larger than that of the Aztecs. (See Zooming In: Doña Marina, page 558.) Much of the Inca elite, according to a recent study, "actually welcomed the Spanish invaders as liberators and willingly settled down with them to share rule of Andean farmers and miners."[3] A violent dispute between two rival contenders for the Inca throne, the brothers Atahualpa and Huáscar, certainly helped the European invaders recruit allies to augment their own minimal forces. In short, Spanish military victories were not solely of their own making, but the product of alliances with local peoples, who supplied the bulk of the Europeans' conquering armies.

Perhaps the most significant of European advantages lay in their germs and diseases, with which Native Americans had no familiarity. Those diseases decimated society after society, sometimes in advance of the Europeans' actual arrival. In particular regions such as the Caribbean, Virginia, and New England, the rapid buildup of immigrant populations, coupled with the sharply diminished native numbers, allowed Europeans to actually outnumber local peoples within a few decades.

The Great Dying and the Little Ice Age

Whatever combination of factors explains the European acquisition of empires in the Americas, there is no doubting their global significance. Chief among the consequences was the demographic collapse of Native American societies. Although precise figures remain the subject of much debate, scholars generally agree that the

Doña Marina: Between Two Worlds

In her brief life, she was known variously as Malinal, Doña Marina, and La Malinche.[4] By whatever name, she was a woman who experienced the encounter of the Old World and the New in particularly intimate ways, even as she became a bridge between them. Born around 1505, Malinal was the daughter of an elite and cultured family in the borderlands between the Maya and Aztec cultures in what is now southern Mexico. Two dramatic events decisively shaped her life. The first occurred when her father died and her mother remarried, bearing a son to her new husband. To protect this boy's inheritance, Malinal's family sold her into slavery. Eventually, she came into the possession of a Maya chieftain in Tabasco on the Gulf of Mexico.

Here her second life-changing event took place in March 1519, when the Spanish conquistador Hernán Cortés landed his troops and inflicted a sharp military defeat on Tabasco. In the negotiations that followed, Tabasco authorities gave lavish gifts to the Spanish, including twenty women, one of whom was Malinal.

Doña Marina (center left) translating for Cortés.

Described by Bernal Díaz, one of Cortés's associates, as "good-looking, intelligent, and self-assured," the teenage Malinal soon found herself in service to Cortés himself. Since Spanish men were not supposed to touch non-Christian women, these newcomers were distributed among his officers, quickly baptized, and given Christian names. Thus Malinal became Doña Marina.

With a ready ear for languages and already fluent in Mayan and Nahuatl, the language of the Aztecs, Doña Marina soon picked up Spanish and quickly became indispensable to Cortés as an interpreter, cross-cultural broker, and strategist. She accompanied him on his march inland to the Aztec capital, Tenochtitlán, and on several occasions her language skills and cultural awareness allowed her to uncover spies and plots that might well have seriously impeded Cortés's defeat of the Aztec Empire. Díaz reported that "Doña Marina, who understood full well what was happening, told [Cortés] what

photo: Biblioteca Nacional Madrid/Giraudon/Bridgeman Images

pre-Columbian population of the Western Hemisphere was substantial, perhaps 60 to 80 million. The greatest concentrations of people lived in the Mesoamerican and Andean zones, which were dominated by the Aztec and Inca empires. Long isolation from the Afro-Eurasian world and the lack of most domesticated animals meant the absence of acquired immunities to Old World diseases such as smallpox, measles, typhus, influenza, malaria, and, later, yellow fever.

Therefore, when Native American peoples came into contact with these European and African diseases, they died in appalling numbers, in many cases losing up to 90 percent of the population. As one recent historian has noted, "It was as if the suffering these diseases had caused in Eurasia over the past millennia were concentrated into the span of decades."[5] The densely settled peoples of Caribbean islands

was going on." In the Aztec capital, where Cortés took the emperor Moctezuma captive, it fell to Doña Marina to persuade him to accept this humiliating position and surrender his wealth to the Spanish. Even Cortés, who was never very gracious with his praise for her, acknowledged that "after God, we owe this conquest of New Spain to Doña Marina." Aztecs soon came to see this young woman as the voice of Cortés, referring to her as La Malinche, a Spanish approximation of her original name. So paired did Cortés and La Malinche become in Aztec thinking that Cortés himself was often called "Malinche."

More than an interpreter for Cortés, Doña Marina also became his mistress and bore him a son. But after the initial conquest of Mexico was complete and he no longer needed her skills, Cortés married Doña Marina off to another Spanish conquistador, Juan Jaramillo, with whom she lived until her death, probably around 1530. Cortés did provide her with several pieces of land, one of which, ironically, had belonged to Moctezuma. Her son, however, was taken from her and raised in Spain.

In 1523, Doña Marina performed one final service for Cortés, accompanying him on a mission to Honduras to suppress a rebellion. There her personal life seemed to come full circle, for near her hometown she encountered her mother, who had sold her into slavery, and her half brother. Díaz reported that they "were very much afraid of Doña Marina," thinking that they would surely be put to death by their now-powerful and well-connected relative. But in a replay of the biblical story of Joseph and his brothers, Doña Marina quickly reassured and forgave them, while granting them "many golden jewels and some clothes."

In the centuries since her death, Doña Marina has been highly controversial. For much of the colonial era, she was viewed positively as an ally of the Spanish. But after independence, some came to see her as a traitor to her own people, shunning her heritage and siding with the invaders. Still others have considered her as the mother of Mexico's mixed-race, or mestizo, culture. Should she be understood primarily as a victim or as a skillful survivor negotiating hard choices under difficult circumstances?

Whatever the judgments of later generations, Doña Marina herself seems to have made a clear choice to cast her lot with the Europeans. Even when Cortés had given her to another man, Doña Marina expressed no regret. According to Díaz, she declared, "Even if they were to make me mistress of all the provinces of New Spain, I would refuse the honor, for I would rather serve my husband and Cortés than anything else in the world."

Questions: How might you define the significance of Doña Marina's life? In what larger contexts might that life find a place?

---

virtually vanished within fifty years of Columbus's arrival. Central Mexico, with a population estimated at some 10 to 20 million before the Spanish conquest, declined to about 1 million by 1650. A native Nahuatl (nah-watl) account depicted the social breakdown that accompanied the smallpox pandemic: "A great many died from this plague, and many others died of hunger. They could not get up to search for food, and everyone else was too sick to care for them, so they starved to death in their beds."[6]

The situation was similar in Dutch and British territories of North America. A Dutch observer in New Netherland (later New York) reported in 1656 that "the Indians . . . affirm that before the arrival of the Christians, and before the small pox broke out amongst them, they were ten times as numerous as they are now, and that their population had been melted down by this disease, whereof nine-tenths of them have died."[7] To Governor Bradford of Plymouth colony (in present-day Massachusetts), such conditions represented the "good hand of God" at work, "sweeping away great multitudes of the natives . . . that he might make room for us."[8] Not until the late seventeenth century did native numbers begin to recuperate somewhat from this catastrophe, and even then, they did not recover everywhere.

As the Great Dying took hold in the Americas, it interacted with another natural phenomenon, this time one of genuinely global proportions. Known as the Little Ice Age, it was a period of unusually cool temperatures that spanned much of the early modern period, most prominently in the Northern Hemisphere. Scholars continue to debate its causes. Some have suggested a low point in sunspot activity, leading to less intense solar irradiation of the earth, while others have argued that the chief cause was volcanic eruptions, whose ash and gases blocked the sun's warming energy in the upper atmosphere. More recently, some scientists have linked the Little Ice Age to the demographic collapse in the Americas. The Great Dying, they argue, resulted in the desertion of large areas of Native American farmland and ended the traditional practices of forest management through burning in many regions. These changes sparked a resurgence of plant life, which in turn took large amounts of carbon dioxide, a greenhouse gas, out of the atmosphere, contributing to global cooling. Whatever the causes, shorter growing seasons and less hospitable weather conditions adversely affected food production in regions across the globe.

While the onset, duration, and effects of the Little Ice Age varied from region to region, the impact of a cooler climate reached its peak in many regions in the mid-seventeenth century, helping to spark what scholars term the General Crisis. Much of China, Europe, and North America experienced record or near-record cold winters during this period. Regions near the equator in the tropics and Southern Hemisphere also experienced extreme conditions and irregular rainfall, resulting, for instance, in the growth of the Sahara Desert. Wet, cold summers reduced harvests dramatically in Europe, while severe droughts ruined crops in many other regions, especially China, which suffered its worst years of drought in the previous five centuries between 1637 and 1641. Difficult weather conditions accentuated other stresses in societies, leading to widespread famines, epidemics, uprisings, and wars in which millions perished. Eurasia did not escape lightly from these stresses: the collapse of the Ming dynasty in China, nearly constant warfare in Europe, and civil war in Mughal India all occurred in the context of the General Crisis, which only fully subsided when more favorable weather patterns returned in the eighteenth century.

Nor were the Americas, already devastated by the Great Dying, spared the suffering that accompanied the Little Ice Age and the General Crisis of the seventeenth century. In central Mexico, heartland of the Aztec Empire and the center of Spanish colonial rule in the area, severe drought in the five years after 1639 sent the price of maize skyrocketing, left granaries empty and many people without water, and prompted an unsuccessful plot to declare Mexico's independence from Spain.

Continuing drought years in the decades that followed witnessed repeated public processions of the statue of Our Lady of Guadalupe, who had gained a reputation for producing rain. The Caribbean region during the 1640s experienced the opposite condition — torrential rains that accompanied more frequent El Niño weather patterns — which provided ideal conditions for the breeding of mosquitoes that carried both yellow fever and malaria. A Maya chronicle for 1648 noted, "There was bloody vomit and we began to die."[9]

Like the Great Dying, the General Crisis reminds us that climate often plays an important role in shaping human history. But it also reminds us that human activity — the importation of deadly diseases to the Americas, in this case — may also help shape the climate, and that this has been true long before the twenty-first century.

The Columbian Exchange

In sharply diminishing the population of the Americas, the Great Dying and the impact of the Little Ice Age created an acute labor shortage and certainly did make room for immigrant newcomers, both colonizing Europeans and enslaved Africans. Over the several centuries of the colonial era and beyond, various combinations of indigenous, European, and African peoples created entirely new societies in the Americas, largely replacing the many and varied cultures that had flourished before 1492. To those colonial societies, Europeans and Africans brought not only their

germs and their people but also their plants and animals. Wheat, rice, sugarcane, grapes, and many garden vegetables and fruits, as well as numerous weeds, took hold in the Americas, where they transformed the landscape and made possible a recognizably European diet and way of life. Even more revolutionary were their animals — horses, pigs, cattle, goats, sheep — all of which were new to the Americas and multiplied spectacularly in an environment largely free of natural predators. These domesticated animals made possible the ranching economies and cowboy cultures of both North and South America. Horses also transformed many Native American societies, particularly in the North American West as settled farming peoples such

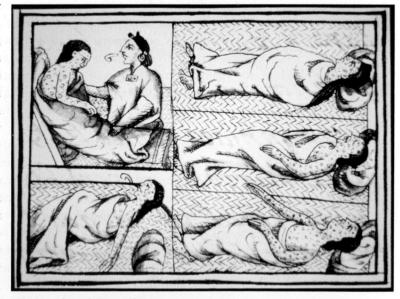

Disease and Death among the Aztecs
Smallpox, which accompanied the Spanish to the Americas, devastated native populations. This image, drawn by an Aztec artist and contained in the sixteenth-century *Florentine Codex*, illustrates the impact of the disease in Mesoamerica. (Private Collection/Peter Newark American Pictures/Bridgeman Images)

as the Pawnee abandoned their fields to hunt bison from horseback. In the process, women lost much of their earlier role as food producers as a male-dominated hunting and warrior culture emerged. Both environmentally and socially, these changes were nothing less than revolutionary.

■ Change
What large-scale transformations did European empires generate?

In the other direction, American food crops such as corn, potatoes, and cassava spread widely in the Eastern Hemisphere, where they provided the nutritional foundation for the immense population growth that became everywhere a hallmark of the modern era. In Europe, calories derived from corn and potatoes helped push human numbers from some 60 million in 1400 to 390 million in 1900. Those Amerindian crops later provided cheap and reasonably nutritious food for millions of industrial workers. Potatoes, especially, allowed Ireland's population to grow enormously and then condemned many of the Irish to starvation or emigration when an airborne fungus, also from the Americas, destroyed the crop in the mid-nineteenth century. In China, corn, peanuts, and especially sweet potatoes supplemented the traditional rice and wheat to sustain China's modern population explosion. By the early twentieth century, food plants of American origin represented about 20 percent of total Chinese food production. In Africa, corn took hold quickly and was used as a cheap food for the human cargoes of the transatlantic trade. Scholars have speculated that corn, together with peanuts and cassava, underwrote some of Africa's population growth and partially offset the population drain of the slave trade.

Beyond food crops, American stimulants such as tobacco and chocolate were soon used around the world. By the seventeenth century, how-to manuals instructed Chinese users on smoking techniques, and tobacco had become, in the words of one enamored Chinese poet, "the gentleman's companion, it warms my heart and leaves my mouth feeling like a divine furnace."[10] Tea from China and coffee from the Islamic world also spread globally, contributing to this worldwide biological exchange. Never before in human history had such a large-scale and consequential diffusion of plants and animals operated to remake the biological environment of the planet.

Furthermore, the societies that developed within the American colonies drove the processes of globalization and reshaped the world economy of the early modern era (see Chapter 14 for a more extended treatment). The silver mines of Mexico and Peru fueled both transatlantic and transpacific commerce, encouraged Spain's unsuccessful effort to dominate Europe, and enabled Europeans to buy the Chinese tea, silk, and porcelain that they valued so highly. The plantation owners of the tropical lowland regions needed workers and found them by the millions in Africa. The Atlantic slave trade, which brought these workers to the colonies, and the sugar and cotton trade, which distributed the fruits of their labor abroad, created a lasting link among Africa, Europe, and the Americas, while scattering peoples of African origin throughout the Western Hemisphere.

This enormous network of communication, migration, trade, disease, and the transfer of plants and animals, all generated by European colonial empires in the

Americas, has been dubbed the "Columbian exchange." It gave rise to something wholly new in world history: an interacting Atlantic world connecting four continents. Millions of years ago, the Eastern and Western hemispheres had physically drifted apart, and, ecologically speaking, they had remained largely apart. Now these two "old worlds" were joined, increasingly creating a single biological regime, a "new world" of global dimensions.

The long-term benefits of this Atlantic network were very unequally distributed. Western Europeans were clearly the dominant players in the Atlantic world, and their societies reaped the greatest rewards. Mountains of new information flooded into Europe, shaking up conventional understandings of the world and contributing to a revolutionary new way of thinking known as the Scientific Revolution. The wealth of the colonies—precious metals, natural resources, new food crops, slave labor, financial profits, colonial markets—provided one of the foundations on which Europe's Industrial Revolution was built. The colonies also provided an outlet for the rapidly growing population of European societies and represented an enormous extension of European civilization. In short, the colonial empires of the Americas greatly facilitated a changing global balance of power, which now thrust the previously marginal Western Europeans into an increasingly central and commanding role on the world stage. "Without a New World to deliver economic balance in the Old," concluded a prominent world historian, "Europe would have remained inferior, as ever, in wealth and power, to the great civilizations of Asia."[11]

Comparing Colonial Societies in the Americas

What the Europeans had encountered across the Atlantic was another "old world," but their actions surely gave rise to a "new world" in the Americas. Their colonial empires—Spanish, Portuguese, British, and French alike—did not simply conquer and govern established societies, but rather generated wholly new societies, born of the decimation of Native American populations and the introduction of European and African peoples, cultures, plants, and animals.

Furthermore, all the European rulers of these empires viewed their realms through the lens of the prevailing economic theory known as mercantilism. This view held that European governments served their countries' economic interests best by encouraging exports and accumulating bullion (precious metals such as silver and gold), believed to be the source of national prosperity. In this scheme of things, colonies provided closed markets for the manufactured goods of the "mother country" and, if they were lucky, supplied great quantities of bullion as well. Mercantilist thinking thus fueled European wars and colonial rivalries around the world in the early modern era. Particularly in Spanish America, however, it was a theory largely ignored or evaded in practice. Spain had few manufactured goods to sell, and piracy and smuggling allowed Spanish colonists to exchange goods with Spain's rivals.

But variations across the immense colonial world of the Western Hemisphere were at least as noticeable as these similarities. Some differences grew out of the societies of the colonizing power, such as the contrast between a semi-feudal and Catholic Spain and a more rapidly changing Protestant England. The kind of economy established in particular regions—settler-dominated agriculture, slave-based plantations, ranching, or mining—likewise influenced their development. So too did the character of the Native American cultures—the more densely populated and urbanized Mesoamerican and Andean civilizations differed greatly from the more sparsely populated rural villages of North America, for example.

Furthermore, women and men often experienced colonial intrusion in quite distinct ways. Beyond the common burdens of violent conquest, epidemic disease, and coerced labor, both Native American and enslaved African women had to cope with the additional demands made on them as females. Conquest was often accompanied by the transfer of women to the new colonial rulers. Cortés, for example, marked his alliance with the city of Tlaxcala (tlah-SKAH-lah) against the Aztecs by an exchange of gifts in which he received hundreds of female slaves and eight daughters of elite Tlaxcalan families, whom he distributed to his soldiers. And he commanded the Aztec ruler: "You are to deliver women with light skins, corn, chicken, eggs, and tortillas."[12]

Soon after conquest, many Spanish men married elite native women. It was a long-standing practice in Amerindian societies and was encouraged by both Spanish and indigenous male authorities as a means of cementing their new relationship. It was also advantageous for some of the women involved. One of Aztec emperor Moctezuma's daughters, who was mistress to Cortés and eventually married several other Spaniards, wound up with the largest landed estate in the valley of Mexico. Below this elite level of interaction, however, far more women experienced sexual violence and abuse. Rape accompanied conquest in many places, and dependent or enslaved women working under the control of European men frequently found themselves required to perform sexual services. This was tragedy and humiliation for native and enslaved men as well, for they were unable to protect their women from such abuse. Such variations in culture, policy, economy, and gender generated quite different colonial societies in several major regions of the Americas.

In the Lands of the Aztecs and the Incas

The Spanish conquest of the Aztec and Inca empires in the early sixteenth century gave Spain access to the most wealthy, urbanized, and densely populated regions of the Western Hemisphere. Within a century and well before the British had even begun their colonizing efforts in North America, the Spanish in Mexico and Peru had established nearly a dozen major cities; several impressive universities; hundreds of cathedrals, churches, and missions; an elaborate administrative bureaucracy; and a network of regulated international commerce.

■ **Change**
What was the economic foundation of colonial rule in Mexico and Peru? How did it shape the kinds of societies that arose there?

The economic foundation for this emerging colonial society lay in commercial agriculture, much of it on large rural estates, and in silver and gold mining. In both cases, native peoples, rather than African slaves or European workers, provided most of the labor, despite their much-diminished numbers. Almost everywhere it was forced labor, often directly required by colonial authorities. In a legal system known as *encomienda*, the Spanish Crown granted to particular Spanish settlers a number of local native people from whom they could require labor, gold, or agricultural produce and to whom they owed "protection" and instruction in the Christian faith. It turned into an exploitative regime not far removed from slavery and was replaced by a similar system, *repartimiento*, with slightly more control by the Crown and Spanish officials. By the seventeenth century, the *hacienda* system had taken shape by which the owners of large estates directly employed native workers. With low wages, high taxes, and large debts to the landowners, the *peons* who worked these estates enjoyed little control over their lives or their livelihood.

On this economic base, a distinctive social order grew up, replicating something of the Spanish class and gender hierarchy while accommodating the racially and culturally different Indians and Africans as well as growing numbers of racially mixed people. At the top of this colonial society were the male Spanish settlers, who were politically and economically dominant and seeking to become a landed aristocracy. One Spanish official commented in 1619: "The Spaniards, from the able and rich to the humble and poor, all hold themselves to be lords and will not serve [do manual labor]."[13] Politically, they increasingly saw themselves not as colonials, but as residents of a Spanish kingdom, subject to the Spanish monarch, yet separate and distinct from Spain itself and deserving of a large measure of self-government. Therefore, they chafed under the heavy bureaucratic restrictions imposed by the Crown. "I obey but I do not enforce" was a slogan that reflected local authorities' resistance to orders from Spain.

But the Spanish minority, never more than 20 percent of the population, was itself a divided community. Descendants of the original conquistadores sought to protect their privileges against immigrant newcomers; Spaniards born in the Americas (*creoles*) resented the pretensions to superiority of those born in Spain (*peninsulares*); landowning Spaniards felt threatened by the growing wealth of commercial and mercantile groups practicing less prestigious occupations. Spanish missionaries and church authorities

Racial Mixing in Colonial Mexico
This eighteenth-century painting by the famous Zapotec artist Miguel Cabrera shows a Spanish man, a *mestiza* woman, and their child, who was labeled as *castiza*. By the twentieth century, such mixed-race people represented the majority of the population of Mexico, and cultural blending had become a central feature of the country's identity. (Museo de América, Madrid, Spain/Bridgeman Images)

were often sharply critical of how these settlers treated native peoples. While Spanish women shared the racial privileges of their husbands, they were clearly subordinate in gender terms, unable to hold public office and viewed as weak and in need of male protection. But they were also regarded as the "bearers of civilization," and through their capacity to produce legitimate children, they were the essential link for transmitting male wealth, honor, and status to future generations. This required strict control of their sexuality and a continuation of the Iberian obsession with "purity of blood." In Spain, that concern had focused on potential liaisons with Jews and Muslims; in the colonies, the alleged threat to female virtue derived from Native American and African men.

From a male viewpoint, the problem with Spanish women was that there were very few of them. This demographic fact led to the most distinctive feature of these new colonial societies in Mexico and Peru—the emergence of a *mestizo* (mehs-TEE-zoh), or mixed-race, population, initially the product of unions between Spanish men and Indian women. Rooted in the sexual imbalance among Spanish immigrants (seven men to one woman in early colonial Peru, for example), the emergence of a mestizo population was facilitated by the desire of many surviving Indian women for the relative security of life in a Spanish household, where they and their children would not be subject to the abuse and harsh demands made on native peoples. Over the 300 years of the colonial era, mestizo numbers grew substantially, becoming the majority of the population in Mexico sometime during the nineteenth century. Such mixed-race people were divided into dozens of separate groups known as *castas* (castes), based on their racial heritage and skin color.

Mestizos were largely Hispanic in culture, but Spaniards looked down on them during much of the colonial era, regarding them as illegitimate, for many were not born of "proper" marriages. Despite this attitude, their growing numbers and the economic usefulness of their men as artisans, clerks, supervisors of labor gangs, and lower-level officials in both church and state bureaucracies led to their recognition as a distinct social group. *Mestizas*, women of mixed racial background, worked as domestic servants or in their husbands' shops, wove cloth, and manufactured candles and cigars, in addition to performing domestic duties. A few became quite wealthy. An illiterate mestiza named Mencia Perez married successively two reasonably well-to-do Spanish men and upon their deaths took over their businesses, becoming in her own right a very rich woman by the 1590s. At that point, no one would have referred to her as a mestiza.[14] Particularly in Mexico, mestizo identity blurred the sense of sharp racial difference between Spanish and Indian peoples and became a major element in the identity of modern Mexico.

At the bottom of Mexican and Peruvian colonial societies were the indigenous peoples, known to Europeans as "Indians." Traumatized by the Great Dying, they were subject to gross abuse and exploitation as the primary labor force for the mines and estates of the Spanish Empire and were required to render tribute payments to their Spanish overlords. Their empires dismantled by Spanish conquest, their religions attacked by Spanish missionaries, and their diminished numbers forcibly relocated into larger settlements, many Indians gravitated toward the world of their conquerors. Many learned Spanish; converted to Christianity; moved to cities to work for wages; ate the meat of cows, chickens, and pigs; used plows and draft animals rather than traditional digging sticks; and took their many grievances to Spanish courts. Indian women endured some distinctive conditions as Spanish legal codes generally defined them as minors rather than responsible adults. As those codes took hold, Indian women were increasingly excluded from the courts or represented by their menfolk. This made it more difficult to maintain female property rights. In 1804, for example, a Maya legal petition identified eight men and ten women from a particular family as owners of a piece of land, but the Spanish translation omitted the women's names altogether.[15]

But much that was indigenous persisted. At the local level, Indian male authorities retained a measure of autonomy, and traditional markets operated regularly. Both Andean and Maya women continued to leave personal property to their female descendants. Maize, beans, and squash persisted as the major elements of Indian diets in Mexico. Christian saints in many places blended easily with specialized indigenous gods, while belief in magic, folk medicine, and communion with the dead remained strong. Memories of the past also endured. The Tupac Amaru revolt in Peru during 1780–1781 was made in the name of the last independent Inca emperor. In that revolt, the wife of the leader, Micaela Bastidas, was referred to as La Coya, the female Inca, evoking the parallel hierarchies of male and female officials who had earlier governed the Inca Empire (see Chapter 12, pages 528–29).

Thus Spaniards, mestizos, and Indians represented the major social categories in the colonial lands of what had been the Inca and Aztec empires, while African slaves and freemen were less numerous than elsewhere in the Americas. Despite the sharp divisions among these groups, some movement was possible. Indians who acquired an education, wealth, and some European culture might "pass" as mestizo. Likewise, more fortunate mestizo families might be accepted as Spaniards over time. Colonial Spanish America was a vast laboratory of ethnic mixing and cultural change. It was dominated by Europeans, to be sure, but with a rather more fluid and culturally blended society than in the racially rigid colonies of British North America.

Colonies of Sugar

Another and quite different kind of colonial society emerged in the lowland areas of Brazil, ruled by Portugal, and in the Spanish, British, French, and Dutch colonies in the Caribbean. These regions lacked the great civilizations of Mexico and Peru. Nor did they provide much mineral wealth until the Brazilian gold rush of the 1690s and the discovery of diamonds a little later. Still, Europeans found a very profitable substitute in sugar, which was much in demand in Europe, where it was used as a medicine, a spice, a sweetener, a preservative, and in sculptured forms as a decoration that indicated high status. Although commercial agriculture in the

Spanish Empire served a domestic market in its towns and mining camps, these sugar-based colonies produced almost exclusively for export, while importing their food and other necessities.

■ Comparison
How did the plantation societies of Brazil and the Caribbean differ from those of southern colonies in British North America?

Large-scale sugar production had been pioneered by Arabs, who had introduced it in the Mediterranean. Europeans learned the technique and transferred it to their Atlantic island possessions and then to the Americas. For a century (1570–1670), Portuguese planters along the northeast coast of Brazil dominated the world market for sugar. Then the British, French, and Dutch turned their Caribbean territories into highly productive sugar-producing colonies, breaking the Portuguese and Brazilian monopoly.

Sugar decisively transformed Brazil and the Caribbean. Its production, which involved both growing the sugarcane and processing it into usable sugar, was very labor-intensive and could most profitably occur in a large-scale, almost industrial setting. It was perhaps the first modern industry in that it produced for an international and mass market, using capital and expertise from Europe, with production facilities located in the Americas. However, its most characteristic feature—the massive use of slave labor—was an ancient practice. In the absence of a Native American population, which had been almost totally wiped out in the Caribbean or had fled inland in Brazil, European sugarcane planters turned to Africa and the Atlantic slave trade for an alternative workforce. The vast majority of the African captives transported across the Atlantic, some 80 percent or more, ended up in Brazil and the Caribbean. (See Chapter 14 for a more extensive description of the Atlantic slave trade.)

Slaves worked on sugar-producing estates in horrendous conditions. The heat and fire from the cauldrons, which turned raw sugarcane into crystallized sugar, reminded many visitors of scenes from Hell. These conditions, combined with disease, generated a high death rate, perhaps 5 to 10 percent per year, which required plantation owners to constantly import fresh slaves. A Jesuit observer in 1580 aptly summarized the situation: "The work is great and many die."[16]

More male slaves than female slaves were imported from Africa into the sugar economies of the Americas, leading to major and persistent gender imbalances. Nonetheless, female slaves did play distinctive roles in these societies. Women made up about half of the field gangs that did the heavy work of planting and harvesting sugarcane. They were subject to the same brutal punishments and received the same rations as their male counterparts, though they were seldom permitted to undertake the more skilled labor inside the sugar mills. Women who worked in urban areas, mostly for white female owners, did domestic chores and were often hired out as laborers in various homes, shops, laundries, inns, and brothels. Discouraged from establishing stable families, women had to endure, often alone, the wrenching separation from their children that occurred when they were sold. Mary Prince, a Caribbean slave who wrote a brief account of her life, recalled the pain of families torn apart: "The great God above alone knows the thoughts of the poor slave's heart, and the bitter pains which follow such separations as these. All that we love taken away from us—oh, it is sad, sad! and sore to be borne!"[17]

The extensive use of African slave labor gave these plantation colonies a very different ethnic and racial makeup than that of highland Spanish America, as the Snapshot on page 570 indicates. Thus, after three centuries of colonial rule, a substantial majority of Brazil's population was either partially or wholly of African descent. In the French Caribbean colony of Haiti in 1790, the corresponding figure was 93 percent.

As in Spanish America, a considerable amount of racial mixing took place in Brazil. Cross-racial unions accounted for only about 10 percent of all marriages in Brazil, but the use of concubines and informal liaisons among Indians, Africans, and Portuguese produced a substantial mixed-race population. From their ranks derived much of the urban skilled workforce and many of the supervisors in the sugar industry. *Mulattoes*, the product of Portuguese-African unions, predominated, but as many as forty separate and named groups, each indicating a different racial mixture, emerged in colonial Brazil.

The plantation complex of the Americas, based on African slavery, extended beyond the Caribbean and Brazil to encompass the southern colonies of British North America, where tobacco, cotton, rice, and indigo were major crops, but the social outcomes of these plantation colonies were quite different from those farther south. Because European women had joined the colonial migration to North

Plantation Life in the Caribbean
This painting from 1823 shows the use of slave labor on a plantation in Antigua, a British-ruled island in the Caribbean. Notice the overseer with a whip supervising the tilling and planting of the field. (Breaking Up the Land, from *Ten Views in the Island of Antigua*, 1823, color engraving by William Clark [fl. 1823]/British Library, London, UK/© British Library Board. All Rights Reserved/Bridgeman Images)

SNAPSHOT Ethnic Composition of Colonial Societies in Latin America (1825)[18]		
	Highland Spanish America	**Portuguese America (Brazil)**
Europeans	18.2 percent	23.4 percent
Mixed-race	28.3 percent	17.8 percent
Africans	11.9 percent	49.8 percent
Native Americans	41.7 percent	9.1 percent

America at an early date, these colonies experienced less racial mixing and certainly demonstrated less willingness to recognize the offspring of such unions and accord them a place in society. A sharply defined racial system (with black Africans, "red" Native Americans, and white Europeans) evolved in North America, whereas both Portuguese and Spanish colonies acknowledged a wide variety of mixed-race groups.

Slavery too was different in North America than in the sugar colonies. By 1750 or so, slaves in what became the United States proved able to reproduce themselves, and by the time of the Civil War almost all North American slaves had been born in the New World. That was never the case in Latin America, where large-scale importation of new slaves continued well into the nineteenth century. Nonetheless, many more slaves were voluntarily set free by their owners in Brazil than in North America, and free blacks and mulattoes in Brazil had more economic opportunities than did their counterparts in the United States. At least a few among them found positions as political leaders, scholars, musicians, writers, and artists. Some were even hired as slave catchers.

Does this mean, then, that racism was absent in colonial Brazil? Certainly not, but it was different from racism in North America. For one thing, in North America, any African ancestry, no matter how small or distant, made a person "black"; in Brazil, a person of African and non-African ancestry was considered not black, but some other mixed-race category. Racial prejudice surely persisted, for white characteristics were prized more highly than black features, and people regarded as white had enormously greater privileges and opportunities than others. Nevertheless, skin color in Brazil, and in Latin America generally, was only one criterion of class status, and the perception of color changed with the educational or economic standing of individuals. A light-skinned mulatto who had acquired some wealth or education might well pass as a white. One curious visitor to Brazil was surprised to find a darker-skinned man serving as a local official. "Isn't the governor a mulatto?" inquired the visitor. "He was, but he isn't any more," was the reply. "How can a governor be a mulatto?"[19]

Settler Colonies in North America

Yet another distinctive type of colonial society emerged in the northern British colonies of New England, New York, and Pennsylvania. Because the British were the last of the European powers to establish a colonial presence in the Americas, a full century after Spain, they found that "only the dregs were left."[20] The lands they acquired were widely regarded in Europe as the unpromising leftovers of the New World, lacking the obvious wealth and sophisticated cultures of the Spanish possessions. Until at least the eighteenth century, these British colonies remained far less prominent on the world stage than those of Spain or Portugal.

The British settlers came from a more rapidly changing society than did those from an ardently Catholic, semi-feudal, authoritarian Spain. When Britain launched its colonial ventures in the seventeenth century, it had already experienced considerable conflict between Catholics and Protestants, the rise of a merchant capitalist class distinct from the nobility, and the emergence of Parliament as a check on the authority of kings. Although they brought much of their English culture with them, many of the British settlers—Puritans in Massachusetts and Quakers in Pennsylvania, for example—sought to escape aspects of an old European society rather than to re-create it, as was the case for most Spanish and Portuguese colonists. The easy availability of land and the outsider status of many British settlers made it even more difficult to follow the Spanish or Portuguese colonial pattern of sharp class hierarchies, large rural estates, and dependent laborers.

Thus men in Puritan New England became independent heads of family farms, a world away from Old England, where most land was owned by nobles and gentry and worked by servants, tenants, and paid laborers. But if men escaped the class restrictions of the old country, women were less able to avoid its gender limitations. While Puritan Christianity extolled the family and a woman's role as wife and mother, it reinforced largely unlimited male authority. "Since he is thy Husband," declared Boston minister Benjamin Wadsworth in 1712 to the colony's women, "God has made him the Head and set him above thee."[21] Women were prosecuted for the crime of "fornication" far more often than their male companions; the inheritance of daughters was substantially less than that of sons; few girls attended school; and while women were the majority of church members, they could never become ministers.

Furthermore, British settlers were far more numerous than their Spanish counterparts, outnumbering them five to one by 1750. This disparity was the most obvious distinguishing feature of the New England and middle Atlantic colonies. By the time of the American Revolution, some 90 percent or more of these colonies' populations were Europeans. Devastating diseases and a highly aggressive military policy had largely cleared the colonies of Native Americans, and their numbers, which were far smaller to start with than those of their Mesoamerican and Andean counterparts, did not rebound in subsequent centuries as they did in the lands of the Aztecs and the Incas. Moreover, slaves were not needed in an agricultural economy

■ **Comparison**
What distinguished the British settler colonies of North America from their counterparts in Latin America?

dominated by numerous small-scale independent farmers working their own land, although elite families, especially in urban areas, sometimes employed household slaves. These were almost pure settler colonies, without the racial mixing that was so prominent in Spanish and Portuguese territories.

Other differences likewise emerged. A largely Protestant England was far less interested in spreading Christianity among the remaining native peoples than were the large and well-funded missionary societies of Catholic Spain. Although religion loomed large in the North American colonies, the church and colonial state were not so intimately connected as they were in Latin America. The Protestant emphasis on reading the Bible for oneself led to a much greater mass literacy than in Latin America, where three centuries of church education still left some 95 percent of the population illiterate at independence. By contrast, well over 75 percent of white males in British North America were literate by the 1770s, although women's literacy rates were somewhat lower. Furthermore, British settler colonies evolved traditions of local self-government more extensively than in Latin America. Preferring to rely on joint stock companies or wealthy individuals operating under a royal charter, Britain had nothing resembling the elaborate imperial bureaucracy that governed Spanish colonies. For much of the seventeenth century, a prolonged power struggle between the English king and Parliament meant that the British government paid little attention to the internal affairs of the colonies. Therefore, elected colonial assemblies, seeing themselves as little parliaments defending "the rights of Englishmen," vigorously contested the prerogatives of royal governors sent to administer their affairs.

The grand irony of the modern history of the Americas lay in the reversal of long-established relationships between the northern and southern continents. For thousands of years, the major centers of wealth, power, commerce, and innovation lay in Mesoamerica and the Andes. That pattern continued for much of the colonial era, as the Spanish and Portuguese colonies seemed far more prosperous and successful than their British or French counterparts in North America. In the nineteenth and twentieth centuries, however, the balance shifted. What had once been the "dregs" of the colonial world became the United States, more politically stable, more democratic, more economically successful, and more internationally powerful than a divided, unstable, and much less prosperous Latin America.

> ### SUMMING UP SO FAR
>
> In what ways might European empire building in the Americas be understood as a single phenomenon? And in what respects should it be viewed as a set of distinct and separate processes?

The Steppes and Siberia: The Making of a Russian Empire

At the same time as Western Europeans were building their empires in the Americas, the Russian Empire, which subsequently became the world's largest state, was beginning to take shape. When Columbus crossed the Atlantic, a small Russian state centered on the city of Moscow was emerging from two centuries of Mongol rule. That state soon conquered a number of neighboring Russian-speaking cities and incorporated them into its expanding territory. Located on the remote, cold, and heavily forested eastern fringe of Christendom, it was perhaps an unlikely candidate for constructing one of the great empires of the modern era. And yet, over the next three centuries, it did precisely that, extending Russian domination over the vast tundra, forests, and grasslands of northern Asia that lay to the south and east of Moscow, all the way to the Pacific Ocean. Furthermore, Russians also expanded westward, bringing numerous Poles, Germans, Ukrainians, Belorussians, and Baltic peoples into the Russian Empire.

Russian attention was drawn first to the grasslands south and east of the Russian heartland, an area long inhabited by various nomadic pastoral peoples, who were organized into feuding tribes and clans and adjusting to the recent disappearance of the Mongol Empire. From the viewpoint of the emerging Russian state, the problem was security because these pastoral peoples, like the Mongols before them, frequently raided their agricultural Russian neighbors and sold many into slavery. To the east, across the vast expanse of Siberia, Russian motives were quite different, for the scattered peoples of its endless forests and tundra posed no threat to Russia. Numbering only some 220,000 in the seventeenth century and speaking more than 100 languages, they were mostly hunting, gathering, and herding people, living in small-scale societies and largely without access to gunpowder weapons. What drew the Russians across Siberia was opportunity—primarily the "soft gold" of fur-bearing animals, whose pelts were in great demand on the world market.

Whatever motives drove it, this enormous Russian Empire took shape in the three centuries between 1500 and 1800 (see Map 13.2). A growing line of wooden forts offered protection to frontier towns and trading centers as well as to mounting numbers of Russian farmers. Empire building was an extended process, involving the Russian state and its officials as well as a variety of private interests—merchants, hunters, peasants, churchmen, exiles, criminals, and adventurers. For the Russian migrants to these new eastern lands, the empire offered "economic and social improvements over what they had known at home—from more and better land to fewer lords and officials."[22] Political leaders and educated Russians generally defined the empire in grander terms: defending Russian frontiers; enhancing the power of the Russian state; and bringing Christianity, civilization, and enlightenment to savages. But what did that empire mean to those on its receiving end?

■ **Description**
What motivated Russian empire building?

Experiencing the Russian Empire

First, of course, empire meant conquest. Although resistance was frequent, especially from nomadic peoples, in the long run Russian military might, based in modern weaponry and the organizational capacity of a state, brought both the steppes and Siberia under Russian control. Everywhere Russian authorities demanded an oath of allegiance by which native peoples swore "eternal submission to the grand tsar,"

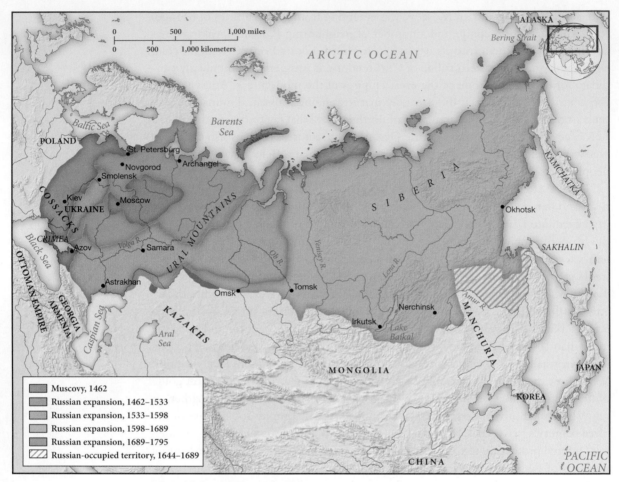

Map 13.2   The Russian Empire

From its beginnings as a small principality under Mongol control, Moscow became the center of a vast Russian Empire during the early modern era.

the monarch of the Russian Empire. They also demanded *yasak*, or "tribute," paid in cash or in kind. In Siberia, this meant enormous quantities of furs, especially the extremely valuable sable, which Siberian peoples were compelled to produce. As in the Americas, devastating epidemics accompanied conquest, particularly in the more remote regions of Siberia, where local people had little immunity to smallpox or measles. Also accompanying conquest was an intermittent pressure to convert to Christianity. Tax breaks, exemptions from paying tribute, and the promise of land or cash provided incentives for conversion, while the destruction of many mosques and the forced resettlement of Muslims added to the pressures. Yet the Russian state did not pursue conversion with the single-minded intensity that Spanish authorities exercised in Latin America, particularly if missionary activity threatened political and social stability. The empress Catherine the Great, for example, established religious tolerance for Muslims in the late eighteenth century and created a state agency to oversee Muslim affairs.

The most profoundly transforming feature of the Russian Empire was the influx of Russian settlers, whose numbers by the end of the eighteenth century had over-whelmed native peoples, giving their lands a distinctively Russian character. By 1720, some 700,000 Russians lived in Siberia, thus reducing the native Siberians to 30 percent of the total population, a proportion that dropped to 14 percent in the nineteenth century. The loss of hunting grounds and pasturelands to Russian agricultural settlers undermined long-standing economies and rendered local people dependent on Russian markets for grain, sugar, tea, tobacco, and alcohol. Pressures to encourage pastoralists to abandon their nomadic ways included the requirement to pay fees and to obtain permission to cross agricultural lands. Kazakh herders responded with outrage: "The grass and the water belong to Heaven, and why should we pay any fees?"[23] Intermarriage, prostitution, and sexual abuse resulted in some mixed-race offspring, but these were generally absorbed as Russians rather than identified as distinctive communities, as in Latin America.

Over the course of three centuries, both Siberia and the steppes were incorporated into the Russian state. Their native peoples were not driven into reservations or eradicated as in the Americas. Many of them, though, were Russified, adopting the Russian language and converting to Christianity, even as their traditional ways of life — hunting and herding — were much disrupted. The Russian Empire represented the final triumph of an agrarian civilization over the hunting societies of Siberia and over the pastoral peoples of the grasslands.

■ **Change**
How did the Russian Empire transform the life of its conquered people and of the Russian homeland itself?

The Cossacks
In the vanguard of Russian expansion across Siberia were the Cossacks, bands of fiercely independent warriors consisting of peasants who had escaped serfdom as well as criminals and other adventurers. Here the sixteenth-century Cossack warrior Yermak is shown leading his troops. (De Agostini Picture Library/akg-images)

Russians and Empire

If the empire transformed the conquered peoples, it also fundamentally changed Russia itself. Within an increasingly multiethnic empire, Russians diminished as a proportion of the overall population, although they remained politically dominant. Among the growing number of non-Russians in the empire, Slavic-speaking Ukrainians and Belorussians predominated, while the vast territories of Siberia and the steppes housed numerous separate peoples, but with quite small populations.[24] The wealth of empire—rich agricultural lands, valuable furs, mineral deposits—played a major role in making Russia one of the great powers of Europe by the eighteenth century, and it has enjoyed that position ever since.

Unlike its expansion to the east, Russia's westward movement occurred in the context of military rivalries with the major powers of the region—the Ottoman Empire, Poland, Sweden, Lithuania, Prussia, and Austria. During the late seventeenth and eighteenth centuries, Russia acquired substantial territories in the Baltic region, Poland, and Ukraine. This contact with Europe also fostered an awareness of Russia's backwardness relative to Europe and prompted an extensive program of westernization, particularly under the leadership of Peter the Great (r. 1689–1725). His massive efforts included vast administrative changes, the enlargement and modernization of Russian military forces, a new educational system for the sons of noblemen, and dozens of manufacturing enterprises. Russian nobles were instructed to dress in European styles and to shave their sacred and much-revered beards. The newly created capital city of St. Petersburg was to be Russia's "window on the West." One of Peter's successors, Catherine the Great (r. 1762–1796), followed up with further efforts to Europeanize Russian cultural and intellectual life, viewing herself as part of the European Enlightenment. Thus Russians were the first of many peoples to measure themselves against the West and to mount major "catch-up" efforts.

But this European-oriented and Christian state had also become an Asian power, bumping up against China, India, Persia, and the Ottoman Empire. It was on the front lines of the encounter between Christendom and the world of Islam. This straddling of Asia and Europe was the source of a long-standing identity problem that has troubled educated Russians for 300 years. Was Russia a backward European country, destined to follow the lead of more highly developed Western European societies? Or was it different, uniquely Slavic or even Asian, shaped by its Mongol legacy and its status as an Asian power? It is a question that Russians have not completely answered even in the twenty-first century. Either way, the very size of that empire, bordering on virtually all of the great agrarian civilizations of outer Eurasia, turned Russia, like many empires before it, into a highly militarized state, "a society organized for continuous war," according to one scholar.[25] It also reinforced the highly autocratic character of the Russian Empire because such a huge state arguably required a powerful monarchy to hold its vast domains and highly diverse peoples together.

Clearly, the Russians had created an empire, similar to those of Western Europe in terms of conquest, settlement, exploitation, religious conversion, and feelings of superiority. Nonetheless, the Russians had acquired their empire under different circumstances than did the Western Europeans. The Spanish and the British had conquered and colonized the New World, an ocean away and wholly unknown to them before 1492. They acquired those empires only after establishing themselves as distinct European states. The Russians, on the other hand, absorbed adjacent territories, and they did so at the same time that a modern Russian state was taking shape. "The British had an empire," wrote historian Geoffrey Hosking. "Russia *was* an empire."[26] Perhaps this helps explain the unique longevity of the Russian Empire. Whereas the Spanish, Portuguese, and British colonies in the Americas long ago achieved independence, the Russian Empire remained intact until the collapse of the Soviet Union in 1991. So thorough was Russian colonization that Siberia and much of the steppes remain still an integral part of the Russian state.

Asian Empires

Even as West Europeans were building their empires in the Americas and the Russians were expanding across Siberia, other imperial projects were likewise under way. The Chinese pushed deep into central Eurasia; Turko-Mongol invaders from Central Asia created the Mughal Empire, bringing much of Hindu South Asia within a single Muslim-ruled political system; and the Ottoman Empire brought Muslim rule to a largely Christian population in southeastern Europe and Turkish rule to largely Arab populations in North Africa and the Middle East. None of these empires had the global reach or worldwide impact of Europe's American colonies; they were regional rather than global in scope. Nor did they have the same devastating and transforming impact on their conquered peoples, for those peoples were not being exposed to new diseases. Nothing remotely approaching the catastrophic population collapse of Native American peoples occurred in these Asian empires. Moreover, the process of building these empires did not transform the imperial homeland as fundamentally as did the wealth of the Americas and to a lesser extent Siberia for European imperial powers. Nonetheless, these expanding Asian empires reflected the energies and vitality of their respective civilizations in the early modern era, and they gave rise to profoundly important cross-cultural encounters, with legacies that echoed for many centuries.

Making China an Empire

In the fifteenth century, China had declined an opportunity to construct a maritime empire in the Indian Ocean, as Zheng He's massive fleet was withdrawn and left to wither away (see Chapter 12, pages 507–9). In the seventeenth and eighteenth centuries, however, China built another kind of empire on its northern and western frontiers that vastly enlarged the territorial size of the country and incorporated a number of non-Chinese peoples. Undertaking this enormous project of imperial expansion was China's Qing, or Manchu, dynasty (1644–1912). Strangely enough, the Qing dynasty was itself of foreign and nomadic origin, hailing from Manchuria, north of the Great Wall. Having conquered China, the Qing rulers sought to maintain their ethnic distinctiveness by forbidding intermarriage between themselves and the Chinese. Nonetheless, their ruling elites also mastered the Chinese language and Confucian teachings and used Chinese bureaucratic techniques to govern the empire. Perhaps because they were foreigners, Qing rulers went to great lengths to reinforce traditional Confucian gender roles, honoring men who were loyal sons, officials, and philanthropists and women who demonstrated loyalty to their spouses by resisting rape or remaining chaste as widows.

For many centuries, the Chinese had interacted with the nomadic peoples, who inhabited the dry and lightly populated regions now known as Mongolia, Xinjiang, and Tibet. Trade, tribute, and warfare ensured that these ecologically and culturally different worlds were well known to each other, quite unlike the New World "discoveries" of the Europeans. Chinese authority in the area had been intermittent and actively resisted. Then, in the early modern era, Qing dynasty China undertook an eighty-year military effort (1680–1760) that brought these huge regions solidly under Chinese control. It was largely security concerns, rather than economic need, that motivated this aggressive posture. During the late seventeenth century, the creation of a substantial state among the western Mongols, known as the Zunghars, revived Chinese memories of an earlier Mongol conquest. As in so many other cases, Chinese expansion was viewed as a defensive necessity. The eastward movement of the Russian Empire likewise appeared potentially threatening, but this

■ **Description**

What were the distinctive features of Chinese empire building in the early modern era?

Chinese Conquests in Central Asia

Painted by the Chinese artist Jin Tingbiao in the mid-eighteenth century, this image portrays Machang, a leading warrior involved in the westward extension of the Chinese empire. The painting was commissioned by the emperor himself and served to honor the bravery of Machang. (Pictures from History/CPA Media)

danger was resolved diplomatically, rather than militarily, in the Treaty of Nerchinsk (1689), which marked the boundary between Russia and China.

Although undertaken by the non-Chinese Manchus, the Qing dynasty campaigns against the Mongols marked the evolution of China into a Central Asian empire. The Chinese, however, have seldom thought of themselves as an imperial power. Rather, they spoke of the "unification" of the peoples of central Eurasia within a Chinese state. Nonetheless, historians have seen many similarities between Chinese expansion and other cases of early modern empire building, while noting some clear differences as well.

Clearly the Qing dynasty takeover of central Eurasia was a conquest, making use of China's more powerful military technology and greater resources. Furthermore, the area was ruled separately from the rest of China through a new office called the Court of Colonial Affairs. Like other colonial powers, the Chinese made active use of local notables—Mongol aristocrats, Muslim officials, Buddhist leaders—as they attempted to govern the region as inexpensively as possible. Sometimes these native officials abused their authority, demanding extra taxes or labor service from local people and thus earning their hostility. In places, those officials imitated Chinese ways by wearing peacock feathers, decorating their hats with gold buttons, or adopting a Manchu hairstyle that was much resented by many Chinese who were forced to wear it.

More generally, however, Chinese or Qing officials did not seek to assimilate local people into Chinese culture and showed considerable respect for the Mongolian, Tibetan, and Muslim cultures of the region. People of noble rank, Buddhist monks, and those associated with monasteries were excused from the taxes and labor service required of ordinary people. Nor was the area flooded with Chinese settlers. In parts of Mongolia, for example, Qing authorities sharply restricted the entry of Chinese merchants and other immigrants in an effort to preserve the area as a source of recruitment for the Chinese military. They feared that the "soft" and civilized Chinese ways might erode the fighting spirit of the Mongols.

The long-term significance of this new Chinese imperial state was tremendous. It greatly expanded the territory of China and added a small but important minority of non-Chinese people to the empire's vast population (see Map 13.3). The borders of contemporary China are essentially those created during the Qing dynasty. Some of those peoples, particularly those in Tibet and Xinjiang, have retained their older identities and in recent decades have actively sought greater autonomy or even independence from China.

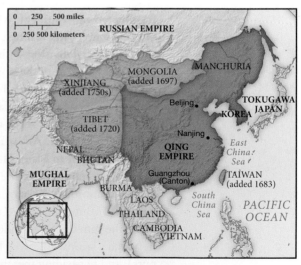

Map 13.3   China's Qing Dynasty Empire
After many centuries of intermittent expansion into Central Asia, the Qing dynasty brought this vast region firmly within the Chinese empire.

Even more important, Chinese conquests, together with the expansion of the Russian Empire, utterly transformed Central Asia. For centuries, that region had been the cosmopolitan crossroads of Eurasia, hosting the Silk Road trading network, welcoming all the major world religions, and generating an enduring encounter between the nomads of the steppes and the farmers of settled agricultural regions. Now under Russian or Chinese rule, it became the backward and impoverished region known to nineteenth- and twentieth-century observers. Land-based commerce across Eurasia increasingly took a backseat to oceanic trade. Indebted Mongolian nobles lost their land to Chinese merchants, while nomads, no longer able to herd their animals freely, fled to urban areas, where many were reduced to begging. The incorporation of inner Eurasia into the Russian and Chinese empires "eliminated permanently as a major actor on the historical stage the nomadic pastoralists, who had been the strongest alternative to settled agricultural society since the second millennium B.C.E."[27] It was the end of a long era.

Muslims and Hindus in the Mughal Empire

If the creation of a Chinese imperial state in the early modern era provoked a final clash of nomadic pastoralists and settled farmers, India's Mughal Empire hosted a different kind of encounter—a further phase in the long interaction of Islamic and Hindu cultures in South Asia. That empire was the product of Central Asian warriors, who were Muslims in religion and Turkic in culture and who claimed descent from Chinggis Khan and Timur (see Chapters 11 and 12). Their brutal conquests in the sixteenth century provided India with a rare period of relative political unity (1526–1707), as Mughal emperors exercised a fragile control over a diverse and fragmented subcontinent, which had long been divided into a bewildering variety of small states, principalities, tribes, castes, sects, and ethno-linguistic groups.

■ Change

How did Mughal attitudes and policies toward Hindus change from the time of Akbar to that of Aurangzeb?

The central division within Mughal India was religious. The ruling dynasty and perhaps 20 percent of the population were Muslims; most of the rest practiced some form of Hinduism. Mughal India's most famous emperor, Akbar (r. 1556–1605), clearly recognized this fundamental reality and acted deliberately to accommodate the Hindu majority. After conquering the warrior-based and Hindu Rajputs of northwestern India, Akbar married several of their princesses but did not require them to convert to Islam. He incorporated a substantial number of Hindus into the political-military elite of the empire and supported the building of Hindu temples as well as mosques, palaces, and forts. (See Working with Evidence, Source 13.1, page 590.) But Akbar acted to soften some Hindu restrictions on women, encouraging the remarriage of widows, discouraging child marriages and *sati* (the practice in which a widow followed her husband to death by throwing herself on his funeral pyre), and persuading merchants to set aside special market days for women so as to moderate their seclusion in the home. Nur Jahan, the twentieth and favorite wife of Emperor Jahangir (r. 1605–1627), was widely regarded as the power behind the throne of her alcohol- and opium-addicted husband, giving audiences to visiting dignitaries, consulting with ministers, and even having a coin issued in her name.

In directly religious matters, Akbar imposed a policy of toleration, deliberately restraining the more militantly Islamic *ulama* (religious scholars) and removing the special tax (*jizya*) on non-Muslims. He constructed a special House of Worship where he presided over intellectual discussion with representatives of many religions—Muslim, Hindu, Christian, Buddhist, Jewish, Jain, and Zoroastrian. His son Jahangir wrote proudly of his father: "He associated with the good of every race and creed and persuasion. . . . The professors of various faiths had room in the broad expanse of his incomparable sway."[28] Akbar went so far as to create his own state cult, a religious faith aimed at the Mughal elite, drawing on Islam, Hinduism, and Zoroastrianism and emphasizing loyalty to the emperor himself. The

The Mughal Empire

overall style of the Mughal Empire was that of a blended elite culture in which both Hindus and various Muslim groups could feel comfortable. Thus Persian artists and writers were welcomed into the empire, and the Hindu epic *Ramayana* was translated into Persian, while various Persian classics appeared in Hindi and Sanskrit. In short, Akbar and his immediate successors downplayed a distinctly Islamic identity for the Mughal Empire in favor of a cosmopolitan and hybrid Indian-Persian-Turkic culture.

Such policies fostered sharp opposition among some Muslims. The philosopher Shaykh Ahmad Sirhindi (1564–1624), claiming to be a "renewer" of authentic Islam in his time, strongly objected to this cultural synthesis. The worship of saints, the sacrifice of animals, and support for Hindu religious festivals all represented impure intrusions of Sufi Islam or Hinduism that needed to be rooted out. In Sirhindi's view, it was primarily women who had introduced these deviations: "Because of their utter stupidity women pray to stones and idols and ask for their help. This practice is common, especially when small pox strikes, and there is hardly a woman who is not involved in this polytheistic practice. Women participate in the holidays of Hindus and Jews. They celebrate Diwali [a major Hindu festival] and send their sisters and daughters presents similar to those exchanged by the infidels."[29] It was therefore the duty of Muslim rulers to impose the sharia (Islamic law), to enforce the jizya, and to remove non-Muslims from high office.

This strain of Muslim thinking found a champion in the emperor Aurangzeb (ow-rang-ZEHB) (r. 1658–1707), who reversed Akbar's policy of accommodation and sought to impose Islamic supremacy. While Akbar had discouraged the Hindu practice of sati, Aurangzeb forbade it outright. Music and dance were now banned at court, and previously tolerated vices such as gambling, drinking, prostitution, and narcotics were actively suppressed. Dancing girls were ordered to get married or leave the empire altogether. Some Hindu temples were destroyed, and the jizya was reimposed. "Censors of public morals," posted to large cities, enforced Islamic law.

Aurangzeb's religious policies, combined with intolerable demands for taxes to support his many wars of expansion, antagonized Hindus and prompted various movements of opposition to the Mughals. "Your subjects are trampled underfoot," wrote one anonymous protester. "Every province of your empire is impoverished. . . . God is the God of all mankind, not the God of Mussalmans [Muslims] alone."[30] These opposition movements, some of them self-consciously Hindu, fatally fractured the Mughal Empire, especially after Aurangzeb's death in 1707, and opened the way for a British takeover in the second half of the eighteenth century.

Thus the Mughal Empire was the site of a highly significant encounter between two of the world's great religious traditions. It began with an experiment in multicultural empire building and ended in growing antagonism between Hindus and Muslims. In the centuries that followed, both elements of the Mughal experience would be repeated.

Muslims and Christians in the Ottoman Empire

Like the Mughal state, the Ottoman Empire was also the creation of Turkic warrior groups, whose aggressive raiding of agricultural civilization was now legitimized in Islamic terms. Beginning around 1300 from a base area in northwestern Anatolia, these Ottoman Turks over the next three centuries swept over much of the Middle East, North Africa, and southeastern Europe to create the Islamic world's most significant empire (see Map 13.4). During those centuries, the Ottoman state was transformed from a small frontier principality to a prosperous, powerful, cosmopolitan empire, heir both to the Byzantine Empire and to leadership within the Islamic world. Its sultan combined the roles of a Turkic warrior prince, a Muslim caliph, and a conquering emperor, bearing the "strong sword of Islam" and serving as chief defender of the faith.

Gaining such an empire transformed Turkish social life as well. The relative independence of Central Asian pastoral women, their open association with men, and their political influence in society all diminished as the Turks adopted Islam, beginning in the tenth century, and later acquired an empire in the heartland of ancient and patriarchal Mediterranean civilizations. Now elite Turkish women found themselves secluded and often veiled; slave women from the Caucasus Mountains and the Sudan grew more numerous; official imperial censuses did not count women; and orthodox Muslim reformers sought to restrict women's religious gatherings.

And yet within the new constraints of a settled Islamic empire, Turkish women retained something of the social power they had enjoyed in pastoral societies. From around 1550 to 1650, women of the royal court had such an influence in political matters that their critics referred to the "sultanate of women." Islamic law permitted women important property rights, which enabled some to become quite

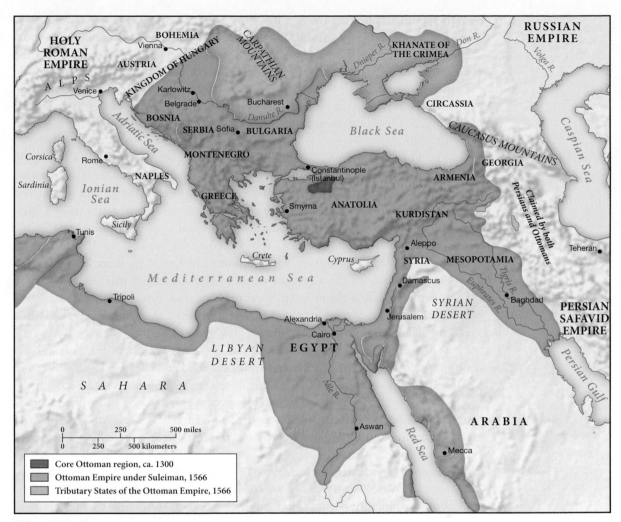

Map 13.4   The Ottoman Empire

At its high point in the mid-sixteenth century, the Ottoman Empire encompassed a vast diversity of peoples; straddled Europe, Africa, and Asia; and battled both the Austrian and Safavid empires.

wealthy, endowing religious and charitable institutions. Many women actively used the Ottoman courts to protect their legal rights in matters of marriage, divorce, and inheritance, sometimes representing themselves or acting as agents for female relatives. In 1717, the wife of an English ambassador to the Ottoman Empire compared the lives of Turkish and European women, declaring, "'Tis very easy to see that they have more liberty than we have."[31]

Within the Islamic world, the Ottoman Empire represented the growing prominence of Turkic people, for their empire now incorporated a large number of

■ **Significance**

In what ways was the Ottoman Empire important for Europe in the early modern era?

Arabs, among whom the religion had been born. The responsibility and the prestige of protecting Mecca, Medina, and Jerusalem—the holy cities of Islam—now fell to the Ottoman Empire. A century-long conflict (1534–1639) between the Ottoman Empire, espousing the Sunni version of Islam, and the Persian Safavid Empire, holding fast to the Shia form of the faith, expressed a deep and enduring division within the Islamic world. Nonetheless, Persian culture, especially its poetry, painting, and traditions of imperial splendor, occupied a prominent position among the Ottoman elite.

The Ottoman Empire, like its Mughal counterpart, was the site of a highly significant cross-cultural encounter in the early modern era, adding yet another chapter to the long-running story of interaction between the Islamic world and Christendom. As the Ottoman Empire expanded across Anatolia, its mostly Christian population converted in large numbers to Islam as the Byzantine state visibly weakened and large numbers of Turks settled in the region. By 1500, some 90 percent of Anatolia's inhabitants were Muslims and Turkic speakers. The climax of this Turkic assault on the Christian world of Byzantium occurred in 1453, when Constantinople fell to the invaders. Renamed Istanbul, that splendid Christian city became the capital of the Ottoman Empire. Byzantium, heir to the glory of Rome and the guardian of Orthodox Christianity, was no more.

In the empire's southeastern European domains, known as the Balkans, the Ottoman encounter with Christian peoples unfolded quite differently than it had in Anatolia. In the Balkans, Muslims ruled over a large Christian population, but the scarcity of Turkish settlers and the willingness of the Ottoman authorities to accommodate the region's Christian churches led to far fewer conversions. By the early sixteenth century, only about 19 percent of the area's people were Muslims, and 81 percent were Christians.

Many of these Christians had welcomed Ottoman conquest because taxes were lighter and oppression less pronounced than under their former Christian rulers. Christian communities such as the Eastern Orthodox and Armenian Churches were granted considerable autonomy in regulating their internal social, religious, educational, and charitable affairs. Nonetheless, many Christian and Jewish women appealed legal cases dealing with marriage and inheritance to Muslim courts, where their property rights were greater. A substantial number of Christian men—Balkan landlords, Greek merchants, government officials, and high-ranking clergy—became part of the Ottoman elite, sometimes without converting to Islam. Jewish refugees, fleeing Christian persecution in a Spain recently "liberated" from Islamic rule, likewise found greater opportunity in the Ottoman Empire, where they became prominent in trade and banking circles. In these ways, Ottoman dealings with the Christian and Jewish populations of their empire broadly resembled Akbar's policies toward the Hindu majority of Mughal India. In another way, however, Turkish rule bore heavily on Christians. Through a process known as the *devshirme* (devv-shirr-MEH) (the collecting or gathering), Ottoman authorities siphoned off

many thousands of young boys from Christian families into the service of the state. (See Zooming In: Devshirme, page 586.)

Even though Ottoman authorities were relatively tolerant toward Christians within their borders, the empire itself represented an enormous threat to Christendom generally. The seizure of Constantinople, the conquest of the Balkans, Ottoman naval power in the Mediterranean, and the siege of Vienna in 1529 and again in 1683 raised anew "the specter of a Muslim takeover of all of Europe."[32] (See Working with Evidence, Source 13.2, page 593.) One European ambassador reported fearfully in 1555 from the court of the Turkish ruler Suleiman:

> He tramples the soil of Hungary with 200,000 horses, he is at the very gates of Austria, threatens the rest of Germany, and brings in his train all the nations that extend from our borders to those of Persia.[33]

Indeed, the "terror of the Turk" inspired fear across much of Europe and placed Christendom on the defensive, even as Europeans were expanding aggressively across the Atlantic and into the Indian Ocean.

The Ottoman Siege of Vienna, 1683
In this late seventeenth-century painting by the Flemish artist Frans Geffels, the last Ottoman incursion into the Austrian Empire is pushed back with French and Polish help, marking the end of a serious Muslim threat to Christian Europe. (Wien Museum Karlsplatz, Vienna, Austria/ Erich Lessing/Art Resource, NY)

Devshirme: The "Gathering" of Christian Boys in the Ottoman Empire

Every few years, Ottoman official recruiters descended on rural Christian villages in the Balkan provinces of the empire, mostly among Serbs, Greeks, and Albanians. There they required the village priest to present the birth records of the village and to assemble boys of about ten to eighteen years of age. Then they selected a certain number of these boys, dressed them in red uniforms, and marched them off to Constantinople. Once the boys arrived, they were circumcised, converted to Islam, given a Muslim name, and enrolled in a long training program to prepare them for administrative or military positions within the Ottoman government.

Ottoman officials selecting Christian boys, in red, for the devshirme.

This was the *devshirme*, or "gathering," of Christian boys, a distinctive practice that began in the mid- to late fourteenth century when the rapid expansion of the Ottoman Empire required more soldiers and officials. It extended a much older Islamic tradition of using prisoners captured in war as slave soldiers. The devshirme enabled the sultan to create a cadre of civil and military officials personally loyal to and dependent upon him,

thus avoiding reliance on the Turkish nobility. Boys with the greatest potential received a prestigious education, lasting some fourteen years, in Arabic, Turkish, and Persian languages; mathematics; Islamic studies; horsemanship; weaponry; and more. They were tracked into civil administrative careers, often in the palace itself. Others entered a rigorous training for military service and generally ended up in the Janissary corps, an elite military unit responsible directly to the sultan.

Technically, the devshirme recruits were slaves, but they were quite different from ordinary purchased slaves. They were absorbed into Ottoman society in distinctive and privileged roles, and some of them were able to rise to very prominent positions, including that of grand vizier, the chief adviser to the sultan himself. One such official recalled that he was taken "weeping and in distress," but also reported with some pride that "a shepherd may be [transported] to a sultan's domain."[34]

photo: From the "Suleymanname" (Mss Hazine, 1517 f. 31v.), 1558 (ink and gold leaf on vellum)/Topkapi Palace Museum, Istanbul, Turkey/Bridgeman Images

But the Ottoman encounter with Christian Europe spawned admiration and cooperation as well as fear and trembling. Italian Renaissance artists portrayed the splendor of the Islamic world. (See Working with Evidence, Chapter 12, page 536.) The sixteenth-century French philosopher Jean Bodin praised the religious tolerance of the Ottoman sultan in contrast to Christian intolerance: "The King of the Turks who rules over a great part of Europe safeguards the rites of religion as well as any prince in this world. Yet he constrains no-one, but on the contrary permits everyone to live as his conscience dictates."[35] The French government on occasion found it useful to ally with the Ottoman Empire against their common enemy of Habsburg Austria, while European merchants willingly violated a papal ban on selling firearms to the Turks. Cultural encounter involved more than conflict.

So prestigious were such positions—or so desperate were impoverished Christians—that some Christian families voluntarily offered their sons to the recruiters, and some free Muslim families schemed to get their children into the exalted ranks of the devshirme.

Yet there is little doubt that the devshirme system brought great suffering to the empire's Christian subjects and was widely hated and resisted. In 1395, an Eastern Orthodox metropolitan, or archbishop, named Isidore Glabas from Thessaloniki in Greece delivered a scathing public sermon denouncing the practice, no doubt reflecting the views of his parishioners. "My eyes are filled with tears and can no longer bear to see my beloved ones," he began. Then he outlined the various ways that the devshirme brought grief to his people: their children were "forced to change over to alien customs and to become a vessel of barbaric garb, speech, impiety, and other contaminations, all in a moment." His words reflected the Greeks' view of Turks as "barbarians" and their fear that their children might be subjected to castration as eunuchs or exposed to the homosexuality widely regarded as a part of Janissary life. Furthermore, according to the archbishop, the devshirme threatened the continuity of family life, for a father "will not have his son to send him to his grave in fitting manner." And who, he asked, would not "lament his son because a free child becomes a slave?" Worst of all, in the archbishop's view, was the danger to the immortal soul of a Christian boy who was circumcised and converted to Islam, for "he is shamefully separated from God and has become miserably entangled with the devil, and in the end will be sent to darkness and hell with the demons."[36]

It was no wonder then that Ottoman Christians deployed many strategies to avoid the devshirme. Some communities required their boys to formally marry at a very young age; parish priests might conveniently lose names from the parish registries; families sometimes fled to avoid the recruiters; Eastern Orthodox Christians on occasion appealed to the pope or to Catholic military orders for help, "lest we lose our children." On several occasions, villagers murdered the recruiters and many times sought to bribe them.

By the mid-seventeenth century, the devshirme system had been largely abandoned, as recruitment to these positions was opened to free Muslim Turks. But the memory lingered well into the twentieth century as an irritant in the conflicted relations of Greeks and Turks. A song recently sung in northern Greece recalled the memory: "Be Dammed, Emperor, thrice be dammed. . . . You catch and shackle the old and the archpriests, in order to take the children as janissaries. Their parents weep, their sisters and brothers, too."[37]

Questions: How might you summarize the origins and outcomes of the devshirme system? How does this practice alter your understanding of slavery?

The Centrality of Context in World History

World history is, to put it mildly, a big subject. To teachers and students alike, it can easily seem overwhelming in its detail. And yet the central task of world history is *not* the inclusion of endless facts or particular cases. It is rather to establish contexts or frameworks within which carefully selected facts and cases take on new meaning. In world history, every event, every process, every historical figure, and every culture, society, or civilization gain significance from their incorporation into some larger context or framework. Contextual thinking is central to world history.

The broad outlines of European colonization in the Americas are familiar to most American and European students. And yet, when that story is set in the context of other empire-building projects of the early modern era, it takes on new and different meanings. Such a context helps to counter any remaining Eurocentrism in our thinking about the past by reminding us that Western Europe was not the only center of vitality and expansion and that the interaction of culturally different peoples, so characteristic of the modern age, derived from multiple sources. How often do we notice that a European Christendom creating empires across the Atlantic was also the victim of Ottoman imperial expansion in the Balkans?

This kind of contextualizing also allows us to see more clearly the distinctive features of European empires as we view them in the mirror of other imperial creations. The Chinese, Mughal, and Ottoman empires continued older patterns of historical development, while those of Europe represented something wholly new in human history — an interacting Atlantic world of Europe, Africa, and the Americas. Furthermore, the European empires had a far greater impact on the peoples they incorporated than did other empires. Nowhere else did empire building generate such a catastrophic population collapse as in the Americas. Nor did Asian empires foster the kind of slave-based societies and transcontinental trade in slaves that were among the chief outcomes of Europe's American colonies. Finally, Europe was enriched and transformed by its American possessions far more than China and the Ottomans were by their territorial acquisitions. Europeans gained enormous new biological resources from their empires — corn, potatoes, tomatoes, chocolate, tobacco, timber, and much more — as well as enormous wealth in the form of gold, silver, and land.

Should we need a motto for world history, consider this one: in world history, nothing stands alone; context is everything.

Second Thoughts

What's the Significance?

Big Picture Questions

1. The experience of empire for conquered peoples was broadly similar whoever their rulers were. Does the material in this chapter support or challenge this idea?

2. In thinking about the similarities and differences among the empires of the early modern era, what categories of comparison might be most useful to consider?

3. Have a look at the maps in this chapter with an eye to the areas of the world that were not incorporated into a major empire. Pick one or more of them and do a little research as to what was happening there in the early modern era.

4. **Looking Back:** Compared to the world of the fifteenth century, what new patterns of development are visible in the empire-building projects of the centuries that followed?

Next Steps: For Further Study

Jane Burbank and Frederick Cooper, *Empires in World History* (2010). Chapters 5–7 of this recent work describe and compare the empires of the early modern world.

Jorge Canizares-Esguerra and Erik R. Seeman, eds., *The Atlantic in Global History* (2007). A collection of essays that treats the Atlantic basin as a single interacting region.

Alfred W. Crosby, *The Columbian Voyages, the Columbian Exchange, and Their Historians* (1987). A brief and classic account of changing understandings of Columbus and his global impact.

John Kicza, *Resilient Cultures: America's Native Peoples Confront European Colonization, 1500–1800* (2003). An account of European colonization in the Americas that casts the native peoples as active agents rather than passive victims.

Charles C. Mann, *1493: Uncovering the New World Columbus Created* (2011). A global account of the Columbian exchange that presents contemporary scholarship in a very accessible fashion.

Peter Perdue, *China Marches West: The Qing Conquest of Central Eurasia* (2005). Describes how China became an empire as it incorporated the non-Chinese people of Central Asia.

Willard Sutherland, *Taming the Wild Fields: Colonization and Empire on the Russian Steppe* (2004). An up-to-date account of Russian expansion in the steppes.

"Discover the Ottomans," http://www.theottomans.org/english/index.asp. A series of essays and images that traces the history of the Ottoman Empire over six centuries.

"1492: An Ongoing Voyage," http://www.ibiblio.org/expo/1492.exhibit/Intro.html. An interactive Web site based on an exhibit from the Library of Congress that provides a rich context for exploring the meaning of Columbus and his voyages.

WORKING WITH EVIDENCE

State Building in the Early Modern Era

The empires of the early modern era were the projects of states, though these states often made use of various private groups—missionaries, settlers, merchants, mercenaries—to achieve the goals of empire. Such imperial states—Mughal India, the Ottoman Empire, France, and the Inca Empire, for example—were invariably headed by kings or emperors who were the source of ultimate political authority in their lands. Each of those rulers sought to govern societies divided by religion, region, ethnicity, or class.

During the three centuries between 1450 and 1750, all of these states, and a number of non-imperial states as well, moved toward greater political integration and centralization. In all of them, more effective central bureaucracies curtailed, though never eliminated, entrenched local interests; royal courts became more elaborate; and the role of monarchs grew more prominent. The growth of empire accompanied this process of political integration, and perhaps helped cause it. However, efforts at state building differed considerably across the early modern world, depending on variations in historical backgrounds, the particular problems and circumstances that each state faced, the cultural basis of political authority, and the policies that individual leaders followed.

The documents that follow allow us to examine this state-building effort in several distinct settings. Two of them were written by monarchs themselves and two by outside observers. What similarities and variations in this process of state building can you notice as you study the documents? How did these early modern states differ from the states of later centuries or those of today? To what extent was government personal rather than institutional? In what ways was power exercised—through coercion and violence, through accommodation with established elites, through the operation of new bureaucratic structures, or by persuading people that the central authority was in fact legitimate?

Source 13.1
The Memoirs of Emperor Jahangir

The peoples of India had only rarely experienced a political system that encompassed most of the subcontinent. Its vast ethnic and cultural diversity and the division between its Hindu and Muslim peoples usually generated a fragmented political order of many competing states and principalities. But in the early modern era, the Mughal Empire gave to South Asia a rare period of substantial political unity. Source 13.1 offer excerpts from the memoirs of Jahangir, who ruled the Mughal state from 1605 to 1627, following the reign of his more famous father Akbar (see pages 580–81). Written in Persian, the literary language of the eastern Islamic world, Jahangir's account of his reign followed the tradition of earlier Mughal emperors in noting major events of his lifetime, but it departed from that tradition in reflecting personally on art, politics, family life, and more.

- Why do you think Jahangir mounted such an elaborate coronation celebration for himself?

- In what ways did Jahangir seek to ensure the effective authority of the state he led?

- In what ways was Jahangir a distinctly Muslim ruler? In what respects did he and his father depart from Islamic principles?

- Based on these selections, what concrete problems of governance can you infer were facing Jahangir?

JAHANGIR

Memoirs

1605–1627

At the age of thirty-eight, I became Emperor. . . . As at the very instant that I seated myself on the throne, the sun rose from the horizon; I accepted this as the omen of victory, and as indicating a reign of unvarying prosperity. Hence I assumed the titles of . . . the world-subduing emperor, the world-subduing king.

On this occasion I made use of the throne prepared by my father, and enriched at an expense without parallel for the celebration of the festival of the new year. . . . Having thus seated myself on the throne of my expectations and wishes, I caused also the imperial crown, which my father had caused to be made after the manner of that which was worn by the great kings of Persia, to be brought before me, and then, in the presence of the whole assembled Emirs, having placed it on my brows, as an omen auspicious to the stability and happiness of my reign, kept it there for the space of a full astronomical hour. . . .

For forty days and forty nights I caused the . . . great imperial state drum, to strike up, without ceasing, the strains of joy and triumph; and . . . around my throne, the ground was spread by my directions with the most costly brocades and gold embroidered carpets. Censers [containers for burning incense] of gold and silver were disposed in different directions for the purpose of burning odoriferous drugs, and nearly three thousand camphorated wax lights . . . illuminated the scene from night till morning. Numbers of blooming youths, beautiful as young Joseph in the pavilions of Egypt, clad in dresses of the most costly materials . . . awaited my commands, rank after rank, and in attitude most respectful. And finally, the Emirs of the empire . . . covered from head to foot in gold and jewels, and shoulder to shoulder, stood round in brilliant array, also waiting for the commands of their sovereign. For forty days and forty nights did I keep open to the world these scenes of festivity and splendor, furnishing altogether an example of imperial magnificence seldom paralleled in this stage of earthly existence. . . .

I instituted . . . special regulations . . . as rules of conduct, never to be deviated from in their respective stations.

1. I remitted [canceled] altogether to my subjects three sources of revenue taxes or duties. . . .

2. I directed, when the district lay waste or destitute of inhabitants, that towns should be built. . . . I charged the Jaguir-daurs [local rulers granted a certain territory by the emperor], or feudatories of the empire, in such deserted places to erect mosques and substantial . . . stations for the accommodation of travelers, in order to render the district once more an inhabited country, and that wayfaring men might again be able to pass and repass in safety.

3. Merchants traveling through the country were not to have their bales or packages of any kind opened without their consent. But when they were perfectly willing to dispose of any article of merchandise, purchasers were permitted to deal with them, without, however, offering any species of molestation. . . .

5. No person was permitted either to make or sell either wine or any other kind of intoxicating liquor. I undertook to institute this regulation, although it is sufficiently notorious that I have myself the strongest inclination for wine, in which from the age of sixteen I have liberally indulged. . . .

6. No person [official] was permitted to take up his abode obtrusively in the dwelling of any subject of my realm. . . .

7. No person was to suffer, for any offense, the loss of a nose or ear. If the crime were theft, the offender was to be scourged with thorns, or deterred from further transgression by an attestation on the Koran.

8. [High officials] were prohibited from possessing themselves by violence of the lands of the subject, or from cultivating them on their own account. . . .

10. The governors in all the principal cities were directed to establish infirmaries or hospitals, with competent medical aid for the relief of the sick. . . .

11. During the month of my birth . . . the use of all animal food was prohibited both in town and country; and at equidistant periods throughout the year a day was set apart, on which all slaughtering of animals was strictly forbidden.

[H]aving on one occasion asked my father [Akbar] the reason why he had forbidden any one to prevent or interfere with the building of these haunts of idolatry [Hindu temples], his reply was in the following terms: "My dear child," said he, "I find myself a powerful monarch, the shadow of God upon earth. I have seen that he bestows the blessings of his gracious providence upon all his creatures without distinction. Ill should I discharge the duties of my exalted station, were I to withhold my compassion and indulgence from any of those entrusted to my charge. With all of the human race, with all of God's creatures, I am at peace: why then should I permit myself, under any consideration, to be the cause of molestation or aggression to any one? Besides, are not five parts in six of mankind either Hindus or aliens to the faith; and were I to be governed by motives of the kind suggested in your inquiry, what alternative can I have but to put them all to death! I have thought it therefore my wisest plan to let these men alone. Neither is it to be forgotten, that the class of whom we are speaking . . . are usefully engaged, either in the pursuits of science or the arts, or of improvements for the benefit of mankind, and have in numerous instances arrived at the highest distinctions in the state, there being, indeed, to be found in this city men of every description, and of every religion on the face of the earth."

Source: *The Memoirs of the Emperor Jahangir*, translated from the Persian by Major David Price (London: Oriental Translation Committee, 1829), 1–3, 5–8, 15.

Source 13.2
An Outsider's View of the Ottoman Empire

Under Suleiman I (r. 1520–1566), the Ottoman Empire reached its greatest territorial extent and perhaps its golden age in terms of culture and economy (see Map 13.4, page 583). A helpful window into the life of this most powerful of Muslim states comes from the writings of Ogier Ghiselin de Busbecq, a Flemish nobleman who served as a diplomat for the Austrian Empire, which then felt under great threat from Ottoman expansion into Central Europe. Busbecq's letters to a friend, excerpted in Source 13.2, present his view of the Ottoman court and his reflections on Ottoman military power.

- How do you think Busbecq's outsider status shaped his perceptions of Ottoman political and military life? To what extent does his role as a foreigner enhance or undermine the usefulness of his account for historians?

- How did he define the differences between the Ottoman Empire and Austria? What do you think he hoped to accomplish by highlighting these differences?

- What sources of Ottoman political authority are apparent in Busbecq's account?

- What potential problems of the Ottoman Empire does this document imply or state?

OGIER GHISELIN DE BUSBECQ
The Turkish Letters
1555–1562

On his [Suleiman's] arrival we were admitted to an audience. . . . His air [attitude], was by no means gracious, and his face wore a stern, though dignified, expression. On entering we were separately conducted into the royal presence by the chamberlains, who grasped our arms. This has been the Turkish fashion of admitting people to the Sovereign ever since a Croat, in order to avenge the death of his master . . . asked Amurath [an earlier Sultan] for an audience, and took advantage of it to slay him. After having gone through a pretense of kissing his hand, we were conducted backward to the wall opposite his seat, care being taken that we should never turn our backs on him. . . .

The Sultan's hall was crowded with people, among whom were several officers of high rank. Besides these there were all the troopers of the Imperial guard and a large force of Janissaries; but there was not in all that great assembly a single man who owed his position to aught save his valor and his merit. No distinction is attached to birth among the Turks. . . . In making his appointments the Sultan pays no regard to any pretensions on the score of wealth or rank, nor does he take into consideration recommendations or popularity. . . . It is by merit that men rise in the service, a system which ensures that posts should only be assigned to the competent. . . . Those who receive the highest offices from the Sultan are for the most part the sons of shepherds or herdsmen, and so far from being ashamed of their parentage, they actually glory in it, and consider it a matter of boasting that they owe nothing to the accident of birth. . . .

Among the Turks, therefore, honors, high posts, and judgeships are the rewards of great ability and good service. If a man be dishonest, or lazy, or careless, he remains at the bottom of the ladder, an object of contempt; for such qualities there are no honors in Turkey! This is the reason that they are successful in their undertakings, that they lord it over others, and are daily extending the bounds of their empire. These are not our ideas, with us [Europeans] there is no opening left for merit; birth is the standard for everything; the prestige of birth is the sole key to advancement in the public service. . . .

[T]ake your stand by my side, and look at the sea of turbaned heads, each wrapped in twisted folds of the whitest silk; look at those marvelously handsome dresses of every kind and every color; time would fail me to tell how all around is glittering with gold, with silver, with purple, with silk, and with velvet; words cannot convey an adequate idea of that strange and wondrous sight: it was the most beautiful spectacle I ever saw.

With all this luxury, great simplicity and economy are combined; every man's dress, whatever his position may be, is of the same pattern; no fringes or useless points are sewn on, as is the case with us, appendages which cost a great deal of money, and are worn out in three days. . . . I was greatly struck with the silence and order that prevailed in this great crowd. There were no cries, no hum of voices, the usual accompaniments of a motley gathering, neither was there any jostling; without the slightest disturbance each man took his proper place according to his rank. . . .

On leaving the assembly we had a fresh treat in the sight of the household cavalry returning to their quarters; the men were mounted on splendid horses, excellently groomed, and gorgeously accoutred. And so we left the royal presence, taking with us but little hope of a successful issue to our embassy.

The Turkish monarch going to war takes with him over 40,000 camels and nearly as many baggage mules, of which a great part, when he is invading Persia, are loaded with rice and other kinds of grain. . . . The invading army carefully abstains from encroaching on its magazines [supplies] at the outset. . . . The Sultan's magazines are opened, and a ration just sufficient to sustain life is daily weighed out to the Janissaries and other troops of the royal household.

From this you will see that it is the patience, self-denial, and thrift of the Turkish soldier that enable him to face the most trying circumstances. . . . What a contrast to our men! Christian soldiers on a campaign refuse to put up with their ordinary food, and call for thrushes, beccaficos [small birds], and such like dainty dishes! If these are not supplied they grow mutinous and work their own ruin; and, if they are supplied, they are ruined all the same. For each man is his own worst enemy, and has no foe more deadly than his own intemperance, which is sure to kill him, if the enemy be not quick.

It makes me shudder to think of what the result of a struggle between such different systems must be; one of us must prevail and the other be destroyed. . . . On their side is the vast wealth of their empire, unimpaired resources, experience and practice in arms, a veteran soldiery, an uninterrupted series of victories, readiness to endure hardships, union, order, discipline, thrift, and watchfulness. On ours are found an empty exchequer, luxurious habits, exhausted resources, broken spirits, a raw and insubordinate soldiery, and greedy generals; there is no regard for discipline, license runs riot, the men indulge in drunkenness and debauchery, and, worst of all, the enemy are accustomed to victory, we, to defeat. Can we doubt what the result must be? The only obstacle is Persia, whose position on his rear forces the invader to take precautions. The fear of Persia gives us a respite, but it is only for a time. When he has secured himself in that quarter, he will fall upon us with all the resources of the East. How ill prepared we are to meet such an attack it is not for me to say.

[*In the following passage, Busbecq reflects on a major problem of the Ottoman state, succession to the throne.*]

The sons of Turkish Sultans are in the most wretched position in the world, for, as soon as one of them succeeds his father, the rest are doomed to certain death. The Turk can endure no rival to the throne, and, indeed, the conduct of the Janissaries renders it impossible for the new Sultan to spare his brothers; for if one of them survives, the Janissaries are forever asking largesses. If these are refused, forthwith the cry is heard, "Long live the brother!" "God preserve the brother!"—a tolerably broad hint that they intend to place him on the throne. So that the Turkish Sultans are compelled to celebrate their succession by imbruing their hands in the blood of their nearest relatives.

Source: Charles Thornton Forester and F. H. Blackburne Daniell, *The Life and Letters of Ogier Ghiselin de Busbecq* (London: C. Kegan Paul, 1881), 114–15, 152–56, 219–22.

Source 13.3
French State Building and Louis XIV

Like their counterparts in the Middle East and Asia, a number of European states in the early modern era also pursued the twin projects of imperial expansion abroad and political integration at home. But consolidating central authority was a long and difficult task. Obstacles to the ambitions of kings in Europe were many—the absence of an effective transportation and communication infrastructure; the difficulty of acquiring information about the population and resources; the entrenched interests of privileged groups such as the nobility, church, town councils, and guilds; and the division between Catholics and Protestants.

Perhaps the most well-known example of such European state-building efforts is that of France under the rule of Louis XIV (r. 1643–1715). Louis and other European monarchs, such as those in Spain and Russia, operated under a set of assumptions known as absolutism, which held that kings ruled by "divine right" and could legitimately claim sole and uncontested authority in their realms. Louis's famous dictum *"L'état, c'est moi"* ("I am the state") summed up the absolutist ideal. Source 13.3 illustrates at least one way in which Louis attempted to realize this ideal.

Written by Louis himself, this document focuses on the importance of "spectacle" and public display in solidifying the exalted role of the monarch. The "carousel" described here was an extravagant pageant, held in Paris in June 1662. It featured various exotic animals, slaves, princes, and nobles arrayed in fantastic costumes representing distant lands, as well as many equestrian competitions. Unifying this disparate assembly was King Louis himself, dressed as a Roman emperor, while on the shields of the nobles was that grand symbol of the monarchy, the sun.

- What posture does Louis take toward his subjects in this document?

- How does he understand the role of spectacle in general and the carousel in particular?

- What does the choice of the sun as a royal symbol suggest about Louis's conception of his role in the French state and empire?

LOUIS XIV

Memoirs

1670

It was necessary to conserve and cultivate with care all that which, without diminishing the authority and the respect due to me, linked me by bonds of affection to my peoples and above all to the people of rank, so as to make them see by this very means that it was neither aversion for them nor affected severity, nor harshness of spirit, but simply reason and duty, that made me more reserved and more exact toward them in other matters. That sharing of pleasures, which gives people at court a respectable familiarity with us, touches them and charms them more than can be expressed. The common people, on the other hand, are delighted by shows in which, at bottom, we always have the aim of pleasing them; and all our subjects, in general, are delighted to see that we like what they like, or what they excel in. By this means we hold on to their hearts and their minds, sometimes more strongly perhaps than by recompenses and gifts; and with regard to foreigners, in a state they see flourishing and well ordered, that which is spent on expenses and which could be called superfluous, makes a very favorable impression on them, of magnificence, of power, of grandeur. . . .

The carousel, which has furnished me the subject of these reflections, had only been conceived at first as a light amusement; but little by little, we were carried away, and it became a spectacle that was fairly grand and magnificent, both in the number of exercises, and by the novelty of the costumes and the variety of the [heraldic] devices. It was

then that I began to employ the one that I have always kept since and which you see in so many places . . . it ought to represent in some way the duties of a prince, and constantly encourage me to fulfill them. For the device they chose the sun, which . . . is the most noble of all, and which, by its quality of being unique, by the brilliance that surrounds it, by the light that it communicates to the other stars which form for it a kind of court, by the just and equal share that the different climates of the world receive of this light, by the good it does in all places, ceaselessly producing as it does, in every sphere of life, joy and activity, by its unhindered movement, in which it nevertheless always appears calm, by its constant and invariable course, from which it never departs nor wavers, is the most striking and beautiful image of a great monarch.

Those who saw me governing with a good deal of ease and without being confused by anything, in all the numerous attentions that royalty demands, persuaded me to add the earth's globe, and for motto, *nec pluribus impar* (not unequal to many things): by which they meant something that flattered the aspirations of a young king, namely that, being sufficient to so many things, I would doubtless be capable of governing other empires, just as the sun was capable of lighting up other worlds if they were exposed to its rays.

Source: Robert Campbell, *Louis XIV* (London: Longmans, 1993), 117–18.

Source 13.4

An Outsider's View of the Inca Empire

Pedro de Cieza de León (1520–1554), a Spanish chronicler of the Inca Empire of the early sixteenth century, came to the Americas as a boy at the age of thirteen. For the next seventeen years, Cieza took part as a soldier in a number of expeditions that established Spanish rule in various parts of South America. Along the way, he collected a great deal of information, especially about the Inca Empire, which he began to publish on his return to Spain in 1550. Despite a very limited education, Cieza wrote a series of works that have become a major source for historians about the workings of the Inca Empire and about the Spanish conquest of that land. The selection that follows focuses on the techniques that the Incas used to govern their huge empire.

■ How would you describe Cieza's posture toward the Inca Empire? What in particular did he seem to appreciate about it?

■ Based on this account, what difficulties did the Inca rulers face in governing their large and diverse realm?

■ What policies or practices did the Inca authorities follow in seeking to integrate their empire?

■ Some modern observers have described the Inca Empire as "totalitarian" or "socialist." Do such terms seem appropriate? How else might you describe the Inca state?

■ How does Cieza's relationship to the Inca Empire compare to that of Busbecq to the Ottoman Empire?

PEDRO DE CIEZA DE LEÓN
Chronicles of the Incas
ca. 1550

The Incas had the seat of their empire in the city of Cuzco, where the laws were given and the captains set out to make war. . . . As soon as one of these large provinces was conquered, ten or twelve thousand of the men and their wives, or six thousand, or the number decided upon were ordered to leave and remove themselves from it. These were transferred to another town or province of the same climate and nature as that which they left. . . . And they had another device to keep the natives from hating them, and this was that they never divested the natural chieftains of their power. If it so happened that one of them committed a crime or in some way deserved to be stripped of his power, it was vested in his sons or brothers, and all were ordered to obey them. . . .

One of the things most to be envied in these rulers is how well they knew to conquer such vast lands. . . .

[T]hey entered many lands without war, and the soldiers who accompanied the Inca were ordered to do no damage or harm, robbery or violence. If there was a shortage of food in the province, he ordered supplies brought in from other regions so that those newly won to his service would not find his rule and acquaintance irksome. . . .

In many others, where they entered by war and force of arms, they ordered that the crops and houses of the enemy be spared. . . . But in the end the Incas always came out victorious, and when they had vanquished the others, they did not do them further harm, but released those they had taken prisoner, if there were any, and restored the booty, and put them back in possession of their property and rule, exhorting them not to be foolish and try to compete with his royal majesty nor abandon his friendship, but to be his friends as their neighbors were. And saying this, he gave them a number of beautiful women and fine pieces of wool or gold. . . .

They never deprived the native chieftains of their rule. They were all ordered to worship the sun as God, but they were not prohibited from observing their own religions and customs. . . .

It is told for a fact of the rulers of this kingdom that in the days of their rule they [the Incas] had their representatives in the capitals of all the provinces. . . . They served as head of the provinces or regions, and from every so many leagues around the tributes were brought to one of these capitals. . . . This was so well organized that there was not a village that did not know where it was to send its tribute. In all these capitals the Incas had temples of the sun, mints, and many silversmiths who did nothing but work rich pieces of gold or fair vessels of silver. . . . The tribute paid by each of these districts where the capital was situated, and that turned over by the natives, whether gold, silver, clothing, arms, and all else they gave, was entered in the accounts of the [quipu-] camayocs, who kept the quipus and did everything ordered by the governor in the matter of finding the soldiers or supplying whomever the Inca ordered, or making delivery to Cuzco; but when they came from the city of Cuzco to go over the accounts, or they were ordered to go to Cuzco to give an accounting, the accountants themselves gave it by the quipus, or went to give it where there could be no fraud, but everything had to come out right. Few years went by in which an accounting of all these things was not made. . . .

When the Incas set out to visit their kingdom, it is told that they traveled with great pomp, riding in rich litters set upon smooth, long poles of the finest wood and adorned with gold and silver. . . .

So many people came to see his passing that all the hills and slopes seemed covered with them, and all called down blessings upon him. . . .

He [the Inca] traveled four leagues each day, or as much as he wished; he stopped wherever he liked to inquire into the state of his kingdom; he willingly listened to those who came to him with complaints, righting wrongs and punishing those who had committed an injustice. . . .

[T]hese rulers, as the best measure, ordered and decreed, with severe punishment for failure to obey, that all the natives of their empire should know

and understand the language of Cuzco, both they and their women. . . . This was carried out so faithfully that in the space of a very few years a single tongue was known and used in an extension of more than 1,200 leagues; yet, even though this language was employed, they all spoke their own [languages], which were so numerous that if I were to list them it would not be credited. . . .

[The Inca] appointed those whose duty it was to punish wrongdoers, and to this end they were always traveling about the country. The Incas took such care to see that justice was meted out that nobody ventured to commit a felony or theft. This was to deal with thieves, ravishers of women, or conspirators against the Inca; however, there were many provinces that warred on one another, and the Incas were not wholly able to prevent this. By the river [Huatanay] that runs through Cuzco justice was executed on those who were caught or brought in as prisoners from some other place. There they had their heads cut off, or were put to death in some other manner which they chose. Mutiny and conspiracy were severely punished, and, above all, those who were thieves and known as such; even their wives and children were despised and considered to be tarred with the same brush. . . .

[I]n each of the many provinces there were many storehouses filled with supplies and other needful things; thus, in times of war, wherever the armies went they draw upon the contents of these storehouses, without ever touching the supplies of their confederates or laying a finger on what they had in their settlements. And when there was no war, all this stock of supplies and food was divided up among the poor and the widows. These poor were the aged, or the lame, crippled, or paralyzed, or those afflicted with some other diseases. . . . If there came a lean year, the storehouses were opened and the provinces were lent what they needed in the way of supplies; then, in a year of abundance, they paid back all they had received.

Source: *The Incas of Pedro de Cieza de León*, translated by Harriet de Onis (Norman: University of Oklahoma Press, 1959), 56–57, 158–60, 165–73, 177–78.

DOING HISTORY

State Building in the Early Modern Era

1. **Making comparisons:** To what extent did these four early modern states face similar problems and devise similar solutions? How did they differ? In particular, how did the rulers of these states deal with subordinates? How did they use violence? What challenges to imperial authority did they face?

2. **Assessing spectacle:** In what different ways was spectacle, royal splendor, or public display evident in the documents? How would you define the purpose of such display? How effective do you think spectacle has been in consolidating state authority?

3. **Distinguishing power and authority:** Some scholars have made a distinction between "power," the ability of a state to coerce its subjects into some required behavior, and "authority," the ability of a state to persuade its subjects to do its bidding voluntarily by convincing them that it is proper, right, or natural to do so. What examples of power and authority can you find in these documents? How were power and authority related? What are the advantages and disadvantages of each, from the viewpoint of ambitious rulers?

4. **Comparing past and present:** It is important to recognize that early modern states differed in many ways from twentieth- or twenty-first-century states. How would you define those differences? Consider, among other things, the personal role of the ruler, the use of violence, the means of establishing authority, and the extent to which the state could shape the lives of its citizens.

5. **Comparing insiders' and outsiders' accounts:** What differences do you notice between the two passages written by monarchs themselves and the two composed by foreign observers? What advantages and limitations do these two types of sources offer to historians seeking to use them as evidence?

Slave Merchant in Gorée Island, Senegal, from *Encyclopédie des Voyages*, engraved by L. F. Labrousse, 1796/Bibliothèque des Arts Décoratifs, Paris, France/Archives Charmet/Bridgeman Images

Economic Transformations

Commerce and Consequence
1450–1750

"I have come full circle back to my destiny: from Africa to America and back to Africa. I could hear the cries and wails of my ancestors. I weep with them and for them."[1] This is what an African American woman from Atlanta wrote in 2002 in the guest book of the Cape Coast Castle, one of the many ports of embarkation for slaves located along the coast of Ghana in West Africa. There she no doubt saw the whips and leg irons used to discipline the captured Africans as well as the windowless dungeons in which hundreds were crammed while waiting for the ships that would carry them across the Atlantic to the Americas. Almost certainly she also caught sight of the infamous "gate of no return," through which the captives departed to their new life as slaves.

This visitor's emotional encounter with the legacy of the Atlantic slave trade reminds us of the enormous significance of this commerce in human beings for the early modern world and of its continuing echoes even in the twenty-first century. The slave trade, however, was only one component of those international networks of exchange that shaped human interactions during the centuries between 1450 and 1750. Europeans now smashed their way into the ancient spice trade of the Indian Ocean, developing new relationships with Asian societies as a result. Silver, obtained from mines in Spanish America, enriched Western Europe, even as much of it made its way to China, where it allowed Europeans to participate more fully in the rich commerce of East Asia. Furs from North America and Siberia found a ready market in Europe and China, while the hunting and trapping of those fur-bearing animals transformed

---

The Atlantic Slave Trade   This eighteenth-century French engraving shows the sale of slaves at Gorée, a major slave-trading port in what is now Dakar in Senegal. A European merchant and an African authority figure negotiate the arrangement, while the shackled victims themselves wait for their fate to be decided.

both natural environments and human societies. Despite their growing prominence in long-distance exchange, Europeans were far from the only actors in early modern commerce. Southeast Asians, Chinese, Indians, Armenians, Arabs, Africans, and Native Americans likewise played major roles in the making of the world economy during the early modern era.

Thus commerce joined empire as the twin creators of a global network during these centuries. Together they gave rise to new relationships, disrupted old patterns, brought distant peoples into contact with one another, enriched some, and impoverished or enslaved others. They also generated new ways of expressing status, as the Working with Evidence feature on pages 634–41 illustrates. From the various "old worlds" of the premodern era, a single "new world" emerged—slowly, amid much suffering, and accompanied by growing inequalities. What was gained and what was lost in the transformations born of global commerce have been the subject of great controversy ever since.

SEEKING THE MAIN POINT

In what different ways did global commerce transform human societies and the lives of individuals during the early modern era?

Europeans and Asian Commerce

Schoolchildren everywhere know that European empires in the Western Hemisphere grew out of an accident—Columbus's unknowing encounter with the Americas—and that new colonial societies and new commercial connections across the Atlantic were the result. In Asia, it was a very different story. The voyage (1497–1499) of the Portuguese mariner Vasco da Gama, in which Europeans sailed to India for the first time, was certainly no accident. It was the outcome of a deliberate, systematic, century-long Portuguese effort to explore a sea route to the East, by creeping slowly down the West African coast, around the tip of South Africa, up the East African coast, and finally across the Indian Ocean to Calicut in southern India in 1498. There Europeans encountered an ancient and rich network of commerce that stretched from East Africa to China. They were certainly aware of the wealth of that commercial network, but largely ignorant of its workings.

■ **Causation**
What drove European involvement in the world of Asian commerce?

The most immediate motivation for this massive effort was the desire for tropical spices—cinnamon, nutmeg, mace, cloves, and, above all, pepper—which were widely used as condiments and preservatives and were sometimes regarded as aphrodisiacs. A fifteenth-century English book declared: "Pepper [from Java] is black and has a good smack, And every man doth buy it."[2] Other products of the East, such as Chinese silk, Indian cottons, rhubarb for medicinal purposes, emeralds, rubies, and sapphires, were also in great demand.

Underlying this growing interest in Asia was the more general recovery of European civilization following the disaster of the Black Death in the early fourteenth century. During the fifteenth century, Europe's population was growing again, and its national monarchies—in Spain, Portugal, England, and France—were learning how to tax their subjects more effectively and to build substantial military forces equipped with gunpowder weapons. Its cities were growing too. Some of them—

A MAP OF TIME

Early 15th century	Beginning of Portuguese voyages along the coast of West Africa
1440s	First European export of slaves from West Africa
1492	Columbus reaches the Americas
1497	Vasco da Gama reaches India
1545	Founding of Potosí as silver mining town in Bolivia
1565	Beginning of Spanish takeover of the Philippines
1570s	Beginning of silver shipments from Mexico to Manila
17th century	Russian conquest of Siberia
1601–1602	British and Dutch East India companies established in Asia
18th century	Peak of the transatlantic slave trade
1750s	British begin military conquest of India

in England, the Netherlands, and northern Italy, for example—were becoming centers of international commerce, giving birth to economies based on market exchange, private ownership, and the accumulation of capital for further investment.

For many centuries, Eastern goods had trickled into the Mediterranean through the Middle East from the Indian Ocean commercial network. From the viewpoint of an increasingly dynamic Europe, several major problems accompanied this pattern of trade. First, of course, the source of supply for these much-desired goods lay solidly in Muslim hands. Most immediately, Muslim Egypt was the primary point of transfer into the Mediterranean basin and its European Christian customers. The Italian commercial city of Venice largely monopolized the European trade in Eastern goods, annually sending convoys of ships to Alexandria in Egypt. Venetians resented the Muslim monopoly on Indian Ocean trade, and other European powers disliked relying on Venice as well as on Muslims. Circumventing these monopolies was yet another impetus—both religious and political—for the Portuguese to attempt a sea route to India that bypassed both Venetian and Muslim intermediaries. In addition, many Europeans of the time were persuaded that a mysterious Christian monarch, known as Prester John, ruled somewhere in Asia or Africa. Joining with his mythical kingdom to continue the Crusades and combat a common Islamic enemy was likewise a goal of the Portuguese voyages.

A further problem for Europeans lay in paying for Eastern goods. Few products of an economically less developed Europe were attractive in Eastern markets. Thus Europeans were required to pay cash—gold or silver—for Asian spices or textiles.

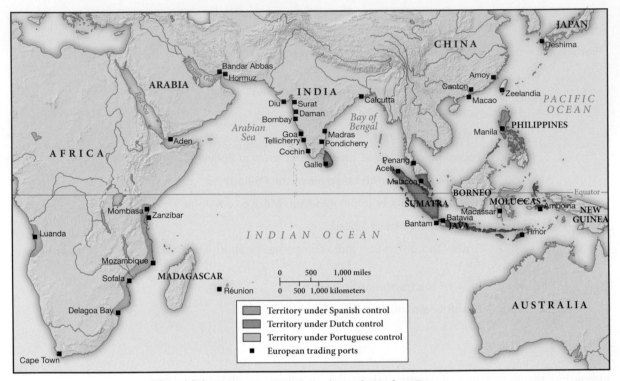

Map 14.1   Europeans in Asia in the Early Modern Era

The early modern era witnessed only very limited territorial control by Europeans in Asia. Trade, rather than empire, was the chief concern of the Western newcomers, who were not, in any event, a serious military threat to major Asian states.

This persistent trade deficit contributed much to the intense desire for precious metals that attracted early modern European explorers, traders, and conquerors. Portuguese voyages along the West African coast, for example, were seeking direct access to African goldfields. The enormously rich silver deposits of Mexico and Bolivia provided at least a temporary solution to this persistent European problem.

First the Portuguese and then the Spanish, French, Dutch, and British found their way into the ancient Asian world of Indian Ocean commerce (see Map 14.1). How they behaved in that world and what they created there differed considerably among the various European countries, but collectively they contributed much to the new regime of globalized trade.

A Portuguese Empire of Commerce

The arena of Indian Ocean commerce into which Vasco da Gama and his Portuguese successors sailed was a world away from anything they had known. It was vast, both in geographic extent and in the diversity of those who participated in it. East Africans, Arabs, Persians, Indians, Malays, Chinese, and others traded freely.

Most of them were Muslims, though hailing from many separate communities, but Hindus, Buddhists, Christians, Jews, and Chinese likewise had a role in this commercial network. Had the Portuguese sought simply to participate in peaceful trading, they certainly could have done so, but it was quickly apparent that European trade goods were crude and unattractive in Asian markets and that Europeans would be unable to compete effectively. Moreover, the Portuguese soon learned that most Indian Ocean merchant ships were not heavily armed and certainly lacked the onboard cannons that Portuguese ships carried. Since the withdrawal of the Chinese fleet from the Indian Ocean early in the fifteenth century, no major power was in a position to dominate the sea lanes, and the many smaller-scale merchants generally traded openly, although piracy was sometimes a problem.

Given these conditions, the Portuguese saw an opening, for their ships could outgun and outmaneuver competing naval forces, while their onboard cannons could devastate coastal fortifications. Although their overall economy lagged behind that of Asian producers, Europeans had more than caught up in the critical area of naval technology and naval warfare. This military advantage enabled the Portuguese to quickly establish fortified bases at several key locations within the Indian Ocean world—Mombasa in East Africa, Hormuz at the entrance to the Persian Gulf, Goa on the west coast of India, Malacca in Southeast Asia, and Macao on the south coast of China. With the exception of Macao, which had been obtained through bribery and negotiations with Chinese authorities, these Portuguese bases were obtained forcibly against small and weak states. In Mombasa, for example, the commander of a Portuguese fleet responded to local resistance in 1505 by burning and sacking the city, killing some 1,500 people, and seizing large quantities of cotton and silk textiles and carpets. The king of Mombasa wrote a warning to a neighboring city:

> This is to inform you that a great lord has passed through the town, burning it and laying it waste. He came to the town in such strength and was of such a cruelty that he spared neither man nor woman, or old nor young—nay, not even the smallest child. . . . Nor can I ascertain nor estimate what wealth they have taken from the town.[3]

What the Portuguese created in the Indian Ocean is commonly known as a "trading post empire," for they aimed to control commerce, not large territories or populations, and to do so by force of arms rather than by economic competition. Seeking to monopolize the spice trade, the Portuguese king grandly titled himself "Lord of the Conquest, Navigation, and Commerce of Ethiopia, Arabia, Persia, and India." Portuguese authorities in the East tried to require all merchant vessels to purchase a *cartaz*, or pass, and to pay duties of 6 to 10 percent on their cargoes. They partially blocked the traditional Red Sea route to the Mediterranean and for a century or so monopolized the highly profitable route around Africa to Europe. Even so, they never succeeded in controlling much more than half of the spice trade to Europe.

■ **Connection**
To what extent did the Portuguese realize their own goals in the Indian Ocean?

The Spice Trade
For thousands of years, spices were a major trade item in the Indian Ocean commercial network, as this fifteenth-century French depiction of the gathering of pepper in southern India illustrates. In the early modern era, Europeans gained direct access to this ancient network for the first time. (From the *Livres des Merveilles du Monde*, ca. 1410–1412, by Master Boucicaut [fl. 1390–1430] and workshop/Bibliothèque Nationale, Paris, France /Archives Charmet/Bridgeman Images)

Failing to dominate Indian Ocean commerce as they had hoped, the Portuguese gradually assimilated themselves to its ancient patterns. They became heavily involved in carrying Asian goods to Asian ports, selling their shipping services because they were largely unable to sell their goods. Even in their major settlements, the Portuguese were outnumbered by Asian traders, and many married Asian women. Hundreds of Portuguese escaped the control of their government altogether and settled in Asian or African ports, where they learned local languages, sometimes converted to Islam, and became simply one more group in the diverse trading culture of the East.

By 1600, the Portuguese trading post empire was in steep decline. This small European country was overextended, and rising Asian states such as Japan, Burma, Mughal India, Persia, and the sultanate of Oman actively resisted Portuguese commercial control. Unwilling to accept a dominant Portuguese role in the Indian Ocean, other European countries also gradually contested Portugal's efforts to monopolize the rich spice trade to Europe.

Spain and the Philippines

Spain was the first to challenge Portugal's position. As precious and profitable spices began to arrive in Europe on Portuguese ships in the early sixteenth century, the Spanish soon realized that they were behind in the race to gain access to the riches of the East. In an effort to catch up, they established themselves on what became the Philippine Islands, named after the Spanish king Philip II. The Spanish first encountered the region during the famous round-the-world voyage (1519–1521) of Ferdinand Magellan, a Portuguese mariner sailing on behalf of the Spanish Crown. There they found an archipelago of islands, thousands of them, occupied by culturally diverse peoples and organized in small and highly competitive chiefdoms. One of the local chiefs later told the Spanish: "There is no king and no sole authority in this land; but everyone holds his own view and opinion, and does as he prefers."[4] Some were involved in tribute trade with China, and a small number of Chinese settlers lived in the port towns. Nonetheless, the region was of little interest to the governments of China and Japan, the major powers in the area.

These conditions — proximity to China and the spice islands, small and militarily weak societies, the absence of competing claims — encouraged the Spanish to establish outright colonial rule on the islands, rather than to imitate a Portuguese-style trading post empire. Accomplished largely from Spanish Mexico, conquest and colonization involved small-scale military operations, gunpowder weapons, local alliances, gifts and favors to chiefs, and the pageantry of Catholic ritual, all of which contributed to a relatively easy and often-bloodless Spanish takeover of the islands in the century or so after 1565. They remained a Spanish colonial territory until the end of the nineteenth century, when the United States assumed control following the Spanish-American War of 1898.

Accompanying Spanish rule was a major missionary effort, which turned Filipino society into the only major outpost of Christianity in Asia. That effort also opened up a new front in the long encounter of Christendom and Islam, for on the southern island of Mindanao, Islam was gaining strength and provided an ideology of resistance to Spanish encroachment for 300 years. Indeed, Mindanao remains a contested part of the Philippines into the twenty-first century.

Beyond the missionary enterprise, other features of Spanish colonial practice in the Americas found expression in the Philippines. People living in scattered settlements were persuaded or forced to relocate into more concentrated Christian communities. Tribute, taxes, and unpaid labor became part of ordinary life. Large landed estates emerged, owned by Spanish settlers, Catholic religious orders, or prominent Filipinos. Women who had played major roles as ritual specialists, healers, and midwives were now displaced by male Spanish priests, and the ceremonial instruments of these women were deliberately defiled and disgraced. Short-lived revolts and flight to interior mountains were among the Filipino responses to colonial oppression.

Yet others fled to Manila, the new capital of the colonial Philippines. By 1600, it had become a flourishing and culturally diverse city of more than 40,000 inhabitants and was home to many Spanish settlers and officials and growing numbers of Filipino migrants. Its rising prosperity also attracted some 3,000 Japanese and more than 20,000 Chinese. Serving as traders, artisans, and sailors, the Chinese in particular became an essential element in the Spanish colony's growing economic

■ Comparison
How did the Portuguese, Spanish, Dutch, and British initiatives in Asia differ from one another?

relationship with China; however, their economic prominence and their resistance to conversion earned them Spanish hostility and clearly discriminatory treatment. Periodic Chinese revolts, followed by expulsions and massacres, were the result. On one occasion in 1603, the Spanish killed about 20,000 people, nearly the entire Chinese population of the island.

The East India Companies

Far more important than the Spanish as European competitors for the spice trade were the Dutch and English, both of whom entered Indian Ocean commerce in the early seventeenth century. Together they quickly overtook and displaced the Portuguese, often by force, even as they competed vigorously with each other as well. These rising Northern European powers were both militarily and economically stronger than the Portuguese. During the sixteenth century, the Dutch had become a highly commercialized and urbanized society, and their business skills and maritime shipping operations were the envy of Europe. Around 1600, both the British and the Dutch, unlike the Portuguese, organized their Indian Ocean ventures through private trading companies, which were able to raise money and share risks among a substantial number of merchant investors. The British East India Company and the Dutch East India Company received charters from their respective governments granting them trading monopolies and the power to make war and to govern conquered peoples. Thus they established their own parallel and competing trading post empires, with the Dutch focused on the islands of Indonesia and the English on India. Somewhat later, a French company also established settlements in the Indian Ocean basin.

■ **Change**
To what extent did the British and Dutch trading companies change the societies they encountered in Asia?

Operating in a region of fragmented and weak political authority, the Dutch acted to control not only the shipping of cloves, cinnamon, nutmeg, and mace but also their production. With much bloodshed, the Dutch seized control of a number of small spice-producing islands, forcing their people to sell only to the Dutch and destroying the crops of those who refused. On the Banda Islands, famous for their nutmeg, the Dutch killed, enslaved, or left to starve virtually the entire population of some 15,000 people and then replaced them with Dutch planters, using a slave labor force to produce the nutmeg crop. One Indonesian sultan asked a Dutch commander, "Do you believe that God has preserved for your trade alone islands which lie so far from your homeland?"[5] Apparently the Dutch did. And for a time in the seventeenth century, they were able to monopolize the trade in nutmeg, mace, and cloves and to sell these spices in Europe and India at fourteen to seventeen times the price they paid in Indonesia.[6] While Dutch profits soared, the local economy of the Spice Islands was shattered, and their people were impoverished.

The Dutch East India Company also established itself briefly on the large island of Taiwan, off the coast of southern China, between 1624 and 1662, hoping to produce deerskins, rice, and sugar for export. Finding the local people unwilling to take part in commercial agriculture, the Dutch opened the island to large-scale

Chinese immigration. Thus, under a regime of Dutch and Chinese "co-colonization," Taiwan became ethnically Chinese. Later in the century, Chinese forces expelled the Dutch, bringing Taiwan into China politically as well. And so Taiwan emerged as a site of intersection between European and Chinese expansion in the early modern era.[7]

The British East India Company operated differently from its Dutch counterpart. Less well financed and less commercially sophisticated, the British were largely excluded from the rich Spice Islands by the Dutch monopoly. Thus they fell back on India, where they established three major trading settlements during the seventeenth century: Bombay (now Mumbai), on India's

A European View of Asian Commerce
The various East India companies (British, French, and Dutch) represented the major vehicle for European commerce in Asia during the early modern era. This wall painting, dating from 1778 and titled *The East Offering Its Riches to Britannia*, hung in the main offices of the British East India Company. (*The East Offering Its Riches to Britannia*, by Roma Spiridione [d. 1787]/British Library, London, UK/© British Library Board. All Rights Reserved/Bridgeman Images)

west coast, and Calcutta and Madras, on the east coast. Although British naval forces soon gained control of the Arabian Sea and the Persian Gulf, largely replacing the Portuguese, on land they were no match for the powerful Mughal Empire, which ruled most of the Indian subcontinent. Therefore, the British were unable to practice "trade by warfare," as the Dutch did in Indonesia.[8] Rather, they secured their trading bases with the permission of Mughal authorities or local rulers, with substantial payments and bribes as the price of admission to the Indian market. When some independent English traders plundered a Mughal ship in 1636, local authorities detained British East India Company officials for two months and forced them to pay a whopping fine. Although pepper and other spices remained important in British trade, British merchants came to focus much more heavily on Indian cotton textiles, which were becoming widely popular in England and its American colonies. Hundreds of villages in the interior of southern India became specialized producers for this British market.

Like the Portuguese before them, both the Dutch and English became heavily involved in trade within Asia. The profits from this "carrying trade" enabled them to purchase Asian goods without paying for them in gold or silver from Europe. Dutch and English traders also began to deal in bulk goods for a mass market — pepper, textiles, and later, tea and coffee — rather than just luxury goods for an elite market. In the second half of the eighteenth century, both the Dutch and British trading post empires slowly evolved into a more conventional form of colonial domination, in which the British came to rule India and the Dutch controlled Indonesia.

Asians and Asian Commerce

The attention of historians often falls disproportionately on what is new. Although European commerce in the Indian Ocean and the South China Sea certainly qualifies as "something new," the European presence was far less significant in Asia than it was in the Americas or Africa during these centuries. European political control was limited to the Philippines, parts of Java, and a few of the Spice Islands. The small Southeast Asian state of Siam was able to expel the French in 1688, outraged by their aggressive religious efforts at conversion and their plotting to extend French influence. To the great powers of Asia—Mughal India, China, and Japan—Europeans represented no real military threat and played minor roles in their large and prosperous economies. Japan provides a fascinating case study in the ability of major Asian powers to control the European intruders.

When Portuguese traders and missionaries first arrived in that island nation in the mid-sixteenth century, soon followed by Spanish, Dutch, and English merchants, Japan was plagued by endemic conflict among numerous feudal lords, known as *daimyo*, each with his own cadre of *samurai* warriors. In these circumstances, the European newcomers found a hospitable welcome, for their military technology, shipbuilding skills, geographic knowledge, commercial opportunities, and even religious ideas proved useful or attractive to various elements in Japan's fractious and competitive society. The second half of the sixteenth century, for example, witnessed the growth of a substantial Christian movement, with some 300,000 converts and a Japanese-led church organization.

By the early seventeenth century, however, a series of remarkable military figures had unified Japan politically, under the leadership of a supreme military commander known as the *shogun*, who hailed from the Tokugawa clan. With the end of Japan's civil wars, successive shoguns came to view Europeans as a threat to the country's newly established unity rather than an opportunity. They therefore expelled Christian missionaries and violently suppressed the practice of Christianity. This policy included the execution, often under torture, of some sixty-two missionaries and thousands of Japanese converts. Shogunate authorities also forbade Japanese from traveling abroad and banned most European traders altogether, permitting only the Dutch, who appeared less interested in spreading Christianity, to trade at a single site. Thus, for two centuries (1650–1850), Japanese authorities of the Tokugawa shogunate largely closed their country off from the emerging world of European commerce, although they maintained their trading ties to China, Korea, and Southeast Asia.

In the early seventeenth century, a large number of Japanese traders began to operate in Southeast Asia, where they behaved much like the newly arriving Europeans, frequently using force in support of their commercial interests. But unlike European states, the Japanese government of the Tokugawa shogunate explicitly disavowed any responsibility for or connection with these Japanese merchants. In one of many letters to rulers of Southeast Asian states, the Tokugawa shogun wrote to officials in Cambodia in 1610: "Merchants from my country [Japan] go to several places in your country [Cambodia] as well as Cochinchina and Champa [Vietnam]. There they become cruel and ferocious. . . . These men cause terrible damage. . . . They commit crimes and cause suffering. . . . Their offenses are extremely serious. Please punish them immediately according to the laws of your country. It is not necessary to have any reservations in this regard."[9] Thus Japanese merchants lacked the kind of support from their government that European merchants consistently received, but they did not refrain from trading in Southeast Asia.

Nor did other Asian merchants disappear from the Indian Ocean, despite European naval dominance. Arab, Indian, Chinese, Javanese, Malay, Vietnamese, and other traders benefited from the upsurge in seaborne commerce. Resident communities of Chinese merchants inhabited many Southeast Asian port cities and dominated the growing spice trade between that region and China. Southeast Asian merchants, many of them women, continued a long tradition of involvement in international trade. Malay proverbs from the sixteenth century, for example, encouraged "teaching daughters how to calculate and make a profit."[10] Overland trade within Asia remained wholly in Asian hands and grew considerably. Christian merchants from Armenia were particularly active in the commerce linking Europe, the Middle East, and Central Asia. Tens of thousands of Indian merchants and moneylenders, mostly Hindus representing sophisticated family firms, lived throughout Central Asia, Persia, and Russia, thus connecting this vast region to markets in India. These international Asian commercial networks, equivalent in their commercial sophistication to those of Europe, continued to operate successfully even as Europeans militarized the seaborne commerce of the Indian Ocean.

Within India, large and wealthy family firms, such as the one headed by Virji Vora during the seventeenth century, were able to monopolize the buying and selling of particular products, such as pepper or coral, and thus dictate terms and prices to the European trading companies. "He knoweth that wee must sell," complained one English trader about Vora, "and so beats us downe till we come to his owne rates." Furthermore, Vora was often the only source of loans for the cash-strapped Europeans, forcing them to pay interest rates as high as 12 to 18 percent annually. Despite their resentments, Europeans had little choice, because "none but Virji Vora hath moneye to lend or will lend."[11]

Silver and Global Commerce

Even more than the spice trade of Eurasia, it was the silver trade that gave birth to a genuinely global network of exchange (see Map 14.2). As one historian put it, silver "went round the world and made the world go round."[12] The mid-sixteenth-century discovery of enormously rich silver deposits in Bolivia, and simultaneously in Japan, suddenly provided a vastly increased supply of that precious metal. Spanish America alone produced perhaps 85 percent of the world's silver during the early modern era. Spain's sole Asian colony, the Philippines, provided a critical link in

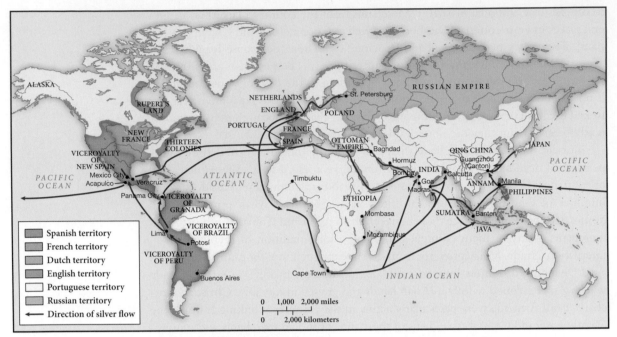

Map 14.2   The Global Silver Trade

Silver was one of the first major commodities to be exchanged on a genuinely global scale.

■ **Connection**

What was the significance of the silver trade in the early modern era of world history?

this emerging network of global commerce. Manila, the colonial capital of the Philippines, was the destination of annual Spanish shipments of silver, which were drawn from the rich mines of Bolivia, transported initially to Acapulco in Mexico, and from there shipped across the Pacific to the Philippines. This trade was the first direct and sustained link between the Americas and Asia, and it initiated a web of Pacific commerce that grew steadily over the centuries.

At the heart of that Pacific web, and of early modern global commerce generally, was China's huge economy, especially its growing demand for silver. In the 1570s, Chinese authorities consolidated a variety of tax levies into a single tax, which its huge population was now required to pay in silver. This sudden new demand for the white metal caused its value to skyrocket. It meant that foreigners with silver could now purchase far more of China's silks and porcelains than before.

This demand set silver in motion around the world, with the bulk of the world's silver supply winding up in China and much of the rest elsewhere in Asia. The routes by which this "silver drain" operated were numerous. Chinese, Portuguese, and Dutch traders flocked to Manila to sell Chinese goods in exchange for silver. European ships carried Japanese silver to China. Much of the silver shipped across the Atlantic to Spain was spent in Europe generally and then used to pay for the Asian goods that the French, British, and Dutch so greatly desired. Silver paid for some African slaves and for spices in Southeast Asia. The standard Spanish silver coin, known as a "piece of eight," was used by merchants in North America, Europe, India, Russia, and West Africa as a medium of exchange. By 1600, it circulated widely in southern China. A Portuguese merchant in 1621 noted that silver "wanders throughout all the world . . . before flocking to China, where it remains as if at its natural center."[13]

In its global journeys, silver transformed much that it touched, and nowhere more profoundly than at Potosí, the site of a huge silver-mining operation in what is now Bolivia. (See Zooming In: Potosí, page 614.) In Spain itself, which was the initial destination for much of Latin America's silver, the precious metal vastly enriched the Crown, making Spain the envy of its European rivals during the sixteenth century. Spanish rulers could now pursue military and political ambitions in both Europe and the Americas far beyond the country's own resource base. "New World mines," concluded several prominent historians, "supported the Spanish empire."[14] Nonetheless, this vast infusion of wealth did not fundamentally transform the Spanish economy, because it generated more inflation of prices than real economic growth. A rigid economy laced with monopolies and regulations, an aristocratic class that preferred leisure to enterprise, and a crusading insistence on religious uniformity all prevented the Spanish from using their silver windfall in a productive fashion. When the value of silver dropped in the early seventeenth century, Spain lost its earlier position as the dominant Western European power. More generally, the flood of American silver that circulated in Europe drove prices higher, further impoverished many, stimulated uprisings across the continent, and, together with the Little Ice Age of global cooling, contributed to what historians sometimes call a "General Crisis" of upheaval and instability in the seventeenth century. (For a broader discussion of the General Crisis, see Chapter 13, page 560.)

Japan, another major source of silver production in the sixteenth century, did better. Its military rulers, the Tokugawa shoguns, used silver-generated profits to defeat hundreds of rival feudal lords and unify the country. Unlike their Spanish counterparts, the shoguns allied with the country's vigorous domestic merchant class to develop a market-based economy and to invest heavily in agricultural and industrial enterprises. Japanese state and local authorities alike acted vigorously to protect and renew Japan's dwindling forests, while millions of families in the eighteenth century took steps to have fewer children by practicing late marriages, contraception, abortion, and infanticide. The outcome was the dramatic slowing of Japan's population growth, the easing of an impending ecological crisis, and a flourishing, highly commercialized economy. These were the foundations for Japan's remarkable nineteenth-century Industrial Revolution.

In China, silver deepened the already-substantial commercialization of the country's economy. To obtain the silver needed to pay their taxes, more and more people had to sell something—either their labor or their products. Communities that devoted themselves to growing mulberry trees, on which silkworms fed, had to buy their rice from other regions. Thus the Chinese economy became more

Potosí, a Mountain of Silver

China's insatiable demand for silver during the early modern period drove global commerce, transforming the economies and societies of far distant lands. Perhaps nowhere did the silver trade have a greater impact than at Cerro de Potosí, a mountain located in a barren and remote stretch of Andean highlands, ten weeks' travel by mule from Lima, Peru. In 1545, Spanish prospectors discovered the richest deposit of silver in history at Potosí, and within a few decades this single mountain was producing over half of the silver mined in the world each year. At its foot, the city of Potosí grew rapidly. "New people arrive by the hour, attracted by the smell of silver," commented a Spanish observer in the 1570s. Within just a few decades, Potosí's population had reached 160,000 people, making it the largest city in the Americas and equivalent in size to London, Amsterdam, or Seville.

The mines of Potosí.

The silver was mined and processed at great human and environmental cost. The Spanish authorities forced Native American villages across a wide region of the Andes to supply workers for the mines, with as many as 14,000 to 16,000 at a time laboring in horrendous conditions. A Spanish priest observed, "Once inside, they spend the whole week in there without emerging, working with tallow candles. They are in great danger inside there, for one very small stone that falls injures or kills anyone it strikes. If 20 healthy Indians enter on Monday, half may emerge crippled on Saturday."[15] Work aboveground, often undertaken by slaves of African descent, was also dangerous because extracting silver from the mined ore required mixing it with the toxic metal mercury. Many thousands died. Mortality rates were so high that some families held funeral

regionally specialized. Particularly in southern China, this surging economic growth resulted in the loss of about half the area's forest cover as more and more land was devoted to cash crops. No Japanese-style conservation program emerged to address this growing problem. An eighteenth-century Chinese poet, Wang Dayue, gave voice to the fears that this ecological transformation generated:

Rarer, too, their timber grew, and rarer still and rarer
As the hills resembled heads now shaven clean of hair.
For the first time, too, moreover, they felt an anxious mood
That all their daily logging might not furnish them with fuel.[16]

China's role in the silver trade is a useful reminder of Asian centrality in the world economy of the early modern era. Its large and prosperous population,

services for men drafted to work in the mines before they embarked for Potosí. Beyond the human cost, the environment suffered as well when highly intensive mining techniques deforested the region and poisoned and eroded the soil.

Although some indigenous merchants, muleteers, and chiefs were enriched by mining, much of the wealth generated flowed to the Europeans who owned the mines and to the Spanish government, which impounded one-fifth of the silver as well as collecting other taxes and duties. European elites in Potosí lived in luxury, with all the goods of Europe and Asia at their disposal. Merchants brought to Potosí French hats, Venetian glass, German swords, Persian carpets, Southeast Asian spices, and Chinese porcelain and silks. Potosí also imported almost all of its basic needs because the dry, cold region was unable to support the city. Pack trains of llamas brought large quantities of foodstuffs, cloth, and other necessities from Ecuador, Peru, Chile, and Argentina. By the early seventeenth century, the economies of many regions in Spanish South America were structured to supply this huge mining operation.

While the mines caused much suffering, the silver-fueled economy of Potosí also offered opportunity to groups beyond the mine-owning European elite, not least to women. To earn a few pesos for the household, Spanish women might rent out buildings they owned for commercial purposes or send their slaves into the streets as small-scale traders. Less well-to-do Spanish women often ran stores, pawnshops, bakeries, and taverns. Indian and *mestiza* women likewise opened businesses that provided the city with beverages, food, clothing, and credit. The wealth created a hive of commercial activity in this otherwise-barren backwater.

But the silver that created Potosí also caused its decline. After a century of intensive mining, all that remained were lower-quality ores that were difficult to extract from the ground. This led the mines to shut down. By 1800, Potosí, which had once rivaled the largest cities in Europe, was just a shadow of its former self. The history of this remote region of the Andes reminds us of the profound and often-conflicting results of world trade during the early modern period. While many suffered in the hellish conditions of the mines, others grew wealthy off the demand for silver.

Question: What can Potosí tell us about the consequences of global trade in the early modern period?

increasingly operating within a silver-based economy, fueled global commerce, vastly increasing the quantity of goods exchanged and the geographic range of world trade. Despite their obvious physical presence in the Americas, Africa, and Asia, economically speaking Europeans were essentially middlemen, funneling American silver to Asia and competing with one another for a place in the rich markets of the East. The productivity of the Chinese economy was evident in Spanish America, where cheap and well-made Chinese goods easily outsold those of Spain. In 1594, the Spanish viceroy of Peru observed that "a man can clothe his wife in Chinese silks for [25 pesos], whereas he could not provide her with clothing of Spanish silks with 200 pesos."[17] Indian cotton textiles likewise outsold European woolen or linen textiles in the seventeenth century to such an extent that French laws in 1717 prohibited the wearing of Indian cotton or Chinese silk clothing as a means of protecting French industry.

"The World Hunt": Fur in Global Commerce

In the early modern era, furs joined silver, textiles, and spices as major items of global commerce.[18] Their production had an important environmental impact as well as serious implications for the human societies that generated and consumed them. Furs, of course, had long provided warmth and conveyed status in colder regions of the world, but the integration of North America and of northern Asia (Siberia) into a larger world economy vastly increased their significance in global trade.

By 1500, European population growth and agricultural expansion had sharply diminished the supply of fur-bearing animals, such as beaver, rabbits, sable, marten, and deer. Furthermore, much of the early modern era witnessed a period of cooling temperatures and harsh winters, known as the Little Ice Age, which may well have increased the demand for furs. "The weather is bitterly cold and everyone is in furs although we are almost in July," observed a surprised visitor from Venice while in London in 1604.[19] These conditions pushed prices higher. The cost of a good-quality beaver pelt, for example, quadrupled in France between 1558 and 1611. This price increase translated into strong economic incentives for European traders to tap the immense wealth of fur-bearing animals found in North America. At the same time, the collapse of Native American populations in North America caused by the Great Dying led to the regrowth of forest habitats for fur-bearing animals and deer herds.

Like other aspects of imperial expansion, the fur trade was a highly competitive enterprise. The French were most prominent in the St. Lawrence valley, around the Great Lakes, and later along the Mississippi River; British traders pushed into the Hudson Bay region; and the Dutch focused their attention along the Hudson River in what is now New York. They were frequently rivals for the great prize of North American furs. In the southern colonies of British North America, deerskins by the hundreds of thousands found a ready market in England's leather industry (see Map 14.3).

Only a few Europeans directly engaged in commercial trapping or hunting. They usually waited for Indians to bring the furs or skins initially to their coastal settlements and later to their fortified trading posts in the interior of North America. European merchants paid for the furs with a variety of trade goods, including guns, blankets, metal tools, rum, and brandy, amid much ceremony, haggling over prices, and ritualized gift giving. Native Americans represented a cheap labor force in this international commercial effort, but they were not a directly coerced labor force.

Over the three centuries of the early modern era, enormous quantities of furs and deerskins found their way to Europe, where they considerably enhanced the standard of living in those cold climates. The environmental price was paid in the Americas, and it was high. A consistent demand for beaver hats led to the near extinction of that industrious animal in much of North America by the early nineteenth century and with it the degradation or loss of many wetland habitats. Other

■ **Change**
Describe the impact of the fur trade on North American native societies.

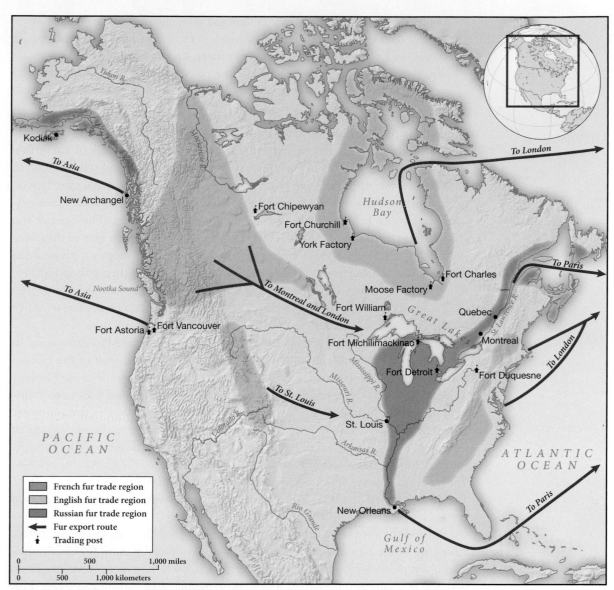

Map 14.3   The North American Fur Trade

North America, as well as Russian Siberia, funneled an apparently endless supply of furs into the circuits of global trade during the early modern era.

fur-bearing species were also seriously depleted as the trade moved inexorably west-ward. By the 1760s, hunters in southeastern British colonies took about 500,000 deer every year, seriously diminishing the deer population of the region. As early as 1642, Miantonomo, a chief of the New England Narragansett people, spoke of the environmental consequences of English colonialism:

You know our fathers had plenty of deer and skins and our plains were full of game and turkeys, and our coves and rivers were full of fish. But, brothers, since these Englishmen have seized our country, they have cut down the grass with scythes, and the trees with axes. Their cows and horses eat up the grass, and their hogs spoil our bed of clams; and finally we shall all starve to death.[20]

For the Native American peoples who hunted, trapped, processed, and transported these products, the fur trade bore various benefits, particularly at the beginning. The Hurons, for example, who lived on the northern shores of Lakes Erie and Ontario in the early seventeenth century, annually exchanged some 20,000 to 30,000 pelts, mostly beaver, and in return received copper pots, metal axes, knives, cloth, firearms, and alcohol. Many of these items were of real value, which strengthened the Hurons in their relationships with neighboring peoples. These goods also enhanced the authority of Huron chiefs by providing them with gifts to distribute among their followers. At least initially, competition among Europeans ensured that Native American leaders could negotiate reasonable prices for their goods. Furthermore, their important role in the lucrative fur trade protected them for a time from the kind of extermination, enslavement, or displacement that was the fate of native peoples in Portuguese Brazil.

Nothing, however, protected them against the diseases carried by Europeans. In the 1630s and 1640s, to cite only one example of many, about half of the Hurons perished from influenza, smallpox, and other European-borne diseases. Furthermore, the fur trade generated warfare beyond anything previously known. Competition among Native American societies became more intense as the economic stakes grew higher. Catastrophic population declines owing to disease stimulated "mourning wars," designed to capture people who could be assimilated into much-diminished societies. A century of French-British rivalry for North America (1664–1763) forced Native American societies to take sides, to fight, and to die in these European imperial conflicts. Firearms, of course, made warfare far more deadly than before.

Beyond the fur trade, many Native American peoples sought actively to take advantage of the new commercial economy now impinging upon them. The Iroquois, for example, began to sell new products such as ginseng root, much in demand in China as a medicine. They also rented land to Europeans, worked for wages in various European enterprises, and started to use currency, when barter was ineffective. But as they became enmeshed in these commercial relationships, Native Americans grew dependent on European trade goods. Among the Algonquians, for example, iron tools and cooking pots replaced those of stone, wood, or bone; gunpowder weapons took the place of bows and arrows; European textiles proved more attractive than traditional beaver and deerskin clothing; and flint and steel were found to be more effective for starting fires than wooden drills. A wide range of traditional crafts were thus lost, while the native peoples did not gain a corresponding ability to manufacture the new items for themselves. Enthusiasm for these imported goods and continued European demands for furs and skins frequently eroded the customary restraint that characterized traditional hunting practices, resulting in the depletion of many species. One European observer wrote of the Creek Indians: "[They] wage eternal war against deer and bear . . . which is indeed carried to an unreasonable and perhaps criminal excess, since the white people have dazzled their senses with foreign superfluities."[21]

Alongside germs and guns, yet another highly destructive European import was alcohol—rum and brandy, in particular. Whiskey, a locally produced grain-based alcohol, only added to the problem. With no prior experience of alcohol and little time to adjust to its easy availability, these drinks "hit Indian societies with explosive force."[22] Binge drinking, violence among young men, promiscuity, and addiction followed in many places. In 1753, Iroquois leaders complained bitterly to European authorities in Pennsylvania: "These wicked Whiskey Sellers, when they have once got the Indians in liquor, make them sell their very clothes from their backs. . . . If this practice be continued, we must be inevitably ruined."[23] In short, it was not so much the fur trade itself that decimated Native American societies, but all that accompanied it—disease, dependence, guns, alcohol, and the growing encroachment of European colonial empires.

All of this had particular implications for women. A substantial number of native women married European traders according to the "custom of the country"—with no sanction from civil or church authorities. Such marriages eased the difficulties of this cross-cultural exchange, providing traders with guides, interpreters, and negotiators. But sometimes these women were left abandoned when their husbands returned to Europe. More generally, the fur trade enhanced the position of men in their societies since hunting or trapping animals was normally a male occupation. Among the Ojibwa, a gathering and hunting people in the northern Great Lakes region, women had traditionally acquired economic power by creating

Fur and the Russians
This colored engraving shows a sixteenth-century Russian ambassador and his contingent arriving at the court of the Holy Roman Emperor and bearing gifts of animal pelts, the richest fruit of the expanding Russian Empire. (Contemporary color line engraving, 1576/The Granger Collection, NYC —All rights reserved)

food, utensils, clothing, and decorations from the hides and flesh of the animals that their husbands caught. With the fur trade in full operation, women spent more time processing those furs for sale than in producing household items, some of which were now available for purchase from Europeans. And so, as one scholar put it, "women lost authority and prestige." At the same time, however, women generated and controlled the trade in wild rice and maple syrup, both essential to the livelihood of European traders.[24] Thus the fur trade offered women a mix of opportunities and liabilities.

Paralleling the North American fur trade was the one simultaneously taking shape within a rapidly expanding Russian Empire, which became a major source of furs for Western Europe, China, and the Ottoman Empire. The profitability of that trade in furs was the chief incentive for Russia's rapid expansion during the sixteenth and seventeenth centuries across Siberia, where the "soft gold" of fur-bearing animals was abundant. The international sale of furs greatly enriched the Russian state as well as many private merchants, trappers, and hunters. Here the silver trade and the fur trade intersected, as Europeans paid for Russian furs largely with American gold and silver.

■ **Comparison**
How did the North American and Siberian fur trades differ from each other? What did they have in common?

The consequences for native Siberians were similar to those in North America as disease took its toll, as indigenous people became dependent on Russian goods, as the settler frontier encroached on native lands, and as many species of fur-bearing mammals were seriously depleted. In several ways, however, the Russian fur trade was unique. Whereas several European nations competed in North America and generally obtained their furs through commercial negotiations with Indian societies, no such competition accompanied Russian expansion across Siberia. Russian authorities imposed a tax or tribute, payable in furs, on every able-bodied Siberian

SUMMING UP SO FAR

What differences can you identify in the operation and impact of the spice, silver, and fur trades?

male between eighteen and fifty years of age. To enforce the payment, they took hostages from Siberian societies, with death as a possible outcome if the required furs were not forthcoming. A further difference lay in the large-scale presence of private Russian hunters and trappers, who competed directly with their Siberian counterparts.

Commerce in People: The Atlantic Slave Trade

Of all the commercial ties that linked the early modern world into a global network of exchange, none had more profound or enduring human consequences than the Atlantic slave trade. Between 1500 and 1866, this trade in human beings took an estimated 12.5 million people from African societies, shipped them across the Atlantic in the infamous Middle Passage, and deposited some 10.7 million of them in the Americas, where they lived out their often-brief lives as slaves. About 1.8 million (14.4 percent) died during the transatlantic crossing, while countless others perished in the process of capture and transport to the African coast.[25] (See Map 14.4.)

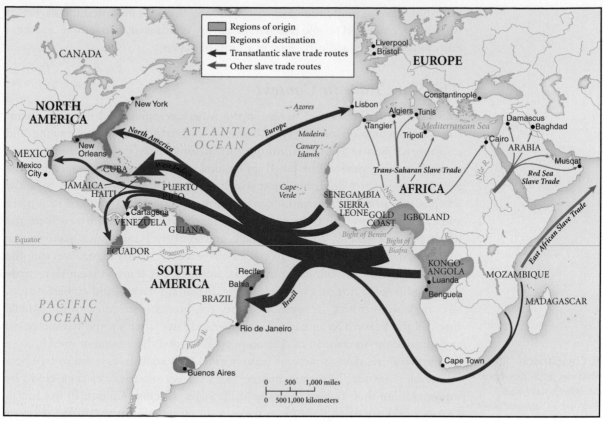

Map 14.4   The Atlantic Slave Trade
Stimulated by the plantation complex of the Americas, the Atlantic slave trade represented an enormous extension of the ancient practice of people owning and selling other people.

Beyond the multitude of individual tragedies that it spawned—capture and sale, displacement from home cultures, forced labor, beatings and brandings, broken families—the Atlantic slave trade transformed all of its participants. Within Africa itself, that commerce thoroughly disrupted some societies, strengthened others, and corrupted many. Elites often enriched themselves, while the slaves, of course, were victimized almost beyond imagination.

In the Americas, the slave trade added a substantial African presence to the mix of European and Native American peoples. This African diaspora (the global spread of African peoples) injected into these new societies issues of race that endure still in the twenty-first century. It also introduced elements of African culture, such as religious ideas, musical and artistic traditions, and cuisine, into the making of American cultures. The profits from the slave trade and the forced labor of African slaves certainly enriched European and Euro-American societies, even as the practice of slavery contributed much to the racial stereotypes of European peoples. Finally, slavery became a metaphor for many kinds of social oppression, quite different from plantation slavery, in the centuries that followed. Workers protested the slavery of wage labor, colonized people rejected the slavery of imperial domination, and feminists sometimes defined patriarchy as a form of slavery.

The Slave Trade in Context

The Atlantic slave trade and slavery in the Americas represented the most recent large-scale expression of a very widespread human practice—the owning and exchange of human beings. It was present in some early gathering and hunting societies, among some village-based agricultural peoples, and in pastoral communities. But the practice flourished most widely in civilizations where it was generally accepted as a perfectly normal human enterprise and was closely linked to warfare and capture. Before 1500, the Mediterranean and Indian Ocean basins were the major arenas of the Old World slave trade, and southern Russia was a major source of slaves. Many African societies likewise both practiced slavery themselves and sold slaves into these international commercial networks. A trans-Saharan slave trade had long funneled African captives into Mediterranean slavery, and an East African slave trade from at least the seventh century C.E. brought Africans into the Middle East and the Indian Ocean basin. Both operated largely within the Islamic world and initiated the movement of African peoples beyond the continent itself.

■ Comparison

What was distinctive about the Atlantic slave trade? What did it share with other patterns of slave owning and slave trading?

Furthermore, slavery came in many forms. Although slaves were everywhere vulnerable "outsiders" to their masters' societies, in many places they could be integrated into their owners' households, lineages, or communities. In the Indian Ocean world, for example, African slaves were often assimilated into the societies of their owners and lost the sense of a distinctive identity that was so prominent in North America. In some places, children inherited the slave status of their parents; elsewhere those children were free persons. Within the Islamic world, where most slaves worked in domestic settings, the preference was for female slaves by a two-to-one margin, while the later Atlantic slave trade, which funneled captives into plantation labor, favored males by a similar margin. Not all slaves, however, occupied degraded positions. Some in the Islamic world acquired prominent military or political status. Most slaves in the premodern world worked in their owners' households, farms, or shops, with smaller numbers laboring in large-scale agricultural or industrial enterprises.

The slavery that emerged in the Americas was distinctive in several ways. One was simply the immense size of the traffic in slaves and its centrality to the economies of colonial America. Furthermore, this New World slavery was largely based on plantation agriculture and treated slaves as a form of dehumanized property, lacking any rights in the society of their owners. Slave status throughout the Americas was inherited across generations, and there was little hope of eventual freedom for the vast majority. Nowhere else, with the possible exception of ancient Greece, was widespread slavery associated with societies that affirmed values of human freedom and equality. Perhaps most distinctive was the racial dimension: Atlantic slavery came to be identified wholly with Africa and with "blackness." How did this exceptional form of slavery emerge?

The origins of Atlantic slavery clearly lie in the Mediterranean world and with that now-common sweetener known as sugar. Until the Crusades, Europeans knew nothing of sugar and relied on honey and fruits to sweeten their bland diets. However, as they learned from the Arabs about sugarcane and the laborious techniques for producing usable sugar, Europeans established sugar-producing plantations within the Mediterranean and later on various islands off the coast of West Africa. It was a "modern" industry, perhaps the first one, in that it required huge capital investment, substantial technology, an almost factory-like discipline among workers, and a mass market of consumers. The immense difficulty and danger of the work, the limitations attached to serf labor, and the general absence of wageworkers all pointed to slavery as a source of labor for sugar plantations.

Initially, Slavic-speaking peoples from the Black Sea region furnished the bulk of the slaves for Mediterranean plantations, so much so that "Slav" became the basis for the word "slave" in many European languages. In 1453, however, when the Ottoman Turks seized Constantinople, the supply of Slavic slaves was effectively cut off. At the same time, Portuguese mariners were exploring the coast of West Africa; they were looking primarily for gold, but they also found there an alternative source of slaves available for sale. Thus, when sugar, and later tobacco and cotton, plantations took hold in the Americas, Europeans had already established links to a West African source of supply. They also now had religious justification for their actions, for in 1452 the pope formally granted to the kings of Spain and Portugal "full and free permission to invade, search out, capture, and subjugate the Saracens [Muslims] and pagans and any other unbelievers . . . and to reduce their persons into perpetual slavery."[26] Largely through a process of elimination, Africa became the primary source of slave labor for the plantation economies of the Americas. Slavic peoples were no longer available; Native Americans quickly perished from European diseases; marginal Europeans were Christians and therefore supposedly exempt from slavery; and European indentured servants, who agreed to work for a fixed period in return for transportation, food, and shelter, were expensive and temporary. Africans, on the other hand, were skilled farmers; they had some immunity to both tropical and European diseases; they were not Christians; they were, relatively speaking, close at hand; and they were readily available in substantial numbers through African-operated commercial networks.

Moreover, Africans were black. The precise relationship between slavery and European racism has long been a much-debated subject. Historian David Brion Davis has suggested the controversial view that "racial stereotypes were transmitted, along with black slavery itself, from Muslims to Christians."[27] For many centuries, Muslims had drawn on sub-Saharan Africa as one source of slaves and in the process had developed a form of racism. The fourteenth-century Tunisian scholar

■ Causation
What explains the rise of the Atlantic slave trade?

Ibn Khaldun wrote that black people were "submissive to slavery, because Negroes have little that is essentially human and have attributes that are quite similar to those of dumb animals."[28]

Other scholars find the origins of racism within European culture itself. For the English, argues historian Audrey Smedley, the process of conquering Ireland had generated by the sixteenth century a view of the Irish as "rude, beastly, ignorant, cruel, and unruly infidels," perceptions that were then transferred to Africans enslaved on English sugar plantations of the West Indies.[29] Whether Europeans borrowed such images of Africans from their Muslim neighbors or developed them independently, slavery and racism soon went hand in hand. "Europeans were better able to tolerate their brutal exploitation of Africans," writes a prominent world historian, "by imagining that these Africans were an inferior race, or better still, not even human."[30]

The Slave Trade in Practice

The European demand for slaves was clearly the chief cause of this tragic commerce, and from the point of sale on the African coast to the massive use of slave labor on American plantations, the entire enterprise was in European hands. Within Africa itself, however, a different picture emerges, for over the four centuries of the Atlantic slave trade, European demand elicited an African supply. A few early efforts by the Portuguese at slave raiding along the West African coast convinced Europeans that such efforts were unwise and unnecessary, for African societies were quite capable of defending themselves against European intrusion, and many were willing to sell their slaves peacefully. Furthermore, Europeans died like flies when they entered the interior because they lacked immunities to common tropical diseases. Thus the slave trade quickly came to operate largely with Europeans waiting on the coast, either on their ships or in fortified settlements, to purchase slaves from African merchants and political elites. Certainly, Europeans tried to exploit African rivalries to obtain slaves at the lowest possible cost, and the firearms they funneled into West Africa may well have increased the warfare from which so many slaves were derived. But from the point of initial capture to sale on the coast, the entire enterprise was normally in African hands. Almost nowhere did Europeans attempt outright military conquest; instead they generally dealt as equals with local African authorities.

■ **Connection**
What roles did Europeans and Africans play in the unfolding of the Atlantic slave trade?

An arrogant agent of the British Royal Africa Company in the 1680s learned the hard way who was in control when he spoke improperly to the king of Niumi, a small state in what is now Gambia. The company's records describe what happened next:

> [O]ne of the grandees [of the king], by name Sambalama, taught him better manners by reaching him a box on the ears, which beat off his hat, and a few thumps on the back, and seizing him . . . and several others, who together with the agent were taken and put into the king's pound and stayed there three or four days till their ransom was brought, value five hundred bars.[31]

In exchange for slaves, African sellers sought both European and Indian textiles, cowrie shells (widely used as money in West Africa), European metal goods, firearms and gunpowder, tobacco and alcohol, and various decorative items such as beads. Europeans purchased some of these items—cowrie shells and Indian textiles, for example—with silver mined in the Americas. Thus the slave trade connected with commerce in silver and textiles as it became part of an emerging worldwide network of exchange. Issues about the precise mix of goods African authorities desired, about the number and quality of slaves to be purchased, and always about the price of everything were settled in endless negotiation. Most of the time, a leading historian concluded, the slave trade took place "not unlike international trade anywhere in the world of the period."[32]

For the slaves themselves—seized in the interior, often sold several times on the harrowing journey to the coast, sometimes branded, and held in squalid slave dungeons while awaiting transportation to the New World—it was anything but a normal commercial transaction. One European engaged in the trade noted that "the negroes are so willful and loath to leave their own country, that they have often leap'd out of the canoes, boat, and ship, into the sea, and kept under water till they were drowned, to avoid being taken up and saved by our boats."[33]

Over the four centuries of the slave trade, millions of Africans underwent such experiences, but their numbers varied considerably over time. During the sixteenth century, slave exports from Africa averaged fewer than 3,000 annually. In those years, the Portuguese were at least as much interested in African gold, spices, and textiles. Furthermore, as in Asia, they became involved in transporting African goods, including slaves, from one African port to another, thus becoming the "truck drivers" of coastal West African commerce.[34] In the seventeenth century, the pace picked up as the slave trade became highly competitive, with the

The Middle Passage
This mid-nineteenth-century painting of slaves held belowdecks on a Spanish slave ship illustrates the horrendous conditions of the transatlantic voyage, a journey experienced by many millions of captured Africans. (Watercolor by Lt. Francis Meinelli, British Royal Navy/The Granger Collection, NYC—All rights reserved)

British, Dutch, and French contesting the earlier Portuguese monopoly. The century and a half between 1700 and 1850 marked the high point of the slave trade as the plantation economies of the Americas boomed. (See Snapshot, opposite.)

Where did these Africans come from, and where did they go? Geographically, the slave trade drew mainly on the societies of West and South-Central Africa, from present-day Mauritania in the north to Angola in the south. Initially focused on the coastal regions, the slave trade progressively penetrated into the interior as the demand for slaves picked up. Socially, slaves were mostly drawn from various marginal groups in African societies—prisoners of war, criminals, debtors, people who had been "pawned" during times of difficulty. Thus Africans did not generally sell "their own people" into slavery. Divided into hundreds of separate, usually small-scale, and often rival communities—cities, kingdoms, microstates, clans, and villages—the various peoples of West Africa had no concept of an "African" identity. Those whom they captured and sold were normally outsiders, vulnerable people who lacked the protection of membership in an established community. When short-term economic or political advantage could be gained, such people were sold. In this respect, the Atlantic slave trade was little different from the experience of enslavement elsewhere in the world.

The destination of enslaved Africans, half a world away in the Americas, was very different. The vast majority wound up in Brazil or the Caribbean, where the labor demands of the plantation economy were most intense. Smaller numbers found themselves in North America, mainland Spanish America, or in Europe itself. Their journey across the Atlantic was horrendous, with the Middle Passage having an overall mortality rate of more than 14 percent.

Enslaved Africans frequently resisted their fates in a variety of ways. About 10 percent of the transatlantic voyages experienced a major rebellion by desperate captives, and resistance continued in the Americas, taking a range of forms from surreptitious slowdowns of work to outright rebellion. One common act was to flee. Many who escaped joined free communities of former slaves known as maroon societies, which were founded in remote regions, especially in South America and the Caribbean. The largest such settlement was Palmares in Brazil, which endured for most of the seventeenth century, housing 10,000 or more people, mostly of African descent but also including Native Americans, mestizos, and renegade whites. While slave owners feared wide-scale slave rebellions, these were rare, and even small-scale rebellions were usually crushed with great brutality. It was only with the Haitian Revolution of the 1790s that a full-scale slave revolt brought lasting freedom for its participants.

Consequences: The Impact of the Slave Trade in Africa

From the viewpoint of world history, the chief outcome of the slave trade lay in the new transregional linkages that it generated as Africa became a permanent part of an interacting Atlantic world. Millions of its people were now compelled to make

SNAPSHOT   The Slave Trade in Numbers (1501–1866)[35]

The Rise and Decline of the Slave Trade

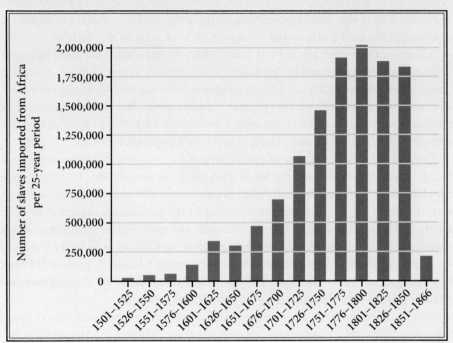

The Destinations of Slaves

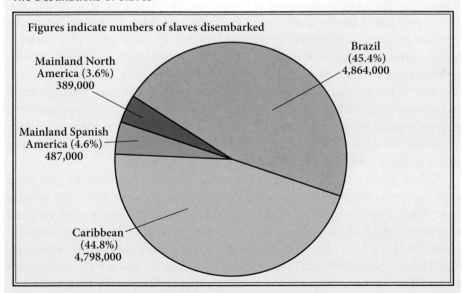

Figures indicate numbers of slaves disembarked

Brazil
(45.4%)
4,864,000

Mainland North
America (3.6%)
389,000

Mainland Spanish
America (4.6%)
487,000

Caribbean
(44.8%)
4,798,000

their lives in the Americas, where they made an enormous impact both demo-graphically and economically. Until the nineteenth century, they outnumbered European immigrants to the Americas by three or four to one, and West African societies were increasingly connected to an emerging European-centered world economy. These vast processes set in motion a chain of consequences that have transformed the lives and societies of people on both sides of the Atlantic.

■ **Change**
In what different ways did the Atlantic slave trade transform African societies?

Although the slave trade did not cause Africa to experience the kind of popu-lation collapse that occurred in the Americas, it certainly slowed Africa's growth at a time when Europe, China, and other regions were expanding demographically. Scholars have estimated that sub-Saharan Africa represented about 18 percent of the world's population in 1600, but only 6 percent in 1900.[36] A portion of that dif-ference reflects the slave trade's impact on Africa's population history.

Beyond the loss of millions of people over four centuries, the slave trade pro-duced economic stagnation and social disruption. Economically, the slave trade stimulated little positive change in Africa because those Africans who benefited most from the traffic in people were not investing in the productive capacities of their societies. Although European imports generally did not displace traditional artisan manufacturing, no technological breakthroughs in agriculture or industry increased the wealth available to these societies. Maize and manioc (cassava), introduced from the Americas, added a new source of calories to African diets, but the international demand was for Africa's people, not its agricultural products.

Socially too, the slave trade shaped African societies. It surely fostered moral corruption, particularly as judicial proceedings were manipulated to generate vic-tims for the slave trade. A West African legend that cowrie shells, a major currency of the slave trade, grew on corpses of the slaves was a symbolic recognition of the corrupting effects of this commerce in human beings. During the seventeenth cen-tury, a movement known as the Lemba cult appeared along the lower and middle stretches of the Congo River. It brought together the mercantile elite—chiefs, traders, caravan leaders—of a region heavily involved in the slave trade. Com-plaining about stomach pains, breathing problems, and sterility, they sought protec-tion against the envy of the poor and the sorcery that it provoked. Through ritual and ceremony as well as efforts to control markets, arrange elite marriages, and police a widespread trading network, Lemba officials sought to counter the disrup-tive impact of the slave trade and to maintain elite privileges in an area that lacked an overarching state authority.

African women felt the impact of the slave trade in various ways, beyond those who numbered among its transatlantic victims. Since far more men than women were shipped to the Americas, the labor demands on those women who remained increased substantially, compounded by the growing use of cassava, a labor-intensive import from the New World. Unbalanced sex ratios also meant that far more men than before could marry multiple women. Furthermore, the use of female slaves within West African societies also grew as the export trade in male slaves expanded. Retaining female slaves for their own use allowed warriors and nobles in the Senegambia region to distinguish themselves more clearly from ordinary peasants. In the Kongo, female slaves provided a source of dependent laborers for the plantations that sustained the lifestyle of urban elites. A European merchant on the Gold Coast in the late eighteenth century observed that every free man had at least one or two slaves.

For much smaller numbers of women, the slave trade provided an opportunity to exercise power and accumulate wealth. In the Senegambia region, where women had long been involved in politics and commerce, marriage to European traders offered advantage to both partners. For European male merchants, as for fur traders in North America, such marriages afforded access to African-operated commercial networks as well as the comforts of domestic life. Some of the women involved in these cross-cultural marriages, known as *signares*, became quite wealthy, operating their own trading empires, employing large numbers of female slaves, and acquiring elaborate houses, jewelry, and fashionable clothing.

Furthermore, the state-building enterprises that often accompanied the slave trade in West Africa offered yet other opportunities to a few women. As the Kingdom of Dahomey (deh-HOH-mee) expanded during the eighteenth century, the royal palace, housing thousands of women and presided over by a powerful Queen Mother, served to integrate the diverse regions of the state. Each lineage was required to send a daughter to the palace even as well-to-do families sent additional girls to increase their influence at court. In the Kingdom of Kongo, women held lower-level administrative positions, the head wife of a nobleman exercised authority over hundreds of junior wives and slaves, and women served on the council that advised the monarch. The neighboring region of Matamba was known for its female rulers, most notably the powerful Queen Nzinga (1626–1663), who guided the state amid the complexities and intrigues of various European and African rivalries and gained a reputation for her resistance to Portuguese imperialism.

Within particular African societies, the impact of the slave trade differed considerably from place to place and over time. Many small-scale kinship-based societies, lacking the protection of a strong state, were thoroughly disrupted by raids from more powerful neighbors, and insecurity was pervasive. Oral traditions in southern Ghana, for example, reported that "there was no rest in the land," that people went about in groups rather than alone, and that mothers kept their children inside when European ships appeared.[37] Some larger kingdoms such as Kongo and Oyo slowly disintegrated as access to trading opportunities and firearms enabled outlying regions to establish their independence. (For an account of one young man's journey to slavery and back, see Zooming In: Ayuba Suleiman Diallo, page 630.)

However, African authorities also sought to take advantage of the new commercial opportunities and to manage the slave trade in their own interests. The Kingdom of Benin, in the forest area of present-day Nigeria, successfully avoided a deep involvement in the trade while diversifying the exports with which it purchased European firearms and other goods. As early as 1516, its ruler began to

Ayuba Suleiman Diallo: To Slavery and Back

February 1730 found Ayuba Suleiman Diallo, less than thirty years of age, living between the Gambia and Senegal rivers in West Africa among the Fulbe-speaking people.[38] Like his father, a prominent Islamic scholar and teacher, Ayuba was a Muslim who was literate in Arabic, a prayer leader in the local mosque, and a *hafiz*, someone who had memorized the entire Quran. He was also husband to two wives and father to four children. Now his father sent the young man on an errand. He was to take several of their many slaves to a location some 200 miles away, where an English trading ship had anchored, and exchange them for paper and other goods. The paper was especially important, for his father's income depended on inscribing passages from the Quran on small slips of paper and selling them as protective charms.

To put it mildly, things did not go as planned. Unable to reach an agreement with the English merchant Captain

Ayuba Suleiman Diallo.

Stephen Pike, Ayuba traveled farther south and traded his slaves for a number of cows in the land of the Mandinka people. Well beyond the safety of his own country, he was in dangerous territory. As he and his companions stopped to rest on the journey home, they were seized, their heads were shaved, and they were sold as slaves to the very same Captain Pike. Although Ayuba was able to send a message to his father asking to be ransomed in exchange for some of their slaves, the ship sailed before a reply was received. And so Ayuba, along with 168 other slaves, both men and women, headed for the British American colony of Maryland, where 150 of them arrived alive.

Sold to a local planter, Ayuba was immediately sent to the tobacco fields, but when he became ill from this heavy and unaccustomed work, his owner assigned him

photo: By William Hoare of Bath (1707–1792), 1733, oil on canvas/photo © Christie's Images/Bridgeman Images

restrict the slave trade and soon forbade the export of male slaves altogether, a ban that lasted until the early eighteenth century. By then, the ruler's authority over outlying areas had declined, and the country's major exports of pepper and cotton cloth had lost out to Asian and then European competition. In these circumstances, Benin felt compelled to resume limited participation in the slave trade. The neighboring kingdom of Dahomey, on the other hand, turned to a vigorous involvement in the slave trade in the early eighteenth century under strict royal control. The army conducted annual slave raids, and the government soon came to depend on the trade for its essential revenues. The slave trade in Dahomey became the chief business of the state and remained so until well into the nineteenth century.

the less arduous and more familiar task of tending cattle. Alone with the cattle, Ayuba was able to withdraw into a nearby forest to pray, but he was spotted by a young white boy who mocked him and threw dirt in his face. Sometime later, no doubt in despair, Ayuba ran away, but he was soon captured and housed in the county jail, located in the back room of a tavern. There he became something of a local curiosity and attracted the attention of a lawyer named Thomas Bluett. When Ayuba refused wine, wrote a few lines in Arabic, and mentioned "Allah" and "Muhammad," Bluett realized that he was "no common slave." After locating an old slave who could translate for him, Bluett became fascinated by Ayuba's story, and he initiated a process that took both of them to England in 1733, where philanthropists purchased Ayuba's freedom.

Ayuba's reception in England was amazing. Now fluent in English, Ayuba was received by the English royal family and various members of the nobility, hosted by leading scholars, and entertained by wealthy merchants, eager to tap his knowledge of economic conditions in West Africa. The prominent artist William Hoare painted his portrait, complete with a small Quran hanging from his neck.

In 1734, he finally set off for home, loaded with gifts from his English friends. There he encountered, quite by chance, the same Mandinka men who had sold him only a few years before. Francis Moore, a European trader accompanying Ayuba, wrote that he "fell into a most terrible passion and was for killing them" and was restrained from doing so only with difficulty. He arrived in his hometown to find that his father had recently died. His wives and children, however, were all alive and welcomed him warmly. One of his wives had remarried, believing him gone forever, but her new husband readily gave way, and Ayuba resumed his place of prominence in his own community until his death in 1773.

He also resumed his life as a slave owner. Selling some of the gifts he had acquired in England, he purchased a woman slave and two horses soon after his arrival back in West Africa. According to Moore, he "spoke always very handsomely of the English," and he continued his association with the Royal African Company, the primary English trading firm in West Africa, in their rivalry with French traders.[39] The last mention of Ayuba in the records of that company noted that he was seeking compensation for the loss of two slaves and a watch, probably the one given him in England by Queen Caroline.

Questions: What might you infer about Ayuba's own view of slavery and the slave trade? What insights or questions about the slave trade does his remarkable story suggest?

REFLECTIONS

Economic Globalization—Then and Now

The study of history reminds us of two quite contradictory truths. One is that our lives in the present bear remarkable similarities to those of people long ago. We are perhaps not so unique as we might think. The other is that our lives are very different from theirs and that things have changed substantially. This chapter about global commerce—long-distance trade in spices and textiles, silver and gold, beaver pelts and deerskins, slaves and sugar—provides both perspectives.

If we are accustomed to thinking about globalization as a product of the late twentieth century, early modern world history provides a corrective. Those three centuries reveal much that is familiar to people of the twenty-first century—the global circulation of goods; an international currency; production for a world market; the growing economic role of the West on the global stage; private enterprise, such as the British and Dutch East India companies, operating on a world scale; national governments eager to support their merchants in a highly competitive environment. By the eighteenth century, many Europeans dined from Chinese porcelain dishes called "china," wore Indian-made cotton textiles, and drank chocolate from Mexico, tea from China, and coffee from Yemen while sweetening these beverages with sugar from the Caribbean or Brazil. The millions who worked to produce these goods, whether slave or free, were operating in a world economy. Some industries were thoroughly international. New England rum producers, for example, depended on molasses imported from the Caribbean, while the West Indian sugar industry used African labor and European equipment to produce for a global market.

Nonetheless, early modern economic globalization was a far cry from that of the twentieth century. The most obvious differences, perhaps, were scale and speed. By 2000, immensely more goods circulated internationally, and far more people produced for and depended on the world market than was the case even in 1750. Back-and-forth communications between England and India that took eighteen months in the eighteenth century could be accomplished in an hour by telegraph in the late nineteenth century and almost instantaneously via the Internet in the late twentieth century. Moreover, by 1900 globalization was firmly centered in the economies of Europe and North America. In the early modern era, by contrast, Asia in general and China in particular remained major engines of the world economy, despite the emerging presence of Europeans around the world. By the end of the twentieth century, the booming economies of Turkey, Brazil, India, and China suggested at least a partial return to that earlier pattern.

Early modern globalization differed in still other ways from that of the contemporary world. Economic life then was primarily preindustrial: it was still powered by human and animal muscles, wind, and water and lacked the enormous productive capacity that accompanied the later technological breakthrough of the steam engine and the Industrial Revolution. Finally, the dawning of a genuinely global economy in the early modern era was tied unapologetically to empire building and to slavery, both of which had been discredited by the late twentieth century. Slavery lost its legitimacy during the nineteenth century, and formal territorial empires largely disappeared in the twentieth. Most people during the early modern era would have been surprised to learn that a global economy, as it turned out, could function effectively without either of these long-standing practices.

Second Thoughts

What's the Significance?

Big Picture Questions

1. To what extent did Europeans transform earlier patterns of commerce, and in what ways did they assimilate into those older patterns?

2. How should we distribute the moral responsibility for the Atlantic slave trade? Is this an appropriate task for historians?

3. What lasting legacies of early modern globalization are evident in the twenty-first century? Pay particular attention to the legacies of the slave trade.

4. **Looking Back:** Asians, Africans, and Native Americans experienced early modern European expansion in quite different ways. Based on Chapters 13 and 14, how might you describe and explain those differences? In what respects were they active agents in the historical process rather than simply victims of European actions?

Next Steps: For Further Study

Glenn J. Ames, *The Globe Encompassed: The Age of European Discovery, 1500–1700* (2007). An up-to-date survey of European expansion in the early modern era.

Andre Gunder Frank, *ReOrient: Global Economy in the Asian Age* (1998). An account of the early modern world economy that highlights the centrality of Asia.

Erik Gilbert and Jonathan Reynolds, *Trading Tastes: Commodity and Cultural Exchange to 1750* (2006). A world historical perspective on transcontinental and transoceanic commerce.

David Northrup, ed., *The Atlantic Slave Trade* (2002). A fine collection of essays about the origins, practice, impact, and abolition of Atlantic slavery.

John Richards, *The Endless Frontier* (2003). Explores the ecological consequences of early modern commerce.

John K. Thornton, *A Cultural History of the Atlantic World, 1250–1820* (2012). A recent account of the intersection of European, African, and Native American people by a highly respected historian.

"Atlantic Slave Trade and Slave Life in the Americas: A Visual Record," http://hitchcock.itc.virginia.edu /Slavery/index.php. An immense collection of maps and images, illustrating the slave trade and the life of slaves in the Americas.

"The Spice of Life: Pepper, the Master Spice," https://www.youtube.com/watch?v=NuZujx-LMfg. A BBC film that presents the history of pepper, so central to the spice trade of the early modern era.

WORKING WITH EVIDENCE

Exchange and Status in the Early Modern World

In many cultures across many centuries, the possession of scarce foreign goods has served not only to meet practical needs and desires but also to convey status. For centuries, Chinese silk signified rank, position, or prestige across much of Eurasia. Pepper and other spices from South and Southeast Asia likewise appealed to elite Romans and Chinese, eager to demonstrate their elevated position in society. In the late twentieth century, American blue jeans were much in demand among Russian young people who sought to display their independence from an oppressive communist regime, while Americans who could afford a German Porsche or an Italian Ferrari acquired an image of sophistication or glamour, setting them apart from others.

As global commerce expanded in the early modern era, so too did the exchange of foods, fashions, finery, and more. Already in 1500, according to a recent study, "it would be possible for a person in the Persian Gulf to wear cotton cloth from India while eating a bowl of rice also from India while sitting under a roof made of timber imported from East Africa. As he finished the rice he would see a Chinese character—the bowl itself came from China."[40] In the centuries that followed, growing numbers of people all across the world, particularly in elite social circles, had access to luxury goods from far away with which they could display, and perhaps enhance, their status. Some of these goods—sugar, pepper, tobacco, tea, and Indian cotton textiles, for example—gradually dropped in price, becoming more widely available. The images that follow illustrate this relationship between global trade and the display of status during the several centuries after 1500.

More than the peoples of other major civilizations, Europeans in the early modern era embraced the goods of the world. They had long been fascinated by and impressed with the wealth and splendor of Asia, which Marco Polo had described in the early fourteenth century after returning from his famous sojourn in China. Now in the early modern era, Western Europe was increasingly at the hub of a growing network of global commerce with access to products from around the world. Tea, porcelain, and silk from China; cotton textiles and spices from India and Southeast Asia; sugar, chocolate, and tobacco from the Americas; coffee from the Middle East—all of this and much more flooded into Europe. By the eighteenth century, a fascination for things Chinese had seized the elite classes of Europe—Chinese textiles, porcelains, tea, wallpaper, furniture, gardens, and artistic styles. The son of King George II of England built a "Mandarin yacht" resembling a Chinese pleasure boat to sail on a large artificial lake near London.

Source 14.1, which shows a German painting from the early eighteenth century, illustrates the growing popularity of tea as a beverage of choice in Europe as well as Chinese teacups. Long popular in China and Japan, tea made its entry into Europe in the sixteenth century aboard Portuguese ships. Initially, it was extremely expensive and limited to the very wealthy, but the price dropped as the supply increased, and by the eighteenth century it was widely consumed in Europe. Chinese teacups without handles also became popular and arrived packed in tea or rice via European merchant vessels. Like many other porcelains, these teacups had been created by Chinese artisans

Staadliche Schloesser und Gaerton, Karlsruhe, Germany/Erich Lessing/Art Resource, NY

Source 14.1 Tea and Porcelain in Europe

specifically for a European market. Those sitting on the table in the fore-ground of the image were manufactured in China between 1662 and 1722. Notice the practice of pouring the tea into the saucer to cool it.

- What foreign trade items can you identify in this painting?

- Note the European house on the teacup at the bottom left. What does this indicate about the willingness of the Chinese to cater to the tastes of European customers?

- From what social class do you think the woman in the image comes?

- How might you explain the great European interest in Chinese products and styles during the eighteenth century? Why might their possession have suggested status?

Like tea from China and coffee from Ethiopia, chocolate from Meso-america also became an elite beverage and an indicator of high status in Europe during the early modern era. It was the Olmecs, the Maya, and the Aztecs who first discovered how to process the seeds of the cacao tree into a choco-late drink. After the Spanish conquest of the Aztec Empire, that drink was introduced into Spain, where it became highly fashionable in court and aris-tocratic circles. And from Spain it spread to much of the rest of Europe, also limited to the elite social classes, who could afford to purchase this expensive import. Not until the Industrial Revolution made it possible to produce solid chocolate candy for mass consumption did this Mesoamerican acquisition become more widely available. Unlike tobacco and coffee, however, choco-late did not take hold in the Islamic world or China until more recent times.

A part of the larger Columbian exchange, chocolate in Europe lost the religious or ritual associations with which the Aztecs had invested it, becom-ing a medicine, sometimes an aphrodisiac, and in general a recreational bev-erage. Hernán Cortés, the Spanish conqueror of the Aztecs, described choco-late as "the divine drink which builds up resistance and fights fatigue" and reported, "A cup of this precious drink permits a man to walk for a whole day without food."[41] After some debate, the Church approved it as a nutri-tional substitute during times of fasting, when taking solid food was forbid-den. Europeans also innovated with the beverage, adding sugar, cinnamon, and other spices, and later milk. With ingredients from the Americas and Asia, some of them produced by African slave labor, chocolate illustrated the process by which Europe was becoming the center of an emerging world economy.

Source 14.2, a painted tile panel from the early eighteenth century, shows a *chocolatada*, or "chocolate party," in Valencia, Spain. Notice the saucer, or *mancerina*, also a European innovation, for drinking chocolate without spill-ing it.

Museu de Ceramica, Barcelona, Spain/Album/Art Resource, NY

Source 14.2 A Chocolate Party in Spain

- What marks this event as an upper-class occasion?

- What steps in the preparation of the chocolate drink can you observe in the image?

- Why do you think Europeans embraced a practice of people they regarded as uncivilized, bloodthirsty, and savage? What does this suggest about the process of cultural borrowing?

Europeans, of course, were not the only people to embrace foreign tastes newly available in the early modern era. Tobacco and coffee, like tea, soon found a growing range of consumers all across Eurasia. Originating in the Americas, tobacco smoking spread quickly to Europe and Asia. Well before 1700, it had become perhaps the first global recreation. In the Ottoman Empire, as elsewhere, it provoked strenuous opposition on the grounds that it was an intoxicant, like wine, and was associated with unwholesome and promiscuous behavior. It was also associated with coffee, which had entered the Ottoman Empire in the sixteenth century from its place of origin in Ethiopia and Yemen. Coffee too encountered considerable opposition, partly because it was consumed in the new social arena of the coffeehouse. To moralists and other critics, the coffeehouse was a "refuge of Satan," which drew people away from the mosques even as it drew together all different classes. Authorities suspected that coffeehouses were places of political intrigue. None of this stopped the spread of either tobacco or coffee, and the coffeehouse, in the Ottoman Empire and in Europe, came to embody a new "public culture of fun" as it wore away at earlier religious restrictions on the enjoyment of life.[42]

Source 14.3 is a sixteenth-century miniature painting depicting a Turkish coffeehouse in the Ottoman Empire.

■ What activities can you identify in the painting?

■ Would you read this painting as critical of the coffeehouse, as celebrating it, or as a neutral description? Notice that the musicians and those playing board games at the bottom were engaged in activities considered rather disreputable. How would you describe the general demeanor of the men in the coffeehouse?

■ Notice the cups that the patrons are using and those stacked in the upper right. Do they look similar to those shown in Source 14.1? Certainly Ottoman elites by the sixteenth century preferred Chinese porcelain to that manufactured within their own empire.

The emerging colonial societies of Spanish and Portuguese America gave rise to a wide variety of recognized mixed-race groups known as *castas*, or "castes," defined in terms of the precise mixture of Native American, European, and African ancestry that an individual possessed. While this system slotted people into a hierarchical social order defined by race and heritage, it did allow for some social mobility. If individuals managed to acquire some education, land, or money, they might gain in social prestige and even pass as members of a more highly favored category (see Chapter 13, pages 565–67). Adopting the dress and lifestyle of higher-ranking groups could facilitate this process.

Source 14.4 shows a woman of Indian ancestry and a man of African/Indian descent as well as their child, who is categorized as a *loba*, or "wolf." It comes from a series of "casta paintings" created in eighteenth-century Mexico by the well-known Zapotec artist Miguel Cabrera to depict some eighteen or more mixed-race couples and their children, each with a distinct designation. The woman in this image is wearing a lovely *huipil*, a traditional Maya tunic or blouse, while the man is dressed in a European-style waistcoat, vest, and lace shirt, while holding a black tricorne hat, widely popular in Europe during the seventeenth and eighteenth centuries. Interest in such

Source 14.3 An Ottoman Coffeehouse

De Chino-cambujoy dIndia ; Loba

Source 14.4 Clothing and Status in Colonial Mexico

paintings reflected both a Spanish fascination with race and a more general European concern with classification, which was characteristic of eighteenth-century scientific thinking.

- What indications of status ambition or upward mobility can you identify in this image? Keep in mind that status here is associated with race and gender as well as the possession of foreign products.

- Why do you think the woman is shown in more traditional costume, while the man is portrayed in European dress?

- Notice the porcelain items at the bottom right. Where might they have come from?

- In what cultural tradition do you think this couple raised their daughter? What problems might they have experienced in the process?

DOING HISTORY

Exchange and Status in the Early Modern World

1. **Analyzing the display of status:** In what different ways did the possession of foreign objects convey status in the early modern world? Toward whom were these various claims of status directed? Notice the difference between the display of status in public and private settings.

2. **Noticing gender differences:** In what ways are men and women portrayed in these visual sources? Why might women be absent in Sources 14.2 and 14.3?

3. **Exploring the functions of trade:** How might you use these images to support the idea that trade served more than economic needs?

4. **Raising questions about cultural borrowing:** What issues about cross-cultural borrowing do these visual sources suggest?

5. **Evaluating images as evidence:** What are the strengths and limitations of visual sources as a means of understanding the relationship of trade and status in the early modern era? What other kinds of sources would be useful for pursuing this theme?

National Palace, Mexico City, Mexico/The Art Archive at Art Resource, NY

CHAPTER 15

Cultural Transformations

Religion and Science

1450–1750

Nigerian pastor Daniel Ajayi-Adeniran is a missionary to the United States, with his mission field in the Bronx. The church he represents, the Redeemed Christian Church of God, began in Nigeria in 1952. It has acquired millions of members in Nigeria and boasts a missionary network with a presence in 100 countries. According to its leader, the church was "made in heaven, assembled in Nigeria, exported to the world." And the Redeemed Church of God is not alone. As secularism and materialism born of the Scientific Revolution and modern life have eroded religious faith in the West, many believers in Asia, Africa, and Latin America have felt called to reinvigorate a declining Christianity in Europe and North America. In a remarkable reversal of an earlier pattern, they now seek to "re-evangelize" the West, from which they originally received the faith. After all, more than 60 percent of the world's professing Christians now live outside Europe and North America, and, within the United States, one in six Catholic diocesan priests and one in three seminary students are foreign-born. For example, hundreds of Filipino priests, nuns, and lay workers now serve churches in the West. "We couldn't just throw up our hands and see these churches turned into nightclubs or mosques," declared Tokunboh Adeyemo, another Nigerian church leader seeking to minister to an "increasingly godless West."[1]

The early modern era of world history gave birth to two intersecting cultural trends that continue to play out in the twenty-first century. The first was the spread of Christianity to Asians, Africans, and Native Americans, some of whom now seem to be returning the favor. The second was the emergence of a modern scientific outlook, which sharply challenged Western Christianity even as it too acquired a global presence.

The Virgin of Guadalupe   According to Mexican tradition, a dark-skinned Virgin Mary appeared to an indigenous peasant named Juan Diego in 1531, an apparition reflected in this Mexican painting from 1720. Belief in the Virgin of Guadalupe represented the incorporation of Catholicism into the emerging culture and identity of Mexico.

And so, alongside new empires and new patterns of commerce, the early modern centuries also witnessed novel cultural transformations that likewise connected distant peoples. Riding the currents of European empire building and commercial expansion, Christianity was established solidly in the Americas and the Philippines; far more modestly in Siberia, China, Japan, and India; and hardly at all within the vast and still-growing domains of Islam. A cultural tradition largely limited to Europe in 1500 now became a genuine world religion, spawning a multitude of cultural encounters. While this ancient faith was spreading, a new understanding of the universe and a new approach to knowledge were taking shape among European thinkers of the Scientific Revolution, giving rise to another kind of cultural encounter— that between science and religion. Science was a new and competing worldview, and for some it became almost a new religion. In time, it grew into a defining feature of global modernity, achieving a worldwide acceptance that exceeded that of Christianity or any other religious tradition.

Although Europeans were central players in the globalization of Christianity and the emergence of modern science, they did not act alone in the cultural transformations of the early modern era. Asian, African, and Native American peoples largely determined how Christianity would be accepted, rejected, or transformed as it entered new cultural environments. Science emerged within an international and not simply a European context, and it met varying receptions in different parts of the world. Islam continued a long pattern of religious expansion and renewal, even as Christianity began to compete with it as a world religion. Buddhism maintained its hold in much of East Asia, as did Hinduism in South Asia and numerous smaller-scale religious traditions in Africa. And Europeans themselves were certainly affected by the many "new worlds" that they now encountered. The cultural interactions of the early modern era, in short, did not take place on a one-way street.

> ### SEEKING THE MAIN POINT
>
> To what extent did the cultural changes of the early modern world derive from cross-cultural interaction? And to what extent did they grow from within particular societies or civilizations?

The Globalization of Christianity

Despite its Middle Eastern origins and its earlier presence in many parts of the Afro-Asian world, Christianity was largely limited to Europe at the beginning of the early modern era. In 1500, the world of Christendom stretched from Spain and England in the west to Russia in the east, with small and beleaguered communities of various kinds in Egypt, Ethiopia, southern India, and Central Asia. Internally, the Christian world was seriously divided between the Roman Catholics of Western and Central Europe and the Eastern Orthodox of Eastern Europe and Russia. Externally, it was very much on the defensive against an expansive Islam. Muslims had ousted Christian Crusaders from their toeholds in the Holy Land by 1300, and with the Ottoman seizure of Constantinople in 1453, they had captured the prestigious capital of Eastern Orthodoxy. The Ottoman siege of Vienna in 1529 marked a Muslim advance into the heart of Central Europe. Except in Spain and Sicily,

A MAP OF TIME

1453	Ottoman conquest of Constantinople
1469–1539	Life of Guru Nanak; beginning of Sikh tradition
1472–1529	Life of Wang Yangming in China
1498–1547	Life of Mirabai, bhakti poet of India
1517	Luther's Ninety-Five Theses; beginning of Protestant Reformation
1543	Publication of Copernicus's masterwork about a sun-centered universe
1545–1563	Council of Trent
1560s	Taki Onqoy movement in Peru
1582–1610	Matteo Ricci in China
1598	Edict of Nantes proclaiming religious toleration in France
Early 17th century	European missionaries expelled from Japan
1618–1648	Thirty Years' War in Europe
1642–1727	Life of Isaac Newton; culmination of European Scientific Revolution
18th century	European Enlightenment
Early 18th century	Missionaries lost favor in the Chinese court
1740–1818	Wahhabi movement of Islamic reform in Arabia

which had recently been reclaimed for Christendom after centuries of Muslim rule, the future, it must have seemed, lay with Islam rather than Christianity.

Western Christendom Fragmented: The Protestant Reformation

As if these were not troubles enough, in the early sixteenth century the Protestant Reformation shattered the unity of Roman Catholic Christianity, which for the previous 1,000 years had provided the cultural and organizational foundation of an emerging Western European civilization. The Reformation began in 1517 when a German priest, Martin Luther (1483–1546), publicly invited debate about various abuses within the Roman Catholic Church by issuing a document, known as the Ninety-Five Theses, allegedly nailing it to the door of a church in Wittenberg. In itself, this was nothing new, for many people were critical of the luxurious life of the popes, the corruption and immorality of some clergy, the Church's selling of

The Protestant Reformation
An engraving of Martin Luther nailing his Ninety-Five Theses to the door of the Wittenberg castle church in 1517, thus launching the Protestant Reformation. (Photo © Tarker/ Bridgeman Images)

indulgences (said to remove the penalties for sin), and other aspects of church life and practice.

■ **Change**
In what ways did the Protestant Reformation transform European society, culture, and politics?

What made Luther's protest potentially revolutionary, however, was its theological basis. A troubled and brooding man anxious about his relationship with God, Luther had recently come to a new understanding of salvation: he believed that it came through faith alone. Neither the good works of the sinner nor the sacraments of the Church had any bearing on the eternal destiny of the soul, for faith was a free gift of God, graciously granted to his needy and undeserving people. To Luther, the source of these beliefs, and of religious authority in general, was not the teaching of the Church, but the Bible alone, interpreted according to the individual's conscience. All of this challenged the authority of the Church and called into question the special position of the clerical hierarchy and of the pope in particular. In sixteenth-century Europe, this was the stuff of revolution. (See the Snapshot, opposite, for a brief summary of Catholic and Protestant differences.)

Contrary to Luther's original intentions, his ideas provoked a massive schism within the world of Catholic Christendom, for they came to express a variety of political, economic, and social tensions as well as religious differences. Some kings and princes, many of whom had long disputed the political authority of the pope, found in these ideas a justification for their own independence and an opportunity to gain the lands and taxes previously held by the Church. In the Protestant idea

SNAPSHOT   Catholic/Protestant Differences in the Sixteenth Century

	Catholic	Protestant
Religious authority	Pope and church hierarchy	The Bible, as interpreted by individual Christians
Role of the pope	Ultimate authority in faith and doctrine	Authority of the pope denied
Ordination of clergy	Apostolic succession: direct line between original apostles and all subsequently ordained clergy	Apostolic succession denied; ordination by individual congregations or denominations
Salvation	Importance of church sacraments as channels of God's grace	Importance of faith alone; God's grace is freely and directly granted to believers
Status of Mary	Highly prominent, ranking just below Jesus; provides constant intercession for believers	Less prominent; Mary's intercession on behalf of the faithful denied
Prayer	To God, but often through or with Mary and saints	To God alone; no role for Mary and saints
Holy Communion	Transubstantiation: bread and wine become the actual body and blood of Christ	Transubstantiation denied; bread and wine have a spiritual or symbolic significance
Role of clergy	Priests are generally celibate; sharp distinction between priests and laypeople; priests are mediators between God and humankind	Ministers may marry; priesthood of all believers; clergy have different functions (to preach, administer sacraments) but no distinct spiritual status
Role of saints	Prominent spiritual exemplars and intermediaries between God and humankind	Generally disdained as a source of idolatry; saints refer to all Christians

that all vocations were of equal merit, middle-class urban dwellers found a new religious legitimacy for their growing role in society, since the Roman Catholic Church was associated in their eyes with the rural and feudal world of aristocratic privilege. For common people, who were offended by the corruption and luxurious living of some bishops, abbots, and popes, the new religious ideas served to express their opposition to the entire social order, particularly in a series of German peasant revolts in the 1520s. Although large numbers of women were attracted to Protestantism, Reformation teachings and practices did not offer them a substantially greater role in the church or society. In Protestant-dominated areas, the veneration of Mary and female saints ended, leaving the male Christ figure as the sole

Map 15.1
Reformation Europe in the Sixteenth Century

The rise of Protestantism added yet another set of religious divisions, both within and between states, to the world of Christendom, which was already sharply divided between the Roman Catholic Church and the Eastern Orthodox Church.

Protestant dominant
Some Protestant influence
Catholic
Eastern Orthodox Christian
Boundary of the Holy Roman Empire

object of worship. Protestant opposition to celibacy and monastic life closed the convents, which had offered some women an alternative to marriage. Nor were Protestants (except the Quakers) any more willing than Catholics to offer women an official role within their churches. The importance that Protestants gave to reading the Bible for oneself stimulated education and literacy for women, but given the emphasis on women as wives and mothers subject to male supervision, they had little opportunity to use that education outside of the family.

Reformation thinking spread quickly both within and beyond Germany, thanks in large measure to the recent invention of the printing press. Luther's many pamphlets and his translation of the New Testament into German were soon widely available. "God has appointed the [printing] Press to preach, whose voice the pope is never able to stop," declared one Reformation leader.[2] As the movement spread to France, Switzerland, England, and elsewhere, it also splintered, amoeba-like, into a variety of competing Protestant churches—Lutheran, Calvinist, Anglican, Quaker, Anabaptist—many of which subsequently subdivided, producing a bewildering array of Protestant denominations. Each was distinctive, but none gave allegiance to Rome or the pope.

Thus to the sharp class divisions and the fractured political system of Europe was now added the potent brew of religious difference, operating both within and between states (see Map 15.1). For more than thirty years (1562–1598), French society was torn by violence between Catholics and the Protestant minority known as Huguenots (HYOO-guh-naht). On a single day, August 24, 1572, Catholic mobs in Paris massacred some 3,000 Huguenots, and thousands more perished in provincial towns in the weeks that followed. Finally, a war-weary monarch, Henry IV, issued the Edict of Nantes (nahnt) in 1598, granting a substantial measure of religious toleration to French Protestants, though with the intention that they would soon return to the Catholic Church. The culmination of European religious conflict took shape in the Thirty Years' War (1618–1648), a Catholic–Protestant struggle that began in the Holy Roman Empire but eventually engulfed most of Europe. It was a horrendously destructive war, during which, scholars estimate, between 15 and 30 percent of the German population perished from violence, famine, or disease. Finally, the Peace of Westphalia (1648) brought the conflict to an end, with some reshuffling of boundaries and an agreement that each state was sovereign, authorized to control religious affairs within its own territory. Whatever religious unity Catholic Europe had once enjoyed was now permanently splintered.

The Protestant breakaway, combined with reformist tendencies within the Catholic Church itself, provoked a Catholic Reformation, or Counter-Reformation. In the Council of Trent (1545–1563), Catholics clarified and reaffirmed their unique doctrines and practices, such as the authority of the pope, priestly celibacy, the veneration of saints and relics, and the importance of church tradition and good works, all of which Protestants had rejected. Moreover, they set about correcting the abuses and corruption that had stimulated the Protestant movement by placing a new emphasis on the education of priests and their supervision by bishops. A crackdown on dissidents included the censorship of books, fines, exile, penitence, and occasionally the burning of heretics. Renewed attention was given to individual spirituality and personal piety. New religious orders, such as the Society of Jesus (Jesuits), provided a dedicated brotherhood of priests committed to the renewal of the Catholic Church and its extension abroad.

Although the Reformation was profoundly religious, it encouraged a skeptical attitude toward authority and tradition, for it had, after all, successfully challenged the immense prestige and power of the pope and the established Church. Protestant

Map 15.2
The Globalization
of Christianity

The growing Christian
presence in Asia, Africa,
and especially the Ameri-
cas, combined with older
centers of that faith, gave
the religion derived from
Jesus a global dimension
during the early modern
era.

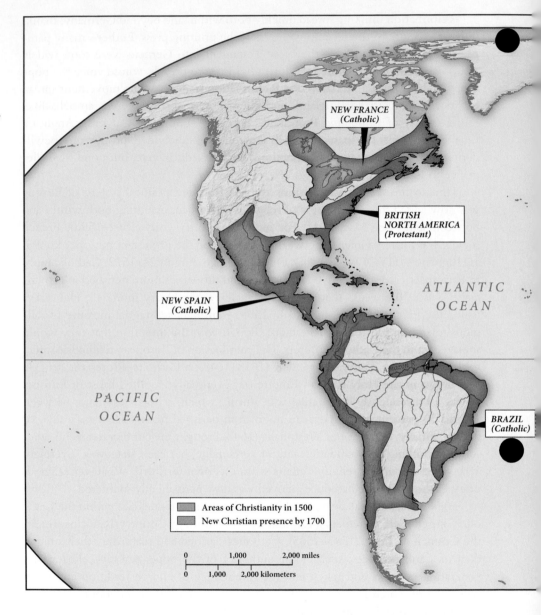

reformers fostered religious individualism, as people were now encouraged to read
and interpret the scriptures for themselves and to seek salvation without the media-
tion of the Church. In the centuries that followed, some people turned that skepticism and the habit of thinking independently against all conventional religion.
Thus the Protestant Reformation opened some space for new directions in European intellectual life.

    In short, it was a more highly fragmented but also a renewed and revitalized Chris-
tianity that established itself around the world in the several centuries after 1500
(see Map 15.2).

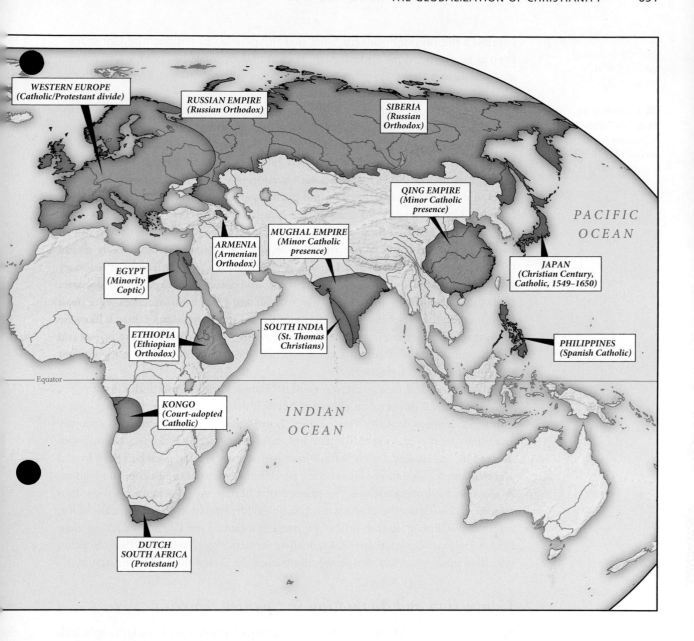

Christianity Outward Bound

Christianity motivated European political and economic expansion and also benefited from it. The resolutely Catholic Spanish and Portuguese both viewed their movement overseas as a continuation of a long crusading tradition, which only recently had completed the liberation of their countries from Muslim control. When Vasco da Gama's small fleet landed in India in 1498, local authorities understandably asked, "What brought you hither?" The reply: they had come "in search of Christians and of spices."[3] Likewise, Columbus, upon arriving in the Americas, expressed the no doubt sincere hope that the people "might become Christians," even as he promised his Spanish patrons an abundant harvest of gold, spice, cotton, aloe wood, and slaves.[4] Neither man sensed any contradiction or hypocrisy in this blending of religious and material concerns.

■ **Connection**
How was European imperial expansion related to the spread of Christianity?

If religion drove and justified European ventures abroad, it is difficult to imagine the globalization of Christianity (see Map 15.2) without the support of empire. Colonial settlers and traders, of course, brought their faith with them and sought to replicate it in their newly conquered homelands. New England Puritans, for example, planted a distinctive Protestant version of Christianity in North America, with an emphasis on education, moral purity, personal conversion, civic responsibility, and little tolerance for competing expressions of the faith. They did not show much interest in converting native peoples but sought rather to push them out of their ancestral territories. It was missionaries, mostly Catholic, who actively spread the Christian message beyond European communities. Organized in missionary orders such as the Dominicans, Franciscans, and Jesuits, Portuguese missionaries took the lead in Africa and Asia, while Spanish and French missionaries were most prominent in the Americas. Missionaries of the Russian Orthodox Church likewise accompanied the expansion of the Russian Empire across Siberia, where priests and monks ministered to Russian settlers and trappers, who often donated their first sable furs to a church or monastery.

Missionaries had their greatest success in Spanish America and in the Philippines, areas that shared two critical elements beyond their colonization by Spain. Most important, perhaps, was an overwhelming European presence, experienced variously as military conquest, colonial settlement, missionary activity, forced labor, social disruption, and disease. Surely it must have seemed as if the old gods had been bested and that any possible future lay with the powerful religion of the European invaders. A second common factor was the absence of a literate world religion in these two regions. Throughout the modern era, peoples solidly rooted in Confucian, Buddhist, Hindu, or Islamic traditions proved far more resistant to the Christian message than those who practiced more localized, small-scale, orally based religions. (See Working with Evidence, page 679, for images illustrating the global spread of Christianity.)

Conversion and Adaptation in Spanish America

Spanish America and China illustrate the difference between those societies in which Christianity became widely practiced and those that largely rejected it. Both cases, however, represent major cultural encounters of a kind that was becoming more frequent as European expansion brought the Christian faith to distant peoples with very different cultural traditions.

■ **Connection**
In what ways was European Christianity assimilated into the Native American cultures of Spanish America?

The decisive conquest of the Aztec and Inca empires and all that followed from it — disease, population collapse, loss of land to Europeans, forced labor, resettlement into more compact villages — created a setting in which the religion of the victors took hold in Spanish American colonies. Europeans saw their political and military success as a demonstration of the power of the Christian God. Native American peoples generally agreed, and by 1700 or earlier the vast majority had been baptized and saw themselves in some respects as Christians. After all, other conquerors such as the Aztecs and the Incas had always imposed their gods in some fashion on defeated peoples. So it made sense, both practically and spiritually, to affiliate with the Europeans' God, saints, rites, and rituals. Many millions accepted baptism, contributed to the construction of village churches, attended services, and embraced images of saints. Despite the prominence of the Virgin Mary as a religious figure across Latin America, the cost of conversion was high, especially for women. Many women, who had long served as priests, shamans, or ritual specialists, had no corresponding role in a Catholic church, led by an all-male clergy. And, with a few exceptions, convent life, which had provided some outlet for female authority and education in Catholic Europe, was reserved largely for Spanish women in the Americas. (See Zooming In: Úrsula de Jesús, page 654, for an exception.)

Earlier conquerors had made no attempt to eradicate local deities and religious practices. The flexibility and inclusiveness of Mesoamerican and Andean religions had made it possible for subject people to accommodate the gods of their new rulers while maintaining their own traditions. But Europeans were different. They claimed an exclusive religious truth and sought the utter destruction of local gods and everything associated with them. Operating within a Spanish colonial regime that actively encouraged conversion, missionaries often proceeded by persuasion and patient teaching. At times, though, their frustration with the persistence of "idolatry, superstition,

Andean Christianity
In 1753, Marcos Zapata, a native Peruvian artist trained in European techniques, painted this rendering of Jesus' Last Supper with his disciples, which included a number of Andean elements. The central dish on the table was a roasted guinea pig, a traditional sacrificial animal, while a local fermented corn drink called *chicha* was also part of the meal. Side dishes featured pomegranates, a Eurasian fruit brought to Peru by the Columbian exchange symbolizing the passion of Christ. At the bottom right, looking away from Jesus while grasping a money bag, is the figure of Judas, painted, some say, to resemble Francisco Pizarro, the Spanish conqueror of the Inca Empire. (© Yadid Levy/age fotostock)

ZOOMING IN

Úrsula de Jesús, an Afro-Peruvian Slave and Christian Visionary

Úrsula de Jesús was born in the prosperous Spanish colonial city of Lima, Peru, in 1606, the daughter of a slave mother. Thus she entered life at the lowest rung of Spanish colonial society. But among enslaved people, Úrsula was fortunate. Her mother's owner was a wealthy aristocratic woman, and at age eight Úrsula was sent to live in the home of another elite woman with a reputation for piety and religious visions. Five years later, Úrsula accompanied a third woman into the Convent of Santa Clara, where she spent the rest of her life. There Úrsula found a place for herself in the world of colonial Peru and Latin American Christianity—but not easily or immediately.[5]

For the next quarter of a century, Úrsula was one of more than a hundred slaves in the convent, where she attended to the personal needs of her mistress and participated in communal labor—cooking, cleaning, and attending the sick. In the convent, as in the larger society, Úrsula was at the bottom of the social ladder as nuns, novices, and *doñadas* (religious laywomen) all

A wealthy white Peruvian woman and her African slave.

enjoyed a higher status. But the wealth of her mistress or perhaps her own day labor allowed her to dress well and to elevate herself above common slaves. She later noted that she went about "beautifully adorned from head to toe." She recalled, "I used to wear fancy clothes and parade about the choir."

The year 1642 marked a dramatic turning point in Úrsula's life, when she almost fell into a deep well. Crediting her deliverance from certain death to the Virgin of Carmen, Úrsula turned decisively away from her earlier vain and self-centered ways and embraced an ever-deepening spirituality. She sold her lovely clothes, devoted every spare moment to prayer, and sought out the most onerous tasks such as caring for contagious patients and washing soiled garments. She took to whipping herself twice daily, wearing a coarse and painful hair shirt, and placing a crown of thorns beneath her hair. In Catholic

and error" boiled over into violent campaigns designed to uproot old religions once and for all. In 1535, the bishop of Mexico proudly claimed that he had destroyed 500 pagan shrines and 20,000 idols. During the seventeenth and early eighteenth centuries, church authorities in the Andean region periodically launched movements of "extirpation," designed to fatally undermine native religion. They destroyed religious images and ritual objects, publicly urinated on native "idols," desecrated the remains of ancestors, flogged "idolaters," and held religious trials and "processions of shame" aimed at humiliating offenders.

It is hardly surprising that such aggressive action generated resistance. Writing around 1600, the native Peruvian nobleman Guaman Poma de Ayala commented on the posture of native women toward Christianity: "They do not confess; they

religious thinking of the time, such "mortification" of the body served to enhance identification with Jesus' suffering.

Úrsula's new religious fervor incurred the displeasure of her mistress, who felt neglected by her slave. By 1645, a deeply unhappy Úrsula determined to leave the convent and find a new owner. Then one of the nuns, hoping to retain her pious services, purchased Úrsula's freedom. Nonetheless, Úrsula chose to stay in the convent as a *doñada*. Doing so represented a modest elevation in her social status, an opportunity to pursue her spiritual life with fewer restrictions, and a measure of social and economic security.

Still, she continued to perform the same exhausting tasks she had as a slave and complained frequently about them. "I was up to my ears with cooking and other things," she confided to her diary, "desiring only to be in the mountains where there are no people." Even as she struggled with the restrictions of her position in the convent, Úrsula enhanced her reputation as a "servant of God," a woman of extraordinary devotion and humility, and as a visionary and a mystic.

In her diary, Úrsula recounted numerous direct encounters with God, Jesus, Mary, and with dead souls seeking her intervention to shorten their time in the purifying fires of purgatory. These visions frequently reflected the tensions of class, race, and position within the convent and in the larger society. Several priests, suffering in purgatory for their sexual sins, luxurious living, and mistreatment of slaves, appealed to Úrsula. So too did nuns who had been lax in their spiritual practices or placed their business interests above their religious duties. Úrsula had a special concern for the female slaves and servants who asked for her intercession. One feared becoming an "orphan" in purgatory with no one to remember her. Another confessed to a lesbian love affair with a nun. Although Úrsula once questioned "whether black women went to heaven," it was later revealed to her as an abode of "great harmony," but not of social equality, for "everyone had their place . . . in accordance with their standing and the obligations of their class." By the end of her life, however, Úrsula was able to affirm the spiritual equality of all. "In memory, understanding, and will," she declared, "they [blacks and whites] are all one."

When Úrsula died in 1666, a prominent nun confirmed that she had entered Heaven directly, with no intervening time in purgatory. Her funeral was attended by many high officials of both state and church, and she was buried beneath the chapel of the convent she had served.

Question: To what extent did Úrsula shape her own life, and in what way was it shaped by larger historical forces?

do not attend catechism classes . . . nor do they go to mass. . . . And resuming their ancient customs and idolatry, they do not want to serve God or the crown."[6] Occasionally, overt resistance erupted. One such example was the religious revivalist movement in central Peru in the 1560s, known as Taki Onqoy (dancing sickness). Possessed by the spirits of local gods, or *huacas*, traveling dancers and teachers predicted that an alliance of Andean deities would soon overcome the Christian God, inflict the intruding Europeans with the same diseases that they had brought to the Americas, and restore the world of the Andes to an imagined earlier harmony. They called on native peoples to cut off all contact with the Spanish, to reject Christian worship, and to return to traditional practices. "The world has turned about," one member declared, "and this time God and the Spaniards [will be] defeated and all the Spaniards killed and their cities drowned; and the sea will rise and overwhelm them, so that there will remain no memory of them."[7]

More common than such frontal attacks on Christianity, which colonial authorities quickly smashed, were efforts at blending two religious traditions, reinterpreting Christian practices within an Andean framework, and incorporating local elements into an emerging Andean Christianity. Even female dancers in the Taki Onqoy movement sometimes took the names of Christian saints, seeking to appropriate for themselves the religious power of Christian figures. Within Andean Christian communities, women might offer the blood of a llama to strengthen a village church or make a cloth covering for the Virgin Mary and a shirt for an image of a huaca with the same material. Although the state cults of the Incas faded away, missionary attacks did not succeed in eliminating the influence of local huacas. Images and holy sites might be destroyed, but the souls of the huacas remained, and their representatives gained prestige. One resilient Andean resident inquired of a Jesuit missionary: "Father, are you tired of taking our idols from us? Take away that mountain if you can, since that is the God I worship."[8]

In Mexico as well, an immigrant Christianity was assimilated into patterns of local culture. Parishes were organized largely around precolonial towns or regions. Churches built on or near the sites of old temples became the focus of community identity. *Cofradias*, church-based associations of laypeople, organized community processions and festivals and made provisions for proper funerals and burials for their members. Central to an emerging Mexican Christianity were the saints who closely paralleled the functions of precolonial gods. Saints were imagined as parents of the local community and the true owners of its land, and their images were paraded through the streets on the occasion of great feasts and were collected by individual households. Mexico's Virgin of Guadalupe neatly combined both Mesoamerican and Spanish notions of Divine Motherhood (see the chapter-opening photo on page 642). Although parish priests were almost always Spanish, the *fiscal*, or leader of the church staff, was a native Christian of great local prestige, who carried on the traditions and role of earlier religious specialists.

Throughout the colonial period and beyond, many Mexican Christians also took part in rituals derived from the past, with little sense of incompatibility with Christian practice. Incantations to various gods for good fortune in hunting, farming, or healing; sacrifices of self-bleeding; offerings to the sun; divination; the use of hallucinogenic drugs—all of these practices provided spiritual assistance in those areas of everyday life not directly addressed by Christian rites. Conversely, these practices also showed signs of Christian influence. Wax candles, normally used in Christian services, might now appear in front of a stone image of a precolonial god. The anger of a neglected saint, rather than that of a traditional god, might explain someone's illness and require offerings, celebration, or a new covering to regain his or her favor. In such ways did Christianity take root in the new cultural environments of Spanish America, but it was a distinctly Andean or Mexican Christianity, not merely a copy of the Spanish version.

An Asian Comparison: China and the Jesuits

The Chinese encounter with Christianity was very different from that of Native Americans in Spain's New World empire. The most obvious difference was the political context. The peoples of Spanish America had been defeated, their societies thoroughly disrupted, and their cultural confidence sorely shaken. China, on the other hand, encountered European Christianity between the sixteenth and eighteenth centuries during the powerful and prosperous Ming (1368–1644) and Qing (1644–1912) dynasties. Although the transition between these two dynasties occasioned several decades of internal conflict, at no point was China's political independence or cultural integrity threatened by the handful of European missionaries and traders working there.

The reality of a strong, independent, confident China required a different missionary strategy, for Europeans needed the permission of Chinese authorities to operate in the country. Whereas Spanish missionaries working in a colonial setting sought primarily to convert the masses, the leading missionary order in China, the Jesuits, took deliberate aim at the official Chinese elite. Following the example of their most famous missionary, Matteo Ricci (in China 1582–1610), many Jesuits learned Chinese, became thoroughly acquainted with classical Confucian texts, and dressed like Chinese scholars. Initially, they downplayed their mission to convert and instead emphasized their interest in exchanging ideas and learning from China's ancient culture. As highly educated men, the Jesuits carried the recent secular knowledge of Europe—science, technology, geography, mapmaking—to an audience of curious Chinese scholars. In presenting Christian teachings, Jesuits were at pains to be respectful of Chinese culture, pointing out parallels between Confucianism and Christianity rather than portraying it as something new and foreign. They chose to define Chinese rituals honoring the emperor or venerating ancestors as secular or civil observances rather than as religious practices that had to be abandoned. Such efforts to accommodate Chinese culture contrast sharply with the frontal attacks on Native American religions in the Spanish Empire undertaken by many missionaries.

The religious and cultural outcomes of the missionary enterprise likewise differed greatly in the two regions. Nothing approaching mass conversion to Christianity took place in China, as it had in Latin America. During the sixteenth and seventeenth centuries, a modest number of Chinese scholars and officials did become Christians, attracted by the personal lives of the missionaries, by their interest in Western science, and by the moral certainty that Christianity offered. Jesuit missionaries found favor for a time at the Chinese imperial court, where their mathematical, astronomical, technological, and mapmaking skills rendered them useful. For more than a century, they were appointed to head the Chinese Bureau of Astronomy. Among ordinary people, Christianity spread very modestly amid tales of miracles attributed to the Christian God, while missionary teachings about "eternal life" sounded to some like Daoist prescriptions for immortality. At most, though,

■ **Comparison**
Why were missionary efforts to spread Christianity so much less successful in China than in Spanish America?

Jesuits in China
In this seventeenth-century Dutch engraving, two Jesuit missionaries hold a map of China. Their mapmaking skills were among the reasons that the Jesuits were initially welcomed among the educated elite of that country. (Frontispiece [engraving] from *China Monumentis* by Athanasius Kircher, 1667/Private Collection/Bridgeman Images)

missionary efforts over the course of some 250 years (1550–1800) resulted in 200,000 to 300,000 converts, a minuscule number in a Chinese population approaching 300 million by 1800. What explains the very limited acceptance of Christianity in early modern China?

Fundamentally, the missionaries offered little that the Chinese really wanted. Confucianism for the elites and Buddhism, Daoism, and a multitude of Chinese gods and spirits at the local level adequately supplied the spiritual needs of most Chinese. Furthermore, it became increasingly clear that Christianity was an all-or-nothing faith that required converts to abandon much of traditional Chinese culture. Christian monogamy, for example, seemed to require Chinese men to put away their concubines. What would happen to these deserted women?

By the early eighteenth century, the papacy and competing missionary orders came to oppose the Jesuit policy of accommodation. The pope claimed authority over Chinese Christians and declared that sacrifices to Confucius and the veneration of ancestors were "idolatry" and thus forbidden to Christians. The pope's pronouncements represented an unacceptable challenge to the authority of the emperor and an affront to Chinese culture. In 1715, an outraged Emperor Kangxi wrote:

> I ask myself how these uncultivated Westerners dare to speak of the great precepts of China. . . . [T]heir doctrine is of the same kind as the little heresies of the Buddhist and Taoist monks. . . . These are the greatest absurdities that have ever been seen. As from now I forbid the Westerners to spread their doctrine in China; that will spare us a lot of trouble.[9]

This represented a major turning point in the relationship of Christian missionaries and Chinese society. Many were subsequently expelled, and missionaries lost favor at court.

In other ways as well, missionaries played into the hands of their Chinese opponents. Their willingness to work under the Manchurian Qing dynasty, which came to power in 1644, discredited them with those Chinese scholars who viewed the Qing as uncivilized foreigners and their rule in China as disgraceful and illegitimate. Missionaries' reputation as miracle workers further damaged their standing as men of science and rationality, for elite Chinese often regarded miracles and supernatural religion as superstitions, fit only for the uneducated masses. Some viewed the Christian ritual of Holy Communion as a kind of cannibalism. Others came to see missionaries as potentially subversive, for various Christian groups met in secret, and such religious sects had often provided the basis for peasant rebellion. Nor did it escape Chinese notice that European Christians had taken over the Philippines and that their warships were active in the Indian Ocean. Perhaps the missionaries, with their great interest in maps, were spies for these aggressive foreigners. All of this contributed to the general failure of Christianity to secure a prominent presence in China.

Persistence and Change in Afro-Asian Cultural Traditions

Although Europeans were central players in the globalization of Christianity, theirs was not the only expanding or transformed culture of the early modern era. African religious ideas and practices, for example, accompanied slaves to the Americas. Common African forms of religious revelation—divination, dream interpretation, visions, spirit possession—found a place in the Africanized versions of Christianity that emerged in the New World. Europeans frequently perceived these practices as evidence of sorcery, witchcraft, or even devil worship and tried to suppress them. Nonetheless, syncretic (blended) religions such as Vodou in Haiti, Santeria in Cuba, and Candomblé and Macumba in Brazil persisted. They derived from various West African traditions and featured drumming, ritual dancing, animal sacrifice, and spirit possession. Over time, they incorporated Christian beliefs and practices such as church attendance, the search for salvation, and the use of candles and crucifixes and often identified their various spirits or deities with Catholic saints.

Expansion and Renewal in the Islamic World

The early modern era likewise witnessed the continuation of the "long march of Islam" across the Afro-Asian world. In sub-Saharan Africa, in the eastern and western wings of India, and in Central and Southeast Asia, the expansion of the Islamic frontier, a process already a thousand years in the making, extended farther still. Conversion to Islam generally did not mean a sudden abandonment of old religious practices in favor of the new. Rather, it was more often a matter of "assimilating Islamic rituals, cosmologies, and literatures into . . . local religious systems."[10]

Continued Islamization was not usually the product of conquering armies and expanding empires. It depended instead on wandering Muslim holy men or Sufis, Islamic scholars, and itinerant traders, none of whom posed a threat to local rulers. In fact, such people often were useful to those rulers and their village communities.

■ **Explanation**
What accounts for the continued spread of Islam in the early modern era and for the emergence of reform or renewal movements within the Islamic world?

They offered literacy in Arabic, established informal schools, provided protective charms containing passages from the Quran, served as advisers to local authorities and healers to the sick, often intermarried with local people, and generally did not insist that new converts give up their older practices. What they offered, in short, was connection to the wider, prestigious, prosperous world of Islam. Islamization extended modestly even to the Americas, where enslaved African Muslims practiced their faith in North America, particularly in Brazil, where Muslims led a number of slave revolts in the early nineteenth century. (See Zooming In: Ayuba Suleiman Diallo in Chapter 14, page 630.)

The islands of Southeast Asia illustrate the diversity of belief and practice that accompanied the spread of Islam in the early modern era. During the seventeenth century in Aceh, a Muslim sultanate on the northern tip of Sumatra, authorities sought to enforce the dietary codes and almsgiving practices of Islamic law. After four successive women ruled the area in the late seventeenth century, women were forbidden from exercising political power. On Muslim Java, however, numerous women served in royal courts, and women throughout Indonesia continued their longtime role as buyers and sellers in local markets. Among ordinary Javanese, traditional animistic practices of spirit worship coexisted easily with a tolerant and accommodating Islam, while merchants often embraced a more orthodox version of the religion in line with Middle Eastern traditions.

To such orthodox Muslims, religious syncretism, which accompanied Islamization almost everywhere, became increasingly offensive, even heretical. Such sentiments played an important role in movements of religious renewal and reform that emerged throughout the vast Islamic world of the eighteenth century. The leaders of such movements sharply criticized those practices that departed from earlier patterns established by Muhammad and from the authority of the Quran. For example, in India, which was governed by the Muslim Mughal Empire, religious resistance to official policies that accommodated Hindus found concrete expression during the reign of the emperor Aurangzeb (r. 1658–1707) (see Chapter 13, page 581). A series of religious wars in West Africa during the eighteenth and early nineteenth centuries took aim at corrupt Islamic practices and the rulers, Muslim and non-Muslim alike, who permitted them. In Southeast and Central Asia, tension grew between practitioners of localized and blended versions of Islam and those who sought to purify such practices in the name of a more authentic and universal faith.

The most well-known and widely visible of these Islamic renewal movements took place during the mid-eighteenth century in Arabia itself, where the religion had been born more than 1,000 years earlier. This movement originated in the teachings of the Islamic scholar Muhammad Ibn Abd al-Wahhab (1703–1792). The growing difficulties of the Islamic world, such as the weakening of the Ottoman Empire, were directly related, he argued, to deviations from the pure faith of early Islam. Al-Wahhab was particularly upset by common religious practices in central Arabia that seemed to him idolatry—the widespread veneration of Sufi saints and their tombs, the adoration of natural sites, and even the respect paid to Muhammad's tomb at Medina. All of this was a dilution of the absolute monotheism of authentic Islam.

The Wahhabi movement took a new turn in the 1740s when it received the political backing of Muhammad Ibn Saud, a local ruler who found al-Wahhab's ideas compelling. With Ibn Saud's support, the religious movement became an expansive state in central Arabia. Within that state, offending tombs were razed; "idols" were eliminated; books on logic were destroyed; the use of tobacco, hashish, and musical instruments was forbidden; and certain taxes not authorized by religious teaching were abolished.

Al-Wahhab's ideas about the role of women have attracted considerable attention in light of the highly restrictive practices of Wahhabi Islam in contemporary Saudi Arabia. He did on one occasion reluctantly authorize the stoning of a woman who persisted in an adulterous sexual relationship after numerous warnings, but more generally he emphasized the rights of women within a patriarchal Islamic framework. These included the right to consent to and stipulate conditions for a marriage, to control her dowry, to divorce, and to engage in commerce. Such rights, long embedded in Islamic law, had apparently been forgotten or ignored in eighteenth-century Arabia. Furthermore, he did not insist on head-to-toe covering of women in public and allowed for the mixing of unrelated men and women for business or medical purposes.

Map 15.3   The Expansion of Wahhabi Islam

From its base in central Arabia, the Wahhabi movement represented a challenge to the Ottoman Empire, while its ideas subsequently spread widely within the Islamic world.

By the early nineteenth century, this new reformist state encompassed much of central Arabia, with Mecca itself coming under Wahhabi control in 1803 (see Map 15.3). Although an Egyptian army broke the power of the Wahhabis in 1818, the movement's influence continued to spread across the Islamic world. Together with the ongoing expansion of the religion, these movements of reform and renewal signaled the continuing cultural vitality of the "abode of Islam," even as the European presence on the world stage assumed larger dimensions. In the nineteenth and twentieth centuries, such movements persisted and became associated with resistance to the political, military, and cultural intrusion of the European West into the affairs of the Islamic world.

China: New Directions in an Old Tradition

Neither China nor India experienced cultural or religious change as dramatic as that of the Reformation in Europe, nor did Confucian or Hindu cultures during the early modern era spread widely, as did Christianity and Islam. Nonetheless, neither of these traditions remained static. As in Christian Europe, challenges to established orthodoxies in China and India emerged as commercial and urban life, as well as political change, fostered new thinking.

■ **Change**
What kinds of cultural changes occurred in China and India during the early modern era?

China during the Ming and Qing dynasties continued to operate broadly within a Confucian framework, enriched now by the insights of Buddhism and Daoism to generate a system of thought called Neo-Confucianism. Chinese Ming dynasty rulers, in their aversion to the despised Mongols, embraced and actively supported this native Confucian tradition, whereas the foreign Manchu or Qing rulers did so to woo Chinese intellectuals to support the new dynasty. Within this context, a considerable amount of controversy, debate, and new thinking emerged during the early modern era.

During late Ming times, for example, the influential thinker Wang Yangming (1472–1529) argued that "intuitive moral knowledge exists in people . . . even robbers know that they should not rob."[11] Thus anyone could achieve a virtuous life by introspection and contemplation, without the extended education, study of classical texts, and constant striving for improvement that traditional Confucianism prescribed for an elite class of "gentlemen." Such ideas figured prominently among Confucian scholars of the sixteenth century, although critics later contended that such thinking promoted an excessive individualism. They also argued that Wang Yangming's ideas had undermined the Ming dynasty and contributed to China's conquest by the foreign Manchus. Some Chinese Buddhists as well sought to make their religion more accessible to ordinary people, by suggesting that laypeople at home could undertake practices similar to those performed by monks in monasteries. Withdrawal from the world was not necessary for enlightenment. This kind of moral or religious individualism bore some similarity to the thinking of Martin Luther, who argued that individuals could seek salvation by "faith alone," without the assistance of a priestly hierarchy.

Another new direction in Chinese elite culture took shape in a movement known as *kaozheng*, or "research based on evidence." Intended to "seek truth from facts," kaozheng was critical of the unfounded speculation of conventional Confucian philosophy and instead emphasized the importance of verification, precision, accuracy, and rigorous analysis in all fields of inquiry. During the late Ming years, this emphasis generated works dealing with agriculture, medicine, pharmacology, botany, craft techniques, and more. In the Qing era, kaozheng was associated with the recovery and critical analysis of ancient historical documents, which sometimes led to sharp criticism of Neo-Confucian orthodoxy. It was a genuinely scientific approach to knowledge, but it was applied more to the study of the past than to the natural world of astronomy, physics, or anatomy, which was the focus in the West.

While such matters occupied the intellectual elite of China, in the cities a lively popular culture emerged among the less educated. For city-dwellers, plays, paintings, short stories, and especially novels provided diversion and entertainment that were a step up from what could be found in teahouses and wineshops. Numerous "how-to" painting manuals allowed a larger public to participate in this favorite

Chinese art form. Even though Confucian scholars disdained popular fiction, a vigorous printing industry responded to the growing demand for exciting novels. The most famous was Cao Xueqin's mid-eighteenth-century novel *The Dream of the Red Chamber*, a huge book that contained 120 chapters and some 400 characters, most of them women. It explored the social life of an eighteenth-century elite family with connections to the Chinese court.

India: Bridging the Hindu/Muslim Divide

In a largely Hindu India, ruled by the Muslim Mughal Empire, several significant cultural departures took shape in the early modern era that brought Hindus and Muslims together in new forms of religious expression. At the level of elite culture, the Mughal ruler Akbar formulated a state cult that combined elements of Islam, Hinduism, and Zoroastrianism (see Chapter 13, page 581). The Mughal court also embraced Renaissance Christian art, and soon murals featuring Jesus, Mary, and Christian saints appeared on the walls of palaces, garden pavilions, and harems. The court also commissioned a prominent Sufi spiritual master to compose an illustrated book describing various Hindu yoga postures. Intended to bring this Hindu tradition into Islamic Sufi practice, the book, known as the *Ocean of Life*, portrayed some of the yogis in a Christ-like fashion.

Within popular culture, the flourishing of a devotional form of Hinduism known as *bhakti* also bridged the gulf separating Hindu and Muslim. Through songs, prayers, dances, poetry, and rituals, devotees sought to achieve union with one or another of India's many deities. Appealing especially to women, the bhakti movement provided an avenue for social criticism. Its practitioners often set aside caste distinctions and disregarded the detailed rituals of the Brahmin priests in favor of direct contact with the Divine. This emphasis had much in common with mystical Sufi forms of Islam and helped blur the distinction between these two traditions in India.

Among the most beloved of bhakti poets was Mirabai (1498–1547), a high-caste woman from northern India who abandoned her upper-class family and conventional Hindu practice. Upon her husband's death, tradition asserts, she declined to burn herself on his funeral pyre (a practice known as *sati*). She further offended caste restrictions by

Guru Nanak

This painting shows a seated Guru Nanak, the founder of Sikhism, disputing with four kneeling Hindu holy men. (British Library, London, UK/© British Library Board. All Rights Reserved/Robena/Art Resource, NY)

taking as her guru (religious teacher) an old untouchable shoemaker. To visit him, she apparently tied her saris together and climbed down the castle walls at night. Then she would wash his aged feet and drink the water from these ablutions. Much of her poetry deals with her yearning for union with Krishna, a Hindu deity she regarded as her husband, lover, and lord. She wrote:

> What I paid was my social body, my town body, my family body, and all my inherited jewels. Mirabai says: The Dark One [Krishna] is my husband now.[12]

Yet another major cultural change that blended Islam and Hinduism emerged with the growth of Sikhism as a new and distinctive religious tradition in the Punjab region of northern India. Its founder, Guru Nanak (1469–1539), had been involved in the bhakti movement but came to believe that "there is no Hindu; there is no Muslim; only God." His teachings and those of subsequent gurus also generally ignored caste distinctions and untouchability and ended the seclusion of women, while proclaiming the "brotherhood of all mankind" as well as the essential equality of men and women. Drawing converts from Punjabi peasants and merchants, both Muslim and Hindu, the Sikhs gradually became a separate religious community. They developed their own sacred book, known as the Guru Granth (teacher book); created a central place of worship and pilgrimage in the Golden Temple of Amritsar; and prescribed certain dress requirements for men, including keeping hair and beards uncut, wearing a turban, and carrying a short sword. During the seventeenth century, Sikhs encountered hostility from both the Mughal Empire and some of their Hindu neighbors. In response, Sikhism evolved from a peaceful religious movement, blending Hindu and Muslim elements, into a militant community whose military skills were highly valued by the British when they took over India in the late eighteenth century.

SUMMING UP SO FAR

In what ways did religious changes in Asia and the Middle East parallel those in Europe, and in what ways were they different?

A New Way of Thinking: The Birth of Modern Science

While some Europeans were actively attempting to spread the Christian faith to distant corners of the world, others were nurturing an understanding of the cosmos at least partially at odds with traditional Christian teaching. These were the makers of Europe's Scientific Revolution, a vast intellectual and cultural transformation that took place between the mid-sixteenth and early eighteenth centuries. These men of science would no longer rely on the external authority of the Bible, the Church, the speculations of ancient philosophers, or the received wisdom of cultural tradition. For them, knowledge would be acquired through rational inquiry based on evidence, the product of human minds alone. Those who created this revolution—Copernicus from Poland, Galileo from Italy, Descartes from France,

Newton from England, and many others—saw themselves as departing radically from older ways of thinking. "The old rubbish must be thrown away," wrote a seventeenth-century English scientist. "These are the days that must lay a new Foundation of a more magnificent Philosophy."[13]

The long-term significance of the Scientific Revolution can hardly be overestimated. Within early modern Europe, it fundamentally altered ideas about the place of humankind within the cosmos and sharply challenged both the teachings and the authority of the Church. Over the past several centuries, it has substantially eroded religious belief and practice in the West, particularly among the well educated. When applied to the affairs of human society, scientific ways of thinking challenged ancient social hierarchies and political systems and played a role in the revolutionary upheavals of the modern era. But science was also used to legitimize racial and gender inequalities, giving new support to old ideas about the natural inferiority of women and enslaved people. When married to the technological innovations of the Industrial Revolution, science fostered both the marvels of modern production and the horrors of modern means of destruction. By the twentieth century, science had become so widespread that it largely lost its association with European culture and became the chief marker of global modernity. Like Buddhism, Christianity, and Islam, modern science became a universal worldview, open to all who could accept its premises and its techniques.

The Question of Origins: Why Europe?

Why did the breakthrough of the Scientific Revolution occur first in Europe and during the early modern era? The realm of Islam, after all, had generated the most advanced science in the world during the centuries between 800 and 1400. Arab scholars could boast of remarkable achievements in mathematics, astronomy, optics, and medicine, and their libraries far exceeded those of Europe.[14] And what of China? Its elite culture of Confucianism was both sophisticated and secular, less burdened by religious dogma than that of the Christian or Islamic worlds; its technological accomplishments and economic growth were unmatched anywhere in the several centuries after 1000. In neither civilization, however, did these achievements lead to the kind of intellectual innovation that occurred in Europe.

Europe's historical development as a reinvigorated and fragmented civilization arguably gave rise to conditions particularly favorable to the scientific enterprise. By the twelfth and thirteenth centuries, Europeans had evolved a legal system that guaranteed a measure of independence for a variety of institutions—the Church, towns and cities, guilds, professional associations, and universities. This legal revolution was based on the idea of a "corporation," a collective group of people that was treated as a unit, a legal person, with certain rights to regulate and control its own members.

Most important for the development of science in the West was the autonomy of its emerging universities. By 1215, the University of Paris was recognized as a

■ **Comparison**
Why did the Scientific Revolution occur in Europe rather than in China or the Islamic world?

"corporation of masters and scholars," which could admit and expel students, establish courses of instruction, and grant a "license to teach" to its faculty. Such universities—for example, in Paris, Bologna, Oxford, Cambridge, and Salamanca—became "neutral zones of intellectual autonomy" in which scholars could pursue their studies in relative freedom from the dictates of church or state authorities. Within them, the study of the natural order began to slowly separate itself from philosophy and theology and to gain a distinct identity. Their curricula featured "a basically scientific core of readings and lectures" that drew heavily on the writings of the Greek thinker Aristotle, which had only recently become available to Western Europeans. Most of the major figures in the Scientific Revolution had been trained in and were affiliated with these universities.

In the Islamic world, by contrast, science was patronized by a variety of local authorities, but it occurred largely outside the formal system of higher education. Within colleges known as madrassas, Quranic studies and religious law held the central place, whereas philosophy and natural science were viewed with great suspicion. To religious scholars, the Quran held all wisdom, and scientific thinking might well challenge it. An earlier openness to free inquiry and religious toleration was increasingly replaced by a disdain for scientific and philosophical inquiry, for it seemed to lead only to uncertainty and confusion. "May God protect us from useless knowledge" was a saying that reflected this outlook. Nor did Chinese authorities permit independent institutions of higher learning in which scholars could conduct their studies in relative freedom. Instead, Chinese education focused on preparing for a rigidly defined set of civil service examinations and emphasized the humanistic and moral texts of classical Confucianism. "The pursuit of scientific subjects," one recent historian concluded, "was thereby relegated to the margins of Chinese society."[15]

Beyond its distinctive institutional development, Western Europe was in a position to draw extensively on the knowledge of other cultures, especially that of the Islamic world. Arab medical texts, astronomical research, and translations of Greek classics played a major role in the birth of European natural philosophy (as science was then called) between 1000 and 1500. Then, in the sixteenth through the eighteenth centuries, Europeans found themselves at the center of a massive new exchange of information as they became aware of lands, peoples, plants, animals, societies, and religions from around the world. This tidal wave of new knowledge, uniquely available to Europeans, shook up older ways of thinking and opened the way to new conceptions of the world. The sixteenth-century Italian doctor, mathematician, and writer Girolamo Cardano (1501–1576) clearly expressed this sense of wonderment: "The most unusual [circumstance of my life] is that I was born in this century in which the whole world became known; whereas the ancients were familiar with but a little more than a third part of it." He worried, however, that amid this explosion of knowledge, "certainties will be exchanged for uncertainties."[16] It was precisely those uncertainties—skepticism about established views—that provided such a fertile cultural ground for the emergence of modern science.

The Reformation too contributed to that cultural climate in its challenge to author-ity, its encouragement of mass literacy, and its affirmation of secular professions.

Science as Cultural Revolution

Before the Scientific Revolution, educated Europeans held a view of the world that derived from Aristotle, perhaps the greatest of the ancient Greek philosophers, and from Ptolemy, a Greco-Egyptian mathematician and astronomer who lived in Alexandria during the second century C.E. To medieval European thinkers, the earth was stationary and at the center of the universe, and around it revolved the sun, moon, and stars embedded in ten spheres of transparent crystal. This under-standing coincided well with the religious outlook of the Catholic Church because the attention of the entire universe was centered on the earth and its human inhab-itants, among whom God's plan for salvation unfolded. It was a universe of divine purpose, with angels guiding the hierarchically arranged heavenly bodies along their way while God watched over the whole from his realm beyond the spheres. The Scientific Revolution was revolutionary because it fundamentally challenged this understanding of the universe.

The initial breakthrough in the Scientific Revolution came from the Polish mathematician and astronomer Nicolaus Copernicus, whose famous book *On the Revolutions of the Heavenly Spheres* was published in the year of his death, 1543. Its essential argument was that "at the middle of all things lies the sun" and that the earth, like the other planets, revolved around it. Thus the earth was no longer unique or at the obvious center of God's attention.

■ **Change**
What was revolutionary about the Scientific Revolution?

Other European scientists built on Copernicus's central insight, and some even argued that other inhabited worlds and other kinds of humans existed. Less specula-tively, in the early seventeenth century Johannes Kepler, a German mathematician, showed that the planets followed elliptical orbits, undermining the ancient belief that they moved in perfect circles. The Italian Galileo (gal-uh-LAY-oh) developed an improved telescope, with which he made many observations that undermined estab-lished understandings of the cosmos. (See Zooming In: Galileo and the Telescope, page 668.) Some thinkers began to discuss the notion of an unlimited universe in which humankind occupied a mere speck of dust in an unimaginable vastness. The French mathematician and philosopher Blaise Pascal (1623–1662) perhaps spoke for many when he wrote, "The eternal silence of infinite space frightens me."[17]

The culmination of the Scientific Revolution came in the work of Sir Isaac Newton (1642–1727), the Englishman who formulated the modern laws of motion and mechanics, which remained unchallenged until the twentieth century. At the core of Newton's thinking was the concept of universal gravitation. "All bodies whatsoever," Newton declared, "are endowed with a principle of mutual gravita-tion."[18] Here was the grand unifying idea of early modern science. The radical implication of this view was that the heavens and the earth, long regarded as separate and distinct spheres, were not so different after all, for the motion of a cannonball

Galileo and the Telescope: Reflecting on Science and Religion

The Scientific Revolution was predicated on the idea that knowledge of how the universe worked was acquired through a combination of careful observations, controlled experiments, and the formulation of general laws, expressed in mathematical terms. New scientific instruments capable of making precise empirical observations underpinned some of the most important break-

Galileo on trial.

throughs of the period. Perhaps no single invention produced more dramatic discoveries than the telescope, the first of which were produced in the early seventeenth century by Dutch eyeglass makers.

The impact of new instruments depended on how scientists employed them. In the case of the telescope, it was the brilliant Italian mathematician and astronomer Galileo Galilei (1564–1642) who unlocked its potential when he used it to observe the night sky. Within months of creating his own telescope, which improved on earlier designs, Galileo made a series of discoveries that put into question well-established understandings of the cosmos. He observed craters on the moon and sunspots, or blemishes, moving across the face of the sun, which challenged the traditional notion that no imperfection or change

marred the heavenly bodies. Moreover, his discovery of the moons of Jupiter and many new stars suggested a cosmos far larger than the finite universe of traditional astronomy. In 1610, Galileo published his remarkable findings in a book titled *The Starry Messenger*, where he emphasized time and again that his precise observations provided irrefutable evidence of a cosmos unlike that described by traditional authorities. "With the aid of the telescope," he argued, "this has been scrutinized so directly and with such ocular certainty that all the disputes which have vexed the philosophers through so many ages have been resolved, and we are at last freed from wordy debates about it."[19]

Galileo's empirical evidence transformed the debate over the nature of the cosmos. His dramatic and unexpected discoveries were readily grasped, and with the aid of a telescope anyone could confirm their veracity. His initial findings were heralded by many in the scientific community, including Christoph Clavius, the Church's leading astronomer in Rome. Galileo's findings led him

photo: *Trial of Galileo*, 1633, oil on canvas, Italian/Private Collection/Bridgeman Images

or the falling of an apple obeyed the same natural laws that governed the orbiting planets.

By the time Newton died, a revolutionary new understanding of the physical universe had emerged among educated Europeans: the universe was no longer propelled by supernatural forces but functioned on its own according to scientific principles that could be described mathematically. Articulating this view, Kepler wrote, "The machine of the universe is not similar to a divine animated being but similar to a clock."[20] Furthermore, it was a machine that regulated itself, requiring neither God nor angels to account for its normal operation. Knowledge of that universe could be obtained through human reason alone—by observation, deduction, and experimentation—without the aid of ancient authorities or divine reve-

to conclude that Copernicus (1473–1543), an earlier astronomer and mathematician, had been correct when he had advanced the theory that the sun rather than the earth was at the center of the solar system. But Galileo's evidence could not definitively prove Copernicus's theory to the satisfaction of critics, leading Galileo to study other phenomena, such as the tides, that could provide further evidence that the earth was in motion.

When the Church condemned Copernicus's theory in 1616, it remained silent on Galileo's astronomical observations, instead warning him to refrain from teaching or promoting Copernicus's ideas. Ultimately, though, Galileo came into conflict with church authorities when in 1629 he published, with what he thought was the consent of the Church, the *Dialogue Concerning the Two Chief World Systems*, a work sympathetic to Copernicus's sun-centric system. In 1632, Galileo was tried by the Roman Inquisition, an ecclesiastical court charged with maintaining orthodoxy, and convicted of teaching doctrines against the express orders of the Church. He recanted his beliefs and at the age of sixty-nine was sentenced to house arrest.

Although Galileo was formally convicted of disobeying the Church's order to remain silent on the issue of Copernicus's theory, the question most fundamentally at stake in the trial was "What does it mean, 'to know something'?"[21] This question of the relationship between scientific knowledge, primarily concerned with how the universe works, and other forms of "knowledge," derived from divine revelation or mystical experience, has persisted in the West. Over 350 years after the trial, Pope John Paul II spoke of Galileo's conviction in a public speech in 1992, declaring it a "sad misunderstanding" that belongs to the past, but one with ongoing resonance because "the underlying problems of this case concern both the nature of science and the message of faith." Addressing the central question of what it means to know something, the pope declared scientific and religious knowledge to be compatible: "There exist two realms of knowledge, one which has its source in Revelation and one which reason can discover by its own power. . . . The distinction between the two realms of knowledge ought not to be understood as opposition. . . . The methodologies proper to each make it possible to bring out different aspects of reality."[22]

Strangely enough, Galileo himself had expressed something similar centuries earlier. "Nor is God," he wrote, "any less excellently revealed in Nature's actions than in the sacred statements of the Bible."[23] Finding the place of new scientific knowledge in a constellation of older wisdom traditions proved a fraught but highly significant development in the emergence of the modern world.

Question: What can Galileo's discoveries with his telescope and his conviction by the Inquisition tell us about the Scientific Revolution?

lation. The French philosopher René Descartes (day-KAHRT) resolved "to seek no other knowledge than that which I might find within myself, or perhaps in the book of nature."[24]

Like the physical universe, the human body also lost some of its mystery. The careful dissections of cadavers and animals enabled doctors and scientists to describe the human body with much greater accuracy and to understand the circulation of the blood throughout the body. The heart was no longer the mysterious center of the body's heat and the seat of its passions; instead it was just another machine, a complex muscle that functioned as a pump.

The movers and shakers of this enormous cultural transformation were almost entirely male. European women, after all, had been largely excluded from the

The Telescope
Johannes Hevelius, an astronomer of German Lutheran background living in what is now Poland, constructed extraordinarily long telescopes in the mid-seventeenth century with which he observed sunspots, charted the surface of the moon, and discovered several comets. Such telescopes played a central role in transforming understandings of the universe during the Scientific Revolution. (© World History Archive/Alamy)

universities where much of the new science was discussed. A few aristocratic women, however, had the leisure and connections to participate informally in the scientific networks of their male relatives. Through her marriage to the Duke of Newcastle, Margaret Cavendish (1623–1673) joined in conversations with a circle of "natural philosophers," wrote six scientific texts, and was the only seventeenth-century English woman to attend a session of the Royal Society of London, created to foster scientific learning. In Germany, a number of women took part in astronomical work as assistants to their husbands or brothers. Maria Winkelman, for example, discovered a previously unknown comet, though her husband took credit for it. After his death, she sought to continue his work in the Berlin Academy of Sciences but was refused on the grounds that "mouths would gape" if a woman held such a position.

Much of this scientific thinking developed in the face of strenuous opposition from the Catholic Church, for both its teachings and its authority were under attack. The Italian philosopher Giordano Bruno, proclaiming an infinite universe and many worlds, was burned at the stake in 1600, and Galileo was compelled by the Church to publicly renounce his belief that the earth moved around an orbit and rotated on its axis.

But scholars have sometimes exaggerated the conflict of science and religion, casting it in military terms as an almost unbroken war. None of the early scientists rejected Christianity. Copernicus in fact published his famous book with the support of several leading Catholic churchmen and dedicated it to the pope. After all, several earlier Catholic writers had proposed the idea of the earth in motion. He more likely feared the criticism of fellow scientists than that of the church hierarchy. Galileo himself proclaimed the compatibility of science and faith, and his lack of diplomacy in dealing with church leaders was at least in part responsible for his quarrel with the Church.[25] Newton was a serious biblical scholar and saw no inherent contradiction between his ideas and belief in God. "This most beautiful system of the sun, planets, and comets," he declared, "could only proceed from the counsel and dominion of an intelligent Being."[26] Thus the Church gradually accommodated as well as resisted the new ideas, largely by compartmentalizing them. Science might prevail in its limited sphere of describing the physical universe, but religion was still the arbiter of truth about those ultimate questions concerning human salvation, righteous behavior, and the larger purposes of life.

Science and Enlightenment

Initially limited to a small handful of scholars, the ideas of the Scientific Revolution spread to a wider European public during the eighteenth century. That process was aided by novel techniques of printing and bookmaking, by a popular press, by growing literacy, and by a host of scientific societies. Moreover, the new approach to knowledge—rooted in human reason, skeptical of authority, expressed in natural laws—was now applied to human affairs, not just to the physical universe. The Scottish professor Adam Smith (1723–1790), for example, formulated laws that accounted for the operation of the economy and that, if followed, he believed, would generate inevitably favorable results for society. Growing numbers of people believed that the long-term outcome of scientific development would be "enlightenment," a term that has come to define the eighteenth century in European history. If human reason could discover the laws that governed the universe, surely it could uncover ways in which humankind might govern itself more effectively.

"What is Enlightenment?" asked the prominent German intellectual Immanuel Kant (1724–1804). "It is man's emergence from his self-imposed . . . inability to use one's own understanding without another's guidance. . . . Dare to know! 'Have the courage to use your own understanding' is therefore the motto of the enlightenment."[27] Although they often disagreed sharply with one another, European Enlightenment thinkers shared this belief in the power of knowledge to transform human society. They also shared a satirical, critical style, a commitment to open-mindedness and inquiry, and in various degrees a hostility to established political and religious authority. Many took aim at arbitrary governments, the "divine right of kings," and the aristocratic privileges of European society. The English philosopher John Locke (1632–1704) offered principles for constructing a constitutional government, a contract between rulers and ruled that was created by human ingenuity rather than divinely prescribed. Much of Enlightenment thinking was directed against the superstition, ignorance, and corruption of established religion. In his *Treatise on Toleration*, the French writer Voltaire (1694–1778) reflected the outlook of the Scientific Revolution as he commented sarcastically on religious intolerance:

■ **Change**
In what ways did the Enlightenment challenge older patterns of European thinking?

> This little globe, nothing more than a point, rolls in space like so many other globes; we are lost in its immensity. Man, some five feet tall, is surely a very small part of the universe. One of these imperceptible beings says to some of his neighbors in Arabia or Africa: "Listen to me, for the God of all these worlds has enlightened me; there are nine hundred million little ants like us on the earth, but only my anthill is beloved of God; He will hold all others in horror through all eternity; only mine will be blessed, the others will be eternally wretched."[28]

Voltaire's own faith, like that of many others among the "enlightened," was deism. Deists believed in a rather abstract and remote Deity, sometimes compared to a clockmaker, who had created the world, but not in a personal God who intervened

The Philosophers of the Enlightenment
This painting shows the French philosopher Voltaire with a group of intellectual luminaries at the summer palace of the Prussian king Frederick II. Such literary gatherings, sometimes called salons, were places of lively conversation among mostly male participants and came to be seen as emblematic of the European Enlightenment. (Painting by Adolph Menzel [1815–1905], 1850/© akg-images/The Image Works)

in history or tampered with natural law. Others became *pantheists*, who believed that God and nature were identical. Here was a conception of religion shaped by the outlook of science. Sometimes called "natural religion," it was devoid of mystery, revelation, ritual, and spiritual practice, while proclaiming a God that could be "proven" by human rationality, logic, and the techniques of scientific inquiry. In this view, all else was superstition. Among the most radical of such thinkers were the several Dutchmen who wrote the *Treatise of Three Imposters*, which claimed that Moses, Jesus, and Muhammad were fraudulent impostors who based their teachings on "the ignorance of Peoples [and] resolved to keep them in it."[29]

Prominent among the debates spawned by the Enlightenment was the question of women's nature, their role in society, and the education most appropriate for them. Although well-to-do Parisian women hosted in their elegant salons many gatherings of the largely male Enlightenment figures, most of those men were anything but ardent feminists. The male editors of the famous *Encyclopédie*, a vast compendium of Enlightenment thought, included very few essays by women. One of the male authors expressed a common view: "[Women] constitute the principal ornament of the world. . . . May they, through submissive discretion and . . . artless cleverness, spur us [men] on to virtue." In his treatise *Emile*, Jean-Jacques Rousseau described women as fundamentally different from and inferior to men and urged that "the whole education of women ought to be relative to men."

Such views were sharply contested by any number of other Enlightenment figures—men and women alike. The *Journal des Dames* (Ladies Journal), founded in Paris in 1759, aggressively defended women. "If we have not been raised up in the sciences as you have," declared Madame Beaulmer, the *Journal*'s first editor, "it is you [men] who are the guilty ones; for have you not always abused . . . the bodily strength that nature has given you?"[30] The philosopher Condorcet looked forward to the "complete destruction of those prejudices that have established an inequality of rights between the sexes." And in 1792, the British writer Mary Wollstonecraft directly confronted Rousseau's view of women and their education: "What nonsense! . . . Til women are more rationally educated, the progress of human virtue and improvement in knowledge must receive continual checks." Thus was initiated a debate that echoed throughout the centuries that followed.

Though solidly rooted in Europe, Enlightenment thought was influenced by the growing global awareness of its major thinkers. Voltaire, for example, idealized China as an empire governed by an elite of secular scholars selected for their talent, which stood in sharp contrast to continental Europe, where aristocratic birth and military prowess were far more important. The example of Confucianism—supposedly secular, moral, rational, and tolerant—encouraged Enlightenment thinkers to imagine a future for European civilization without the kind of supernatural religion that they found so offensive in the Christian West.

The central theme of the Enlightenment—and what made it potentially revolutionary—was the idea of progress. Human society was not fixed by tradition or divine command but could be changed, and improved, by human action guided by reason. No one expressed this soaring confidence in human possibility more clearly than the French thinker the Marquis de Condorcet (1743–1794), who boldly declared that "the perfectibility of humanity is indefinite." Belief in progress was a sharp departure from much of premodern social thinking, and it inspired those who later made the great revolutions of the modern era in the Americas, France, Russia, China, and elsewhere. Born of the Scientific Revolution, that was the faith of the Enlightenment. For some, it was virtually a new religion.

The age of the Enlightenment, however, also witnessed a reaction against too much reliance on human reason. Jean-Jacques Rousseau (1712–1778) minimized the importance of book learning for the education of children and prescribed instead an immersion in nature, which taught self-reliance and generosity rather than the greed and envy fostered by "civilization." The Romantic movement in art and literature appealed to emotion, intuition, passion, and imagination rather than cold reason and scientific learning. Religious awakenings—complete with fiery sermons, public repentance, and intense personal experience of sin and redemption—shook Protestant Europe and North America in the eighteenth and early nineteenth centuries. The Methodist movement—with its emphasis on Bible study, confession of sins, fasting, enthusiastic preaching, and resistance to worldly pleasures—was a case in point.

Various forms of "enlightened religion" also arose in the early modern centuries, reflecting the influence of Enlightenment thinking. Quakers, for example, emphasized tolerance, an absence of hierarchy and ostentation, a benevolent God, and an "inner light" available to all people. Unitarians denied the Trinity, original sin, predestination, and the divinity of Jesus, but honored him as a great teacher and a moral prophet. Later, in the nineteenth century, proponents of the "social gospel" saw the essence of Christianity not in personal salvation but in ethical behavior. Science and the Enlightenment surely challenged religion, and for some they eroded religious belief and practice. Just as surely, though, religion persisted, adapted, and revived for many others.

Looking Ahead: Science in the Nineteenth Century and Beyond

The perspectives of the Enlightenment were challenged not only by romanticism and religious "enthusiasm" but also by the continued development of European science itself. This remarkable phenomenon justifies a brief look ahead at several scientific developments in the nineteenth and twentieth centuries.

■ **Change**

How did nineteenth-century developments in the sciences challenge the faith of the Enlightenment?

Modern science was a cumulative and self-critical enterprise, which in the nineteenth century and later was applied to new domains of human inquiry in ways that undermined some of the assumptions of the Enlightenment. In the realm of biology, for example, Charles Darwin (1809–1882) laid out a complex argument that all life was in constant change, that an endless and competitive struggle for survival over millions of years constantly generated new species of plants and animals, while casting others into extinction. Human beings were not excluded from this vast process, for they too were the work of evolution operating through natural selection. Darwin's famous books *The Origin of Species* (1859) and *The Descent of Man* (1871) were threatening to many traditional Christian believers, perhaps more so than Copernicus's ideas about a sun-centered universe had been several centuries earlier.

At the same time, Karl Marx (1818–1883) articulated a view of human history that likewise emphasized change and struggle. Conflicting social classes—slave owners and slaves, nobles and peasants, capitalists and workers—successively drove the process of historical transformation. Although he was describing the evolution of human civilization, Marx saw himself as a scientist. He based his theories on extensive historical research; like Newton and Darwin, he sought to formulate general laws that would explain events in a rational way. Nor did he believe in heavenly intervention, chance, or the divinely endowed powers of kings. The coming of socialism, in this view, was not simply a good idea; it was inscribed in the laws of historical development. (See Working with Evidence, Source 17.1, page 776.)

Like the intellectuals of the Enlightenment, Darwin and Marx believed strongly in progress, but in their thinking, conflict and struggle rather than reason and education were the motors of progress. The Enlightenment image of the thoughtful, rational, and independent individual was fading. Individuals—plant, animal, and human alike—were now viewed as enmeshed in vast systems of biological, economic, and social conflict.

The work of the Viennese doctor Sigmund Freud (1856–1939) applied scientific techniques to the operation of the human mind and emotions and in doing so cast further doubt on Enlightenment conceptions of human rationality. At the core of each person, Freud argued, lay primal impulses toward sexuality and aggression, which were only barely held in check by the thin veneer of social conscience derived from civilization. Our neuroses arose from the ceaseless struggle between our irrational drives and the claims of conscience. This too was a far cry from the Enlightenment conception of the human condition.

And in the twentieth century, developments in physics, such as relativity and quantum theory, called into question some of the established verities of the Newtonian view of the world, particularly at the subatomic level and at speeds approaching that of light. In this new physics, time is relative to the position of the observer; space can warp and light can bend; matter and energy are equivalent; black holes and dark matter abound; and probability, not certain prediction, is the best that scientists can hope for. None of this was even on the horizon of those who made the original Scientific Revolution in the early modern era.

European Science beyond the West

In the long run, the achievements of the Scientific Revolution spread globally, becoming the most widely sought-after product of European culture and far more desired than Christianity, democracy, socialism, or Western literature. In the early modern era, however, interest in European scientific thinking within major Asian societies was both modest and selective. The telescope provides an example. Invented in early seventeenth-century Europe and endlessly improved in the centuries that followed, the telescope provoked enormous excitement in European scientific circles. It made possible any number of astronomical discoveries, including the rugged surface of the moon, the moons of Jupiter, the rings of Saturn, and the phases of Venus. "We are here . . . on fire with these things," wrote an English astronomer in 1610.[31] Soon the telescope was available in China, Mughal India, and the Ottoman Empire. But in none of these places did it evoke much interest or evolve into the kind of "discovery machine" that it was rapidly becoming in Europe.

In China, Qing dynasty emperors and scholars were most interested in European techniques, derived largely from Jesuit missionaries, for predicting eclipses, reforming the calendar, and making accurate maps of the empire. European medicine, however, was of little importance for Chinese physicians before the nineteenth century. But the reputation of the Jesuits suffered when it became apparent in the 1760s that for two centuries the missionaries had withheld information about Copernican views of a sun-centered solar system because those ideas had been condemned by the Church. Nonetheless, European science had a substantial impact on

■ **Connection**

In what ways was European science received in the major civilizations of Asia in the early modern era?

a number of Chinese scholars as it seemed compatible with the data-based kaozheng movement, described by one participant as "an ant-like accumulation of facts."[32] European mathematics was of particular interest to kaozheng researchers who were exploring the history of Chinese mathematics. To convince their skeptical colleagues that the barbarian Europeans had something to offer in this field, some Chinese scholars argued that European mathematics had in fact grown out of much earlier Chinese ideas and could therefore be adopted with comfort.[33] In such ways, early modern Chinese thinkers selectively assimilated Western science very much on their own terms.[34]

Although Japanese authorities largely closed their country off from the West in the early seventeenth century (see Chapter 14), one window remained open. Alone among Europeans, the Dutch were permitted to trade in Japan at a single location near Nagasaki, but not until 1720 did the Japanese lift the ban on importing Western books. Then a number of European texts in medicine, astronomy, geography, mathematics, and other disciplines were translated and studied by a small group of Japanese scholars. They were especially impressed with Western anatomical studies, for in Japan dissection was work fit only for outcasts. Returning from an autopsy conducted by Dutch physicians in the mid-eighteenth century, several Japanese observers reflected on their experience: "We remarked to each other how amazing the autopsy had been, and how inexcusable it had been for us to be ignorant of the anatomical structure of the human body."[35] Nonetheless, this small center of "Dutch learning," as it was called, remained isolated amid a pervasive Confucian-based culture. Not until the mid-nineteenth century, when Japan was forcibly opened to Western penetration, would European-style science assume a prominent place in Japanese culture.

Like China and Japan, the Ottoman Empire in the sixteenth and seventeenth centuries was an independent, powerful, successful society whose intellectual elites saw no need for a wholesale embrace of things European. Ottoman scholars were conscious of the rich tradition of Muslim astronomy and chose not to translate the works of major European scientists such as Copernicus, Kepler, or Newton, although they were broadly aware of European scientific achievements by 1650. Insofar as they were interested in these developments, it was for their practical usefulness in making maps and calendars rather than for their larger philosophical implications. In any event, the notion of a sun-centered solar system did not cause the kind of upset that it did in Europe.

More broadly, theoretical science of any kind—Muslim or European—faced an uphill struggle in the face of a conservative Islamic educational system. In 1580, for example, a highly sophisticated astronomical observatory was dismantled under pressure from conservative religious scholars and teachers, who interpreted an outbreak of the plague as God's disapproval with those who sought to understand his secrets. As in Japan, the systematic embrace of Western science would have to await the nineteenth century, when the Ottoman Empire was under far more intense European pressure and reform seemed more necessary.

REFLECTIONS

Cultural Borrowing and Its Hazards

Ideas are important in human history. They shape the mental or cultural worlds that people everywhere inhabit, and they often influence behavior as well. Many of the ideas developed or introduced during the early modern era have had enormous and continuing significance in the centuries that followed. The Western Hemisphere was solidly incorporated into Christendom. A Wahhabi version of Islam remains the official faith of Saudi Arabia into the twenty-first century and has influenced many contemporary Islamic revival movements, including al-Qaeda. Modern science and the associated notions of progress have become for many people something approaching a new religion.

Accompanying the development of these ideas has been a great deal of cultural borrowing. Filipinos, Siberians, and many Native American peoples borrowed elements of Christianity from Europeans. Numerous Asian and African peoples borrowed Islam from the Arabs. North Indian Sikhs drew on both Hindu and Muslim teachings. Europeans borrowed scientific and medical ideas from the Islamic world and subsequently contributed their own rich scientific thinking to the entire planet.

In virtually every case, though, borrowing was selective rather than wholesale, even when it took place under conditions of foreign domination or colonial rule. Many peoples who appropriated Christianity or Islam certainly did not accept the rigid exclusivity and ardent monotheism of more orthodox versions of those faiths. Elite Chinese were far more interested in European mapmaking and mathematics than in Western medicine, while Japanese scholars became fascinated with the anatomical work of the Dutch. Neither, however, adopted Christianity in a widespread manner.

Borrowing was frequently the occasion for serious conflict. Some objected to much borrowing at all, particularly when it occurred under conditions of foreign domination or foreign threat. Thus members of the Taki Onqoy movement in Peru sought to wipe out Spanish influence and control, while Chinese and Japanese authorities clamped down firmly on European missionaries, even as they maintained some interest in European technological and scientific skills. Another kind of conflict derived from the efforts to control the terms of cultural borrowing. For example, European missionaries and Muslim reformers alike sought to root out "idolatry" among native converts.

To ease the tensions of cultural borrowing, efforts to "domesticate" foreign ideas and practices proliferated. Thus the Jesuits in China tried to point out similarities between Christianity and Confucianism, and Native American converts identified Christian saints with their own gods and spirits. By the late seventeenth century, some local churches in central Mexico had come to associate Catholicism less with the Spanish than with ancient pre-Aztec communities and beliefs that were now, supposedly, restored to their rightful position.

The pace of global cultural borrowing and its associated tensions stepped up even more as Europe's modern transformation unfolded in the nineteenth century and as its imperial reach extended and deepened around the world.

Second Thoughts

What's the Significance?

Big Picture Questions

1. Why did Christianity take hold in some places more than in others?
2. In what ways was the missionary message of Christianity shaped by the cultures of Asian and American peoples?
3. In what ways did the spread of Christianity, Islam, and modern science give rise to culturally based conflicts?
4. **Looking Back:** Based on Chapters 13 through 15, how might you challenge a Eurocentric understanding of the early modern era while acknowledging the growing role of Europeans on the global stage?

Next Steps: For Further Study

Natana J. Delong-Bas, *Wahhabi Islam: From Revival and Reform to Global Jihad* (2004). A careful study of the origins of Wahhabi Islam and its subsequent development.

Patricia Buckley Ebrey et al., *East Asia: A Cultural, Social, and Political History* (2005). A broad survey by major scholars in the field.

Geoffrey C. Gunn, *First Globalization: The Eurasian Exchange, 1500–1800* (2003). Explores the two-way exchange of ideas between Europe and Asia in the early modern era.

Toby E. Huff, *The Rise of Early Modern Science* (2003). A fascinating and controversial explanation as to why modern science arose in the West rather than in China or the Islamic world.

Úrsula de Jesús, *The Souls of Purgatory: The Spiritual Diary of a Seventeenth-Century Afro-Peruvian Mystic* (2004). A scholarly introduction by Nancy E. van Deusen places Úrsula in a broader context.

Diarmaid MacCulloch, *Christianity: The First Three Thousand Years* (2009). A masterful exploration of global Christianity with extensive coverage of the early modern era.

Deva Sobel, *A More Perfect Heaven: How Copernicus Revolutionized the Cosmos* (2011). A fascinating account of a major breakthrough in the Scientific Revolution.

"Christianity: A History of 'Dark Continents,' " http://vimeo.com/15944175.

Internet Modern History Sourcebook, "The Scientific Revolution," http://www.fordham.edu/halsall/mod/modsbook09.html. A collection of primary-source documents dealing with the breakthrough to modern science in Europe.

Global Christianity in the Early Modern Era

During the early modern centuries, the world of European Christendom, long divided between its Roman Catholic and Eastern Orthodox branches, underwent two major transformations. First, the Reformation sharply divided Western Christendom into bitterly hostile Protestant and Catholic halves. And while that process was unfolding in Europe, missionaries—mostly Roman Catholic—rode the tide of European expansion to establish the faith in the Americas and parts of Africa and Asia. In those places, native converts sometimes imitated European patterns and at other times adapted the new religion to their own cultural traditions. Furthermore, smaller but ancient Christian communities persisted in Ethiopia, Armenia, Egypt, southern India, and elsewhere. Thus the Christian world of the early modern era was far more globalized and much more varied than before 1500. That variety found expression in both art and architecture, as the sources that follow illustrate.

Some of the differences between Protestant and Catholic Christianity become apparent in the interiors of their churches. To Martin Luther, the founder of Protestant Christianity, elaborate church interiors, with their many sculptures and paintings, represented a spiritual danger, for he feared that the wealthy few who endowed such images would come to believe that they were buying their way into Heaven rather than relying on God's grace. "It would be better," he wrote, "if we gave less to the churches and altars, . . . and more to the needy."[36] John Calvin, the prominent French-born Protestant theologian, went even further, declaring that "God forbade . . . the making of any images representing him."[37]

Behind such statements lay different understandings of the church building. While Roman Catholics generally saw a church as a temple or "house of God," sacred because it is where God dwells on earth, Protestants viewed churches more as meetinghouses, gathering places for a congregation. They were not sacred in themselves as places, but only on account of the worship that occurred within them.[38] Furthermore, to Protestants, images of the saints were an invitation to idolatry. Acting on such ideas, Protestants in various places stripped older churches of the offending images, decapitated statues, and sometimes ritually burned statues and paintings at the stake. The new

Interior of the Choir of St. Bavo's Church at Haarlem, 1660 (oil on panel), by Pieter Jansz Saenredam (1597–1665)/Worcester Art Museum, Massachusetts, USA/Bridgeman Images

Source 15.1 Interior of a Dutch Reformed Church

churches they created were often quite different from their Catholic counter-parts. Source 15.1, a painting by the seventeenth-century Dutch artist Pieter Saenredam, portrays the interior of a Dutch Reformed (Protestant) church in the city of Haarlem.

Roman Catholic response to the Reformation took shape in the Catholic Reformation, or Counter-Reformation (see page 649). That vigorous move-ment found expression in a style of church architecture known as Baroque, which emerged powerfully in Catholic Europe as well as in the Spanish and Portuguese colonies of Latin America during the seventeenth and eighteenth

centuries. The interiors of such churches were ornately adorned with paintings, ceiling frescoes, and statues, depicting Jesus on the cross, the Virgin and
child, numerous saints, and biblical stories. The exuberant art of these church
interiors appealed to the senses, seeking to provoke an emotional response of
mystery, awe, and grandeur while kindling the faith of the worshippers and
binding them firmly to the Catholic Church in the face of Protestant competition. Source 15.2 is a photograph of the interior of the Pilgrimage Church
of Mariazell, located in present-day Austria. A church site since the twelfth
century, the building was enlarged and refurbished in Baroque style in the
seventeenth century.

Erich Lessing/Art Resource, NY

Source 15.2 Catholic Baroque, Interior of Pilgrimage Church, Mariazell, Austria

■ What obvious differences do you notice between these two church interiors? What kind of emotional responses would each of them have evoked?

■ In what ways do these church interiors reflect differences between Protestant and Catholic theology? (See Snapshot, page 647.)

■ How might Protestants and Catholics have reacted upon entering each other's churches?

■ Keep in mind that Source 15.1 is a painting. Why do you think the artist showed the people disproportionately small?

Throughout Latin America, Christianity was established in the context of European conquest and colonial rule (see pages 652–56). As the new faith took hold across the region, it incorporated much that was of European origin, as the construction of many large and ornate Baroque churches illustrates. But local communities also sought to blend this European Catholic Christianity with religious symbols and concepts drawn from their own traditions in a process that historians call syncretism. In the Andes, for example, Inca religion featured a supreme creator god (Viracocha); a sun god (Inti), regarded as the creator of the Inca people; a moon goddess (Killa), who was the wife of Inti and was attended by an order of priestesses; and an earth mother goddess (Pachamama), associated with mountain peaks and fertility. Those religious figures found their way into Andean understanding of Christianity, as Source 15.3 illustrates.

Painted around 1740 by an unknown artist, this striking image shows the Virgin Mary placed within the "rich mountain" of Potosí in Bolivia, from which the Spanish had extracted so much silver (see Chapter 14, page 614). Thus Christianity was visually expressed in an Andean tradition that viewed mountains as the embodiment of the gods. A number of smaller figures within the mountain represent the native miners whose labor had enriched their colonial rulers. A somewhat larger figure at the bottom of the mountain is an Inca ruler dressed in royal garb receiving tribute from his people. At the bottom left are the pope and a cardinal, while on the right stand the Habsburg emperor Charles V and perhaps his wife.

■ What is Mary's relationship to the heavenly beings standing above her (God the Father on the right; the dove, symbolizing the Holy Spirit, in the center; and Jesus on the left) as well as to the miners at work in the mountain? What is the significance of the crown above her head and her outstretched arms?

■ The European figures at the bottom are shown in a posture of prayer or thanksgiving. What might the artist have been trying to convey? How would you interpret the relative size of the European and Andean figures?

■ Why do you think the artist placed Mary actually inside the mountain rather than on it, while depicting her dress in a mountain-like form?

Museo de la Casa de la Moneda, Potosí, Bolivia/Gilles Mermet/akg-images

15.3 Cultural Blending in Andean Christianity

■ What marks this painting and the one on page 653 as examples of syncretism?

■ Do you read these two images from the Andes as subversive of the colonial order or as supportive of it? Do you think the artist who painted Source 15.3 was a European or a Native American Christian?

In China, unlike in Latin America, Christian missionaries operated in a setting wholly outside of European political control, bringing their faith to a powerful and proud civilization, long dominant in eastern Asia, where Confucianism, Daoism, and Buddhism had for many centuries mixed and mingled. The outcome of those missionary efforts was far more modest and much less successful than in the Americas. Nonetheless, in China too the tendency toward syncretism was evident. Jesuit missionaries themselves sought to present the Christian message within a Chinese cultural context to the intellectual and political elites who were their primary target audience. And Chinese Christians often transposed the new religion into more familiar cultural concepts. European critics of the Jesuit approach, however, feared that syncretism watered down the Christian message and risked losing its distinctive character.

Source 15.4 provides an example of Christianity becoming Chinese.[39] In the early seventeenth century, the Jesuits published several books in the Chinese language describing the life of Christ and illustrated them with a series of woodblock prints created by Chinese artists affiliated with the Jesuits. Although they were clearly modeled on European images, those prints cast Christian

Roma, ARSI, Jap. Sin I 43

Source 15.4 Making Christianity Chinese

figures into an altogether Chinese setting. The print in Source 15.4 portrays the familiar biblical story of the Annunciation, when an angel informs Mary that she will be the mother of Jesus. The house and furniture shown in the print suggest the dwelling of a wealthy Chinese scholar. The reading table in front of Mary was a common item in the homes of the literary elite of the time. The view from the window shows a seascape, mountains in the distance, a lone tree, and a "scholar's rock"—all of which were common features in Chinese landscape painting. The clouds that appear at the angel's feet and around the shaft of light shining on Mary are identical to those associated with sacred Buddhist and Daoist figures. To Chinese eyes, the angel might well appear as a Buddhist bodhisattva, while Mary may resemble a Ming dynasty noblewoman or perhaps Kuanyin, the Chinese Buddhist goddess of mercy and compassion.

- What specifically Chinese elements can you identify in this image?

- To whom might this image have been directed?

- How might educated Chinese have responded to this image?

- The European engraving on which this Chinese print was modeled included in the background the scene of Jesus' crucifixion. Why might the Chinese artist have chosen to omit that scene from his image?

- How would European critics of the Jesuits' approach to missionary work have reacted to this image? To what extent has the basic message of Catholic Christianity been retained or altered in this Chinese cultural setting?

As Chinese emperors welcomed Jesuit missionaries at court, so too did the rulers of Mughal India during the time of Akbar (r. 1556–1605) and Jahangir (r. 1605–1627). But while Chinese elite circles received the Jesuits for their scientific skills, especially in astronomy, the Mughal court seemed more interested in the religious and artistic achievements of European civilization. Akbar invited the Jesuits to take part in cross-religious discussions that included Muslim, Hindu, Jain, and Zoroastrian scholars. Furthermore, the Mughal emperors eagerly embraced the art of late Renaissance Europe, which the Jesuits provided to them, much of it devotional and distinctly Christian. Mughal artists quickly learned to paint in the European style, and soon murals featuring Jesus, Mary, and Christian saints appeared on the walls of palaces, garden pavilions, and harems of the Mughal court, while miniature paintings adorned books, albums, and jewelry.

In religious terms, however, the Jesuit efforts were "a fantastic and extravagant failure,"[40] for these Muslim rulers of India were not in the least interested in abandoning Islam for the Christian faith, and few conversions of any kind occurred. Akbar and Jahangir, however, were cosmopolitan connoisseurs of art, which they collected, reproduced, and displayed. European religious art also had propaganda value in enhancing their status. Jesus and Mary, after all, had a prominent place within Islam. Jesus was seen both as an earlier prophet and as a mystical figure, similar to the Sufi masters who were so important in Indian Islam. Mughal paintings, pairing the adult Jesus and Mary side by side, were placed above the imperial throne as well as on the emperor's jewelry and his official seal, suggesting an identification of Jesus and a semi-divine emperor. That the mothers of both Akbar and Jahangir were named Mary only added to the appeal. Thus Akbar and Jahangir sought to incorporate European-style Christian art into their efforts to create a blended and tolerant religious culture for the elites of their vast and diverse realm. It was a culture that drew on Islam, Hinduism, Zoroastrianism, and Christianity.

But as Catholic devotional art was reworked by Mughal artists, it was also subtly changed. Source 15.5 shows an early seventeenth-century depiction of the Holy Family painted by an Indian artist.

The Free Library of Philadelphia/Bridgeman Images

Source 15.5 Christian Art at the Mughal Court

- Why do you think that this Mughal painter portrayed Mary and Joseph as rather distinguished and educated persons rather than as the humble carpenter and his peasant wife, as in so many European images? Why might he have placed the family in rather palatial surroundings instead of a stable?

- How do you imagine European missionaries responded to this representation of the Holy Family?

- How might more orthodox Muslims have reacted to the larger project of creating a blended religion making use of elements from many traditions?

- What similarities can you identify between this Indian image and the Chinese print in Source 15.4? Pay attention to the setting, the clothing, the class status of the human figures, and the scenes outside the windows.

DOING HISTORY

Global Christianity in the Early Modern Era

1. **Making comparisons:** What common Christian elements can you identify in these visual sources? What differences in the expression of Christianity can you define?

2. **Considering Mary:** The Catholic Christian tradition as it developed in Latin America, China, and India as well as Europe assigned a very important role to representations of the Virgin Mary. Why might such images of Mary have been so widely appealing? But in what ways does the image of the Holy Mother differ in Sources 15.3, 15.4, and 15.5? In what ways were those images adapted to the distinctive cultures in which they were created?

3. **Pondering syncretism:** From a missionary viewpoint, develop arguments for and against religious syncretism using these visual sources as points of reference.

4. **Considering visual sources as evidence:** What are the strengths and limitations of these visual sources, as opposed to texts, as historians seek to understand the globalization of Christianity in the early modern era? What other visual sources might be useful?

PART FIVE

THE EUROPEAN MOMENT IN WORLD HISTORY

1750–1914

Contents

photos: left, Musée de la Ville de Paris, Musée Carnavalet, Paris, France/© RMN–Grand Palais/Art Resource, NY; center, © Topham/The Image Works; right, The Chinese Cake, from *Le Petit Journal*, 1898, lithograph by Henri Meyer (1844–1899)/Private Collection/Roger-Viollet, Paris, France/Bridgeman Images

EUROPEAN CENTRALITY AND THE PROBLEM OF EUROCENTRISM

During the century and a half between 1750 and 1914, sometimes referred to as the "long nineteenth century," two new and related phenomena held center stage in the global history of humankind and represent the major themes of the four chapters that follow. The first of these, explored in Chapters 16 and 17, was the creation of a new kind of human society, commonly called "modern." It emerged from the intersection of the Scientific, French, and Industrial Revolutions, all of which took shape initially in Western Europe. Those societies generated many of the transformative ideas that have guided human behavior over the past several centuries: that movement toward social equality and the end of poverty was possible; that ordinary people might participate in political life; that nations might trump empires; that women could be equal to men; that slavery was no longer necessary.

The second theme of this long nineteenth century, which is addressed in Chapters 18 and 19, was the growing ability of these modern societies to exercise enormous power and influence over the rest of humankind. In some places, this occurred within expanding European empires, such as those that governed India, Southeast Asia, Africa, and Pacific Oceania. Elsewhere, it took place through less formal means—economic penetration, military intervention, diplomatic pressure, missionary activity—in states that remained officially independent, such as China, Japan, the Ottoman Empire, and various countries in Latin America.

Together, these two phenomena thrust Western Europe, and to a lesser extent North America, into a new and far more prominent role in world history than ever before. While various regions had experienced sprouts of modernity during the "early modern" centuries, it was in Western European societies that these novel ways of living emerged most fully. Those societies, and their North American offspring, also came to exercise a wholly unprecedented role in world affairs, as they achieved, collectively, something approaching global dominance by the early twentieth century.

But if Europeans were moving toward dominance over other peoples, they were also leading a human intervention in the natural order of unprecedented dimensions, largely the product of industrialization. The demand for raw materials to supply new factories and to feed their workers drove developments across the globe, leaving a mark on such remote regions as the high peaks of the Andes, the guano islands of the Pacific, and the plains of Kansas and Argentina as well as on the industrial cities of Western Europe and North America. Growing numbers of scientists and other scholars now argue that humankind was then entering a new era, not only in human history but also in the history of the planet—its biological regime, its atmosphere, its climate, even its geology. They have called it the Anthropocene, or the "age of man."

Historically, scientists have viewed human activity as incidental to the larger processes that have shaped the physical and biological evolution of the earth. But now they are suggesting that over the past several centuries, humankind itself has become an active agent of change in this domain, rapidly reshaping the planet. While these changes became more pronounced and obvious in the second half of the twentieth century, the European moment of the long nineteenth century takes on an added significance as the starting point of an epic transformation in the relationship of humanity to the earth, equivalent perhaps to the early stages of the Agricultural Revolution. While human beings have long felt themselves vulnerable to nature, in recent centuries unprecedented numbers of humans, possessing unprecedented powers and material desires, have left nature increasingly vulnerable to humans.

Eurocentric Geography and History

The unprecedented power that Europeans accumulated during the long nineteenth century included the ability to rewrite geography and history in ways that centered the human story on Europe and to convey those views powerfully to other people. Thus flat maps placed Europe at the center of the world, while dividing Asia in half. Europe was granted continental status, even though it was more accurately only the western peninsula of Asia, much as India was its southern peninsula. Other regions of the world, such as the Far East or the Near (Middle) East, were defined in terms of their distance from Europe. The entire world came to measure longitude from a line, known as the prime meridian, which passes through the Royal Astronomical Observatory in Greenwich, England.

History textbooks as well often reflected a Europe-centered outlook, sometimes blatantly. In 1874, the American author William O. Swinton wrote *An Outline of the World's History*, a book intended for use in high school and college classes, in which he flatly declared that "the race to which we belong, the Aryan, has always played the leading part in the great drama of the world's progress."[1] Other peoples and civilizations, by contrast, were long believed to be static or stagnant, thus largely lacking any real history. Most Europeans assumed that these "backward" peoples and regions must either imitate the Western model or face further decline and possible extinction. Until the mid-twentieth century, such ideas went largely unchallenged in the Western world.

They implied that history was a race toward the finish line of modernity. The fact that Europeans arrived there first seemed to suggest something unique, special, or superior about them or their culture, while everyone else struggled to overcome their inadequacy and catch up.

As the discipline of world history took shape in the decades after World War II, scholars and teachers actively sought to counteract such Eurocentric understandings of the past, but they faced a special problem in dealing with recent centuries. How can we avoid Eurocentrism when dealing with a phase of world history in which Europeans were in fact central? The long nineteenth century, after all, was "the European moment," a time when Europeans were clearly the most powerful, most innovative, most prosperous, most expansive, and most widely imitated people on the planet.

Countering Eurocentrism

At least five answers to this dilemma are reflected in the chapters that follow. The first is simply to remind ourselves how recent and perhaps how brief the European moment in world history has been. Other peoples too had times of "cultural flowering" that granted them a period of primacy or influence—for example, the Greeks (500 B.C.E.–200 C.E.), Indians of South Asia (200–600 C.E.), Arabs (600–1000), Chinese (1000–1500), Mongols (1200–1350), and Incas and Aztecs (fifteenth century)—but all of these were limited to particular regions of Afro-Eurasia or the Americas.[2] Even though the European moment operated on a genuinely global scale, Western peoples have enjoyed their worldwide primacy for at most two centuries. Some scholars have suggested that the events of the late twentieth and early twenty-first centuries—the end of colonial empires, the rise of India and especially China, and the assertion of Islam—mark the end, or at least the erosion, of the age of European predominance.

Second, we need to remember that the rise of Europe occurred within an international context. It was the withdrawal of the Chinese naval fleet that allowed Europeans to enter the Indian Ocean in the sixteenth century, while Native Americans' lack of immunity to European diseases and their own divisions and conflicts greatly assisted the European takeover of the Western Hemisphere. The Industrial Revolution, explored in Chapter 17, likewise benefited from New World resources and markets and from the stimulus of superior Asian textile and pottery production. Chapters 18 and 19 make clear that European control of other regions everywhere depended on the cooperation of local elites. Such observations remind us that the remarkable—indeed revolutionary—transformations of the European moment in world history did not derive wholly from some special European genius or long-term advantage. Rather, they emerged from a unique intersection of European historical development with that of other peoples, regions, and cultures. Europeans, like everyone else, were embedded in a web of relationships that shaped their own histories.

A third reminder is that the rise of Europe to a position of global dominance was not an easy or automatic process. Frequently it occurred in the face of ferocious resistance and rebellion, which often required Europeans to modify their policies and practices. The so-called Indian mutiny in mid-nineteenth-century South Asia, a massive uprising against British colonial rule, did not end British control, but it substantially transformed the character of the colonial experience. In Africa, fear of offending Muslim sensibilities persuaded the British to keep European missionaries and mission schools out of northern Nigeria during the colonial era. Even when Europeans exercised political power, they could not do so precisely as they pleased. Empire, formal and informal alike, was always in some ways a negotiated arrangement.

Fourth, peoples the world over made active use of Europeans and European ideas for their own purposes, seeking to gain advantage over local rivals or to benefit themselves in light of new conditions. In Southeast Asia, for example, a number of highland minority groups, long oppressed by the dominant lowland Vietnamese, viewed the French invaders as liberators and assisted in their takeover of Vietnam. Hindus in India used the railroads, introduced by the British, to go on pilgrimages to holy sites more easily, while the printing press made possible the more widespread distribution of their sacred texts. During the Haitian Revolution, examined in Chapter 16, enslaved Africans made use of radical French ideas about "the rights of man" in ways that most Europeans never intended. The leaders of a massive Chinese peasant upheaval in the mid-nineteenth century adopted a unique form of Christianity to legitimate their revolutionary assault on an ancient social order. Recognizing that Asian and African peoples remained active agents, pursuing their own interests even in oppressive conditions, is another way of countering residual Eurocentrism.

Moreover, what was borrowed from Europe was always adapted to local circumstances. Thus Japanese or Russian industrial development did not wholly follow the pattern of England's Industrial Revolution. The Christianity that took root in the Americas or later in Africa evolved in culturally distinctive ways. Ideas of nationalism, born in Europe, were used to oppose European imperialism throughout Asia and Africa. Russian and Chinese socialism in the twentieth century departed in many ways from the vision of Karl Marx. The most interesting stories of modern world history are not simply those of European triumph or the imposition of Western ideas and practices but those of encounters, though highly unequal, among culturally different peoples. It was from these encounters, not just from the intentions and actions of Europeans, that the dramatic global changes of the modern era arose.

A fifth and final antidote to Eurocentrism in an age of European centrality lies in the recognition that although Europeans gained an unprecedented prominence on the world stage, they were not the only game in town, nor were they the sole preoccupation of Asian, African, and Middle Eastern peoples. While China confronted Western aggression in the nineteenth century, it was also absorbing a huge population increase and experiencing massive peasant rebellions that grew out of distinctly Chinese conditions. The long relationship of Muslim and Hindu cultures in India continued to evolve under British colonial rule, as it had for centuries under other political systems. West African societies in the nineteenth century experienced a wave of religious wars that created new states and extended and transformed the practice of Islam, and that faith continued its centuries-long spread on the continent even under European colonial rule. A further wave of wars and state formation in southern Africa transformed the political and ethnic landscape, even as European penetration picked up speed.

None of this diminishes the significance of the European moment in world history, but it sets that moment in a larger context of continuing patterns of historical development and of interaction and exchange with other peoples.

MAPPING PART FIVE

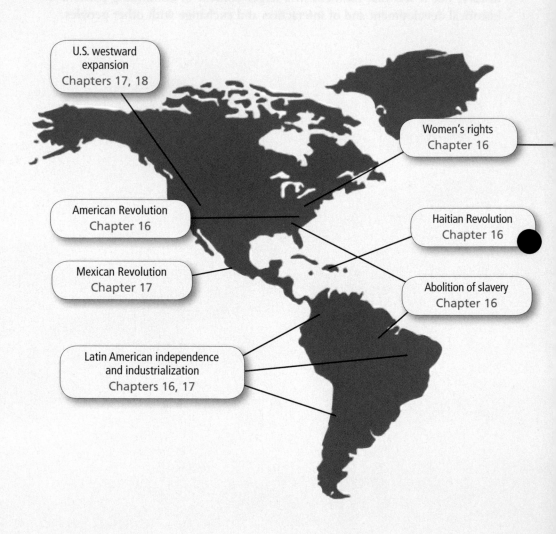

U.S. westward
expansion
Chapters 17, 18

Women's rights
Chapter 16

American Revolution
Chapter 16

Haitian Revolution
Chapter 16

Mexican Revolution
Chapter 17

Abolition of slavery
Chapter 16

Latin American independence
and industrialization
Chapters 16, 17

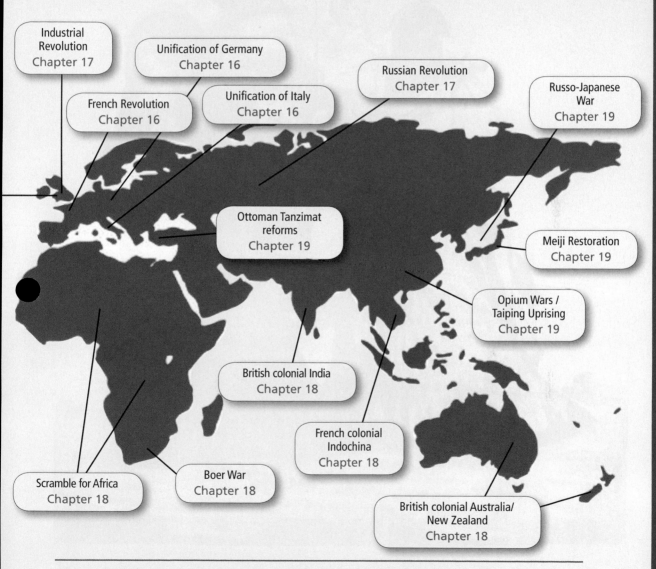

Industrial Revolution
Chapter 17

Unification of Germany
Chapter 16

Unification of Italy
Chapter 16

French Revolution
Chapter 16

Russian Revolution
Chapter 17

Russo-Japanese War
Chapter 19

Ottoman Tanzimat reforms
Chapter 19

Meiji Restoration
Chapter 19

Opium Wars /
Taiping Uprising
Chapter 19

British colonial India
Chapter 18

French colonial Indochina
Chapter 18

Scramble for Africa
Chapter 18

Boer War
Chapter 18

British colonial Australia/
New Zealand
Chapter 18

Vive le Roi, Vive la Nation.

J savois ben Qu'jaurions not tour.

CHAPTER 16

Atlantic Revolutions, Global Echoes

1750–1914

The Haitian earthquake of January 2010 not only devastated an already-impoverished country but also reawakened issues deriving from that country's revolution against slavery and French colonial rule, which finally succeeded in 1804. Twenty-one years later, the French government demanded from Haiti a payment of 150 million gold francs in compensation for the loss of its richest colony and its "property" in slaves. With French warships hovering offshore, Haitian authorities agreed. To make the heavy payments, even after they were somewhat reduced, Haiti took out major loans from French, German, and North American banks. Repaying those loans, finally accomplished only in 1947, represented a huge drain on the country's budget, costing 80 percent of the government's revenue in 1915. In 2010, with the country in ruins, an international petition signed by over 100 prominent people called on the French government to repay some $17 billion, effectively returning the "independence debt" extorted from Haiti 185 years earlier. While the French government dismissed those claims, the issue provided a reminder of the continuing echoes of events from an earlier age of revolution.

The Haitian Revolution was part of and linked to a much larger set of upheavals that shook both sides of the Atlantic world between 1775 and 1825. Haitians had drawn inspiration from the earlier North American and French revolutions, even as their successful overthrow of French rule helped shape the Latin American independence struggles that followed. These four closely related upheavals reflect the new connections among Europe, Africa,

Revolution and the Reversal of Class Roles   Three French female figures, representing from right to left the clergy, nobility, and commoners (Third Estate), show the reversal of class roles that the revolution generated. Now the commoner rides on the back of the noblewoman and is shown in a dominant position over the nun.

697

SEEKING THE MAIN POINT

What were the most important out-comes of the Atlantic revolutions, both immediately and in the century that followed?

North America, and South America, which took shape in the wake of Columbus's voyages and the European conquests that followed. Together, they launched a new chapter in the history of the Atlantic world, while the echoes of those revolutions reverberated in the larger world.

Atlantic Revolutions in a Global Context

Writing to a friend in 1772, before any of the Atlantic revolutions had occurred, the French intellectual Voltaire asked, "My dear philosopher, doesn't this appear to you to be the century of revolutions?"[1] He was certainly on target, and not only for the European/Atlantic world. From the early eighteenth century to the mid-nineteenth, many parts of the world witnessed political and social upheaval, leading some historians to think in terms of a "world crisis" or "converging revolutions." By the 1730s, the Safavid dynasty that had ruled Persia (now Iran) for several centuries had completely collapsed, even as the powerful Mughal Empire governing India also fragmented. About the same time, the Wahhabi movement in Arabia seriously threatened the Ottoman Empire, and its religious ideals informed major political upheavals in Central Asia and elsewhere (see Chapter 15, pages 659–61). The Russian Empire under Catherine the Great experienced a series of peasant uprisings, most notably one led by the Cossack commander Pugachev in 1773–1774, which briefly proclaimed the end of serfdom before that rebellion was crushed. China too in the late eighteenth and early nineteenth centuries hosted a number of popular though unsuccessful rebellions, a prelude perhaps to the huge Taiping revolution of 1850–1864. Beginning in the early nineteenth century, a wave of Islamic revolutions shook West Africa, while in southern Africa a series of wars and migrations known as the *mfecane* (the breaking or crushing) involved widespread and violent disruptions as well as the creation of new states and societies.

Thus the Atlantic revolutions in North America, France, Haiti, and Latin America took place within a larger global framework. Like many of the other upheavals, they too occurred in the context of expensive wars, weakening states, and destabilizing processes of commercialization. But compared to upheavals elsewhere, the Atlantic revolutions were distinctive in various ways. The costly wars that strained European imperial states—Britain, France, and Spain in particular—were global rather than regional. In the so-called Seven Years' War (1754–1763), Britain and France joined battle in North America, the Caribbean, West Africa, and South Asia. The expenses of those conflicts prompted the British to levy additional taxes on their North American colonies and the French monarchy to seek new revenue from its landowners. These actions contributed to the launching of the North American and French revolutions, respectively.

Furthermore, the Atlantic revolutions were distinctive in that they were closely connected to one another. The American revolutionary leader Thomas Jefferson

A MAP OF TIME

1775–1787	North American Revolution
1780s	Beginnings of antislavery movement
1789–1799	French Revolution
1791–1804	Haitian Revolution
1793–1794	Execution of Louis XVI; the Terror in France
1799–1814	Reign of Napoleon
1807	End of slave trade in British Empire
1808–1825	Latin American wars of independence
1810–1811	Hidalgo-Morelos rebellion in Mexico
1822	Brazil gains independence from Portugal
1848	Women's Rights Convention, Seneca Falls, New York
1861	Emancipation of serfs in Russia
1861–1865	Civil War and abolition of slavery in United States
1870–1871	Unification of Germany and Italy
1886–1888	Cuba and Brazil abolish slavery
1920	Women gain the vote in United States

was the U.S. ambassador to France on the eve of the French Revolution. While there, he provided advice and encouragement to French reformers and revolutionaries. Simón Bolívar, a leading figure in Spanish American struggles for independence, twice visited Haiti, where he received military aid from the first black government in the Americas.

Beyond such direct connections, the various Atlantic revolutionaries shared a set of common ideas. The Atlantic basin had become a world of intellectual and cultural exchange as well as one of commercial and biological interaction. The ideas that animated the Atlantic revolutions derived from the European Enlightenment and were shared across the ocean in newspapers, books, and pamphlets. At the heart of these ideas was the radical notion that human political and social arrangements could be engineered, and improved, by human action. Thus conventional and long-established ways of living and thinking—the divine right of kings, state control of trade, aristocratic privilege, the authority of a single church—were no longer sacrosanct and came under repeated attack. New ideas of liberty, equality, free trade, religious tolerance, republicanism, and human rationality were in the air. Politically, the core notion was "popular sovereignty," which meant that the authority to govern derived from the people rather than from God or from established tradition. As the Englishman John Locke (1632–1704) had argued, the "social contract" between ruler and ruled should last only as long as it served the people well. In short, it was both possible and desirable to start over in the construction of human communities. In the late eighteenth and early nineteenth centuries, these ideas were largely limited to the Atlantic world. While all of the Atlantic revolutions involved the elimination of monarchs, at least temporarily, across Asia and the Middle East such republican political systems were virtually inconceivable until much later. There the only solution to a bad monarch was a new and better one.

In the world of the Atlantic revolutions, ideas born of the Enlightenment generated endless controversy. Were liberty and equality compatible? What kind of government—unitary and centralized or federal and decentralized—best ensured freedom? And how far should liberty be extended? Except in Haiti, the chief beneficiaries of these revolutions were propertied white men of the "middling classes." Although women, slaves, Native Americans, and men without property did not gain much from these revolutions, the ideas that accompanied those upheavals gave them ammunition for the future. Because their overall thrust was to extend political rights further than ever before, these Atlantic movements have often been referred to as "democratic revolutions."

A final distinctive feature of the Atlantic revolutions lies in their immense global impact, extending well beyond the Atlantic world. The armies of revolutionary France, for example, invaded Egypt, Germany, Poland, and Russia, carrying seeds of change. The ideals that animated these Atlantic revolutions inspired efforts in many countries to abolish slavery, to extend the right to vote, to develop constitutions, and to secure greater equality for women. Nationalism, perhaps the most potent ideology of the modern era, was nurtured in the Atlantic revolutions and shaped much of nineteenth- and twentieth-century world history. The ideas of human equality articulated in these revolutions later found expression in feminist, socialist, and communist movements. The Universal Declaration of Human Rights, adopted by the United Nations in 1948, echoed and amplified those principles while providing the basis for any number of subsequent protests against oppression, tyranny, and deprivation. In 1989, a number of Chinese students, fleeing the suppression of a democracy movement in their own country, marched at the head of a huge parade in Paris, celebrating the bicentennial of the French Revolution. And in 2011, the Middle Eastern uprisings known as the Arab Spring initially prompted numerous comparisons with the French Revolution. The Atlantic revolutions had a long reach.

■ Causation

In what ways did the ideas of the Enlightenment contribute to the Atlantic revolutions?

Comparing Atlantic Revolutions

Despite their common political vocabulary and a broadly democratic character, the Atlantic revolutions differed substantially from one another. They were triggered by different circumstances, expressed quite different social and political tensions,

and varied considerably in their outcomes. Liberty, noted Simón Bolívar, "is a suc-
culent morsel, but one difficult to digest."[2] "Digesting liberty" occurred in quite
distinct ways in the various sites of the Atlantic revolutions.

The North American Revolution, 1775–1787

Every schoolchild in the United States learns early that the American Revolution
was a struggle for independence from oppressive British rule. That struggle was
launched with the Declaration of Independence in 1776, resulted in an unlikely
military victory by 1781, and generated a federal constitution in 1787, joining thirteen formerly separate colonies into a new nation (see Map 16.1). It was the first in
a series of upheavals that rocked the Atlantic world and beyond in the century that
followed. But was it a genuine revolution? What, precisely, did it change?

By effecting a break with Britain, the American Revolution marked a decisive
political change, but in other ways it was, strangely enough, a conservative movement, because it originated in an effort to preserve the existing liberties of the colonies rather than to create new ones. For much of the seventeenth and eighteenth
centuries, the British colonies in North America enjoyed a considerable degree of
local autonomy, as the British government was embroiled in its own internal conflicts and various European wars. Furthermore, Britain's West Indian colonies seemed
more profitable and of greater significance than those of North America. In these
circumstances, local elected assemblies in North America, dominated by the wealthier property-owning settlers, achieved something close to self-government. Colonists came to regard such autonomy as a birthright and part of their English heritage.
Thus, until the mid-eighteenth century, almost no one in the colonies thought of
breaking away from England because participation in the British Empire provided
many advantages—protection in war, access to British markets, and confirmation
of the settlers' continuing identity as "Englishmen"—and few drawbacks.

There were, however, real differences between Englishmen in England and
those in the North American colonies. Within the colonies, English settlers had
developed societies described by a leading historian as "the most radical in the contemporary Western world." Certainly class distinctions were real and visible, and a
small class of wealthy "gentlemen"—the Adamses, Washingtons, Jeffersons, and
Hancocks—wore powdered wigs, imitated the latest European styles, were prominent in political life, and were generally accorded deference by ordinary people.
But the ready availability of land following the dispossession of Native Americans,
the scarcity of people, and the absence of both a titled nobility and a single established church meant that social life was far more open than in Europe. No legal
distinctions differentiated clergy, aristocracy, and commoners, as they did in France.
All free men enjoyed the same status before the law, a situation that excluded black
slaves and, in some ways, white women as well. These conditions made for less
poverty, more economic opportunity, fewer social differences, and easier relationships among the classes than in Europe. The famous economist Adam Smith observed

■ **Change**
What was revolutionary
about the American Revo-
lution, and what was not?

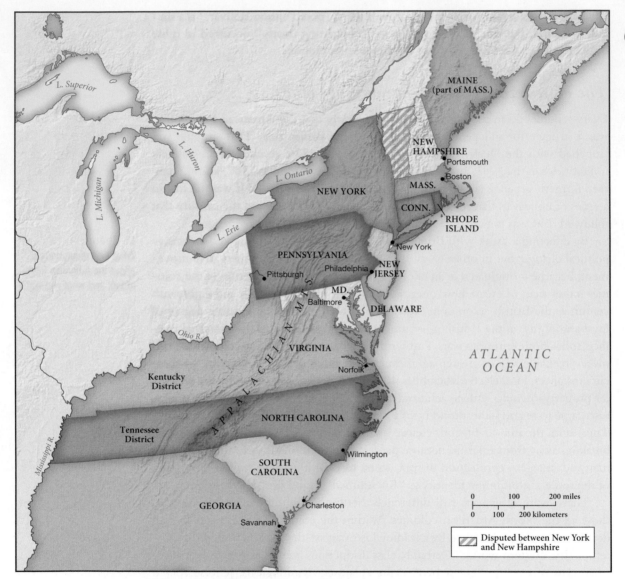

Map 16.1   The United States after the American Revolution

The union of the thirteen British colonies in North America created the embryonic United States, shown here in 1788. Over the past two centuries and more of anticolonial struggles, it was the only example of separate colonies joining together after independence to form a larger and enduring nation.

that British colonists were "republican in their manners . . . and their government" well before their independence from England.[3]

Thus the American Revolution grew not from social tensions within the colonies, but from a rather sudden and unexpected effort by the British government to tighten its control over the colonies and to extract more revenue from them. As

Britain's global struggle with France drained its treasury and ran up its national debt, British authorities, beginning in the 1760s, looked to America to make good these losses. Abandoning its neglectful oversight of the colonies, Britain began to act like a genuine imperial power, imposing a variety of new taxes and tariffs on the colonies without their consent, for they were not represented in the British Parliament. Many of the colonists were infuriated, because such measures challenged their economic interests, their established traditions of local autonomy, and their identity as true Englishmen. Armed with the ideas of the Enlightenment—popular sovereignty, natural rights, the consent of the governed—they went to war, and by 1781 they had prevailed, with considerable aid from the French, who were only too pleased to harm the interests of their British rivals.

What was revolutionary about the American experience was not so much the revolution itself but the kind of society that had already emerged within the colonies. Independence from Britain was not accompanied by any wholesale social transformation. Rather, the revolution accelerated the established democratic tendencies of the colonial societies. Political authority remained largely in the hands of existing elites who had led the revolution, although property requirements for voting were lowered and more white men of modest means, such as small farmers and urban artisans, were elected to state legislatures.

This widening of political participation gradually eroded the power of traditional gentlemen, but no women or people of color shared in these gains. Land was not seized from its owners, except in the case of pro-British loyalists who had fled the country. Although slavery was gradually abolished in the northern states, where it counted for little, it remained firmly entrenched in the southern states, where it counted for much. Chief Justice John Marshall later gave voice to this conservative understanding of the American Revolution: "All contracts and rights, respecting property, remained unchanged by the Revolution."[4] In the century that followed independence, the United States did become the world's most democratic country, but this development was less the direct product of the revolution and more the gradual working out in a reformist fashion of earlier practices and the principles of equality announced in the Declaration of Independence.

Nonetheless, many American patriots felt passionately that they were creating "a new order for the ages." James Madison in the *Federalist Papers* made the point clearly: "We pursued a new and more noble course . . . and accomplished a revolution that has no parallel in the annals of human society." Supporters abroad agreed. On the eve of the French Revolution, a Paris newspaper proclaimed that the United States was "the hope and model of the human race."[5] In both cases, they were referring primarily to the political ideas and practices of the new country. The American Revolution, after all, initiated the political dismantling of Europe's New World empires. The "right to revolution," proclaimed in the Declaration of Independence and made effective only in a great struggle, inspired revolutionaries and nationalists from Simón Bolívar in nineteenth-century Latin America to Ho Chi Minh in twentieth-century Vietnam. Moreover, the new U.S. Constitution—with its Bill of Rights, checks and balances, separation of church and state, and federalism—was one of the first sustained efforts to put the political ideas of the Enlightenment into practice. That document, and the ideas that it embraced, echoed repeatedly in the political upheavals of the century that followed.

The French Revolution, 1789–1815

Act Two in the drama of the Atlantic revolutions took place in France, beginning in 1789, although it was closely connected to Act One in North America. Thousands of French soldiers had provided assistance to the American colonists and now returned home full of republican enthusiasm. Thomas Jefferson, the U.S. ambassador in Paris, reported that France "has been awakened by our revolution."[6] More immediately, the French government, which had generously aided the Americans in an effort to undermine its British rivals, was teetering on the brink of bankruptcy and had long sought reforms that would modernize the tax system and make it more equitable. In a desperate effort to raise taxes against the opposition of the privileged classes, the French king, Louis XVI, had called into session an ancient representative body, the Estates General. It consisted of male representatives of the three "estates," or legal orders, of prerevolutionary France: the clergy, the nobility, and the commoners. The first two estates comprised about 2 percent of the population, and the Third Estate included everyone else. When that body convened in 1789, representatives of the Third Estate soon organized themselves as the National Assembly, claiming the sole authority to make laws for the country. A few weeks later, they drew up the Declaration of the Rights of Man and Citizen, which forthrightly declared that "men are born and remain free and equal in rights." These actions, unprecedented and illegal in the *ancien régime* (the old regime), launched the French Revolution and radicalized many of the participants in the National Assembly.

■ **Comparison**

How did the French Revolution differ from the American Revolution?

The French Revolution was quite different from its North American predecessor. Whereas the American Revolution expressed the tensions of a colonial relationship with a distant imperial power, the French insurrection was driven by sharp conflicts within French society. Members of the titled nobility—privileged, prestigious, and wealthy—resented and resisted the monarchy's efforts to subject them to new taxes. Educated middle-class men such as doctors, lawyers, lower-level officials, and merchants were growing in numbers and sometimes in wealth and were offended by the remaining privileges of the aristocracy, from which they were excluded. Ordinary urban men and women, many of whose incomes had declined for a generation, were hit particularly hard in the late 1780s by the rapidly rising price of bread and widespread unemployment. Peasants in the countryside, though largely free of serfdom, were subject to hated dues imposed by their landlords, taxes from the state, obligations to the Church, and the requirement to work without pay on public roads. As Enlightenment ideas penetrated French society, more and more people, mostly in the Third Estate but also including some priests and nobles, found a language with which to articulate these grievances. The famous French writer Jean-Jacques Rousseau had told them that it was "manifestly contrary to the law of nature . . . that a handful of people should gorge themselves with superfluities while the hungry multitude goes in want of necessities."[7]

These social conflicts gave the French Revolution, especially during its first five years, a much more violent, far-reaching, and radical character than its American counterpart. It was a profound social upheaval, more comparable to the revolutions of Russia and China in the twentieth century than to the earlier American Revolution. Initial efforts to establish a constitutional monarchy and promote harmony among the classes (see Working with Evidence, Source 16.1, page 731) gave way to more radical measures, as internal resistance and foreign opposition produced a fear that the revolution might be overturned. In the process, urban crowds organized insurrections. Some peasants attacked the residences of their lords, burning the documents that recorded their dues and payments. The National Assembly decreed the end of all legal privileges and eliminated what remained of feudalism in France. Even slavery was abolished, albeit briefly. Church lands were sold to raise revenue, and priests were put under government authority. (See Sources 16.2 and 16.3, pages 732 and 733, for images reflecting this more radical phase of the revolution.)

In 1793, King Louis XVI and his queen, Marie Antoinette, were executed, an act of regicide that shocked traditionalists all across Europe and marked a new stage in revolutionary violence. (See Source 16.4, page 734.) What followed was the Terror of 1793–1794. Under the leadership of Maximilien Robespierre (ROHBS-pee-air) and his Committee of Public Safety, tens of thousands deemed enemies of the revolution lost their lives on the guillotine. Shortly thereafter, Robespierre himself was arrested and guillotined, accused of leading France into tyranny and dictatorship. "The revolution," remarked one of its victims, "was devouring its own children."

Accompanying attacks on the old order were efforts to create a wholly new society, symbolized by a new calendar with the Year 1 in 1792, marking a fresh start for France. Unlike the Americans, who sought to restore or build on earlier freedoms, French revolutionaries perceived themselves to be starting from scratch and looked to the future. For the first time in its history, the country became a republic and briefly passed universal male suffrage, although it was never implemented. The old administrative system was rationalized into eighty-three territorial departments, each with a new name. As revolutionary France

The Execution of Robespierre
The beheading of the radical leader Robespierre, who had himself brought thousands of others to the guillotine, marked a decisive turning point in the unfolding of the French Revolution and the end of its most violent phase. (Musée de la Ville de Paris, Musée Carnavalet, Paris, France/Bridgeman Images)

prepared for war against its threatened and threatening neighbors, it created the world's largest army, with some 800,000 men, and all adult males were required to serve. Led by officers from the middle and even lower classes, this was an army of citizens representing the nation.

In terms of gender roles, the French Revolution did not create a new society, but it did raise the question of female political equality far more explicitly than the American Revolution had done. Partly this was because French women were active in the major events of the revolution. In July 1789, they took part in the famous storming of the Bastille, a large fortress, prison, and armory that had come to symbolize the oppressive old regime. In October of that year, some 7,000 Parisian women, desperate about the shortage of bread, marched on the palace at Versailles, stormed through the royal apartments searching for the despised Queen Marie Antoinette, and forced the royal family to return with them to Paris.

Backed by a few male supporters, women also made serious political demands. They signed petitions detailing their complaints: lack of education, male competition in female trades, the prevalence of prostitution, the rapidly rising price of bread and soap. One petition, reflecting the intersection of class and gender, referred to women as the "Third Estate of the Third Estate." Another demanded the right to bear arms in defense of the revolution. Over sixty women's clubs were established throughout the country. A small group called the Cercle Social (Social Circle) campaigned for women's rights, noting that "the laws favor men at the expense of women, because everywhere power is in your hands."[8] The French playwright and journalist Olympe de Gouges appropriated the language of the Declaration of Rights to insist that "woman is born free and lives equal to man in her rights."

But the assertion of French women in the early years of the revolution seemed wildly inappropriate and threatening to most men, uniting conservatives and revolutionaries alike in defense of male privileges. And so in late 1793, the country's all-male legislative body voted to ban all women's clubs. "Women are ill-suited for elevated thoughts and serious meditation," declared one of the male representatives. "A woman should not leave her family to meddle in affairs of government." Here was a conception of gender that defined masculinity in terms of exercising political power. Women who aspired to do so were, in the words of one revolutionary orator, "denatured *viragos*" (domineering women), in short, not really women at all.[9] Thus French revolutionaries were distinctly unwilling to offer any political rights to women, even though they had eliminated class restrictions, at least in theory; granted religious freedom to Jews and Protestants; and abolished slavery. Nonetheless, according to a leading historian, "the French Revolution, more than any other event of its time, opened up the question of women's rights for consideration" and thus laid the foundations for modern feminism.[10]

If not in terms of gender, the immediate impact of the revolution was felt in many other ways. Streets got new names; monuments to the royal family were destroyed; titles vanished; people referred to one another as "citizen so-and-so." Real politics in the public sphere emerged for the first time as many people joined political clubs, took part in marches and demonstrations, served on local committees, and ran for public office. Ordinary men and women, who had identified primarily with their local communities, now began to think of themselves as belonging to a nation. The state replaced the Catholic Church as the place for registering births, marriages, and deaths, and revolutionary festivals substituted for church holidays.

More radical revolutionary leaders deliberately sought to convey a sense of new beginnings and endless possibilities. At a Festival of Unity held in 1793 to mark the first anniversary of the end of monarchy, participants burned the crowns and scepters of the royal family in a huge bonfire while releasing a cloud of 3,000 white doves. The Cathedral of Notre Dame was temporarily turned into the Temple of Reason, while the "Hymn to Liberty" combined traditional church music with the explicit message of the Enlightenment:

> Oh Liberty, sacred Liberty
> Goddess of an enlightened people
> Rule today within these walls.
> Through you this temple is purified.
> Liberty! Before you reason chases out deception,
> Error flees, fanaticism is beaten down.
> Our gospel is nature
> And our cult is virtue.
> To love one's country and one's brothers, To serve the Sovereign People—
> These are the sacred tenets
> And pledge of a Republican.[11]

Elsewhere too the French Revolution evoked images of starting over. Witnessing that revolution in 1790, the young William Wordsworth, later a famous British Romantic poet, imagined "human nature seeming born again." "Bliss it was in that dawn to be alive," he wrote. "But to be young was very heaven."

The French Revolution also differed from the American Revolution in the way its influence spread. At least until the United States became a world power at the end of the nineteenth century, what inspired others was primarily the example of its revolution and its constitution. French influence, by contrast, spread through conquest, largely under the leadership of Napoleon Bonaparte (r. 1799–1814). A highly successful general who seized power in 1799, Napoleon is often credited with taming the revolution in the face of growing disenchantment with its more radical features and with the social conflicts it generated. He preserved many of its more moderate elements, such as civil equality, a secular law code, religious freedom, and promotion by merit, while reconciling with the Catholic Church and suppressing the revolution's more democratic elements in a military dictatorship. In short, Napoleon kept the revolution's emphasis on social equality for men but dispensed with liberty.

Like many of the revolution's ardent supporters, Napoleon was intent on spreading its benefits far and wide. In a series of brilliant military campaigns, his forces

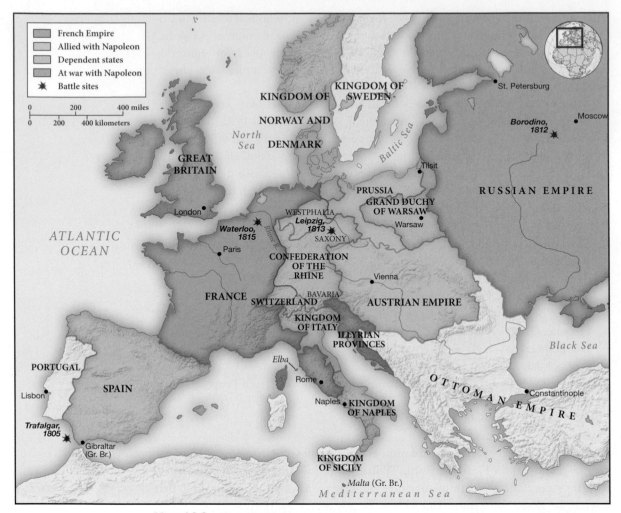

Map 16.2 Napoleon's European Empire
The French Revolution spawned a French empire, under Napoleon's leadership, that encompassed most of Europe and served to spread the principles of the revolution.

subdued most of Europe, thus creating the continent's largest empire since the days of the Romans (see Map 16.2). Within that empire, Napoleon imposed such revolutionary practices as ending feudalism, proclaiming equality of rights, insisting on religious toleration, codifying the laws, and rationalizing government administration. In many places, these reforms were welcomed, and seeds of further change were planted. But French domination was also resented and resisted, stimulating national consciousness throughout Europe. That too was a seed that bore fruit in the century that followed. More immediately, national resistance, particularly from Russia and Britain, brought down Napoleon and his amazing empire by 1815 and marked an end to the era of the French Revolution, though not to the potency of its ideas.

The Haitian Revolution, 1791–1804

Nowhere did the example of the French Revolution echo more loudly than in the French Caribbean colony of Saint Domingue, later renamed Haiti (see Map 16.3, page 712). Widely regarded as the richest colony in the world, Saint Domingue boasted 8,000 plantations, which in the late eighteenth century produced some 40 percent of the world's sugar and perhaps half of its coffee. A slave labor force of about 500,000 people made up the vast majority of the colony's population. Whites numbered about 40,000, sharply divided between very well-to-do plantation owners, merchants, and lawyers and those known as *petits blancs* (peh-TEE blahnk), or poor whites. A third social group consisted of some 30,000 *gens de couleur libres* (free people of color), many of them of mixed-race background. Saint Domingue was a colonial society very different from the New England colonies or even the southern colonies of British North America. Given its enormous inequalities and its rampant exploitation, this Caribbean colony was primed for explosion.

In such a volatile setting, the ideas and example of the French Revolution lit several fuses and set in motion a spiral of violence that engulfed the colony for more than a decade. The principles of the revolution, however, meant different things to different people. To the *grands blancs*—the rich white landowners—it suggested greater autonomy for the colony and fewer economic restrictions on trade, but they resented the demands of the *petits blancs*, who sought equality of citizenship for all whites. Both white groups were adamantly opposed to the insistence of free people of color that the "rights of man" meant equal treatment for all free people regardless of race. To the slaves, the promise of the French Revolution was a personal freedom that challenged the entire slave labor system. In a massive revolt beginning in 1791, triggered by rumors that the French king had already declared an end to slavery, slaves burned 1,000 plantations and killed hundreds of whites as well as mixed-race people.

Soon warring factions of slaves, whites, and free people of color battled one another. Spanish and British forces, seeking to enlarge their own empires at the expense of the French, only added to the turmoil. Amid the confusion, brutality, and massacres of the 1790s, power gravitated toward the slaves, now led by the astute Toussaint Louverture, himself a former slave. He and his successor overcame internal resistance, outmaneuvered the foreign powers, and even defeated an attempt by Napoleon to reestablish French control.

When the dust settled in the early years of the nineteenth century, it was clear that something remarkable and unprecedented had taken place, a revolution unique in the Atlantic world and in world history. Socially, the last had become first. In the only completely successful slave revolt in world history, "the lowest order of the society—slaves—became equal, free, and independent citizens."[12] Politically, they had thrown off French colonial rule, creating the second independent republic in the Americas and the first non-European state to emerge from Western colonialism. They renamed their country "Haiti," a term meaning "mountainous" or "rugged" in the language of the original Taino people. It was a symbolic break with

■ **Comparison**

What was distinctive about the Haitian Revolution, both in world history generally and in the history of Atlantic revolutions?

The Haitian Revolution
This early nineteenth-century engraving, titled *Revenge Taken by the Black Army*, shows black Haitian soldiers hanging a large number of French soldiers, thus illustrating both the violence and the racial dimension of the upheaval in Haiti. (From *An Historic Account of the Black Empire of Haiti*, engraving by Marcus Rainsford [ca. 1750–1805]/Private Collection/Bridgeman Images)

Europe and represented an effort to connect with the long-deceased native inhabitants of the land. Some, in fact, referred to themselves as "Incas." At the formal declaration of Haiti's independence on January 1, 1804, Jean-Jacques Dessalines, the new country's first head of state, declared: "I have given the French cannibals blood for blood; I have avenged America."[13] In defining all Haitian citizens as "black" and legally equal regardless of color or class, Haiti directly confronted elite preferences for lighter skin even as it disallowed citizenship for most whites. Economically, the country's plantation system, oriented wholly toward the export of sugar and coffee, had been largely destroyed. As whites fled or were killed, both private and state lands were redistributed among former slaves and free blacks, and Haiti became a nation of small-scale farmers producing mostly for their own needs, with a much smaller export sector.

The destructiveness of the Haitian Revolution, its bitter internal divisions of race and class, and continuing external opposition contributed much to Haiti's abiding poverty as well as to its authoritarian and unstable politics. So too did the enormous "independence debt" that the French forced on the fledgling republic in 1825, a financial burden that endured for well over a century (see page 697). "Freedom" in Haiti came to mean primarily the end of slavery rather than the establishment of political rights for all. In the early nineteenth century, however, Haiti was a source of enormous hope and of great fear. Within weeks of the Haitian slave uprising in 1791, Jamaican slaves had composed songs in its honor, and it was not long before slave owners in the Caribbean and North America observed a new "insolence" in their slaves. Certainly, its example inspired other slave rebellions, gave a boost to the dawning abolitionist movement, and has been a source of pride for people of African descent ever since.

To whites throughout the hemisphere, the cautionary saying "Remember Haiti" reflected a sense of horror at what had occurred there and a determination not to allow political change to reproduce that fearful outcome again. Particularly in Latin America, the events in Haiti injected a deep caution and social conservatism in the elites who led their countries to independence in the early nineteenth century. Ironically, though, the Haitian Revolution also led to a temporary expansion of slavery elsewhere. Cuban plantations and their slave workers considerably increased their production of sugar as that of Haiti declined. Moreover, Napoleon's defeat in Haiti persuaded him to sell to the United States the French territories known as the Louisiana Purchase, from which a number of "slave states" were carved out. Nor did the example of Haiti lead to successful independence struggles in the rest of the thirty or so Caribbean colonies. Unlike mainland North and South America, Caribbean decolonization had to await the twentieth century. In such contradictory ways did the echoes of the Haitian Revolution reverberate in the Atlantic world.

Spanish American Revolutions, 1808–1825

The final act in a half century of Atlantic revolutionary upheaval took place in the Spanish and Portuguese colonies of mainland Latin America (see Map 16.3). Their revolutions were shaped by preceding events in North America, France, and Haiti as well as by their own distinctive societies and historical experiences. As in British North America, native-born elites (known as *creoles*) in the Spanish colonies were offended and insulted by the Spanish monarchy's efforts during the eighteenth century to exercise greater power over its colonies and to subject them to heavier taxes and tariffs. Creole intellectuals had also become familiar with ideas of popular sovereignty, republican government, and personal liberty derived from the European Enlightenment. But these conditions, similar to those in North America, led initially only to scattered and uncoordinated protests rather than to outrage, declarations of independence, war, and unity, as had occurred in the British colonies. Why did Spanish colonies win their independence almost fifty years later than those of British North America?

Spanish colonies had long been governed in a rather more authoritarian fashion than their British counterparts and were more sharply divided by class. In addition, whites throughout Latin America were vastly outnumbered by Native Americans, people of African ancestry, and those of mixed race. All of this inhibited the growth of a movement for independence, notwithstanding the example of North America and similar provocations.

Despite their growing disenchantment with Spanish rule, creole elites did not so much generate a revolution as have one thrust upon them by events in Europe. In 1808, Napoleon invaded Spain and Portugal, deposing the Spanish king Ferdinand VII and forcing the Portuguese royal family into exile in Brazil. With legitimate royal authority now in disarray, Latin Americans were forced to take action. The outcome, ultimately, was independence for the various states of Latin America, established almost everywhere by 1826. But the way in which independence occurred and the kind of societies it generated differed greatly from the experience of both North America and Haiti.

The process lasted more than twice as long as it did in North America, partly because Latin American societies were so divided by class, race, and region. In North America, violence was directed almost entirely against the British and seldom

■ **Connection**

How were the Spanish American revolutions shaped by the American, French, and Haitian revolutions that happened earlier?

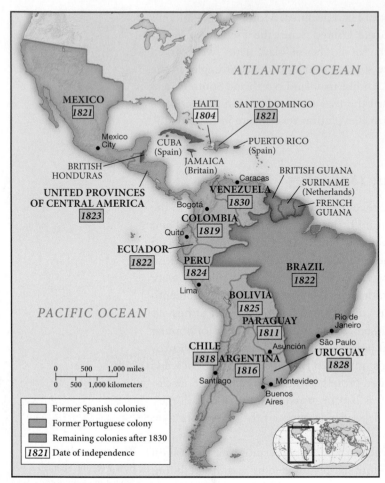

Map 16.3   Latin American Independence

With the exception of Haiti, Latin American revolutions brought independence to new states but offered little social change or political opportunity for the vast majority of people.

spilled over into domestic disputes, except for some bloody skirmishes with loyalists. Even then, little lasting hostility occurred, and some loyalists were able to reenter U.S. society after independence was achieved. In Mexico, by contrast, the move toward independence began in 1810 in a peasant insurrection, driven by hunger for land and by high food prices and led successively by two priests, Miguel Hidalgo and José Morelos. Alarmed by the social radicalism of the Hidalgo-Morelos rebellion, creole landowners, with the support of the Church, raised an army and crushed the insurgency. Later that alliance of clergy and creole elites brought Mexico to a more socially controlled independence in 1821. Such violent conflict among Latin Americans, along lines of race, class, and ideology, accompanied the struggle against Spain in many places.

The entire independence movement in Latin America took place under the shadow of a great fear—the dread of social rebellion from below—that had little counterpart in North America. The extensive violence of the French and Haitian revolutions was a lesson to Latin American elites that political change could easily get out of hand and was fraught with danger to themselves. An abortive rebellion of Native Americans in Peru in the early 1780s, led by a man who claimed direct descent from the last Inca emperor, Tupac Amaru, reminded whites that they sat atop a potentially explosive society, most of whose members were exploited and oppressed people of color. So too did the Hidalgo-Morelos rebellion in Mexico.

And yet the creole sponsors of independence movements, both regional military leaders such as Simón Bolívar and José de San Martín and their civilian counterparts, required the support of "the people," or at least some of them, if they were to prevail against Spanish forces. The answer to this dilemma was found in nativism, which cast all of those born in the Americas—creoles, Indians, mixed-race people, free blacks—as Americanos, while the enemy was defined as those born in

Spain or Portugal.[14] This was no easy task, because many creole whites and mestizos saw themselves as Spanish and because great differences of race, culture, and wealth divided the Americanos. Nonetheless, nationalist leaders made efforts to mobilize people of color into the struggle with promises of freedom, the end of legal restrictions, and social advancement. Many of these leaders were genuine liberals, who had been influenced by the ideals of the Enlightenment, the French Revolution, and Spanish liberalism. In the long run, however, few of those promises were kept. Certainly, the lower classes, Native Americans, and slaves benefited little from independence. "The imperial state was destroyed in Spanish America," concluded one historian, "but colonial society was preserved."[15]

Nor did women as a group gain much from the independence struggle, though they had participated in it in various ways. Upper-class or wealthy women gave and raised money for the cause and provided safe havens for revolutionary meetings. In Mexico, some women disguised themselves as men to join the struggle, while numerous working-class and peasant women served as cooks and carriers of supplies in a "women's brigade." A considerable number of women were severely punished for their disloyalty to the Crown, with some forty-eight executed in Colombia. Yet, after independence, few social gains attended these efforts. General San Martín of Argentina accorded national recognition to a number of women, and modest improvement in educational opportunities for women appeared. But Latin American women continued to be wholly excluded from political life and remained under firm legal control of the men in their families.

A further difference in the Latin American situation lay in the apparent impossibility of uniting the various Spanish colonies, so much larger than the small British territories of North America, despite several failed efforts to do so. Thus no United States of Latin America emerged. Distances among the colonies and geographic obstacles to effective communication were certainly greater than in the Eastern Seaboard colonies of North America, and their longer colonial experience had given rise to distinct and deeply rooted regional identities. Shortly before his death in 1830, the "great liberator" Bolívar, who so admired George Washington and had so ardently hoped for greater unity, wrote in despair to a friend: "[Latin] America is ungovernable. Those who serve the revolution plough the sea."[16]

Simón Bolívar
Among the heroic figures of Spanish American independence movements, none was more significant than Simón Bolívar, shown here in a moment of triumph entering his hometown of Caracas in present-day Venezuela. But Bolívar was immensely disappointed in the outcomes of independence as his dream of a unified South America perished amid the rivalries of separate countries. (By R. Weibezahl, 1829/Sammlung Archiv für Kunst und Geschichte/akg-images)

The aftermath of independence in Latin America marked a reversal in the earlier relationship of the two American continents. The United States, which began its history as the leftover "dregs" of the New World, grew increasingly wealthy, industrialized, democratic, internationally influential, and generally stable, with the major exception of the Civil War. The Spanish colonies, which took shape in the wealthiest areas and among the most sophisticated cultures of the Americas, were widely regarded as the more promising region compared to England's North American territories, which had a backwater reputation. But in the nineteenth century, as newly independent countries in both regions launched a new phase of their histories, those in Latin America became relatively underdeveloped, impoverished, undemocratic, politically unstable, and dependent on foreign technology and investment (see Chapter 17, pages 766–72). Begun in broadly similar circumstances, the Latin American and North American revolutions occurred in very different societies and gave rise to very different historical trajectories.

SUMMING UP SO FAR

Compare the North American, French, Haitian, and Spanish American revolutions. What are the most significant categories of comparisons?

Echoes of Revolution

The repercussions of the Atlantic revolutions reverberated far beyond their places of origin and persisted long after those upheavals had been concluded. Britain's loss of its North American colonies, for example, fueled its growing interest and interventions in Asia, contributing to British colonial rule in India and the Opium Wars in China. Napoleon's brief conquest of Egypt opened the way for a modernizing regime to emerge in that ancient land and stimulated westernizing reforms in the Ottoman Empire (see Chapter 19, pages 844–49). During the nineteenth century, the idea of a "constitution" found advocates in Poland, Latin America, the Spanish-ruled Philippines, China, the Ottoman Empire, and British-governed India.

Within Europe, which was generally dominated by conservative governments following Napoleon's final defeat, smaller revolutionary eruptions occurred in 1830, more widely in 1848, and in Paris in 1870. They reflected ideas of republicanism, greater social equality, and national liberation from foreign rule. Such ideas and social pressures pushed the major states of Western Europe, the United States, and Argentina to enlarge their voting publics, generally granting universal male suffrage by 1914. An abortive attempt to establish a constitutional regime even broke out in autocratic Russia in 1825. (See Zooming In: The Russian Decembrist Revolt, page 716.) More generally, the American and French revolutions led sympathetic elites in Central Europe and elsewhere to feel that they had fallen behind, that their countries were "sleeping." As early as 1791, a Hungarian poet gave voice to such sentiments: "O you still in the slave's collar . . . And you too! Holy consecrated kings . . . turn your eyes to Paris! Let France set out the fate of both king and shackled slave."[17]

Beyond these echoes of the Atlantic revolutions, three major movements arose to challenge continuing patterns of oppression or exclusion. Abolitionists sought the end of slavery; nationalists hoped to foster unity and independence from foreign rule; and feminists challenged male dominance. Each of these movements bore the marks of the Atlantic revolutions, and although they took root first in Europe and the Americas, each came to have a global significance in the centuries that followed.

The Abolition of Slavery

In little more than a century, from roughly 1780 to 1890, a remarkable transformation occurred in human affairs as slavery, widely practiced and little condemned since at least the beginning of civilization, lost its legitimacy and was largely ended. In this amazing process, the ideas and practices of the Atlantic revolutions played an important role.

Enlightenment thinkers in eighteenth-century Europe had become increasingly critical of slavery as a violation of the natural rights of every person, and the public pronouncements of the American and French revolutions about liberty and equality likewise focused attention on this obvious breach of those principles. To this secular antislavery thinking was added an increasingly vociferous religious voice, expressed first by Quakers and then by Protestant evangelicals in Britain and the United States. To them, slavery was "repugnant to our religion" and a "crime in the sight of God."[18] What made these moral arguments more widely acceptable was the growing belief that, contrary to much earlier thinking, slavery was not essential for economic progress. After all, England and New England were among the most prosperous regions of the Western world in the early nineteenth century, and both were based on free labor. Slavery in this view was out of date, unnecessary in the new era of industrial technology and capitalism. Thus moral virtue and economic success were joined. It was an attractive argument. The actions of slaves themselves likewise hastened the end of slavery. The dramatically successful Haitian Revolution was followed by three major rebellions in the British West Indies, all of which were harshly crushed, in the early nineteenth century. The Great Jamaica Revolt of 1831–1832 was particularly important in prompting Britain to abolish slavery throughout its empire in 1833. These revolts demonstrated clearly that slaves were hardly "contented," and the brutality with which they were suppressed appalled British public opinion. Growing numbers of the British public came to believe that slavery was "not only morally wrong and economically inefficient, but also politically unwise."[19]

These various strands of thinking—secular, religious, economic, and political—came together in abolitionist movements, most powerfully in Britain, which brought growing pressure on governments

■ **Change**
What accounts for the end of Atlantic slavery during the nineteenth century?

Abolitionism
This antislavery medallion was commissioned in the late eighteenth century by English Quakers, who were among the earliest participants in the abolitionist movement. Its famous motto, "Am I not a man and a brother," reflected both Enlightenment and Christian values of human equality. (The Art Archive at Art Resource, NY)

The Russian Decembrist Revolt

It must surely rank among the world's shortest and least impressive revolts. On December 26, 1825, a group of radicalized military officers persuaded around 3,000 Russian soldiers stationed in the capital of St. Petersburg to stage an uprising, refusing to swear an oath of allegiance to the new tsar, Nicholas I. But expected reinforcements never arrived, and several of their leaders deserted the cause. Soon some 9,000 soldiers loyal to the tsar had reached the square where the rebels were assembled, together with the tsar himself. After some hesitation and failed negotiations, Nicholas ordered artillery fire, and soon about seventy of the rebels lay dead. The rest scattered and the uprising was over, in less than a day. This was the Decembrist revolt, named for the month in which it occurred.

Many of those who planned and executed this uprising were well-educated, often French-speaking, army officers from aristocratic families. They had accompanied the Russian forces that had chased Napoleon out of their country, serving in France itself or elsewhere in Europe. There they had been exposed to the ideas of the European Enlightenment and the French Revolution, and

The Decembrists in Siberian exile.

some had become intoxicated with these ideas. The contrast between the backwardness of Russia and what they witnessed in Europe was striking indeed. Russia was still ruled by an absolute monarch, backed by the Church; it had no constitution and no representative assemblies to provide an outlet for grievances; and the ancient institution of serfdom still persisted.

When these officers returned to Russia, some of them formed a secret society known as the Union of Salvation, whose goals were to bring Enlightenment sensibilities to life in their homeland. But they differed on precisely how to do so. Some favored gradual change toward a constitutional monarchy along British lines. Others were more radical, seeking to overthrow the tsarist regime altogether: they wanted to kill the royal family, establish a republic, abolish class distinctions, and end serfdom immediately. Growing frustration with the reactionary and repressive policies of Tsar Alexander I inclined this small cadre of revolutionaries to action. Alexander's death in November 1825, followed by a confusing succession struggle,

photo: © Mary Evans Picture Library/John Massey Stewart Russian Collection/ The Image Works

to close down the trade in slaves and then to ban slavery itself. In the late eighteenth century, such a movement gained wide support among middle- and working-class people in Britain. Its techniques included pamphlets with heartrending descriptions of slavery, numerous petitions to Parliament, lawsuits, and boycotts of slave-produced sugar. Frequent public meetings dramatically featured the testimony of Africans who had experienced the horrors of slavery firsthand. In 1807, Britain forbade the sale of slaves within its empire and in 1834 emancipated those who remained enslaved. Over the next half century, other nations followed suit, responding to growing international pressure, particularly from Britain, then the world's leading economic and military power. British naval vessels patrolled the Atlantic,

provided the occasion for that action. And so they struck in the abortive uprising of December 1825. The revolt itself marked the first open breach between a section of the educated Russian nobility and the tsarist regime, a gulf that grew much wider over the next century. But its quick failure demonstrated how little social support the rebels enjoyed.

Russian authorities arrested hundreds of participants in the revolt, and the tsar himself interrogated their leaders. Five were executed, others were imprisoned, and over 100 were sent to live in exile in Siberia, including a number of high-ranking nobles. Some months later, after a ceremonial ritual to remove the stain of bloodshed and treason, the tsar declared: "The fatherland is cleansed of the marks of infection." Nicholas now forbade all mention of the Decembrists and sought to erase the memory of the uprising, while defining himself as "conqueror," a defender of Russia and the monarchy from the insidious forces of revolution.

But erasing memory is more easily declared than accomplished. The Decembrists in fact gained a nearly mythic status among a segment of the Russian intelligentsia, many of whom felt increasingly alienated from their autocratic regime. Through veiled references in literary publications, in letters among members of the elite, and by word of mouth, the Decembrists came to symbolize an untarnished heroic morality in sharp contrast to a corrupt and repressive society.[20] They provided inspiration when the revolutionary impulse resurfaced in the 1860s to 1870s.

This shining image of the rebels also gained strength from their behavior in Siberian exile. While sentenced to hard labor and living under close supervision, they were able to establish schools, clinics, theaters, and libraries; organize symposia and concerts; and introduce modern agricultural innovations. To identify with the poor, some dressed like peasants and refused to trim their beards in proper aristocratic fashion.

The wives of these upper-class Siberian exiles likewise gained notoriety for voluntarily joining their husbands in exile. A special law after the revolt permitted the wives of the revolutionaries to be considered widows and to remarry. But a number refused the privilege, leaving their children, titles, and wealth behind. "Whatever your fate, I will share it," declared Maria Volkonskaya in a letter to her exiled husband. And she did. These women came to personify the self-sacrificial loyalty of the ideal Russian feminine. All of this generated a legendary image of the Decembrists in various parts of Siberia.

Although an obvious failure at the time, the Decembrist uprising looked both backward and forward. It represented a distant echo of the earlier French Revolution, and it marked the beginning of a Russian revolutionary movement that came to fruition only in 1917.

Question: Are failures or dead ends in history worthy of the same consideration as more successful ventures? Why or why not?

intercepted illegal slave ships, and freed their human cargoes in a small West African settlement called Freetown, in present-day Sierra Leone. Following their independence, most Latin American countries abolished slavery by the 1850s. Brazil, in 1888, was the last to do so, bringing more than four centuries of Atlantic slavery to an end. A roughly similar set of conditions—fear of rebellion, economic inefficiency, and moral concerns—persuaded the Russian tsar (zahr) to free the many serfs of that huge country in 1861, although there it occurred by fiat from above rather than from growing public pressure.

None of this happened easily. Slave economies continued to flourish well into the nineteenth century, and plantation owners vigorously resisted the onslaught of abolitionists. So did slave traders, both European and African, who together shipped millions of additional captives, mostly to Cuba and Brazil, long after the trade had been declared illegal. Osei Bonsu, the powerful king of the West African state of Asante, was puzzled as to why the British would no longer buy his slaves. "If they think it bad now," he asked a local British representative in 1820, "why did they think it good before?"[21] Nowhere was the persistence of slavery more evident and resistance to abolition more intense than in the southern states of the United States. It was the only slaveholding society in which the end of slavery occurred through such a bitter, prolonged, and highly destructive civil war (1861–1865).

■ **Change**
How did the end of slavery affect the lives of the former slaves?

The end of Atlantic slavery during the nineteenth century surely marked a major and quite rapid turn in the world's social history and in the moral thinking of humankind. Nonetheless, the outcomes of that process were often surprising and far from the expectations of abolitionists or the newly freed slaves. In most cases, the economic lives of the former slaves did not improve dramatically. Nowhere in the Atlantic world, except Haiti, did a redistribution of land follow the end of slavery. But freedmen everywhere desperately sought economic autonomy on their own land, and in parts of the Caribbean such as Jamaica, where unoccupied land was available, independent peasant agriculture proved possible for some. Elsewhere, as in the southern United States, various forms of legally free but highly dependent labor, such as sharecropping, emerged to replace slavery and to provide low-paid and often-indebted workers for planters. The understandable reluctance of former slaves to continue working in plantation agriculture created labor shortages and set in motion a huge new wave of global migration. Large numbers of indentured servants from India and China were imported into the Caribbean, Peru, South Africa, Hawaii, Malaya, and elsewhere to work in mines, on plantations, and in construction projects. There they often toiled in conditions not far removed from slavery itself.

Newly freed people did not achieve anything close to political equality, except in Haiti. White planters, farmers, and mine owners retained local authority in the Caribbean, where colonial rule persisted until well into the twentieth century. In the southern United States, a brief period of "radical reconstruction," during which newly freed blacks did enjoy full political rights and some power, was followed by harsh segregation laws, denial of voting rights, a wave of lynching, and a virulent racism that lasted well into the twentieth century. For most former slaves, emancipation usually meant "nothing but freedom."[22] Unlike the situation in the Americas, the end of serfdom in Russia transferred to the peasants a considerable portion of the nobles' land, but the need to pay for this land with "redemption dues" and the rapid growth of Russia's rural population ensured that most peasants remained impoverished and politically volatile.

In both West and East Africa, the closing of the external slave trade decreased the price of slaves and increased their use within African societies to produce the export crops that the world economy now sought. Thus, as Europeans imposed colonial rule on Africa in the late nineteenth century, one of their justifications for doing so was the need to emancipate enslaved Africans. The fact that Europeans proclaimed the need to end slavery in a continent from which they had extracted slaves for more than four centuries was surely among the more ironic outcomes of the abolitionist process.

In the Islamic world, where slavery had long been practiced and elaborately regulated, the freeing of slaves, though not required, was strongly recommended as a mark of piety. Some nineteenth-century Muslim authorities opposed slavery altogether on the grounds that it violated the Quran's ideals of freedom and equality. But unlike Europe and North America, the Islamic world generated no popular grassroots antislavery movements. There slavery was outlawed gradually only in the twentieth century under the pressure of international opinion.

Nations and Nationalism

In addition to contributing to the end of slavery, the Atlantic revolutions also gave new prominence to a relatively recent kind of human community—the nation. By the end of the twentieth century, the idea that humankind was divided into separate nations, each with a distinct culture and territory and deserving an independent political life, was so widespread as to seem natural and timeless. And yet for most of human experience, states did not usually coincide with the culture of a particular people, for all the great empires and many smaller states governed culturally diverse societies. Few people considered rule by foreigners itself a terrible offense because the most important identities and loyalties were local, limited to clan, village, or region, with only modest connection to the larger state or empire that governed them. People might on occasion consider themselves part of larger religious communities (such as Christians or Muslims) or ethno-linguistic groupings such as Greek, Arab, or Maya, but such identities rarely provided the basis for enduring states.

All of that began to change during the era of Atlantic revolutions. Independence movements in both North and South America were made in the name of new nations. The French Revolution declared that sovereignty lay with "the people," and its leaders mobilized this people to defend the "French nation" against its external enemies. In 1793, the revolutionary government of France declared a mass conscription (*levée en masse*) with a stirring call to service:

> Henceforth, until the enemies have been driven from the territory of the Republic, all the French are in permanent requisition for army service. The young men shall go to battle; the married men shall forge arms and transport provisions; the women shall make tents and clothes, and shall serve in the hospitals; the children shall turn old linen into lint; the old men shall repair to the public places, to stimulate the courage of the warriors and preach the unity of the Republic and the hatred of kings.[23]

Napoleon's conquests likewise stimulated national resistance in many parts of Europe. European states had long competed and fought with one another, but increasingly

■ **Explanation**
What accounts for the growth of nationalism as a powerful political and personal identity in the nineteenth century?

Second Thoughts

What's the Significance?

North American Revolution, 701–4

Declaration of the Rights of Man and
Citizen, 704

French Revolution, 704–8

Napoleon Bonaparte, 707–8

Haitian Revolution, 709–11

Spanish American revolutions, 711–14

abolitionist movement, 715–19

Decembrists, 716–17

nationalism, 719–23

Vindication of the Rights of Woman, 723

Elizabeth Cady Stanton, 724

maternal feminism, 725

Kartini, 726–27

Big Picture Questions

1. Do revolutions originate in oppression and injustice, in the weakening of political authorities, in new ideas, or in the activities of small groups of determined activists?

2. "The influence of revolutions endured long after they ended and far beyond where they started." To what extent does this chapter support or undermine this idea?

3. Did the Atlantic revolutions fulfill or betray the goals of those who made them? Consider this question in both short- and long-term perspectives.

4. **Looking Back:** To what extent did the Atlantic revolutions reflect the influence of early modern historical developments (1450–1750)?

Next Steps: For Further Study

Benedict Anderson, *Imagined Communities: Reflections on the Origins and Spread of Nationalism* (1991). A now-classic though controversial examination of the process by which national identities were created.

Bonnie S. Anderson, *Joyous Greetings: The First International Women's Movement, 1830–1860* (2000). Describes the beginnings of transatlantic feminism.

David Armitage and Sanjay Subrahmanyam, eds., *The Age of Revolutions in Global Context, c. 1760–1840* (2010). A recent collection of scholarly essays that seeks to explore revolutions within a global framework.

Laurent Dubois and John Garrigus, *Slave Revolution in the Caribbean, 1789–1804* (2006). A brief and up-to-date summary of the Haitian Revolution, combined with a number of documents.

Eric Hobsbawm, *The Age of Revolution, 1789–1848* (1999). A highly respected survey by a well-known British historian.

Lynn Hunt, ed., *The French Revolution and Human Rights* (1996). A collection of documents, with a fine introduction by a prominent scholar.

Égalité for All: Toussaint Louverture and the Haitian Revolution, http://www.youtube.com/watch?v=IOGVgQYX6SU. A thoughtful PBS documentary on the Haitian Revolution, focusing on its principal leader.

"Liberty, Equality, Fraternity: Exploring the French Revolution," http://chnm.gmu.edu/revolution/. A collection of cartoons, paintings, and artifacts illustrating the French Revolution.

Representing the French Revolution

The era of the French Revolution, generally reckoned to have lasted from 1789 to 1815, unfolded as a complex and varied process. Its first several years were relatively moderate, but by 1792 it had become far more radical and violent. After 1795, a reaction set in against the chaos and upheaval that it had generated, culminating in the seizure of power in 1799 by the successful general Napoleon Bonaparte. Nor was the revolution a purely French affair. Conservative opposition in the rest of Europe prompted prolonged warfare, and French efforts under Napoleon to spread the revolution led to a huge French empire in Europe and much resistance to it (see pages 704–8).

All of this provoked enormous controversy, which found visual expression in paintings, cartoons, drawings, and portraits. The four visual sources that follow suggest something of the changing nature of the revolution and the varied reactions it elicited.

Like all major social upheavals, the French Revolution unleashed both enormous hopes and great fears, largely depending on an individual's position in French society. Nonetheless, in the early stages of the revolution (1789–1791), many people believed that France could become a constitutional monarchy with a far more limited role for the king and that the three estates—clergy, nobility, and commoners—could live together in harmony. Source 16.1 represents this phase of the revolution as it depicts the peaceful interaction of members of the three estates. The text that originally accompanied this image read: "Then Messieur we drink to the health of our good King and the Fatherland, that we may be in agreement, at least for this life. And that virtue may be our guide and we will taste together the true pleasures of life."

- What changes during the first year of the French Revolution does this image reveal? Consider the activity portrayed in the painting and the posture of the three figures. What continuities with the past does it also suggest?

- How does the image portray the ideal of national unity?

- How are the representatives of the three estates distinguished from one another?

Musée de la Ville de Paris, Musée Carnavalet, Paris, France/Giraudon/Bridgeman Images

Source 16.1 The Patriotic Snack, Reunion of the Three Estates, August 4, 1789

■ Notice the peasants hunting in the background. Keep in mind that before the revolution peasants who hunted on the estates of the nobility were subject to harsh punishment or even death. Why do you suppose the artist chose to include them in the painting?

Despite the hope for harmony, many soon came to see the revolution as a sharp reversal of class roles. Source 16.2, titled *The Awakening of the Third Estate*, illustrates this stage of the revolution. In the foreground are male figures representing the three estates of old France. While a member of the Third Estate breaks his chains and takes up arms, members of the clergy and nobility recoil in horror. In the background is the Bastille, the fortress/prison and symbol of the old regime, which was seized by a crowd in July 1789 and subsequently demolished. Also displaying this reversal of class roles is the painting on page 696. Here three female figures symbolize the three estates, with the

Source 16.2 A Reversal of Roles: The Three Estates of Revolutionary France

Third Estate, holding a child, now riding on the back of the nobility and in a superior position to that of the clergy. The caption reads: "I really knew we would have our turn."

■ What different impressions of the revolution are conveyed by these images as compared to that of Source 16.1?

■ What particular fears might animate the horror with which the clergy and nobility greet the awakening of the Third Estate?

■ Notice that the woman representing the Third Estate in the chapter-opening image holds a distaff, a tool used for spinning, as well as a child. What does this suggest about the roles of women in the new order?

© Musée Carnavalet/Roger-Viollet/The Image Works

Source 16.3 Revolution and Religion: "Patience, Monsignor, your turn will come."

In its more radical phase, the French Revolution witnessed not only serious class conflict but also a vigorous attack on the Catholic Church and on Christianity itself. The Church was brought under state control, and members of the clergy were required to swear an oath of allegiance to the revolution. The revolutionary government closed many church buildings or sold them to the highest bidder. The government also seized church property to finance France's wars. For a time, revolutionaries tried to establish a Cult of Reason to replace the Christian faith. This attack on the Church also involved the closure of monasteries and efforts to force priests to abandon their vocation and even to marry. Source 16.3 suggests some of the reasons that ardent revolutionaries were so opposed to supernatural religion in general and the Catholic Church in particular.

- How does this visual source reflect the outlook of the Enlightenment? (See Chapter 15, pages 671–74.)

- What criticisms of the Church are suggested by this image? Why is the bishop on the left portrayed as a fat, even bloated, figure? What is the significance of efforts to "squeeze" the priests? Based on their dress, what class do you think the pressmen represent?

- The caption reads: "Patience, Monsignor, your turn will come." What do you imagine was the reaction of devout Catholics to such images and to the policies of de-Christianization?

Library of Congress, Prints and Photographs Division, LC-DIG-ppmsca-10742

HELL BROKE LOOSE, OR, THE MURDER OF LOUIS.

Source 16.4 An English Response to Revolution: "Hell Broke Loose, or, The Murder of Louis"

Attacks on the Church and religion in general were among the actions of the revolution that prompted fear, outrage, and revulsion, both within France and in the more conservative societies of Europe. So too was the execution of Louis XVI and Marie Antoinette, as well as the widespread violence of the Terror. Source 16.4, a British political cartoon, conveys this highly critical, indeed horrified, outlook on the French Revolution. Captioned "Hell Broke Loose," it depicts the execution of Louis XVI and was printed shortly after his death in January 1793. The flying demonic figures in the image are repeating popular slogans of the revolution: "*Vive la nation*" ("Long live the nation") and "*Ca ira*" ("That will go well," or more loosely, "We will win").

■ What is the significance of the demons and dragons in the cartoon? Notice how the soldiers at the bottom of the image are portrayed.

■ What meaning would you attribute to the caption, "Hell Broke Loose"? What disasters might critics of the revolution have imagined coming in its wake?

■ How do you understand the beam of light from Heaven that falls on Louis XVI?

■ Why was regicide regarded with such horror in England in the 1790s?

DOING HISTORY

Representing the French Revolution

1. **Considering political art as evidence:** Based on these four visual sources, together with those in the text itself, what are the advantages and limitations of political or satirical art in understanding a complex phenomenon such as the French Revolution?

2. **Making comparisons:** In what different ways was the French Revolution portrayed in these visual sources? How might you account for those differences? Consider issues of class, nationality, religious commitment, time period, and gender.

3. **Defining the French Revolution:** Based on these visual sources, what was revolutionary about the French Revolution? And what earlier patterns of French life persisted?

4. **Identifying opponents of the revolution:** Based on these visual sources and the text narrative, which groups of people likely opposed the revolution? Why?

Vivian's copper foundry, Swansea, Wales, engraving by Durand-Brager/Bibliothèque des Arts décoratifs, Paris, France/Gianni Dagli Orti/The Art Archive at Art Resource, NY

CHAPTER 17

Revolutions of Industrialization

1750–1914

"Industrialization is, I am afraid, going to be a curse for mankind. . . . God forbid that India should ever take to industrialism after the manner of the West. The economic imperialism of a single tiny island kingdom (England) is today [1928] keeping the world in chains. If an entire nation of 300 millions took to similar economic exploitation, it would strip the world bare like locusts. . . . Industrialization on a mass scale will necessarily lead to passive or active exploitation of the villagers. . . . The machine produces much too fast."[1]

Such were the views of the famous Indian nationalist and spiritual leader Mahatma Gandhi, who subsequently led his country to independence from British colonial rule by 1947, only to be assassinated a few months later. However, few people anywhere have agreed with the heroic Indian figure's views on industrialization. Since its beginning in Great Britain in the late eighteenth century, the idea of industrialization, if not always its reality, has been embraced in every kind of society, both for the wealth it generates and for the power it conveys. Even Gandhi's own country, once it achieved its independence, largely abandoned its founding father's vision of small-scale, village-based handicraft manufacturing in favor of modern industry. As the twenty-first century dawned, India was moving rapidly to develop a major high-technology industrial sector. At that time, across the river from the site in New Delhi where Gandhi was cremated in 1948, a large power plant belched black smoke.

No element of Europe's modern transformation held a greater significance for the history of humankind than the Industrial Revolution, which took place initially in the century and a half

---

Industrial Britain   The dirt, smoke, and pollution of early industrial societies are vividly conveyed in this nineteenth-century engraving of a copper foundry in Wales.

between 1750 and 1900. It drew on the Scientific Revolution and accompanied the unfolding legacy of the French Revolution to utterly transform European society and to propel Europe into a temporary position of global dominance. Not since the breakthrough of the Agricultural Revolution some 12,000 years ago had human ways of life been so fundamentally altered. Also transformed was the human relationship to the natural world as our species learned to access energy resources derived from outside of the biosphere—coal, oil, gas, and the nucleus of atoms. But the Industrial Revolution, unlike its agricultural predecessor, began independently in only one place, Western Europe, and more specifically Great Britain. From there, it spread much more rapidly than agriculture, though very unevenly, to achieve a worldwide presence in less than 250 years. Far more than Christianity, democracy, or capitalism, Europe's Industrial Revolution has been enthusiastically welcomed virtually everywhere.

In any long-term reckoning, the history of industrialization is very much an unfinished story. It is hard to know whether we are at the beginning of a movement leading to worldwide industrialization, stuck in the middle of a world permanently divided into rich and poor countries, or approaching the end of an environmentally unsustainable industrial era. Whatever the future holds, this chapter focuses on the early stages of an immense transformation in the global condition of humankind.

> **SEEKING THE MAIN POINT**
>
> In what ways did the Industrial Revolution mark a sharp break with the past? In what ways did it continue earlier patterns?

Explaining the Industrial Revolution

The global context for this epochal economic transformation lies in a very substantial increase in human numbers from about 375 million people in 1400 to about 1 billion in the early nineteenth century. Accompanying this growth in population was an emerging energy crisis, most pronounced in Western Europe, China, and Japan, as wood and charcoal, the major industrial fuels, became scarcer and their prices rose. In short, "global energy demands began to push against the existing local and regional ecological limits."[2] In broad terms, the Industrial Revolution marks a human response to that dilemma as nonrenewable fossil fuels such as coal, oil, and natural gas replaced the endlessly renewable energy sources of wind, water, wood, and the muscle power of people and animals. It was a breakthrough of unprecedented proportions that made available for human use, at least temporarily, immensely greater quantities of energy. Sustaining the Industrial Revolution was another breakthrough, which lay in the exploitation of guano, or seabird excrement, from the islands off the coast of Peru as well as various mineral sources of nitrates and phosphates in South America and Pacific Oceania. This was an agricultural breakthrough, as these substances made excellent fertilizers, enriching the soils and enabling highly productive input-intensive farming. In much of Western Europe, North America, Australia, and New Zealand, they sustained the produc-

A MAP OF TIME

1712	Early steam engine in Britain
1780s	Beginning of British Industrial Revolution
1812	Locomotives first used to haul coal in England
1832	Reform Bill gives vote to middle-class men in England
1848	Karl Marx, *The Communist Manifesto*
1850s	Beginning of railroad building in Argentina, Cuba, Chile, Brazil
1861	Freeing of serfs in Russia
1864–1876	First International socialist organization in Europe
After 1865	Rapid growth of U.S. industrialization
After 1868	Takeoff of Japanese industrialization
1869	Opening of transcontinental railroad across United States
1871	Unification of Germany
1889–1916	Second International socialist organization in Europe
1890s	Rapid growth of Russian industrialization
1891–1916	Building of trans-Siberian railroad
1905	Failed revolution in Russia
1910–1920	Mexican Revolution
1917	Russian Revolution

tion of food to feed both the draft animals and the growing human populations of the industrializing world.[3]

All of this wrought, of course, a mounting impact on the environment. The massive extraction of nonrenewable raw materials to feed and to fuel industrial machinery—coal, iron ore, petroleum, guano, and much more—altered the landscape in many places. Sewers and industrial waste emptied into rivers, turning them into poisonous cesspools. In 1858, the Thames River running through London smelled so bad that the British House of Commons had to suspend its session. Smoke from coal-fired industries and domestic use polluted the air in urban areas and sharply increased the incidence of respiratory illness. (See the chapter-opening image on page 736.) Against these conditions a number of individuals and small groups raised their voices. Romantic poets such as William Blake and William Wordsworth inveighed against the "dark satanic mills" of industrial England and nostalgically urged a return to the "green and pleasant land" of an earlier time. Here were early and local signs of what became by the late twentieth century an issue of unprecedented and global proportions. For many historians, the Industrial Revolution marked a new era in both human history and the history of the planet that scientists increasingly call the Anthropocene, or the "age of man." More and more, human industrial activity left a mark not only on human society but also on the ecological, atmospheric, and geological history of the earth.

More immediately and more obviously, however, access to huge new sources of energy gave rise to an enormously increased output of goods and services. In Britain, where the Industrial Revolution began, industrial output increased some fiftyfold between 1750 and 1900. It was a wholly unprecedented and previously unimaginable jump in the capacity of human societies to produce wealth. Lying behind it was a great acceleration in the rate of technological innovation, not simply this or that invention—the spinning jenny, power loom, steam engine, or cotton gin—but a "culture of innovation," a widespread and almost obsessive belief that things could be endlessly improved.

Early signs of the technological creativity that spawned the Industrial Revolution appeared in eighteenth-century Britain, where a variety of innovations transformed cotton textile production. It was only in the nineteenth century, though, that Europeans in general and the British in particular more clearly forged ahead of the rest of the world. The great breakthrough was the coal-fired steam engine, which provided an inanimate and almost limitless source of power beyond that of wind, water, or muscle and could be used to drive any number of machines as well as locomotives and oceangoing ships. Soon the Industrial Revolution spread beyond the textile industry to iron and steel production, railroads and steamships, food processing, and construction. Later in the nineteenth century, a so-called second Industrial Revolution focused on chemicals, electricity, precision machinery, the telegraph and telephone, rubber, printing, and much more. Agriculture too was affected as mechanical reapers, chemical fertilizers, pesticides, and refrigeration transformed this most ancient of industries. Technical innovation occurred in more modest ways as well. Patents for horseshoes in the United States, for example, grew from fewer than five per year before 1840 to thirty to forty per year by the end of the century. Furthermore, industrialization soon spread beyond Britain to continental Western Europe and then, in the second half of the century, to the United States, Russia, and Japan.

In the twentieth century, the Industrial Revolution became global as a number of Asian, African, and Latin American countries developed substantial industrial sectors. Oil, natural gas, and nuclear reactions joined coal as widely available sources of energy, and new industries emerged in automobiles, airplanes, consumer durable goods, electronics, computers, and on and on. It was a cumulative process that, despite periodic ups and downs, accelerated over time. More than anything else, this continuous emergence of new techniques of production, together with the massive economic growth they made possible and the environmental impact they generated, marks the past 250 years as a distinct phase of human history.

Why Europe?

The Industrial Revolution has long been a source of great controversy among scholars. Why did it occur first in Europe? Within Europe, why did it occur earliest in Great Britain? And why did it take place in the late eighteenth and nineteenth centuries? Some explanations have sought the answer in unique and deeply rooted features of European society, history, or culture. One recent account, for example, argued that Europeans have been distinguished for several thousand years by a restless, creative, and freedom-loving culture with its roots in the aristocratic warlike societies of early Indo-European invaders.[4] While not denying certain distinctive qualities of the West, many world historians have challenged views that seem to suggest that Europe alone was destined to lead the way to modern economic life. Such an approach, they argue, not only is Eurocentric and deterministic but also flies in the face of much recent research.

Historians now know that other areas of the world had experienced times of great technological and scientific flourishing. Between 750 and 1100 C.E., the Islamic world generated major advances in shipbuilding, the use of tides and falling water to generate power, papermaking, textile production, chemical technologies, water mills, clocks, and much more.[5] India had long been the world center of cotton textile production, the first place to turn sugarcane juice into crystallized sugar, and the source of many agricultural innovations and mathematical inventions. To the Arabs of the ninth century C.E., India was a "place of marvels."[6] More than either of these, China was clearly the world leader in technological innovation between 700 and 1400 C.E., prompting various scholars to suggest that China was on the edge of an industrial revolution by 1200 or so. For reasons much debated among historians, all of these flowerings of technological creativity had slowed down considerably or stagnated by the early modern era, when the pace of technological change in Europe began to pick up. But these earlier achievements certainly suggest that Europe was not alone in its capacity for technological innovation.

Nor did Europe enjoy any overall economic advantage as late as 1750. Over the past several decades, historians have carefully examined the economic conditions of various Eurasian societies in the eighteenth century and found "a world of surprising resemblances." Economic indicators such as life expectancies, patterns of consumption and nutrition, wage levels, general living standards, widespread free markets, and prosperous merchant communities suggest broadly similar conditions across the major civilizations of Europe and Asia.[7] Thus Europe had no obvious economic lead, even on the eve of the Industrial Revolution. Rather, according to one leading scholar, "there existed something of a global economic parity between the most advanced regions in the world economy."[8]

A final reason for doubting a unique European capacity for industrial development lies in the relatively rapid spread of industrial techniques to many parts of the world over the past 250 years, a fairly short time by world history standards. Although the process has been highly uneven, industrialization has taken root, to one degree

■ **Change**

In what respects did the roots of the Industrial Revolution lie within Europe? In what ways did that transformation have global roots?

or another, in Japan, China, India, Brazil, Mexico, Turkey, Indonesia, South Africa, Saudi Arabia, Thailand, South Korea, and elsewhere. Such a pattern weakens any suggestion that European culture or society was exceptionally compatible with industrial development.

Thus, while sharp debate continues, many contemporary historians are inclined to see the Industrial Revolution erupting rather quickly and quite unexpectedly between 1750 and 1850 (see Map 17.1). Two intersecting factors help explain why this process occurred in Europe rather than elsewhere. One lies in certain patterns of Europe's internal development that favored innovation. Its many small and highly competitive states, taking shape in the twelfth or thirteenth centuries, arguably provided an "insurance against economic and technological stagnation," which the larger Chinese, Ottoman, or Mughal empires perhaps lacked.[9] If so, then Western Europe's failure to re-create the earlier unity of the Roman Empire may have acted as a stimulus to innovation.

Furthermore, the relative newness of these European states and their monarchs' desperate need for revenue in the absence of an effective tax-collecting bureaucracy pushed European royals into an unusual alliance with their merchant classes. Small groups of merchant capitalists might be granted special privileges, monopolies, or even tax-collecting responsibilities in exchange for much-needed loans or payments to the state. It was therefore in the interest of governments to actively encourage commerce and innovation. Thus states granted charters and monopolies to private trading companies, and governments founded scientific societies and offered prizes to promote innovation. In this way, European merchants and other innovators from the fifteenth century onward gained an unusual degree of freedom from state control and in some places a higher social status than their counterparts in more established civilizations. In Venice and Holland, merchants actually controlled the state. By the eighteenth century, major Western European societies were highly commercialized and governed by states generally supportive of private commerce. In short, they were well on their way toward capitalist economies—where buying and selling on the market was a widely established practice—before they experienced industrialization. Such internally competitive economies, coupled with a highly competitive system of rival states, arguably fostered innovation in the new civilization taking shape in Western Europe.

Europe's societies, of course, were not alone in developing market-based economies by the eighteenth century. Japan, India, and especially China were likewise highly commercialized or market driven. However, in the several centuries after 1500, Western Europe was unique in a second way. That region alone "found itself at the hub of the largest and most varied network of exchange in history."[10] Widespread contact with culturally different peoples was yet another factor that historically has generated extensive change and innovation. This new global network, largely the creation of Europeans themselves, greatly energized commerce and brought Europeans into direct contact with peoples around the world.

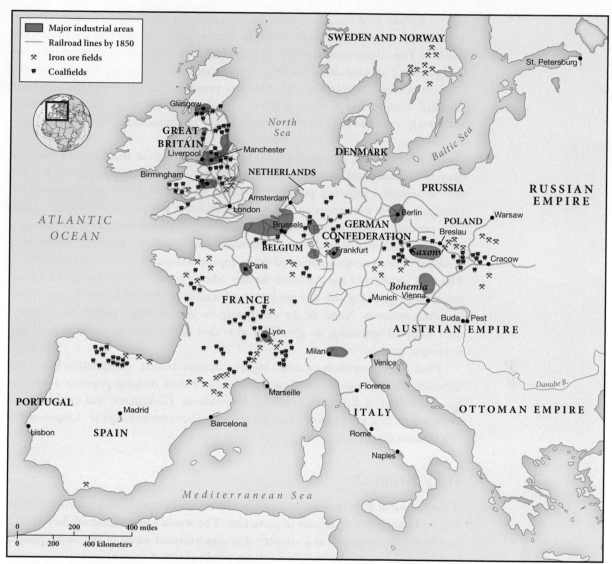

Map 17.1   The Early Phase of Europe's Industrial Revolution

From its beginning in Great Britain, industrialization had spread by 1850 across Western Europe to include parts of France, Germany, Belgium, Bohemia, and Italy.

For example, Asia, home to the world's richest and most sophisticated societies, was the initial destination of European voyages of exploration. The German philosopher Gottfried Wilhelm Leibniz (1646–1716) encouraged Jesuit missionaries in China "not to worry so much about getting things European to the Chinese but rather about getting remarkable Chinese inventions to us."[11] Inexpensive and well-made Indian textiles began to flood into Europe, causing one English observer to note: "Almost everything that used to be made of wool or silk, relating either to dress of the women or the furniture of our houses, was supplied by the Indian trade."[12] The competitive stimulus of these Indian cotton textiles was certainly one factor driving innovation in the British textile industry. Likewise, the popularity of Chinese porcelain and Japanese lacquerware prompted imitation and innovation in England, France, and Holland.[13] Thus competition from desirable, high-quality, and newly available Asian goods played a role in stimulating Europe's Industrial Revolution.

In the Americas, Europeans found a windfall of silver that allowed them to operate in Asian markets. They also found timber, fish, maize, potatoes, and much else to sustain a growing population. Later, slave-produced cotton supplied an emerging textile industry with its key raw material at low prices, while sugar, similarly produced with slave labor, furnished cheap calories to European workers. "Europe's Industrial Revolution," concluded historian Peter Stearns, "stemmed in great part from Europe's ability to draw disproportionately on world resources."[14] The new societies of the Americas further offered a growing market for European machine-produced goods and generated substantial profits for European merchants and entrepreneurs. None of the other empires of the early modern era enriched their imperial heartlands so greatly or provided such a spur to technological and economic growth.

Thus the intersection of new, highly commercialized, competitive European societies with the novel global network of their own making provides a context for understanding Europe's Industrial Revolution. Commerce and cross-cultural exchange, acting in tandem, sustained the impressive technological changes of the first industrial societies.

Why Britain?

If the Industrial Revolution was initially a Western European phenomenon generally, it clearly began in Britain in particular. The world's first Industrial Revolution unfolded spontaneously in a country that concentrated some of the more general features of European society. It was both unplanned and unexpected.

■ **Comparison**

What was distinctive about Britain that may help explain its status as the breakthrough point of the Industrial Revolution?

With substantial imperial possessions in the Caribbean, in North America, and, by the late eighteenth century, in India as well, Britain was the most highly commercialized of Europe's larger countries. Its landlords had long ago "enclosed" much agricultural land, pushing out the small farmers and producing for the market. A series of agricultural innovations—crop rotation, selective breeding of animals, lighter plows, higher-yielding seeds—increased agricultural output, kept food prices low, and freed up labor from the countryside. The guilds, which earlier had protected Britain's urban artisans, had largely disappeared by the eighteenth century, allowing employers to run their manufacturing enterprises as they saw fit. Coupled with a rapidly growing population, these processes ensured a ready supply of industrial workers who had few alternatives available to them. Furthermore, British aristocrats, unlike their counterparts in Europe, had long been interested in the world of business, and some took part in new mining and manufacturing enterprises. British commerce, moreover, extended around the world, its large merchant fleet protected by the Royal Navy. The wealth of empire and global commerce, however, were not themselves sufficient for spawning the Industrial Revolution, for Spain, the earliest beneficiary of American wealth, was one of the slowest-industrializing European countries into the twentieth century.

British political life encouraged commercialization and economic innovation. Its policy of religious toleration, formally established in 1688, welcomed people with technical skills regardless of their faith, whereas France's persecution of its Protestant minority had chased out some of its most skilled workers. The British government favored men of business with tariffs that kept out cheap Indian textiles, with laws that made it easy to form companies and to forbid workers' unions, with roads and canals that helped create a unified internal market, and with patent laws that served to protect the interests of inventors. Checks on royal prerogative—trial by jury and the growing authority of Parliament, for example—provided a freer arena for private enterprise than elsewhere in Europe.

Europe's Scientific Revolution also took a distinctive form in Great Britain in ways that fostered technological innovation.[15] Whereas science in continental Europe was largely based on logic, deduction, and mathematical reasoning, in Britain it was much more concerned with observation, experiment, precise measurements, mechanical devices, and practical commercial applications. This kind of science played a role in the invention and improvement of the steam engine. Even though most inventors were artisans or craftsmen rather than scientists, in eighteenth-century Britain, they were in close contact with scientists, makers of scientific instruments, and entrepreneurs, whereas in continental Europe these groups were largely separate. The British Royal Society, an association of "natural philosophers" (scientists) established in 1660, saw its role as promoting "useful knowledge." To this end, it established "mechanics' libraries," published broadsheets and pamphlets on recent scientific advances, and held frequent public lectures and demonstrations. The integration of science and technology became widespread and permanent after 1850, but for a century before, it was largely a British phenomenon.

Finally, several accidents of geography and history contributed something to Britain's Industrial Revolution. The country had a ready supply of coal and iron ore, often located close to each other and within easy reach of major industrial centers. Although Britain took part in the wars against Napoleon, the country's island location protected it from the kind of invasions that so many continental European states experienced during the era of the French Revolution. Moreover, Britain's relatively fluid society allowed for adjustments in the face of social changes without widespread revolution. By the time the dust settled from the immense disturbance of the French Revolution, Britain was well on its way to becoming the world's first industrial society.

The First Industrial Society

Wherever it took hold, the Industrial Revolution generated, within a century or less, an economic miracle, at least in comparison with earlier technologies. The British textile industry, which used 52 million pounds of cotton in 1800, consumed 588 million pounds in 1850. Britain's output of coal soared from 5.23 million tons in 1750 to 68.4 million tons a century later.[16] Railroads crisscrossed Britain and much of Europe like a giant spider web (see Map 17.1, page 743). Most of this dramatic increase in production occurred in mining, manufacturing, and services. Thus agriculture, for millennia the overwhelmingly dominant economic sector in every civilization, shrank in relative importance. In Britain, for example, agriculture generated only 8 percent of national income in 1891 and employed fewer than 8 percent of working Britons in 1914. Accompanying this vast economic change was an epic transformation of social life. "In two centuries," wrote one prominent historian, "daily life changed more than it had in the 7,000 years before."[17] Nowhere were the revolutionary dimensions of industrialization more apparent than in Great Britain, the world's first industrial society.

The social transformation of the Industrial Revolution both destroyed and created. Referring to the impact of the Industrial Revolution on British society, historian Eric Hobsbawm wrote: "In its initial stages it destroyed their old ways of living and left them free to discover or make for themselves new ones, if they could and knew how. But it rarely told them how to set about it."[18] For many people, it was an enormously painful, even traumatic process, full of social conflict, insecurity, and false starts as well as new opportunities, an eventually higher standard of living, and greater participation in public life. Scholars, politicians, journalists, and ordinary people have endlessly debated the gains and losses associated with the Industrial Revolution. Amid the controversy, however, one thing is clear: not everyone was affected in the same way.

Railroads
The popularity of railroads, long a symbol of the Industrial Revolution, is illustrated in this early nineteenth-century watercolor, which shows a miniature train offered as a paid amusement for enthusiasts in London's Euston Square. (*Richard Trevithick's Railroad, Euston Square in 1809*, by Thomas Rowlandson [1756–1827]/Science Museum, London, UK/Bridgeman Images)

The British Aristocracy

Individual landowning aristocrats, long the dominant class in Britain, suffered little in material terms from the Industrial Revolution. In the mid-nineteenth century, a few thousand families still owned more than half of the cultivated land in Britain, most of it leased to tenant farmers, who in turn employed agricultural wage laborers to work it. Rapidly growing population and urbanization sustained a demand for food products grown on that land. For most of the nineteenth century, landowners continued to dominate the British Parliament.

As a class, however, the British aristocracy declined as a result of the Industrial Revolution, as have large landowners in every industrial society. As urban wealth became more important, landed aristocrats had to make way for the up-and-coming businessmen, manufacturers, and bankers, newly enriched by the Industrial Revolution. The aristocracy's declining political clout was demonstrated in the 1840s when high tariffs on foreign agricultural imports, designed to protect the interests of British landlords, were finally abolished. By the end of the century, landownership had largely ceased to be the basis of great wealth, and businessmen, rather than aristocrats, led the major political parties. Even so, the titled nobility of dukes, earls, viscounts, and barons retained great social prestige and considerable personal wealth. Many among them found an outlet for their energies and opportunities for status and enrichment in the vast domains of the British Empire, where they went as colonial administrators or settlers. Famously described as a "system of outdoor relief for the aristocracy," the empire provided a cushion for a declining class.

■ **Change**
How did the Industrial Revolution transform British society?

The Middle Classes

Those who benefited most conspicuously from industrialization were members of that amorphous group known as the middle class. At its upper levels, this middle class contained extremely wealthy factory and mine owners, bankers, and merchants. Such rising businessmen readily assimilated into aristocratic life, buying country houses, obtaining seats in Parliament, sending their sons to Oxford or Cambridge University, and gratefully accepting titles of nobility from Queen Victoria.

Far more numerous were the smaller businessmen, doctors, lawyers, engineers, teachers, journalists, scientists, and other professionals required in any industrial society. Such people set the tone for a distinctly middle-class society with its own values and outlooks. Politically they were liberals, favoring constitutional government, private property, free trade, and social reform within limits. Their agitation resulted in the Reform Bill of 1832, which broadened the right to vote to many men of the middle class, but not to middle-class women. Ideas of thrift and hard work, a rigid morality, and cleanliness characterized middle-class culture. The central value of that culture was "respectability," a term that combined notions of social status and virtuous behavior. Nowhere were these values more effectively displayed than in the Scotsman Samuel Smiles's famous book *Self-Help*, published in 1859. Individuals are responsible for their own destiny, Smiles argued. An hour a day devoted to self-improvement "would make an ignorant man wise in a few years." According to Smiles, this enterprising spirit was what distinguished the prosperous middle class from Britain's poor. The misery of the poorer classes was

■ **Change**
How did Britain's middle classes change during the nineteenth century?

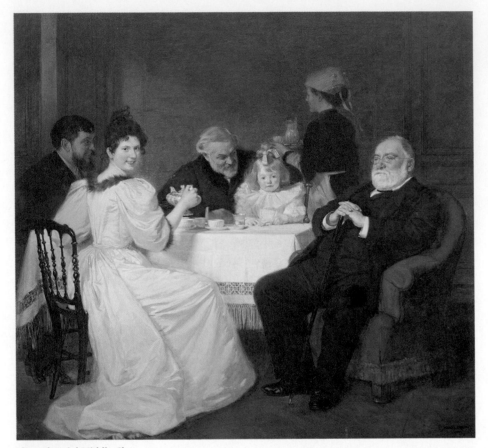

The Industrial Middle Class
This late nineteenth-century painting shows a prosperous French middle-class family, attended by a servant. (*Family Reunion at the Home of Madame Adolphe Brisson*, 1893, by Marcel André Baschet [1862–1941]/Château de Versailles, France/ Giraudon/Bridgeman Images)

"voluntary and self-imposed—the results of idleness, thriftlessness, intemperance, and misconduct."[19] Women in such middle-class families were increasingly cast as homemakers, wives, and mothers, charged with creating an emotional haven for their men and a refuge from a heartless and cutthroat capitalist world. They were also expected to be the moral centers of family life, the educators of "respectability," and the managers of household consumption as "shopping"—a new concept in eighteenth-century Britain—became a central activity for the middle classes. An "ideology of domesticity" defined homemaking, child rearing, charitable endeavors, and "refined" activities such as embroidery, music, and drawing as the proper sphere for women, while paid employment and the public sphere of life outside the home beckoned to men.

Male elites in many civilizations had long established their status by detaching women from productive labor. The new wealth of the Industrial Revolution now allowed larger numbers of families to aspire to that kind of status. With her husband as "provider," such a woman was now a "lady." "She must not work for profit," wrote the Englishwoman Margaretta Greg in 1853, "or engage in any occupation that money can command."[20] Employing even one servant became a proud marker of such middle-class status. But the withdrawal of middle-class women from the labor force turned out to be only a temporary phenomenon. By the late nineteenth century, some middle-class women began to enter the teaching, clerical, and nursing professions, and in the second half of the twentieth century, educated middle-class women flooded into the labor force. By contrast, the withdrawal of children from productive labor into schools has proved a more enduring phenomenon as industrial economies increasingly required a more educated workforce.

As Britain's industrial economy matured, it also gave rise to a sizable lower middle class, which included people employed in the growing service sector as clerks, salespeople, bank tellers, hotel staff, secretaries, telephone operators, police officers, and the like. By the end of the nineteenth century, this growing segment of the middle class represented about 20 percent of Britain's population and provided new employment opportunities for women as well as men. In just twenty years (1881–1901), the number of female secretaries in Britain rose from 7,000 to 90,000. Almost all were single and expected to return to the home after marriage. Telephone operators had initially been boys or men, but by the end of the nineteenth century in both Britain and the United States that work had become a wholly female occupation. For both men and women, such employment represented a claim on membership in the larger middle class and a means of distinguishing themselves clearly from a working class tainted by manual labor. The mounting ability of these middle classes to consume all manner of material goods—and their appetite for doing so—was among the factors that sustained the continuing growth of the industrializing process.

The Laboring Classes

The overwhelming majority of Britain's nineteenth-century population—some 70 percent or more—were neither aristocrats nor members of the middle classes. They were manual workers in the mines, ports, factories, construction sites, workshops, and farms of an industrializing Britain. Although their conditions varied considerably and changed over time, it was the laboring classes who suffered most and benefited least from the epic transformations of the Industrial Revolution. Their efforts to accommodate, resist, protest, and change those conditions contributed much to the texture of the first industrial society.

The lives of the laboring classes were shaped primarily by the new working conditions of the industrial era. Chief among those conditions was rapid urbanization. Liverpool's population alone grew from 77,000 to 400,000 in the first half of the nineteenth century. By 1851, a majority of Britain's population lived in towns and cities, an enormous change from the overwhelmingly rural life of almost all

DEATH'S DISPENSARY.
OPEN TO THE POOR, GRATIS, BY PERMISSION OF THE PARISH.

The Urban Poor of Industrial Britain
This 1866 political cartoon shows an impoverished urban family forced to draw its drinking water from a polluted public well, while a figure of Death operates the pump.

previous civilizations. By the end of the century, London was the world's largest city, with more than 6 million inhabitants.

These cities were vastly overcrowded and smoky, with wholly insufficient sanitation, periodic epidemics, endless row houses and warehouses, few public services or open spaces, and inadequate and often-polluted water supplies. This was the environment in which most urban workers lived in the first half of the nineteenth century. By 1850, the average life expectancy in England was only 39.5 years, less than it had been some three centuries earlier. Nor was there much personal contact between the rich and the poor of industrial cities. Benjamin Disraeli's novel *Sybil*, published in 1845, described these two ends of the social spectrum as "two nations between whom there is no intercourse and no sympathy; who are ignorant of each other's habits, thoughts and feelings, as if they were dwellers in different zones or inhabitants of different planets."

The industrial factories to which growing numbers of desperate people looked for employment offered a work environment far different from the artisan's shop or the tenant's farm. Long hours, low wages, and child labor were nothing new for the poor, but the routine and monotony of work, dictated by the factory whistle and the needs of machines, imposed novel and highly unwelcome conditions of labor. Also objectionable were the direct and constant supervision and the rules and fines aimed at enforcing work discipline. The ups and downs of a capitalist economy made industrial work insecure as well as onerous.

In the early decades of the nineteenth century, Britain's industrialists favored girls and young unmarried women as employees in the textile mills, for they were often willing to accept lower wages, while male owners believed them to be both docile and more suitable for repetitive tasks such as tending machines. (See Zooming In: Ellen Johnston, page 752.) A gendered hierarchy of labor emerged in these factories, with men in supervisory and more skilled positions while women occupied the less skilled and "lighter" jobs that offered little opportunity for advancement. Nor were women welcome in the unions that eventually offered men some ability to shape the conditions under which they labored.

Thus, unlike their middle-class counterparts, many girls and young women of the laboring classes engaged in industrial work or found jobs as domestic servants for upper- and middle-class families to supplement meager family incomes. But after marriage, they too usually left outside paid employment because a man who could not support his wife was widely considered a failure. Within the home, however, many working-class women continued to earn money by taking in boarders, doing laundry, or sewing clothes in addition to the domestic and child-rearing responsibilities long assigned to women.

Social Protest

For workers of the laboring classes, industrial life "was a stony desert, which they had to make habitable by their own efforts."[21] Such efforts took many forms. By 1815, about 1 million workers, mostly artisans, had created a variety of "friendly societies." With dues contributed by members, these working-class self-help groups provided insurance against sickness, a decent funeral, and an opportunity for social life in an otherwise-bleak environment. Other skilled artisans, who had been displaced by machine-produced goods and forbidden to organize in legal unions, sometimes wrecked the offending machinery and burned the mills that had taken their jobs. (See Zooming In: The English Luddites and Machine Breaking, page 758.) The class consciousness of working people was such that one police informer reported that "most every creature of the lower order both in town and country are on their side."[22] Others acted within the political arena by joining movements aimed at obtaining the vote for working-class men, a goal that was gradually achieved in the second half of the nineteenth century. When trade unions were legalized in 1824, growing numbers of factory workers joined these associations in their efforts to achieve better wages and working conditions. Initially their strikes, attempts at nationwide organization, and threat of violence made them fearful indeed to the upper classes. One British newspaper in 1834 described unions as "the most dangerous institutions that were ever permitted to take root, under shelter of law, in any country,"[23] although they later became rather more "respectable" organizations.

Socialist ideas of various kinds gradually spread within the working class, challenging the assumptions of a capitalist society. Robert Owen (1771–1858), a wealthy British cotton textile manufacturer, urged the creation of small industrial communities where workers and their families would be well treated. He established one such community, with a ten-hour workday, spacious housing, decent wages, and education for children, at his mill in New Lanark in Scotland.

Of more lasting significance was the socialism of Karl Marx (1818–1883). German by birth, Marx spent much of his life in England, where he witnessed the brutal conditions of Britain's Industrial Revolution and wrote voluminously about history and economics. His probing analysis led him to the conclusion that industrial capitalism was an inherently unstable system, doomed to collapse in a revolutionary

Ellen Johnston,
Factory Worker and Poet

Born around 1835 to a working-class family in an industrializing Scotland, Ellen Johnston worked in a variety of textile mills throughout her life, lived as a single mother, and, most unusually, became a published poet with a modest local reputation. Through her brief autobiography and her poetry, we can catch a glimpse of one working-class woman's experience during Britain's Industrial Revolution.[24]

Shortly after her birth, Ellen's father, a stonemason, decided to emigrate to America. Her mother, however, refused to join him and returned with her young daughter to her father's house, where she supported her small family as a dressmaker. Ellen remembered with pleasure those early years, in which she wandered the area with her doll and her dog. When she was eight, her mother remarried, to an abusive man who forced young Ellen into factory work a few years later. "No language can paint the suffering," she wrote about her stepfather, "which I afterwards endured from my tormentor." She repeatedly ran away from his home and entered into

A young British woolen factory worker in a setting similar to that in which Ellen Johnston labored.

a love affair that left her a single mother at age seventeen. Nonetheless, in a time of expanding literacy, Ellen read widely, calling herself a "self-taught scholar." She especially liked to read "love adventures" and developed a romantic image of herself as a "heroine of the modern style." She also began to write poetry for the "penny press," inexpensive newspapers of the region.

Ellen's troubled home life made her resistant to the emerging ideology of domesticity, which defined women's roles as tranquil homemakers, wives, and mothers, a view that was taking hold even within the working classes by the mid-nineteenth century. "Fallen women"—those who gave birth outside of marriage—were considered beyond the confines of "true womanhood" and were generally expected to withdraw from public life in disgrace. Ellen Johnston, however, was unrepentant. "I did not . . . feel inclined to die," she wrote, "when I could no longer conceal what

photo: Science and Society/SuperStock

upheaval that would give birth to a classless socialist society, thus ending forever the ancient conflict between rich and poor. (See Working with Evidence, page 775, for the various voices of a socialist tradition inspired by Marx.)

In his writings, the combined impact of Europe's industrial, political, and scientific revolutions found expression. Industrialization created both the social conditions against which Marx protested so bitterly and the enormous wealth he felt would make socialism possible. The French Revolution, still a living memory in Marx's youth, provided evidence that grand upheavals, giving rise to new societies, had in fact taken place and could do so again. Moreover, Marx regarded himself as a scientist, discovering the laws of social development in much the same fashion as

■ **Change**
How did Karl Marx understand the Industrial Revolution? In what ways did his ideas have an impact in the industrializing world of the nineteenth century?

the world falsely calls a woman's shame." Descriptions of home life in her writing are almost always negative. Referring to her aunt's marriage to an alcoholic, she wrote: "Now the dark cup of sorrow embitters thy life / To a hard hearted drunkard, ah! thou art a wife."

Johnston supported herself and her daughter by working intermittently in the textile mills of industrial Scotland, occasionally withdrawing for health reasons or to write poetry that she signed as "the factory girl." Through her poetry, Johnston made clear her awareness of the inequalities and exploitation of industrial life, writing in one poem: "It is the puir [poor] man's hard-won toil that fills the rich man's purse . . . / What care the gentry if they're well, though all the poor would die." Another poem urged unionization for boatbuilders and boilermakers.

In response to industrial misery, however, Johnston did not advocate for socialism or revolutionary upheaval. Rather, she implicitly called on the "master" of the mill to behave in a benevolent fashion toward his employees and to create within the factory a sense of community. At times she recited her poetry at factory-organized gatherings, sometimes toasting the owner: "May he still have wealth; may we still have health / To remain his servants of toil."

On a personal level, this "factory girl" stood up for herself, at one point taking her foreman to court to recover a week's wages when she was fired without notice. But it was within the factory, not the family, that Johnston found emotional and personal satisfaction. In the mills, she discovered camaraderie, an emotional and spiritual home, and a status higher than that of domestic labor, which was the lot of so many young working-class women. Celebrating one of the factories where she worked, Johnston proclaimed: "I would not leave thee, dear beloved place / A crown, a sceptre, or a throne to grace, / To be a queen—the nation's flag unfurl—/ A thousand times I'd be a Factory Girl!"

Johnston had hoped to make her living as a poet and thus escape the poverty to which factory wages condemned her. She did receive occasional financial support from upper-class benefactors, including a small gift from Queen Victoria, and a published collection of her work appeared in 1867. She was, however, aware that both class and gender made it difficult for her to win acceptance among middle- and upper-class members of the literary establishment, a recognition expressed in her writing. "I am so small I cannot shine / Amidst the great that read my rhyme." In 1870, only a year after the publication of the second edition of her book of poetry, she had to apply for "poor relief," and in 1874, Ellen Johnston died in a Scottish poorhouse, not yet forty years of age.

Question: How would you describe Ellen Johnston's outlook on industrial Britain?

Newton discovered the laws of motion. His was therefore a "scientific socialism," embedded in these laws of historical change; revolution was a certainty and the socialist future was inevitable.

It was a grand, compelling, prophetic, utopian vision of human freedom and community—and it inspired socialist movements of workers and intellectuals amid the grim harshness of Europe's industrialization in the second half of the nineteenth century. Socialists established political parties in most European states and linked them together in international organizations as well. These parties recruited members, contested elections as they gained the right to vote, agitated for reforms, and in some cases plotted revolution.

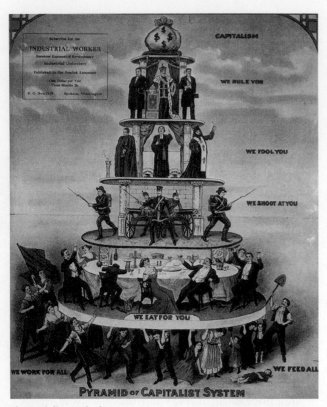

The Socialist Outlook
This 1911 poster was first published in the newspaper of the Industrial Workers of the World, a radical American trade union organization. It illustrates a socialist perspective on capitalist societies. At the bottom of the pyramid, supporting the entire social edifice, are the workers, while above them are arrayed the various oppressive layers of the social hierarchy: the bourgeoisie, the police and militias, religious figures, and state officials. (From *Pyramid of Capitalist System*, issued by Nedelkovich, Brashick and Kuharich, Cleveland [International Publishing Company, 1911]/photo: IAM/akg-images)

In the later decades of the nineteenth century, such ideas echoed among more radical trade unionists and some middle-class intellectuals in Britain, and even more so in a rapidly industrializing Germany and elsewhere. By then, however, the British working-class movement was not overtly revolutionary. When a working-class political party, the Labour Party, was established in the 1890s, it advocated a reformist program and a peaceful democratic transition to socialism, largely rejecting the class struggle and revolutionary emphasis of classical Marxism. Generally known as "social democracy," this approach to socialism was especially prominent in Germany during the late nineteenth century and spread more widely in the twentieth century when it came into conflict with the more violent and revolutionary movements calling themselves "communist."

Improving material conditions during the second half of the nineteenth century helped move the working-class movement in Britain, Germany, and elsewhere away from a revolutionary posture. Marx had expected industrial capitalist societies to polarize into a small wealthy class and a huge and increasingly impoverished proletariat. However, standing between "the captains of industry" and the workers was a sizable middle and lower middle class, constituting perhaps 30 percent of the population, most of whom were not really wealthy but were immensely proud that they were not manual laborers. Marx had not foreseen the development of this intermediate social group, nor had he imagined that workers could better their standard of living within a capitalist framework. But they did. Wages rose under pressure from unions; cheap imported food improved working-class diets; infant mortality rates fell; and shops and chain stores catering to working-class families multiplied. As English male workers gradually obtained the right to vote, politicians had an incentive to legislate in their favor, by abolishing child labor, regulating factory conditions, and even, in 1911, inaugurating a system of relief for the unemployed. Sanitary reform considerably cleaned up the "filth and stink" of early nineteenth-century cities, and urban parks made a modest appearance. Contrary to Marx's expectations, capitalist societies demonstrated some capacity for reform.

Further eroding working-class radicalism was a growing sense of nationalism, which bound workers in particular countries to their middle-class employers and compatriots, offsetting to some extent the economic and social antagonism between them. When World War I broke out, the "workers of the world," far from uniting against their bourgeois enemies as Marx had urged them, instead set off to slaughter one another in enormous numbers on the battlefields of Europe. National loyalty had trumped class loyalty.

Nonetheless, as the twentieth century dawned, industrial Britain was hardly a stable or contented society. Immense inequalities still separated the classes. Some 40 percent of the working class continued to live in conditions then described as "poverty." A mounting wave of strikes from 1910 to 1913 testified to the intensity of class conflict. The Labour Party was becoming a major force in Parliament. Some socialists and some feminists were becoming radicalized. "Wisps of violence hung in the English air," wrote Eric Hobsbawm, "symptoms of a crisis in economy and society, which the [country's] self-confident opulence . . . could not quite conceal."[25] The world's first industrial society remained dissatisfied and conflicted.

It was also a society in economic decline relative to industrial newcomers such as Germany and the United States. Britain paid a price for its early lead, for its businessmen became committed to machinery that became obsolete as the century progressed. Latecomers invested in more modern equipment and in various ways had surpassed the British by the early twentieth century.

Europeans in Motion

Europe's Industrial Revolution prompted a massive migratory process that uprooted many millions, setting them in motion both internally and around the globe. Within Europe itself, the movement of men, women, and families from the countryside to the cities involved half or more of the region's people by the mid-nineteenth century. More significant for world history was the exodus between 1815 and 1939 of fully 20 percent of Europe's population, some 50 to 55 million people, who left home for the Americas, Australia, New Zealand, South Africa, and elsewhere (see Map 17.2). They were pushed by poverty, a rapidly growing population, and the displacement of peasant farming and artisan manufacturing. And they were pulled abroad by the enormous demand for labor overseas, the ready availability of land in some places, and the relatively cheap transportation of railroads and steamships. But not all found a satisfactory life in their new homes, and perhaps 7 million returned to Europe.[26]

This huge process had a transformative global impact, temporarily increasing Europe's share of the world's population and scattering Europeans around the world. In 1800, less than 1 percent of the total world population consisted of overseas Europeans and their descendants; by 1930, they represented 11 percent.[27] In particular regions, the impact was profound. Australia and New Zealand became settler colonies, outposts of European civilization in the South Pacific that overwhelmed their native populations through conquest, acquisition of their lands, and disease. In Australia, the initial settlers derived from the unwanted of British

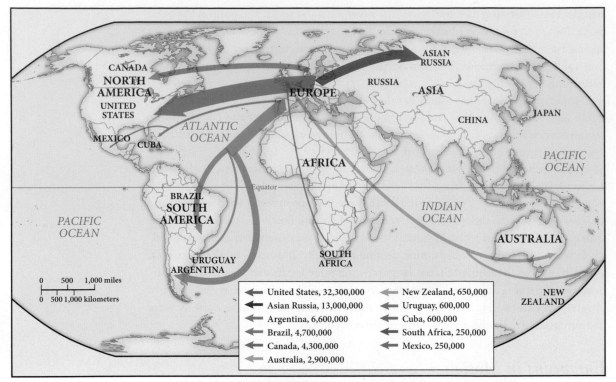

← United States, 32,300,000	← New Zealand, 650,000
← Asian Russia, 13,000,000	← Uruguay, 600,000
← Argentina, 6,600,000	← Cuba, 600,000
← Brazil, 4,700,000	← South Africa, 250,000
← Canada, 4,300,000	← Mexico, 250,000
← Australia, 2,900,000	

Map 17.2   European Migration in the Industrial Age

The Industrial Revolution not only transformed European society but also scattered millions of Europeans to the far corners of the world.

society: convicts were sentenced to penal colonies on the island continent, and by 1867 over 165,000 of them had arrived. By the end of the nineteenth century, New Zealand's European population, based on immigration of free people, out-numbered the native Maori by 700,000 to 40,000. Smaller numbers of Europeans found their way to South Africa, Kenya, Rhodesia, Algeria, and elsewhere, where they injected a sharp racial divide into those colonized territories.

But it was the Americas that felt the brunt of this huge movement of people. Latin America received about 20 percent of the European migratory stream, mostly from Italy, Spain, and Portugal, with Argentina and Brazil accounting for some 80 percent of those immigrants. Considered "white," they enhanced the social weight of the European element in those countries and thus enjoyed economic advantages over the mixed-race, Indian, and African populations.

In several ways the immigrant experience in the United States was distinctive. It was far larger and more diverse than elsewhere, with some 32 million newcomers arriving from all over Europe between 1820 and 1930. Furthermore, the United

States offered affordable land to many and industrial jobs to many more, neither of which was widely available in Latin America. And the United States was unique in turning the immigrant experience into a national myth—that of the melting pot. Despite this ideology of assimilation, the earlier immigrants, mostly Protestants from Britain and Germany, were anything but welcoming to Catholics and Jews from Southern and Eastern Europe who arrived later. The newcomers were seen as distinctly inferior, even "un-American," and blamed for crime, labor unrest, and socialist ideas. Nonetheless, this surge of immigration contributed much to the westward expansion of the United States, to the establishment of a European-derived culture in a vast area of North America, and to the displacement of the Native American peoples of the region.

In the vast domains of the Russian Empire, a parallel process of European migration likewise unfolded. After the freeing of the serfs in 1861, some 13 million Russians and Ukrainians migrated to Siberia, where they overwhelmed the native population of the region, while millions more settled in Central Asia. By the end of the century, native Siberians totaled only 10 percent of that region's population. The availability of land, the prospect of greater freedom from tsarist restrictions and from the exploitation of aristocratic landowners, and the construction of the trans-Siberian railroad—all of this facilitated the continued Europeanization of Siberia. As in the United States, the Russian government encouraged and aided this process, hoping to forestall Chinese pressures in the region and relieve growing population pressures in the more densely settled western lands of the empire.

Variations on a Theme: Industrialization in the United States and Russia

Not for long was the Industrial Revolution confined to Britain. It soon spread to continental Western Europe, and by the end of the nineteenth century it was well under way in the United States, Russia, and Japan. The globalization of industrialization had begun. Everywhere it took hold, industrialization bore a range of broadly similar outcomes. New technologies and sources of energy generated vast increases in production and spawned an unprecedented urbanization as well. Class structures changed as aristocrats, artisans, and peasants declined as classes, while the middle classes and a factory working class grew in numbers and social prominence. Middle-class women generally withdrew from paid labor altogether, and their working-class counterparts sought to do so after marriage. Working women usually received lower wages than their male counterparts, had difficulty joining unions, and were accused of taking jobs from men. Working-class frustration and anger gave rise to trade unions and socialist movements, injecting a new element of social conflict into industrial societies.

Nevertheless, different histories, cultures, and societies ensured that the Industrial Revolution unfolded variously in the diverse countries in which it became

The English Luddites and Machine Breaking

> If you do Not Cause those Dressing Machines to be Remov'd Within the Bounds of Seven Days . . . your factory and all that it Contains Will and Shall Surely Be Set on fire . . . it is Not our Desire to Do you the Least Injury, But We are fully Determin'd to Destroy Both Dressing Machines and Steam Looms.[28]

Between 1811 and 1813, this kind of warning was sent to hundreds of English workshops in the woolen and cotton industry, where more efficient machines, some of them steam powered, threatened the jobs and livelihood of workers. Over and over, that threat was carried out as well-organized bands of skilled artisans destroyed the offending machines, burned buildings, and on occasion attacked employers. These were the Luddites, taking their name from a mythical Robin Hood–like figure, Ned Ludd. A song called "General Ludd's Triumph" expressed their sentiments: "These Engines of mischief were sentenced to die / By unanimous vote of the Trade / And Ludd who can all opposition defy / Was the Grand executioner made."

So widespread and serious was this Luddite uprising that the British government sent 12,000 troops to sup-

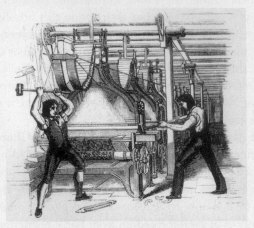

Luddites smashing a loom.

press it, more than it was then devoting to the struggle against Napoleon in continental Europe. And a new law, rushed through Parliament as an "emergency measure" in 1812, made those who destroyed mechanized looms subject to the death penalty. Some sixty to seventy alleged Luddites were in fact hanged, and sometimes beheaded as well, for machine breaking.

In the governing circles of England, Luddism was widely regarded as blind protest, an outrageous, unthinking, and futile resistance to progress. It has remained in more recent times a term of insult applied to those who resist or reject technological innovation. And yet, a closer look suggests that we might view that movement with some sympathy as an understandable response to a painful transformation of social life when few alternatives for expressing grievances were available.

At the time of the Luddite uprising, England was involved in an increasingly unpopular war with Napoleon's France, and mutual blockades substantially reduced trade and hurt the textile industry. The country was also

photo: © Mary Evans Picture Library/Alamy

established. Differences in the pace and timing of industrialization, the size and shape of major industries, the role of the state, the political expression of social conflict, and many other factors have made this process rich in comparative possibilities. French industrialization, for example, occurred more slowly and perhaps less disruptively than did that of Britain. Germany focused initially on heavy industry—iron, steel, and coal—rather than on the textile industry with which Britain had begun. Moreover, German industrialization was far more highly concentrated in huge companies called cartels, and it generated a rather more militant and Marxist-oriented labor movement than in Britain.

in the early phase of an Industrial Revolution in which mechanized production was replacing skilled artisan labor. All of this, plus some bad weather and poor harvests, combined to generate real economic hardship, unemployment, and hunger. Bread riots and various protests against high prices proliferated.

Furthermore, English elites were embracing new laissez-faire, or free market, economic principles, which eroded customary protections for the poor and working classes. Over the previous several decades, many laws that had regulated wages and apprenticeships and prohibited certain laborsaving machines had been repealed, despite repeated workers' appeals to Parliament to maintain some minimal protections for their older way of life. A further act of Parliament in 1799 had forbidden trade unions and collective bargaining. In these circumstances, some form of direct action is hardly surprising.

At one level, the Luddite machine-breaking movement represented "collective bargaining by riot," a way of pressuring employers when legal negotiations with them had been outlawed. And the issues involved more than laborsaving machines. Luddites also argued for price reductions, minimum wages, and prohibitions on the flooding of their industry by unapprenticed workers. They wanted to return to a time when "full fashioned work at the old fashioned price is established by custom and law," according to one of their songs. More generally, Luddites sought to preserve elements of an older way of life in which industry existed to provide a live-lihood for workers, in which men could take pride in their craft, in which government and employers felt some paternalistic responsibility to the lower classes, and in which journeymen workers felt some bonds of attachment to a larger social and moral order. All of this was rapidly eroding in the new era of capitalist industrialization. In these ways, the Luddite movement looked backward to idealized memories of an earlier time.

And yet in other ways, the rebels anticipated the future with their demands for minimum wage and an end to child labor, their concern about inferior-quality products produced by machines, and their desire to organize trade unions. At the height of the Luddite movement, some among them began to move beyond local industrial action toward a "general insurrection" that might bring real political change to the entire country. In one letter from a Luddite in 1812, the writer expressed "hope for assistance from the French emperor [Napoleon] in shaking off the yoke of the rottenest, wickedest, and most tyranious government that ever existed." He continued, "Then we will be governed by a just republic."

After 1813, the organized Luddite movement faded away. But it serves as a cautionary reminder that what is hailed as progress claims victims as well as beneficiaries.

Questions: To what extent did the concerns of the Luddites come to pass as the Industrial Revolution unfolded? How does your understanding of the Luddites affect your posture toward technological change in our time?

Nowhere were the variations in the industrializing process more apparent than in those two vast countries that lay on the periphery of Europe. To the west across the Atlantic Ocean was the United States, a young, vigorous, democratic, expanding country, populated largely by people of European descent, along with a substantial number of slaves of African origin. To the east was Russia, with its Eastern Orthodox Christianity, an autocratic tsar, a huge population of serfs, and an empire stretching across all of northern Asia. In the 1830s, the French observer Alexis de Tocqueville famously commented on these two emerging giants in his book *Democracy in America*:

> The Anglo-American relies upon personal interest to accomplish his ends and
> gives free scope to the unguided strength and common sense of the people; the
> Russian centers all the authority of society in a single arm. . . . Their starting-
> point is different and their courses are not the same; yet each of them seems
> marked out by the will of Heaven to sway the destinies of half the globe.

By the early twentieth century, his prediction seemed to be coming true. Industrialization had turned the United States into a major global power and had spawned
in Russia an enormous revolutionary upheaval that made that country the first outpost of global communism.

The United States: Industrialization without Socialism

American industrialization began in the textile factories of New England during
the 1820s but grew explosively in the half century following the Civil War (1861–
1865) (see Map 17.3). The country's huge size, the ready availability of natural
resources, its expanding domestic market, and its relative political stability combined to make the United States the world's leading industrial power by 1914. At
that time, it produced 36 percent of the world's manufactured goods, compared to
16 percent for Germany, 14 percent for Great Britain, and 6 percent for France.
Furthermore, U.S. industrialization was closely linked to that of Europe. About
one-third of the capital investment that financed its remarkable growth came from
British, French, and German capitalists. But unlike Latin America, which also received
much foreign investment, the United States was able to use those funds to generate
an independent Industrial Revolution of its own.

■ **Comparison**

What were the differences
between industrialization
in the United States and
that in Russia?

As in other second-wave industrializing countries, the U.S. government played
an important role, though less directly than in Germany or Japan. Tax breaks, huge
grants of public land to the railroad companies, laws enabling the easy formation of
corporations, and the absence of much overt regulation of industry all fostered the
rise of very large business enterprises. The U.S. Steel Corporation, for example, by
1901 had an annual budget three times the size of that of the federal government.
In this respect, the United States followed the pattern of Germany but differed
from that of France and Britain, where family businesses still predominated.

The United States also pioneered techniques of mass production, using inter-
changeable parts, the assembly line, and "scientific management" to produce for a
mass market. The nation's advertising agencies, Sears Roebuck's and Montgomery
Ward's mail-order catalogs, and urban department stores generated a middle-class
"culture of consumption." When the industrialist Henry Ford in the early twentieth century began producing the Model T at a price that many ordinary people
could afford, he famously declared: "I am going to democratize the automobile."
More so than in Europe, with its aristocratic traditions, self-made American industrialists of fabulous wealth such as Henry Ford, Andrew Carnegie, and John D.

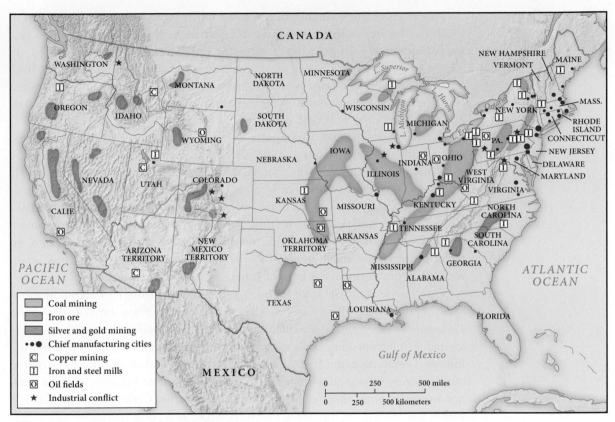

Map 17.3   The Industrial United States in 1900

By the early twentieth century, manufacturing industries were largely in the Northeast and Midwest, whereas mining operations were more widely scattered across the country.

Rockefeller became cultural heroes, widely admired as models of what anyone could achieve with daring and hard work in a land of endless opportunity.

Nevertheless, well before the first Model T rolled off the assembly line, serious social divisions of a kind common to European industrial societies mounted. Preindustrial America had boasted of a relative social equality, quite unlike that of Europe, but by the end of the nineteenth century a widening gap separated the classes. In Carnegie's Homestead steel plant near Pittsburgh, employees worked every day except Christmas and the Fourth of July, often for twelve hours a day. In Manhattan, where millions of European immigrants disembarked, many lived in five- or six-story buildings with four families and two toilets on each floor. In every large city, such conditions prevailed close by the mansions of elite neighborhoods. To some, the contrast was a betrayal of American ideals, while others saw it as a natural outcome of competition and "the survival of the fittest."

■ **Explanation**
Why did Marxist socialism not take root in the United States?

As elsewhere, such conditions generated much labor protest, the formation of unions, and strikes, sometimes leading to violence. In 1877, when the eastern railroads announced a 10 percent wage cut for their workers, strikers disrupted rail service across the eastern half of the country, smashed equipment, and rioted. Both state militias and federal troops were called out to put down the movement. Class consciousness and class conflict were intense in the industrial America of the late nineteenth and early twentieth centuries.

Unlike in many European countries, however, no major political party emerged in the United States to represent the interests of the working class. Nor did the ideas of socialism, especially those of Marxism, appeal to American workers nearly as much as they did to European laborers. At its high point, the Socialist Party of America garnered just 6 percent of the vote for its presidential candidate in the 1912 election, whereas socialists at the time held more seats in Germany's Parliament than any other party. Even in the depths of the Great Depression of the 1930s, no major socialist movement emerged to champion American workers. How might we explain this distinctive feature of American industrial development?

One answer lies in the relative conservatism of major American union organizations, especially the American Federation of Labor. Its focus on skilled workers excluded the more radical unskilled laborers, and its refusal to align with any party limited its influence in the political arena. Furthermore, massive immigration from Europe, beginning in the 1840s, created a very diverse industrial labor force on top of the country's sharp racial divide. This diversity contrasted sharply with the more homogeneous populations of many European countries. Catholics and Protestants; whites and blacks; English, Irish, Germans, Slavs, Jews, and Italians—such differences undermined the class solidarity of American workers, making it far more difficult to sustain class-oriented political parties and a socialist labor movement. Moreover, the country's remarkable economic growth generated on average a higher standard of living for American workers than their European counterparts experienced. Land was cheaper, and home ownership was more available. Workers with property generally found socialism less attractive than those without. By 1910, a particularly large group of white-collar workers in sales, services, and offices outnumbered factory laborers. Their middle-class aspirations further diluted impulses toward radicalism.

But political challenges to the abuses of capitalist industrialization did arise. In the 1890s, among small farmers in the U.S. South, West, and Midwest, "populists" railed against banks, industrialists, monopolies, the existing money system, and both major political parties, all of which they thought were dominated by the corporate interests of the eastern elites. More successful, especially in the early twentieth century, were the Progressives, who pushed for specific reforms, such as wages-and-hours legislation, better sanitation standards, antitrust laws, and greater governmental intervention in the economy. Socialism, however, came to be defined as fundamentally "un-American" in a country that so valued individualism and so feared "big government." It was a distinctive feature of the American response to industrialization.

Russia: Industrialization and Revolution

As a setting for the Industrial Revolution, it would be hard to imagine two more different environments than the United States and Russia. If the United States was the Western world's most exuberant democracy during the nineteenth century, Russia remained the sole outpost of absolute monarchy, in which the state exercised far greater control over individuals and society than anywhere in the Western world.

At the beginning of the twentieth century, Russia still had no national parliament, no legal political parties, and no nationwide elections. The tsar, answerable to God alone, ruled unchecked. Furthermore, Russian society was dominated by a titled nobility of various ranks. Its upper levels included great landowners, who furnished the state with military officers and leading government officials. Until 1861, most Russians were peasant serfs, bound to the estates of their masters, subject to sale, greatly exploited, and largely at the mercy of their owners. A vast cultural gulf separated these two classes. Many nobles were highly westernized, some speaking French better than Russian, whereas their serfs were steeped in a backwoods Orthodox Christianity that incorporated pre-Christian spirits, spells, curses, and magic.

A further difference between Russia and the United States lay in the source of social and economic change. In the United States, such change bubbled up from society as free farmers, workers, and businessmen sought new opportunities and operated in a political system that gave them varying degrees of expression. In autocratic Russia, change was far more often initiated by the state itself, in its continuing

Russian Serfdom
This nineteenth-century cartoon by the French artist Gustave Doré shows Russian noblemen gambling with tied bundles of stiff serfs. Serfdom was not finally abolished in Russia until 1861. (The Granger Collection, NYC—All rights reserved)

efforts to catch up with the more powerful and innovative states of Europe. This kind of "transformation from above" found an early expression in the reign of Peter the Great (r. 1689–1725). (See Chapter 13, page 576.) Such state-directed change continued in the nineteenth century with the freeing of the serfs in 1861, an action stimulated by military defeat at the hands of British and French forces in the Crimean War (1854–1856). To many thoughtful Russians, serfdom seemed incompatible with modern civilization and held back the country's overall development, as did its economic and industrial backwardness. Thus, beginning in the 1860s, Russia began a program of industrial development, which was more heavily directed by the state than was the case in Western Europe or the United States.

■ **Change**
What factors contributed to the making of a revolutionary situation in Russia by the beginning of the twentieth century?

By the 1890s, Russia's Industrial Revolution was launched and growing rapidly. It focused particularly on railroads and heavy industry and was fueled by a substantial amount of foreign investment. By 1900, Russia ranked fourth in the world in steel production and had major industries in coal, textiles, and oil. Its industrial enterprises, still modest in comparison to those of Europe, were concentrated in a few major cities—Moscow, St. Petersburg, and Kiev, for example—and took place in factories far larger than in most of Western Europe.

All of this contributed to the explosive social outcomes of Russian industrialization. A growing middle class of businessmen and professionals increasingly took shape. As modern and educated people, many in the middle class objected strongly to the deep conservatism of tsarist Russia and sought a greater role in political life, but they were also dependent on the state for contracts and jobs and for suppressing the growing radicalism of the workers, which they greatly feared. Although factory workers constituted only about 5 percent of Russia's total population, they quickly developed a radical class consciousness, based on harsh conditions and the absence of any legal outlet for their grievances. As in Western Europe, millions flocked to the new centers of industrial development. By 1897, over 70 percent of the population in Moscow and St. Petersburg were recent migrants from the rural areas. Their conditions of life resembled those of industrial migrants in New York or Berlin. One observer wrote: "People live in impossible conditions: filth, stench, suffocating heat. They lie down together barely a few feet apart; there is no division between the sexes and adults sleep with children."[29] Until 1897, a thirteen-hour working day was common, while ruthless discipline and overt disrespect from supervisors created resentment. In the absence of legal unions or political parties, these grievances often erupted in the form of large-scale strikes.

In these conditions, a small but growing number of educated Russians found in Marxist socialism a way of understanding the changes they witnessed daily as well as hope for the future in a revolutionary upheaval of workers. In 1898, they created an illegal Russian Social-Democratic Labor Party and quickly became involved in workers' education, union organizing, and, eventually, revolutionary action. By the early twentieth century, the strains of rapid change and the state's continued intransigence had reached the bursting point, and in 1905, following its defeat in a naval war with Japan, Russia erupted in spontaneous insurrection (see Map 17.4). Workers in Moscow and St. Petersburg went on strike and created their own representative councils, called soviets. Peasant uprisings, student demonstrations, revolts of non-Russian nationalities, and mutinies in the military all contributed to the upheaval. Recently formed political parties, representing intellectuals of various persuasions, came out into the open.

The 1905 revolution, though brutally suppressed, forced the tsar's regime to make more substantial reforms than it had ever contemplated. It granted a constitution, legalized both trade unions and political parties, and permitted the election of a national assembly, called the Duma. Censorship was eased, and plans were under way for universal primary education. Industrial development likewise continued at a rapid rate, so that by 1914 Russia stood fifth in the world in terms of overall output. But in the first half of that year, some 1,250,000 workers, representing about 40 percent of the entire industrial workforce, went out on strike.

Thus the tsar's limited political reforms, which had been granted with great reluctance and were often reversed in practice, failed to tame working-class radicalism or to bring social stability to Russia. In Russian political life, the people generally, and even the middle class, had only a very limited voice. Representatives of even the privileged classes had become so alienated by the government's intransigence that many felt revolution was inevitable. Various revolutionary groups, many of them socialist, published pamphlets and newspapers, organized trade unions, and spread their messages among workers and peasants. Particularly in the cities, these revolutionary parties had an impact. They provided a language through which workers could express their grievances; they created links among workers from different factories; and they furnished leaders who were able to act when the revolutionary moment arrived.

World War I provided that moment. The enormous hardships of that war, coupled with the immense social tensions of industrialization within a still-autocratic political system, sparked the Russian Revolution of 1917 (see Chapter 21). That massive upheaval quickly brought to power the most radical of the socialist groups operating in the country—the Bolsheviks, led by the charismatic Vladimir Ilyich Ulyanov, better known as Lenin. Only in Russia was industrialization associated

Map 17.4 **Industrialization and Revolution in Russia, 1905**
Only in Russia did industrialization lead to violent revolutionary upheavals, both in 1905 and more successfully in 1917.

SUMMING UP SO FAR

What was common to industrialization everywhere, and in what ways did it vary from place to place?

with violent social revolution. This was the most distinctive feature of Russia's modern historical development. And only in Russia was a socialist political party, inspired by the teachings of Karl Marx, able to seize power, thus launching the modern world's first socialist society, with enormous implications for the twentieth century.

The Industrial Revolution and Latin America in the Nineteenth Century

Beyond the world of Europe and North America, only Japan underwent a major industrial transformation during the nineteenth century, part of that country's overall response to the threat of European aggression. (See Chapter 19, pages 852–60, for a more detailed examination of Japan's industrialization.) Elsewhere—in colonial India, Egypt, the Ottoman Empire, China, and Latin America—very modest experiments in modern industry were undertaken, but nowhere did they drive the kind of major social transformation that had taken place in Britain, Europe, North America, and Japan. However, even in societies that did not experience their own Industrial Revolution, the profound impact of European and North American industrialization was hard to avoid. Such was the case in Latin America during the nineteenth century. (See Snapshot, opposite, for the global economic divisions that accompanied industrialization.)

After Independence in Latin America

The struggle for independence in Latin America had lasted far longer and proved far more destructive than in North America. Decimated populations, diminished herds of livestock, flooded or closed silver mines, abandoned farms, shrinking international trade and investment capital, and empty national treasuries—these were the conditions that greeted Latin Americans upon independence. Furthermore, the four major administrative units (viceroyalties) of Spanish America ultimately dissolved into eighteen separate countries, and regional revolts wracked Brazil in the early decades of its independent life. A number of international wars in the post-independence century likewise shook these new nations. Peru and Bolivia briefly united and then broke apart in a bitter conflict (1836–1839); Mexico lost huge territories to the United States (1846–1848); and an alliance of Argentina, Brazil, and Uruguay went to war with Paraguay (1864–1870) in a conflict that devastated Paraguay's small population.

Within these new countries, political life was turbulent and unstable. Conservatives favored centralized authority and sought to maintain the social status quo of the colonial era in alliance with the Catholic Church, which at independence owned perhaps half of all productive land. Their often-bitter opponents were liberals, who attacked the Church in the name of Enlightenment values, sought at least

SNAPSHOT The Industrial Revolution and the Global Divide

During the nineteenth century, the Industrial Revolution generated an enormous and unprecedented economic division in the world, as measured by the share of manufacturing output. What patterns can you see in this table?[30]

SHARE OF TOTAL WORLD MANUFACTURING OUTPUT (percentage)

	1750	1800	1860	1880	1900
EUROPE AS A WHOLE	**23.2**	**28.1**	**53.2**	**61.3**	**62.0**
United Kingdom	1.9	4.3	19.9	22.9	18.5
France	4.0	4.2	7.9	7.8	6.8
Germany	2.9	3.5	4.9	8.5	13.2
Russia	5.0	5.6	7.0	7.6	8.8
UNITED STATES	**0.1**	**0.8**	**7.2**	**14.7**	**23.6**
JAPAN	**3.8**	**3.5**	**2.6**	**2.4**	**2.4**
THE REST OF THE WORLD	**73.0**	**67.7**	**36.6**	**20.9**	**11.0**
China	32.8	33.3	19.7	12.5	6.2
South Asia (India/Pakistan)	24.5	19.7	8.6	2.8	1.7

modest social reforms, and preferred federalism. In many countries, conflicts between these factions, often violent, enabled military strongmen known as *caudillos* (kaw-DEE-yos) to achieve power as defenders of order and property, although they too succeeded one another with great frequency. One of them, Antonio López de Santa Anna of Mexico, was president of his country at least nine separate times between 1833 and 1855. Constitutions too replaced one another with bewildering speed. Bolivia had ten constitutions during the nineteenth century, while Ecuador and Peru each had eight.

Social life did not change fundamentally in the aftermath of independence. As in Europe and North America, women remained disenfranchised and wholly outside of formal political life. Slavery, it is true, was abolished in most of Latin America by midcentury, although it persisted in both Brazil and Cuba until the late 1880s. Most of the legal distinctions among various racial categories also disappeared, and all free people were considered, at least officially, equal citizens. Nevertheless, productive economic resources such as businesses, ranches, and plantations remained overwhelmingly in the hands of creole white men, who were culturally oriented toward Europe. The military provided an avenue of mobility for a few skilled and ambitious mestizo men, some of whom subsequently became caudillos. Other mixed-race men and women found a place in a small middle class as teachers, shopkeepers, or artisans. The vast majority—blacks, Indians, and many mixed-race people of both sexes—remained impoverished, working small subsistence farms or laboring in the mines or on the *haciendas* (ah-see-EHN-duhz) (plantations) of the well-to-do. Only rarely did the poor and dispossessed actively rebel against their social betters. One such case was the Caste War of Yucatán (1847–1901), a prolonged struggle of the Maya people of Mexico, aimed at cleansing their land of European and mestizo intruders.

Facing the World Economy

During the second half of the nineteenth century, a measure of political consolidation took hold in Latin America, and countries such as Mexico, Peru, and Argentina entered periods of greater stability. At the same time, Latin America as a whole became more closely integrated into a world economy driven by the industrialization of Western Europe and North America. The new technology of the steamship cut the sailing time between Britain and Argentina almost in half, while the underwater telegraph instantly brought the latest news and fashions of Europe to Latin America.

■ **Connection**

In what ways was Latin America linked to the global economy of the nineteenth century, and what was the impact of these links?

The most significant economic outcome of this growing integration was a rapid growth of Latin American exports to the industrializing countries, which now needed the food products, raw materials, and markets of these new nations. Latin American landowners, businessmen, and governments proved eager to supply those needs, and in the sixty years or so after 1850, an export boom increased the value of Latin American goods sold abroad by a factor of ten.

Mexico continued to produce large amounts of silver, providing more than half the world's new supply until 1860. Now added to the list of raw materials flowing out of Latin America were copper from Chile, a metal that the growing electrical industry required; tin from Bolivia, which met the mounting demand for tin cans; and nitrates from Chile and guano (bird droppings) from Peru, both of which were used for fertilizer. Wild rubber from the Amazon rain forest was in great demand for bicycle and automobile tires, as was sisal from Mexico, used to make binder twine for the proliferating mechanical harvesters of North America. Bananas from Central America, beef from Argentina, cacao from Ecuador, coffee from Brazil and Guatemala, and sugar from Cuba also found eager markets in the rapidly growing and increasingly prosperous world of industrializing countries. In return for these primary products, Latin Americans imported the textiles, machinery, tools, weapons, and luxury goods of Europe and the United States (see Map 17.5).

Accompanying this burgeoning commerce was large-scale investment of European capital in Latin America, $10 billion alone between 1870 and 1919. Most of this capital came from Great Britain, which invested more in Argentina in the late nineteenth century than in its colony of India, although France, Germany, Italy, and the United States also contributed to this substantial financial transfer. By 1910, U.S. business interests controlled 40 percent of Mexican property and produced

U.S. Interventions

→ Puerto Rico, 1898–on
→ Panama, 1903
→ Cuba, 1898–1902, 1905–09, 1917–21
→ Haiti, 1915–34
→ Mexico, 1846–48, 1914, 1916–17
→ Nicaragua, 1909, 1912–25, 1927–32
→ Dominican Republic, 1916–24

MEXICO
$1329

CUBA
$471
$11 $16 $44
$42
$99
$19 $12 $61 $28

VENEZUELA
$161

COLOMBIA
$77

ECUADOR
$41

PERU
$197

BOLIVIA
$59

BRAZIL
$1913

PARAGUAY
$27

ARGENTINA
$4001

CHILE
$668

URUGUAY
$475

EXPORTS

Bananas	Oil
Cacao	Rubber
Cattle	Sheep
Coffee	Silver
Copper and tin	Sisal
Cotton	Sugar
Guano	Tobacco
Nitrate	Wheat

$161   Foreign investment
(in millions of U.S. dollars around 1914)

← European immigration

Map 17.5   Latin America and the World, 1825–1935

During the nineteenth and early twentieth centuries, Latin American countries interacted with the industrializing world via investment, trade, immigration, and military intervention from the United States.

half of its oil. Much of this capital was used to build railroads, largely to funnel Latin American exports to the coast, where they were shipped to overseas markets. Mexico had only 390 miles of railroad in 1876; it had 15,000 miles in 1910. By 1915, Argentina, with 22,000 miles of railroad, had more track per person than the United States had.

Becoming like Europe?

To the economic elites of Latin America, intent on making their countries resemble Europe or the United States, all of this was progress. In some respects, they were surely right. Economies were growing, producing more than ever before. The population was also burgeoning; it increased from about 30 million in 1850 to more than 77 million in 1912 as public health measures (such as safe drinking water, inoculations, sewers, and campaigns to eliminate mosquitoes that carried yellow fever) brought down death rates.

■ **Comparison**
Did Latin America follow or diverge from the historical path of Europe during the nineteenth century?

Urbanization also proceeded rapidly. By the early twentieth century, wrote one scholar, "Latin American cities lost their colonial cobblestones, white-plastered walls, and red-tiled roofs. They became modern metropolises, comparable to urban giants anywhere. Streetcars swayed, telephones jangled, and silent movies flickered from Montevideo and Santiago to Mexico City and Havana."[31] Buenos Aires, Argentina's metropolitan center, boasted 750,000 people in 1900 and billed itself as the "Paris of South America." There the educated elite, just like the English, drank tea in the afternoon, while discussing European literature, philosophy, and fashion, usually in French.

To become more like Europe, Latin America sought to attract more Europeans. Because civilization, progress, and modernity apparently derived from Europe, many Latin American countries actively sought to increase their "white" populations by deliberately recruiting impoverished Europeans with the promise, mostly unfulfilled, of a new and prosperous life in the New World. Argentina received the largest wave of European immigrants (some 2.5 million between 1870 and 1915), mostly from Spain and Italy. Brazil and Uruguay likewise attracted substantial numbers of European newcomers.

Only a quite modest segment of Latin American society saw any great benefits from the export boom and all that followed from it. Upper-class landowners certainly gained as exports flourished and their property values soared. Middle-class urban dwellers—merchants, office workers, lawyers, and other professionals—also grew in numbers and prosperity as their skills proved valuable in a modernizing society. As a percentage of the total population, however, these were narrow elites. In Mexico in the mid-1890s, for example, the landowning upper class made up no more than 1 percent and the middle classes perhaps 8 percent of the population. Everyone else was lower class, and most of them were impoverished.[32]

A new but quite small segment of this vast lower class emerged among urban workers who labored in the railroads, ports, mines, and a few factories. They initially organized themselves in a variety of mutual aid societies, but by the end of the nineteenth century they were creating unions and engaging in strikes. To authoritarian governments interested in stability and progress, such activity was highly provocative and threatening, and they acted harshly to crush or repress unions and strikes. In 1906, the Mexican dictator Porfirio Díaz invited the Arizona Rangers to suppress a strike at Cananea, near the U.S. border, an action that resulted in dozens of deaths. The following year in the Chilean city of Iquique, more than 1,000 men, women, and children were slaughtered by police when nitrate miners protested their wages and working conditions.

The vast majority of the lower class lived in rural areas, where they suffered the most and benefited the least from the export boom. Government attacks on communal landholding and peasant indebtedness to wealthy landowners combined to push many farmers off their land or into remote and poor areas where they could barely make a living. Many wound up as dependent laborers or peons on the haciendas of the wealthy, where their wages were often too meager to support a family. Thus women and children, who had earlier remained at home to tend the family plot, were required to join their menfolk as field laborers. Many immigrant Italian farmworkers in Argentina and Brazil were unable to acquire their own farms, as they had expected, and so drifted into the growing cities or returned to Italy.

Although local protests and violence were frequent, only in Mexico did these vast inequalities erupt into a nationwide revolution. There, in the early twentieth century, middle-class reformers joined with workers and peasants to overthrow the long dictatorship of Porfirio Díaz (r. 1876–1911). What followed was a decade of bloody conflict (1910–1920) that cost Mexico some 1 million lives, or roughly 10 percent of the population. Huge peasant armies under charismatic leaders such as Pancho Villa and Emiliano Zapata helped oust Díaz. Intent on seizing land and redistributing it to the peasants, they then went on to attack many of Mexico's large haciendas. But unlike the leaders of the later Russian and Chinese revolutions, whose most radical elements seized state power, Villa and Zapata proved unable to do so on a long-term basis, in part because they were hobbled by factionalism and focused on local or regional issues. Despite this

The Mexican Revolution
Women were active participants in the Mexican Revolution. They prepared food, nursed the wounded, washed clothes, and at times served as soldiers on the battlefield, as illustrated in this cover image from a French magazine in 1913. (© Archivio Iconografico, S.A./Corbis)

limitation and its own internal conflicts, the Mexican Revolution transformed the country. When the dust settled, Mexico had a new constitution (1917) that proclaimed universal male suffrage; provided for the redistribution of land; stripped the Catholic Church of any role in public education and forbade it to own land; announced unheard-of rights for workers, such as a minimum wage and an eight-hour workday; and placed restrictions on foreign ownership of property. Much of Mexico's history in the twentieth century involved working out the implications of these nationalist and reformist changes. The revolution's direct influence, however, was largely limited to Mexico itself and a few places in Central America and the Andes; the upheaval did not have the wider international impact of the Russian and Chinese revolutions.

Perhaps the most significant outcome of the export boom lay in what did *not* happen, for nowhere in Latin America did it jump-start a thorough Industrial Revolution, despite a few factories that processed foods or manufactured textiles, clothing, and building materials. The reasons are many. A social structure that relegated some 90 percent of its population to an impoverished lower class generated only a very small market for manufactured goods. Moreover, economically powerful groups such as landowners and cattlemen benefited greatly from exporting agricultural products and had little incentive to invest in manufacturing. Domestic manufacturing enterprises could only have competed with cheaper and higher-quality foreign goods if they had been protected for a time by high tariffs. But Latin American political leaders had thoroughly embraced the popular European doctrine of prosperity through free trade, and many governments depended on taxing imports to fill their treasuries.

Instead of its own Industrial Revolution, Latin Americans developed a form of economic growth that was largely financed by capital from abroad and dependent on European and North American prosperity and decisions. Brazil experienced this kind of dependence when its booming rubber industry suddenly collapsed in 1910–1911, after seeds from the wild rubber tree had been illegally exported to Britain and were used to start competing and cheaper rubber plantations in Malaysia.

Later critics saw this "dependent development" as a new form of colonialism, expressed in the power exercised by foreign investors. The influence of the U.S.-owned United Fruit Company in Central America was a case in point. Allied with large landowners and compliant politicians, the company pressured the governments of these "banana republics" to maintain conditions favorable to U.S. business. This indirect or behind-the-scenes imperialism was supplemented by repeated U.S. military intervention in support of American corporate interests in Cuba, Haiti, the Dominican Republic, Nicaragua, and Mexico. The United States also controlled the Panama Canal and acquired Puerto Rico as a territory in the aftermath of the Spanish-American War (see Map 17.5, page 769).

Thus, despite Latin America's domination by people of European descent and its close ties to the industrializing countries of the Atlantic world, that region's historical trajectory in the nineteenth century diverged considerably from that of Europe and North America.

REFLECTIONS

History and Horse Races

Historians and students of history seem endlessly fascinated by "firsts"—the first breakthrough to agriculture, the first domestication of horses, the first civilization, the first use of gunpowder, the first printing press, and so on. Each of these firsts presents a problem of explanation: why did it occur in some particular time and place rather than somewhere else or at some other time? Such questions have assumed historical significance because "first achievements" represent something new in the human journey and because many of them conveyed unusual power, wealth, status, or influence on their creators.

Nonetheless, the focus on firsts can be misleading as well. Those who accomplished something first may see themselves as generally superior to those who embraced that innovation later. Historians too can sometimes adopt a winners-and-losers mentality, inviting a view of history as a horse race toward some finish line of accomplishment. Most first achievements in history, however, were not the result of intentional efforts but rather the unexpected outcome of converging circumstances.

The Industrial Revolution is a case in point. Understanding the European beginnings of this immense breakthrough is certainly justified by its pervasive global consequences and its global spread over the past several centuries. In terms of human ability to dominate the natural environment and to extract wealth from it, the Industrial Revolution marks a decisive turning point in the history of our species. But Europeans' attempts to explain their Industrial Revolution have at times stated or implied their own unique genius. In the nineteenth century, many Europeans saw their technological mastery as a sure sign of their cultural and racial superiority as they came to use "machines as the measure of men."[33] In pondering the "why Europe?" question, historians too have sometimes sought an answer in some distinct or even superior feature of European civilization.

In emphasizing the unexpectedness of the first Industrial Revolution, and the global context within which it occurred, world historians have attempted to avoid a "history as horse race" outlook. Clearly, the first industrial breakthrough in Britain was not a self-conscious effort to win a race; it was the surprising outcome of countless decisions by many people to further their own interests. Subsequently, however, other societies and their governments quite deliberately tried to catch up, seeking the wealth and power that the Industrial Revolution promised.

The rapid spread of industrialization across the planet, though highly uneven, may diminish the importance of the "why Europe?" issue. Just as no one views agriculture as a Middle Eastern phenomenon even though it occurred first in that region, it seems likely that industrialization will be seen increasingly as a global process rather than one uniquely associated with Europe. If industrial society proves to be a sustainable future for humankind—and this is presently an open question—historians of the future may well be more interested in the pattern of its global spread and in efforts to cope with its social and environmental consequences than in its origins in Western Europe.

Second Thoughts

What's the Significance?

steam engine, 740
Indian cotton textiles, 743–44
middle-class values, 747–49
lower middle class, 749
Karl Marx, 751–53
Ellen Johnston, 752–53
Labour Party, 754–55
Luddites, 758–59

socialism in the United States, 762
Progressives, 762
Russian Revolution of 1905, 764–65
caudillos, 767
Latin American export boom, 768
Mexican Revolution, 771–72
dependent development, 772

Big Picture Questions

1. What did humankind gain from the Industrial Revolution, and what did it lose?
2. In what ways might the Industrial Revolution be understood as a global rather than simply a European phenomenon?
3. How might you situate the Industrial Revolution in the long history of humankind? How do you think the material covered in this chapter will be viewed 50, 100, or 200 years into the future?
4. **Looking Back:** How did the Industrial Revolution interact with the Scientific Revolution and the French Revolution to generate Europe's modern transformation?

Next Steps: For Further Study

John Charles Chasteen, *Born in Blood and Fire* (2006). A lively and well-written account of Latin America's turbulent history since the sixteenth century.

Jack Goldstone, *Why Europe? The Rise of the West in World History, 1500–1850* (2009). An original synthesis of recent research provided by a leading world historian.

David S. Landes, *The Wealth and Poverty of Nations* (1998). An argument that culture largely shapes the possibilities for industrialization and economic growth.

Robert B. Marks, *The Origins of the Modern World* (2007). An effective summary of new thinking about the origins of European industrialization.

Peter Stearns, *The Industrial Revolution in World History* (1998). A global and comparative perspective on the Industrial Revolution.

Peter Waldron, *The End of Imperial Russia, 1855–1917* (1997). A brief account of Russian history during its early industrialization.

Bridging World History, Units 18 and 19, http://www.learner.org/channel/courses/worldhistory. An innovative world history Web site that provides pictures, video, and text dealing with "Rethinking the Rise of the West" and "Global Industrialization."

"A History of Women in Industry," http://www.nwhm.org/online-exhibits/industry/womenindustry_intro .html. An exhibit of the National Women's History Museum that provides commentary, images, and primary sources about the lives of American women during the Industrial Revolution.

WORKING WITH EVIDENCE

Voices of European Socialism

Among the ideologies and social movements that grew out of Europe's Industrial Revolution, none was more important than socialism. The socialist dream of equality, justice, and community has an ancient pedigree, but the early currents of modern socialism took shape during the first quarter of the nineteenth century in the minds of various thinkers—the Englishman Robert Owen and the Frenchman Charles Fourier, for example—both of whom were appalled by the social divisions that industrial society generated. As an alternative, they proposed small-scale, voluntary, and cooperative communities, and their followers actually established a number of such experimental groups in Europe and the United States. But they seldom lasted long and never spread widely.

Far more important were the socialist ideas and movements inspired by the writings of Karl Marx, who disdained the voluntary communities as merely "utopian." The historical significance of Marxist socialism was immense. It offered an exuberant and thoroughly modern praise of the Industrial Revolution, embracing the new science and technology that generated such amazing wealth. But Marx also provided a devastating critique of the social inequalities, the economic instability, and the blatant exploitation that accompanied this process. In short, Marx distinguished sharply between the technological achievements of industrialization and the capitalist socioeconomic system in which it occurred. Marxist thinking sharpened the social conflicts that characterized industrializing Europe by dramatically highlighting, and simplifying, those conflicts. On one side of this great divide was the wealthy industrial business class, the bourgeoisie, those who owned and managed the mines, factories, and docks of an industrializing Europe. On the other stood the proletariat, the workers in those enterprises—often impoverished, exploited, and living in squalid conditions.

In the political realm, Marx's ideas inspired a variety of movements and parties that aimed to create the socialist society that he predicted. By the end of the nineteenth century, socialism had become a major element of European political and intellectual life, and it enjoyed a modest presence in the United States and Japan and among a handful of intellectuals elsewhere. For many people, those ideas also served as a way of understanding the world, perhaps akin to a religion, or as a substitute for religion. Marxism offered an alternative model for industrializing societies, imagining a future that would

775

more fully realize the promise of modern industry and more equally distribute its benefits. Thus nineteenth-century Marxism provided the foundation for twentieth-century world communism as it took shape in Russia, China, Vietnam, Cuba, and elsewhere.

The documents that follow illustrate some of the ways that Marxist socialism was expressed and debated within a nineteenth-century European context.

Source 17.1
Socialism According to Marx

The life of Karl Marx (1818–1883) coincided with perhaps the harshest phase of capitalist industrialization in Europe. At that time, an encompassing market economy was rudely shattering older institutions and traditions, but the benefits of this new and highly productive system were not yet widely shared (see pages 746–66). But in this brutal process, Marx discerned the inevitable approach of a new world. Source 17.1 presents excerpts from the most famous of Marx's writings, *The Communist Manifesto*, first published in 1848. In this effort and throughout much of his life, Marx was assisted by another German thinker, Friedrich Engels (1820–1895), the son of a successful textile manufacturer. Engels became radicalized as he witnessed the devastating social results of capitalist industrialization. Marx and Engels's *Manifesto* begins with a summary description of the historical process. Much of the document then analyzes what the authors call the "bourgeoisie" or the "bourgeois epoch," terms that refer to the age of industrial capitalism.

■ How do Marx and Engels understand the motor of change in human history? How do they view the role of class?

■ What are their criticisms of the existing social system? What do they see as its major achievements?

■ Why do they believe that the capitalist system is doomed?

■ What kind of society do Marx and Engels envisage after the collapse of capitalism? Why do they believe that only a revolution, "the forcible overthrow of all existing social conditions," will enable the creation of a socialist society?

■ Which of Marx and Engels's descriptions and predictions ring true even now? In what respects was their analysis disproved by later developments?

KARL MARX AND FRIEDRICH ENGELS

The Communist Manifesto

1848

The history of all hitherto existing society is the history of class struggles. Freeman and slave, patrician and plebeian, lord and serf, guild-master and journeyman, in a word, oppressor and oppressed, stood in constant opposition to one another, carried on an uninterrupted, now hidden, now open fight, a fight that each time ended, either in a revolutionary reconstitution of society at large, or in the common ruin of the contending classes. . . .

Our epoch, the epoch of the bourgeoisie, possesses, however, this distinct feature: it has simplified class antagonisms. Society as a whole is more and more splitting up into two great hostile camps, into two great classes directly facing each other — bourgeoisie and proletariat.

Modern industry has established the world market, for which the discovery of America paved the way. This market has given an immense development to commerce, to navigation, to communication by land. . . .

[T]he bourgeoisie has at last, since the establishment of Modern Industry and of the world market, conquered for itself, in the modern representative state, exclusive political sway. The executive of the modern state is but a committee for managing the common affairs of the whole bourgeoisie. . . .

The bourgeoisie, wherever it has got the upper hand, has put an end to all feudal, patriarchal, idyllic relations. It has pitilessly torn asunder the motley feudal ties that bound man to his "natural superiors," and has left no other nexus between people than naked self-interest, than callous "cash payment." It has drowned out the most heavenly ecstasies of religious fervor, of chivalrous enthusiasm, of philistine sentimentalism, in the icy water of egotistical calculation. It has resolved personal worth into exchange value, and in place of the numberless indefeasible chartered freedoms, has set up that single, unconscionable freedom — Free Trade. In one word, for exploitation, veiled by religious and political illusions, it has substituted naked, shameless, direct, brutal exploitation.

The bourgeoisie has stripped of its halo every occupation hitherto honored and looked up to with reverent awe. It has converted the physician, the lawyer, the priest, the poet, the man of science, into its paid wage laborers.

The bourgeoisie has torn away from the family its sentimental veil, and has reduced the family relation into a mere money relation. . . .

It has been the first to show what man's activity can bring about. It has accomplished wonders far surpassing Egyptian pyramids, Roman aqueducts, and Gothic cathedrals. . . .

The need of a constantly expanding market for its products chases the bourgeoisie over the entire surface of the globe. It must nestle everywhere, settle everywhere, establish connections everywhere. . . .

All old-established national industries have been destroyed or are daily being destroyed. They are dislodged by new industries, whose introduction becomes a life and death question for all civilized nations, by industries that no longer work up indigenous raw material, but raw material drawn from the remotest zones; industries whose products are consumed, not only at home, but in every quarter of the globe. In place of the old wants, satisfied by the production of the country, we find new wants, requiring for their satisfaction the products of distant lands and climes. In place of the old local and national seclusion and self-sufficiency, we have intercourse in every direction, universal interdependence of nations. . . .

The bourgeoisie, by the rapid improvement of all instruments of production, by the immensely facilitated means of communication, draws all, even the most barbarian, nations into civilization.

The cheap prices of commodities are the heavy artillery with which it forces the barbarians' intensely obstinate hatred of foreigners to capitulate. It compels all nations, on pain of extinction, to adopt the bourgeois mode of production; it compels them to introduce what it calls civilization into their midst, i.e., to become bourgeois themselves. In one word, it creates a world after its own image.

The bourgeoisie has subjected the country to the rule of the towns. It has created enormous cities, has greatly increased the urban population as compared with the rural, and has thus rescued a considerable part of the population from the idiocy of rural life. Just as it has made the country dependent on the towns, so it has made barbarian and semibarbarian countries dependent on the civilized ones, nations of peasants on nations of bourgeois, the East on the West. . . . The bourgeoisie, during its rule of scarce one hundred years, has created more massive and more colossal productive forces than have all preceding generations together. Subjection of nature's forces to man, machinery, application of chemistry to industry and agriculture, steam navigation, railways, electric telegraphs, clearing of whole continents for cultivation, canalization of rivers, whole populations conjured out of the ground—what earlier century had even a presentiment that such productive forces slumbered in the lap of social labor? . . .

It is enough to mention the commercial crises that, by their periodical return, put the existence of the entire bourgeois society on its trial, each time more threateningly. . . . In these crises, there breaks out an epidemic that, in all earlier epochs, would have seemed an absurdity—the epidemic of overproduction. . . .

But not only has the bourgeoisie forged the weapons that bring death to itself; it has also called into existence the men who are to wield those weapons—the modern working class—the proletarians. . . .

These laborers, who must sell themselves piecemeal, are a commodity, like every other article of commerce, and are consequently exposed to all the vicissitudes of competition, to all the fluctuations of the market.

Owing to the extensive use of machinery, and to the division of labor, the work of the proletarians has lost all individual character, and, consequently, all charm for the workman. He becomes an appendage of the machine, and it is only the most simple, most monotonous, and most easily acquired knack, that is required of him. . . .

Masses of laborers, crowded into the factory, are organized like soldiers. As privates of the industrial army, they are placed under the command of a perfect hierarchy of officers and sergeants. Not only are they slaves of the bourgeois class, and of the bourgeois state; they are daily and hourly enslaved by the machine, by the overlooker, and, above all, by the individual bourgeois manufacturer himself. . . .

The lower strata of the middle class—the small tradespeople, shopkeepers, and retired tradesmen generally, the handicraftsmen and peasants—all these sink gradually into the proletariat. . . . Thus, the proletariat is recruited from all classes of the population. . . .

This organization of the proletarians into a class, and, consequently, into a political party, is continually being upset again by the competition between the workers themselves. But it ever rises up again, stronger, firmer, mightier. . . .

Finally, in times when the class struggle nears the decisive hour, . . . a small section of the ruling class cuts itself adrift, and joins the revolutionary class, the class that holds the future in its hands. . . . What the bourgeoisie therefore produces, above all, are its own grave-diggers. Its fall and the victory of the proletariat are equally inevitable. . . .

We have seen above that the first step in the revolution by the working class is to raise the proletariat to the position of ruling class, to win the battle of democracy.

The proletariat will use its political supremacy to wrest, by degree, all capital from the bourgeoisie, to centralize all instruments of production in the hands of the state, i.e., of the proletariat organized as the ruling class; and to increase the total productive forces as rapidly as possible.

Of course, in the beginning, this cannot be effected except by means of despotic inroads on the rights of property. . . .

These measures will, of course, be different in different countries. Nevertheless, in most advanced countries, the following will be pretty generally applicable.

1. Abolition of property in land and application of all rents of land to public purposes.
2. A heavy progressive or graduated income tax.
3. Abolition of all rights of inheritance.
4. Confiscation of the property of all emigrants and rebels.
5. Centralization of credit in the banks of the state, by means of a national bank with state capital and an exclusive monopoly.
6. Centralization of the means of communication and transport in the hands of the state.
7. Extension of factories and instruments of production owned by the state; the bringing into cultivation of waste lands, and the improvement of the soil generally in accordance with a common plan.
8. Equal obligation of all to work. Establishment of industrial armies, especially for agriculture.
9. Combination of agriculture with manufacturing industries; gradual abolition of all the distinction between town and country by a more equable distribution of the populace over the country.
10. Free education for all children in public schools. Abolition of children's factory labor in its present form. Combination of education with industrial production, etc.

When, in the course of development, class distinctions have disappeared, and all production has been concentrated in the hands of a vast association of the whole nation, the public power will lose its political character. Political power, properly so called, is merely the organized power of one class for oppressing another. If the proletariat during its contest with the bourgeoisie is compelled, by the force of circumstances, to organize itself as a class; if, by means of a revolution, it makes itself the ruling class, and, as such, sweeps away by force the old conditions of production, then it will, along with these conditions, have swept away the conditions for the existence of class antagonisms and of classes generally, and will thereby have abolished its own supremacy as a class.

In place of the old bourgeois society, with its classes and class antagonisms, we shall have an association in which the free development of each is the condition for the free development of all. . . .

The Communists disdain to conceal their views and aims. They openly declare that their ends can be attained only by the forcible overthrow of all existing social conditions. Let the ruling classes tremble at a communist revolution. The proletarians have nothing to lose but their chains. They have a world to win.

Source: John E. Toews, ed., *The Communist Manifesto by Karl Marx and Frederick Engels with Related Documents* (Boston: Bedford/St. Martin's, 1999), 63–96.

Source 17.2
Socialism without Revolution

Karl Marx and Friedrich Engels provided the set of ideas that informed much of the European socialist movement during the second half of the nineteenth century. Organized in various national parties and joined together in international organizations as well, socialists usually referred to themselves as social democrats, for they were seeking to extend the principles of democracy from the political arena (voting rights, for example) into the realm of the economy and society. By the 1890s, however, some of them had begun to question at least part of Marx's teachings, especially the need for violent revolution. The chief spokesperson for this group of socialists, known as "revisionists," was Eduard Bernstein (1850–1932), a prominent member of the German Social Democratic Party. His ideas provoked a storm of controversy within European socialist circles. Source 17.2 is drawn from the preface of Bernstein's 1899 book, *Evolutionary Socialism*.

- In what ways and for what reasons was Bernstein critical of Marx and Engels's analysis of capitalism?

- Why do you think Bernstein refers so often to Engels?

- What strategy does Bernstein recommend for the German Social Democratic Party?

- What does he mean by saying that "the movement means everything for me and . . . 'the final aim of socialism' is nothing"?

- Why would some of Marx's followers have considered Bernstein a virtual traitor to the socialist cause?

EDUARD BERNSTEIN

Evolutionary Socialism
1899

It has been maintained in a certain quarter that the practical deductions from my treatises would be the abandonment of the conquest of political power by the proletariat organized politically and economically. That [idea] . . . I altogether deny.

I set myself against the notion that we have to expect shortly a collapse of the bourgeois economy. . . .

The adherents of this theory of a catastrophe base it especially on the conclusions of the *Communist Manifesto*. This is a mistake. . . .

Social conditions have not developed to such an acute opposition of things and classes as is depicted in the *Manifesto*. It is not only useless, it is the greatest folly to attempt to conceal this from ourselves. The number of members of the possessing classes is today not smaller but larger. The enormous increase of social wealth is not accompanied by a decreasing number of large capitalists but by an increasing number of capitalists of all degrees. The middle classes change their character but they do not disappear from the social scale.

The concentration in productive industry is not being accomplished even today in all its departments with equal thoroughness and at an equal rate. . . . Trade statistics show an extraordinarily elaborated graduation of enterprises in regard to size. . . .

In all advanced countries we see the privileges of the capitalist bourgeoisie yielding step by step to democratic organizations. Under the influence of this, and driven by the movement of the working classes which is daily becoming stronger, a social reaction has set in against the exploiting tendencies of capital. . . . Factory legislation, the democratizing of local government, and the extension of its area of work, the freeing of trade unions and systems of cooperative trading from legal restrictions, the consideration of standard conditions of labor in the work undertaken by public authorities—all these characterize this phase of the evolution.

But the more the political organizations of modern nations are democratized, the more the needs and opportunities of great political catastrophes are diminished. . . .

[Engels] points out in conformity with this opinion that the next task of the party should be "to work for an uninterrupted increase of its votes" or to carry on a slow *propaganda of parliamentary activity*. . . .

Shall we be told that he [Engels] abandoned the conquest of political power by the working classes . . . ?

[F]or a long time yet the task of social democracy is, instead of speculating on a great economic crash, "to organize the working classes politically and develop them as a democracy and to fight for all reforms in the State which are adapted to raise the working classes and transform the State in the direction of democracy." . . .

[T]he movement means everything for me and that what is *usually* called "the final aim of socialism" is nothing. . . .

The conquest of political power by the working classes, the expropriation of capitalists, are not ends themselves but only means for the accomplishment of certain aims and endeavors. . . . But the conquest of political power necessitates the possession of political *rights*; German social democracy [must] devise the best ways for the extension of the political and economic rights of the German working classes.

Source: Eduard Bernstein, *Evolutionary Socialism*, translated by Edith C. Harvey (New York: Schocken Books, 1961), xxiv–xxx.

Source 17.3
Socialism and Women

Marxist socialism focused largely on issues of class, but that movement coincided with the emergence of feminism, giving rise to what many socialists called "the woman question." The main theoretical issue was the source of female subjugation. Did it derive from private property and the class structure of capitalist society, or was it the product of deeply rooted cultural attitudes independent of class? While middle-class feminists generally assumed the second view, orthodox Marxist thinking aligned with the first one, believing that the lack of economic independence was the root cause of women's subordination. Their liberation would follow, more or less automatically, after the creation of socialist societies. On a more practical level, the question was whether socialist parties should seek to enroll women by actively supporting their unique concerns—suffrage, equal pay, education, maternity insurance. Or did such efforts divide the working class and weaken the socialist movement? Should socialists treat women as members of an oppressed class or as members of an oppressed sex? Among the leading figures addressing such issues was Clara Zetkin (1857–1933), a prominent German socialist and feminist. In Source 17.3, Zetkin outlines the efforts of the German Social Democratic Party to reach out to women and describes the party's posture toward middle-class feminism.

■ How would you describe Zetkin's view of the relationship between socialism and feminism? Which one has priority, in her thinking?

- Why is she so insistent that the Social Democratic Party of Germany address the concerns of women? How precisely did it do so?

- Why does she believe that women's issues will be better served within a socialist framework than in a bourgeois women's rights movement?

- How might critics—both feminist and socialist—argue with Zetkin?

CLARA ZETKIN

The German Socialist Women's Movement

1909

In 1907 the Social-Democratic Party of Germany [SDP] embraced 29,458 women members, in 1908 they numbered 62,257. . . . One hundred and fifty lecture and study circles for women have been established. . . . Socialist propaganda amongst the workers' wives and women wage-earners has been carried on by many hundred public meetings, in which women comrades addressed more particularly working-class women. . . .

The women's office works now in conjunction with the Party's Executive. . . . They are to make a vigorous propaganda that the wage-earning women shall in large numbers exercise the franchise to the administrative bodies of the State Sick-Insurance, the only kind of franchise women possess in Germany. The women comrades were further engaged to form local committees for the protection of children. . . . Besides this, Socialist women were reminded to found and improve protective committees for women workers, and collect their grievances on illegal and pernicious conditions of labor, forwarding them to the factory inspector.

Besides their activity in that line, the Socialist women have continued their propaganda in favor of the full political emancipation of their sex. The struggle for universal suffrage . . . was a struggle for adult suffrage for both sexes, vindicated in meetings and leaflets. . . . The work of our trade unions to enlighten, train, and organize wage-earning women is not smaller nor less important than what

the S.D.P. has done to induce women to join in political struggles of the working class. . . .

The most prominent feature of the Socialist women's movement in Germany is its clearness and revolutionary spirit as to Socialist theories and principles. The women who head it are fully conscious that the social fate of their sex is indissolubly connected with the general evolution of society. . . . The integral human emancipation of all women depends in consequence on the social emancipation of labor; that can only be realized by the class-war of the exploited majority. Therefore, our Socialist women oppose strongly the bourgeois women righters' credo that the women of all classes must gather into an unpolitical, neutral movement striving exclusively for women's rights. In theory and practice they maintain the conviction that the class antagonisms are much more powerful, effective, and decisive than the social antagonisms between the sexes. . . . [T]hus the working-class women will [only] win their full emancipation . . . in the class war of all the exploited, without difference of sex, against all who exploit, without difference of sex. That does not mean at all that they undervalue the importance of the political emancipation of the female sex. On the contrary, they employ much more energy than the German women-righters to conquer the suffrage. But the vote is, according to their views, not the last word and term of their aspirations, but only a weapon—a means in struggle for a revolutionary aim—the Socialistic order.

The Socialist women's movement in Germany . . . strives to help change the world by awakening the consciousness and the will of working-class women to join in performing the most Titanic deed that history will know: the emancipation of labor by the laboring class themselves.

Source: Clara Zetkin, *The German Socialist Women's Movement* (1909; Marxists Internet Archive, 2007), http://www.marxists.org /archive/zetkin/1909/10/09.htm.

Source 17.4
Lenin and Russian Socialism

By the late nineteenth century, most West European socialist parties were operating in a more or less democratic environment in which they could organize legally, contest elections, and serve in parliament. Some of them, following Eduard Bernstein, had largely abandoned any thoughts of revolution in favor of a peaceful and democratic path to socialism. For others, this amounted to a betrayal of the Marxist vision. This was particularly the case for Vladimir Ilyich Ulyanov, better known as Lenin, then a prominent figure in the small Russian Social Democratic Labor Party, established in 1898. Lenin was particularly hostile to what he called "economism" or "trade-unionism," which focused on immediate reforms such as higher wages, shorter hours, and better working conditions. He was operating in a still-autocratic Russian state, where neither political parties nor trade unions were legal and where no national parliament or elections allowed for the expression of popular grievances.

In a famous pamphlet titled *What Is to Be Done?* (1902), Lenin addressed many of these issues, well before he became the leader of the world's first successful socialist revolution in 1917.

■ What were Lenin's objections to economism?

■ What kind of party organization did he favor?

■ Why did Lenin believe that workers were unlikely to come to a revolutionary consciousness on their own? What was necessary to move them in that direction?

■ Was Lenin more faithful to the views of Marx himself than the revisionists and economists were?

■ In what ways did Lenin's views reflect the specific conditions of Russia?

LENIN
What Is to Be Done?
1902

The history of all countries shows that the working class, exclusively by its own effort, is able to develop only trade union consciousness, i.e., it may itself realize the necessity for combining in unions, for fighting against the employers, and for striving to compel the government to pass necessary labor legislation, etc. The theory of socialism, however, grew out of the philosophic, historical, and economic theories that were elaborated by the educated representatives of the propertied classes, the intellectuals. . . . [I]n Russia . . . it arose as a natural and inevitable outcome of the development of ideas among the revolutionary socialist intelligentsia.

It is only natural that a Social Democrat, who conceives the political struggle as being identical with the "economic struggle against the employers and the government," should conceive of an "organization of revolutionaries" as being more or less identical with an "organization of workers." . . .

[O]n questions of organization and politics, the Economists are forever lapsing from Social Democracy into trade unionism. The political struggle carried on by the Social Democrats is far more extensive and complex than the economic struggle the workers carry on against the employers and the government. Similarly . . . the organization of a revolutionary Social Democratic Party must inevitably *differ* from the organizations of the workers designed for the latter struggle. A workers' organization . . . must be as wide as possible; and . . . it must be as public as conditions will allow. . . . On the other hand, the organizations of revolutionaries must consist first and foremost of people whose profession is that of a revolutionary. . . . Such an organization must of necessity be not too extensive and as secret as possible. . . .

I assert:

1. that no movement can be durable without a stable organization of leaders to maintain continuity;

2. that the more widely the masses are spontaneously drawn into the struggle and form the basis of the movement and participate in it, the more necessary is it to have such an organization. . . .
3. that the organization must consist chiefly of persons engaged in revolutionary activities as a profession;
4. that in a country with an autocratic government, the more we restrict the membership of this organization to persons who are engaged in revolutionary activities as a profession and who have been professionally trained in the art of combating the political police, the more difficult will it be to catch the organization. . . .

The centralization of the more secret functions in an organization of revolutionaries will not diminish, but rather increase the extent and the quality of the activity of a large number of other organizations intended for wide membership. . . . [I]n order to "serve" the mass movement we must have people who will devote themselves exclusively to Social Democratic activities, and that such people must *train* themselves patiently and steadfastly to be professional revolutionaries. . . .

Let no active worker take offense at these frank remarks, for as far as insufficient training is concerned, I apply them first and foremost to myself. I used to work in a circle that set itself great and all-embracing tasks; and every member of that circle suffered to the point of torture from the realization that we were proving ourselves to be amateurs at a moment in history when we might have been able to say, paraphrasing a well-known epigram: "Give us an organization of revolutionaries, and we shall overturn the whole of Russia!"

Source: V. I. Lenin, *What Is to Be Done?* (Pamphlet, 1902; Marxists Internet Archive, 1999), https://www.marxists.org/archive/lenin/works/1901/witbd/index.htm.

Voices of European Socialism

1. **Comparing socialisms:** While the various strands of Marxist socialism in nineteenth-century Europe shared some common views and values, it was also a sharply divided movement. How would you describe those commonalities as well as the divisions and controversies?

2. **Connecting socialist thinking with the Atlantic revolutions:** To what extent did socialist thinking reflect the concerns of the Atlantic revolutions explored in Chapter 16? In what ways did it diverge from those earlier revolutionary movements?

3. **Considering the appeal of Marxism:** These documents were written by intellectuals within the socialist movement. In what ways might their ideas have appealed to ordinary workers?

4. **Considering responses to socialism:** With which of the variant forms of socialism might Marx himself have been most and least sympathetic? Which of them do you think would have had the most appeal in the United States? How might a manager or owner of an industrial enterprise respond to these ideas?

CHAPTER 18

Colonial Encounters in Asia, Africa, and Oceania

1750–1950

In mid-1967, I (Robert Strayer) was on summer break from a teaching assignment with the Peace Corps in Ethiopia and was traveling with some friends in neighboring Kenya, just four years after that country had gained its independence from British colonial rule. The bus we were riding on broke down, and I found myself hitchhiking across Kenya, heading for Uganda. Soon I was picked up by a friendly Englishman, one of Kenya's many European settlers who had stayed on after independence. At one point, he pulled off the road to show me a lovely view of Kenya's famous Rift Valley, and we were approached by a group of boys selling baskets and other tourist items. They spoke to us in good English, but my British companion replied to them in Swahili. He later explained that Europeans generally did not speak English with the "natives." I was puzzled, but reluctant to inquire further.

Several years later, while conducting research about British missionaries in Kenya in the early twentieth century, I found a clue about the origins of this man's reluctance to speak his own language with Kenyans. It came in a letter from a missionary in which the writer argued against the teaching of English to Africans. Among his reasons were "the danger in which such a course would place our white women and girls" and "the danger of organizing against the government and Europeans."[1] Here, clearly displayed, was the European colonial insistence on maintaining distance and distinction between whites and blacks, for both sexual and political reasons. Such monitoring of racial boundaries was a central feature of many nineteenth- and

---

The Imperial Durbar of 1903 To mark the coronation of British monarch Edward VII and his installation as the Emperor of India, colonial authorities in India mounted an elaborate assembly, or durbar. The durbar was intended to showcase the splendor of the British Empire, and its pageantry included sporting events; a state ball; a huge display of Indian arts, crafts, and jewels; and an enormous parade in which a long line of British officials and Indian princes passed by on bejeweled elephants.

early twentieth-century colonial societies and, in the case of my new British acquaintance, a practice that persisted even after the colonial era had ended.

For many millions of Africans, Asians, and Pacific Islanders, colonial rule—by the British, French, Germans, Italians, Belgians, Portuguese, Russians, or Americans—was the major new element in their historical experience during the long nineteenth century (1750–1914). Of course, no single colonial experience characterized this vast region. Much depended on the cultures and prior history of various colonized people. Policies of the colonial powers sometimes differed sharply and changed over time. Men and women experienced the colonial era differently, as did traditional elites, Western-educated groups, artisans, peasant farmers, and migrant laborers. Furthermore, the varied actions and reactions of such people, despite their oppression and exploitation, shaped the colonial experience, perhaps as much as the policies, practices, and intentions of their temporary European rulers. All of them—colonizers and colonized alike—were caught up in the flood of change that accompanied this new burst of European imperialism.

SEEKING THE MAIN POINT

In what ways did colonial rule transform the societies that it encompassed?

Industry and Empire

Behind much of Europe's nineteenth-century expansion lay the massive fact of its Industrial Revolution, a process that gave rise to new economic needs, many of which found solutions abroad. The enormous productivity of industrial technology and Europe's growing affluence now created the need for extensive raw materials and agricultural products: wheat from the American Midwest and southern Russia; meat from Argentina; bananas from Central America; rubber from Brazil; cocoa and palm oil from West Africa; tea, copra, and coconut oil from Ceylon; gold and diamonds from South Africa; gutta-percha, a natural latex used to insulate underwater telegraph lines, from Southeast Asia. This demand radically changed patterns of economic and social life in the countries of their origin.

■ **Change**
In what ways did the Industrial Revolution shape the character of nineteenth-century European imperialism?

Furthermore, Europe needed to sell its own products. One of the peculiarities of industrial capitalism was that it periodically produced more manufactured goods than its own people could afford to buy. By 1840, for example, Britain was exporting 60 percent of its cotton-cloth production, annually sending 200 million yards to Europe, 300 million yards to Latin America, and 145 million yards to India. This last figure is particularly significant because for centuries Europe had offered little that Asian societies were willing to buy. Part of European and American fascination with China during the nineteenth and twentieth centuries lay in the enormous market potential represented by its huge population.

Much the same could be said for capital, for European investors often found it more profitable to invest their money abroad than at home. Between 1910 and

A MAP OF TIME

1750s	Beginnings of British takeover of India
1788	Initial British settlement of Australia
1798	Napoleon's invasion of Egypt
1830	French invasion of Algeria
1840s	Beginning of major British settlement in New Zealand
1857–1858	Indian Rebellion
1858–1893	French conquest of Indochina
1869	Opening of Suez Canal
1875–1900	Scramble for Africa
1898	United States acquires the Philippines from Spain and annexes Hawaii
1899–1902	Boer War in South Africa
1901–1910	Completion of Dutch conquest of Indonesia
1904–1905	Maji Maji rebellion in East Africa
1910	Japan annexes Korea
Twentieth century	Spread of Christianity in non-Muslim Africa
1920s–1947	Gandhi's leadership of Indian National Congress

1913, Britain was sending about half of its savings overseas as foreign investment. In 1914, it had some 3.7 billion pounds sterling invested abroad, about equally divided between Europe, North America, and Australia on the one hand and Asia, Africa, and Latin America on the other.

Wealthy Europeans also saw social benefits to foreign markets, which served to keep Europe's factories humming and its workers employed. The English imperialist Cecil Rhodes confided his fears to a friend in the late nineteenth century:

Yesterday I attended a meeting of the unemployed in London and having listened to the wild speeches which were nothing more than a scream for bread, I returned home convinced more than ever of the importance of imperialism. . . . In order to save the 40 million inhabitants of the United Kingdom from a murderous civil war, the colonial politicians must open up new areas to absorb the excess population and create new markets for the products of the mines and factories. . . . The British Empire is a matter of bread and butter. If you wish to avoid civil war, then you must become an imperialist.[2]

THE DEVILFISH IN EGYPTIAN WATERS.

An American View of British Imperialism
In this American cartoon dating to 1882, the British Empire is portrayed as an octopus whose tentacles are already attached to many countries, while one tentacle is about to grasp yet another colony, Egypt.

Thus imperialism promised to solve the class conflicts of an industrializing society while avoiding revolution or the serious redistribution of wealth.

But what made imperialism so broadly popular in Europe, especially in the last quarter of the nineteenth century, was the growth of mass nationalism. By 1871, the unification of Italy and Germany made Europe's already-competitive international relations even more so, and much of this rivalry spilled over into the struggle for colonies or economic concessions in Asia, Africa, and Pacific Oceania. Colonies and spheres of influence abroad became symbols of "Great Power" status for a nation, and their acquisition was a matter of urgency, even if they possessed little immediate economic value. After 1875, it seemed to matter, even to ordinary people, whether some remote corner of Africa or some obscure Pacific island was in British, French, or German hands. Imperialism, in short, appealed on economic and social grounds to the wealthy or ambitious, seemed politically and strategically necessary in the game of international power politics, and was emotionally satisfying to almost everyone. This was a potent mix!

If the industrial era made overseas expansion more desirable or even urgent, it also provided new means for achieving those goals. Steam-driven ships, moving through the new Suez Canal, completed in 1869, allowed Europeans to reach distant Asian, African, and Pacific ports more quickly and predictably and to penetrate interior rivers as well. The underwater telegraph made possible almost instant communication with far-flung outposts of empire. The discovery of quinine to prevent malaria greatly reduced European death rates in the tropics. Breech-loading rifles and machine guns vastly widened the military gap between Europeans and everyone else.

Industrialization also occasioned a marked change in the way Europeans perceived themselves and others. In earlier centuries, Europeans had defined others largely in religious terms. "They" were heathen; "we" were Christian. Even as they held on to this sense of religious superiority, Europeans nonetheless adopted many of the ideas and techniques of more advanced societies. They held many aspects of Chinese and Indian civilization in high regard; they freely mixed and mingled with

Asian and African elites and often married their women; some even saw more technologically simple peoples as "noble savages."

With the advent of the industrial age, however, Europeans developed a secular arrogance that fused with or in some cases replaced their notions of religious superiority. They had, after all, unlocked the secrets of nature, created a society of unprecedented wealth, and used both to produce unsurpassed military power. These became the criteria by which Europeans judged both themselves and the rest of the world.

■ Change
What contributed to changing European views of Asians and Africans in the nineteenth century?

By such standards, it is not surprising that their opinions of other cultures dropped sharply. The Chinese, who had been highly praised in the eighteenth century, were reduced in the nineteenth century to the image of "John Chinaman"—weak, cunning, obstinately conservative, and, in large numbers, a distinct threat, represented by the "yellow peril" in late nineteenth-century European thinking. African societies, which had been regarded even in the slave-trade era as nations, and their leaders, who had been regarded as kings, were demoted in nineteenth-century European eyes to the status of tribes led by chiefs as a means of emphasizing their "primitive" qualities.

Peoples of Pacific Oceania and elsewhere could be regarded as "big children," who lived "closer to nature" than their civilized counterparts and correspondingly distant from the high culture with which Europeans congratulated themselves. Upon visiting Tahiti in 1768, the French explorer Bougainville concluded: "I thought I was walking in the Garden of Eden."[3] Such views could be mobilized to criticize the artificiality and materialism of modern European life, but they could also serve to justify the conquest of people who were, apparently, doing little to improve what nature had granted them. Writing in 1854, a European settler in Australia declared: "The question comes to this; which has the better right—the savage, born in a country, which he runs over but can scarcely be said to occupy . . . or the civilized man, who comes to introduce into this . . . unproductive country, the industry which supports life?"[4]

Increasingly, Europeans viewed the culture and achievements of Asian and African peoples through the prism of a new kind of racism, expressed now in terms of modern science. Although physical differences had often been a basis of fear or dislike, in the nineteenth century Europeans increasingly used the prestige and apparatus of science to support their

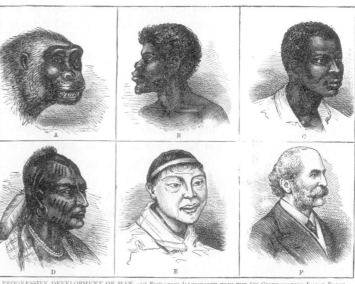

PROGRESSIVE DEVELOPMENT OF MAN.—(a) EVOLUTION ILLUSTRATED WITH THE SIX CORRESPONDING LIVING FORMS.

European Racial Images
This nineteenth-century chart, depicting the "Progressive Development of Man" from apes to modern Europeans, reflected the racial categories that were so prominent at the time. It also highlights the influence of Darwin's evolutionary ideas as they were applied to varieties of human beings. (The Granger Collection, NYC—All rights reserved)

racial preferences and prejudices. Phrenologists, craniologists, and sometimes physicians used allegedly scientific methods and numerous instruments to classify the
size and shape of human skulls and concluded, not surprisingly, that those of whites
were larger and therefore more advanced. Nineteenth-century biologists, who
classified the varieties of plants and animals, applied these notions of rank to varieties of human beings as well. The result was a hierarchy of races, with the whites
on top and the less developed "child races" beneath them. Race, in this view,
determined human intelligence, moral development, and destiny. "Race is everything," declared the British anatomist Robert Knox in 1850. "Civilization depends
on it."[5] Furthermore, as the germ theory of disease took hold in nineteenth-
century Europe, it was accompanied by fears that contact with "inferiors" threatened the health and even the biological future of more advanced or "superior"
peoples.

These ideas influenced how Europeans viewed their own global expansion.
Almost everyone saw it as inevitable, a natural outgrowth of a superior civilization.
For many, though, this viewpoint was tempered with a genuine, if condescending,
sense of responsibility to the "weaker races" that Europe was fated to dominate.
"Superior races have a right, because they have a duty," declared the French politician Jules Ferry in 1883. "They have the duty to civilize the inferior races."[6] That
"civilizing mission" included bringing Christianity to the heathen, good government to disordered lands, work discipline and production for the market to "lazy
natives," a measure of education to the ignorant and illiterate, clothing to the
naked, and health care to the sick, all while suppressing "native customs" that ran
counter to Western ways of living. In European thinking, this was "progress" and
"civilization."

A harsher side to the ideology of imperialism derived from an effort to apply,
or perhaps misapply, the evolutionary thinking of Charles Darwin to an understanding of human societies. The key concept of this "social Darwinism," though
not necessarily shared by Darwin himself, was "the survival of the fittest," suggesting that European dominance inevitably involved the displacement or destruction
of backward peoples or "unfit" races. Referring to native peoples of Australia, a
European bishop declared:

> Everyone who knows a little about aboriginal races is aware that those races
> which are of a low type mentally and who are at the same time weak in con-
> stitution rapidly die out when their country comes to be occupied by a differ-
> ent race much more rigorous, robust, and pushing than themselves.[7]

Such views made imperialism, war, and aggression seem both natural and progressive, for they were predicated on the notion that weeding out "weaker" peoples of
the world would allow the "stronger" to flourish. These were some of the ideas
with which industrializing and increasingly powerful Europeans confronted the
peoples of Asia and Africa in the nineteenth century.

A Second Wave of European Conquests

If the sixteenth- and seventeenth-century takeover of the Americas represented the first phase of European colonial conquests, the century and a half between 1750 and 1914 was a second and quite distinct round of that larger process. Now it was focused in Asia, Africa, and Oceania rather than in the Western Hemisphere. And it featured a number of new players—Germany, Italy, Belgium, the United States, and Japan—who were not at all involved in the earlier phase, while the Spanish and Portuguese now had only minor roles. In general, Europeans preferred informal control, which operated through economic penetration and occasional military intervention but without a wholesale colonial takeover. Such a course was cheaper and less likely to provoke wars. But where rivalry with other European states made it impossible or where local governments were unable or unwilling to cooperate, Europeans proved more than willing to undertake the expense and risk of conquest and outright colonial rule.

The construction of these new European empires in the Afro-Asian world, like empires everywhere, involved military force or the threat of it. Initially, the European military advantage lay in organization, drill and practice, and command structure. Increasingly in the nineteenth century, the Europeans also possessed overwhelming advantages in firepower, deriving from the recently invented repeating rifles and machine guns. A much-quoted jingle by the English writer Hilaire Belloc summed up the situation:

> Whatever happens we have got
> The Maxim gun [an automatic machine gun] and they have not.

Nonetheless, Europeans had to fight, often long and hard, to create their new empires, as countless wars of conquest attest. In the end, though, they prevailed almost everywhere, largely against adversaries who did not have Maxim guns or in some cases any guns at all. Thus were African, Asian, and Oceanic peoples of all kinds incorporated within one or another of the European empires. Gathering and hunting bands in Australia, agricultural village societies or chiefdoms on Pacific islands and in parts of Africa, pastoralists of the Sahara and Central Asia, residents of states large and small, and virtually everyone in the large and complex civilizations of India and Southeast Asia—all of them alike lost the political sovereignty and freedom of action they had previously exercised. For some, such as Hindus governed by the Muslim Mughal Empire, it was an exchange of one set of foreign rulers for another. But now all were subjects of a European colonial state.

The passage to colonial status occurred in various ways. For the peoples of India and Indonesia, colonial conquest grew out of earlier interaction with European trading firms. Particularly in India, the British East India Company, rather than the British government directly, played the leading role in the colonial takeover of South Asia. The fragmentation of the Mughal Empire and the absence of any overall

■ Comparison

In what different ways was colonial rule established in various parts of Africa and Asia?

sense of cultural or political unity both invited and facilitated European penetration. A similar situation of many small and rival states assisted the Dutch acquisition of Indonesia. However, neither the British nor the Dutch had a clear-cut plan for conquest. Rather, it evolved slowly as local authorities and European traders made and unmade a variety of alliances over roughly a century in India (1750–1850). In Indonesia, a few areas held out until the early twentieth century (see Map 18.1).

For most of Africa, mainland Southeast Asia, and the Pacific islands, colonial conquest came later, in the second half of the nineteenth century, and rather more abruptly and deliberately than in India or Indonesia. The "scramble for Africa," for example, pitted half a dozen European powers against one another as they partitioned the entire continent among themselves in only about twenty-five years (1875–1900). (See Working with Evidence: The Scramble for Africa, page 825, for various perspectives on the "scramble.") European leaders themselves were surprised by the intensity of their rivalries and the speed with which they acquired huge territories, about which they knew very little (see Map 18.2).

That process involved endless but peaceful negotiations among the competing Great Powers about "who got what" and extensive and bloody military action, sometimes lasting decades, to make their control effective on the ground. It took the French sixteen years (1882–1898) to finally conquer the recently created West African empire led by Samori Toure. Among the most difficult to subdue were those decentralized societies without any formal state structure. In such cases, Europeans confronted no central authority with which they could negotiate or that they might decisively defeat. It was a matter of village-by-village conquest against extended resistance. As late as 1925, one British official commented on the process as it operated in central Nigeria: "I shall of course go on walloping them until they surrender. It's a rather piteous sight watching a village being knocked to pieces and I wish there was some other way, but unfortunately there isn't."[8] Another very difficult situation for the British lay in South Africa, where they were initially defeated by a Zulu army in 1879 at the Battle of Isandlwana. And twenty years later, in what became known as the Boer War (1899–1902), the Boers, white descendants of the earlier Dutch settlers in South Africa, fought bitterly for three years before succumbing to British forces. Perhaps the great disparity in military forces made the final outcome of European victory inevitable, but the conquest of Africa was intensely contested.

Europeans and Americans had been drawn into the world of Pacific Oceania during the eighteenth century through exploration and scientific curiosity, by the missionary impulse for conversion, and by their economic interests in sperm whale oil, coconut oil, guano, mineral nitrates and phosphates, sandalwood, and other products. Primarily in the second half of the nineteenth century, these entanglements morphed into competitive annexations as Britain, France, the Netherlands, Germany, and the United States, now joined by Australia, claimed control of all the islands of Oceania. Chile too, in search of valuable guano and nitrates, entered the fray and gained a number of coastal islands as well as Rapa Nui (Easter Island), the easternmost island of Polynesia.

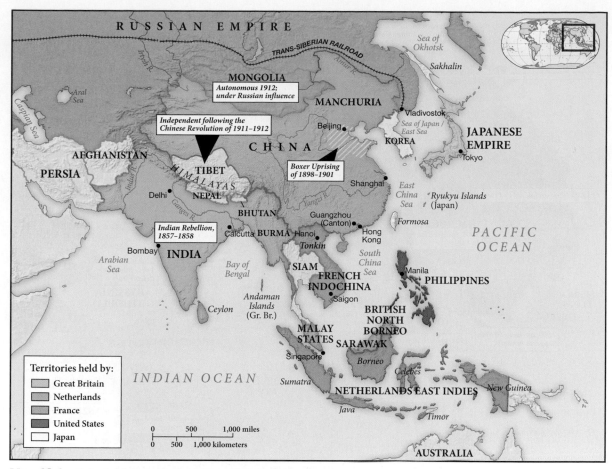

Map 18.1   Colonial Asia in the Early Twentieth Century

By the early twentieth century, several of the great population centers of Asia had come under the colonial control of Britain, the Netherlands, France, the United States, or Japan.

The colonization of the South Pacific territories of Australia and New Zealand, both of which were taken over by the British during the nineteenth century, was more similar to the earlier colonization of North America than to contemporary patterns of Asian and African conquest. In both places, conquest was accompanied by large-scale European settlement and diseases that reduced native numbers by 75 percent or more by 1900. Like Canada and the United States, these became settler colonies, "neo-European" societies in the Pacific. Aboriginal Australians constituted only about 2.4 percent of their country's population in the early twenty-first century, and the indigenous Maori were a minority of about 15 percent in New Zealand. In other previously isolated regions as well—Polynesia, Amazonia, Siberia— disease took a terrible toll on peoples who lacked immunities to European pathogens. For example, in Polynesia the population of Hawaii declined from around 142,000 in 1823 to only 39,000 in 1896, while in Rapa Nui the number of residents dropped

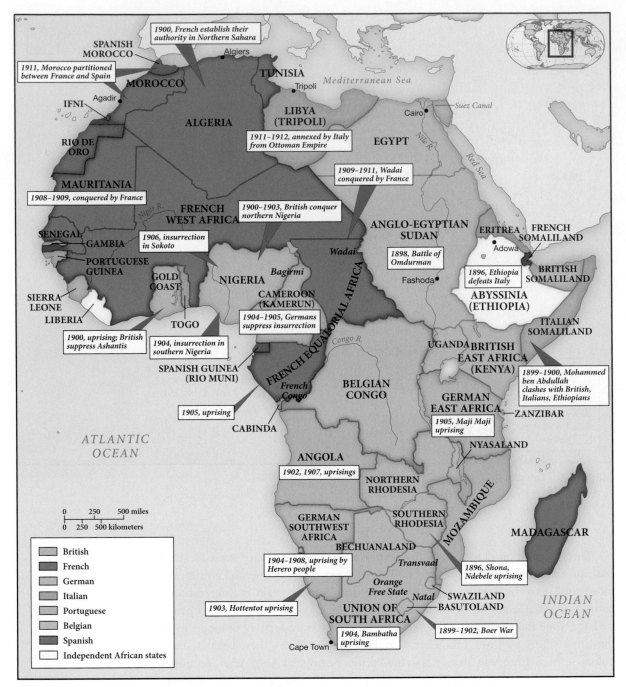

Map 18.2   Conquest and Resistance in Colonial Africa

By the early twentieth century, the map of Africa reflected the outcome of the "scramble for Africa," a conquest that was heavily resisted in many places. The boundaries established during that process still provide the political framework for Africa's independent states.

from around 3,000 in 1863 to 111 in 1877. Unlike these remote areas, most of Africa and Asia shared with Europe a broadly similar disease environment and so were less susceptible to the pathogens of the conquerors.

Elsewhere other variations on the theme of imperial conquest unfolded. The westward expansion of the United States, for example, overwhelmed Native American populations and involved the country in an imperialist war with Mexico. Seeking territory for white settlement, the United States practiced a policy of removing, sometimes almost exterminating, Indian peoples. On the "reservations" to which Indians were confined and in boarding schools to which many of their children were removed, reformers sought to "civilize" the remaining Native Americans, eradicating tribal life and culture, under the slogan "Kill the Indian and Save the Man."

Japan's takeover of Taiwan and Korea bore marked similarities to European actions, as that East Asian nation joined the imperialist club. Russian penetration of Central Asia brought additional millions under European control as the Russian Empire continued its earlier territorial expansion. Filipinos acquired new colonial rulers when the United States took over from Spain following the Spanish-American War of 1898. Some 13,000 freed U.S. slaves, seeking greater freedom than was possible at home, migrated to West Africa, where they became, ironically, a colonizing elite in the land they named Liberia. Ethiopia and Siam (Thailand) were notable for avoiding the colonization to which their neighbors succumbed. Those countries' military and diplomatic skills, their willingness to make modest concessions to the Europeans, and the rivalries of the imperialists all contributed to these exceptions to the rule of colonial takeover in East Africa and Southeast Asia. Ethiopia, in fact, considerably expanded its own empire, even as it defeated Italy at the famous Battle of Adowa in 1896. (See Zooming In: The Battle of Adowa in Chapter 19, page 850, for an account of Ethiopia's defeat of Italian forces.)

These broad patterns of colonial conquest dissolved into thousands of separate encounters as the target societies of Western empire builders were confronted with decisions about how to respond to encroaching European power in the context of their local circumstances. Many initially sought to enlist Europeans in their own internal struggles for power or in their external rivalries with neighboring states or peoples. As pressures mounted and European demands escalated, some tried to play off imperial powers against one another, while others resorted to military action. Many societies were sharply divided between those who wanted to fight and those who believed that resistance was futile. After extended resistance against French aggression, the nineteenth-century Vietnamese emperor Tu Duc argued with those who wanted the struggle to go on:

> Do you really wish to confront such a power with a pack of [our] cowardly soldiers? It would be like mounting an elephant's head or caressing a tiger's tail. . . . With what you presently have, do you really expect to dissolve the enemy's rifles into air or chase his battleships into hell?[9]

Still others negotiated, attempting to preserve as much independence and power as possible. The rulers of the East African kingdom of Buganda, for example, saw opportunity in the British presence and negotiated an arrangement that substantially enlarged their state and personally benefited the kingdom's elite class.

Under European Rule

In many places and for many people, incorporation into European colonial empires was a traumatic experience. Especially for small-scale societies, the loss of life, homes, cattle, crops, and land was devastating. In 1902, a British soldier in East Africa described what happened in a single village: "Every soul was either shot or bayoneted. . . . We burned all the huts and razed the banana plantations to the ground."[10]

For the Vietnamese elite, schooled for centuries in Chinese-style Confucian thinking, conquest meant that the natural harmonies of life had been badly disrupted; it was a time when "water flowed uphill." Nguyen Khuyen (1835–1909), a senior Vietnamese official, retired to his ancestral village to farm and write poetry after the French conquest. In his poems he expressed his anguish at the passing of the world he had known:

> Fine wine but no good friends,
> So I buy none though I have the money.
> A poem comes to mind, but I choose not to write it down.
> If it were written, to whom would I give it?
> The spare bed hangs upon the wall in cold indifference.
> I pluck the lute, but it just doesn't sound right.[11]

Many others also withdrew into private life, feigning illness when asked to serve in public office under the French.

Cooperation and Rebellion

Although violence was a prominent feature of colonial life both during conquest and after, various groups and many individuals willingly cooperated with colonial authorities to their own advantage. Many men found employment, status, and security in European-led armed forces. The shortage and expense of European administrators and the difficulties of communicating across cultural boundaries made it necessary for colonial rulers to rely heavily on a range of local intermediaries. Thus Indian princes, Muslim emirs, and African rulers, often from elite or governing families, found it possible to retain much of their earlier status and many of their privileges while gaining considerable wealth by exercising authority, legally and otherwise, at the local level. For example, in French West Africa, an area eight times the size of France and with a population of about 15 million in the late 1930s, the colonial state consisted of just 385 French administrators and more than 50,000

African "chiefs." Thus colonial rule rested on and reinforced the most conservative segments of colonized societies.

Both colonial governments and private missionary organizations had an interest in promoting a measure of European education. From this process arose a small Western-educated class, whose members served the colonial state, European businesses, and Christian missions as teachers, clerks, translators, and lower-level administrators. A few received higher education abroad and returned home as lawyers, doctors, engineers, or journalists. As colonial governments and business enterprises became more sophisticated, Europeans increasingly depended on the Western-educated class at the expense of the more traditional elites.

If colonial rule enlisted the willing cooperation of some, it provoked the bitter opposition of many others. Thus periodic rebellions, both large and small, erupted in colonial regimes everywhere. The most famous among them was the Indian Rebellion of 1857–1858, which was triggered by the introduction into the colony's military forces of a new cartridge smeared with animal fat from cows and pigs. Because Hindus venerated cows and Muslims regarded pigs as unclean, both groups viewed the innovation as a plot to render them defiled and to convert them to Christianity. Behind this incident were many groups of people with a whole series of grievances generated by the British colonial presence: local rulers who had lost power; landlords deprived of their estates or their rent; peasants overtaxed and exploited by urban moneylenders and landlords alike; unemployed weavers displaced by machine-manufactured textiles; and religious leaders outraged by missionary preaching. A mutiny among Indian troops in Bengal triggered the rebellion, which soon spread to other regions of the colony and other social groups. Soon much of India was aflame. Some rebel leaders presented their cause as an effort to revive an almost-vanished Mughal Empire and thereby attracted support from those with strong resentments against the British. Although it was crushed in 1858, the rebellion greatly widened the racial divide in colonial India and eroded British tolerance for those they viewed as "nigger natives" who had betrayed their trust. Fear of provoking another rebellion made the British more conservative and cautious about deliberately trying to change Indian society. Moreover, the rebellion convinced the British government to assume direct control over India, ending the era of British East India Company rule in the subcontinent.

Colonial Empires with a Difference

At one level, European colonial empires were but the latest in a very long line of imperial creations, all of which had enlisted cooperation and experienced resistance from their subject peoples, but the nineteenth-century European version of empire was distinctive in several remarkable ways. One was the prominence of race in distinguishing rulers and ruled, as the high tide of "scientific racism" in Europe coincided with the acquisition of Asian and African colonies. In East Africa, for

■ **Explanation**
Why might subject people choose to cooperate with the colonial regime? What might prompt them to violent rebellion or resistance?

example, white men expected to be addressed as *bwana* (Swahili for "master"), whereas Europeans regularly called African men "boy." Education for colonial subjects was both limited and skewed toward practical subjects rather than scientific and literary studies, which were widely regarded as inappropriate for the "primitive mind" of "natives." Particularly affected by European racism were those whose Western education and aspirations most clearly threatened the racial divide. Europeans were exceedingly reluctant to allow even the most highly educated Asians and Africans to enter the higher ranks of the colonial civil service. A proposal in 1883 to allow Indian judges to hear cases involving whites provoked outrage and massive demonstrations among European inhabitants of India.

■ **Comparison**

What was distinctive about European colonial empires of the nineteenth century?

In those colonies that had a large European settler population, the pattern of racial separation was much more pronounced than in places such as Nigeria, which had few permanently settled whites. The most extreme case was South Africa, where a large European population and the widespread use of African labor in mines and industries brought blacks and whites into closer and more prolonged contact than elsewhere. The racial fears that were aroused resulted in extraordinary efforts to establish race as a legal, not just a customary, feature of South African society. This racial system provided for separate "homelands," educational systems, residential areas, public facilities, and much more. In what was eventually known as apartheid, South African whites attempted the impossible task of creating an industrializing economy based on cheap African labor, while limiting African social and political integration in every conceivable fashion.

A further distinctive feature of nineteenth-century European empires lay in the extent to which colonial states were able to penetrate the societies they governed. Centralized tax-collecting bureaucracies, new means of communication and transportation, imposed changes in landholding patterns, integration of colonial economies into a global network of exchange, public health and sanitation measures, and the activities of missionaries—all of this touched the daily lives of many people far more deeply than in earlier empires. Not only were Europeans foreign rulers, but they also bore the seeds of a very different way of life, which grew out of their own modern transformation.

Nineteenth-century European colonizers were extraordinary as well in their penchant for counting and classifying their subject people. With the assistance of anthropologists and missionaries, colonial governments collected a vast amount of information, sought to organize it "scientifically," and used it to manage the unfamiliar, complex, varied, and fluctuating societies that they governed. In India, the British found in classical texts and Brahmin ideology an idealized description of the caste system, based on the notion of four ranked and unchanging varnas, which made it possible to bring order out of the immense complexity and variety of caste as it actually operated. Thus the British invented or appropriated a Brahmin version of "traditional India" that they favored and sought to preserve, while scorning as "non-Indian" the new elite who had been educated in European schools and were enthusiastic about Western ways of life. This view of India reflected the great influence of Brahmins on British thinking and clearly served the interests of this Indian upper class.

Likewise, within African colonies Europeans identified, and sometimes invented, distinct tribes, each with its own clearly defined territory, language, customs, and chief. The notion of a "tribal Africa" expressed the Western view that African societies were primitive or backward, representing an earlier stage of human development. It was also a convenient idea, for it reduced the enormous complexity and fluidity of African societies to a more manageable state and thus made colonial administration easier.

Gender too entered into the efforts of Europeans to define both themselves and their newly acquired subject peoples. European colonizers—mostly male—took pride in their "active masculinity" while defining the "conquered races" as soft, passive, and feminine. Indian Bengali men, wrote a British official in 1892, "are disqualified for political enfranchisement by the possession of essentially feminine characteristics."[12] By linking the inferiority of women with that of people of color, gender ideology and race prejudice were joined in support of colonial rule. But the intersection of race, gender, and empire was complex and varied. European men in the colonies often viewed their own women as the bearers and emblems of civilization, "upholding the moral dignity of the white community" amid the darkness of inferior peoples.[13] As such, European women had to be above reproach in sexual matters, protected against the alleged lust of native men by their separation from local African or Asian societies. Furthermore, certain colonized people, such as the Sikhs and Gurkhas in India, the Kamba in Kenya, and the Hausa in Nigeria, were gendered as masculine or "martial races" and targeted for recruitment into British military or police forces.

Finally, the colonial policies of Europeans contradicted their own core values and their practices at home to an unusual degree. While nineteenth-century Britain and France were becoming more democratic, their colonies were essentially dictatorships, offering perhaps order and stability, but certainly not democratic government, because few colonial subjects were participating citizens. Empire, of course, was wholly at odds with European notions of national independence, and ranked racial classifications went against the grain of both Christian and Enlightenment ideas of human equality. Furthermore, many Europeans were distinctly reluctant to encourage within their colonies the kind of modernization—urban growth, industrialization, individual values, religious skepticism—that was sweeping their own societies. They feared that this kind of social change, often vilified as "detribalization," would encourage unrest and challenge colonial rule. As a model for social development, they much preferred "traditional" rural society, with its established authorities and social hierarchies, though shorn of abuses such as slavery and *sati* (widow burning). Such contradictions between what Europeans embraced at home and what they practiced in the colonies became increasingly apparent to many Asians and Africans and played a major role in undermining the foundations of colonial rule in the twentieth century.

Ways of Working: Comparing Colonial Economies

Colonial rule affected the lives of its subject people in many ways, but the most pronounced change was in their ways of working. The colonial state—with its power to tax, to seize land for European enterprises, to compel labor, and to build railroads, ports, and roads—played an important role in these transformations. Even more powerful was the growing integration of colonized societies into a world economy that increasingly demanded their gold, diamonds, copper, tin, rubber, coffee, cotton, sugar, cocoa, and many other products. But the economic transformations born of these twin pressures were far from uniform. Various groups— migrant workers and cash-crop farmers, plantation laborers and domestic servants, urban elites and day laborers, men and women—experienced the colonial era differently as their daily working lives underwent profound changes.

To various degrees, old ways of working were eroded almost everywhere in the colonial world. Subsistence farming, in which peasant families produced largely for their own needs, diminished as growing numbers directed at least some of their energies to working for wages or selling what they produced for a cash income. That money was both necessary to pay taxes and school fees and useful for buying the various products—such as machine-produced textiles, bicycles, and kerosene— that the industrial economies of Europe sent their way. As in Europe, artisans suffered greatly when cheaper machine-manufactured merchandise displaced their own handmade goods. A flood of inexpensive textiles from Britain's new factories ruined the livelihood of tens of thousands of India's handloom weavers. Iron smelting largely disappeared in Africa, and occupations such as blacksmithing and tanning lost ground. Furthermore, Asian and African merchants, who had earlier handled the trade between their countries and the wider world, were squeezed out by well-financed European commercial firms.

Economies of Coercion: Forced Labor and the Power of the State

Many of the new ways of working that emerged during the colonial era derived directly from the demands of the colonial state. The most obvious was required and unpaid labor on public projects, such as building railroads, constructing government buildings, and transporting goods. In French Africa, all "natives" were legally obligated for "statute labor" of ten to twelve days a year, a practice that lasted through 1946. It was much resented. A resident of British West Africa, interviewed in 1996, bitterly recalled this feature of colonial life: "They [British officials] were rude, and they made us work for them a lot. They came to the village and just rounded us up and made us go off and clear the road or carry loads on our heads."[14]

The most infamous cruelties of forced labor occurred during the early twentieth century in the Congo Free State, then governed personally by King Leopold II of Belgium. Private companies in the Congo, operating under the authority of the

■ **Connection**
How did the policies of colonial states change the economic lives of their subjects?

state, forced villagers to collect rubber, which was much in demand for bicycle and automobile tires, with a reign of terror and abuse that cost millions of lives. One refugee from these horrors described the process:

> We were always in the forest to find the rubber vines, to go without food, and our women had to give up cultivating the fields and gardens. Then we starved. . . . We begged the white man to leave us alone, saying we could get no more rubber, but the white men and their soldiers said "Go. You are only beasts yourselves. . . ." When we failed and our rubber was short, the soldiers came to our towns and killed us. Many were shot, some had their ears cut off; others were tied up with ropes round their necks and taken away.[15]

Eventually such outrages were widely publicized in Europe, where they created a scandal, forcing the Belgian government to take control of the Congo in 1908 and ending Leopold's reign of terror.

Meanwhile, however, this late nineteenth- and early twentieth-century commerce in rubber and ivory, made possible by the massive use of forced labor in both the Congo and the neighboring German colony of Cameroon, laid the foundations for

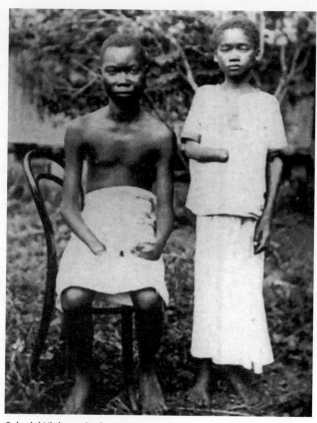

Colonial Violence in the Congo
These young boys with severed hands were among the victims of a brutal regime of forced labor undertaken in the Congo during the late nineteenth and early twentieth centuries. Such mutilation was punishment for their villages' inability to supply the required amount of wild rubber. (Universal History Archive/ Universal Images Group/UIG via Getty Images)

the modern AIDS epidemic. It was in southeastern Cameroon that the virus causing AIDS made the jump from chimpanzees to humans, and it was in the crowded and hectic Congolese city of Kinshasa, with its new networks of sexual interaction, where that disease found its initial breakout point, becoming an epidemic. "Without the scramble [for Africa]," concludes a recent account, "it's hard to see how HIV could have made it out of southeastern Cameroon to eventually kill tens of millions of people."[16]

A variation on the theme of forced labor took shape in the so-called cultivation system of the Netherlands East Indies (Indonesia) during the nineteenth century. Peasants were required to cultivate 20 percent or more of their land in cash crops such as sugar or coffee to meet their tax obligation to the state. Sold to government contractors at fixed and low prices, those crops, when resold on the world market, proved highly profitable for Dutch traders and shippers as well as for the Dutch state and its citizens. According to one scholar, the cultivation system "performed a miracle for the Dutch economy," enabling it to avoid taxing its own people and providing capital for its Industrial Revolution.[17] It also enriched and strengthened the position of those "traditional authorities" who enforced the system, often by using lashings and various tortures, on behalf of the Dutch. For the peasants of Java, however, it meant a double burden of obligations to the colonial state as well as to local lords. Many became indebted to moneylenders when they could not meet those obligations. Those demands, coupled with the loss of land and labor now excluded from food production, contributed to a wave of famines during the mid-nineteenth century in which hundreds of thousands perished.

On occasion, the forced cultivation of cash crops was successfully resisted. In German East Africa, for example, colonial authorities in the late nineteenth century imposed the cultivation of cotton, which seriously interfered with production of local food crops. Here is how one man remembered the experience:

> The cultivation of cotton was done by turns. Every village was allotted days on which to cultivate. . . . After arriving you all suffered very greatly. Your back and your buttocks were whipped and there was no rising up once you stooped to dig. . . . And yet he [the German] wanted us to pay him tax. Were we not human beings?[18]

Such conditions prompted a massive rebellion in 1904–1905, known as Maji Maji, and persuaded the Germans to end the forced growing of cotton. In Mozambique, where the Portuguese likewise brutally enforced cotton cultivation, a combination of peasant sabotage, the planting of unauthorized crops, and the smuggling of cotton across the border to more profitable markets ensured that Portugal never achieved its goal of becoming self-sufficient in cotton production. Thus the actions of colonized peoples could alter or frustrate the plans of the colonizers.

Economies of Cash-Crop Agriculture: The Pull of the Market

Many Asian and African peoples had produced quite willingly for an international market long before they were enclosed within colonial societies. They offered for trade items such as peanuts and palm oil in West Africa, cotton in Egypt, spices in Indonesia, and pepper and textiles in India. In some places, colonial rule created conditions that facilitated and increased cash-crop production to the advantage of local farmers. British authorities in Burma, for example, acted to encourage rice production among small farmers by ending an earlier prohibition on rice exports, providing irrigation and transportation facilities, and enacting land tenure laws that facilitated private ownership of small farms. Under these conditions, the population of the Irrawaddy Delta boomed, migrants from Upper Burma and India poured into the region, and rice exports soared. Local small farmers benefited considerably because they were now able to own their own land, build substantial houses, and buy imported goods. For several decades in the late nineteenth century, standards of living improved sharply, and huge increases in rice production fed millions of people in other parts of Asia and elsewhere. It was a very different situation from that of peasants forced to grow crops that seriously interfered with their food production.

But that kind of colonial development, practiced also in the Mekong River delta of French-ruled Vietnam, had important environmental consequences. It involved the destruction of mangrove forests and swamplands along with the fish and shellfish that supplemented local diets. New dikes and irrigation channels inhibited the depositing of silt from upstream and thus depleted soils in the deltas of these major river systems. And, unknown to anyone at the time, this kind of agriculture generates large amounts of methane gas, a major contributor to global warming.

■ **Change**
How did cash-crop agriculture transform the lives of colonized peoples?

Profitable cash-crop farming also developed in the southern Gold Coast (present-day Ghana), a British territory in West Africa. Unlike in Burma, it was African farmers themselves who took the initiative to develop export agriculture. Planting cacao trees in huge quantities, they became the world's leading supplier of cocoa, used to make chocolate, by 1911. Cacao was an attractive crop because, unlike cotton, it was compatible with the continued production of foods and did not require so much labor time. In the early twentieth century, it brought a new prosperity to many local farmers. "A hybrid society was taking shape," wrote one scholar, "partly peasant, in that most members farmed their own land with family labor . . . and partly capitalist, in that a minority employed wage laborers, produced chiefly for the market, and reinvested profits."[19]

That success brought new problems in its wake. A shortage of labor fostered the employment of former slaves as dependent and exploited workers and also generated tensions between the sexes when some men married women for their labor power but refused to support them adequately. Moreover, the labor shortage brought a huge influx of migrants from the drier interior parts of West Africa, generating ethnic and class tensions. Furthermore, many colonies came to specialize in one or two cash crops, creating an unhealthy dependence when world market prices dropped. Thus African and Asian farmers were increasingly subject to the uncertain rhythms of the international marketplace as well as to those of weather and climate.

Economies of Wage Labor: Migration for Work

Yet another new way of working in colonial societies involved wage labor in some European enterprise. Driven by the need for money, by the loss of land adequate to support their families, or sometimes by the orders of colonial authorities, millions of colonial subjects across Asia, Africa, and Oceania sought employment in European-owned plantations, mines, construction projects, and homes. Often this required migration to distant work sites, many of them overseas. In this process, colonized migrants were joined by millions of Chinese, Japanese, and others, who lived in more independent states. Together they generated vast streams of migration

Economic Change in the Colonial World
These workers on a Ceylon tea plantation in the early twentieth century are moving sacks of tea into a drying house in preparation for export. The Lipton label on the bags is a reminder of the role of large-scale foreign investment in the economic transformations of the colonial era. (© Hulton-Deutsch Collection/Corbis)

that paralleled and at least equaled in numbers the huge movement of Europeans during the nineteenth and early twentieth centuries (see Chapter 17, pages 755–57). For Europeans, Asians, and Africans alike, the globalizing world of the colonial era was one of people in motion. (See the Snapshot on long-distance migration, opposite.)

The African segment of this migratory stream moved in several directions. For much of the nineteenth century, the Atlantic slave trade continued, funneling well over 3 million additional people to the Americas, mostly to Brazil. As the slave trade diminished and colonial rule took shape in Africa, internal migration mounted within or among particular colonies. More than in Asia, Africans migrated to European farms or plantations because they had lost their own land. In the settler colonies of Africa — Algeria, Kenya, Southern Rhodesia (Zimbabwe), and South Africa, for example — permanent European communities, with the help of colonial governments, obtained huge tracts of land, much of which had previously been home to African societies. A 1913 law in South Africa legally defined 88 percent of the land as belonging to whites, who were then about 20 percent of the population. Much of highland Kenya, an enormously rich agricultural region that was home to the Gikuyu and Kamba peoples, was taken over by some 4,000 white farmers. In

SNAPSHOT Long-Distance Migration in an Age of Empire, 1846–1940

The age of empire was also an age of global migration. Beyond the three major patterns of long-distance migration shown here, shorter migrations within particular regions or colonies set millions more into motion.[20]

Origins	Destination	Numbers
Europe	Americas	55–58 million
India, southern China	Southeast Asia, Indian Ocean rim, South Pacific	48–52 million
Northeast Asia, Russia	Manchuria, Siberia, Central Asia, Japan	46–51 million

such places, some Africans stayed on as "squatters," working for the new landowners as the price of remaining on what had been their own land. Others were displaced to "native reserves," limited areas that could not support their growing populations, and many were thus forced to work for wages on European farms. Most notably in South Africa, such reserved areas, known as Bantustans, became greatly overcrowded: soil fertility declined, hillsides were cleared, forests shrank, and erosion scarred the land. This kind of ecological degradation was among the environmental consequences of African wage labor on European farms and estates.

The gold and diamond mines of South Africa likewise set in motion a huge pattern of labor migration that encompassed all of Africa south of the Belgian Congo. With skilled and highly paid work reserved for white miners, Africans worked largely as unskilled laborers at a fraction of the wages paid to whites. Furthermore, they were recruited on short-term contracts, lived in all-male prison-like barracks that were often surrounded by barbed wire, and were forced to return home periodically to prevent them from establishing a permanent family life near the mines.

Asians too were in motion and in large numbers. Some 29 million Indians and 19 million Chinese migrated variously to Southeast Asia, the South Pacific, East and South Africa, the Caribbean islands, or the lands around the Indian Ocean basin. All across Southeast Asia in the later nineteenth and early twentieth centuries, huge plantations sprouted, which were financed from Europe and which grew sugarcane, rubber, tea, tobacco, sisal (used for making rope), and more. Impoverished workers by the hundreds of thousands came from great distances (India, China, Java) to these plantations, where they were subject to strict control, often housed in barracks, and paid poorly, with women receiving 50 to 75 percent of a man's wage. Disease was common, and death rates were at least double that of the colony as a whole. In 1927 in southern Vietnam alone, one in twenty plantation workers died. British colonial authorities in India facilitated the migration of millions of Indians to work sites elsewhere in the British Empire—Trinidad, Jamaica, Fiji, Malaysia, Ceylon, South Africa, Kenya, and Uganda, for example—with some working as indentured laborers, receiving free passage and enough money to survive in return for five to seven years of heavy labor. Others operated as independent merchants. Particularly in the Caribbean region, Indian migration rose as the end of slavery created a need for additional labor. Since the vast majority of these Asian migrants were male, it altered gender ratios in the islands and in their countries of origin, where women faced increased workloads.

■ Change
What kinds of wage labor were available in the colonies? Why might people take part in it? How did doing so change their lives?

Mines were another source of wage labor for many Asians. In the British-ruled Malay States (Malaysia), tin mining accelerated greatly in the late nineteenth century, and by 1895 that colony produced some 55 percent of the world's tin. Operated initially by Chinese and later by European entrepreneurs, Malaysian tin mines drew many millions of impoverished Chinese workers on strictly controlled three-year contracts. Appalling living conditions, disease, and accidents generated extraordinarily high death rates.

Beyond Southeast Asia, Chinese migrants moved north to Manchuria in substantial numbers, encouraged by a Chinese government eager to prevent Russian encroachment in the area. The gold rushes of Australia and California also attracted hundreds of thousands of Chinese, who often found themselves subject to sharp discrimination from local people, including recently arrived European migrants. For example, Dennis Kearney, who led a California anti-immigrant labor organization with the slogan "The Chinese must go," was himself an Irish-born immigrant. Canada, Australia, New Zealand, and the United States all enacted measures to restrict or end Chinese immigration in the late nineteenth century.

A further destination of African and Asian migrants lay in the rapidly swelling cities of the colonial world—Lagos, Nairobi, Cairo, Calcutta, Rangoon, Batavia, Singapore, Saigon. Racially segregated, often unsanitary, and greatly overcrowded, these cities nonetheless were seen as meccas of opportunity for people all across the social spectrum. Traditional elites, absentee landlords, and wealthy Chinese businessmen occupied the top rungs of Southeast Asian cities. Western-educated people everywhere found opportunities as teachers, doctors, and professional specialists, but more often as clerks in European business offices and government bureaucracies. Skilled workers on the railways or in the ports represented a working-class elite, while a few labored in the factories that processed agricultural goods or manufactured basic products such as beer, cigarettes, cement, and furniture. Far more numerous were the construction workers, rickshaw drivers, food sellers, domestic servants, prostitutes, and others who made up the urban poor of colonial cities. In 1955, a British investigating commission described life in Nairobi, the capital of Kenya, one of Britain's richest colonies:

> The wages of the majority of African workers are too low to enable them to obtain accommodation which is adequate to any standard. The high cost of housing relative to wages is in itself a cause of overcrowding, because housing is shared to lighten the cost. This, with the high cost of food in towns, makes family life impossible for the majority.[21]

Thus, after more than half a century of colonial rule, British authorities themselves acknowledged that normal family life in the colony's major urban center proved out of reach for the vast majority. It was quite an admission.

Women and the Colonial Economy: Examples from Africa

If economic life in European empires varied greatly from place to place, even within the same colony, it also offered a different combination of opportunities and hardships to women than it did to men, as the experience of colonial Africa shows.[22] In precolonial Africa, women were almost everywhere active farmers, with responsibility for planting, weeding, and harvesting in addition to food preparation and child care. Men cleared the land, built houses, herded the cattle, and in some cases assisted with field work. Within this division of labor, women were expected to feed their own families and were usually allocated their own fields for that purpose. Many were also involved in local trading activity. Though clearly subordinate to men, African women nevertheless had a measure of economic autonomy.

As the demands of the colonial economy grew, women's lives increasingly diverged from those of men. In colonies where cash-crop agriculture was dominant, men often withdrew from subsistence production in favor of more lucrative export crops. Among the Ewe people of southern Ghana, men almost completely dominated the highly profitable cacao farming, whereas women assumed near total responsibility for domestic food production. In neighboring Ivory Coast, women had traditionally grown cotton for their families' clothing, but when that crop acquired a cash value, men insisted that cotton grown for export be produced on their own personal fields. Thus men acted to control the most profitable aspects of cash-crop agriculture and in doing so greatly increased the subsistence workload of women. One study from Cameroon estimated that women's working hours increased from forty-six per week in precolonial times to more than seventy by 1934.

Further increasing women's workload and differentiating their lives from those of men was labor migration. As growing numbers of men sought employment in the cities, on settler farms, or in the mines, their wives were left to manage the domestic economy almost alone. In many cases, women also had to supply food to men in the cities to compensate for very low urban wages. They often took over such traditionally male tasks as breaking the ground for planting, milking the cows, and supervising the herds, in addition to their normal responsibilities. In South Africa, where the demands of the European economy were particularly heavy, some 40 to 50 percent of able-bodied adult men were absent from the rural areas, and women headed 60 percent of households. In Botswana, which supplied much male labor to South Africa, married couples by the 1930s rarely lived together for more than two months at a time. Increasingly, men and women lived in different worlds, with one focused on the cities and working for wages and the other on village life and subsistence agriculture. (See Zooming In: Wanjiku of Kenya, page 810).

■ **Change**
How were the lives of African women altered by colonial economies?

Wanjiku of Kenya

Born in 1910 among the Gikuyu people of East Africa, Wanjiku witnessed almost the entire twentieth century.[23] Her life encompassed the dramatic intrusion of British colonialism, the coming of Christianity, the Mau Mau rebellion against European rule, the achievement of independence for Kenya in 1963, and the challenges of modernization in the decades that followed.

Women of Kenya forming a Home Guard.

photo: © Bettmann/Corbis

And yet, the first thirty years or more of Wanjiku's life were shaped far more by the customary patterns of rural Gikuyu culture than by the transformations of colonial rule. She grew up in her father's compound, where her mother, three other wives, and more than a dozen children also lived. As a child, she began contributing to the household—fetching water, firewood, and vegetables—even as she learned the stories, riddles, and proverbs of Gikuyu folklore. At age fourteen, she had her ears pierced, thus achieving a "new stage of maturity."

Far more important, however, was her "circumcision," a procedure that involved the cutting of her genitals and the excision of the clitoris. For Wanjiku, as for virtually all Gikuyu girls, this procedure was a prerequisite for becoming "a grown-up person" and eligible for marriage. Described as "buying maturity with pain," the operation was, as Wanjiku later recalled, "like being slaughtered." Circumcision also marked Wanjiku's entry into an age-set, a group of girls who had undergone this initiation into womanhood together. As adults, they worked together in the fields, provided help and gifts at the birth of children, and protected one another from sexual abuse by men.

Now Wanjiku was also able to attend the evening dances where young men and women mingled. There she met her first husband, Wamai, who initiated the long process of negotiation between families and the payment of numerous goats and cows to the bride's father. She said of her marriage, "[It] was a big change—learning about sex and my husband's habits." Tragedy struck, however, when both her husband and her first child died. A few years later, Wanjiku married Kamau, the younger brother of her first husband, with whom she had three sons. Her second marriage, unlike the first, was accompanied by a church service and a wedding ring,

Women coped with these difficult circumstances in a number of ways. Many sought closer relations with their families of birth rather than with their absent husbands' families, as would otherwise have been expected. Among the Luo of Kenya, women introduced laborsaving crops, adopted new farm implements, and earned some money as traders. In the cities, they established a variety of self-help associations, including those for prostitutes and for brewers of beer.

The colonial economy sometimes provided a measure of opportunity for enterprising women, particularly in small-scale trade and marketing. In some parts of West Africa, women came to dominate this sector of the economy by selling food-

signs of encroaching Western culture. Both marriages were apparently relatively satisfying, and she reported with pride that neither man mistreated or beat her.

During the 1940s and 1950s, the new realities of colonial life began to touch Wanjiku more personally than before. She and Kamau became Christians around 1940, and in 1948 Wanjiku "became saved." "The saved ones," she declared, "do not take tobacco nor drink. And they don't abuse anybody." She then joined a church-based "Mother's Union," vowing "never again to carry out old Gikuyu customs." For Wanjiku, this group became a major source of social support that operated outside of traditional Gikuyu culture.

In 1952, Wanjiku found herself caught up in the Gikuyu-based Mau Mau rebellion against colonial rule. To separate the general population from the Mau Mau "freedom fighters" in the surrounding forests, the colonial government forced most Gikuyu to relocate into compact villages where they were closely and brutally supervised by the Home Guard, local African police appointed by European authorities. Wanjiku and many others were required to dig a large trench around the village to keep the rebels out. "We were like prisoners," Wanjiku reported. "If we started to drag behind working, we were beaten." Caught between the opposing forces of the Home Guard and the Mau Mau fighters, Wanjiku lived in fear. "If you made a mistake with the Home Guard, you would die. If you made a mistake with the Mau Mau, you would die too."

The British crushed the Mau Mau rebellion by 1956, but by 1963 Kenya, like dozens of other African countries, had achieved its independence. Wanjiku remembered the day with exhilaration. "We spent the whole night singing and dancing. We were so happy because we would never be ruled by foreigners again. It also meant the end of the beatings." It was perhaps the high point of Wanjiku's consciousness as a public person and a participant in a new nation.

In the decades following independence, Wanjiku experienced still further changes. She and her husband began to grow tea as a cash crop, an undertaking that had been limited to European farmers for much of the colonial era. Kenya's new government tried to forbid female circumcision, and, as young people were increasingly drawn to the larger cities, older rural social patterns broke down. Boys and girls of different age-sets mingled far more freely than before. Educated young people felt superior and sometimes behaved disrespectfully to illiterate elders such as Wanjiku.

By the 1990s, Wanjiku was an old woman afflicted with arthritis and much-diminished vision. She saw herself less as a Kenyan than as a Gikuyu. No longer able to farm, she counseled her children, looked after her grandchildren, and enjoyed recounting her life story to a visiting anthropologist.

Question: How does Wanjiku's life reflect both the continuities and changes of the twentieth century in African history?

stuffs, cloth, and inexpensive imported goods, while men or foreign firms controlled the more profitable wholesale and import-export trade. Such opportunities sometimes gave women considerable economic autonomy. By the 1930s, for example, Nupe women in northern Nigeria had gained sufficient wealth as itinerant traders that they were contributing more to the family income than their husbands and frequently lent money to them. Among some Igbo groups in southern Nigeria, men were responsible for growing the prestigious yams, but women's crops—especially cassava—came to have a cash value during the colonial era, and women were entitled to keep the profits from selling them. "What is man? I have my own money" was a popular saying that expressed the growing economic independence of such women.[24]

At the other end of the social scale, women of impoverished rural families, by necessity, often became virtually independent heads of household in the absence of their husbands. Others took advantage of new opportunities in mission schools, towns, and mines to flee the restrictions of rural patriarchy. Such challenges to patriarchal values elicited various responses from men, including increased accusations of witchcraft against women and fears of impotence. Among the Shona in Southern Rhodesia, and no doubt elsewhere, senior African men repeatedly petitioned the colonial authorities for laws and regulations that would criminalize adultery and restrict women's ability to leave their rural villages. The control of women's sexuality and mobility was a common interest of European and African men.

Assessing Colonial Development

Beyond the many and varied changes that transformed the working lives of millions in the colonial world lies the difficult and highly controversial question of the overall economic impact of colonial rule on Asian and African societies. Defenders, both then and now, praise it for jump-starting modern economic growth, but numerous critics cite a record of exploitation and highlight the limitations and unevenness of that growth.

Amid the continuing debates, three things seem reasonably clear. First, colonial rule served, for better or worse, to further the integration of Asian and African economies into a global network of exchange, now centered in Europe. In many places, that process was well under way before conquest imposed foreign rule, and elsewhere it occurred without formal colonial control. Nonetheless, it is apparent that within the colonial world far more land and labor were devoted to production for the global market at the end of the colonial era than at its beginning. Many colonized groups and individuals benefited from their new access to global markets—Burmese rice farmers and West African cocoa farmers, for example. Others were devastated. In India, large-scale wheat exports to Britain continued unchecked—or even increased—despite a major drought and famine that claimed between 6 and 10 million lives in the late 1870s. A colonial government committed to free market principles declined to interfere with those exports or to provide much by way of relief. One senior official declared it "a mistake to spend so much money to save a lot of black fellows."[25]

■ **Change**
Did colonial rule bring "economic progress" in its wake?

Second, Europeans could hardly avoid conveying to the colonies some elements of their own modernizing process. It was in their interests to do so, and many felt duty bound to "improve" the societies they briefly governed. Modern administrative and bureaucratic structures facilitated colonial control; communication and transportation infrastructure (railroads, motorways, ports, telegraphs, postal services) moved products to the world market; schools trained the army of intermediaries on which colonial rule depended; and modest health care provisions fulfilled some of the "civilizing mission" to which many Europeans felt committed. These elements of modernization made an appearance, however inadequately, during the colonial era.

Third, nowhere in the colonial world did a major breakthrough to modern industrial society occur. When India became independent after two centuries of colonial rule by the world's first industrial society, it was still one of the poorest of the world's developing countries. The British may not have created Indian poverty, but neither did they overcome it to any substantial degree. Scholars continue to debate the reasons for that failure: was it the result of deliberate British policies, or was it due to the conditions of Indian society? The nationalist movements that surged across Asia and Africa in the twentieth century had their own answer. To their many millions of participants, colonial rule, whatever its earlier promise, had become an economic dead end, whereas independence represented a grand opening to new and more hopeful possibilities. Paraphrasing a famous teaching of Jesus, Kwame Nkrumah, the first prime minister of an independent Ghana, declared, "Seek ye first the political kingdom, and all these other things [schools, factories, hospitals, for example] will be added unto you."

SUMMING UP SO FAR

In what different ways did the colonial experience reshape the economic lives of Asian and African societies?

Believing and Belonging: Identity and Cultural Change in the Colonial Era

The experience of colonial rule—its racism, its exposure to European culture, its social and economic upheavals—contributed much to cultural change within Asian, African, and Oceanic societies. Coping with these enormous disruptions induced many colonized peoples to alter the ways they thought about themselves and their communities. Cultural identities, of course, are never static, but the transformations of the colonial era catalyzed substantial and quite rapid changes in what people believed and in how they defined the societies to which they belonged. Those transformed identities continued to echo long after European rule had ended.

Education

For an important minority, it was the acquisition of Western education, obtained through missionary or government schools, that generated a new identity. To many European colonizers, education was a means of "uplifting native races," a paternalistic obligation of the superior to the inferior. To previously illiterate people, the knowledge of reading and writing of any kind often suggested an almost magical power. Within the colonial setting, it could mean an escape from some of the most onerous obligations of living under European control, such as forced labor. More positively, it meant access to better-paying positions in government bureaucracies, mission organizations, or business firms and to the exciting imported goods that their salaries could buy. Moreover, education often provided social mobility and elite status within their own communities and an opportunity to achieve, or at least approach, equality with whites in racially defined societies. An African man from colonial Kenya described an encounter he had as a boy in 1938 with a relative who was a teacher in a mission school:

> Aged about 25, he seems to me like a young god with his smart clothes and shoes, his watch, and a beautiful bicycle. I worshipped in particular his bicycle that day and decided that I must somehow get myself one. As he talked with us, it seemed to me that the secret of his riches came from his education, his knowledge of reading and writing, and that it was essential for me to obtain this power.[26]

■ **Change**
What impact did Western education have on colonial societies?

Many such people ardently embraced European culture, dressing in European clothes, speaking French or English, building European-style houses, getting married in long white dresses, and otherwise emulating European ways. Some of the early Western-educated Bengalis from northeastern India boasted about dreaming in English and deliberately ate beef, to the consternation of their elders. In a well-known poem titled "A Prayer for Peace," Léopold Senghor, a highly educated West African writer and political leader, enumerated the many crimes of colonialism and yet confessed, "I have a great weakness for France." Asian and African colonial societies now had a new cultural divide: between the small numbers who had mastered to varying degrees the ways of their rulers and the vast majority who had not. Literate Christians in the East African kingdom of Buganda referred with contempt to their "pagan" neighbors as "those who do not read."

Many among the Western-educated elite saw themselves as a modernizing vanguard, leading the regeneration of their societies in association with colonial authorities. For them, at least initially, the colonial enterprise was full of promise for a better future. The Vietnamese teacher and nationalist Nguyen Thai Hoc, while awaiting execution in 1930 by the French for his revolutionary activities, wrote about his earlier hopes: "At the beginning, I had thought to cooperate with the French in Indochina in order to serve my compatriots, my country, and my people, particularly in the areas of cultural and economic development."[27] Senghor too wrote wistfully about an earlier time when "we could have lived in harmony [with Europeans]."

In nineteenth-century India, Western-educated men organized a variety of reform societies, which drew inspiration from the classic texts of Hinduism while seeking a renewed Indian culture that was free of idolatry, caste restrictions, and other "errors" that had entered Indian life over the centuries. Much of this reform effort centered on improving the status of women. Thus reformers campaigned against *sati*, the ban on remarriage of widows, female infanticide, and child marriages, while advocating women's education and property rights. For a time, some of these Indian reformers saw themselves working in tandem with British colonial authorities. One of them, Keshub Chunder Sen (1838–1884), spoke to his fellow Indians in 1877: "You are bound to be loyal to the British government that came

The Educated Elite
Throughout the Afro-Asian world of the nineteenth century, the European presence generated a small group of people who enthusiastically embraced the culture and lifestyle of Europe. Here King Chulalongkorn of Siam poses with the crown prince and other young students, all of them impeccably garbed in European clothing. (© Hulton-Deutsch Collection/Corbis)

to your rescue, as God's ambassador, when your country was sunk in ignorance and superstition. . . . India in her present fallen condition seems destined to sit at the feet of England for many long years, to learn western art and science."[28] Such fond hopes for the modernization or renewal of Asian and African societies within a colonial framework would be bitterly disappointed. Europeans generally declined to treat their Asian and African subjects—even those with a Western education— as equal partners in the enterprise of renewal. The frequent denigration of their cultures as primitive, backward, uncivilized, or savage certainly rankled, particularly among the well educated. "My people of Africa," wrote the West African intellectual James Aggrey in the 1920s, "we were created in the image of God, but men have made us think that we are chickens, and we still think we are; but we are eagles. Stretch forth your wings and fly."[29] In the long run, the educated classes in colonial societies everywhere found European rule far more of an obstacle to their countries' development than a means of achieving it. Turning decisively against a now-despised foreign imperialism, they led the many struggles for independence that came to fruition in the second half of the twentieth century.

Religion

Religion too provided the basis for new or transformed identities during the colonial era. Most dramatic were those places where widespread conversion to Christianity took place, such as Pacific Oceania and especially non-Muslim Africa. Some 10,000 missionaries had descended on Africa by 1910; by the 1960s, about 50 million Africans, roughly half of the non-Muslim population, claimed a Christian identity. The attractions of the new faith were many. As in the Americas centuries earlier, military defeat shook confidence in the old gods and local practices, fostering openness to new sources of supernatural power that could operate in the wider world now impinging on Oceanic and African societies. Furthermore, Christianity was widely associated with modern education, and, especially in Africa, mission schools were the primary providers of Western education. The young, the poor, and many women—all of them oppressed groups in many African societies— found new opportunities and greater freedom in some association with missions. Moreover, the spread of the Christian message was less the work of European missionaries than of those many thousands of African teachers, catechists, and pastors who brought the new faith to remote villages as well as the local communities that begged for a teacher and supplied the labor and materials to build a small church or school. In Oceania, local authorities, such as those in Fiji, Tonga, and Hawaii, sought to strengthen their position by associating with Christian missionaries, widely regarded as linked to the growing influence of European or American power in the region. In many of these small island societies, mission Christianity with its schools, clinics, political counsel, and new social conventions provided a measure of social cohesion for peoples devastated by disease and other disruptions that accompanied Western incursions.

■ **Change**

What were the attractions of Christianity within some colonial societies?

But missionary teaching and practice also generated conflict and opposition, particularly when they touched on gender roles. A wide range of issues focusing on the lives of women proved challenging for missionaries and spawned opposition from converts or potential converts. Female nudity offended Western notions of modesty. Polygyny contradicted Christian monogamy, though such prescriptions sat uneasily beside Old Testament practices, and the question of what male converts should do with their additional wives was always difficult. Bride wealth made marriage seem "a mere mercantile transaction." Marriages between Christians and non-Christians remained problematic. Sexual activity outside of monogamous marriage often resulted in disciplinary action or expulsion from the church. Missionaries' efforts to enforce Western gender norms were in part responsible for considerable turnover in the ranks of African church members.

Among the more explosive issues that agitated nascent Christian communities in colonial Kenya was that of "female circumcision," the excision of a pubescent

The Missionary Factor
Among the major change agents of the colonial era were the thousands of Christian missionaries who brought not only a new religion but also elements of European medicine, education, gender roles, and culture. Here is an assembly at a mission school for girls in New Guinea in the early twentieth century.

girl's clitoris and adjacent genital tissue as a part of initiation rites marking her coming-of-age.[30] To the Gikuyu people, among whom it was widely practiced, it was a prerequisite for adult status and marriage. To missionaries, it was physically damaging to girls and brought "unnecessary attention . . . to the non-spiritual aspects of sex." When missionaries in 1929 sought to enforce a ban on the practice among their African converts, outrage ensued. Thousands abandoned mission schools and churches, but they did not abandon Christianity or modern education. Rather, they created a series of independent schools and churches in which they could practice their new faith and pursue their educational goals without missionary intrusion. Some recalled that the New Testament itself had declared that "circumcision is nothing and uncircumcision is nothing." Accordingly, wrote one angry convert to a local missionary, "Has God spoken to you this time and informed you that those who circumcise will not enter in to God's place? It is better for a European like you to leave off speaking about such things because you can make the Gospel to be evil spoken of." (See Zooming In: Wanjiku, page 810, for the experience of a Gikuyu woman.)

As elsewhere, Christianity in Africa soon became Africanized. Within mission-based churches, many converts continued using protective charms and medicines and consulting local medicine men, all of which caused their missionary mentors to

Vivekananda, a Hindu Monk in America

The modern colonial era is associated with the "westernization" of the peoples of Asia, Africa, and the Middle East. Less frequently noticed has been traffic in the other direction, as Eastern, and especially Indian, religious culture penetrated Europe and the Americas. The Transcendentalist writers of early nineteenth-century New England warmly welcomed the translations of Hindu texts that derived from British scholars in colonial India. At his cabin on Walden Pond, Henry David Thoreau remarked, "In the morning I bathe my intellect in the stupendous . . . philosophy of the Bhagavad Gita . . . in comparison with which our modern world and its literature seem puny and trivial."[31] Since then, many Americans and Europeans have embraced elements of the universal and inclusive Hindu philosophical system known as Vedanta, and far more have practiced the physical and mental disciplines of yoga, both of which derive from ancient India.

A seminal moment in the coming of Indian spirituality to the United States occurred in Chicago during September 1893. The occasion was the World's Parlia-

Swami Vivekananda.

ment of Religions, an interfaith gathering that drew representatives from many of the world's religious traditions. The man who made the most vivid impression at the conference was a handsome thirty-year-old Hindu monk known as Swami Vivekananda. Appearing in an orange robe and a yellow turban and speaking fluent and eloquent English, he had only recently arrived from India, where he had received an excellent European education as well as a deep immersion in Hindu philosophy and practice.

In his initial speech to the parliament on its opening day, Vivekananda began by addressing his audience as "sisters and brothers of America." The intimacy of his greeting alone prompted prolonged applause. "I am proud," he continued, "to belong to a religion which has taught the world both tolerance and universal acceptance. . . . We accept all religions as true." He concluded with a plea that the parliament might mark the end of sectarianism, fanaticism, and persecution "between persons wending their way to the same goal."

photo: Roland and Sabrina Michaud/akg-images

speak frequently of "backsliding." Other converts continued to believe in their old gods and spirits but now deemed them evil and sought their destruction. Furthermore, thousands of separatist movements established a wide array of independent churches, which were thoroughly Christian but under African rather than missionary control and which in many cases incorporated African cultural practices and modes of worship. It was a twentieth-century "African Reformation."

In India, where Christianity made only very modest inroads, leading intellectuals and reformers began to define their region's endlessly varied beliefs, practices, sects, rituals, and philosophies as a more distinct, unified, and separate religion now

In further speeches at the parliament and in subsequent travels around the country, Vivekananda expressed the major themes of his modernized Vedanta outlook: that all human beings possess a divine nature; that awakening to that nature can be pursued through a variety of paths; and that spiritual practice and realization are far more important than dogma or doctrine. He argued that the disciplines of the mind and body that derived from Hindu tradition represented a psychological, experimental, and almost scientific approach to spiritual development and certainly did not require "conversion" to an alien faith. On occasion, he was sharply critical of Christian missionaries for their emphasis on conversion. "The people of India have more than religion enough," he declared. "What they want is bread." He described England as "the most prosperous Christian nation in the world with her foot on the neck of 250 million Asiatics."

Vivekananda emerged from the parliament a sensation and a celebrity, widely acclaimed but also widely criticized. His critique of Christian missionaries offended many. More conservative Christians objected to his assertion of the equality of all religious traditions. "We believe that Christianity is to supplant all other religions," declared the leading organizer of the parliament.

Vivekananda's time in the United States represented India speaking back to the West. After a century of European missionary activity and colonial rule in his country, he was declaring that India could offer spiritual support to a Western world mired in materialism and militarism. He proclaimed, "The whole of the Western world is a volcano which may burst tomorrow. . . . Now is the time to work so that India's spiritual ideas may penetrate deep into the West."[32]

And so he established a number of Vedanta Societies, some of which have persisted to the present day. In exposing Americans to Indian spirituality, Vivekananda's followers did not seek converts, but invited participants to apply Vedanta principles and practices within their own religious traditions. They also spoke about Jesus with great respect and displayed his image along with that of the Buddha and various Hindu sacred figures. In the early twentieth century, these Vedanta centers attracted a modest following among Americans who were disillusioned with the superficiality of modern life as well as with the rigidity of Christian doctrine and the many divisions and conflicts among Christian churches. In the 1960s and later, interest in Eastern religion exploded in the West as hundreds of Indian teachers arrived, many of them bearing the same universal message that Vivekananda had presented in Chicago. The growing numbers of Americans who claim to be "spiritual but not religious" are following in the path of that orange-robed monk.

Question: What accounts for the appeal of Vivekananda's message, and what accounts for opposition to it?

known as Hinduism. It was in part an effort to provide for India a religion wholly equivalent to Christianity, "an accessible tradition and a feeling of historical worth when faced with the humiliation of colonial rule."[33] To Swami Vivekananda (1863–1902), one of nineteenth-century India's most influential religious figures, as well as others active in reform movements, a revived Hinduism, shorn of its distortions, offered a means of uplifting the country's village communities, which were the heart of Indian civilization. In his famous travels to America, Vivekananda focused his attention on the cultivation of an inner life rather than on service and social reform as he did in India. (See Zooming In: Vivekananda, above.)

■ **Change**
How and why did Hinduism emerge as a distinct religious tradition during the colonial era in India?

This new notion of Hinduism provided a cultural foundation for emerging ideas of India as a nation, but it also contributed to a clearer sense of Muslims as a distinct community in India. Before the British takeover, little sense of commonality united the many diverse communities who practiced Islam—urban and rural dwellers; nomads and farmers; artisans, merchants, and state officials. But the British had created separate inheritance laws for all Muslims and others for all Hindus; in their census taking, they counted the numbers of people within these now sharply distinguished groups; and they allotted seats in local councils according to these artificial categories. As some anti-British patriots began to cast India in Hindu terms, the idea of Muslims as a separate community, which was perhaps threatened by the much larger number of Hindus, began to make sense to some who practiced Islam. In the early twentieth century, a young Hindu Bengali schoolboy noticed that "our Muslim school-fellows were beginning to air the fact of their being Muslims rather more consciously than before and with a touch of assertiveness."[34] Here were the beginnings of what became in the twentieth century a profound religious and political division within the South Asian peninsula.

"Race" and "Tribe"

In Africa as well, intellectuals and ordinary people alike forged new ways of belonging as they confronted the upheavals of colonial life. Central to these new identities were notions of race and ethnicity. By the end of the nineteenth century, a number of African thinkers, familiar with Western culture, began to define the idea of an "African identity." Previously, few if any people on the continent had regarded themselves as Africans. Rather, they were members of particular local communities, usually defined by language; some were also Muslims; and still others inhabited some state or empire. Now, however, influenced by the common experience of colonial oppression and by a highly derogatory European racism, well-educated Africans began to think in broader terms, similar to those of Indian reformers who were developing the notion of Hinduism. It was an effort to revive the cultural self-confidence of their people by articulating a larger, common, and respected "African tradition," equivalent to that of Western culture.

■ **Change**
In what ways were "race" and "tribe" new identities in colonial Africa?

This effort took various shapes. One line of argument held that African culture and history in fact possessed the very characteristics that Europeans exalted. Knowing that Europeans valued large empires and complex political systems, African intellectuals pointed with pride to the ancient kingdoms of Ethiopia, Mali, Songhay, and others. C. A. Diop, a French-educated scholar from Senegal, insisted that Egyptian civilization was in fact the work of black Africans. Reversing European assumptions, Diop argued that Western civilization owed much to Egyptian influence and was therefore derived from Africa. Black people, in short, had a history of achievement fully comparable to that of Europe and therefore deserved just as much respect and admiration.

An alternative approach to defining an African identity lay in praising the differences between African and European cultures. The most influential proponent of such views was Edward Blyden (1832–1912), a West African born in the West Indies and educated in the United States who later became a prominent scholar and political official in Liberia. Blyden accepted the assumption that the world's various races were different but argued that each had its own distinctive contribution to make to world civilization. The uniqueness of African culture, Blyden wrote, lay in its communal, cooperative, and egalitarian societies, which contrasted sharply with Europe's highly individualistic, competitive, and class-ridden societies; in its harmonious relationship with nature as opposed to Europe's efforts to dominate and exploit the natural order; and particularly in its profound religious sensibility, which Europeans had lost in centuries of attention to material gain. Like Vivekananda in India, Blyden argued that Africa had a global mission "to be the spiritual conservatory of the world."[35]

In the twentieth century, such ideas resonated with a broader public. Hundreds of thousands of Africans took part in World War I, during which they encountered other Africans as well as Europeans. Some were able to travel widely. Contact with American black leaders, such as Booker T. Washington, W. E. B. DuBois, and Marcus Garvey, as well as various West Indian intellectuals further stimulated among a few a sense of belonging to an even larger pan-African world. Such notions underlay the growing nationalist movements that contested colonial rule as the twentieth century unfolded.

For the vast majority, however, the most important new sense of belonging that evolved from the colonial experience was not the notion of "Africa"; rather, it was the idea of "tribe" or, in the language of contemporary scholars, that of ethnic identity. African peoples, of course, had long recognized differences among themselves based on language, kinship, clan, village, or state, but these were seldom clearly defined. Boundaries fluctuated and were hazy; local communities often incorporated a variety of culturally different peoples. The idea of an Africa sharply divided into separate and distinct "tribes" was in fact a European notion that facilitated colonial administration and reflected Europeans' belief in African primitiveness. For example, when the British began to rule the peoples living along the northern side of Lake Tanganyika, in present-day Tanzania, they found a series of communities that were similar to one another in language and customs but that governed themselves separately and certainly had not regarded themselves as a distinct "tribe." It was British attempts to rule them as a single people, first through a "paramount chief" and later through a council of chiefs and elders, that resulted in their being called, collectively, the Nyakyusa. A tribe had been born. By requiring people to identify their tribe on applications for jobs, schools, and identity cards, colonial governments spread the idea of tribe widely within their colonies.

New ethnic identities were not simply imposed by Europeans, for Africans themselves increasingly found ethnic or tribal labels useful. This was especially true in rapidly growing urban areas. Surrounded by a bewildering variety of people and in a setting where competition for jobs, housing, and education was very intense, migrants to the city found it helpful to categorize themselves and others in larger ethnic terms. Thus, in many colonial cities, people who spoke similar languages, shared a common culture, or came from the same general part of the country began to think of themselves as a single people—a new tribe. They organized a rich variety of ethnic or tribal associations to provide mutual assistance while in the cities and to send money back home to build schools or clinics. Migrant workers, far from home and concerned about protecting their rights to land and to their wives and families, found a sense of security in being part of a recognized tribe, with its chiefs, courts, and established authority.

The Igbo people of southeastern Nigeria represent a case in point. Prior to the twentieth century, they were organized in a series of independently governed village groups. Although they spoke related languages, they had no unifying political system and no myth of common ancestry. Occupying a region of unusually dense population, many of these people eagerly seized on Western education and moved in large numbers to the cities and towns of colonial Nigeria. There they gradually discovered what they had in common and how they differed from the other peoples of Nigeria. By the 1940s, they were organizing on a national level and calling on Igbos everywhere to "sink all differences" to achieve "tribal unity, cooperation, and progress of all the Igbos." Fifty years earlier, however, no one had regarded himself or herself as an Igbo. One historian summed up the process of creating African ethnic identities in this way: "Europeans believed Africans belonged to tribes; Africans built tribes to belong to."[36]

REFLECTIONS

Who Makes History?

Winners may write history, but they do not make history, at least not alone. Dominant groups everywhere—slave owners, upper classes, men generally, and certainly colonial rulers—have found their actions constrained and their choices limited by the sheer presence of subordinated people and the ability of those people to act. Europeans who sought to make their countries self-sufficient in cotton by requiring colonized Africans to grow it generally found themselves unable to achieve that goal. Missionaries who tried to impose their own understanding of Christianity in the colonies found their converts often unwilling to accept missionary authority or the cultural framework in which the new religion was presented. In the twentieth century, colonial rulers all across Asia and Africa found that their most highly educated subjects became the leaders of those movements seeking to end colonial rule. Clearly, this was not what they had intended.

In recent decades, historians have been at pains to uncover the ways in which subordinated people—slaves, workers, peasants, women, the colonized—have been able to act in their own interests, even within the most oppressive conditions. This kind of "history from below" found expression in a famous book about American slavery that was subtitled *The World the Slaves Made*. Historians of women's lives have sought to show women not only as victims of patriarchy but also as historical actors in their own right.

Likewise, colonized people in any number of ways actively shaped the history of the colonial era. On occasion, they resisted and rebelled; in various times and places, they embraced, rejected, and transformed a transplanted Christianity; many eagerly sought Western education but later turned it against the colonizers; women both suffered from and creatively coped with the difficulties of colonial life; and everywhere people created new ways of belonging. None of this diminishes the hardships, the enormous inequalities of power, or the exploitation and oppression of the colonial experience. Rather, it suggests that history is often made through the struggle of unequal groups and that the outcome corresponds to no one's intentions.

Perhaps we might let Karl Marx have the last word on this endlessly fascinating topic: "Men make their own history," he wrote, "but they do not make it as they please nor under conditions of their own choosing." In the colonial experience of the nineteenth and early twentieth centuries, both the colonizers and the colonized "made history," but neither was able to do so as they pleased.

Second Thoughts

What's the Significance?

European racism, 790–92
scramble for Africa, 794
Indian Rebellion, 1857–1858, 799
Congo Free State / Leopold II, 802–3
cultivation system, 803–4
cash-crop agriculture, 804–5

Wanjiku, 810–11
Western-educated elite, 813–16
Africanization of Christianity, 816–18
Swami Vivekananda, 818–19
Edward Blyden, 821

Big Picture Questions

1. In what ways did colonial rule rest on violence and coercion, and in what ways did it elicit voluntary cooperation or generate benefits for some people?

2. In what respects were colonized people more than victims of colonial conquest and rule? To what extent could they act in their own interests within the colonial situation?

3. Was colonial rule a transforming, even a revolutionary, experience, or did it serve to freeze or preserve existing social and economic patterns? What evidence can you find to support both sides of this argument?

4. **Looking Back:** How would you compare the colonial experience of Asian and African peoples during the long nineteenth century to the earlier colonial experience in the Americas?

Next Steps: For Further Study

A. Adu Boahen, *African Perspectives on Colonialism* (1987). An examination of the colonial experience by a prominent African scholar.

Alice Conklin and Ian Fletcher, *European Imperialism, 1830–1930* (1999). A collection of both classical reflections on empire and examples of modern scholarship.

Scott B. Cook, *Colonial Encounters in the Age of High Imperialism* (1996). Seven case studies of the late nineteenth-century colonial experience.

Adam Hochschild, *King Leopold's Ghost* (1999). A journalist's evocative account of the horrors of early colonial rule in the Congo.

Douglas Peers, *India under Colonial Rule* (2006). A concise and up-to-date exploration of colonial India.

Bonnie Smith, ed., *Imperialism* (2000). A fine collection of documents, pictures, and commentary on nineteenth- and twentieth-century empires.

Margaret Strobel, *Gender, Sex, and Empire* (1994). A brief account of late twentieth-century historical thinking about colonial life and gender.

Bridging World History, Unit 21: "Colonial Identities," http://www.learner.org/courses/worldhistory/unit_main_21.html. Provides text, primary and secondary sources, images, and video to explore the question of identity during the colonial era via clothing.

"The Magnificent African Cake," http://www.youtube.com/watch?v=irDWdqOvjVA. A thoughtful documentary on the colonial experience in Africa, from the series *Africa: A Voyage of Discovery* by the well-known historian Basil Davidson.

The Scramble for Africa

The centerpiece of Europe's global expansion during the nineteenth century occurred in the so-called scramble for Africa, during which a half dozen or so European countries divided up almost the entire continent into colonial territories (see Map 18.2, page 796). The "scramble" took place very quickly (between roughly 1875 and 1900), surprising even the European leaders who initiated it, as well as the many African societies that suddenly found themselves confronting highly aggressive and well-armed foreign forces. Each of the rival powers—Britain, France, Germany, Belgium, Portugal, Spain, and Italy—sought to get a piece of a continent that many believed held the promise of great wealth. Given Europe's wars over colonial possessions in the early modern era, it is remarkable that the entire partition of Africa took place without any direct military conflict between the competing imperial countries. But in establishing their control on the ground, Europeans faced widespread African resistance, making the scramble an extremely bloody process of military conquest. The images that follow illustrate some of the distinctive features of the scramble for Africa as well as the differing ways in which it was perceived and represented.

As the Atlantic slave trade diminished over the course of the nineteenth century, Europeans began to look at Africa in new ways—as a source of raw materials, as an opportunity for investment, as a market for industrial products, as a field for exploration, and as an opportunity to spread Christianity. But it was not until the last quarter of the nineteenth century that Europeans showed much interest in actually acquiring territory and ruling large populations in Africa. Source 18.1, from a late nineteenth-century French board game, illustrates the widespread interest in the growing missionary enterprise in Africa as well as in the celebrated adventures of the intrepid explorers who penetrated the dangerous interior of the continent. This game, featuring the travels of David Livingstone and Henry Stanley, enabled ordinary Europeans to participate in exciting events in distant lands. Livingstone (1813–1873) was a British missionary and explorer of Central Africa whose work in exposing the horrors of the Arab slave trade gave him an almost mythic status among Europeans. Stanley (1841–1904), a British journalist and explorer, gained lasting fame by finding Livingstone, long out of touch with his homeland, deep in the African interior.

Private Collection/Archives Charmet/Bridgeman Images

Source 18.1 Prelude to the Scramble

- What images of Africa are suggested by this board game? Notice carefully the landscape, the animals, and the activities in which people are engaged.

- How does the game depict European activities in Africa?

- What might be the meaning of the large sun arising at the top of the image?

- What nineteenth-century realities are missing from this portrayal of Africa?

As the scramble for Africa got under way in earnest in the 1880s and 1890s, it became a highly competitive process. French designs on Africa, for example, focused on obtaining an uninterrupted east-west link from the Red Sea to the Atlantic Ocean. But the British, entrenched in Egypt and in control of the

Suez Canal, were determined that no major European power should be allowed to control the headwaters of the Nile on which Egypt depended. Those conflicting goals came to a head in 1898, when British forces moving south from Egypt met a French expedition moving northeast from the Atlantic coast of what is now Gabon. That encounter took place along the Nile River at Fashoda in present-day Sudan, threatening war between France and Great Britain. In the end, negotiations persuaded the French to withdraw.

Source 18.2, the cover of a French publication, shows the commander of the French expedition, Jean-Baptiste Marchand, who gained heroic stature in leading his troops on an epic journey across much of Africa for more than eighteen months.

- How did the artist portray Marchand? How might a British artist have portrayed him?

- What does this source suggest about the role of violence in the scramble for Africa?

- Notice the large number of African troops among Marchand's forces. What does that suggest about the process of colonial conquest? Why might Africans have agreed to fight on behalf of a European colonial power?

- How do you understand the fallen soldier lying between Marchand's legs?

Nowhere did the vaulting ambition of European colonial powers in Africa emerge more clearly than in the British vision of a north-south corridor of British territories along the eastern side of the continent stretching from South Africa to Egypt, or in the popular phrase of the time, "from the Cape to Cairo." A part of this vision was an unbroken railroad line running the entire length of the African continent. That grand idea was popularized by Cecil Rhodes, a British-born businessman and politician who made a fortune in South African diamonds and became an enthusiastic advocate of British imperialism. Source 18.3, an 1892 cartoon published in the popular British magazine of satire and humor named *Punch*, shows Rhodes bestriding the continent with one foot in Egypt and the other in South Africa.

- Is this famous image criticizing or celebrating Rhodes's Cape-to-Cairo dream? Explain your reasoning.

- What does this source suggest about the purpose of the Cape-to-Cairo scheme and the means to achieve it? Notice the telegraph wire in Rhodes's hands and the rifle on his shoulder.

- How did the artist portray the African continent? What does the absence of African people suggest? How does this image compare to Source 18.1?

Source 18.2 Conquest and Competition

THE RHODES COLOSSUS
STRIDING FROM CAPE TOWN TO CAIRO.

Source 18.3 From the Cape to Cairo

■ Scholars have sometimes argued that the scramble for Africa was driven less by concrete economic interests than by emotional, even romantic, notions of national grandeur and personal adventure. In what ways do Sources 18.2 and 18.3 support or challenge this interpretation?

In North Africa, the primary European rivalries for territory involved Great Britain, which occupied Egypt in 1881; France, which came to control Tunisia, Algeria, and Morocco; and Italy, which seized Libya in 1912. Source 18.4 portrays two of these rivals—Britain, on the right, and France, on the left—toasting one another while standing on piles of skeletons. This image appeared in the Cairo *Punch*, a British-owned magazine in Egypt published in Arabic, probably around 1910.

A. H. Zaki/© Corbis

Source 18.4 British and French in North Africa

This image refers specifically to two incidents. On the British side, the cartoon evokes a 1906 quarrel between British soldiers hunting pigeons and local villagers of Denshway that resulted in the death of one of the soldiers. In response, outraged British authorities hanged several people and flogged dozens of others. The following year in Morocco, French civilians building a small railway near the harbor of Casablanca dug up parts of a Muslim cemetery, "churning up piles of bones." When attacks against European laborers followed, killing eight, the French bombarded the Arab quarter of the city, with many casualties—European and Arab alike—in the fighting that ensued. Both incidents stimulated nationalist feelings in these two North African countries.

- What references to the incidents described here can you find in Source 18.4?

- The British and French generally saw themselves as rivals in the scramble for Africa. How are they portrayed here?

- What criticisms of colonial rule does this image contain? While the artist remains unknown, do you think it more likely to have been an Egyptian or a European?

The Scramble for Africa

1. **Distinguishing viewpoints:** From what different perspectives do these sources represent the scramble for Africa? What criticisms of the scramble can you read in them?

2. **Portraying Africans and Europeans:** Both Africans and Europeans are portrayed variously in these images. What differences can you identify?

3. **Using images selectively:** In what ways might sources such as these be most useful to historians seeking to understand the scramble for Africa? For what kinds of questions about the scramble might they have little to offer?

4. **Considering moral visions:** How do these visual sources deal with issues of morality or visions of right and wrong?

The Chinese Cake, from *Le Petit Journal*, 1898, lithograph by Henri Meyer (1844–1899)/Private Collection/Roger-Viollet, Paris, France/Bridgeman Images

CHAPTER 19

Empires in Collision

Europe, the Middle East, and East Asia
1800–1914

"In the 170-plus years since the Opium War of 1840, our great country has weathered untold hardships. . . . Following the Opium War, China gradually became a semi-colonial . . . society, and foreign powers stepped up their aggression against China."[1] Speaking in 2011, Chinese president Hu Jintao thus reminded his listeners of Britain's violent intrusion into China's history in order to sell highly addictive opium to China's people. This conflict marked the beginning of what the Chinese still describe as a "century of humiliation." In Hu Jintao's view, it was only the victory of the Chinese Communist Party that enabled his country to finally escape from that shameful past. Memories of the Opium War remain a central element of China's "patriotic education" for the young, serve as a warning against uncritical admiration of the West, and provide a rejoinder to any Western criticism of China. Some 170 years after that clash between the Chinese and British empires, the Opium War retains an emotional resonance for many Chinese and offers a politically useful tool for the country's government.

China was among the countries that confronted an aggressive and industrializing West while maintaining its formal independence, unlike the colonized areas discussed in Chapter 18. So too did Japan, the Ottoman Empire, Persia (now Iran), Ethiopia, and Siam (now Thailand). Latin America also falls in this category (see Chapter 17, pages 766–72). These states avoided outright incorporation into European colonial empires, retaining some ability to resist European aggression and to reform or transform their

---

Carving Up the Pie of China   In this French cartoon from the late 1890s, the Great Powers of the day (from left to right: Great Britain's Queen Victoria, Germany's Kaiser Wilhelm, Russia's Tsar Nicholas II, a female figure representing France, and the Meiji emperor of Japan) participate in dividing China, while a Chinese figure behind them tries helplessly to stop the partition of his country.

own societies. But they shared with their colonized counterparts the need to deal with four dimensions of the European moment in world history. First, they faced the immense military might and political ambitions of rival European states. Second, they became enmeshed in networks of trade, investment, and sometimes migration that arose from an industrializing and capitalist Europe to generate a new world economy. Third, they were touched by various aspects of traditional European culture, as some among them learned the French, English, or German language; converted to Christianity; or studied European literature and philosophy. Fourth, and finally, they too engaged with the culture of modernity—its scientific rationalism; its technological achievements; its belief in a better future; and its ideas of nationalism, socialism, feminism, and individualism. In those epic encounters, they sometimes resisted, at other times accommodated, and almost always adapted what came from the West. They were active participants in the global drama of nineteenth-century world history, not simply its passive victims or beneficiaries.

Dealing with Europe, however, was not the only item on their agendas. Population growth and peasant rebellion wracked China; internal social and economic changes eroded the stability of Japanese public life; the great empires of the Islamic world shrank or disappeared; rivalry among competing elites troubled Latin American societies; Ethiopia launched its own empire-building process even as it resisted European intrusions. (See Zooming In: 1896: The Battle of Adowa, page 850.)

SEEKING THE MAIN POINT

What differences can you identify in how China, the Ottoman Empire, and Japan experienced Western imperialism and responded to it? How might you account for those differences?

Encounters with an expansive Europe were conditioned everywhere by particular local circumstances. Among those societies that remained independent, albeit sometimes precariously, while coping simultaneously with their internal crises and the threat from the West, this chapter focuses primarily on China, the Ottoman Empire, and Japan. Together with Latin America, they provide a range of experiences, responses, and outcomes and many opportunities for comparison.

Reversal of Fortune: China's Century of Crisis

In 1793, just a decade after King George III of Britain lost his North American colonies, he received yet another rebuff, this time from China. In a famous letter to the British monarch, the Chinese emperor Qianlong (chyan-loong) sharply rejected British requests for a less restricted trading relationship with his country. "Our Celestial Empire possesses all things in prolific abundance," he declared. "There was therefore no need to import the manufactures of outside barbarians." Qianlong's snub simply continued the pattern of the previous several centuries, during which Chinese authorities had strictly controlled and limited the activities of European missionaries and merchants. But by 1912, little more than a century later, China's long-established imperial state had collapsed, and the country had been transformed from a central presence in the global economy to a weak and dependent

A MAP OF TIME

1793	Chinese reject British requests for open trade
1798	Napoleon invades Egypt
1830s	Famine and rebellions in Japan
1838–1842	First Opium War in China
1839–1876	Tanzimat reforms in the Ottoman Empire
1850–1864	Taiping Uprising in China
1853	Admiral Perry arrives in Japan
1856–1858	Second Opium War in China
1868	Meiji Restoration in Japan
1894–1895	Japanese war against China
1896	Ethiopian defeat of Italy preserves Ethiopia's independence
1898–1901	Boxer Uprising in China
1904–1905	Russo-Japanese War
1908	Young Turk takeover in Ottoman Empire
1910	Japan annexes Korea
1911–1912	Chinese revolution; end of Qing dynasty

participant in a European-dominated world system in which Great Britain was the major economic and political player. It was a stunning reversal of fortune for a country that in Chinese eyes was the civilized center of the entire world—in their terms, the Celestial Empire or the Middle Kingdom.

The Crisis Within

In many ways, China was the victim of its own earlier success. Its robust economy and American food crops had enabled substantial population growth, from about 100 million people in 1685 to some 430 million in 1853. Unlike in Europe, though, where a similar population spurt took place, no Industrial Revolution accompanied this vast increase in the number of people, nor was agricultural production able to keep up. Neither did China's internal expansion to the west and south generate anything like the wealth and resources that derived from Europe's overseas empires. The result was growing pressure on the land, smaller farms for China's huge peasant population, and, in all too many cases, unemployment, impoverishment, misery, and starvation.

■ **Causation**
What accounts for the massive peasant rebellions of nineteenth-century China?

Furthermore, China's famed centralized and bureaucratic state did not enlarge itself to keep pace with the growing population. Thus the state was increasingly unable to effectively perform its many functions, such as tax collection, flood control, social welfare, and public security. Gradually the central state lost power to provincial officials and local gentry. Among such officials, corruption was endemic, and harsh treatment of peasants was common. According to an official report issued in 1852, "Day and night soldiers are sent out to harass taxpayers. Sometimes corporal punishments are imposed upon tax delinquents; some of them are so badly beaten to exact the last penny that blood and flesh fly in all directions."[2] Finally, European military pressure and economic penetration during the first half of the nineteenth century (see pages 838–41) disrupted internal trade routes, created substantial unemployment, and raised peasant taxes.

This combination of circumstances, traditionally associated with a declining dynasty, gave rise to growing numbers of bandit gangs roaming the countryside and, even more dangerous, to outright peasant rebellion. Beginning in the late eighteenth century, such rebellions drew on a variety of peasant grievances and found leadership in charismatic figures proclaiming a millenarian religious message. Increasingly they also expressed opposition to the Qing dynasty because of its foreign Manchu origins. "We wait only for the northern region to be returned to a Han emperor," declared one rebel group in the early nineteenth century.[3]

The culmination of China's internal crisis lay in the Taiping Uprising, which set much of the country aflame between 1850 and 1864. This was a different kind of peasant upheaval. Its leaders largely rejected Confucianism, Daoism, and Buddhism alike, finding their primary ideology in a unique form of Christianity. Its leading figure, Hong Xiuquan (1814–1864), proclaimed himself the younger brother of Jesus, sent to cleanse the world of demons and to establish a "heavenly kingdom of great peace." Nor were these leaders content to restore an idealized Chinese society; instead they insisted on genuinely revolutionary change. They called for the abolition of private property, a radical redistribution of land, the end of prostitution and opium smoking, and the organization of society into sexually segregated military camps of men and women. Hong fiercely denounced the Qing dynasty as foreigners who had "poisoned China" and "defiled the emperor's throne." His cousin, Hong

Taiping Uprising
The Taiping rebels captured the city of Nanjing in 1853, making it their capital. Eleven years later, in 1864, imperial forces retook the city as illustrated in this Chinese print, effectively ending the Taiping Uprising. (School of Oriental and African Studies/Eileen Tweedy/The Art Archive at Art Resource, NY)

Rengan, developed plans for transforming China into an industrial nation, complete with railroads, health insurance for all, newspapers, and widespread public education.

Among the most revolutionary dimensions of the Taiping Uprising was its posture toward women and gender roles. This outlook reflected its origins among the minority Hakka people of southern China, where women were notably less restricted than Confucian orthodoxy prescribed. During the uprising, Hakka women, whose feet had never been bound, fought as soldiers in their own regiments; in liberated regions, Taiping officials ordered that the feet of other women be unbound. The Taiping land reform program promised women and men equal shares of land. Women were now permitted to sit for civil service examinations and were appointed to supervisory positions, though usually ones in which they exercised authority over other women rather than men. Mutual attraction rather than family interests was promoted as a basis for marriage.

None of these reforms were consistently implemented during the short period of Taiping power, and the movement's leadership demonstrated considerable ambivalence about equality for women. Hong himself reflected a much more traditional understanding of elite women's role when he assembled a large personal harem and declared: "The duty of the palace women is to attend to the needs of their husbands; and it is arranged by Heaven that they are not to learn of the affairs outside."[4] Nonetheless, the Taiping posture toward women represented a sharp challenge to long-established gender roles and contributed to the hostility that the movement generated among many other Chinese, including women.

With a rapidly swelling number of followers, Taiping forces swept out of southern China and established their capital in Nanjing in 1853. For a time, the days of the Qing dynasty appeared to be over. But divisions and indecisiveness within the Taiping leadership, along with their inability to link up with several other rebel groups also operating separately in China, provided an opening for Qing dynasty loyalists to rally and by 1864 to crush this most unusual of peasant rebellions. Western military support for pro-Qing forces likewise contributed to their victory. It was not, however, the imperial military forces of the central government that defeated the rebels. Instead provincial military leaders, fearing the radicalism of the Taiping program, mobilized their own armies, which in the end crushed the rebel forces.

Thus the Qing dynasty was saved, but it was also weakened as the provincial gentry consolidated their power at the expense of the central state. The intense conservatism of both imperial authorities and their gentry supporters postponed any resolution of China's peasant problem, delayed any real change for China's women, and deferred vigorous efforts at modernization until the communists came to power in the mid-twentieth century. More immediately, the devastation and destruction occasioned by this massive civil war seriously disrupted and weakened China's economy. Estimates of the number of lives lost range from 20 to 30 million. In human terms, it was the most costly conflict in the world during the nineteenth century, and it took China more than a decade to recover from its devastation. China's internal crisis in general and the Taiping Uprising in particular also provided a highly unfavorable setting for the country's encounter with a Europe newly invigorated by the Industrial Revolution.

Western Pressures

Nowhere was the shifting balance of global power in the nineteenth century more evident than in China's changing relationship with Europe, a transformation that registered most dramatically in the famous Opium Wars. Derived from Arab traders in the eighth century or earlier, opium had long been used on a small scale as a drinkable medicine; it was regarded as a magical cure for dysentery and described by one poet as "fit for Buddha."[5] It did not become a serious problem until the late eighteenth century, when the British began to use opium, grown and processed in India, to cover their persistent trade imbalance with China. By the 1830s, British, American, and other Western merchants had found an enormous, growing, and very profitable market for this highly addictive drug. From 1,000 chests (each weighing roughly 150 pounds) in 1773, China's opium imports exploded to more than 23,000 chests in 1832. (See Snapshot, below.)

SNAPSHOT   Chinese/British Trade at Canton, 1835–1836

What do these figures suggest about the role of opium in British trade with China? Calculate opium exports as a percentage of British exports to China, Britain's trade deficit without opium, and its trade surplus with opium. What did this pattern mean for China?[6]

	Item	Value (in Spanish dollars)
British Exports to Canton	Opium	17,904,248
	Cotton	8,357,394
	All other items (sandalwood, lead, iron, tin, cotton yarn and piece goods, tin plates, watches, clocks)	6,164,981
	Total	32,426,623
British Imports from Canton	Tea (black and green)	13,412,243
	Raw silk	3,764,115
	Vermilion	705,000
	All other goods (sugar products, camphor, silver, gold, copper, musk)	5,971,541
	Total	23,852,899

By then, Chinese authorities recognized a mounting problem on many levels. Because opium importation was illegal, it had to be smuggled into China, thus flouting Chinese law. Bribed to turn a blind eye to the illegal trade, many officials were corrupted. Furthermore, a massive outflow of silver to pay for the opium reversed China's centuries-long ability to attract much of the world's silver supply, and this imbalance caused serious economic problems. Finally, China found itself with many millions of addicts—men and women, court officials, students preparing for exams, soldiers going into combat, and common laborers seeking to overcome the pain and drudgery of their work. Following an extended debate at court in 1836 on whether to legalize the drug or crack down on its use, the emperor decided on suppression. An upright official, Commissioner Lin Zexu (lin zuh-SHOO), led the campaign against opium use as a kind of "drug czar." (See Zooming In: Lin Zexu, page 840.) The British, offended by the seizure of their property in opium and emboldened by their new military power, sent a large naval expedition to China, determined to end the restrictive conditions under which they had long traded with that country. In the process, they would teach the Chinese a lesson about the virtues of free trade and the "proper" way to conduct relations among countries. Thus began the first Opium War, in which Britain's industrialized military might proved decisive. The Treaty of Nanjing, which ended the war in 1842, largely on British terms, imposed numerous restrictions on Chinese sovereignty and opened five ports to European traders. Its provisions reflected the changed balance of global power that had emerged with Britain's Industrial Revolution. To the Chinese, that agreement represented the first of the "unequal treaties" that seriously eroded China's independence by the end of the century.

But it was not the last of those treaties. Britain's victory in a second Opium War (1856–1858) was accompanied by the brutal vandalizing of the emperor's exquisite Summer Palace outside Beijing and resulted in further humiliations. Still more ports were opened to foreign traders. Now those foreigners were allowed to travel freely and buy land in China, to preach Christianity under the protection of Chinese authorities, and to patrol some of China's rivers. Furthermore, the Chinese were forbidden to use the character for "barbarians" to refer to the

Connection
How did Western pressures stimulate change in China during the nineteenth century?

Addiction to Opium
Throughout the nineteenth century, opium imports created a massive addiction problem in China, as this photograph of an opium den from around 1900 suggests. Not until the early twentieth century did the British prove willing to curtail the opium trade from their Indian colony. (© Hulton-Deutsch Collection/Corbis)

Lin Zexu: Confronting the Opium Trade

When the Chinese emperor decided in 1838 on firm measures to suppress the opium trade, he selected Lin Zexu to enforce that policy.[7] Born in 1785, Lin was the son of a rather poor but scholarly father, who had never achieved an official position. Lin, however, excelled academically, passing the highest-level examinations in 1811 after two failed attempts and then rising rapidly in the ranks of China's bureaucracy. In the process, he gained a reputation as a strict and honest official; he was immune to bribery, genuinely concerned with the welfare of the peasantry, and unafraid to confront the corruption and decadence of rich and poor alike.

And so in December of 1838, after some nineteen personal audiences with the emperor, Lin found himself in Canton, the center of the opium trade and the only Chinese city legally open to foreign merchants. He was facing the greatest challenge of his professional life. Undertaken with the best of intentions, his actions propelled the country into a cen-

Commissioner Lin Zexu.

photo: Commissioner Lin Zexu. From Alexander Murray, *Doings in China: Being the personal narrative of an officer engaged in the late Chinese Expedition, from the Recapture of Chusan in 1841, to the Peace of Nankin in 1842* (London: Richard Bentley, New Burlington Street, Publisher in Ordinary to Her Majesty, 1843), pl. ii/Visual Connection Archive

tury of humiliating subservience to an industrializing Europe and forced growing numbers of Chinese to question their vaunted civilization.

In established Confucian fashion, Lin undertook his enormous task with a combination of moral appeals, reasoned argument, political pressure, and coercion, while hoping to avoid outright armed conflict. It was an approach that focused on both the demand and supply sides of the problem. In dealing with Chinese opium users, Lin emphasized the health hazards of the drug and demanded that people turn in their supplies of opium and the pipes used to smoke it. By mid-1839, he had confiscated some 50,000 pounds of the drug together with over 70,000 pipes and arrested some 1,700 dealers. Hundreds of local students were summoned to an assembly where they were invited to identify opium

British in official documents. Following military defeats at the hands of the French (1885) and Japanese (1895), China lost control of Vietnam, Korea, and Taiwan. By the end of the century, the Western nations plus Japan and Russia had all carved out spheres of influence within China, granting themselves special privileges to establish military bases, extract raw materials, and build railroads. Many Chinese believed that their country was being "carved up like a melon" (see Map 19.1 and the chapter-opening photo on page 832).

Coupled with its internal crisis, China's encounter with European imperialism had reduced the proud Middle Kingdom to dependency on the Western pow-

distributors and to suggest ways of dealing with the problem. Opium-using officials became the target of investigations, and five-person teams were established to enforce the ban on opium smoking on one another.

Lin applied a similar mix of methods to the foreign suppliers of opium. A moralistic appeal to Queen Victoria argued that the articles the English imported from China—silk, tea, and rhubarb—were all beneficial. "By what right," he asked, "do [the barbarians] use this poisonous drug to injure Chinese people?" He pointedly reminded Europeans that new regulations, applying to Chinese and foreigners alike, fixed the penalty for dealing in opium at "decapitation or strangling." Then he demanded that foreign traders hand over their opium, and without compensation. When the merchants hesitated, Lin tightened the screws, ordering all Chinese employed by foreigners to leave their jobs and blockading the Europeans in their factories. After six weeks of negotiations, the Europeans capitulated, turning over some 3 million pounds of raw opium to Lin Zexu.

Disposing of the drug was an enormous task. Workers, stripped and searched daily to prevent looting, dug three huge trenches into which they placed the opium mixed with water, salt, and lime and then flushed the concoction into the sea. Lin offered a sacrifice to the Sea Spirit, apologizing for introducing this poison into its domain and "advising the Spirit to tell the creatures of the water to move away for a time." He informed the emperor that throngs of local people flocked to witness the destruction of the opium. And foreigners too came to observe the spectacle. Lin reported, "[The foreigners] do not dare to show any disrespect, and indeed I should judge from their attitudes that they have the decency to feel heartily ashamed."

Had Lin been correct in his appraisal, history would have taken a very different turn. But neither Lin nor his superiors anticipated the response that these actions provoked from the British government. They were also largely unaware of European industrial and military advances, which had decisively shifted the balance of power between China and the West. Arriving in 1840, a British military expedition quickly demonstrated its superiority and initiated the devastating Opium War that marked Lin's policies in Canton as a failure.

As a punishment for his unsatisfactory performance, the emperor sent Lin to a remote post in western China. Although his career rebounded somewhat after 1845, he died in 1850 while on the way to an appointment aimed at suppressing the Taiping rebellion. While his reputation suffered in the nineteenth century, it recovered in the twentieth as an intensely nationalist China recalled his principled stand against Western imperialism.

Questions: How might Lin Zexu have handled his task differently or more successfully? Or had he been given an impossible mission?

ers as it became part of a European-based "informal empire." China was no longer the center of civilization to which barbarians paid homage and tribute, but just one weak and dependent nation among many others. The Qing dynasty remained in power, but in a weakened condition, which served European interests well and Chinese interests poorly. Restrictions imposed by the unequal treaties clearly inhibited China's industrialization, as foreign goods and foreign investment flooded the country largely unrestricted. Chinese businessmen mostly served foreign firms, rather than developing as an independent capitalist class capable of leading China's own Industrial Revolution.

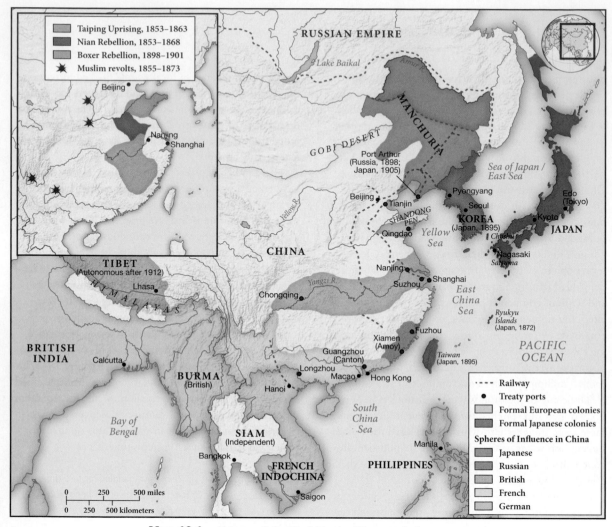

Map 19.1   China and the World in the Nineteenth Century

As China was reeling from massive internal upheavals during the nineteenth century, it also faced external assaults from Russia, Japan, and various European powers. By the end of the century, large parts of China were divided into spheres of influence, each affiliated with one of the major industrial powers of the day.

The Failure of Conservative Modernization

Chinese authorities were not passive in the face of their country's mounting crises, both internal and external. Known as "self-strengthening," their policies during the 1860s and 1870s sought to reinvigorate a traditional China while borrowing cautiously from the West. An overhauled examination system, designed to recruit qualified candidates for official positions, sought the "good men" who could cope with the massive reconstruction that China faced in the wake of the Taiping rebellion. Support for landlords and the repair of dikes and irrigation helped restore rural social and economic order. A few industrial factories producing textiles and steel were established, coal mines were expanded, and a telegraph system was initiated. One Chinese general in 1863 confessed his humiliation that "Chinese weapons are far inferior to those of foreign countries."[8] A number of modern arsenals, shipyards, and foreign-language schools sought to remedy this deficiency.

Self-strengthening as an overall program for China's modernization was inhibited by the fears of conservative leaders that urban, industrial, or commercial development would erode the power and privileges of the landlord class. Furthermore, the new industries remained largely dependent on foreigners for machinery, materials, and expertise. And they served to strengthen local authorities, who largely controlled those industries, rather than the central Chinese state.

The general failure of "self-strengthening" became apparent at the end of the century, when an antiforeign movement known as the Boxer Uprising (1898–1901) erupted in northern China. Led by militia organizations calling themselves the Society of Righteous and Harmonious Fists, the "Boxers" killed numerous Europeans and Chinese Christians and laid siege to the foreign embassies in Beijing. When Western powers and Japan occupied Beijing to crush the rebellion and imposed a huge payment on China as a punishment, it was clear that China remained a dependent country, substantially under foreign control.

No wonder, then, that growing numbers of educated Chinese, including many in official elite positions, became highly disillusioned with the Qing dynasty, which was both foreign and ineffective in protecting China. By the late 1890s, such people were organizing a variety of clubs, study groups, and newspapers to examine China's desperate situation and to explore alternative paths. The names of these organizations reflect their outlook—the National Rejuvenation Study Society, Society to Protect the Nation, and Understand the National Shame Society. They admired not only Western science and technology but also Western political practices that limited the authority of the ruler and permitted wider circles of people to take part in public life. They believed that only a truly unified nation in which rulers and ruled were closely related could save China from dismemberment at the hands of foreign imperialists. Despite the small number of women who took part in these discussions, traditional gender roles became yet another focus of opposition. No one expressed that issue more forcefully than Qiu Jin (1875–1907), the rebellious daughter of a gentry family who left a husband and two children to study in Japan. Upon her return to China, she started a women's journal, arguing that liberated women were essential for a strong Chinese nation, and became involved in revolutionary politics. (For more on Qiu Jin, see Working with Evidence, Source 19.3, page 867.) Thus was born the immensely powerful force of Chinese nationalism, directed alike against Western imperialists, the foreign Qing dynasty, and aspects of China's traditional culture.

The Qing dynasty response to these new pressures proved inadequate. A flurry of progressive imperial edicts in 1898, known as the Hundred Days of Reform, was

■ **Connection**
What strategies did China adopt to confront its various problems? In what ways did these strategies reflect China's own history and culture as well as the new global order?

soon squelched by conservative forces. More extensive reform in the early twentieth century, including the end of the old examination system and the promise of a national parliament, was a classic case of too little too late. (See Working with Evidence: Changing China, page 863.) In 1912 the last Chinese emperor abdicated as the ancient imperial order that had governed China for two millennia collapsed, with only a modest nudge from organized revolutionaries. It was the end of a long era in China and the beginning of an immense struggle over the country's future.

The Ottoman Empire and the West in the Nineteenth Century

Like China, the Islamic world represented a highly successful civilization that felt little need to learn from the "infidels" or "barbarians" of the West until it collided with an expanding and aggressive Europe in the nineteenth century. Unlike China, though, Islamic civilization had been a near neighbor to Europe for 1,000 years. Its most prominent state, the Ottoman Empire, had long governed substantial parts of the Balkans and had posed a clear military and religious threat to Europe in the sixteenth and seventeenth centuries. But if its encounter with the West was less abrupt than that of China, it was no less consequential. Neither the Ottoman Empire nor China fell under direct colonial rule, but both were much diminished as the changing balance of global power took hold; both launched efforts at "defensive modernization" aimed at strengthening their states and preserving their independence; and in both societies, some people held tightly to old identities and values, even as others embraced new loyalties associated with nationalism and modernity.

"The Sick Man of Europe"

In 1750, the Ottoman Empire was still the central political fixture of a widespread Islamic world. From its Turkish heartland in Anatolia, it ruled over much of the Arab world, from which Islam had come. It protected pilgrims on their way to Mecca, governed Egypt and coastal North Africa, and incorporated millions of Christians in the Balkans. Its ruler, the sultan, claimed the role of caliph, successor to the Prophet Muhammad, and was widely viewed as the leader, defender, and primary representative of the Islamic world. But by the middle, and certainly by the end, of the nineteenth century, the Ottoman Empire was no longer able to deal with Europe from a position of equality, let alone superiority. Among the Great Powers of the West, it was now known as "the sick man of Europe." Within the Muslim world, the Ottoman Empire, once viewed as "the strong sword of Islam," was unable to prevent region after region — India, Indonesia, West Africa, Central Asia — from falling under the control of Christian powers.

The Ottoman Empire's own domains shrank considerably at the hands of Russian, British, Austrian, and French aggression (see Map 19.2). In 1798, Napoleon's invasion of Egypt, which had long been a province of the Ottoman Empire, was a

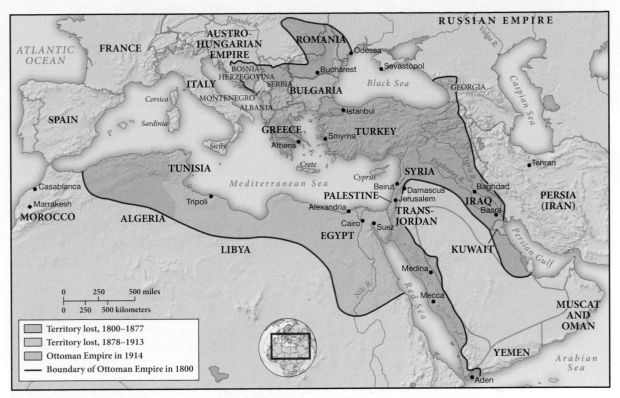

Map 19.2   The Contraction of the Ottoman Empire
Foreign aggression and nationalist movements substantially diminished the Ottoman Empire during the nineteenth century, but they also stimulated a variety of efforts to revive and reform Ottoman society.

particularly stunning blow. A contemporary observer, Abd al-Rahman al-Jabarti, described the French entry into Cairo:

> The French entered the city like a torrent rushing through the alleys and streets without anything to stop them, like demons of the Devil's army. . . . And the French trod in the Mosque of al-Azhar with their shoes, carrying swords and rifles. . . . They plundered whatever they found in the mosque. . . . They treated the books and Quranic volumes as trash. . . . Furthermore, they soiled the mosque, blowing their spit in it, pissing and defecating in it. They guzzled wine and smashed bottles in the central court.[9]

When the French left, a virtually independent Egypt pursued a modernizing and empire-building program of its own during the early and mid-nineteenth century and on one occasion came close to toppling the Ottoman Empire itself.

Beyond territorial losses to stronger European powers, other parts of the empire, such as Greece, Serbia, Bulgaria, and Romania, achieved independence based on their own surging nationalism and support from the British or the Russians. The continued independence of the core region of the Ottoman Empire owed much

■ **Change**
What lay behind the decline of the Ottoman Empire in the nineteenth century?

to the inability of Europe's Great Powers to agree on how to divide it up among themselves.

Behind the contraction of the Ottoman Empire lay other problems. As in China, the central Ottoman state had weakened, particularly in its ability to raise necessary revenue, as provincial authorities and local warlords gained greater power. Moreover, the Janissaries, once the effective and innovative elite infantry units of Ottoman military forces, lost their military edge, becoming a highly conservative force within the empire. The technological and military gap with the West was clearly growing.

Economically, the earlier centrality of the Ottoman and Arab lands in Afro-Eurasian commerce diminished as Europeans achieved direct oceanic access to the treasures of Asia. Competition from cheap European manufactured goods hit Otto-man artisans hard and led to urban riots protesting foreign imports. Furthermore, a series of agreements, known as capitulations, between European countries and the Ottoman Empire granted Westerners various exemptions from Ottoman law and taxation. Like the unequal treaties with China, these agreements facilitated European penetration of the Ottoman economy and became widely resented. Such measures eroded Ottoman sovereignty and reflected the changing position of that empire relative to Europe. So too did the growing indebtedness of the Ottoman Empire, which came to rely on foreign loans to finance its efforts at economic development. By 1881, its inability to pay the interest on those debts led to foreign control of much of its revenue-generating system, while a similar situation in Egypt led to its outright occupation by the British. Like China, the Ottoman Empire had fallen into a position of considerable dependency on Europe.

Reform and Its Opponents

The leadership of the Ottoman Empire recognized many of its problems and dur-ing the nineteenth century mounted increasingly ambitious programs of "defensive modernization" that were earlier, more sustained, and far more vigorous than the timid and halfhearted measures of self-strengthening in China. One reason perhaps lay in the absence of any internal upheaval, such as the Taiping Uprising in China, which threatened the very existence of the ruling dynasty. Nationalist revolts on the empire's periphery, rather than Chinese-style peasant rebellion at the center, represented the primary internal crisis of nineteenth-century Ottoman history. Nor did the Middle East in general experience the explosive population growth that contributed so much to China's nineteenth-century crisis. Furthermore, the long-established Ottoman leadership was Turkic and Muslim, culturally similar to its core population, whereas China's Qing dynasty rulers were widely regarded as foreign-ers from Manchuria.

Ottoman reforms began in the late eighteenth century when Sultan Selim III sought to reorganize and update the army, drawing on European advisers and tech-niques. Even these modest innovations stirred the hostility of powerful factions

■ Change
In what different ways did the Ottoman state respond to its various problems?

among both the *ulama* (religious scholars) and the elite military corps of Janissaries, who saw them in conflict with both Islam and their own institutional interests. Opposition to his measures was so strong that Selim was overthrown in 1807 and then murdered. Subsequent sultans, however, crushed the Janissaries and brought the ulama more thoroughly under state control than elsewhere in the Islamic world.

Then, in the several decades after 1839, more far-reaching reformist measures, known as Tanzimat (tahn-zee-MAHT) (reorganization), took shape as the Ottoman leadership sought to provide the economic, social, and legal underpinnings for a strong and newly recentralized state. Factories producing cloth, paper, and armaments; modern mining operations; reclamation and resettlement of agricultural land; telegraphs, steamships, railroads, and a modern postal service; Western-style law codes and courts; new elementary and secondary schools—all of these new departures began a long process of modernization and westernization in the Ottoman Empire.

Even more revolutionary, at least in principle, were changes in the legal status of the empire's diverse communities, which now gave non-Muslims equal rights under the law. An imperial proclamation of 1856 declared:

> Every distinction or designation tending to make any class whatever of the subjects of my Empire inferior to another class, on account of their religion, language or race shall be forever effaced. . . . No subject of my Empire shall be hindered in the exercise of the religion that he professes. . . . All the subjects of my Empire, without distinction of nationality, shall be admissible to public employment.

This declaration represented a dramatic change that challenged the fundamentally Islamic character of the state. Mixed tribunals with representatives from various religious groups were established to hear cases involving non-Muslims. More Christians were appointed to high office. A mounting tide of secular legislation and secular schools, drawing heavily on European models, now competed with traditional Islamic institutions.

Although Tanzimat-era reforms did not directly address gender issues, they did stimulate modest educational openings for women, mostly in Istanbul, with a training program for midwives in 1842, a girls' secondary school in 1858, and a teacher training college for women in 1870. Furthermore, the reform-minded class that emerged from the Tanzimat era generally favored greater opportunities for women as a means of strengthening the state, and a number of upper- and middle-class women were involved in these discussions. During the 1870s and 1880s, the prominent female poet Sair Nigar Hanim held weekly "salons" in which reformist intellectuals of both sexes participated.

The reform process raised profound and highly contested questions. What was the Ottoman Empire, and who were its people? Were they Ottoman subjects of a dynastic state, Turkish citizens of a national state, or Muslim believers in a religiously defined state? For decades, the answers oscillated as few people wanted to choose decisively among these alternative identities.

■ **Comparison**

In what different ways did various groups define the Ottoman Empire during the nineteenth century?

To those who supported the reforms, the Ottoman Empire was an inclusive state, all of whose people were loyal to the dynasty that ruled it. This was the outlook of a new class spawned by the reform process itself—lower-level officials, military officers, writers, poets, and journalists, many of whom had a modern Western-style education. Dubbed the Young Ottomans, they were active during the middle decades of the nineteenth century, as they sought major changes in the Ottoman political system itself. They favored a more European-style parliamentary and constitutional regime that could curtail the absolute power of the sultan. Only such a political system, they felt, could mobilize the energies of the country to overcome backwardness and preserve the state against European aggression. Known as Islamic modernism, such ideas found expression in many parts of the Muslim world in the second half of the century. Muslim societies, the Young Ottomans argued, needed to embrace Western technical and scientific knowledge, while rejecting its materialism. Islam in their view could accommodate a full modernity without sacrificing its essential religious character. After all, the Islamic world had earlier hosted impressive scientific achievements and had incorporated elements of Greek philosophical thinking.

In 1876, the Young Ottomans experienced a short-lived victory when Sultan Abd al-Hamid II (r. 1876–1909) accepted a constitution and an elected parliament, but not for long. Under the pressure of war with Russia, the sultan soon suspended the reforms and reverted to an older style of despotic rule for the next thirty years,

The First Ottoman Constitution

This Ottoman-era postcard celebrates the short-lived constitutional period of 1876–1878 and the brief political victory of the Young Ottoman reformers. The country is represented by an unveiled woman being released from her chains, while an angel carries a banner inscribed with the slogan of the French Revolution: liberty, equality, fraternity. ("The Ottoman Constitution, December 1895," color postcard. Artist unknown/Visual Connection Archive)

even renewing the claim that he was the caliph, the successor to the Prophet and the protector of Muslims everywhere.

Opposition to this revived despotism soon surfaced among both military and civilian elites known as the Young Turks. Largely abandoning any reference to Islam, they advocated a militantly secular public life, were committed to thorough modernization along European lines, and increasingly thought about the Ottoman Empire as a Turkish national state. "There is only one civilization, and that is European civilization," declared Abdullah Cevdet, a prominent figure in the Young Turk movement. "Therefore we must borrow western civilization with both its rose and its thorn."[10]

A military coup in 1908 finally allowed the Young Turks to exercise real power. They pushed for a radical secularization of schools, courts, and law codes; permitted elections and competing parties; established a single Law of Family Rights for all regardless of religion; and encouraged Turkish as the official language of the empire. They also opened modern schools for women, including access to Istanbul University; allowed women to wear Western clothing; restricted polygamy; and permitted women to obtain divorces in some situations. Women established a number of publications and organizations, some of them linked to British suffrage groups. In the western cities of the empire, some women abandoned their veils.

But the nationalist Turkish conception of Ottoman identity antagonized non-Turkic peoples and helped stimulate Arab and other nationalisms in response. For some, a secular nationality was becoming the most important public loyalty, with Islam relegated to private life. Nationalist sentiments contributed to the complete disintegration of the Ottoman Empire following World War I, but the secularizing and westernizing principles of the Young Turks informed the policies of the Turkish republic that replaced it.

Outcomes: Comparing China and the Ottoman Empire

By the beginning of the twentieth century, both China and the Ottoman Empire, recently centers of proud and vibrant civilizations, had experienced the consequences of a rapidly shifting balance of global power. Now they were "semi-colonies" within the "informal empires" of Europe, although they retained sufficient independence for their governments to launch catch-up efforts of defensive modernization, the Ottomans earlier and the Chinese later. But neither was able to create the industrial economies or strong states required to fend off European intrusion and restore their former status in the world. Despite their diminished power, however, both China and the Ottoman Empire gave rise to new nationalist conceptions of society, which were initially small and limited in appeal but of great significance for the future.

In the early twentieth century, that future witnessed the end of both the Chinese and Ottoman empires. In China, the collapse of the imperial system in 1912 was followed by a vast revolutionary upheaval that by 1949 led to a communist regime within largely the same territorial space as the old empire. By contrast, the

1896: The Battle of Adowa

On March 1, 1896, two armies faced one another near the small town of Adowa in northern Ethiopia. On one side lay the Italian forces, who had intruded into Ethiopia from their adjacent colony of Eritrea, supplemented by a large number of African troops. On the other side stood the much larger Ethiopian army, personally led by Emperor Menelik II, accompanied by his forceful wife, Empress Taytu. The battle that followed proved a decisive victory for the Ethiopians and a rout for the Italians. That victory placed Ethiopia, like China, Persia, the Ottoman Empire, Japan, and Thailand, in the category of countries that retained their independence in an era of rampant European empire building. It was, in fact, the only part of Africa to enjoy that status. How had it happened?

One answer lies in circumstances. Ethiopia's location in the mountainous highlands of eastern Africa made external invasion difficult. Its long tradition of independent statehood and a common Christian culture provided a strong sense of identity alongside the ethnic diversity of its population and the political rivalries of its governing elites. Ethiopia's Italian adversary had become a unified

Emperor Menelik II of Ethiopia
at the Battle of Adowa.

country only in 1871 and possessed a less robust military than Britain, France, or Germany did. Nonetheless, as the scramble for Africa unfolded, the Italians had established colonial rule in both Somalia and Eritrea. Now they were seeking to enlarge their African holdings at the expense of Ethiopia.

Building on these circumstances, Menelik's diplomacy and military strategy proved highly effective. After becoming emperor in 1889, Menelik actively took advantage of European rivalries for territory in northeastern Africa to pursue agreements with and to buy arms from Russia, France, Germany, Britain, and Italy. To obtain an agreement with Italy, he was willing to cede some territory in northern Ethiopia and to acknowledge Italian control of Eritrea in return for financial assistance and military supplies. But a dispute arose when the Italians interpreted the treaty as implying an Italian protectorate over Ethiopia. This, of course, Menelik decisively rejected. When Italian forces moved into Ethiopian territory in early 1895, he prepared for war.

photo: Color lithographic illustration by Louis Fortune Meaulle (1844–1901) from *Le Petit Journal*, 1898/Private Collection/Bridgeman Images

collapse of the Ottoman Empire following World War I led to the creation of the new but much smaller nation-state of Turkey in the Anatolian heartland of the old empire, which lost its vast Arab and European provinces.

China's twentieth-century revolutionaries rejected traditional Confucian culture far more thoroughly than the secularizing leaders of modern Turkey rejected Islam. Almost everywhere in the Islamic world, including Turkey, traditional religion retained its hold on the private loyalties of most people and later in the twentieth century became a basis for social renewal in many places. Islamic civilization, unlike its Chinese counterpart, had many independent centers and was never so

Imposing a special tax to pay for more guns and ammunition, Menelik ordered the expulsion of all Italians from Ethiopia and called for national mobilization. Troops under the command of various regional rulers began to assemble, and in October 1895 a huge force began a five-month, 580-mile march from the capital of Addis Ababa to Adowa, where the decisive battle took place.

The echoes of Adowa resonated far and wide. For Italy, it was a national humiliation, "a shameful scar" according to a leading poet. That wound failed to heal and played a large role in motivating Mussolini's invasion of Ethiopia in 1935, a step on the road to World War II. As the avenger of Adowa, he had a large bust of himself placed on that battlefield.

For Ethiopia itself, Adowa had an immense significance that bears comparison with the experience of Japan. Like Japan, Ethiopia was a long-established independent state, threatened by European expansion, which actually defeated a major European power, and it did so a decade before Japan's victory over Russia in 1905. Both Japan and Ethiopia became beacons of hope and inspiration to societies that had fallen under colonial rule. Furthermore, both nations went on to construct empires of their own. In Ethiopia's case, Menelik practically doubled the territorial size of his country as he expanded Ethiopian control to the south and east. Successfully resisting the European scramble for Africa, he also proceeded to take part in it. These successes enabled

Menelik to solidify his hold on the throne, to unify the country in its modern form, and to emerge with an almost mythic reputation. Within Africa and among African Americans, Ethiopia came to symbolize African bravery and resistance to white oppression. It is no accident that Addis Ababa, the capital of Ethiopia, was chosen as the headquarters of the Organization of African Unity in 1963. A huge stained-glass wall in the main building depicts Ethiopians leading the rest of Africa to independence.

But in another way, Ethiopian and Japanese history sharply diverged. Japan was able to join its political and military success with a thorough economic transformation of the country. Ethiopia was not able to do this and remains one of the least developed countries of the Global South. Menelik did initiate a number of modernizing projects—banks, railroads, schools, hospitals, and a few factories—but nothing approached the scale of Japan's transformation. His success, in fact, strengthened the more conservative forces within Ethiopian society.

When I (Robert Strayer) taught high school history in Ethiopia in the mid-1960s, I was told that Italians were perhaps the most well-liked Europeans in the country, but that they were careful to stay at home on the anniversary of the Battle of Adowa.

Question: How might you describe the significance of the Battle of Adowa in Ethiopian, African, and world history?

---

closely associated with a single state. Furthermore, it was embedded in a deeply religious tradition that was personally meaningful to millions of adherents, in contrast to the more elitist and secular outlook of Confucianism. Many rural Chinese, however, retained traditional Confucian values such as filial piety, and Confucianism has made something of a comeback in China over the past several decades. Nonetheless, Islam retained a hold on its civilization in the twentieth century rather more firmly than Confucianism did in China.

SUMMING UP SO FAR

In what ways were the histories of China and the Ottoman Empire similar during the nineteenth century? And how did they differ?

The Japanese Difference: The Rise of a New East Asian Power

Like China and the Ottoman Empire, the island country of Japan confronted the aggressive power of the West during the nineteenth century, most notably in the form of U.S. commodore Matthew Perry's "black ships," which steamed into Tokyo Bay in 1853 and forcefully demanded that this reclusive nation open up to more "normal" relations with the world. However, the outcome of that encounter differed sharply from the others. In the second half of the nineteenth century, Japan undertook a radical transformation of its society—a "revolution from above," according to some historians—turning it into a powerful, modern, united, industrialized nation. It was an achievement that neither China nor the Ottoman Empire was able to duplicate. Far from succumbing to Western domination, Japan joined the club of imperialist countries by creating its own East Asian empire, at the expense of China and Korea. In building a society that was both modern and distinctly Japanese, Japan demonstrated that modernity was not a uniquely European phenomenon. This "Japanese miracle," as some have called it, was both promising and ominous for the rest of Asia. How had it occurred?

The Tokugawa Background

For 250 years prior to Perry's arrival, Japan had been governed by a shogun (a military ruler) from the Tokugawa family who acted in the name of a revered but powerless emperor, who lived in Kyoto, 300 miles away from the seat of power in Edo (Tokyo). The chief task of this Tokugawa shogunate was to prevent the return of civil war among some 260 rival feudal lords, known as daimyo, each of whom had a cadre of armed retainers, the famed samurai warriors of Japanese tradition.

Based on their own military power and political skills, successive shoguns gave Japan more than two centuries of internal peace (1600–1850). To control the restive daimyo, they required these local authorities to create second homes in Edo, the country's capital, where they had to live during alternate years. When they left for their rural residences, families stayed behind, almost as hostages. Nonetheless, the daimyo, especially the more powerful ones, retained substantial autonomy in their own domains and behaved in some ways like independent states with separate military forces, law codes, tax systems, and currencies. With no national army, no uniform currency, and little central authority at the local level, Tokugawa Japan was "pacified . . . but not really unified."[11] To further stabilize the country, the Tokugawa regime issued highly detailed rules governing the occupation, residence, dress, hairstyles, and behavior of the four hierarchically ranked status groups into which Japanese society was divided—samurai at the top, then peasants, artisans, and, at the bottom, merchants.

Much was changing within Japan during these 250 years of peace in ways that belied the control and orderliness of Tokugawa regulations. For one thing, the samurai, in the absence of wars to fight, evolved into a salaried bureaucratic or administrative class amounting to 5 to 6 percent of the total population, but they were still fiercely devoted to their daimyo lords and to their warrior code of loyalty, honor, and self-sacrifice.

More generally, centuries of peace contributed to a remarkable burst of economic growth, commercialization, and urban development. Entrepreneurial peasants, using fertilizers and other agricultural innovations, grew more rice than ever before and engaged in a variety of rural manufacturing enterprises as well. By 1750, Japan had become perhaps the world's most urbanized country, with about 10 percent of its population living in sizable towns or cities. Edo, with perhaps a million residents, was among the world's largest cities. Well-functioning networks of exchange linked urban and rural areas, marking Japan as an emerging market economy. The influence of Confucianism encouraged education and generated a remarkably literate population, with about 40 percent of men and 15 percent of women able to read and write. Although no one was aware of it at the time, these changes during the Tokugawa era provided a solid foundation for Japan's remarkable industrial growth in the late nineteenth century.

■ **Change**
In what ways was Japan changing during the Tokugawa era?

Such changes also undermined the shogunate's efforts to freeze Japanese society in the interests of stability. Some samurai found the lowly but profitable path of commerce too much to resist. "No more shall we have to live by the sword," declared one of them in 1616 while renouncing his samurai status. "I have seen that great profit can be made honorably. I shall brew *sake* and soy sauce, and we shall prosper."[12] Many merchants, though hailing from the lowest-ranking status group, prospered in the new commercial environment and supported a vibrant urban culture, while not a few daimyo found it necessary, if humiliating, to seek loans from these social inferiors. Thus merchants had money, but little status, whereas samurai enjoyed high status but were often indebted to inferior merchants. Both resented their positions.

Despite prohibitions to the contrary, many peasants moved to the cities, becoming artisans or merchants and imitating the ways of their social betters. A decree of 1788 noted that peasants "have become accustomed to luxury and forgetful of their status." They wore inappropriate clothing, used umbrellas rather than straw hats in the rain, and even left the villages for the city. "Henceforth," declared the shogun, "all luxuries should be avoided by the peasants. They are to live simply and devote themselves to farming."[13] This decree, like many others before it, was widely ignored.

More than social change undermined the Tokugawa regime. Corruption was widespread, to the disgust of many. The shogunate's failure to deal successfully with a severe famine in the 1830s eroded confidence in its effectiveness. At the same time, a mounting wave of local peasant uprisings and urban riots expressed the many grievances of the poor. The most striking of these outbursts left the city of Osaka in flames in 1837. Its leader, Oshio Heihachiro, no doubt spoke for many ordinary people when he wrote:

> We must first punish the officials who torment the people so cruelly; then we must execute the haughty and rich Osaka merchants. Then we must distribute the gold, silver, and copper stored in their cellars, and bands of rice hidden in their storehouses.[14]

From the 1830s on, one historian concluded, "there was a growing feeling that the *shogunate* was losing control."[15]

American Intrusion and the Meiji Restoration

It was foreign intervention that brought matters to a head. Since the expulsion of European missionaries and the harsh suppression of Christianity in the early seventeenth century (see Chapter 14, page 610), Japan had deliberately limited its contact with the West to a single port, where only the Dutch were allowed to trade. By the early nineteenth century, however, various European countries and the United States were knocking at the door. All were turned away, and even shipwrecked sailors or whalers were expelled, jailed, or executed. As it happened, it was the United States that forced the issue, sending Commodore Perry in 1853 to demand

The Black Ships of the United States
The initial occasion for serious Japanese reflection on the West occurred in 1853–1854, in the context of American commodore Matthew Perry's efforts to "open" Japan to regular commercial relationships with the United States. His nine coal-fired steamships, belching black smoke and carrying a crew of some 1,800 men and more than 100 mounted cannons, became known in Japan as the "black ships." Created around 1854, this image represents perhaps the best known of many such Japanese depictions of the American warships. (The Granger Collection, NYC — All rights reserved)

humane treatment for castaways, the right of American vessels to refuel and buy provisions, and the opening of ports for trade. Authorized to use force if necessary, Perry presented his reluctant hosts with, among other gifts, a white flag for surrender should hostilities follow.

In the end, the Japanese avoided war. Aware of what had happened to China as a result of resisting European demands, Japan agreed to a series of unequal treaties with various Western powers. That humiliating capitulation to the demands of the "foreign devils" further eroded support for the shogunate, triggered a brief civil war, and by 1868 led to a political takeover by a group of young samurai from southern Japan. This decisive turning point in Japan's history was known as the Meiji (MAY-jee) Restoration, for the country's new rulers claimed that they were restoring to power the young emperor, then a fifteen-year-old boy whose throne name was Meiji, or Enlightened Rule. Despite his youth, he was regarded as the most recent link in a chain of descent that traced the origins of the imperial family back to the sun goddess Amaterasu. Having eliminated the shogunate, the patriotic young men who led the takeover soon made their goals clear — to save Japan from foreign domination not by futile resistance, but by a thorough transformation of Japanese society drawing on all that the modern West had to offer. "Knowledge shall be sought throughout the world," they declared, "so as to strengthen the foundations of imperial rule."

Japan now had a government committed to a decisive break with the past, and it had acquired that government without massive violence or destruction. By contrast, the defeat of the Taiping Uprising had deprived China of any such opportunity for a fresh start, while saddling it with enormous devastation and massive loss of life. Furthermore, Japan was of less interest to Western powers than either China, with its huge potential market and reputation for riches, or the Ottoman Empire, with its strategic location at the crossroads of Asia, Africa, and Europe. The American Civil War and its aftermath likewise deflected U.S. ambitions in the Pacific for a time, further reducing the Western pressure on Japan.

Modernization Japanese-Style

These circumstances gave Japan some breathing space, and its new rulers moved quickly to take advantage of that unique window of opportunity. Thus they launched a cascading wave of dramatic changes that rolled over the country in the last three decades of the nineteenth century. Like the more modest reforms of China and the Ottoman Empire, Japanese modernizing efforts were defensive, based on fears that Japanese independence was in grave danger. Those reforms, however, were revolutionary in their cumulative effect, transforming Japan far more thoroughly than even the most radical of the Ottoman efforts, let alone the limited "self-strengthening" policies of the Chinese.

The first task was genuine national unity, which required an attack on the power and privileges of both the daimyo and the samurai. In a major break with the past,

■ **Change**
In what respects was Japan's nineteenth-century transformation revolutionary?

the new regime soon ended the semi-independent domains of the daimyo, replacing them with governors appointed by and responsible to the national government. The central state, not the local authorities, now collected the nation's taxes and raised a national army based on conscription from all social classes.

Thus the samurai relinquished their ancient role as the country's warrior class and with it their cherished right to carry swords. The old Confucian-based social order with its special privileges for various classes was largely dismantled, and almost all Japanese became legally equal as commoners and as subjects of the emperor. Limitations on travel and trade likewise fell as a nationwide economy came to parallel the centralized state. Although there was some opposition to these measures, including a brief rebellion of resentful samurai in 1877, it was on the whole a remarkably peaceful process in which a segment of the old ruling class abolished its own privileges. Many, but not all, of these displaced elites found a soft landing in the army, bureaucracy, or business enterprises of the new regime, thus easing a painful transition.

Accompanying these social and political changes was a widespread and eager fascination with almost everything Western. Knowledge about the West—its science and technology; its various political and constitutional arrangements; its legal and educational systems; its dances, clothing, and hairstyles—was enthusiastically sought out by official missions to Europe and the United States, by hundreds of students sent to study abroad, and by many ordinary Japanese at home. Western writers were translated into Japanese; for example, Samuel Smiles's *Self-Help*, which focused on "achieving success and rising in the world," sold a million copies. "Civilization and Enlightenment" was the slogan of the time, and both were to be found in the West. The most prominent popularizer of Western knowledge, Fukuzawa Yukichi, summed up the chief lesson of his studies in the mid-1870s—Japan was backward and needed to learn from the West: "If we compare the knowledge of the Japanese and Westerners, in letters, in technique, in commerce, or in industry, from the largest to the smallest matter, there is not one thing in which we excel. . . . In Japan's present condition there is nothing in which we may take pride vis-à-vis the West."[16]

After this initial wave of uncritical enthusiasm for everything Western receded, Japan proceeded to borrow more selectively and to combine foreign and Japanese elements in distinctive ways. For example, the Constitution of 1889, drawing heavily on German experience, introduced an elected parliament, political parties, and democratic ideals, but that constitution was presented as a gift from a sacred emperor descended from the sun goddess. The parliament could advise, but ultimate power, and particularly control of the military, lay theoretically with the emperor and in practice with an oligarchy of prominent reformers acting in his name. Likewise, a modern educational system, which achieved universal primary schooling by the early twentieth century, was laced with Confucian-based moral instruction and exhortations of loyalty to the emperor. Christianity made little headway in Meiji Japan, but Shinto, an ancient religious tradition featuring ancestors and nature spirits, was elevated to the status of an official state cult. Japan's earlier experience in borrowing massively but selectively from Chinese culture perhaps served it better in these new circumstances than either the Chinese disdain for foreign cultures or the reluctance of many Muslims to see much of value in the infidel West.

Like their counterparts in China and the Ottoman Empire, some reformers in Japan—male and female alike—argued that the oppression of women was an obstacle to the country's modernization and that family reform was essential to gaining the respect of the West. The widely read commentator Fukuzawa Yukichi urged an end to concubinage and prostitution, advocated more education for girls, and called for gender equality in matters of marriage, divorce, and property rights. But most male reformers understood women largely in the context of family life, seeing them as "good wife, wise mother." By the 1880s, however, a small feminist movement arose, demanding—and modeling—a more public role for women. Some even sought the right to vote at a time when only a small fraction of men could do so. A leading feminist, Kishida Toshiko, not yet twenty years old, astonished the country in 1882 when she undertook a two-month speaking tour, where she addressed huge audiences. Only "equality and equal rights," she argued, would allow Japan "to build a new society." Japan must rid itself of the ancient habit of "respecting men and despising women."

While the new Japanese government included girls in their plans for universal education, it was with a gender-specific curriculum and in schools segregated by sex. Any thought of women playing a role in public life was harshly suppressed. A Peace Preservation Law of 1887, in effect until 1922, forbade women from joining political parties and even from attending meetings where political matters were discussed. The Constitution of 1889 made no mention of any political rights for women. The Civil Code of 1898 accorded absolute authority to the male head of the family, while grouping all wives with "cripples and disabled persons" as those who "cannot undertake any legal action." To the authorities of Meiji Japan, a serious transformation of gender roles was more of a threat than an opportunity.

At the core of Japan's effort at defensive modernization lay its state-guided industrialization program. More than in Europe or the United States, the government itself established a number of enterprises, later selling many of them to private investors. It also acted to create a modern infrastructure by building railroads, creating a postal system, and establishing a national currency and banking system. By the early twentieth century, Japan's industrialization, organized around a number of large firms called *zaibatsu*, was well under way. The country became a major exporter of textiles, in part as a way to pay for needed imports of raw materials, such as cotton, owing to its limited natural resources. Soon the country was able to produce its own munitions and industrial goods as well. Its major cities enjoyed mass-circulation newspapers, movie theaters, and electric lights. All of this was accomplished through its own resources and without the massive foreign debt that so afflicted Egypt and the Ottoman Empire. No other country outside of Europe

Japan's Modernization
In Japan, as in Europe, railroads quickly became a popular symbol of the country's modernization, as this woodblock print from the 1870s illustrates. (*Commodore Perry's Gift of a Railway to the Japanese in 1853*, by Ando or Utagawa Hiroshige [1797–1858]/Private Collection/Bridgeman Images)

and North America had been able to launch its own Industrial Revolution in the nineteenth century. It was a distinctive feature of Japan's modern transformation.

Less distinctive, however, were the social results of that process. Taxed heavily to pay for Japan's ambitious modernization program, many peasant families slid into poverty. Their sometimes-violent protests peaked in 1883–1884 as the Japanese countryside witnessed infanticide, the sale of daughters, and starvation.

While state authorities rigidly excluded women from political life and denied them adult legal status, they badly needed female labor in the country's textile industry, which was central to Japan's economic growth. Accordingly, the majority of Japan's textile workers were young women from poor families in the countryside. Recruiters toured rural villages, contracting with parents for their daughters' labor in return for a payment that the girls had to repay from their wages. That pay was low and their working conditions were terrible. Most lived in factory-provided dormitories and worked twelve or more hours per day. While some committed suicide or ran away and many left after earning enough to pay off their contracts, others organized strikes and joined the anarchist or socialist movements that were emerging among a few intellectuals. One such woman, Kanno Sugako, was hanged in 1911 for participating in a plot to assassinate the emperor. Efforts to create unions and organize strikes, both illegal in Japan at the time, were met with harsh repression even as corporate and state authorities sought to depict the company as a family unit to which workers should give their loyalty, all under the beneficent gaze of the divine emperor.

Japan and the World

Japan's modern transformation soon registered internationally. By the early twentieth century, its economic growth, openness to trade, and embrace of "civilization and enlightenment" from the West persuaded the Western powers to revise the unequal treaties in Japan's favor. This had long been a primary goal of the Meiji regime, and the Anglo-Japanese Treaty of 1902 now acknowledged Japan as an equal player among the Great Powers of the world.

Not only did Japan escape from its semi-colonial entanglements with the West, but it also launched its own empire-building enterprise, even as European powers and the United States were carving up much of Asia, Africa, and Pacific Oceania into colonies or spheres of influence. It was what industrializing Great Powers did in the late nineteenth century, and Japan followed suit, in part to compensate for the relative poverty of its natural resource base. Successful wars against China (1894–1895) and Russia (1904–1905) established Japan as a formidable military competitor in East Asia and the first Asian state to defeat a major European power. Through those victories, Japan also gained colonial control of Taiwan and Korea and a territorial foothold in Manchuria. And in the aftermath of World War I, Japan acquired a growing influence in China's Shandong Peninsula and control over a number of Micronesian islands under the auspices of the League of Nations. Japan's entry onto the broader global stage was felt in many places (see Map 19.3). It added yet one more imperialist power to those already burdening a beleaguered China. Defeat at the hands of Japanese upstarts shocked Russia and triggered the 1905 revolution in that country. To Europeans and Americans, Japan was now an economic, political, and military competitor in Asia.

In the world of subject peoples, the rise of Japan and its defeat of Russia generated widespread admiration among those who saw Japan as a model for their own modern development and perhaps as an ally in the struggle against imperialism. Some Poles, Finns, and Jews viewed the Russian defeat in 1905 as an opening for their own liberation from the Russian Empire and were grateful to Japan for the opportunity. Despite Japan's aggression against their country, many Chinese reformers and nationalists found in the Japanese experience valuable lessons for themselves. Thousands flocked to Japan to study its achievements. Newspapers throughout the Islamic world celebrated Japan's victory over Russia as an "awakening of the East," which might herald Muslims' own liberation. Some Turkish women gave their children Japanese names. Indonesian Muslims from Aceh wrote to the Meiji emperor asking for help in their struggle against the Dutch, and Muslim poets wrote odes in his honor. The Egyptian nationalist Mustafa Kamil spoke for many when he declared: "We are amazed by Japan because it is the first Eastern government to utilize Western civilization to resist the shield of European imperialism in Asia."[17]

Those who directly experienced Japanese imperialism in Taiwan or Korea no doubt had a less positive view, for its colonial policies matched or exceeded the

■ **Connection**
How did Japan's relationship to the larger world change during its modernization process?

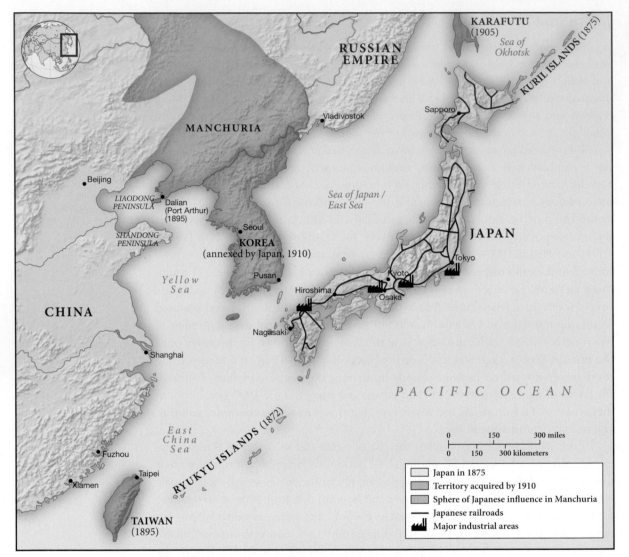

Map 19.3   The Rise of Japan

As Japan modernized after the Meiji Restoration, it launched an empire-building program that provided a foundation for further expansion in the 1930s and during World War II.

brutality of European practices. In the twentieth century, China and much of Southeast Asia suffered bitterly under Japanese imperial aggression. Nonetheless, both the idea of Japan as a liberator of Asia from the European yoke and the reality of Japan as an oppressive imperial power in its own right derived from the country's remarkable modern transformation and its distinctive response to the provocation of Western intrusion.

REFLECTIONS

Success and Failure in History

Beyond describing what happened in the past and explaining why, historians often find themselves evaluating the events they study. When they make judgments about the past, notions of success and failure frequently come into play. Should Europe's Industrial Revolution and its rise to global power be regarded as a success? If so, does that imply that other civilizations were failures? Should we consider Japan more successful than China or the Ottoman Empire during the nineteenth century? Three considerations suggest that we should be very careful in applying these ideas to the complexities of the historical record.

First, and most obviously, is the question of criteria. If the measure of success is national wealth and power, then the Industrial Revolution surely counts as a great accomplishment. But if preservation of the environment, spiritual growth, and the face-to-face relationships of village life are more highly valued, then industrialization, as Gandhi argued, might be more reasonably considered a disaster.

Second, there is the issue of "success for whom?" British artisans who lost their livelihood to industrial machines as well as Japanese women textile workers who suffered through the early stages of industrialization might be forgiven for not appreciating the "success" of their countries' transformation, even if their middle-class counterparts and subsequent generations benefited. In such cases, issues of both social and generational justice complicate any easy assessment of the past.

Third, and finally, success is frequently associated with good judgment and wise choices, yet actors in the historical drama are never completely free in making their decisions, and none, of course, have the benefit of hindsight, which historians enjoy. Did the leaders of China and the Ottoman Empire fail to push industrial development more strongly, or were they not in a position to do so? Were Japanese leaders wiser and more astute than their counterparts elsewhere, or did their knowledge of China's earlier experience and their unique national history simply provide them with circumstances more conducive to modern development? Such questions regarding the possibilities and limitations of human action have no clear-cut answers, but they might caution us about any easy assessment of success and failure.

Second Thoughts

What's the Significance?

Taiping Uprising, 836–38

Opium Wars, 838–40

Commissioner Lin, 839–41

unequal treaties, 839–41

self-strengthening movement, 842–44

Boxer Uprising, 843

Chinese revolution of 1911–1912, 844

"the sick man of Europe," 844–46

Big Picture Questions

1. "The response of each society to European imperialism grew out of its larger historical development and its internal problems." What evidence might support this statement?
2. "Deliberate government policies were more important than historical circumstances in shaping the history of China, the Ottoman Empire, and Japan during the nineteenth century." How might you argue for and against this statement?
3. What kinds of debates, controversies, and conflicts were generated by European intrusion within each of the societies examined in this chapter?
4. **Looking Back:** How did the experiences of China, the Ottoman Empire, Japan, and Latin America, all of which retained their independence despite much European pressure, differ from those of Africa, India, Southeast Asia, and Pacific Oceania, which fell under formal colonial rule?

Next Steps: For Further Study

William Bowman et al., *Imperialism in the Modern World* (2007). A collection of short readings illustrating the various forms and faces of European expansion over the past several centuries.

Carter V. Finley, *The Turks in World History* (2004). A study placing the role of Turkish-speaking peoples in general and the Ottoman Empire in particular in a global context.

Marius B. Jansen, *The Making of Modern Japan* (2002). A well-regarded account of Japan since 1600 by a leading scholar.

Jonathan D. Spence, *The Search for Modern China* (1999). Probably the best single-volume account of Chinese history from about 1600 through the twentieth century.

E. Patricia Tsurumi, *Factory Girls: Women in the Thread Mills of Meiji Japan* (1990). An examination of the lives of women in Japan's nineteenth-century textile factories.

Arthur Waley, *The Opium War through Chinese Eyes* (1968). An older classic that views the Opium War from various Chinese points of view.

"The Decline of the Ottoman Empire," http://www.youtube.com/watch?v=T-SUlb4rwls. A ten-minute video that offers an interpretation of the declining fortunes of the Ottoman Empire.

"Visualizing Cultures: Image-Driven Scholarship," http://ocw.mit.edu/ans7870/21f/21f.027/home/index.html. A collection, provided by MIT, of thoughtful essays and stunning images dealing with China and Japan during the nineteenth century.

WORKING WITH EVIDENCE

Changing China

By the end of the nineteenth century, growing numbers of thoughtful Chinese recognized that their country was in crisis. Repeated European military interventions since the first Opium War in 1839 had humiliated the once-proud Middle Kingdom, reducing it to a semi-colonial dependent of various European powers. A decisive military defeat in a war with Japan in 1894–1895 represented a further humiliation at the hands of a small country long under the cultural influence of China. China also continued to face the enormous problem of widespread poverty among its peasant population, a dilemma reflected in repeated upheavals in the countryside. Both of these issues—foreign imperialism and peasant rebellion—found expression in the Boxer Uprising of 1898–1901 (see page 843). This upheaval demonstrated— once again—the ability of China's vast peasant population to make its presence felt in the political life of the country, as it had in the Taiping Uprising of the 1850s and 1860s (see pages 836–38). The Boxer rebellion's virulent antiforeign and anti-Christian outlook disclosed the depth of feeling against imperialism even among rural people. The outcome of that rebellion—foreign occupation of Beijing and large reparation payments from China's government—revealed China's continuing weakness relative to European and Japanese powers.

In this context, many educated Chinese began to consider alternatives to the status quo and to make plans for changing China. Some of their proposals were reformist and aimed at preserving the Qing dynasty regime; others were more revolutionary and sought to replace dynastic China with a new society and political system altogether. During a brief three-month period in 1898, known as the Hundred Days of Reform, and then again in the decade following the Boxer Uprising, some of the more reformist proposals began to be implemented, including the end of the traditional civil service examination system and the creation of elected provincial assemblies. But more substantial change in China had to await the collapse of the Qing dynasty and the end of the monarchy in 1912, and the most dramatic changes occurred after the communists came to power in 1949. Nonetheless, the proposals of the late nineteenth and early twentieth centuries were significant, for they reveal both the mounting pressures for a new path and the obstacles that confronted those who advocated such changes.

Source 19.1
Toward a Constitutional Monarchy

Among the leading advocates of reform in the aftermath of China's defeat by Japan was Kang Youwei (1858–1927), a brilliant Confucian scholar, whose views informed the Hundred Days of Reform in 1898. Understanding Confucius as a reformer, Kang Youwei argued that the Chinese emperor could be an active agent for China's transformation while operating in a parliamentary and constitutional setting. With its emphasis on human goodness, self-improvement, and the moral example of superiors, Confucianism could provide a framework for real change even as it protected China from "moral degeneration" and an indiscriminate embrace of Western culture. In an appeal to the emperor in early 1898, Kang Youwei spelled out his understanding of what China needed.

■ In what ways does Kang Youwei express a Confucian outlook, and in what respects does he show an awareness of a larger world?

■ What obstacles to reform does Kang Youwei identify?

■ Why does he advocate the Russia of Peter the Great and the Japan of the Meiji reforms as models for China?

KANG YOUWEI
An Appeal to Emperor Guangxu
1898

A survey of all states in the world will show that those states that undertook reforms became stronger while those states which clung to the past perished. . . . If Your Majesty, with your discerning brilliance, observes the trends in other countries, you will see that if we can change, we can preserve ourselves; but if we cannot change, we shall perish.

It is a principle of things that the new is strong but the old is weak. . . . [T]here are no institutions that should remain unchanged for a hundred years. Moreover our present institutions are but unworthy vestiges of the Han, Tang, Yuan, and Ming dynasties. . . . [T]hey are the products of fancy writing and corrupt dealing of the petty officials rather than the original ideas of the ancestors. To

say that they are ancestral institutions is an insult to the ancestors. Furthermore institutions are for the purpose of preserving one's territories. Now that the ancestral territory cannot be preserved, what good is it to maintain the ancestral institutions? . . .

Nowadays the court has been undertaking some reforms, but the action of the emperor is obstructed by the ministers, and the recommendations of the able scholars are attacked by old-fashioned bureaucrats. If the charge is not "using barbarian ways to change China," then it is "upsetting ancestral institutions." Rumors and scandal are rampant, and people fight each other like fire and water. A reform in this way is as effective as attempting a forward march by walking backward. . . . I beg Your Majesty to make up your mind and to decide on the national policy.

After studying ancient and modern institutions, Chinese and foreign, I have found that the institutions of the sage-kings and the Three Dynasties [Xia, Shang, and Zhou dynasties of very ancient times] were excellent, but ancient times were different from today. I hope that Your Majesty will daily read Mencius [a famous Confucian writer] and follow his example of loving the people. The development of the Han, Tang, Song and Ming dynasties may be learned, but it should be remembered that the [present] age of universal unification is different from that of sovereign nations. . . .

As to the republican governments of the United States and France and the constitutional governments of Britain and Germany, these countries are far away and their customs are different from ours. . . . Consequently I beg Your Majesty to adopt the purpose of Peter the Great of Russia as our purpose and to take the Meiji Reform of Japan as the model of our reform. The time and place of Japan's reforms are not remote and her religion and customs are somewhat similar to ours. Her success is manifest; her example can be followed.

Source: Wm. Theodore de Bary and Richard Lufrano, eds., *Sources of Chinese Tradition: From 1600 through the Twentieth Century* (New York: Columbia University Press, 2000), 269–70.

Source 19.2
Education and Examination

At the heart of Chinese elite culture and government lay the country's fabled examination system and the Confucian-based education on which it rested. Those examinations had long been used to select the officials who governed China. The classical texts and rhetorical style that the examinations tested were widely regarded as essential to preserving the essence of Chinese culture while creating common values among the elite. But for those seeking fundamental change in China, the examination system represented everything that was conservative, backward, and out of date, preventing the country from effectively modernizing. In 1905, that ancient examination system was formally and permanently abolished. The two brief selections that follow make the case for educational reform. The first comes from an anonymous editorial in a Chinese newspaper in 1898, while the second was part of an edict from the reforming Emperor Guangxu during the Hundred Days of Reform, also in 1898.

- What criticisms of the old examination system do these excerpts make?
- What kind of education do they advocate?
- How might conservatives respond to these documents?

ANONYMOUS

Editorial on China's Examination System
1898

The dynasty's examination system is extremely annoying and cumbersome. . . . Students go through innumerable hardships before they can obtain the right to wear the robes designating them as officially authorized students. Hence year after year they persist in their studies until their hair turns white. One half of each year is taken up with examinations, and the other half is burdened with wife, children, home, and family. Any spare time is spent trying to master the eight-legged essay. And yet it is very difficult to attain satisfactory competence in the eight-legged style, even though it is considered so vital. What then, if in addition, one wants to read useful books and study useful subjects? . . .

For the court to use poetry, rhyme-prose, and fine script as the criteria for passing or failing the examinations for men of ability is truly vulgar and ridiculous. . . . [T]he multitude of problems on the coast [a reference to European penetration] has steadily weakened the nation. Poetry and rhyme-prose are not adequate to cope with this changing situation, and fine script is not adequate to withstand the enemy. How are we to devise a policy to bring peace and to emulate the wealth and power [of the Western nations]? Every meaningless and extravagant custom should be reformed. . . . Only then will officials of the court . . . be able to devote themselves to useful studies. Their ambitions will no longer be diverted by eight-legged essays, poetry, rhyme-prose and fine script, nor will their minds be disturbed by all the various examinations.

EMPEROR GUANGXU

Edict on Education
1898

Our scholars are now without solid and practical education; our artisans are without scientific instructors; when compared with other countries, we soon see how weak we are. Does anyone think that our troops are as well drilled or as well led as those of the foreign armies? Or that we can successfully stand against them? Changes must be made to accord with the necessities of the times. . . . Keeping in mind the morals of the sages and wise men, we must make them the basis on which to build newer and better structures. We must substitute modern arms and western organization for our old regime; we must select our military officers according to western methods of military education; we must establish elementary and high schools, colleges and universities, in accordance with those of foreign countries; we must abolish the Wen-chang (literary essay) and obtain a knowledge of ancient and modern world-history, a right conception of the present-day state of affairs, with special reference to the governments and institutions of the countries of the five great continents; and we must understand their arts and sciences.

Sources: J. Mason Gentzler, *Changing China* (New York: Praeger, 1977), 88–89; Isaac Taylor Headland, *Court Life in China* (New York: F. H. Revell, 1909).

Source 19.3
Gender, Reform, and Revolution

Among those seeking to change China, the question of women's roles in society frequently arose. Kang Youwei (see Source 19.1), for example, looked forward to the end of traditional marriage, hoping it would be replaced by a series of one-year contracts between a man and woman, which he thought would ensure gender equality. But the most well-known advocate for women was Qiu Jin (1875–1907). Born into a well-to-do family with liberal inclinations, she received a fine literary education, developing a passion for reading as well as for swordplay, horseback riding, and martial arts.

Married to a much older man at age eighteen, she was distinctly unsatisfied in such a conventional life and developed a growing feminist awareness, sometimes dressing in men's clothes and Western styles. "My aim is to dress like a man!" she told a friend. "[I]n China men are strong, and women are oppressed because they're supposed to be weak. . . . If I first take on the form of a man, then I think my mind too will eventually become that of a man. My hair is cut in a foreigner's style, something Chinese aren't supposed to do, and I'm wearing Western clothes."[18]

In 1903, Qiu Jin did something even more unthinkable for a Chinese woman when she left her husband and children to pursue an education in Japan, selling her jewelry to finance the trip. "Cut off from my family I leave my native land," she wrote. "Unbinding my feet I clean out a thousand years of poison."[19]

Returning to China in 1906, she started a women's magazine, the *Chinese Women's Journal*, which was a strong advocate for women's independence and education. "Of the enlightened countries today," declared an article in the *Journal*, "there is not one which does not stress education for women, and thus their countries are strong."[20] Soon Qiu Jin became active in revolutionary circles. For her role in an abortive plot to overthrow the Qing dynasty, she was arrested, tortured, and beheaded in 1907 at the age of thirty-two. Asked to write a confession moments before her execution, she instead penned a short verse of seven characters that included her surname, Qiu, which literally means "autumn" in Chinese: "Autumn rain, autumn wind, they make one die of sorrow."[21]

The selection that follows comes from her most famous appeal for the rights of women.

- How did Qiu Jin describe the difficulties that faced Chinese women?

- How did she account for these sad conditions?

- What did she advocate as a remedy for the problems she identified? Did she seem to have a political agenda?

- To what extent do you think she was writing from personal experience?

Qiu Jin

Address to Two Hundred Million Fellow Countrywomen

1904

Alas, the most unfairly treated things on this earth are the two hundred million who are born as Chinese women. We consider ourselves lucky to be born to a kind father. If we are unlucky, our father will be an ill-tempered and unreasonable person who repeatedly says, "How unlucky I am, yet another useless one," as if at any instant he could pick us up and throw us to our death. He will resent us and say things like "she's eventually going to someone else's family" and give us cold and contemptuous looks. When we grow a few years older, without bothering to ask us our thoughts, they will bind our tender, white and natural feet with a strip of cloth, never loosening them even while we sleep. In the end, the flesh is mangled and the bones broken, all so that relatives, friends and neighbors can say, "the girl from so and so's family has tiny feet."

When the time comes (for the parents) to select a husband, everything is based on the promises of two shameless matchmakers. The daughter's parents will go along with any proposal as long as his family is rich and powerful. Her parents do not bother to ask if the man's family is respectable, or inquire about the groom's temperament and level of education. On the wedding day, one will sit in the brightly decorated bridal sedan chair barely able to breathe. When we arrive at the new home, if the husband is found to be unambitious but even-tempered, her family will say we are blessed with good fortune from a previous life. If he is no good, her family will blame it "on our wrong conduct in a previous life," or simply "bad luck." If we dare complain, or otherwise try to counsel our husbands, then a scolding and beating will befall us. Others who hear of the abuse will say: "She is a woman of no virtue. She does not act as a wife should!" Can you believe such words? These aspersions are cast without the chance for an appeal! Further inequities will follow if the husband dies. The wife will have to wear a mourning dress for three years and will not be allowed to remarry. Yet, if the wife dies, the husband only needs to wear a blue (mourning) braid. Some men find even that unbecoming and do not bother to wear it at all. Even when the wife has only been dead for three days, he can go out and cavort and indulge himself. A new wife is allowed to enter the household even before the official seven weeks of mourning is over. In the beginning, Heaven created all people with no differences between men and women. Ask yourselves this, how could these people have been born without women? Why are things so unjust? Everyday these men say, "We ought to be equal and treat people kindly." Then why do they treat women so unfairly and unequally as if they were African slaves?

A woman has to learn not to depend on others, but to rely on herself instead. . . . Why can't we reject footbinding? Are they afraid of women being educated, knowledgeable, and perhaps surpassing them? Men do not allow us to study. We must not simply go along with their decision without even challenging them. . . .

However, from now on I hope we can leave the past behind us and focus on our future. Assuming we have died in the past and are reincarnated into our next life, the elders should not say "too old to be of any use." If you have a decent husband who wants to establish a school, do not stop him. If you have a fine son who wishes to study abroad, do not stop him. The middle-aged wife should not hinder her husband by causing him to have no ambition and achieve nothing. If you have a son, send him to school. Do the same for your daughter and never bind her feet. If you have a young girl, the best choice would be for her to attend school, but even if she is unable to attend schools, you should teach her to read and write at home. If you come from a family of officials that has money, you should persuade your husband to establish schools and factories and do good deeds that will help common people. If your family is poor, you should work hard to help your husband. Do not be lazy and do nothing. These are my hopes. All of you are aware that we are about to lose our country. Men can scarcely protect themselves. How can we rely on them? We must revitalize ourselves. Otherwise all will be too late when the country is lost. Everybody! Everybody! Please keep my hopes alive!

Source: David G. Atwill and Lurong Y. Atwill, *Sources in Chinese History* (Upper Saddle River, NJ: Prentice Hall, 2010), 140–41.

Source 19.4
Prescriptions for a Revolutionary China

While some advocates for change pressed for various reforms within the framework of Qing dynasty China, others felt that the millennia-old monarchy itself had to be overthrown if China was to modernize and prosper as a nation. The leading figure among China's late nineteenth-century revolutionaries was Sun Yat-sen (1866–1925), a convert to Christianity, a trained medical doctor, and by the 1890s an ardent revolutionary. From exile in Europe, the United States, and Japan, Sun plotted various uprisings against the Qing dynasty and in 1905 created the Revolutionary Alliance in an effort to bring together the various groups seeking to end the ancient imperial system. But what kind of society and political structure did Sun envisage for his country? In 1906, Sun spelled out an early formulation of his "three people's principles"—nationalism, democracy, and people's livelihood—that articulated his vision for China's future.

- Why does Sun Yat-sen believe that China requires a revolution rather than reform?

- In his view, who are the enemies of the Chinese nation?

- What elements of Sun's prescriptions for China's future derive from traditional Chinese practice and which reflect Western influence?

- Is Sun Yat-sen advocating a socialist future for China?

- How might Kang Youwei in Source 19.1 respond to Sun Yat-sen's prescriptions for the future?

SUN YAT-SEN

The Three People's Principles and the Future of the Chinese People

1906

Nationalism . . . has to do with human nature and applies to everyone. Today, more than 260 years have passed since the Manchus entered China proper, yet even as children we Han [ethnic Chinese] would certainly not mistake them for fellow Han. This is the root of nationalism. . . . It simply means not allowing such people [the Manchu rulers of the Qing dynasty] to seize our political power, for only when we Han are in control politically do we have a nation. . . .

Actually we are already a people without a nation. . . . Our nation is the most populous, most ancient, and most civilized in the world, yet today we are a lost nation. . . . We Han are now swiftly being caught up in a tidal wave of nationalist revolution, yet the Manchus continue to discriminate against the Han. They boast that their forefathers conquered the Han because of their superior unity and that they intend . . . to dominate the Han forever. . . . Certainly once we Han unite, our power will be thousands of times greater than theirs and the success of our nationalist revolution will be assured.

As for the Principle of Democracy, it is the foundation of the political revolution. . . . For several thousand years China has been a monarchial autocracy, a type of political system intolerable to those living in freedom and equality. A nationalist revolution is not itself sufficient to get rid of such a system . . . a political revolution is an absolute necessity. The aim of the political revolution is to create a constitutional democratic political system. . . . [Such a] revolution would be necessary even if the monarch were a Han.

As for the Principle of the People's Livelihood . . . , we must try to improve the economic structures of society so as to preclude a social revolution in the future. . . . As civilization advanced, people relied less on physical labor and more on natural forces, since electricity and steam could accomplish things a thousand times faster than physical strength. . . . [N]ow with the development of natural forces that human labor cannot match, agriculture and industry have fallen completely into the hands of capitalists. Unable to compete, the poor have naturally been reduced to destitution. . . . [E]very informed person knows that a social revolution is inevitable in Europe and America.

Indeed this constitutes a lesson for China. . . . Civilization [advanced industrial capitalist countries] yields both good and bad fruits, and we should embrace the good and reject the bad. In Europe and America the rich monopolize the good fruits of civilization, while the poor suffer from its evil fruits. . . .

With respect to a solution . . . the procedure I most favor is land valuation. For example, if a landlord has land worth 1000 dollars, its price can be set at 1000 or even 2000 dollars. Perhaps in the future, after communications have been developed, the value of his land will rise to 10,000 dollars; the owner should receive 2000, which entails a profit and no loss, and the 8000 increment will go to the state. Such an arrangement will greatly benefit both the state and the people's livelihood. Naturally it will also eliminate the shortcomings that have permitted a few people to monopolize wealth. . . .

As to the future constitution I propose that we introduce a new principle, that of the "five separate powers." Under this system there will be two other powers in addition to the [executive, legislative, and judicial]. One is the examination power. . . . American officials are either elected or appointed. Formerly there were no civil service examinations, which led to serious shortcomings. . . . With respect to elections, those endowed with eloquence ingratiated themselves with the public and won elections, while those who had learning and ideals but lacked eloquence were ignored. Consequently members of America's House of Representatives have often been foolish and ignorant people who have made its history quite ridiculous. . . . Therefore the future constitution of the Republic of China must provide for an independent branch expressly responsible for civil service examinations. Furthermore all officials, however high their rank, must undergo examinations in order to determine their qualifications.

The other power is the supervisory power, responsible for monitoring matters involving impeachment. . . . Since ancient times, China had a supervisory organization, the Censorate, to monitor the traditional social order.

Source: Julie Lee Wei et al., *Prescriptions for Saving China: Selected Writings of Sun Yat-sen* (Stanford, CA: Hoover Institution Press, 1994), 41–50.

DOING HISTORY

Changing China

1. **Defining obstacles to change:** What hindrances to China's effective transformation are stated or implied in these documents? Do their authors perceive any positive qualities in Chinese civilization that might facilitate the country's transformation?

2. **Assessing goals:** "China as a culture and a political system must be destroyed in order to preserve China as a nation." To what extent would the authors of these documents have agreed or disagreed with this statement?

3. **Identifying differences:** Imagine a conversation among the authors of these documents. What points of agreement might they find? What conflicts would likely arise among them?

4. **Considering "westernization" and "modernization":** To what extent do these proposals represent plans to "westernize" China? Or might they rather be considered "modernizing" efforts? What is the difference between the two concepts?

PART SIX

THE MOST RECENT CENTURY

1914–2015

Contents

photos: left, Library of Congress, Prints and Photographs Division, LC-USZC4-2119; center, Libor Hajsky/CTK/AP Photo; right, Copyright Andrew Aitchison/In Pictures/Corbis/AP Images

THE BIG PICTURE

SINCE WORLD WAR I:
A NEW PERIOD IN WORLD HISTORY?

Dividing up time into coherent segments—periods, eras, ages—is the way historians mark major changes in the lives of individuals, local communities, social groups, nations, and civilizations and also in the larger story of humankind as a whole. Because all such divisions are artificial, imposed by scholars on a continuously flowing stream of events, they are endlessly controversial and never more so than in the case of the twentieth century. To many historians, that century, and a new era in the human journey, began in 1914 with the outbreak of World War I. That terrible conflict, after all, represented a fratricidal civil war within Western civilization, triggered the Russian Revolution and the beginning of world communism, and stimulated many in the colonial world to work for their own independence. And the way it ended set the stage for an even more terrible struggle in World War II.

But does the century since 1914 represent a separate phase of world history? Granting it that status has become conventional in many world history textbooks, including this one, but there are reasons to wonder whether future generations will agree. One problem, of course, lies in the brevity of this period—only 100 years, compared to the many centuries or millennia that define earlier eras. It is interesting to notice that our time periods get progressively shorter as we approach the present. Perhaps this is because an immense overload of information about the most recent century makes it difficult to distinguish what will prove of lasting significance and what will later seem of only passing importance. Furthermore, because we are so close to the events we study and obviously ignorant of the future, we cannot know if or when this most recent period of world history will end. Or, as some have argued, has it ended already, perhaps with the collapse of the Soviet Union in 1991, with the attacks of September 11, 2001, or with the global economic crisis beginning in 2008? If so, are we now in yet another phase of historical development?

Like all other historical periods, this most recent century both carried on from the past and developed distinctive characteristics as well. Whether that combination of the old and new merits the designation of a separate era in world history will likely be debated for a long time to come. For our purposes, it will be enough to highlight both its continuities with the past and the sharp changes that the last 100 years have witnessed.

One World (p. 1022)

Image created by Reto Stockli, Nazmi El Saleous, and Marit Jentoft-Nilsen, NASA GSFC

Consider, for example, the world wars that played such an important role in the first half of the century. Featured in Chapter 20, they grew out of Europeans' persistent inability to embody their civilization within a single state or empire, as China had long done. They also represent a further stage of European rivalries around the globe that had been going on for four centuries. Nonetheless, the world wars of the twentieth century were also new in the extent to which whole populations were mobilized to fight them and in the enormity of the destruction that they caused. During World War II, for example, Hitler's attempted extermination of the Jews in the Holocaust and the United States' dropping of atomic bombs on Japanese cities marked something new in the history of human conflict.

The communist phenomenon, examined in Chapter 21, provides another illustration of the blending of old and new. The Russian (1917) and Chinese (1949) revolutions, both of which were enormous social upheavals, brought to power regimes committed to remaking their societies from top to bottom along socialist lines. They were the first large-scale attempts in modern world history to undertake such a gigantic task, and in doing so they broke sharply with the capitalist democratic model of the West. They also created a new and global division of humankind, expressed most dramatically in the cold war between the communist East and the capitalist West. On the other hand, the communist experience also drew much from the past. The great revolutions of the twentieth century derived from long-standing conflicts within Russian and Chinese societies, particularly between impoverished and exploited peasants and dominant landlord classes. The ideology of those communist governments came from the thinking of the nineteenth-century German intellectual Karl Marx. Their intentions, like those of their capitalist enemies, were modernization and industrialization. They simply claimed to do it better — more rapidly and more justly.

Another distinguishing feature of the twentieth century lay in the disintegration of its great empires — the Austro-Hungarian, Ottoman, and Russian/Soviet empires and especially the European empires that had encompassed so much of Asia and Africa. In their wake, dozens of new nation-states emerged, fundamentally reshaping the world of this most recent century. Examined in Chapter 22, this enormous process is, at one level, simply the latest turn of the wheel in the endless rise and fall of empires, dating back to the ancient Akkadian Empire, over 4,000 years ago. But in the twentieth century, something new occurred, for the very idea of empire was rendered illegitimate in the twentieth century, much as slavery lost its international acceptance in the nineteenth century. The superpowers of the mid-twentieth century — the Soviet Union and the United States — both claimed an anticolonial ideology, even as both of them constructed their own "empires" of a different kind. By the beginning of the twenty-first century, some 200 nation-states, many of them in the Global South and each claiming sovereignty and legal equality with all the others, provided a distinctly new political order for the planet.

The less visible underlying processes of the twentieth century, just like the more dramatic wars, revolutions, and political upheavals, also had roots in the past as well as new expressions in the new century. Feminism, for example, explored in Chapter 23, had taken root in the West during the nineteenth century but became global in the twentieth, challenging women's subordination more extensively than ever before. Perhaps the most fundamental process of the past century has been explosive population growth, as human numbers more than quadrupled since 1900, leaving the planet with over 7.2 billion people by 2014. This was an absolutely unprecedented rate of growth that conditioned practically every other feature of the century's history. Still, this new element of twentieth-century world history built on earlier achievements, most notably the increased food supply deriving from the global spread of American crops such as corn and potatoes. Improvements in medicine and sanitation, which grew out of the earlier Scientific and Industrial Revolutions, likewise drove down death rates and thus spurred population growth.

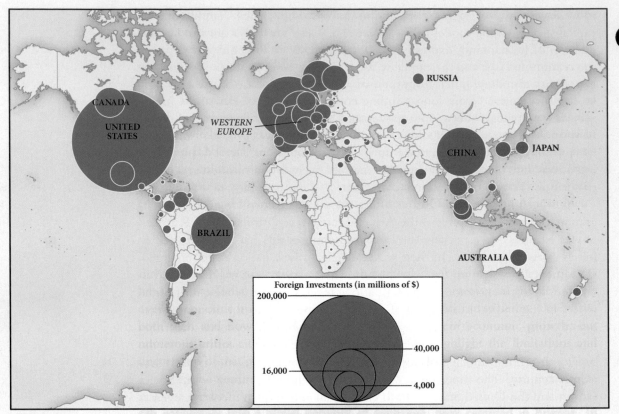

RUSSIA

CANADA

UNITED
STATES

WESTERN
EUROPE

CHINA   JAPAN

BRAZIL

AUSTRALIA

Foreign Investments (in millions of $)

200,000

40,000

16,000

4,000

Globalization in Action: Foreign Direct Investment in the Late Twentieth Century (p. 1027)

While global population increased fourfold in the twentieth century, industrial output grew fortyfold. Despite large variations over time and place, this unprecedented economic growth was associated with a cascading rate of scientific and technological innovation as well as with the extension of industrial production to many regions of the world. This too was a wholly novel feature of twentieth-century world history and, combined with population growth, resulted in an extraordinary and mounting human impact on the environment. Historian J. R. McNeill wrote, "This is the first time in human history that we have altered ecosystems with such intensity, on such a scale, and with such speed. . . . The human race, without intending anything of the sort, has undertaken a gigantic uncontrolled experiment on the earth."[1] By the late twentieth century, that experiment had taken humankind well into what many scientists have been calling the Anthropocene, the "age of man," in which human activity is leaving an enduring and global mark on the geological, atmospheric, and biological history of the planet itself. From a longer-term perspective, of course, these developments represent a continued unfolding of the Scientific and Industrial Revolutions. Both began in Europe, but in the twentieth century they largely lost their unique association with the West as they took hold in many cultures. Furthermore, the human impact on the earth and other living creatures has a history dating back to the extinction of some large mammals at the hands of Paleolithic hunters, although the scope and extent of that impact during the past century is without precedent.

Much the same might be said about that other grand process of contemporary world history—globalization, which is the focus of Chapter 23. It too has a genealogy reaching deep into the past, reflected in the Silk Road trading network; Indian Ocean and trans-Saharan commerce; the spread of Buddhism, Christianity, and Islam; and the Columbian exchange. But the most recent century deepened and extended the connections among the distinct peoples, nations, and regions of the world in ways unparalleled in earlier times. A few strokes on a keyboard can send money racing around the planet; radio, television, and the Internet link the world in an unprecedented network of communication; far more people than ever before produce for and depend on the world market; and global inequalities increasingly surface as sources of international conflict. For good or ill, we live—all of us—in a new phase of an ancient process.

The four chapters of Part Six explore these global themes that have so decisively shaped the history of the past century. Perhaps there is enough that is new about that century to treat it, tentatively, as a distinct era in human history, but only what happens next will determine how this period will be understood by later generations. Will it be regarded as the beginning of the end of the modern age, as human demands on the earth prove unsustainable? Or will it be seen as the midpoint of an ongoing process that extends a full modernity to the entire planet? Will recognition of our common fate as human beings generate shared values, a culture of tolerance, and an easing of international tensions? Or will global inequalities and rivalry over diminishing resources foster even greater and more dangerous conflicts? Like all of our ancestors, every one of them, we too live in a fog when contemplating our futures and see more clearly only in retrospect. In this strange way, our future will shape the telling of the past, even as the past shapes the living of the future.

MAPPING PART SIX

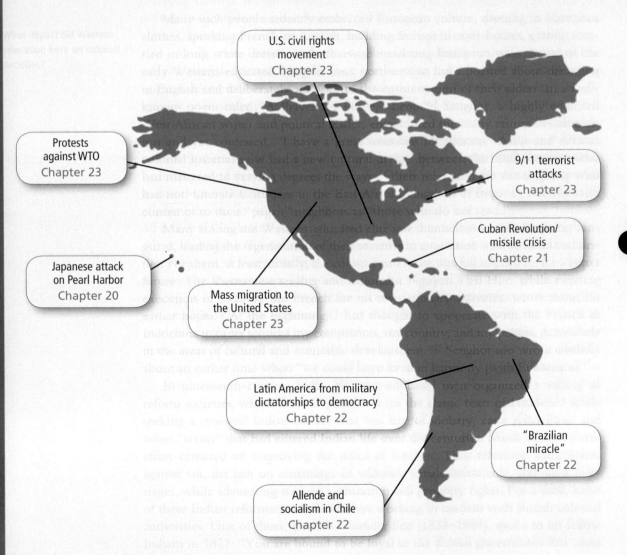

Protests
against WTO
Chapter 23

U.S. civil rights
movement
Chapter 23

9/11 terrorist
attacks
Chapter 23

Japanese attack
on Pearl Harbor
Chapter 20

Mass migration to
the United States
Chapter 23

Cuban Revolution/
missile crisis
Chapter 21

Latin America from military
dictatorships to democracy
Chapter 22

"Brazilian
miracle"
Chapter 22

Allende and
socialism in Chile
Chapter 22

World wars in Europe
Chapter 20

Rise and fall of communism in
Russia and Eastern Eurpope
Chapters 21 and 23

European Union
Chapter 23

Iranian
revolution
Chapter 22

Communist revolution
in China
Chapter 21

Korean War
Chapter 21

Atomic bombs on
Hiroshima and Nagasaki
Chapter 20

Arab uprising
Chapter 23

Israel established
Chapter 22

Vietnam War
Chapter 23

Indian and Pakistani
independence
Chapter 22

End of apartheid
Chapter 22

African independence
from colonialism
Chapter 22

Indonesian independence
Chapter 22

1778   1943

AMERICANS
will always fight for liberty

Collapse at the Center

World War, Depression, and the Rebalancing of Global Power

1914–1970s

"I was told that I was fighting a war that would end all wars, but that wasn't the case." Spoken a few years before his death, these were the thoughts of Alfred Anderson, a World War I veteran who died in Scotland in November 2005, at the age of 109. He was apparently the last survivor of the famous Christmas truce of 1914, when British and German soldiers, enemies on the battlefield of that war, briefly mingled, exchanged gifts, and played football in the no-man's-land that lay between their entrenchments in Belgium. He had been especially dismayed when in 2003 his own unit, the famous Black Watch regiment, was ordered into Iraq along with other British forces.[1] Despite his disappointment at the many conflicts that followed World War I, Anderson's own lifetime had witnessed the fulfillment of the promise of the Christmas truce. By the time he died, the major European nations had put aside their centuries-long hostilities, and war between Britain and Germany, which had erupted twice in the twentieth century, seemed unthinkable.

The "Great War," which came to be called the First World War or World War I (1914–1918), effectively launched the twentieth century, considered as a new phase of world history. That bitter conflict—essentially a European civil war with a global reach—provoked the Russian Revolution and the beginnings of world communism. It was followed by the economic meltdown of the Great Depression, by the rise of Nazi Germany and the horror of the Holocaust, and by World War II, an even bloodier and more destructive struggle that encompassed much of the world. During those three decades, Western Europe—for more than a century

---

The United States and World War II   The Second World War and its aftermath marked the decisive emergence of the United States as a global superpower. In this official 1943 poster, U.S. soldiers march forward to "fight for liberty" against fascism while casting a sideways glance for inspiration at the ragged colonial militiamen of their Revolutionary War.

the dominant and dominating center of the modern "world system"—largely self-destructed, in a process with profound and long-term implications far beyond Europe itself. By 1945, an outside observer might well have thought that Western civilization, which for several centuries was in the ascendancy on the global stage, had damaged itself beyond repair. Certainly, the subsequent emergence of the United States and the Soviet Union as rival superpowers marked a very different balance of global power.

In the second half of the century, however, European civilization proved resilient. Western Europe recovered remarkably from the devastation of war, rebuilt its industrial economy, and set aside its war-prone nationalist passions in a loose European Union. But as Europe revived after 1945, it lost both its overseas colonial possessions and its position as the political, economic, and military core of Western civilization. That role now passed across the Atlantic to the United States, marking a major change in the historical development of the West. The offspring now overshadowed its parent.

SEEKING THE MAIN POINT

In what ways were the world wars and the Great Depression motors of global change in the history of the twentieth century?

The First World War: European Civilization in Crisis, 1914–1918

Since 1500, Europe had assumed an increasingly prominent position on the global stage, driven by its growing military capacity and the marvels of its Scientific and Industrial Revolutions. By 1900, Europeans, or people with European ancestry, largely controlled the world's other peoples through their formal empires, their informal influence, or the weight of their numbers (see Map 20.1). That unique situation provided the foundation for Europeans' pride, self-confidence, and sense of superiority. Few could have imagined that this "proud tower" of European dominance would lie shattered less than a half century later. The starting point in that unraveling was the First World War.

An Accident Waiting to Happen

Europe's modern transformation and its global ascendancy were certainly not accompanied by a growing unity or stability among its own peoples—quite the opposite. The most obvious division was among its competing states, a long-standing feature of European political life. Those historical rivalries further sharpened as both Italy and Germany joined their fragmented territories into two major new powers around 1870. The arrival on the international scene of a powerful and rapidly industrializing Germany, seeking its "place in the sun," was a disruptive new element in European political life, especially for the more established powers, such as Britain, France, and Russia. Since the defeat of Napoleon in 1815, a fragile and fluctuating balance of power had generally maintained the peace among Europe's

A MAP OF TIME

1914–1918	World War I
1917	Bolshevik Revolution in Russia; United States enters World War I
1919	Treaty of Versailles ending World War I; founding of Nazi Party
1920	Treaty of Sèvres, dissolving the Ottoman Empire
1922	Mussolini comes to power in Italy
1929	Beginning of Great Depression
1933	Hitler assumes power in Germany
1937–1938	Japan invades China, beginning World War II in Asia; Rape of Nanjing
1939	Germany invades Poland, beginning World War II in Europe
1939–1945	World War II; the Holocaust
1941	Japanese attack on Pearl Harbor
1945	Atomic bombing of Hiroshima and Nagasaki; United Nations created
1945–1952	U.S. occupation of Japan
1946–1991	Cold war
1948–1952	Marshall Plan for Europe
1957	European Economic Community established
1994	European Union established
2002	Introduction of the euro

major countries. By the early twentieth century, that balance of power was expressed in two rival alliances, the Triple Alliance of Germany, Italy, and the Austro-Hungarian Empire and the Triple Entente of Russia, France, and Britain. Those commitments, undertaken in the interests of national security, transformed a relatively minor incident in the Balkans into a conflagration that consumed almost all of Europe.

That incident occurred on June 28, 1914, when a Serbian nationalist assassinated the heir to the Austro-Hungarian throne, Archduke Franz Ferdinand. To the rulers of Austria-Hungary, the surging nationalism of Serbian Slavs was a mortal threat to the cohesion of their fragile multinational empire, which included other Slavic peoples as well. Thus they determined to crush it. But behind Austria-Hungary lay its far more powerful ally, Germany, and behind tiny Serbia lay Russia, with its self-proclaimed mission of protecting other Slavic peoples. Allied to Russia were

Map 20.1   The World in 1914

A map of the world in 1914 shows an unprecedented situation in which one people—Europeans or those of European descent—exercised enormous control and influence over virtually the entire planet.

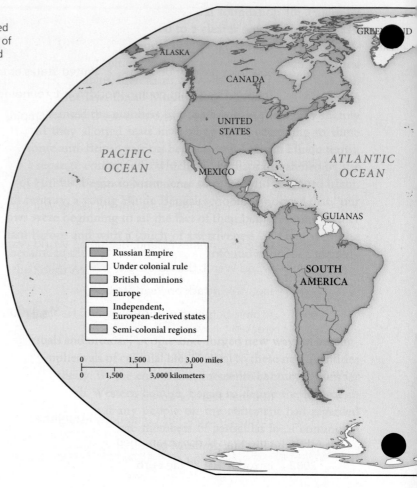

the French and the British. Thus a system of alliances intended to keep the peace created obligations that drew the Great Powers of Europe into a general war by early August 1914 (see Map 20.2).

The outbreak of that war was something of an accident, in that none of the major states planned or predicted the archduke's assassination or deliberately sought a prolonged conflict, but the system of rigid alliances made Europe vulnerable to that kind of accident. Moreover, behind those alliances lay other factors that contributed to the eruption of war and shaped its character. One of them was a mounting popular nationalism (see Chapter 18, pages 790–92). Slavic nationalism and Austro-Hungarian opposition to it certainly lay at the heart of the war's beginning. More importantly, the rulers of the major countries of Europe saw the world as an arena of conflict and competition among rival nation-states. The Great Powers of Europe competed intensely for colonies, spheres of influence, and superiority in armaments. Schools, mass media, and military service had convinced millions of

■ **Explanation**

What aspects of Europe's nineteenth-century history contributed to the First World War?

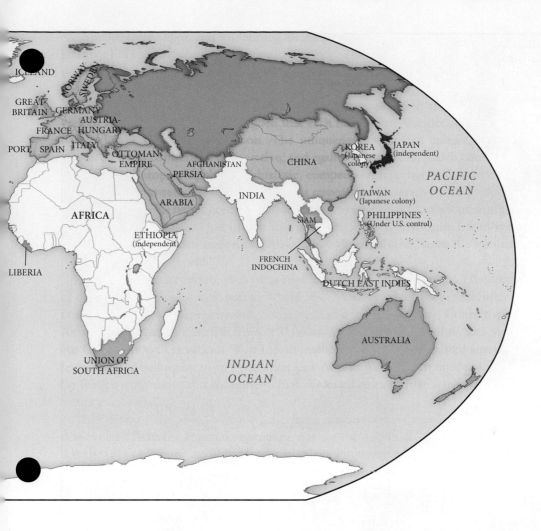

ordinary Europeans that their national identities were profoundly and personally meaningful. The public pressure of these competing nationalisms allowed statesmen little room for compromise and ensured widespread popular support, at least initially, for the decision to go to war. Many men rushed to recruiting offices, fearing that the war might end before they could enlist. Celebratory parades sent them off to the front. British women were encouraged to present a white feather, a symbol of cowardice, to men not in uniform, thus affirming a warrior understanding of masculinity. For conservative governments, the prospect of war was a welcome occasion for national unity in the face of the mounting class- and gender-based conflicts in European societies.

Also contributing to the war was an industrialized militarism. Europe's armed rivalries had long ensured that military men enjoyed great social prestige, and most heads of state wore uniforms in public. All the Great Powers had substantial standing armies and, except for Britain, relied on conscription (compulsory military service)

Map 20.2   Europe on the Eve of World War I

Despite many elements of common culture, Europe in 1914 was a powder keg, with its major states armed to the teeth and divided into two rival alliances. In the early stages of the war, Italy changed sides to join the French, British, and Russians.

to staff them. One expression of the quickening rivalry among these states was a mounting arms race in naval warships, particularly between Germany and Britain. Furthermore, each of the major states had developed elaborate "war plans" that spelled out in great detail the movement of men and materials that should occur immediately upon the outbreak of war. Such plans created a hair-trigger mentality since each country had an incentive to strike first so that its particular strategy could be implemented on schedule and without interruption or surprise. The rapid industrialization of warfare had generated an array of novel weapons, including submarines, tanks, airplanes, poison gas, machine guns, and barbed wire. This new military technology contributed to the staggering casualties of the war, including some 10 million deaths, the vast majority male; perhaps twice that number were wounded, crippled, or disfigured. For countless women, as a result, there would be no husbands or children.

Europe's imperial reach around the world likewise shaped the scope and conduct of the war. It funneled colonial troops and laborers by the hundreds of thousands into the war effort, with men from Africa, India, China, Southeast Asia, Australia, New Zealand, Canada, and South Africa taking part in the conflict. Battles raged in Africa and the South Pacific as British and French forces sought to seize German colonies abroad. Japan, allied with Britain, took various German possessions in China and the Pacific and made heavy demands on China itself. The Ottoman Empire, which entered the conflict on the side of Germany, became the site of intense military actions and witnessed an Arab revolt against Ottoman control. Finally, the United States, after initially seeking to avoid involvement in European quarrels, joined the war in 1917 when German submarines threatened American shipping. Some 2 million Americans took part in the first U.S. military action on European soil and helped turn the tide in favor of the British and French. Thus the war, though centered in Europe, had global dimensions and certainly merited its title as a "world war."

Women and the Great War
World War I temporarily brought a halt to the women's suffrage movement as well as to women's activities on behalf of international peace. Most women on both sides actively supported their countries' war efforts, as suggested by this British wartime poster, inviting women to work in the munitions industry. (Eileen Tweedy/The Art Archive at Art Resource, NY)

Legacies of the Great War

The Great War shattered almost every expectation. Most Europeans believed in the late summer of 1914 that "the boys will be home by Christmas," but instead the war ground relentlessly on for more than four years before ending in a German defeat in November 1918. At the beginning, most military experts expected a war of movement and attack, but armies on the western front soon became bogged down in a war of attrition; combatants engaging in trench warfare experienced enormous casualties while gaining or losing only a few yards of muddy, blood-soaked ground. Extended battles lasting months—such as those at Verdun and the Somme in France—generated casualties of a million or more each, as the destructive potential of industrialized warfare made itself tragically felt. Moreover, everywhere the conflict became a "total war," requiring the mobilization of each country's entire population. Thus the authority of governments expanded greatly. The German state, for example, assumed such control over the economy that its policies became known as "war socialism." Vast propaganda campaigns sought to arouse citizens by depicting a cruel and inhuman enemy who killed innocent children and violated women. Labor unions agreed to suspend strikes and accept sacrifices for the common good, while women, replacing the men who had left the factories for the battlefront, temporarily abandoned the struggle for the vote.

■ **Change**

In what ways did World War I mark new departures in the history of the twentieth century?

No less surprising were the longer-term outcomes of the war. In the European cockpit of that conflict, unprecedented casualties, particularly among elite and well-educated groups, and physical destruction, especially in France, led to a widespread disillusionment among intellectuals with their own civilization. The war seemed to mock the Enlightenment values of progress, tolerance, and rationality. Who could believe any longer that the West was superior or that its vaunted science and technology were unquestionably good things? In the most famous novel to emerge from the war, the German veteran Erich Maria Remarque's *All Quiet on the Western Front*, one soldier expressed what many no doubt felt: "It must all be lies and of no account when the culture of a thousand years could not prevent this stream of blood being poured out."

The aftermath of war also brought substantial social and cultural changes to ordinary Europeans and Americans. Integrating millions of returning veterans into civilian life was no easy task, for they had experienced horrors almost beyond imagination. Governments sought to accommodate them, in Britain for example, with housing programs called "homes for heroes" emphasizing traditional family values. Women were urged to leave factory work and return to their homes, where they would not compete for "men's jobs." French authorities proclaimed Mother's Day as a new holiday, designed to encourage childbearing and thus replace the millions lost in the war.

Nonetheless, the war had loosened the hold of tradition in various ways. Enormous casualties promoted social mobility, allowing the less exalted to move into positions previously dominated by the upper classes. As the war ended, suffrage movements revived and women received the right to vote in a number of countries—Britain, the United States, Germany, the Soviet Union, Hungary, and Poland—in part perhaps because of the sacrifices they had made during the conflict. Young middle-class women, sometimes known as "flappers," began to flout convention by smoking, dancing, appearing at nightclubs, drinking hard liquor, cutting their hair short, wearing revealing clothing, and generally expressing a more open sexuality. A new consumerism encouraged those who could to acquire cars, washing machines, vacuum cleaners, electric irons, gas ovens, and other newly available products. Radio and the movies now became vehicles of popular culture, transmitting American jazz to Europe and turning Hollywood stars into international celebrities.

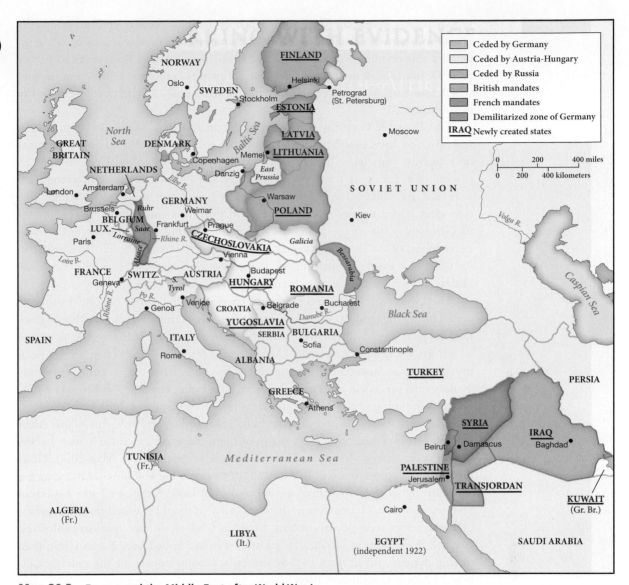

Map 20.3   Europe and the Middle East after World War I

The Great War brought into existence a number of new states that were carved out of the old German, Austro-Hungarian, Russian, and Ottoman empires. Turkey and the new states in Europe were independent, but those in the Middle East—Syria, Palestine, Iraq, and Transjordan—were administered by Britain or France as mandates of the League of Nations.

The war also transformed international political life. From the collapse of the German, Russian, and Austro-Hungarian empires emerged a new map of Central Europe with an independent Poland, Czechoslovakia, Hungary, and Yugoslavia as well as other newly independent nations (see Map 20.3). Such new states were based on the principle of "national self-determination," a concept championed by

U.S. president Woodrow Wilson, but each of them also contained dissatisfied ethnic minorities, who claimed the same principle. In Russia, the strains of war triggered a vast revolutionary upheaval that brought the radical Bolsheviks to power in 1917 and took Russia out of the war. Thus was launched world communism, which was to play such a prominent role in the history of the twentieth century (see Chapter 21).

The Treaty of Versailles, which formally concluded the war in 1919, proved in retrospect to have established conditions that contributed to a second world war only twenty years later. In that treaty, Germany lost its colonial empire and 15 percent of its European territory, was required to pay heavy reparations to the winners, had its military forces severely restricted, and was required to accept sole responsibility for the outbreak of the war. All of this created immense resentment in Germany. One of the country's many demobilized and disillusioned soldiers declared in 1922: "It cannot be that two million Germans should have fallen in vain. . . . No, we do not pardon, we demand—vengeance."[2] His name was Adolf Hitler, and within two decades he had begun to exact that vengeance.

The Great War generated profound changes in the world beyond Europe as well. During the conflict, Ottoman authorities, suspecting that some of their Armenian subjects were collaborating with the Russian enemy, massacred or deported an estimated 1 million Armenians. Although the term "genocide" had not yet been invented, some historians have applied it to those atrocities, arguing that they established a precedent on which the Nazis later built. The war also brought a final end to a declining Ottoman Empire, creating the modern map of the Middle East, with the new states of Turkey, Syria, Iraq, Transjordan, and Palestine. Thus Arabs emerged from Turkish rule, but many of them were governed for a time by the British or French, as "mandates" of the League of Nations (see Map 20.3). Conflicting British promises to both Arabs and Jews regarding Palestine set the stage for an enduring struggle over that ancient and holy land. Although Latin American countries remained bystanders in the war, many of them benefited from the growing demand for their primary products such as Chilean nitrates, used in explosives. But the sharp drop in nitrate exports after the war ended brought to Chile mass unemployment, urban riots, bloody strikes, and some appeal for the newly established Chilean Communist Party.

In the world of European colonies, the war echoed loudly. Millions of Asian and African men had watched Europeans butcher one another without mercy, had gained new military skills and political awareness, and returned home with less respect for their rulers and with expectations for better treatment as a reward for their service. To gain Indian support for the war, the British had publicly promised to put that colony on the road to self-government, an announcement that set the stage for the independence struggle that followed. In East Asia, Japan emerged strengthened from the war, with European support for its claim to take over German territory and privileges in China. That news enraged Chinese nationalists and among a few sparked an interest in Soviet-style communism, for only the new communist rulers of Russia seemed willing to end the imperialist penetration of China.

Finally, the First World War brought the United States to center stage as a global power. Its manpower had contributed much to the defeat of Germany, and its financial resources turned the United States from a debtor nation into Europe's creditor. When the American president Woodrow Wilson arrived in Paris for the peace conference in 1919, he was greeted with an almost religious enthusiasm. His famous Fourteen Points seemed to herald a new kind of international life, one based on moral principles rather than secret deals and imperialist machinations. Particularly appealing to many was his idea for the League of Nations, a new international peacekeeping organization committed to the principle of "collective security" and intended to avoid any repetition of the horrors that had just ended. Wilson's idealistic vision largely failed, however. Germany was treated more harshly than he had wished. And in his own country, the U.S. Senate refused to join the League, on which Wilson had pinned his hopes for a lasting peace. Its opponents feared that Americans would be forced to bow to "the will of other nations." That refusal seriously weakened the League of Nations as a vehicle for a new international order.

Capitalism Unraveling: The Great Depression

Far and away the most influential change of the postwar decades lay in the Great Depression. If World War I represented the political collapse of Europe, this catastrophic downturn suggested that Western capitalism was likewise failing. During the nineteenth century, that economic system had spurred the most substantial economic growth in world history and had raised the living standards of millions, but to many people it was a troubling system. Its very success generated an individualistic materialism that seemed to conflict with older values of community and spiritual life. To socialists and many others, its immense social inequalities were unacceptable. Furthermore, its evident instability—with cycles of boom and bust, expansion and recession—generated profound anxiety and threatened the livelihood of both industrial workers and those who had gained a modest toehold in the middle class.

Never had the flaws of capitalism been so evident or so devastating as during the decade that followed the outbreak of the Great Depression in 1929. All across the Euro-American heartland of the capitalist world, this vaunted economic system seemed to unravel. For the rich, it meant contracting stock prices that wiped out paper fortunes almost overnight. On the day that the American stock market initially crashed (October 24, 1929), eleven Wall Street financiers committed suicide, some jumping out of skyscrapers. Banks closed, and many people lost their life savings. Investment dried up, world trade dropped by 62 percent within a few years, and businesses contracted when they were unable to sell their products. For ordinary people, the worst feature of the Great Depression was the loss of work.

■ **Connection**

In what ways was the Great Depression a global phenomenon?

SNAPSHOT   Comparing the Impact of the Depression

As industrial production dropped during the Depression, unemployment soared.[3] Yet the larger Western capitalist countries differed considerably in the duration and extent of this unemployment. Note especially the differences between Germany and the United States. How might you account for this difference?

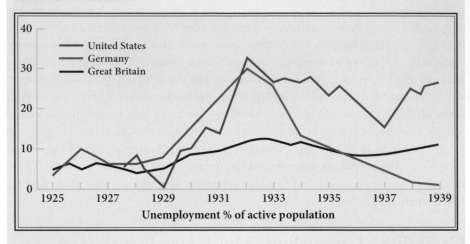

Unemployment % of active population

Unemployment soared everywhere, and in both Germany and the United States it reached 30 percent or more by 1932. (See Snapshot, above.) Beggars, soup kitchens, breadlines, shantytowns, and vacant factories came to symbolize the human reality of this economic disaster.

Explaining its onset, its spread from America to Europe and beyond, and its continuation for a decade has been a complicated task for historians. Part of the story lies in the United States' booming economy during the 1920s. In a country physically untouched by the Great War, wartime demand had greatly stimulated agricultural and industrial capacity. By the end of the 1920s, its farms and factories were producing more goods than could be sold because a highly unequal distribution of income meant that many people could not afford to buy the products that American factories were churning out. Nor were major European countries able to purchase those goods. Germany and Austria had to make huge reparation payments and were able to do so only with extensive U.S. loans. Britain and France, which were much indebted to the United States, depended on those reparations to repay their loans. Furthermore, Europeans generally had recovered enough to begin producing some of their own goods, and their expanding production further reduced the demand for American products. Meanwhile, a speculative stock market frenzy had driven up stock prices to an unsustainable level. When that bubble burst in late 1929, this intricately connected and fragile economic network across the Atlantic collapsed like a house of cards.

Much as Europe's worldwide empires had globalized the Great War, its economic linkages globalized the Great Depression. Countries or colonies tied to exporting one or two products were especially hard-hit. Colonial Southeast Asia, the world's major rubber-producing region, saw the demand for its primary export drop dramatically as automobile sales in Europe and the United States were cut in half. In Britain's West African colony of the Gold Coast (present-day Ghana), farmers who had staked their economic lives on producing cocoa for the world market were badly hurt by the collapse of commodity prices. Latin American countries, whose economies were based on the export of agricultural products and raw materials, were also vulnerable to major fluctuations in the world market. The region as a whole saw the value of its exports cut by half during the Great Depression. In an effort to maintain the price of coffee, Brazil destroyed enough of its crop to have supplied the world for a year. Such conditions led to widespread unemployment and social tensions.

Those tensions of the Depression era often found political expression in Latin America in the form of a military takeover of the state. Such governments sought to steer their countries away from an earlier dependence on exports toward a policy of generating their own industries. Known as import substitution industrialization, such policies hoped to achieve greater economic independence by manufacturing for the domestic market goods that had previously been imported. These efforts were accompanied by more authoritarian and intrusive governments that played a greater role in the economy by enacting tariffs, setting up state-run industries, and favoring local businesses. They often adopted a highly nationalist and populist posture as they sought to extricate themselves from economic domination by the United States and Europe and to respond to the growing urban classes of workers and entrepreneurs.

In Brazil, for example, the Depression discredited the established export elites such as coffee growers and led to the dictatorship of Getúlio Vargas (r. 1930–1945). Supported by the military, his government took steps to modernize the urban industrial sector of the economy, including a state enterprise to manufacture trucks and airplane engines and regulations that gave the state considerable power over both unions and employers. But little was done to alleviate rural poverty. In Mexico, the Depression opened the way to a revival of the principles of the Mexican Revolution under the leadership of Lázaro Cárdenas (r. 1934–1940). He pushed land reform, favored Mexican workers against foreign interests, and nationalized an oil industry dominated by American capital.

These were but two cases of the many political and economic changes stimulated in Latin America by the Great Depression. Many of those changes—the growing role of the army in politics; authoritarian, populist, and interventionist governments; import substitution industrialization; and the assumption that governments should improve economic life—persisted in the decades that followed.

The Great Depression also sharply challenged the governments of industrialized capitalist countries, which generally had believed that the economy would regulate

Contrasts of the Great Depression

This 1937 *Life* magazine image by famed photographer Margaret Bourke-White shows black victims of a flood in Louisville, Kentucky, standing in a bread-line during the Depression while behind them rises a billboard of a happy and prosperous white family. (Margaret Bourke-White/ Time & Life Pictures/Getty Images)

itself through the market. The market's apparent failure to self-correct led many people to look twice at the Soviet Union, the communist state that grew out of the Russian Revolution and encompassed much of the territory of the old Russian Empire (see Chapter 13, pages 572–77). There, the dispossession of the propertied classes and a state-controlled economy had generated an impressive economic growth with almost no unemployment in the 1930s, even as the capitalist world was reeling. No Western country opted for the dictatorial and draconian socialism of the Soviet Union, but in Britain, France, and Scandinavia the Depression energized a "democratic socialism" that sought greater regulation of the economy and a more equal distribution of wealth through peaceful means and electoral politics.

The United States' response to the Great Depression came in the form of President Franklin Roosevelt's New Deal (1933–1942), an experimental combination of reforms seeking to restart economic growth and to prevent similar calamities in the future. These measures reflected the thinking of John Maynard Keynes, a prominent British economist who argued that government actions and spending programs could moderate the recessions and depressions to which capitalist economies were prone. Although this represented a departure from standard economic thinking, none of it was really "socialist," even if some of the New Deal's opponents labeled it as such. Keynes's ideas became capitalist economic orthodoxy in the postwar era.

Nonetheless, Roosevelt's efforts permanently altered the relationship among government, the private economy, and individual citizens. Through immediate programs of public spending (for dams, highways, bridges, and parks), the New Deal sought to prime the pump of the economy and thus reduce unemployment. The New Deal's longer-term reforms, such as the Social Security system, the minimum wage, and various relief and welfare programs, attempted to create a modest economic safety net to sustain the poor, the unemployed, and the elderly. By supporting labor unions, the New Deal strengthened workers in their struggles with business owners or managers. Subsidies for farmers gave rise to a permanent agribusiness that encouraged continued production even as prices fell. Finally, a mounting number of government agencies marked a new degree of federal regulation and supervision of the economy.

Ultimately, none of the New Deal's programs worked very well to end the Great Depression. Not until the massive government spending required by World War II kicked in did that economic disaster abate in the United States. The most successful efforts to cope with the Depression came from unlikely places—Nazi Germany and an increasingly militaristic Japan.

Democracy Denied: Comparing Italy, Germany, and Japan

Despite the victory of the democratic powers in World War I—Britain, France, and the United States—their democratic political ideals and their cultural values celebrating individual freedom came under sharp attack in the aftermath of that bloody conflict. One challenge derived from communism, which was initiated in the Russian Revolution of 1917 and expressed most fully in the cold war during the second half of the twentieth century (see Chapter 21). In the 1920s and 1930s, however, the more immediate challenge to the victors in the Great War came from highly authoritarian, intensely nationalistic, territorially aggressive, and ferociously anticommunist regimes, particularly those that took shape in Italy, Germany, and Japan. (See Working with Evidence: Ideologies of the Axis Powers, page 922, for the ideas underlying these regimes.) Such common features of these three countries drew them together by 1936–1937 in a political alliance directed against the Soviet Union and international communism. In 1940, they solidified their relationship in a formal military alliance, creating the so-called Axis powers. Within this alliance, Germany and Japan clearly stand out, though in quite different ways, in terms of their impact on the larger patterns of world history, for it was their efforts to "establish and maintain a new order of things," as the Axis Pact put it, that generated the Second World War both in East Asia and in Europe.

The Fascist Alternative in Europe

Between 1919 and 1945, a new political ideology, known as fascism, found expression across much of Europe. At the level of ideas, fascism was intensely nationalistic, seeking to revitalize and purify the nation and to mobilize its people for some grand task. Its spokesmen praised violence against enemies as a renewing force in society, celebrated action rather than reflection, and placed their faith in a charismatic leader. Fascists also bitterly condemned individualism, liberalism, feminism, parliamentary democracy, and communism, all of which, they argued, divided and weakened the nation. In their determination to overthrow existing regimes, they were revolutionary; in their embrace of traditional values and their opposition to much of modern life, however, they were conservative or reactionary.

■ **Change**
In what ways did fascism challenge the ideas and practices of European liberalism and democracy?

Such ideas appealed to aggrieved people all across the social spectrum. In the devastation that followed the First World War, the numbers of such people grew substantially. In the aftermath of the Russian Revolution of 1917, some among the middle and upper classes felt the rise of socialism and communism as a dire threat; small-scale merchants, artisans, and farmers feared the loss of their independence to either big business or socialist revolution; demobilized soldiers had few prospects and nursed many resentments; and intellectuals were appalled by the materialism and artificiality of modern life. Such people had lost faith in the capacity of liberal democracy and capitalism to create a good society and to protect their interests. Some among them proved a receptive audience for the message of fascism.

Small fascist movements appeared in many Western European countries, including France, Great Britain, and the Netherlands, but they had little political impact. More substantial movements took shape in Austria, Hungary, and Romania. In Spain, the rise of a fascist movement led to a bitter civil war (1936–1939) and a dictatorial regime that lasted into the 1970s. Conservative and authoritarian regimes or social movements in Latin America sometimes adopted the trappings of fascism — one-man rule, state-controlled parties, youth organizations or militias, a rhetoric of national renewal, anti-Semitic measures — though without implementing its more revolutionary features. But in Italy and Germany, such movements achieved prolonged power in major states, with devastating consequences for Europe and the world.

The fascist alternative took shape first in Italy. That nation had become a unified state only in 1870 and had not yet developed a modern and thoroughly democratic culture. In the early twentieth century, conservative landlords still dominated much of the countryside. Northern Italy, however, had begun to industrialize in the late nineteenth century, generating the characteristic tension between an industrial working class and a substantial middle class. The First World War gave rise to resentful veterans, many of them unemployed, and to patriots who believed that Italy had not gained the territory it deserved from the Treaty of Versailles. During the serious economic downturn after World War I, trade unions, peasant movements, and various communist and socialist parties threatened the established social order with a wave of strikes and land seizures.

Into this setting stepped a charismatic orator and a former journalist with a socialist background, Benito Mussolini (1883–1945). With the help of a private army of disillusioned veterans and jobless men known as the Black Shirts, Mussolini swept to power in 1922, promising an alternative to both communism and ineffective democratic rule. Considerable violence accompanied Mussolini's rise to power as bands of Black Shirts destroyed the offices of socialist newspapers and attacked striking workers. Fearful of communism, big business threw its support to Mussolini, who promised order in the streets, an end to bickering party-based politics, and the maintenance of the traditional social order. That Mussolini's government allegedly made the trains run on time became evidence that these promises might be fulfilled. The symbol of this movement was the *fasces*, a bundle of birch rods bound together around an axe, which represented power and strength in unity and derived from ancient Rome. Thus fascism was born.

The Faces of European Fascism
Benito Mussolini (left) and Adolf Hitler came to symbolize fascism in Europe in the several decades between the two world wars. In this photograph from September 1937, they are reviewing German troops in Munich during Mussolini's visit to Germany, a trip that deepened the growing relationship between their two countries. (Luce/Keystone/Getty Images)

In Mussolini's thinking, fascism was resolutely anticommunist—he called it "the complete opposite . . . of Marxian socialism"—and equally antidemocratic. "Fascism combats the whole complex system of democratic ideology, and repudiates it," he wrote. At the core of Mussolini's fascism was his conception of the state. "Fascism conceives of the State as an absolute, in comparison with which all individuals and groups are relative, only to be conceived of in their relation to the State." To Mussolini, the state was a conscious entity with "a will and a personality," which represented the "spirit of the nation." Its expansion in war and empire building was "an essential manifestation of vitality."[4]

Mussolini promised his mass following major social reforms, though in practice he concentrated on consolidating the power of the central state. His government suspended democracy and imprisoned, deported, or sometimes executed opponents. Italy's fascist regime also disbanded independent labor unions and peasant groups as well as all opposing political parties. In economic life, a "corporate state" took shape, at least in theory, in which workers, employers, and various professional groups were organized into "corporations" that were supposed to settle their disagreements and determine economic policy under the supervision of the state.

Culturally, fascists invoked various aspects of traditional Italian life. Though personally an atheist, Mussolini embraced the Catholic culture of Italy in a series of agreements with the Church, known as the Lateran Accords of 1929, which made the Vatican a sovereign state and Catholicism Italy's national religion. In fascist propaganda, women were portrayed in highly traditional domestic terms, particularly as mothers creating new citizens for the fascist state, with no hint of equality or liberation. Nationalists were delighted when Italy invaded Ethiopia in 1935, avenging the embarrassing defeat that Italians suffered at the hands of Ethiopians in 1896. In the eyes of Mussolini and fascist believers, all of this was the beginning of a "new Roman Empire" that would revitalize Italian society and give it a global mission.

Hitler and the Nazis

Far more important in the long run was the German expression of European fascism, which took shape as the Nazi Party under the leadership of Adolf Hitler (1889–1945). In many respects, German fascism was similar to its Italian counterpart. Both expressions of fascism espoused an extreme nationalism, openly advocated the use of violence as a political tool, generated a single-party dictatorship, were led by charismatic figures, despised parliamentary democracy, hated communism, and viewed war as a positive and ennobling experience.[5] The circumstances that gave rise to the Nazi movement were likewise broadly similar to those that generated Italian fascism, although the Nazis did not achieve national power until 1933.

■ **Comparison**

What was distinctive about the German expression of fascism? What was the basis of popular support for the Nazis?

The end of World War I witnessed the collapse of the German imperial government, itself less than a half century old. It was left to the democratic politicians of a new government—known as the Weimar Republic—to negotiate a peace settlement with the victorious allies. Traditional elites, who had withdrawn from public life in disgrace, never explicitly took responsibility for Germany's defeat; instead they attacked the democratic politicians who had the unenviable task of signing the Treaty of Versailles and enforcing it. In this setting, some began to argue that German military forces had not really lost the war but that civilian socialists, communists, and Jews had betrayed the nation, "stabbing it in the back."

As in postwar Italy, liberal or democratic political leaders during the 1920s faced considerable hostility. Paramilitary groups of veterans known as the Freikorps assassinated hundreds of supporters of the Weimar regime. Gradually, some among the middle classes as well as conservative landowners joined in opposition to the Weimar government, as both groups were threatened by the ruinous inflation of 1923 and then the Great Depression. The German economy largely ground to a halt in the early 1930s amid massive unemployment among workers and the middle class alike. Everyone demanded decisive action from the state. Many industrial workers looked to socialists and communists for solutions; others turned to fascism. Large numbers of middle-class people deserted moderate political parties in favor of conservative and radical right-wing movements.

This was the context in which Adolf Hitler's National Socialist, or Nazi, Party gained growing public support. Founded shortly after the end of World War I, that party under Hitler's leadership proclaimed a message of intense German nationalism cast in terms of racial superiority, bitter hatred for Jews as an alien presence, passionate opposition to communism, a determination to rescue Germany from the humiliating requirements of the Treaty of Versailles, and a willingness to decisively tackle the country's economic problems. Throughout the 1920s, the Nazis were a minor presence in German politics, gaining only 2.6 percent of the vote in the national elections of 1928. Just four years later, however, in the wake of the Depression's terrible impact and the Weimar government's inability to respond effectively, the Nazis attracted 37 percent of the vote. In 1933, Hitler was legally installed as the chancellor of the German government. Thus did the Weimar Republic, a democratic regime that never gained broad support, give way to the Third Reich.

Once in power, Hitler moved quickly to consolidate Nazi control of Germany. All other political parties were outlawed; independent labor unions were ended; thousands of opponents were arrested; and the press and radio came under state control. Far more thoroughly than Mussolini in Italy, Hitler and the Nazis established their control over German society.

By the late 1930s, Hitler apparently had the support of a considerable majority of the population, in large measure because his policies successfully brought Germany out of the Depression. The government invested heavily in projects such as superhighways, bridges, canals, and public buildings and, after 1935, in rebuilding and rearming the country's diminished military forces. These policies drove down the number of unemployed Germans from 6.2 million in 1932 to fewer than 500,000 in 1937. Two years later, Germany had a labor shortage. Erna Kranz, a teenager in the 1930s, later remembered the early years of Nazi rule: "[There was] a glimmer of hope . . . not just for the unemployed but for everybody because we all knew that we were downtrodden. . . . It was a good time . . . there was order and discipline."[6] Millions agreed with her.

Other factors as well contributed to Nazi popularity. Like Italian fascists, Hitler too appealed to rural and traditional values that many Germans feared losing as their country modernized. In Hitler's thinking and in Nazi propaganda, Jews became the symbol of the urban, capitalist, and foreign influences that were undermining traditional German culture. Thus the Nazis reflected and reinforced a broader and long-established current of anti-Semitism that had deep roots in much of Europe. In his book *Mein Kampf* (*My Struggle*), Hitler outlined his case against the Jews and his call for the racial purification of Germany in vitriolic terms. (See Working with Evidence, Source 20.1, page 922, for a statement of Hitler's thinking.)

Far more than elsewhere, this insistence on a racial revolution was a central feature of the Nazi program and differed from the racial attitudes in Italy, where Jews were a tiny minority of the population and deeply assimilated into Italian culture. Early on, Mussolini had ridiculed Nazi racism, but as Germany and Italy drew closer together, Italy too began a program of overt anti-Semitism, though nothing approaching the extremes that characterized Nazi Germany.

Nazi Hatred of the Jews
This picture served as the cover of a highly anti-Semitic book of photographs titled *The Eternal Jew*, published by the Nazis in 1937. It effectively summed up many of the themes of the Nazi case against the Jews, showing them as ugly and sub-human, as the instigators of communism (the hammer and sickle on a map of Russia), as greedy capitalists (coins in one hand), and as seeking to dominate the world (the whip). (akg-images)

Upon coming to power, Hitler implemented policies that increasingly restricted Jewish life. Soon Jews were excluded from universities, professional organizations, and civil employment. In 1935, the Nuremberg Laws ended German citizenship for Jews and forbade marriage or sexual relations between Jews and Germans. On the night of November 9, 1938, known as Kristallnacht, persecution gave way to terror when Nazis smashed and looted Jewish shops. Such actions made clear the Nazis' determination to rid Germany of its Jewish population, thus putting into effect the most radical element of Hitler's program. (See Zooming In: Etty Hillesum, page 902.) Still, it was not yet apparent that this "racial revolution" would mean the mass killing of Europe's Jews. That horrendous development emerged only in the context of World War II.

Beyond race, gender too figured prominently in Nazi thought and policies. Deeply antifeminist and resentful of the liberating changes that modern life had brought to European women, Nazis wanted to limit women largely to the home, removing them from the paid workforce. To Hitler, the state was the natural domain of men, while the home was the realm of women. "Woman in the workplace is an oppressed and tormented being," declared a Nazi publication.[7] Concerned about declining birthrates, Italy and Germany alike promoted a cult of motherhood, glorifying and rewarding women who produced children for the state. Accordingly, fascist regimes in both countries generally opposed abortion, contraception, family planning, and sex education, all of which were associated with feminist thinking.

Yet such an outlook did not necessarily coincide with conservative or puritanical sexual attitudes. In Germany, a state-sponsored system of brothels was initiated in the mid-1930s, for it was assumed that virile men would be promiscuous and that soldiers required a sexual outlet, if they were to contribute to the nation's military strength. Because of this "need," Nazi policy exempted condoms from the ban on birth control. Heinrich Himmler, a leading Nazi official, also openly encouraged illegitimate births among Aryans to augment the nation's numbers. Thus Nazi rhetoric about the chaste Aryan family was trumped—or supplemented—by a desire to use sexuality to advance the cause of the nation.

Also sustaining Nazi rule were massive torchlight ceremonies celebrating the superiority of the German race and its folk culture. In these settings, Hitler was the mystical leader, the Führer, a mesmerizing orator who would lead Germany to national greatness and individual Germans to personal fulfillment.

If World War I and the Great Depression brought about the political and economic collapse of Europe, the Nazi phenomenon represented a moral collapse within the West, deriving from a highly selective incorporation of earlier strands of European culture. On the one hand, the Nazis actively rejected some of the values—rationalism, tolerance, democracy, human equality—that for many people had defined the core of Western civilization since the Enlightenment. On the other hand, they claimed the legacy of modern science, particularly in their concern to classify and rank various human groups. Thus they drew heavily on the "scientific racism" of the late nineteenth century and its expression in phrenology, which linked the size and shape of the skull to human behavior and personality (see Chapter 18, pages 791–92). Moreover, in their effort to purify German society, the Nazis reflected the Enlightenment confidence in the perfectibility of humankind and in the social engineering necessary to achieve it.

Japanese Authoritarianism

In various ways, the modern history of Japan paralleled that of Italy and Germany. All three were newcomers to great power status, with Japan joining the club of industrializing and empire-building states only in the late nineteenth century as its sole Asian member (see Chapter 19, pages 855–60). Like Italy and Germany, Japan had a rather limited experience with democratic politics, for its elected parliament was constrained by a very small electorate (only 1.5 million men in 1917) and by the exalted position of a semi-divine emperor and his small coterie of elite advisers. During the 1930s, Japan too moved toward authoritarian government and a denial of democracy at home, even as it launched an aggressive program of territorial expansion in East Asia.

Despite these broad similarities, Japan's history in the first half of the twentieth century was clearly distinctive. In sharp contrast to Italy and Germany, Japan participated only minimally in World War I, and it experienced considerable economic growth as other industrialized countries were consumed by the European conflict. At the peace conference ending that war, Japan was seated as an equal participant, allied with the winning side of democratic countries such as Britain, France, and the United States.

During the 1920s, Japan seemed to be moving toward more democratic politics and Western cultural values. Universal male suffrage was achieved in 1925; cabinets led by leaders of the major parties, rather than bureaucrats or imperial favorites, governed the country; and a two-party system began to emerge. Supporters of these developments generally embraced the dignity of the individual, free expression of ideas, and greater gender equality. Education expanded; an urban

■ **Comparison**
How did Japan's experience during the 1920s and 1930s resemble that of Germany, and how did it differ?

Etty Hillesum, Witness to the Holocaust

Not often can historians penetrate the inner worlds of the people they study. But in the letters and diary of Etty Hillesum, a young Dutch Jewish woman caught up in the Nazi occupation of her country during the early 1940s, we can catch a glimpse of her expanding interior life even as her external circumstances contracted sharply amid the unfolding of the Holocaust.[8]

Born in 1914, Etty was the daughter of a Dutch academic father and a Russian-born mother. She attended university, tutored students in the Russian language, and hoped to become a writer. The Nazi invasion of the Netherlands in May 1940 found Etty living in Amsterdam with five other people. There she experienced and described Nazi rule and its mounting impact on Jews. "More arrests, more terror, concentration camps; the arbitrary dragging off of fathers, sisters, brothers," she wrote in June 1941. Soon Amsterdam's Jews were required to wear identifying yellow stars and were forbidden from walking on certain streets, riding the tram, visiting particular shops, or eating in cafés. Signs reading "No Admittance to Jews" sprang up across the city.

Etty Hillesum.

Etty initially reacted to these events with hatred and depression. She wrote, "I am suddenly beside myself with anger, cursing and swearing at the Germans," and was even upset with a German woman living in her house who had no connections whatever with the Nazis. "They are out to destroy us completely," she wrote on July 3, 1942. "Today I am filled with despair." Over time, however, her perspective changed. "I really see no other solution than to turn inward and to root out all the rottenness there." One day, with the "sound of fire, shooting, bombs" raging outside, Etty listened to a Bach recording and wrote: "I know and share the many sorrows a human being can experience, but I do not cling to them; they pass through me, like life itself, as a broad eternal stream . . . and life continues. . . . If you have given sorrow the space that its gentle origins demand, then you may say that life is beautiful and so rich . . . that it makes you want to believe in God."

photo: Etty Hillesum. Collection Jewish Historical Museum, Amsterdam

consumer society developed; middle-class women entered new professions; young women known as *moga* (modern girls) sported short hair and short skirts, while dancing with *mobo* (modern boys) at jazz clubs and cabarets. To such people, the Japanese were becoming world citizens and their country was becoming "a province of the world" as they participated increasingly in a cosmopolitan and international culture.

In this environment, the accumulated tensions of Japan's modernizing and industrializing processes found expression. "Rice riots" in 1918 brought more than a million people into the streets of urban Japan to protest the rising price of that essential staple. Union membership tripled in the 1920s as some factory workers began to think in terms of entitlements and workers' rights rather than the benevo-

Meanwhile, Etty had fallen deeply in love with her fifty-five-year-old German Jewish therapist, Julius Spier. She worried that she was becoming overly dependent on a man, particularly since she was already sleeping with another man in whose house she lived. Yet Spier had become her spiritual companion and mentor as well as her lover. When he died in September 1942, she was devastated but determined to go on. "You were the mediator between God and me," she wrote of Spier, "and now you have gone and my path leads straight to God."

Eventually, Etty found herself in Westerbork, a transit camp for Dutch Jews awaiting transport to the east and almost certain death. Friends had offered to hide her, but Etty insisted on voluntarily entering the camp, where she operated as an unofficial social worker and sought to become the "thinking heart of the barracks." In the camp, panic erupted regularly as new waves of Jews were transported east. Babies screamed as they were awakened to board the trains. "The misery here is really indescribable," she wrote in mid-1943. "People live in those big barracks like so many rats in a sewer."

Even there, however, Etty's emerging inner life found expression. "Late at night . . . ," she wrote, "I often walk with a spring in my step along the barbed wire. And then time and again, it soars straight from my heart . . . the feeling that life is glorious and magnificent and that one day we shall be building a whole new world. Against every new outrage and every fresh horror, we shall put up one more piece of love and goodness, drawing strength from within ourselves. We may suffer, but we must not succumb."

Etty's transport came on September 7, 1943, when she, her parents, and a brother boarded a train for Auschwitz. Her parents were gassed immediately upon arrival, and Etty followed on November 30. Her last known writing was a postcard tossed from the train as it departed Westerbork. It read in part: "I am sitting on my rucksack in the middle of a full freight car. Father, mother, and Mischa [her brother] are a few cars behind. . . . We left the camp singing."

Etty Hillesum's public life, like that of most people, left little outward mark on the world she briefly inhabited, except for the small circle of her friends and family. But the record of her inner life, miraculously preserved, remains among the greatest spiritual testaments to emerge from the horrors of the Nazi era, a tribute to the possibilities of human transformation, even amid the most horrendous of circumstances.

Questions: In what ways did Etty experience the Nazi phenomenon? How might you assess Etty's interior response to the Nazis? Was it a "triumph of the human spirit" or an evasion of the responsibility to resist evil more directly?

---

lence of their employers. In rural areas, tenant unions multiplied, and disputes with landowners increased amid demands for a reduction in rents. A mounting women's movement advocated a variety of feminist issues, including suffrage and the end of legalized prostitution. "All the sleeping women are now awake and moving," declared Yosano Akiko, a well-known poet, feminist, and social critic. Within the political arena, a number of "proletarian parties"—the Labor-Farmer Party, the Socialist People's Party, and a small Japan Communist Party—promised radical change, what one of them referred to as "the political, economic and social emancipation of the proletarian class."[9]

For many people in established elite circles—bureaucrats, landowners, industrialists, military officials—all of this was both appalling and alarming, suggesting

Japanese Women Modeling Swimsuits
This photo from around 1930 shows young Japanese women in Western swimwear and clothing during a fashion show in Tokyo. (ullstein bild/The Granger Collection, NYC — All rights reserved)

echoes of the Russian Revolution of 1917. A number of political activists were arrested, and a few were killed. A Peace Preservation Law, enacted in 1925, promised long prison sentences, or even the death penalty, to anyone who organized against the existing imperial system of government or private property.

As in Germany, however, it was the impact of the Great Depression that paved the way for harsher and more authoritarian action. That worldwide economic catastrophe hit Japan hard. The shrinking world demand for silk impoverished millions of rural dwellers who raised silkworms. Japan's exports fell by half between 1929 and 1931, leaving a million or more urban workers unemployed. Many young workers returned to their rural villages only to find food scarce, families forced to sell their daughters to urban brothels, and neighbors unable to offer the customary money for the funerals of their friends. In these desperate circumstances, many began to doubt the ability of parliamentary democracy and capitalism to address Japan's "national emergency." Politicians and business leaders alike were widely regarded as privileged, self-centered, and heedless of the larger interests of the nation.

Such conditions energized a growing movement in Japanese political life known as Radical Nationalism or the Revolutionary Right. Expressed in dozens of small groups, it was especially appealing to younger army officers. The movement's many separate organizations shared an extreme nationalism, hostility to parliamentary democracy, a commitment to elite leadership focused around an exalted emperor, and dedication to foreign expansion. The manifesto of one of those organizations, the Cherry Blossom Society, expressed these sentiments clearly in 1930:

> As we observe recent social trends, top leaders engage in immoral conduct, political parties are corrupt, capitalists and aristocrats have no understanding of the masses, farming villages are devastated, unemployment and depression are serious. . . . The rulers neglect the long term interests of the nation, strive to win only the pleasure of foreign powers and possess no enthusiasm for external expansion. . . . The people are with us in craving the appearance of a vigorous and clean government that is truly based upon the masses, and is genuinely centered around the Emperor.[10]

Members of such organizations managed to assassinate a number of public officials and prominent individuals, in the hope of provoking a return to direct rule by the emperor, and in 1936 a group of junior officers attempted a military takeover of the government, which was quickly suppressed. In sharp contrast to developments in Italy and Germany, however, no right-wing party gained wide popular support, nor was any such party able to seize power in Japan. Although individuals and small groups sometimes espoused ideas similar to those of European fascists, no major fascist party emerged. Nor did Japan produce any charismatic leader on the order of Mussolini or Hitler. People arrested for political offenses were neither criminalized nor exterminated, as in Germany, but instead were subjected to a process of "resocialization" that brought the vast majority of them to renounce their "errors" and return to the "Japanese way." Japan's established institutions of government were sufficiently strong, and traditional notions of the nation as a family headed by the emperor were sufficiently intact, to prevent the development of a widespread fascist movement able to take control of the country.

In the 1930s, though, Japanese public life clearly changed in ways that reflected the growth of right-wing nationalist thinking. Parties and the parliament continued to operate, and elections were held, but major cabinet positions now went to prominent bureaucratic or military figures rather than to party leaders. The military in particular came to exercise a more dominant role in Japanese political life, although military men had to negotiate with business and bureaucratic elites as well as party leaders. Censorship limited the possibilities of free expression, and a single news agency was granted the right to distribute all national and most international news to the country's newspapers and radio stations. An Industrial Patriotic Federation replaced independent trade unions with factory-based "discussion councils" to resolve local disputes between workers and managers.

Established authorities also adopted many of the ideological themes of these radical right-wing groups. In 1937, the Ministry of Education issued a new textbook, *Cardinal Principles of the National Entity of Japan*, for use in all Japanese schools.

(See Working with Evidence, Source 20.2, page 925.) That document proclaimed the Japanese to be "intrinsically quite different from the so-called citizens of the Occidental [Western] countries." Those nations were "conglomerations of separate individuals" with "no deep foundation between ruler and citizen to unite them." In Japan, by contrast, an emperor of divine origin related to his subjects as a father to his children. It was a natural, not a contractual, relationship, expressed most fully in the "sacrifice of the life of a subject for the Emperor." In addition to studying this text, students were now required to engage in more physical training, in which Japanese martial arts replaced baseball in the physical education curriculum.

The erosion of democracy and the rise of the military in Japanese political life reflected long-standing Japanese respect for the military values of the ancient samurai warrior class as well as the relatively independent position of the military in Japan's Meiji constitution. The state's success in quickly bringing the country out of the Depression likewise fostered popular support. As in Nazi Germany, state-financed credit, large-scale spending on armaments, and public works projects enabled Japan to emerge from the Depression more rapidly and more fully than major Western countries. "By the end of 1937," noted one Japanese laborer, "everybody in the country was working."[11] By the mid-1930s, the government increasingly assumed a supervisory or managerial role in economic affairs that included subsidies to strategic industries; profit ceilings on major corporations; caps on wages, prices, and rents; and a measure of central planning. Private property, however, was retained, and the huge industrial enterprises called *zaibatsu* continued to dominate the economic landscape.

Although Japan during the 1930s shared some common features with fascist Italy and Nazi Germany, it remained, at least internally, a less repressive and more pluralistic society than either of those European states. Japanese intellectuals and writers had to contend with government censorship, but they retained some influence in the country. Generals and admirals exercised great political authority as the role of an elected parliament declined, but they did not govern alone. Political prisoners were few and were not subjected to execution or deportation as in European fascist states. Japanese conceptions of their racial purity and uniqueness were directed largely against foreigners rather than an internal minority. Nevertheless, like Germany and Italy, Japan developed extensive imperial ambitions. Those projects of conquest and empire building collided with the interests of established world powers such as the United States and Britain, launching a second, and even more terrible, global war.

A Second World War, 1937–1945

World War II, even more than the Great War, was a genuinely global conflict with independent origins in both Asia and Europe. Their common feature lay in dissatisfied states in both continents that sought to fundamentally alter the international arrangements that had emerged from World War I. Many Japanese, like their counterparts in Italy and Germany, felt stymied by Britain and the United States as they sought empires that they regarded as essential for their national greatness and economic well-being.

The Road to War in Asia

World War II began in Asia before it occurred in Europe. In the late 1920s and the 1930s, Japanese imperial ambitions mounted as the military became more powerful in Japan's political life and as an earlier cultural cosmopolitanism gave way to more nationalist sentiments. An initial problem was the rise of Chinese nationalism, which seemed to threaten Japan's sphere of influence in Manchuria, acquired after the Russo-Japanese War of 1904–1905. Acting independently of civilian authorities in Tokyo, units of the Japanese military seized control of Manchuria in 1931 and established a puppet state called Manchukuo. This action infuriated Western powers, prompting Japan to withdraw from the League of Nations, to break politically with its Western allies, and in 1936 to align more closely with Germany and Italy. By that time, relations with an increasingly nationalist China had deteriorated further, leading to a full-scale attack on heartland China in 1937 and escalating a bitter conflict that would last another eight years. World War II in Asia had begun (see Map 20.4).

As Japan's war against China unfolded, the view of the world held by Japanese authorities and many ordinary people hardened. Increasingly, they felt isolated, surrounded, and threatened. A series of international agreements in the early 1920s that had granted Japan a less robust naval force than Britain or the United States, as well as anti-Japanese immigration policies in the United States, convinced some Japanese that racism prevented the West from acknowledging Japan as an equal power. Furthermore, Japan was quite dependent on foreign, especially American, sources of strategic goods. By the late 1930s, some 73 percent of Japan's scrap iron, 60 percent of its imported machine tools, 80 percent of its oil, and about half of its copper came from the United States, which was becoming increasingly hostile to Japanese ambitions in Asia. Moreover, Western imperialist powers—the British, French, and Dutch—controlled resource-rich colonies in Southeast Asia. Finally, the Soviet Union, proclaiming an alien communist ideology, loomed large in northern Asia. To growing numbers of Japanese, their national survival was at stake.

Thus, in 1940–1941, Japan extended its military operations to the French, British, Dutch, and American colonies of Southeast Asia—Malaya, Burma, Indonesia, Indochina, and the Philippines—in an effort to acquire the resources that would free it from dependence on the West. In carving out this Pacific empire, the Japanese presented themselves as liberators and modernizers, creating an "Asia for Asians" and freeing their continent from European and American dominance. Experience soon showed that Japan was far more concerned with Asia's resources than with its liberation and that Japanese rule exceeded in brutality even that of the Europeans.

■ **Comparison**

In what ways were the origins of World War II in Asia and in Europe similar to each other? How were they different?

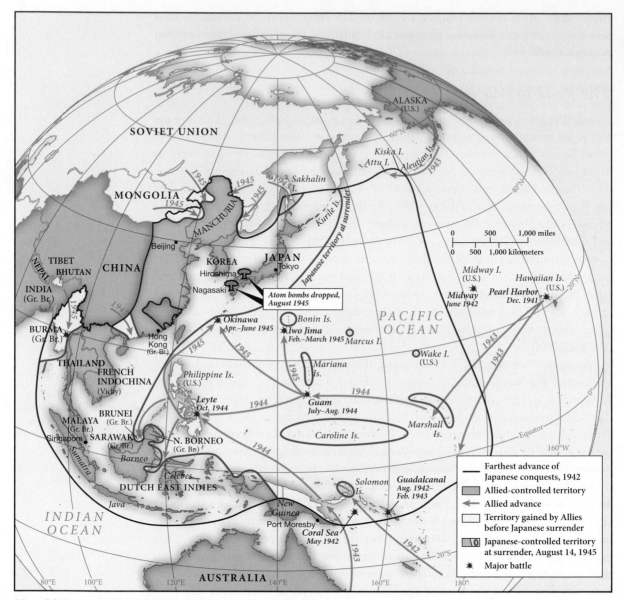

Map 20.4   World War II in Asia and the Pacific

Japanese aggression temporarily dislodged the British, French, Dutch, and Americans from their colonial possessions in Asia, while inflicting vast devastation on China. Much of the American counterattack involved "island hopping" across the Pacific until the dropping of the atomic bombs on Hiroshima and Nagasaki finally prompted the Japanese surrender in August 1945.

A decisive step in the development of World War II in Asia lay in the Japanese attack on the United States at Pearl Harbor in Hawaii in December 1941. Japanese authorities undertook that attack with reluctance and only after negotiations to end American hostility to Japan's empire-building enterprise proved fruitless and an American oil embargo was imposed on Japan in July 1941. American opinion in the 1930s increasingly saw Japan as aggressive, oppressive, and a threat to U.S. economic interests in Asia. In the face of this hostility, Japan's leaders felt that the alternatives for their country boiled down to either an acceptance of American terms, which they feared would reduce Japan to a second- or third-rank power, or a war with an uncertain outcome. Given those choices, the decision for war was made more with foreboding than with enthusiasm. A leading Japanese admiral made the case for war in this way in late 1941: "The government has decided that if there were no war the fate of the nation is sealed. Even if there is a war, the country may be ruined. Nevertheless a nation that does not fight in this plight has lost its spirit and is doomed."[12]

As a consequence of the attack on Pearl Harbor, the United States entered the war in the Pacific, beginning a long and bloody struggle that ended only with the use of atomic bombs against Hiroshima and Nagasaki in 1945. The Pearl Harbor action also joined the Asian theater of the war and the ongoing conflict in Europe into a single global struggle that pitted Germany, Italy, and Japan (the Axis powers) against the United States, Britain, and the Soviet Union (the Allies).

The Road to War in Europe

If Japan was the dissatisfied power in Asia, Nazi Germany clearly occupied that role in Europe. As a consequence of their defeat in World War I and the harsh terms of the Treaty of Versailles, many Germans harbored deep resentments about their country's position in the international arena. Taking advantage of those resentments, the Nazis pledged to rectify the treaty's perceived injustices. Thus, to most historians, the origins of World War II in Europe lie squarely in German aggression, although scholars acknowledge that events took many twists and turns and that German aggression was encouraged by the initial unwillingness of Britain, France, or the Soviet Union to confront it forcefully. If World War I was accidental and unintended, World War II was deliberate and planned—perhaps even desired—by the German leadership and by Hitler in particular.

War was central to the Nazi agenda in several ways. Nazism was born out of World War I, the hated treaty that ended it, and the disillusioned ex-soldiers who emerged from it. Furthermore, the celebration of war as a means of ennobling humanity and enabling the rise of superior peoples was at the core of Nazi ideology. "Whoever would live must fight," Hitler declared. "Only in force lies the right of possession." He consistently stressed the importance for Germany of gaining *lebensraum* (living space) in the east, in the lands of Slavic Poland and Russia. Inevitably, this required war.

Slowly at first and then more aggressively, Hitler prepared the country for war as he also pursued territorial expansion. A major rearmament program began in 1935. The next year, German forces entered the Rhineland, which the Treaty of Versailles had ordered demilitarized. In 1938, Germany annexed Austria and the German-speaking parts of Czechoslovakia. At a famous conference in Munich in that year, the British and the French gave these actions their reluctant blessing, hoping that this "appeasement" of Hitler could satisfy his demands and prevent all-out war. But it did not. On September 1, 1939, Germany unleashed a devastating attack on Poland, triggering the Second World War in Europe, as Britain and France declared war on Germany. Quickly defeating France, the Germans launched a destructive air war against Britain and in 1941 turned their war machine loose on the Soviet Union. By then, most of Europe was under Nazi control (see Map 20.5).

Although Germany was central to both world wars, the second one was quite different from the first. It was not welcomed with the kind of mass enthusiasm across Europe that had accompanied the opening of World War I in 1914. The bitter experience of the Great War suggested to most people that only suffering lay ahead. The conduct of the two wars likewise differed. The first war had quickly bogged down in trench warfare that emphasized defense, whereas in the second war the German tactic of *blitzkrieg* (lightning war) coordinated the rapid movement of infantry, tanks, and airpower over very large areas.

Such military tactics were initially successful and allowed German forces, aided by their Italian allies, to sweep over Europe, the western Soviet Union, and North Africa. The tide began to turn in 1942 when the Soviet Union absorbed the German onslaught and then began to counterattack, slowly and painfully moving westward toward the German heartland. The United States, with its enormous material and human resources, fully joined the struggle against Germany in 1942 and led the invasion of northern France in 1944, opening a long-awaited second front in the struggle against Hitler's Germany. Years of bitter fighting ensued before these two huge military movements ensured German defeat in May 1945.

The Outcomes of Global Conflict

The Second World War was the most destructive conflict in world history, with total deaths estimated at around 60 million, some six times that of World War I. More than half of those casualties were civilians. Partly responsible for this horrendous toll were the new technologies of warfare—heavy bombers, jet fighters, missiles, and atomic weapons. Equally significant, though, was the almost complete blurring of the traditional line between civilian and military targets, as entire cities and whole populations came to be defined as the enemy.

■ **Comparison**

How did World War II differ from World War I?

Nowhere was that blurring more complete than in the Soviet Union, which accounted for more than 40 percent of the total deaths in the war—probably around 25 million, with an equal number made homeless and thousands of towns, villages, and industrial enterprises destroyed. German actions fulfilled Hitler's instructions to

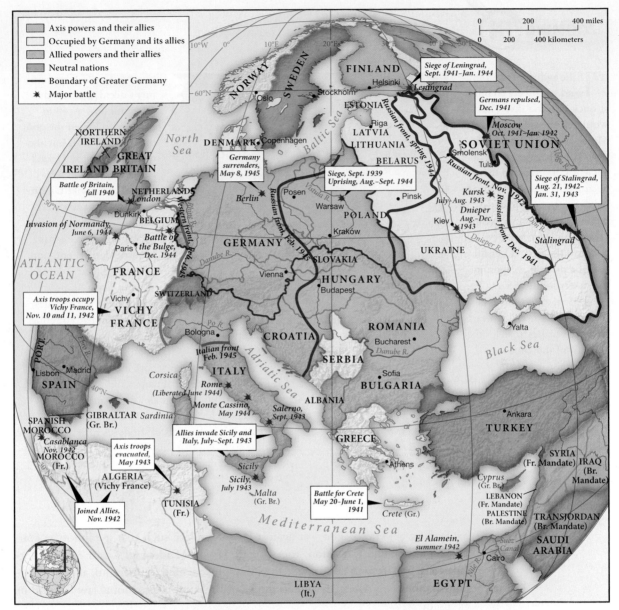

Map 20.5   World War II in Europe and Africa

For a brief moment during World War II, Nazi Germany came close to bringing all of Europe and North Africa under its rule. Then in late 1942, the Allies began a series of counterattacks that led to German surrender in May 1945.

Hiroshima

"If the radiance of a thousand suns were to burst at once into the sky. That would be the splendor of the Mighty One."[13] This passage from the Bhagavad Gita, an ancient Hindu sacred text, occurred to J. Robert Oppenheimer, a leading scientist behind the American push to create a nuclear bomb, as he watched the first successful test of a nuclear weapon in the desert south of Santa Fe, New Mexico, on the evening of July 16, 1945. Years later, he recalled that another verse from the same sacred text had also entered his mind: "I am become Death, the Destroyer of Worlds." And so the atomic age was born amid Oppenheimer's thoughts of divine splendor and divine destruction.

Several weeks later, the whole world became aware of this new era when American forces destroyed the Japanese cities of Hiroshima and Nagasaki with nuclear

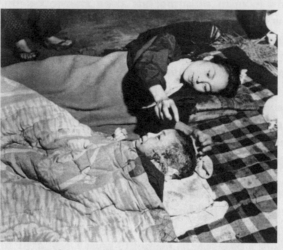

A mother and child, victims of Hiroshima, on the floor of a makeshift hospital, two months after the attack.

photo: Associated Press

bombs. The U.S. government decided to use this powerful new weapon partially to hasten the end of World War II, but also to strengthen the United States' position in relation to the Soviet Union in the postwar world. Whether the bomb was necessary to force Japan to surrender is a question of some historical debate. What is not in dispute was the horrific destruction and human suffering wrought by the two bombs. The centers of both cities were flattened, and as many as 80,000 inhabitants of Hiroshima and 40,000 of Nagasaki perished almost instantly from the force and intense heat of the explosions.

The harrowing accounts of survivors offer some sense of the suffering that followed. Iwao Nakamura,

his leading generals: "The war against Russia will be such that it cannot be conducted in a knightly fashion; the struggle is one of ideologies and racial differences and will have to be conducted with unprecedented, unmerciful, and unrelenting harshness. . . . German soldiers guilty of breaking international law . . . will be excused."[14]

In China as well, perhaps 15 million people died and uncounted numbers became refugees as a result of prolonged Chinese resistance and the shattering Japanese response, including the killing of every person and every animal in many villages. Within a few months, during the infamous Rape of Nanjing in 1937–1938, some 200,000 to 300,000 Chinese civilians were killed and often mutilated, and countless women were sexually assaulted. Indiscriminate German bombing of British cities and the Allied firebombing of Japanese and German cities likewise reflected the new morality of total war, as did the dropping of atomic bombs on Hiroshima

a schoolboy in Hiroshima who lived through the attack, recalled "old people pleading for water, tiny children seeking help, students unconsciously calling for their parents." He remembered that "there was a mother prostrate on the ground, moaning with pain but with one arm still tightly embracing her dead baby."[15] But for many of these survivors, the suffering had only begun. It is estimated that by 1950 as many as 200,000 additional victims had succumbed to their injuries, especially burns and the terrible effects of radiation. Cancer and genetic deformations caused by exposure to radiation continue to affect survivors and their descendants today.

Human suffering on a massive scale was a defining feature of total war during the first half of the twentieth century. In this sense, the atomic bomb was just the latest development in an arms race that drew on advances in manufacturing, technology, and science to create ever more horrific weapons of mass destruction. But no other weapon from that period was as revolutionary as the atomic bomb, which made use of recent discoveries in theoretical physics to harness the fundamental forces of the universe for war. The subsequent development of those weapons has cast an enormous shadow on the world ever since.

That shadow lay in a capacity for destruction previously associated only with an apocalypse of divine origin. Now human beings have acquired that capacity. A single bomb in a single instant can obliterate any major city in the world, and the detonation of even a small fraction of the weapons in existence today would reduce much of the world to radioactive rubble and social chaos. The destructive power of nuclear weapons has led responsible scientists to contemplate the possible extinction of our species—by our own hands. It is hardly surprising that the ongoing threat of nuclear war has led many survivors of the Hiroshima and Nagasaki bombings to push for a world free of nuclear weapons by highlighting the human suffering that they cause. In a speech to a United Nations Special Session on Disarmament in 1982, Senji Yamaguchi, a survivor of the Nagasaki bombing, pleaded, "Please look closely at my [burnt] face and hands. . . . We, atomic bomb survivors, are calling out. I continue calling out as long as I am alive: no more Hiroshima, no more Nagasaki, no more war, no more [victims of nuclear attacks]."[16]

Question: How might you define both the short- and long-term outcomes of the Hiroshima bombing?

and Nagasaki, which in a single instant vaporized tens of thousands of people. This was total war with a scale, intensity, and indiscriminate brutality that exceeded even the horrors of World War I. (See Zooming In: Hiroshima, above.)

A further dimension of total war lay in governments' efforts to mobilize their economies, their people, and their propaganda machines even more extensively than before. Colonial resources were harnessed once again. The British in particular made extensive use of colonial troops and laborers from India and Africa. Japan compelled several hundred thousand women from Korea, China, and elsewhere to serve the sexual needs of Japanese troops as so-called comfort women, who often accommodated twenty to thirty men a day.

As in World War I, though on a much larger scale, the needs of the war drew huge numbers of women into both industry and the military. In the United States, "Rosie the Riveter" represented those women who now took on heavy industrial jobs, which previously had been reserved for men. In the Soviet Union, women constituted more than half of the industrial workforce by 1945 and almost completely dominated agricultural production. Soviet women also participated actively in combat, with some 100,000 of them winning military honors. A much smaller percentage of German and Japanese women were mobilized for factory work, but a Greater Japan Women's Society enrolled some 19 million members, who did volunteer work and promised to lay aside their gold jewelry and abandon extravagant weddings. As always, war heightened the prestige of masculinity, and given the immense sacrifices that men had made, few women were inclined to directly challenge the practices of patriarchy immediately following the war.

But, while women had largely escaped death and injury in the First World War, neither women nor children were able to do so amid the indiscriminate slaughter of World War II. Urban bombing, blockades, mass murder, starvation, concentration camps—all of this affected men, women, and children alike. But women were almost exclusively the victims of the widespread rape that accompanied World War II—Japanese soldiers against Chinese women, Soviet troops against German women, among others. A prominent American observer commented in 1945 on the pervasive victimization of European women: "Europe is now a place where woman has lost her perennial fight for decency because the indecent alone live."[17]

Among the most haunting outcomes of the war was the Holocaust. The outbreak of that war closed off certain possibilities, such as forced emigration, for implementing the Nazi dream of ridding Germany of its Jewish population. It also brought millions of additional Jews in Poland and the Soviet Union under German control and triggered among Hitler's enthusiastic subordinates various schemes for a "final solution" to the Jewish question. From this emerged the death camps that included Auschwitz, Dachau, and Bergen-Belsen. Altogether, some 6 million Jews perished in a technologically sophisticated form of mass murder that set a new standard for human depravity. Millions more whom the Nazis deemed inferior, undesirable, or dangerous—Russians, Poles, and other Slavs; Gypsies, or the Roma; mentally or physically handicapped people; homosexuals; communists; and Jehovah's Witnesses—likewise perished in Germany's efforts at racial purification. (For the personal story of a Holocaust victim, see Zooming In: Etty Hillesum, page 902.)

Although the Holocaust was concentrated in Germany, its significance in twentieth-century world history has been huge. It has haunted postwar Germany in particular and the Western world in general. How could such a thing have occurred in a Europe bearing the legacy of both Christianity and the Enlightenment? More specifically, it sent many of Europe's remaining Jews fleeing to Israel and gave urgency to the establishment of a modern Jewish nation in the ancient Jewish homeland. That action outraged many Arabs, some of whom were displaced by the arrival of the Jews, and has fostered an enduring conflict in the Middle East. Furthermore, the Holocaust defined a new category of crimes against humanity—genocide, the attempted elimination of entire peoples. Universal condemnation of the Holocaust, however, did not end the practice, as cases of mass slaughter in Cambodia, Rwanda, Bosnia, and Sudan have demonstrated.

On an even larger scale than World War I, this second global conflict rearranged the architecture of world politics. As the war ended, Europe was impoverished, its industrial infrastructure was shattered, many of its great cities were in ruins, and millions of its people were homeless or displaced. Within a few years, this much-weakened Europe was effectively divided, with its western half operating under an American security umbrella and its eastern half subject to Soviet control. It was clear that Europe's dominance in world affairs was finished.

Over the next two decades, Europe's greatly diminished role in the world registered internationally as its Asian and African colonies achieved independence. Not only had the war weakened both the will and the ability of European powers to hold on to their colonies, but it had also emboldened nationalist and anticolonial movements everywhere (see Chapter 22). Japanese victories in Southeast Asia had certainly damaged European prestige, for British, Dutch, and American military forces fell to Japanese conquerors, sometimes in a matter of weeks. Japanese authorities staged long and brutal marches of Western prisoners of war, partly to drive home to local people that the era of Western domination was over. Furthermore, tens of thousands of Africans had fought for the British or the French, had seen white people die, had enjoyed the company of white women, and had returned home with very different ideas about white superiority and the permanence of colonial rule. Colonial subjects everywhere were very much aware that U.S. president Franklin Roosevelt and British prime minister Winston Churchill had solemnly declared in 1941: "We respect the right of all peoples to choose the form of government under which they will live." Many asked whether those principles should not apply to people in the colonial world as well as to Europeans.

A further outcome of World War II lay in the consolidation and extension of the communist world. The Soviet victory over the Nazis, though bought at an unimaginable cost in blood and treasure, gave immense credibility to that communist regime and to its leader, Joseph Stalin. In the decades that followed, Soviet authorities nurtured a virtual cult of the war: memorials were everywhere; wedding parties made pilgrimages to them, and brides left their bouquets behind; May 9, Victory Day, saw elaborately orchestrated celebrations; veterans were honored and granted modest privileges. Furthermore, communist parties, largely dominated by the Soviet Union and supported by its armed forces, took power all across Eastern Europe, pushing the communist frontier deep into the European heartland. Even more important was a communist takeover in China in 1949. The Second World War allowed the Chinese Communist Party to gain support and credibility by leading the struggle against Japan. By 1950, the communist world seemed to many in the West very much on the offensive (see Chapter 21).

The horrors of two world wars within a single generation prompted a renewed interest in international efforts to maintain the peace in a world of competing and sovereign states. The chief outcome was the United Nations (UN), established in 1945 as a successor to the moribund League of Nations. As a political body dependent on agreement among its most powerful members, the UN proved more effective as a forum for international opinion than as a means of resolving the major conflicts of the postwar world, particularly the Soviet/American hostility during the cold war decades. Further evidence for a growing internationalism lay in the creation in late 1945 of the World Bank and International Monetary Fund, whose purpose was to regulate the global economy, prevent another depression, and stimulate economic growth, especially in the poorer nations.

What these initiatives shared was the dominant presence of the United States. Unlike the aftermath of World War I, when an isolationist United States substantially withdrew from world affairs, the half century following the end of World War II witnessed the emergence of the United States as a global superpower. This was one of the major outcomes of the Second World War and a chief reason for the remarkable recovery of a badly damaged and discredited Western civilization.

SUMMING UP SO FAR

Is it more useful to view the two world wars as separate and distinct conflicts or as a single briefly interrupted phenomenon?

The Recovery of Europe

The tragedies that afflicted Europe in the first half of the twentieth century— fratricidal war, economic collapse, the Holocaust—were wholly self-inflicted, and yet despite the sorry and desperate state of heartland Europe in 1945, that civilization had not permanently collapsed. In the twentieth century's second half, Europeans rebuilt their industrial economies and revived their democratic political systems, while the United States, a European offshoot, assumed a dominant and often-dominating role both within Western civilization and in the world at large.

■ **Change**
How was Europe able to recover from the devastation of war?

Three factors help to explain this astonishing recovery. One is the apparent resiliency of an industrial society, once it has been established. The knowledge, skills, and habits of mind that enabled industrial societies to operate effectively remained intact, even if the physical infrastructure had been substantially destroyed. Thus even the most terribly damaged countries—Germany, the Soviet Union, and Japan—had largely recovered, both economically and demographically, within a quarter of a century. A second factor lay in the ability of the major Western European countries to integrate their recovering economies. After centuries of military conflict climaxed by the horrors of the two world wars, the major Western European powers were at last willing to put aside some of their prickly nationalism in return for enduring peace and common prosperity.

A third contribution to European recovery derives from the fact that Europe had long ago spawned an overseas extension of its own civilization in what became the United States. In the twentieth century, that country served as a reservoir of military manpower, economic resources, and political leadership for the West as a whole. By 1945, the center of gravity within Western civilization had shifted decisively and had relocated across the Atlantic. With Europe diminished, divided, and on the defensive against the communist threat, leadership of the Western world passed, almost by default, to the United States. It was the only major country physically untouched by the war. Its economy had demonstrated enormous productivity during that struggle and by 1945 was generating fully 50 percent of total world production. Its overall military strength was unmatched, and it was briefly in sole possession of the atomic bomb, the most powerful weapon ever constructed. Thus the United States became the new heartland of the West as well as a global super-power. In 1941, the publisher Henry Luce had proclaimed the twentieth century as "the American century." As the Second World War ended, that prediction seemed to be coming true.

An early indication of the United States' intention to exercise global leadership took shape in its efforts to rebuild and reshape shattered European economies. Known as the Marshall Plan, that effort funneled into Europe some $12 billion, at the time a very large amount, together with numerous advisers and technicians. It was motivated by some combination of genuine humanitarian concern, a desire to prevent a new depression by creating overseas customers for American industrial goods, and an interest in undermining the growing appeal of European communist parties. This economic recovery plan was successful beyond anyone's expectations. Between 1948 and the early 1970s, Western European economies grew rapidly, generating a widespread prosperity and improving living standards. At the same time, Western Europe became both a major customer for American goods and a major competitor in global markets.

The Marshall Plan also required its European recipients to cooperate with one another. After decades of conflict and destruction almost beyond description, many Europeans were eager to do so. That process began in 1951 when Italy, France, West Germany, Belgium, the Netherlands, and Luxembourg created the European Coal and Steel Community to jointly manage the production of these critical items. In 1957, these six countries deepened their level of cooperation by establishing the European Economic Community (EEC), more widely known as the Common Market, whose members reduced their tariffs and developed common trade poli-cies. Over the next half century, the EEC expanded its membership to include almost all of Europe, including many former communist states. In 1994, the EEC was renamed the European Union, and in 2002 twelve of its members, later increased to seventeen, adopted a common currency, the euro (see Map 20.6). All of this sustained Europe's remarkable economic recovery and expressed a larger European identity, although it certainly did not erase deeply rooted national loyal-ties or lead, as some had hoped, to a political union, a United States of Europe. Nor did it generate persistent economic stability as the European financial crisis begin-ning in 2010 called into question the viability of the euro zone and perhaps of the European Union as well. In elections to the European Parliament in 2014, parties skeptical of or outright opposed to the European Union won almost 20 percent of the seats in the body.

Beyond economic assistance, the American commitment to Europe soon came to include political and military security against the distant possibility of renewed German aggression and the more immediate communist threat from the Soviet Union. Without that security, economic recovery was unlikely to continue. Thus

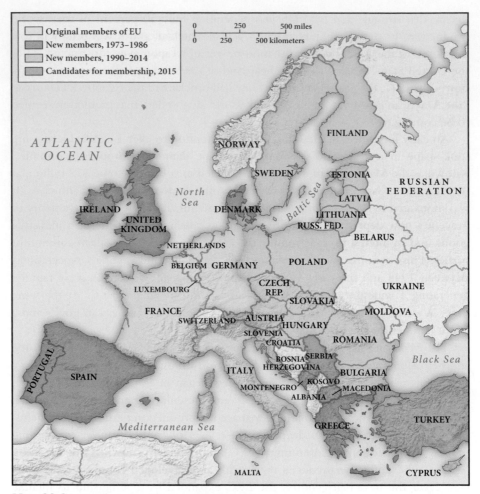

Map 20.6   The Growth of European Integration

During the second half of the twentieth century, Europeans gradually put aside their bitter rivalries and entered into various forms of economic cooperation with one another, although these efforts fell short of complete political union. This map illustrates the growth of what is now called the European Union (EU). Notice the eastward expansion of the EU following the collapse of communism in Eastern Europe and the Soviet Union.

was born the military and political alliance known as the North Atlantic Treaty Organization (NATO) in 1949. It committed the United States and its nuclear arsenal to the defense of Europe against the Soviet Union, and it firmly anchored West Germany within the Western alliance. Thus, as Western Europe revived economically, it did so under the umbrella of U.S. political and military leadership, which Europeans generally welcomed. It was perhaps an imperial relationship, but to historian John Gaddis, it was "an empire by invitation" rather than by imposition.[18]

A parallel process in Japan, which was under American occupation between 1945 and 1952, likewise revived that country's devastated but already industrialized economy. In the two decades following the occupation, Japan's economy grew at the remarkable rate of 10 percent a year, and the nation became an economic giant on the world stage. This "economic miracle" received a substantial boost from some $2 billion in American aid during the occupation and even more from U.S. military purchases in Japan during the Korean War (1950–1953). Furthermore, the democratic constitution imposed on Japan by American occupation authorities required that "land, sea, and air forces, as well as other war potential, will never be maintained." This meant that Japan, even more so than Europe, depended on the United States for its military security. Because it spent only about 1 percent of its gross national product on defense, more was available for productive investment.

The world had changed dramatically during the first seventy years of the twentieth century. That century began with a Europe of rival nations as clearly the dominant imperial center of a global network. But European civilization substantially self-destructed in the first half of the century, though it revived during the second half in a changed form—without its Afro-Asian colonies and with new leadership in the United States. Accompanying this process and intersecting with it was another major theme of twentieth-century world history—the rise and fall of world communism, which is the focus of the next chapter.

REFLECTIONS

War and Remembrance:
Learning from History

When asked about the value of studying history, most students respond with some version of the Spanish-born philosopher George Santayana's famous dictum: "Those who cannot remember the past are condemned to repeat it." At one level, this notion of learning from the "lessons of history" has much to recommend it, for there is, after all, little else except the past on which we can base our actions in the present. And yet historians in general are notably cautious about drawing particular lessons from the past and applying them to present circumstances.

For one thing, the historical record is sufficiently rich and complex to allow many people to draw quite different lessons from it. The world wars of the twentieth century represent a case in point, as writer Adam Gopnik has pointed out:

> The First World War teaches that territorial compromise is better than full-scale war, that an "honor-bound" allegiance of the great powers to small nations is a recipe for mass killing, and that it is crazy to let the blind mechanism of armies and alliances trump common sense. The Second teaches that searching for an accommodation with tyranny by selling out small nations only encourages the tyrant, that refusing to fight now leads to a worse fight later on. . . . The First teaches us never to rush into a fight, the Second never to back down from a bully.[19]

Did the lessons of the First World War lead Americans to ignore the rise of fascism until the country was directly threatened by Japanese attack? Did the lessons of World War II contribute to unnecessary wars in Vietnam and more recently in Iraq? There are no easy answers to such questions, for the lessons of history are many, varied, and changing.

Behind any such lesson is the common assumption that history repeats itself. This too is a notion to which historians bring considerable skepticism. They are generally more impressed with the complexity and particularity of major events such as wars than with their common features. Here is a further basis for caution in easily drawing lessons from the past.

But the wars of the past century perhaps share one broad similarity: all of them led to unexpected consequences. Few people expected the duration and carnage of World War I. The Holocaust was unimaginable when Hitler took power in 1933 or even at the outbreak of the Second World War in 1939. Who would have expected an American defeat at the hands of the Vietnamese? And the invasion of Iraq in 2003 generated a long list of surprises for the United States, including the absence of weapons of mass destruction and a prolonged insurgency. History repeats itself most certainly only in its unexpectedness.

Second Thoughts

What's the Significance?

World War I, 882–91
Treaty of Versailles, 890
Woodrow Wilson / Fourteen Points, 891
Great Depression, 891–95
New Deal, 894–95
fascism, 896–98
Mussolini, 897–98
Nazi Germany, 898–901
Hitler, 899–900
Etty Hillesum, 902–3

Revolutionary Right (Japan), 904–5
World War II in Asia, 907–9
World War II in Europe, 909–10
total war, 910–13
Hiroshima, 912–13
Holocaust, 914
Marshall Plan, 917
European Economic Community, 917
NATO, 918

Big Picture Questions

1. What explains the disasters that befell Europe in the first half of the twentieth century?
2. To what extent did the two world wars settle the issues that caused them? What legacies to the future did they leave?
3. In what ways did Europe's internal conflicts between 1914 and 1945 have global implications?
4. **Looking Back:** In what ways were the major phenomena of the first half of the twentieth century—world wars, the Great Depression, fascism, the Holocaust, the emergence of the United States as a global power—rooted in earlier times?

Next Steps: For Further Study

Michael Burleigh, *The Third Reich: A New History* (2001). A fresh and thorough look at the Nazi era in Germany's history.

John Keegan, *The Second World War* (2005). A comprehensive account by a well-known scholar.

Bernd Martin, *Japan and Germany in the Modern World* (1995). A comparative study of these two countries' modern history and the relationship between them.

Mark Mazower, *Dark Continent* (2000). A history of Europe in the twentieth century that views the era as a struggle among liberal democracy, fascism, and communism.

Michael S. Nieberg, *Fighting the Great War: A Global History* (2006). An exploration of the origins and conduct of World War I.

Dietman Rothermund, *The Global Impact of the Great Depression, 1929–1939* (1996). An examination of the origins of the Depression in America and Europe and its impact in Asia, Africa, and Latin America.

First World War.com, http://www.firstworldwar.com. A Web site rich with articles, documents, photos, diaries, and more that illustrate the history of World War I.

"The Holocaust," http://www.jewishvirtuallibrary.org/jsource/holo.html. A wealth of essays, maps, photographs, and timelines that explores the Holocaust and the context in which it arose.

WORKING WITH EVIDENCE

Ideologies of the Axis Powers

Even more than the Great War of 1914–1918, the Second World War was a conflict of ideas and ideologies as well as a struggle of nations and armies. The ideas of the losing side in that war, repellant as they were to their enemies, had for a time attracted considerable support. Described variously as fascist, authoritarian, right-wing, or radically nationalist, the ideologies of the Axis powers differed in tone and emphasis. But they shared a repudiation of mainstream Western liberalism and democracy, as well as an intense hatred of Marxist communism. The documents that follow provide a taste of this thinking as it took shape in Germany and Japan.

Source 20.1
Hitler on Nazism

Adolf Hitler published his political views well before he came to power. Born in Austria, Hitler absorbed a radical form of German nationalism, which he retained as a profoundly disillusioned veteran of World War I. In 1919, he joined a very small extremist group called the German Workers Party, where he rose quickly to a dominant role based on his powerful oratorical abilities. Inspired by Mussolini's recent victory in Italy, Hitler launched in 1923 an unsuccessful armed uprising in Munich for which he was arrested and imprisoned. During his brief stay in prison (less than a year), he wrote *Mein Kampf* (*My Struggle*), part autobiography and part an exposition of his political and social philosophy. Armed with these ideas, Hitler assumed the leadership of Germany in 1933 (see pages 898–901).

■ What larger patterns in European thinking do Hitler's ideas reflect, and what elements of European thought does he reject? Consider in particular his use of social Darwinism, then an idea with wide popularity in Europe.

■ How does Hitler distinguish between Aryans and Jews? How does he understand the role of race in human affairs?

■ What kind of political system does Hitler advocate?

■ What goals for Germany—both domestic and foreign—did Hitler set forth in *Mein Kampf*?

■ What aspects of Hitler's thinking might have had wide appeal in Germany during the 1930s?

ADOLF HITLER

Mein Kampf (My Struggle)

1925–1926

Nation and Race

There are some truths which are so obvious that for this very reason they are not seen or at least not recognized by ordinary people. . . . Every animal mates only with a member of the same species. . . . Any crossing of two beings not at exactly the same level produces a medium between the level of the two parents. . . . Such mating is contrary to the will of Nature for a higher breeding of all life. . . . The stronger must dominate and not blend with the weaker, thus sacrificing his own greatness. Only the born weakling can view this as cruel . . . , for if this law did not prevail, any conceivable higher development of organic living beings would be unthinkable.

In the struggle for daily bread all those who are weak and sickly or less determined succumb, while the struggle of the males for the female grants the right or opportunity to propagate only to the healthiest. . . . No more than Nature desires the mating of weaker with stronger individuals, even less does she desire the blending of a higher with a lower race, since, if she did, her whole work of higher breeding, over perhaps hundreds of thousands of years, might be ruined with one blow. . . . All great cultures of the past perished only because the originally creative race died out from blood poisoning.

Those who want to live, let them fight, and those who do not want to fight in this world of eternal struggle do not deserve to live. . . .

All the human culture, all the results of art, science, and technology that we see before us today, are almost exclusively the creative product of the Aryan. . . . [H]e alone was the founder of all higher humanity, therefore representing the prototype of all that we understand by the word "man." He is the Prometheus of mankind from whose bright forehead the divine spark of genius has sprung at all times. . . .

All who are not of good race in this world are chaff.

The mightiest counterpart to the Aryan is represented by the Jew. . . . Since the Jew . . . was never in possession of a culture of his own, the foundations of his intellectual work were always provided by others. His intellect at all times developed through the cultural world surrounding him. . . .

He lacks completely the most essential requirement for a cultured people, the idealistic attitude. In the Jewish people the will to self-sacrifice does not go beyond the individual's naked instinct of self-preservation. Their apparently great sense of solidarity is based on the very primitive herd instinct that is seen in many other living creatures in this world. . . . [T]he Jew is led by nothing but the naked egoism of the individual.

With satanic joy in his face, the black-haired Jewish youth lurks in wait for the unsuspecting girl whom he defiles with his blood, thus stealing her from her people. With every means he tries to destroy the racial foundations of the people he has set out to subjugate. . . . And so he tries systematically to lower the racial level by a continuous poisoning of individuals. And in politics he begins to replace the idea of democracy by the dictatorship of the proletariat. In the organized mass of Marxism he has found the weapon which lets him . . . subjugate and govern the peoples with a dictatorial and brutal fist.

In economics he undermines the states until the social enterprises which have become unprofitable are taken from the state and subjected to his financial control.

In the political field he refuses the state the means for its self-preservation, destroys the foundations of all national self-maintenance and defense, destroys faith in the leadership, scoffs at its history and past, and drags everything that is truly great into the gutter.

Culturally he contaminates art, literature, the theater, makes a mockery of natural feeling, overthrows all concepts of beauty and sublimity, of the noble and the good, and instead drags men down into the sphere of his own base nature. Religion is ridiculed, ethics and morality represented as outmoded, until the last props of a nation in its struggle for existence in this world have fallen.

If we pass all the causes of the German collapse [defeat in World War I] in review, the ultimate and most decisive remains the failure to recognize the racial problem and especially the Jewish menace. . . . The lost purity of the blood alone destroys inner happiness forever, plunges man into the abyss for all time, and the consequences can never more be eliminated from body and spirit. . . . All really significant symptoms of decay of the pre-War period can in the last analysis be reduced to racial causes.

The State

The State is only a means to an end. . . . Above all, it must preserve the existence of the race. . . . We, as Aryans, can consider the State only as the living organism of a people, an organism which does not merely maintain the existence of a people, but functions in such a way as to lead its people to a position of supreme liberty by the progressive development of the intellectual and cultural faculties.

We National Socialists know that in holding these views we take up a revolutionary stand in the world of today and that we are branded as revolutionaries. . . .

As a State the German Reich shall include all Germans. Its task is not only to gather in and foster the most valuable sections of our people but to lead them slowly and surely to a dominant position in the world. . . . It will be the task of the People's State to make the race the centre of the life of the community. It must make sure that the purity of the racial strain will be preserved. . . . Those who are physically and mentally unhealthy and unfit must not perpetuate their own suffering in the bodies of their children. . . .

One thing is certain: our world is facing a great revolution. The only question is whether the outcome will be propitious for the Aryan portion of mankind or whether the everlasting Jew will profit by it. By educating the young generation along the right lines, the People's State will have to see to it that a generation of mankind is formed which will be adequate to this supreme combat that will decide the destinies of the world. . . .

[T]he People's State must mercilessly expurgate . . . the parliamentarian principle, according to which decisive power through the majority vote is invested in the multitude. Personal responsibility must be substituted in its stead. . . . The best constitution and the best form of government is that which makes it quite natural for the best brains to reach a position of dominant importance and influence in the community. . . . Genius of an extraordinary stamp is not to be judged by normal standards whereby we judge other men.

There are no decisions made by the majority vote, but only by responsible persons. And the word "council" is once more restored to its original meaning. Every man in a position of responsibility will have councilors at his side, but the decision is made by that individual person alone. . . .

[T]he principle of parliamentarian democracy, whereby decisions are enacted through the majority vote, has not always ruled the world. On the contrary, we find it prevalent only during short periods of history, and those have always been periods of decline in nations and States. . . .

Eastern Orientation or Eastern Policy

[W]e National Socialists must hold unflinchingly to our aim in foreign policy, namely, to secure for the German people the land and soil to which they are entitled on this earth. . . . If we speak of soil in Europe today, we can primarily have in mind only Russia and her vassal border states. . . .

The National Socialist movement must strive to eliminate the disproportion between our population and our area—viewing this latter as a source of food as well as a basis for power politics—between our historical past and the hopelessness of our present impotence. And in this it must remain aware that we, as guardians of the highest humanity on this earth, are bound by the highest obligation, and the more it strives to bring the German people to racial awareness . . . , the more it will be able to meet this obligation. . . .

State boundaries are made by man and changed by man. . . . And in this case, right lies in this strength alone. . . . Just as our ancestors did not receive the soil on which we live today as a gift from Heaven, but had to fight for it at the risk of their lives, in the future no folkish grace will win soil for us . . . but only the might of a victorious sword. . . .

Never forget that the most sacred right on this earth is a man's right to have earth to till with his own hands, and the most sacred sacrifice the blood that a man sheds for this earth.

Source: Adolf Hitler, *Mein Kampf*, translated by Ralph Manheim (Boston: Houghton Mifflin, 1943).

Source 20.2
The Japanese Way

In the Japanese language, the word *kokutai* is an evocative term that refers to the national essence or the fundamental character of the Japanese nation and people. Drawing both on long-established understandings and on recently developed nationalist ideas, the Ministry of Education in 1937 published a small volume, widely distributed in schools and homes throughout the country, titled *Kokutai No Hongi* (*Cardinal Principles of the National Entity of Japan*). That text, excerpted in Source 20.2, defined the uniqueness of Japan and articulated the philosophical foundation of its authoritarian regime. (See pages 901–6 for the background to this document.) When the Americans occupied a defeated and devastated Japan in 1945, they forbade the further distribution of the book.

■ According to *Cardinal Principles*, what was *kokutai*? How did the document define the national essence of Japan? How did its authors compare Japan to the West?

■ What was the ideal role of the individual in Japanese society?

■ To whom might these ideas have been attractive? Why?

■ How might this document have been used to justify Japan's military and territorial expansion?

■ Why do you think the American occupation authorities banned the document?

Cardinal Principles of the National Entity of Japan
1937

The various ideological and social evils of present-day Japan are the result of ignoring the fundamental and running after the trivial, of lack of judgment, and a failure to digest things thoroughly; and this is due to the fact that since the days of *Meiji* so many aspects of European and American culture, systems, and learning, have been imported, and that, too rapidly. As a matter of fact, the foreign ideologies imported into our country are in the main ideologies of the [European] Enlightenment that have come down from the eighteenth century, or extensions of them. The views of the world and of life that form the basis of these ideologies . . . lay the highest value on, and assert the liberty and equality of, individuals. . . .

We have already witnessed the boundless Imperial virtues. Wherever this Imperial virtue of compassion radiates, the Way for the subjects naturally becomes clear. The Way of the subjects exists where the entire nation serves the Emperor united in mind. . . . That is, we by nature serve the Emperor and walk the Way of the Empire. . . .

We subjects are intrinsically quite different from the so-called citizens of the Occidental [Western] countries. . . .

When citizens who are conglomerations of separate individuals independent of each other give support to a ruler, . . . there exists no deep foundation between ruler and citizen to unite them. However, the relationship between the Emperor and his subjects arises from the same fountainhead, and has prospered ever since the founding of the nation as one in essence. . . .

Our country is established with the Emperor. . . . For this reason, to serve the Emperor and to receive the Emperor's great august Will as one's own is the rationale of making our historical "life" live in the present. . . .

Loyalty means to reverence the Emperor as [our] pivot and to follow him implicitly. . . . Hence, offering our lives for the sake of the Emperor does not mean so-called self-sacrifice, but the casting aside of our little selves to live under his august grace and the enhancing of the genuine life of the people of a State. . . . An individual is an existence belonging to the State and her history, which forms the basis of his origin, and is fundamentally one body with it. . . .

We must sweep aside the corruption of the spirit and the clouding of knowledge that arises from setting up one's "self" and from being taken up with one's "self" and return to a pure and clear state of mind that belongs intrinsically to us as subjects, and thereby fathom the great principle loyalty. . . .

Indeed, loyalty is our fundamental Way as subject, and is the basis of our national morality. Through loyalty are we become Japanese subjects;

in loyalty do we obtain life and herein do we find the source of all morality. . . .

In our country filial piety is a Way of the highest importance. Filial piety originates with one's family as its basis, and in its larger sense has the nation for its foundation. . . .

Our country is a great family nation, and the Imperial Household is the head family of the subjects and the nucleus of national life. The subjects revere the Imperial Household, which is the head family, with the tender esteem they have for their ancestors; and the Emperor loves his subjects as his very own. . . .

When we trace the marks of the facts of the founding of our country and the progress of our history, what we always find there is the spirit of harmony. . . . The spirit of harmony is built upon the concord of all things. When people determinedly count themselves as masters and assert their egos, there is nothing but contradictions and the setting of one against the other; and harmony is not begotten. . . . That is, a society of individualism is one of the clashes between [masses of] people . . . and all history may be looked upon as one of class wars. . . .

And this, this harmony is clearly seen in our nation's martial spirit. Our nation is one that holds bushido [the way of the warrior/samurai] in high regard, and there are shrines deifying warlike spirits. . . . Bushido may be cited as showing an outstanding characteristic of our national morality. . . . That is to say, though a sense of obligation binds master and servant, this has developed in a spirit of self-effacement and meeting death with a perfect calmness. In this, it was not that death was made light of so much as that man tempered himself to death and in a true sense regarded it with esteem. In effect, man tried to fulfill true life by the way of death. . . .

To put it in a nutshell, while the strong points of Occidental learning and concepts lie in their analytical and intellectual qualities, the characteristics of Oriental learning and concepts lie in their intuitive and aesthetic qualities. These are natural tendencies that arise through racial and historical differences; and when we compare them with our national spirits, concepts, or mode of living, we cannot help recognizing further great and fundamental differences. Our nation has in the past imported, assimilated, and sublimated Chinese and Indian ideologies, and has therewith supported the Imperial Way, making possible the establishment of an original culture based on her national polity. . . .

Since the *Meiji* restoration our nation has adapted the good elements of the advanced education seen among European and American nations, and has exerted efforts to set up an educational system and materials for teaching. The nation has also assimilated on a wide scale the scholarship of the West, not only in the fields of natural science, but of the mental sciences, and has thus striven to see progress made in our scholastic pursuits and to make education more popular. . . .

However, at the same time, through the infiltration of individualistic concepts, both scholastic pursuits and education have tended to be taken up with a world in which the intellect alone mattered. . . .

In order to correct these tendencies, the only course open to us is to clarify the true nature of our national polity, which is at the very source of our education, and to strive to clear up individualistic and abstract ideas.

Source: J. O. Gauntlett, trans., and R. K. Hall, ed., *Kokutai No Hongi* (*Cardinal Principles of the National Entity of Japan*) (Cambridge, MA: Harvard University Press, 1949), 53–183.

DOING HISTORY

Ideologies of the Axis Powers

1. **Making comparisons:** What aspects of the Japanese document might Hitler have viewed with sympathy, and what parts of it might he have found distasteful or offensive?

2. **Criticizing the West:** In what ways did Hitler and the authors of *Cardinal Principles* find fault with mainstream Western societies and their political and social values?

3. **Considering ideas and circumstances:** From what sources did the ideas expressed in these documents arise? What kinds of people would have found them attractive, and why?

4. **Considering ideas and action:** To what extent did the ideas articulated in these documents find expression in particular actions or policies of political authorities?

5. **Noticing continuity and change:** To what extent were the ideas in these documents new and revolutionary? In what respects did they draw on long-standing traditions in their societies? In what ways did they embrace modern life, and what aspects of it did they reject? Have these ideas been completely discredited, or do they retain some resonance in contemporary political discourse?

ЛЕНИН –
ЖИЛ,
ЛЕНИН –
ЖИВ,
ЛЕНИН –
БУДЕТ ЖИТЬ!

ВЛ. МАЯКОВСКИЙ.

CHAPTER 21

Revolution, Socialism, and Global Conflict

The Rise and Fall of World Communism
1917–present

An upstanding Soviet citizen entered a medical clinic one day and asked to see an ear-and-eye doctor. Asked about his problem, the man replied, "Well, I keep hearing one thing and seeing another."

A Frenchman, an Englishman, and a Soviet Russian are admiring a painting of Adam and Eve in the Garden of Eden. The Frenchman says, "They must be French; they're naked and they're eating fruit." The Englishman says, "Clearly, they're English; observe how politely the woman is offering fruit to the man." The Russian replies, "No, they are Russian communists, of course. They have no house, nothing to wear, little to eat, and they think they are in Paradise."

These are two of an endless array of jokes that had long circulated in the Soviet Union as a means of expressing in private what could not be said in public. A major theme of those jokes involved the hypocrisy of a communist system that promised equality and abundance for all but delivered a dismal and uncertain economic life for the many and great privileges for the few. The growing disbelief in the ability or willingness of the communist regime to provide a decent life for its people was certainly an important factor in the collapse of the Soviet Union in 1991 and the end of communism in the land of its birth. Amid that disillusionment, it was hard to remember that earlier in the century communism had been greeted with enthusiasm by many people—in Russia, China, Cuba, Vietnam, and elsewhere—as a promise of liberation from inequality, oppression, exploitation, and backwardness.

Lenin Vladimir Ulyanov, better known as Lenin, was the Bolshevik leader of the Russian Revolution. He became the iconic symbol of world communism and in his own country was the focus of a semi-religious cult. This widely distributed Soviet propaganda poster reads, "Lenin lived; Lenin lives; Lenin will live."

Communism was a phenomenon of enormous significance in the world of the twentieth century. Communist regimes came to power almost everywhere in the tumultuous wake of war, revolution, or both. Once established, those regimes set about a thorough and revolutionary transformation of their societies—"building socialism," as they so often put it. Internationally, world communism posed a profound military and political/ideological threat to the Western world of capitalism and democracy, particularly during the decades of the cold war from the late 1940s through 1991. That struggle divided continents, countries, and cities into communist and noncommunist halves. It also prompted a global rivalry between the United States and the Soviet Union (USSR) for influence in the Global South. Most hauntingly, it spawned an arms race in horrendously destructive nuclear weapons that sent schoolchildren scrambling under their desks during air raid drills, while sober scientists speculated about the possible extinction of human life, and perhaps all life, in the event of a major war.

Then, to the amazement of everyone, it was over, more with a whimper than a bang. The last two decades of the twentieth century witnessed the collapse of communist regimes or the abandonment of communist principles practically everywhere. The great global struggle of capitalism and communism, embodied in the United States and the Soviet Union, was resolved in favor of the former far more quickly and much more peacefully than anyone had imagined possible.

SEEKING THE MAIN POINT

What was the appeal of communism, both in terms of its promises and its achievements? To what extent did promises match achievements?

Global Communism

Modern communism found its political and philosophical roots in nineteenth-century European socialism, inspired by the teachings of Karl Marx. Although most European socialists came to believe that they could achieve their goals peacefully and through the democratic process, those who defined themselves as communists in the twentieth century disdained such reformism and advocated uncompromising revolution as the only possible route to a socialist future. Russia, later called the Soviet Union, was the first country to experience such a revolution. Other movements that later identified or allied with the Soviet Union likewise defined themselves as communist. In Marxist theory, communism also referred to a final stage of historical development when social equality and collective living would be most fully developed, largely without private property. Socialism was an intermediate stage along the way to that final goal.

By the 1970s, almost one-third of the world's population lived in societies governed by communist regimes. By far the most significant were the Soviet Union, the world's largest country in size, and China, the world's largest country in population. But Mongolia had come under communist rule in 1924 as a spillover of the Russian Revolution. Communist regimes came to power in Eastern Europe in the wake of World War II and the extension of the Soviet military presence there. Fol-

■ Description
When and where did communism exercise influence during the twentieth century?

A MAP OF TIME

1917	Russian Revolution
1921	Founding of Chinese Communist Party
1929–1953	Stalin in power in Soviet Union
1934–1935	Long March in China
1945–1950	Imposition of communist regimes in Eastern Europe
1949	Communist triumph in China
1950–1953	Korean War
1958–1961	China's Great Leap Forward and massive famine
1959	Cuban Revolution
1962	Cuban missile crisis
1965–1973	U.S.-Vietnam war
1966–1976	China's Cultural Revolution
1968	Prague Spring: communist reform movement in Czechoslovakia
1975–1979	Genocide in communist Cambodia
1976–early 1990s	Deng Xiaoping and beginnings of communist reforms in China
1979	Soviet invasion of Afghanistan
1985–1991	Gorbachev reforms in USSR
1989	Collapse of communist regimes in Eastern Europe
1991	Disintegration of Soviet Union
1990s	Economic contraction in the former Soviet Union and economic expansion in China
2007–2009	Communist North Korea acquires nuclear weapons
2008	Fidel Castro steps down as leader of communist Cuba
2014	United States proposes to restore diplomatic relations with Cuba

lowing Japan's defeat in World War II, its Korean colony was partitioned, with the northern half coming under Soviet and therefore communist control. In Vietnam, a much more locally based communist movement, under the leadership of Ho Chi Minh, embodied both a socialist vision and Vietnamese nationalism as it battled Japanese, French, and later American invaders and established communist control first in the northern half of the country and after 1975 throughout the whole country. The victory of the Vietnamese communists spilled over into neighboring Laos and Cambodia, where communist parties took power in the mid-1970s. In Latin America, Fidel Castro led a revolutionary nationalist movement against a repressive, American-backed government in Cuba. On coming to power in 1959, Castro moved toward communism and an alliance with the Soviet Union. Finally, a shaky communist regime took power in Afghanistan in 1979, propped up briefly by massive Soviet military support. None of these countries had achieved the kind of advanced industrial capitalism that Karl Marx had viewed as a prerequisite for revolution and socialism. Indeed, in one of history's strange twists, the communist revolutions of the twentieth century took place in largely agrarian societies. (See Map 21.3, page 950, for a global view of the communist world in the 1970s, the period of its greatest extent.)

In addition to those countries where communist governments controlled state power, communist movements took root in still other places, where they exercised various degrees of influence. In the aftermath of World War II, communist parties played important political roles in Greece, France, and Italy. In the 1950s, a small communist party in the United States became the focus of an intense wave of fear and political repression known as McCarthyism. Revolutionary communist movements threatened established governments in the Philippines, Malaysia, Indonesia, Bolivia, Peru, and elsewhere, sometimes provoking brutal crackdowns by those governments. A number of African states in the 1970s proclaimed themselves Marxist for a time and aligned with the Soviet Union in international affairs. All of this was likewise part of global communism.

These differing expressions of communism were linked to one another in various ways. They shared a common ideology derived from European Marxism, although it was substantially modified in many places. That ideology minimized the claims of national loyalty and looked forward to an international revolutionary movement of the lower classes and a worldwide socialist federation. The Russian Revolution of 1917 served as an inspiration and an example to aspiring revolutionaries elsewhere, and the new Soviet Communist Party and government provided them aid and advice. Through an organization called Comintern (Communist International), Soviet authorities also sought to control their policies and actions.

During the cold war decades, the Warsaw Pact brought the Soviet Union and Eastern European communist states together in a military alliance designed to counter the threat from the Western capitalist countries of the NATO alliance. A parallel organization called the Council on Mutual Economic Assistance tied Eastern European economies tightly to the economy of the Soviet Union. A Treaty of Friendship between the Soviet Union and China in 1950 joined the two communist giants in an alliance that caused many in the West to view communism as a unified international movement aimed at their destruction. Nevertheless, rivalry, outright hostility, and on occasion military conflict marked the communist world as much as or more than solidarity and cooperation. Eastern European nations' resentment of their Soviet overlords boiled over in periodic rebellions, even as the Soviet Union and China came close to war in the late 1960s.

Although the globalization of communism found expression primarily in the second half of the twentieth century, that process began with two quite distinct and different revolutionary upheavals — one in Russia and the other in China — in the first half of the century.

Revolutions as a Path to Communism

Communist movements of the twentieth century quite self-consciously drew on the mystique of the earlier French Revolution, which suggested that new and better worlds could be constructed by human actions. Like their French predecessors, communist revolutionaries ousted old ruling classes and dispossessed landed aristocracies. Those twentieth-century upheavals also involved vast peasant upheavals in the countryside and an educated leadership with roots in the cities. All three revolutions — French, Russian, and Chinese — found their vision of the good society in a modernizing future, not in some nostalgic vision of the past. Communists also worried lest their revolutions end up in a military dictatorship like that of Napoleon following the French Revolution.

But the communist revolutions were distinctive as well. They were made by highly organized parties guided by a Marxist ideology, were committed to an industrial future, pursued economic as well as political equality, and sought the abolition of private property. In doing so, they mobilized, celebrated, and claimed to act on behalf of society's lower classes — exploited urban workers and impoverished rural peasants. The middle classes, who were the chief beneficiaries of the French Revolution, numbered among the many victims of the communist upheavals. And unlike the French or American revolutionaries, communists also carried an explicit message of gender equality. The Russian and Chinese revolutions shared these general features, but in other respects they differed sharply from each other.

■ **Comparison**
Identify the major differences between the Russian and Chinese revolutions.

Russia: Revolution in a Single Year

In Russia, communists came to power on the back of a revolutionary upheaval that took place within a single year, 1917. The immense pressures of World War I, which was going very badly for the Russians, represented the catalyst for that revolution as the accumulated tensions of Russian society exploded. Much exploited and suffering from wartime shortages, workers — men and women alike — took to the streets to express their outrage at the incompetence and privileges of the elites. In St. Petersburg, some 100,000 wives of soldiers demonstrated for bread and peace. Activists from various parties, many of them socialist, recruited members, organized demonstrations, published newspapers, and plotted revolution. By February 1917, Tsar Nicholas II had lost almost all support and was forced to abdicate the throne, thus ending the Romanov dynasty, which had ruled Russia for more than three centuries.

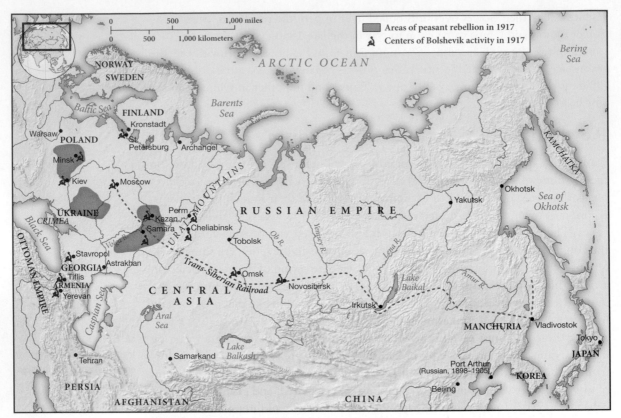

Map 21.1   Russia in 1917

In 1917 during the First World War, the world's largest state, bridging both Europe and Asia, exploded in revolution. The Russian Revolution brought to power the twentieth century's first communist government and launched an international communist movement that eventually incorporated about one-third of the world's people.

That historic event opened the door for a massive social upheaval. Ordinary soldiers, seeking an end to a terrible war and despising their upper-class officers, deserted in substantial numbers. In major industrial centers such as St. Petersburg and Moscow, new trade unions arose to defend workers' interests, and some workers seized control of their factories. Grassroots organizations of workers and soldiers, known as soviets, emerged to speak for ordinary people. Peasants, many of whom had been serfs only a generation or two earlier, seized landlords' estates, burned their manor houses, and redistributed the land among themselves. Non-Russian nationalists in Ukraine, Poland, Muslim Central Asia, and the Baltic region demanded greater autonomy or even independence (see Map 21.1).

This was social revolution, and it quickly demonstrated the inadequacy of the Provisional Government, which had come to power after the tsar abdicated. Consisting of middle-class politicians and some moderate socialist leaders, that government was divided and ineffectual, unable or unwilling to meet the demands of

Russia's revolutionary masses. It was also unwilling to take Russia out of the war, as many were now demanding. Impatience and outrage against the Provisional Government provided an opening for more radical groups. The most effective were the Bolsheviks (BOHL-shih-vehks), a small socialist party with a determined and charismatic leader, Vladimir Ilyich Ulyanov, more commonly known as Lenin. He had long believed that Russia, despite its industrial backwardness, was nonetheless ready for a socialist revolution that would, he expected, spark further revolutions in the more developed countries of Europe. Thus backward Russia would be a catalyst for a more general socialist breakthrough. It was a striking revision of Marxist thinking to accommodate the conditions of a largely agrarian Russian society.

In the desperate circumstances of 1917, his party's message — an end to the war, land for the peasants, workers' control of factories, self-determination for non-Russian nationalities — resonated with an increasingly rebellious public mood, particularly in the major cities. On the basis of this program, the Bolsheviks — claiming to act on behalf of the highly popular soviets — seized power in late October during an overnight coup in the capital city of St. Petersburg.

■ **Change**
Why were the Bolsheviks able to ride the Russian Revolution to power?

Taking or claiming power was one thing; holding on to it was another. A three-year civil war followed in which the Bolsheviks, now officially calling their party "communist," battled an assortment of enemies — tsarist officials, landlords, disaffected socialists, and regional nationalist forces, as well as troops from the United States, Britain, France, and Japan, all of which were eager to crush the fledgling communist regime. Remarkably, the Bolsheviks held on and by 1921 had staggered to victory over their divided and uncoordinated opponents. That remarkable victory was assisted by the Bolsheviks' willingness to sign a separate peace treaty with Germany, thus taking Russia out of World War I in early 1918, but at a great, though temporary, loss of Russian territory.

During the civil war (1918–1921), the Bolsheviks harshly regimented the economy, seized grain from angry peasants, suppressed nationalist rebellions, and perpetrated bloody atrocities, as did their enemies as well. But they also integrated many lower-class men into the Red Army, as Bolshevik military forces were known, and into new local governments, providing them a fresh avenue of social mobility. By battling foreign troops, the Bolsheviks claimed to be defending Russia from imperialists and protecting the downtrodden masses from their exploiters. The civil war exaggerated even further the Bolsheviks' authoritarian tendencies and their inclination to use force. Shortly after that war ended, they renamed their country the Union of Soviet Socialist Republics (USSR or Soviet Union) and set about its transformation.

For the next twenty-five years, the Soviet Union remained a communist island in a capitalist sea. The next major extension of communist control occurred in Eastern Europe in the aftermath of World War II, but it took place quite differently than in Russia. That war ended with Soviet military forces occupying much of Eastern Europe. Stalin, the USSR's longtime leader, determined that Soviet security

The Russian Civil War through Bolshevik Eyes
This Bolshevik poster from 1921, titled "Electrification and Counterrevolution," presents a communist view of the civil war that followed the Russian Revolution. It shows a worker bringing electricity and more generally the light of modernity and progress to a backward country, while depicting their opponents, which include a priest, a general, and a businessman, as seeking to extinguish that light. (The New York Public Library/Art Resource, NY)

required "friendly" governments in the region to permanently end the threat of invasion from the West. When the Marshall Plan seemed to suggest American efforts to incorporate Eastern Europe into a Western economic network, Stalin acted to install fully communist governments, loyal to himself, in Poland, East Germany, Czechoslovakia, Hungary, Romania, and Bulgaria. Backed by the pressure and presence of the Soviet army, communism was largely imposed on Eastern Europe from outside rather than growing out of a domestic revolution, as had happened in Russia itself.

Local communist parties, however, had some domestic support, deriving from their role in the resistance against the Nazis and their policies of land reform. In Hungary and Poland, for example, communist pressures led to the redistribution of much land to poor or landless peasants, and in free elections in Czechoslovakia in 1946 communists received 38 percent of the vote. The situation in Yugoslavia differed sharply from that of the rest of Eastern Europe. There a genuinely popular communist movement had played a leading role in the struggle against Nazi occupation and came to power on its own with little Soviet help. Its leader, Josef Broz, known as Tito, openly defied Soviet efforts to control Yugoslav communism. He proclaimed, "Our goal is that everyone should be master in his own house."[1]

China: A Prolonged Revolutionary Struggle

Communism triumphed in the ancient land of China in 1949, about thirty years after the Russian Revolution, likewise on the heels of war and domestic upheaval. But that revolution, which was a struggle of decades rather than a single year, was far different from its earlier Russian counterpart. The Chinese imperial system had collapsed in 1911, under the pressure of foreign imperialism, its own inadequacies, and mounting internal opposition (see Chapter 19, pages 834–44). Unlike in Russia, where intellectuals had been discussing socialism for half a century or more before the revolution, in China the ideas of Karl Marx were barely known in the early twentieth century. Not until 1921 was a small Chinese Communist Party (CCP) founded, aimed initially at organizing the country's minuscule urban working class.

Over the next twenty-eight years, that small party, with an initial membership of only sixty people, grew enormously, transformed its strategy, found a charismatic leader in Mao Zedong, engaged in an epic struggle with its opponents, fought the Japanese heroically, and in 1949 emerged victorious as the rulers of China. That victory was all the more surprising because the CCP faced a far more formidable foe than the weak Provisional Government over which the Bolsheviks had triumphed in Russia. That opponent was the Guomindang (GWOH-mihn-dahng) (Nationalist Party), which governed China after 1928. Led by a military officer, Chiang Kai-shek, that party promoted a measure of modern development (railroads, light industry, banking, airline services) in the decade that followed. However, the impact of these achievements was limited largely to the cities, leaving the rural areas, where most people lived, still impoverished. The Guomindang's base of support was also narrow, deriving from urban elites, rural landlords, and Western powers.

■ **Change**
What was the appeal of communism in China before 1949?

Chased out of China's cities in a wave of Guomindang-inspired anticommunist terror in 1927, the CCP groped its way toward a new revolutionary strategy, quite at odds with both classical Marxism and Russian practice. Whereas the Bolsheviks had found their primary audience among workers in Russia's major cities, Chinese communists increasingly looked to the country's peasant villages for support. Thus European Marxism was adapted once again, this time to fit the situation of a mostly peasant China. Still, it was no easy sell. Chinese peasants did not rise up spontaneously against their landlords, as Russian peasants had. However, years of guerrilla warfare, experiments with land reform in areas under communist control, and the creation of a communist military force to protect liberated areas slowly gained for the CCP a growing measure of respect and support among China's peasants. In the process, Mao Zedong, the son of a prosperous Chinese peasant family and a professional revolutionary since the early 1920s, emerged as the party's leader.

To recruit women for the revolution, communists drew on a theoretical commitment to the liberation of women and in the areas under communist control established a Marriage Law that outlawed arranged or "purchased" marriages, made divorce easier, and gave women the right to vote and own property. Early experiments with land reform offered equal shares to men and women alike. Women's associations enrolled

Mao Zedong and the Long March
An early member of China's then-minuscule Communist Party, Mao rose to a position of dominant leadership during the Long March of 1934–1935, when beleaguered communists from southeastern China trekked to a new base area in the north. This photograph shows Mao on his horse during that epic journey of some 6,000 miles. (© Collection A. Fox/Magnum Photos)

hundreds of thousands of women and promoted literacy, fostered discussions of women's issues, and encouraged handicraft production, such as making the clothing, blankets, and shoes that were so essential for the revolutionary forces. But resistance to such radical measures from more traditional rural villagers, especially the male peasants and soldiers on whom the communists depended, persuaded the communists to modify these measures. Women were not permitted to seek divorce from men on active military duty. Women's land deeds were often given to male family heads and were regarded as family property. Female party members found themselves limited to work with women or children.

It was Japan's brutal invasion of China that gave the CCP a decisive opening, for that attack destroyed Guomindang control over much of the country and forced it to retreat to the interior, where it became even more dependent on conservative landlords. The CCP, by contrast, grew from just 40,000 members in 1937 to more than 1.2 million in 1945, while the communist-led People's Liberation Army mushroomed to 900,000 men, supported by an additional 2 million militia troops (see Map 21.2). Much of this growing support derived from the vigor with which the CCP waged war against the Japanese invaders. Using guerrilla warfare techniques learned in the struggle against the Guomindang, communist forces established themselves behind enemy lines and, despite periodic setbacks, offered a measure of security to many Chinese faced with Japanese atrocities. The Guomindang, by contrast, sometimes seemed to be more interested in eliminating the communists than in actively fighting the Japanese. Furthermore, in the areas it controlled, the CCP reduced rents, taxes, and interest payments for peasants; established literacy programs for adults; and mobilized women for the struggle. As the war drew to a close, more radical action followed. Teams of activists encouraged poor peasants to "speak bitterness" in public meetings, to "struggle" with landlords, and to "settle accounts" with them.

Thus the CCP frontally addressed both of China's major problems—foreign imperialism and peasant exploitation. It expressed Chinese nationalism as well as a demand for radical social change. It gained a reputation for honesty that contrasted sharply with the massive corruption of Guomindang officials. It put down deep roots among the peasantry in a way that the Bolsheviks never did. And whereas the Bolsheviks gained support by urging Russian withdrawal from the highly unpopular First World War, the CCP won support by aggressively pursuing the struggle against Japanese invaders during World War II. In 1949, four years after the war's end, the Chinese communists swept to victory over the Guomindang, many of whose followers fled to Taiwan. Mao Zedong announced triumphantly in Beijing's Tiananmen Square that "the Chinese people have stood up."

Building Socialism

Once they came to power, communist parties everywhere set about the construction of socialist societies. In the Soviet Union, this massive undertaking occurred under the leadership of Joseph Stalin in the 1920s and 1930s. The corresponding

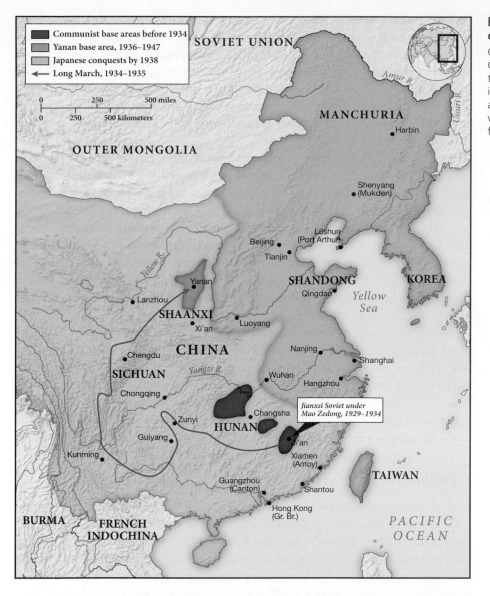

Map 21.2   The Rise of Communism in China

Communism arose in China at the same time as the country was engaged in a terrible war with Japan and in the context of a civil war with Guomindang forces.

Chinese effort took place during the 1950s and 1960s with Mao Zedong at the helm.

To communist regimes, building socialism meant first of all the modernization and industrialization of their backward societies. They sought, however, a distinctly socialist modernity. This involved a frontal attack on long-standing inequalities of class and gender, an effort to prevent the making of new inequalities as the process of modern development unfolded, and the promotion of cultural values of selflessness and collectivism that could support a socialist society.

Those imperatives generated a political system thoroughly dominated by the Communist Party. Top-ranking party members enjoyed various privileges but were expected to be exemplars of socialism in the making by being disciplined, selfless, and utterly loyal to their country's Marxist ideology. The party itself penetrated society in ways that Western scholars called "totalitarian," for other parties were forbidden, the state controlled almost the entire economy, and political authorities ensured that the arts, education, and the media conformed to approved ways of thinking. Mass organizations for women, workers, students, and various professional groups operated under party control, with none of the independence that characterized civil society in the West.

In undertaking these tasks, the Soviet Union and China started from different places, most notably their international positions. In 1917, Russian Bolsheviks faced a hostile capitalist world alone, while Chinese communists, coming to power over thirty years later, had an established Soviet Union as a friendly northern neighbor and ally. Furthermore, Chinese revolutionaries had actually governed parts of their huge country for decades, gaining experience that the new Soviet rulers had altogether lacked, since they had come to power so quickly. And the Chinese communists were firmly rooted in the rural areas and among the country's vast peasant population, while their Russian counterparts had found their support mainly in the cities.

If these comparisons generally favored China in its efforts to "build socialism," in economic terms that country faced even more daunting prospects than did the Soviet Union. Its population was far greater, its industrial base far smaller, and the availability of new agricultural land far more limited than in the Soviet Union. Likewise, in China fewer people were literate, and the education system and transportation network were much less developed. Even more than the Soviets, Chinese communists had to build a modern society from the ground up.

Communist Feminism

Among the earliest and most revolutionary actions of these new communist regimes were efforts at liberating and mobilizing women. Communist countries in fact pioneered forms of women's liberation that only later were adopted in the West. This communist feminism was largely state directed, with the initiative coming from the top rather than bubbling up from grassroots movements as in the West. In the Soviet Union, where a small women's movement had taken shape in pre–World War I Russia, the new communist government almost immediately issued a series of laws and decrees regarding women. These measures declared full legal and political equality for women; marriage became a civil procedure among freely consenting adults; divorce was legalized and made easier, as was abortion; illegitimacy was abolished; women no longer had to take their husbands' surnames; pregnancy leave for employed women was mandated; and women were actively mobilized as workers in the country's drive to industrialization. Addressing a Congress of Women Workers and Peasants, Lenin declared: "Root out old habits. Every cook must learn to rule the state."[2]

In 1919, the party set up a special organization called Zhenotdel (zhen-ut-DEL) (Women's Department), whose radical leaders, all women, pushed a decidedly feminist agenda during the 1920s. They organized numerous conferences for women, trained women to run day-care centers and medical clinics, published newspapers and magazines aimed at a female audience, provided literacy and prenatal classes, and encouraged Muslim women to take off their veils. Alexandra Rodionova, a former streetcar conductor who had played an active role in the revolution, recalled the impact of participation in Zhenotdel: "This former illiterate working girl had been transformed into a person, powerful with the knowledge of her own rights, a consciousness of responsibility for everything happening in the country."[3] Much of this agenda encountered opposition from male communist officials and from ordinary people as well, and Stalin abolished Zhenotdel in 1930. While it lasted, though, it was a remarkable experiment in women's liberation by means of state action, animated by an almost utopian sense of new possibilities set loose by the revolution.

■ **Change**
What changes did communist regimes bring to the lives of women?

Similar policies took shape in communist China. The Marriage Law of 1950 was a direct attack on patriarchal and Confucian traditions. It decreed free choice in marriage, relatively easy divorce, the end of concubinage and child marriage, permission for widows to remarry, and equal property rights for women. A short but intense campaign by the CCP in the early 1950s sought to implement these changes, often against strenuous opposition. The party also launched a Women's Federation, a mass organization that enrolled millions of women. Its leaders, however, were far less radical than the Bolshevik feminists who led Zhenotdel in the 1920s. In China, there was little talk of "free love" or the "withering away of the family," as there had been in the USSR. Nevertheless, like their Soviet counterparts, Chinese women became much more actively involved in production outside the home. By 1978, 50 percent of agricultural workers and 38 percent of nonagricultural laborers were female. "Women can do anything" became a famous party slogan in the 1960s. (See Working with Evidence, Source 21.3, page 971.)

Mobilizing Women for Communism
As the Soviet Union mobilized for rapid economic development in the 1930s, women entered the workforce in great numbers. Here two young women are mastering the skills of driving a tractor on one of the large collective farms that replaced the country's private agriculture. (Sovoto/UIG via Getty Images)

Still, communist-style women's liberation had definite limits. Fearing that the "woman question" would detract from his emphasis on industrial production, Stalin declared it "solved" in 1930. Little direct discussion of women's issues was permitted in the several decades that followed. In neither the Soviet Union nor China did the Communist Party undertake a direct attack on male domination within the family. Thus the double burden of housework and child care plus paid employment continued to afflict most women. Moreover, women appeared only very rarely in the top political leadership of either country.

Socialism in the Countryside

In their efforts to build socialism, both the Soviet Union and China first expropriated landlords' estates and redistributed that land on a much more equitable basis to the peasantry. Such actions, although clearly revolutionary, were not socialist, for peasants initially received their land as private property. In Russia, the peasants had spontaneously redistributed the land among themselves, and the victorious Bolsheviks merely ratified their actions. In China after 1949, land reform was a more prolonged and difficult process. Hastily trained teams were dispatched to the newly liberated areas, where they mobilized the poorer peasants in thousands of separate villages to confront and humiliate the landlords or the more wealthy peasants. Their land, animals, tools, houses, and money were then redistributed to the poorer members of the village. In these villages, land reform teams encountered the age-old deference that peasants traditionally had rendered to their social superiors. One young woman activist described the confrontational meetings intended to break this ancient pattern:

> "Speak bitterness meetings," as they were called, would help [the peasants] to understand how things really had been in the old days, to realize that their lives were not blindly ordained by fate . . . and that far from owing anything to the feudal landlords, it was the feudal landlords who owed them a debt of suffering beyond all reckoning.[4]

It was, as Mao Zedong put it, "not a dinner party." Approximately 1 to 2 million landlords were killed in the process, which was largely over by 1952.

■ **Comparison**
How did the collectivization of agriculture differ between the USSR and China?

A second and more distinctly socialist stage of rural reform sought to end private property in land by collectivizing agriculture. In China, despite brief resistance from richer peasants, collectivization during the 1950s was a generally peaceful process, owing much to the close relationship between the Chinese Communist Party and the peasantry, which had been established during three decades of struggle. This contrasted markedly with the earlier experience of the Soviet Union from 1928 to 1933, when peasants were forced into collective farms and violence was extensive. Russian peasants slaughtered and consumed hundreds of thousands of animals rather than surrender them to the collectives. Stalin singled out the richer peasants, known as *kulaks* (koo-LAHKS), for exclusion from the new collective farms. Some were killed, and many others were deported to remote areas of the country. With little support or experience in the countryside, Soviet communists, who came mostly from the cities, were viewed as intrusive outsiders in Russian peasant villages. A terrible famine ensued, with some 5 million deaths from starvation or malnutrition. China, however, pushed collectivization even further than the Soviet Union did, particularly in huge "people's communes" during the Great Leap Forward in the late 1950s. It was an effort to mobilize China's enormous population for rapid development and at the same time to move toward a more fully communist society with an even greater degree of social equality and collective living. (See Working with Evidence, Source 21.2, page 969, for more on communes.) Administrative chaos, disruption of marketing networks, and bad weather combined to produce a massive famine that killed an amazing 20 million people or more between 1959 and 1962, dwarfing even the earlier Soviet famine.

Communism and Industrial Development

Both the Soviet Union and China defined industrialization as a fundamental task of their regimes. That process was necessary to end humiliating backwardness and poverty, to provide the economic basis for socialism, and to create the military strength that would enable their revolutions to survive in a hostile world. Though strongly anticapitalist, communists everywhere were ardent modernizers.

When the Chinese communists began their active industrialization efforts in the early 1950s, they largely followed the model pioneered by the Soviet Union in the late 1920s and the 1930s. That model involved state ownership of property, centralized planning embodied in successive five-year plans, priority to heavy industry, massive mobilization of the nation's human and material resources, and intrusive Communist Party control of the entire process. Both countries experienced major—indeed unprecedented—economic growth. The Soviet Union constructed the foundations of an industrial society in the 1930s that proved itself in the victory over Nazi Germany in World War II and that by the 1960s and 1970s had generated substantially improved standards of living. China also quickly expanded its output. (See Snapshot, page 944.) In addition, both countries achieved massive improvements in their literacy rates and educational opportunities, allowing far greater social mobility for millions of people than ever before. In both countries, industrialization fostered a similar set of social outcomes: rapid urbanization, exploitation of the countryside to provide resources for modern industry in the cities, and the growth of a privileged bureaucratic and technological elite intent on pursuing their own careers and passing on their new status to their children.

Perhaps the chief difference in the industrial histories of the Soviet Union and China lies in the leadership's response to these social outcomes. In the Soviet Union under Stalin and his successors, they were largely accepted. Industrialization was centered in large urban areas, which pulled from the countryside the most ambitious and talented people. A highly privileged group of state and party leaders emerged in the Stalin era and largely remained the unchallenged ruling class of the country until the 1980s. Even in the 1930s, the outlines of a conservative society, which had discarded much of its revolutionary legacy, were apparent. Stalin himself

■ **Change**
What were the achievements of communist efforts at industrialization? What problems did these achievements generate?

SNAPSHOT   China under Mao, 1949–1976

The following table reveals some of the achievements, limitations, and tragedies of China's communist experience during the era of Mao Zedong.[5]

Steel production	from 1.3 million to 23 million tons
Coal production	from 66 million to 448 million tons
Electric power generation	from 7 million to 133 billion kilowatt-hours
Fertilizer production	from 0.2 million to 28 million tons
Cement production	from 3 million to 49 million tons
Industrial workers	from 3 million to 50 million
Scientists and technicians	from 50,000 to 5 million
"Barefoot doctors" posted to countryside	1 million
Annual growth rate of industrial output	11 percent
Annual growth rate of agricultural output	2.3 percent
Total population	from 542 million to 1 billion
Average population growth rate per year	2 percent
Per capita consumption of rural dwellers	from 62 to 124 yuan annually
Per capita consumption of urban dwellers	from 148 to 324 yuan
Overall life expectancy	from 35 to 65 years
Counterrevolutionaries killed (1949–1952)	between 1 million and 3 million
People labeled "rightists" in 1957	550,000
Deaths from famine during Great Leap Forward	20 million or more
Deaths during Cultural Revolution	500,000
Officials sent down to rural labor camps during Cultural Revolution	3 million or more
Urban youth sent down to countryside	17 million (1967–1976)

endorsed Russian patriotism, traditional family values, individual competition, and substantial differences in wages to stimulate production, as an earlier commitment to egalitarianism was substantially abandoned. Increasingly the invocation of revolutionary values was devoid of real content, and by the 1970s the perception of official hypocrisy was widespread.

The unique feature of Chinese history under Mao Zedong's leadership was a recurrent effort to combat these perhaps inevitable tendencies of any industrializing process and to revive and preserve the revolutionary spirit, which had animated the

Communist Party during its long struggle for power. By the mid-1950s, Mao and some of his followers had become persuaded that the Soviet model of industrialization was leading China away from socialism and toward new forms of inequality, toward individualistic and careerist values, and toward an urban bias that privileged the cities at the expense of the countryside. The Great Leap Forward of 1958–1960 marked Mao's first response to these distortions of Chinese socialism. It promoted small-scale industrialization in the rural areas rather than focusing wholly on large enterprises in the cities; it tried to foster widespread and practical technological education for all rather than relying on a small elite of highly trained technical experts; and it envisaged an immediate transition to full communism in the "people's communes" rather than waiting for industrial development to provide the material basis for that transition. The massive famine that followed temporarily discredited Mao's radicalism.

Nonetheless, in the mid-1960s Mao launched yet another campaign—the Great Proletarian Cultural Revolution—to combat the capitalist tendencies that he believed had penetrated even the highest ranks of the Communist Party itself. The Cultural Revolution also involved new policies to bring health care and education to the countryside and to reinvigorate earlier efforts at rural industrialization under local rather than central control. In these ways, Mao struggled, though without great success, to overcome the inequalities associated with China's modern development and to create a model of socialist modernity quite distinct from that of the Soviet Union.

The Cultural Revolution also rejected feminism, any specific concern with women's issues, and much that was feminine. A popular slogan stated: "The times have changed; men and women are the same." Yet the supposedly gender-neutral model seemed strikingly masculine. Women cut their hair short, wore army clothes, and learned to curse; they were depicted in propaganda posters as "iron girls," strong, muscular, and performing heavy traditionally male work. (See Working with Evidence, Source 21.3, page 971.) Art, literature, ballet, and opera cast them as militant revolutionary participants. And yet, factory managers continued to prefer women workers because of their alleged patience and manual dexterity. Young women sent to the countryside to work with peasants found themselves subject to

The Great Leap Forward
This Chinese poster from 1960 celebrates both the agricultural and industrial efforts of the Great Leap Forward. The caption reads: "Start the movement to increase production and practice thrift, with foodstuffs and steel at the center, with great force!" The great famine that accompanied this "great leap" belied the optimistic outlook of the poster. (Stefan R. Landsberger Collections/International Institute of Social History, Amsterdam/www.chineseposters.net)

sexual abuse by male officials. Thus strenuous Maoist efforts to eliminate differences between classes, between urban and rural life, and between men and women largely failed.

A final commonality among communist industrializers lay in their great confidence in both human rationality and the centralized planning embodied in huge projects—enormous factories, large collective farms, gigantic dams. Soviet officials saw the environment as an enemy, spoke about "the struggle against nature," and looked forward to "a profound rearrangement of the entire living world."[6] This attitude, no less than capitalist assumptions, led to immense environmental devastation and a very difficult legacy for postcommunist regimes. In the Soviet Union, for example, huge industrial complexes such as Magnitogorsk concentrated air and water pollution. A scheme to bring millions of acres of semi-arid land under cultivation in Central Asia depleted and eroded the fragile soil. Diverting the waters of several rivers feeding the Aral Sea for irrigating cotton fields reduced the size of that huge inland sea by 90 percent. By the late 1980s, such environmental heedlessness meant that about half of the cultivated land in the country was endangered by erosion, salinization, or swamping; some 30 percent of food products were contaminated by pesticides or herbicides; 75 percent of the surface water was severely polluted; and 70 million people lived in cities with air pollution five or more times the acceptable level.[7] But nothing brought Soviet environmental problems to public attention more dramatically than the explosion of a nuclear reactor at Chernobyl in 1986. It scattered highly radioactive material over parts of Ukraine and Belorussia, while the cloud from the explosion swept across parts of Eastern Europe and Scandinavia, terrifying millions even much farther away.

The Search for Enemies

Despite their totalitarian tendencies, the communist societies of the Soviet Union and China were laced with conflict. Under both Stalin and Mao, those conflicts erupted in a search for enemies that disfigured both societies. An elastic concept of "enemy" came to include not only surviving remnants from the prerevolutionary elites but also, and more surprisingly, high-ranking members and longtime supporters of the Communist Party who allegedly had been corrupted by bourgeois ideas. Refracted through the lens of Marxist thinking, these people became class enemies who had betrayed the revolution and were engaged in a vast conspiracy, often linked to foreign imperialists, to subvert the socialist enterprise and restore capitalism. In the rhetoric of the leadership, the class struggle continued and even intensified as the triumph of socialism drew closer.

In the Soviet Union, that process culminated in the Terror, or the Great Purges, of the late 1930s, which enveloped tens of thousands of prominent communists, including virtually all of Lenin's top associates, and millions of more ordinary people. (See Zooming In: Anna Dubova, page 948, for an individual experience of the Terror.) Based on suspicious associations in the past, denunciations by colleagues,

■ **Explanation**
Why did communist regimes generate terror and violence on such a massive scale?

connections to foreign countries, or simply bad luck, such people were arrested, usually in the dead of night, and then tried and sentenced either to death or to long years in harsh and remote labor camps known as the gulag. A series of show trials publicized the menace that these "enemies of the people" allegedly posed to the country and its revolution. Close to 1 million people were executed between 1936 and 1941. An additional 4 or 5 million were sent to the gulag, where they were forced to work in horrendous conditions and died in appalling numbers. Victimizers too were numerous: the Terror consumed the energies of a huge corps of officials, investigators, interrogators, informers, guards, and executioners, many of whom were themselves arrested, exiled, or executed in the course of the purges.

In the Soviet Union, the search for enemies occurred under the clear control of the state. In China, however, it became a much more public process, escaping the control of the leadership, particularly during the most violent years of the Cultural Revolution (1966–1969). Mao had become convinced that many within the Communist Party had been seduced by capitalist values of self-seeking and materialism and were no longer animated by the idealistic revolutionary vision of earlier times. Therefore, he called for rebellion, against the Communist Party itself. Millions of young people responded, and, organized as Red Guards, they set out to rid China of those who were "taking the capitalist road." Following gigantic and ecstatic rallies in Beijing, they fanned out across the country and attacked local party and government officials, teachers, intellectuals, factory managers, and others they defined as enemies. (See Working with Evidence, Sources 21.1 and 21.4, pages 968 and 972.) Rival revolutionary groups soon began fighting with one another, violence erupted throughout the country, and civil war threatened China. Mao was forced to call in the military to restore order and Communist Party control. Both the Soviet Terror and the Chinese Cultural Revolution badly discredited the very idea of socialism and contributed to the ultimate collapse of the communist experiment at the end of the century.

> ## SUMMING UP SO FAR
>
> How did the Soviet Union and China differ in terms of the revolutions that brought communists to power and in the construction of socialist societies? What commonalities are also apparent?

East versus West: A Global Divide and a Cold War

Not only did communist regimes bring revolutionary changes to the societies they governed, but their very existence launched a global conflict that restructured international relations and touched the lives of almost everyone, particularly in the twentieth century's second half. That rift began soon after the Russian Revolution when the new communist government became the source of fear and loathing to many in the Western capitalist world. The common threat of Nazi Germany temporarily made unlikely allies of the Soviet Union, Britain, and the United States, but a few years after World War II ended, that division erupted again in what became known as the cold war. Underlying that conflict were the geopolitical and ideological realities of the postwar world. The Soviet Union and the United States

Anna Dubova, a Russian Peasant Girl and Urban Woman

Born into a large peasant family near Smolensk in western Russia in 1916, Anna Dubova lived through the entire communist experience of her country.[8] Hers was a life that illustrates the complexities that ordinary individuals faced as they sought to navigate the communist system.

Anna was one of fourteen children, of whom seven survived. Her family was dominated by a strict, hardworking, and highly religious father, who was choirmaster of the local church. Anna's father was suspicious of the communists when they came to power the year after Anna's birth, but her grandmother was more forthright. "We have a new tsar," she declared. "The forces of the Antichrist have triumphed." Nonetheless, her father accepted an appointment in 1922 as chairman of the village soviet, the new communist organ of local government. During the 1920s, the village and Anna's family flourished under Lenin's New Economic Policy, which briefly permitted a considerable measure of private enterprise and profit making. Her father even opened a small shop in the village where he sold goods purchased in the city.

A 1941 image of a woman factory worker in Moscow.

By 1928, however, everything changed as the Soviet regime, now under Joseph Stalin's leadership, abruptly moved to collectivize agriculture and root out *kulaks*, supposedly wealthy peasants who were thought to bear the germ of a hated capitalism. Because of her father's shop, the family was labeled as kulak and their property was confiscated. "I remember so well how Mama sat and cried when they took away the cow," Anna recalled years later. The family forestalled their expected deportation to the far north of the Soviet Union only by promising Anna, then just thirteen, in marriage to the local Communist Party secretary. The marriage never took place, however, and the family was forced to leave. Later, Anna was permitted to join her older sister in Moscow, but approval for that much-coveted move came at a very high price. Anna recalled, "I had to write out an official statement that I renounced my parents, that I no longer had any ties with them."

were now the world's major political/military powers, replacing the shattered and diminished states of Western Europe, but they represented sharply opposed views of history, society, politics, and international relations. Conflict, in retrospect, seemed almost inevitable.

Military Conflict and the Cold War

The initial arena of the cold war was Eastern Europe, where Soviet insistence on security and control clashed with American and British desires for open and democratic societies with ties to the capitalist world economy. What resulted were rival

Thus Anna, a rural teenager, joined millions of other peasants who flocked to the city to pursue new opportunities that became available as the Soviet Union launched its industrialization drive. In Moscow, she gained a basic education, a vocation in cake decorating, which she enjoyed, and a brief stint as a mechanic and chauffeur, which she detested. All the while the shadow of her kulak label followed her. Had it been discovered, she could have lost her job and her permission to live in Moscow. And so she married a party activist from a poor peasant family, she explained years later, "just so I could cover up my background." Her husband drank heavily, leaving her with a daughter when he went off to war in 1941.

In the Soviet Union, the late 1930s witnessed the Terror when millions of alleged "enemies of the people" were arrested and hauled off to execution or labor camps. Anna recalled what it was like: "You'd come home and they'd say, Yesterday they took away Uncle Lesha. . . . You'd go to see a girlfriend, they'd say, We have an empty room now; they've exiled Andreitsev." Like most people not directly involved, Anna believed in the guilt of these people. And she feared that she herself might be mistakenly accused, for those with a kulak label were particular targets of the search for enemies. "I was only afraid," she remembered, "that I would be raped in prison."

Beyond her kulak background, Anna also felt compelled to hide a deep religious sensibility derived from her childhood. She remembered the disappearance of the village priest, the looting of the churches, and the destruction of icons. And so she never entered a church or prayed in front of others. But she wore a cross under her clothing. "I never stopped [believing]," she recalled. "But I concealed it. Deep down . . . I believed." Nor did she ever seek to join the Communist Party, though it may well have advanced her career prospects and standard of living. Perhaps she feared that the investigations accompanying party membership would have disclosed her compromising social and religious background.

In the decades following World War II and especially after Stalin's death in 1953, Anna's life seemed to stabilize. She entered into a thirty-year relationship with a man and found satisfying work in a construction design office, though the lack of higher education and party connections prevented her from moving into higher-paid jobs. Looking back on her life, she regretted the communist intrusion, particularly in its Stalinist phase, into what she remembered as a happy childhood. She had come to value, perhaps nostalgically, the life of a peasant over that of an urban worker. She reflected, "[As a peasant,] I would have lived on the fruits of my labor. . . . [Instead,] I've lived someone else's life."

Question: In what ways did communism shape Anna's life, and in what respects was she able to construct her own life within that system?

military alliances (NATO and the Warsaw Pact), a largely voluntary American sphere of influence in Western Europe, and an imposed Soviet sphere in Eastern Europe. The heavily fortified border between Eastern and Western Europe came to be known as the Iron Curtain. Thus Europe was bitterly divided. But although tensions flared across this dividing line, particularly in Berlin, no shooting war occurred between the two sides (see Map 21.3).

By contrast, the extension of communism into Asia—China, Korea, and Vietnam—globalized the cold war and occasioned its most destructive and prolonged "hot wars." A North Korean invasion of South Korea in 1950 led to both Chinese and American involvement in a bitter three-year war (1950–1953), which ended in

■ Connection
In what different ways was the cold war expressed?

Map 21.3   The Global Cold War

The cold war witnessed a sharp division between the communist world and the Western democratic world. It also divided the continent of Europe; the countries of China, Korea, Vietnam, and Germany; and the city of Berlin. In many places, it also sparked crises that brought the nuclear-armed superpowers of the United States and the USSR to the brink of war, although in every case they managed to avoid direct military conflict between themselves. Many countries in Africa and Asia claimed membership in a Non-Aligned Movement, which sought to avoid entanglements in cold war conflicts.

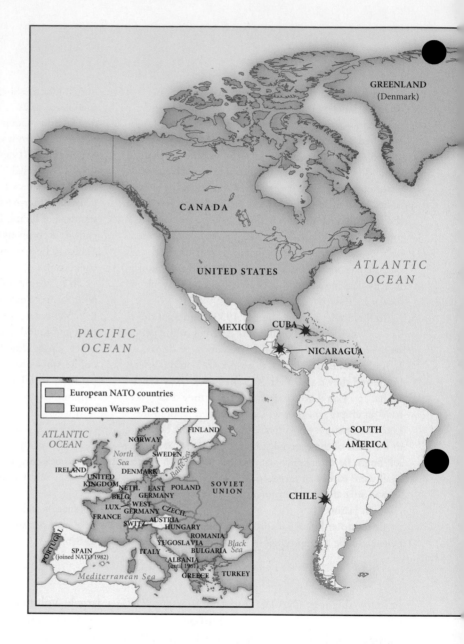

an essential standoff that left the Korean peninsula still divided in the early twenty-first century. Likewise in Vietnam, military efforts by South Vietnamese communists and the already-communist North Vietnamese government to unify their country prompted massive American intervention in the 1960s. To American authorities, a communist victory opened the door to further communist expansion in Asia and beyond. Armed and supported by the Soviets and Chinese and willing to endure enormous losses, the Vietnamese communists bested the Americans, who were

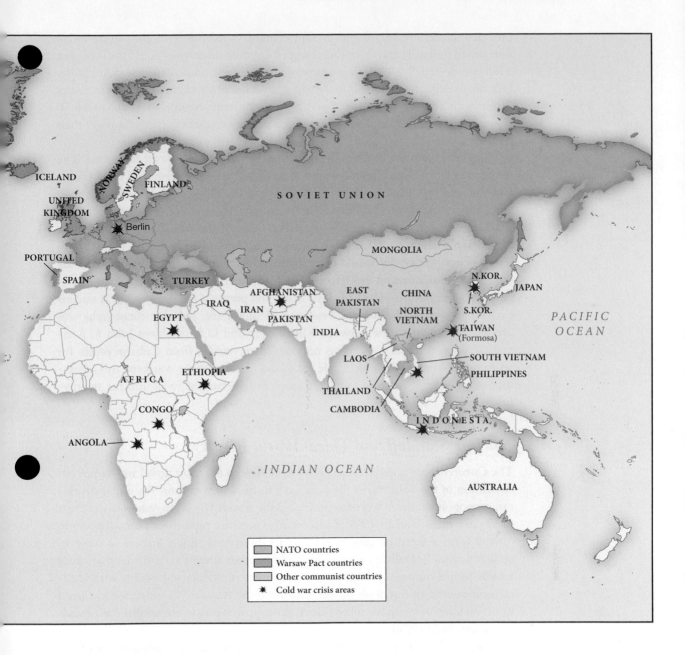

ICELAND

NORWAY

SWEDEN

FINLAND

UNITED KINGDOM

SOVIET UNION

Berlin

PORTUGAL

SPAIN

TURKEY

MONGOLIA

N.KOR.

JAPAN

AFGHANISTAN

EAST PAKISTAN

CHINA

S.KOR.

IRAQ

IRAN

PAKISTAN

EGYPT

INDIA

NORTH VIETNAM

TAIWAN
(Formosa)

PACIFIC OCEAN

AFRICA

ETHIOPIA

LAOS

SOUTH VIETNAM

PHILIPPINES

CONGO

THAILAND

CAMBODIA

ANGOLA

INDONESIA

INDIAN OCEAN

AUSTRALIA

NATO countries	
Warsaw Pact countries	
Other communist countries	
✳	Cold war crisis areas

hobbled by growing protest at home. The Vietnamese united their country under communist control by 1975.

A third major military conflict of the cold war era occurred in Afghanistan, where a Marxist party had taken power in 1978. Soviet leaders were delighted at this extension of communism on their southern border, but radical land reforms and efforts to liberate Afghan women soon alienated much of this conservative Muslim country and led to a mounting opposition movement. Fearing the overthrow of a new communist state and its replacement by Islamic radicals, Soviet forces intervened militarily and were soon bogged down in a war they could not win. For a full decade (1979–1989), that war was a "bleeding wound," sustained in part by U.S. aid to Afghan guerrillas. Under widespread international pressure, Soviet forces finally withdrew in 1989, and the Afghan communist regime soon collapsed. In Vietnam and Afghanistan, both superpowers painfully experienced the limits of their power.

The most haunting battle of the cold war era was one that never happened. The setting was Cuba, where a communist regime under the leadership of Fidel Castro had emerged by the early 1960s. (See Zooming In: The Cuban Revolution, page 954.) Intense American hostility to this nearby outpost of communism prompted the Soviet leader Nikita Khrushchev (KROOSH-chef), who had risen to power after Stalin's death in 1953, to secretly deploy nuclear-tipped Soviet missiles to Cuba, believing that this would deter further U.S. action against Castro. When the missiles were discovered in October 1962, the world held its breath for thirteen days as American forces blockaded the island and prepared for an invasion. A nuclear exchange between the superpowers seemed imminent, but that catastrophe was averted by a compromise between Khrushchev and U.S. president John F. Kennedy. Under its terms, the Soviets removed their missiles from Cuba in return for an American promise not to invade the island. That promise was kept and a communist regime still persists in Cuba, though much changed, well into the twenty-first century.

Nuclear Standoff and Third-World Rivalry

The Cuban missile crisis gave concrete expression to the most novel and dangerous dimension of the cold war—the arms race in nuclear weapons. An initial American monopoly on those weapons prompted the Soviet Union to redouble its efforts to acquire them, and in 1949 it succeeded. Over the next forty years, the world moved from a mere handful of nuclear weapons to a global arsenal of close to 60,000 warheads. Delivery systems included bomber aircraft and missiles that could rapidly propel numerous warheads across whole continents and oceans with accuracies measured in hundreds of feet. During those decades, the entire world lived in the shadow of weapons whose destructive power is scarcely within the bounds of human imagination.

Awareness of this power is surely the primary reason that no shooting war of any kind occurred between the two superpowers. In the two world wars, the participants had been greatly surprised by the destructiveness of modern weapons. During the cold war, however, the leaders of the two superpowers knew beyond any doubt that a nuclear war would produce only losers and utter catastrophe. Already in 1949, Stalin had observed that "atomic weapons can hardly be used without spelling the end of the world."[9] Particularly after the frightening Cuban missile crisis of 1962, both sides carefully avoided further nuclear provocation, even while con-

The Hydrogen Bomb
During the 1950s and early 1960s, tests in the atmosphere of ever larger and more sophisticated hydrogen bombs made images of enormous fireballs and mushroom-shaped clouds the universal symbol of these weapons, which were immensely more powerful than the atomic bombs dropped on Japan. The American test pictured here took place in 1957. (Photo courtesy of National Nuclear Security Administration/Nevada Site Office)

tinuing the buildup of their respective arsenals. Moreover, because they feared that a conventional war would escalate to the nuclear level, they implicitly agreed to sidestep any direct military confrontation at all.

Still, opportunities for conflict abounded as the U.S.-Soviet rivalry spanned the globe. Using military and economic aid, educational opportunities, political pressure, and covert action, both sides courted countries emerging from colonial rule. Cold war fears of communist penetration prompted U.S. intervention, sometimes openly and often secretly, in Iran, the Philippines, Guatemala, El Salvador, Chile, the Congo, and elsewhere. In the process, the United States frequently supported anticommunist but corrupt and authoritarian regimes. However, neither superpower was able to completely dominate its supposed allies, many of whom resisted the role of pawns in superpower rivalries. Some countries, such as India, took a posture of nonalignment in the cold war, while others tried to play off the superpowers against each other. Indonesia received large amounts of Soviet and Eastern European aid, but that did not prevent it from destroying the Indonesian Communist Party in 1965, killing half a million suspected communists in the process. When the Americans refused to assist Egypt in building the Aswan Dam in the mid-1950s, that country developed a close relationship with the Soviet Union. Later, in 1972, Egypt expelled 21,000 Soviet advisers and again aligned more clearly with the United States.

The Cuban Revolution

"You Americans must realize what Cuba means to us old Bolsheviks," declared a high-ranking Soviet official, Anastas Mikoyan, in 1960. "We have been waiting all our lives for a country to go communist without the Red Army. It has happened in Cuba, and it makes us feel like boys again."[10] The triumph of the Cuban revolutionaries must have been exhilarating for communists everywhere because it occurred in such an unlikely place. Located just 90 miles from Florida, Cuba had been a virtual protectorate of the United States in the decades following its independence from Spain in 1902. Moreover, U.S. companies had long exerted considerable influence over the weak and corrupt Cuban government and dominated key sectors of the economy, including sugar, the island's most important export. Nonetheless, Fidel Castro, son of a wealthy sugar plantation owner, led a successful popular insurrection that transformed Cuba into a Marxist socialist state just off the southern coast of the United States.

The armed revolt began disastrously. In 1953, the Cuban army defeated Castro and 123 of his supporters

Fidel Castro fighting in the mountains of Cuba in 1957.

when they attacked two army barracks in what was their first major military operation. Castro himself was captured, sentenced to jail, and then released into exile. However, fortunes shifted in 1956, when Castro slipped back into Cuba and succeeded in bringing together many opponents of the current regime in an armed nationalist insurgency dedicated to radical economic and social reform. Upon seizing power in 1959, Castro and his government acted decisively to implement their revolutionary agenda. Within a year, they had effectively redistributed 15 percent of the nation's wealth by granting land to the poor, increasing wages, and lowering rents. In the following year, the new government nationalized the property of both wealthy Cubans and U.S. corporations. Many Cubans, particularly among the elite, fled into exile. "The revolution," declared Castro, "is the dictatorship of the exploited against the exploiters."[11]

photo: Private Collection/Peter Newark American Pictures/Bridgeman Images

The Cold War and the Superpowers

World War II and the cold war provided the context for the emergence of the United States as a global superpower, playing a role that has often been compared to that of Great Britain in the nineteenth century. Much of that effort was driven by the perceived demands of the cold war, during which the United States spearheaded the Western effort to contain a worldwide communist movement that seemed to be advancing. By 1970, one writer observed, "the United States had more than 1,000,000 soldiers in 30 countries, was a member of four regional defense alliances and an active participant in a fifth, had mutual defense treaties with 42 nations, was

Economic and political pressure from the United States followed, culminating in the Bay of Pigs, a failed invasion of the island in 1961 by Cuban exiles with covert support from the U.S. government. American hostility pushed the revolutionary nationalist Castro closer to the Soviet Union, and gradually he began to think of himself and his revolution as Marxist. In response to Cuban pleas for support against American aggression, the Soviet premier Khrushchev deployed nuclear missiles on the island, sparking the Cuban missile crisis. While the compromise reached between the two superpowers resulted in the withdrawal of the missiles, it did include assurances from the United States that it would not attack Cuba.

In the decades that followed, Cuba sought to export its brand of revolution beyond its borders, especially in Latin America and Africa. Che Guevara, an Argentine who had fought in the Cuban Revolution, declared, "Our revolution is endangering all American possessions in Latin America. We are telling these countries to make their own revolution."[12] Cuba supported revolutionary movements in many regions; however, none succeeded in creating a lasting Cuban-style regime.

The legacy of the Cuban Revolution has been mixed. The new government devoted considerable resources to improving health and education on the island. By the mid-1980s, Cuba possessed both the highest literacy rate and the lowest infant mortality rate in Latin America.

Over the same period, life expectancy increased from fifty-eight to seventy-three years, putting Cuba on a par with the United States. Living standards for most improved as well. Indeed, Cuba became a model for development in other Latin American countries.

However, earlier promises to establish a truly democratic system never materialized. Castro declared in 1959 that elections were unneeded because "this democracy . . . has found its expression, directly, in the intimate union and identification of the government with the people."[13] The state placed limits on free expression and arrested opponents or forced them into exile. Cuba has also failed to achieve the economic development originally envisioned at the time of the revolution. Sugar remains its chief export crop, and by the 1980s Cuba had become almost as economically dependent on the Soviet Union as it had been upon the United States. Desperate consequences followed when the Cuban economy shrank by a third following the collapse of the Soviet Union.

Like communist experiments in the Soviet Union and China, Cuba experienced real improvements in living standards, especially for the poor, but these gains were accompanied by sharp restraints on personal freedoms and mixed results in the economy. Such have been the ambivalent outcomes of many revolutionary upheavals.

Question: Compare the Cuban Revolution to those in Russia and China. What are the similarities and differences?

a member of 53 international organizations, and was furnishing military or economic aid to nearly 100 nations across the face of the globe."[14]

The need for quick and often secret decision making gave rise in the United States to a strong or "imperial" presidency and a "national security state," in which defense and intelligence agencies acquired great power within the government and were often unaccountable to Congress. This served to strengthen the influence of what U.S. president Dwight Eisenhower (r. 1953–1961) called the "military-industrial complex," a coalition of the armed services, military research laboratories, and private defense industries that both stimulated and benefited from increased military spending and cold war tensions.

■ **Connection**
In what ways did the United States play a global role after World War II?

Sustaining this immense military effort was a flourishing U.S. economy and an increasingly middle-class society. The United States was the only major industrial country to escape the physical devastation of war on its own soil. As World War II ended with Europe, the Soviet Union, and Japan in ruins, the United States was clearly the world's most productive economy. "The whole world is hungry for American goods," wrote one American economist in 1945.[15] Beyond their goods, Americans sent their capital abroad in growing amounts—from $19 billion in 1950 to $81 billion in 1965. Huge American firms such as General Motors, Ford, Mobil, Sears, General Electric, and Westinghouse established factories, offices, and subsidiaries in many countries and sold their goods locally. The U.S. dollar replaced the British pound as the most trusted international currency.

Accompanying the United States' political and economic penetration of the world was its popular culture. In musical terms, first jazz, then rock and roll, and most recently rap have found receptive audiences abroad, particularly among the young. By the 1990s, American movies took about 70 percent of the market in Europe, and in 2012 some 33,000 McDonald's restaurants in 119 countries served 68 million customers every day. Various American brand names—Marlboro, Coca-Cola, Jeep, Spam, Nike, Kodak—became common points of reference around the world. English became a global language, while American slang terms—"groovy," "crazy," "cool"—were integrated into many of the world's languages.

On the communist side, the cold war was accompanied by considerable turmoil both within and among the various communist states. Joseph Stalin, Soviet dictator and acknowledged leader of the communist world in general, died in 1953 as that global conflict was mounting. His successor, Nikita Khrushchev, stunned his country and communists everywhere with a lengthy speech delivered to a party congress in 1956 in which he presented a devastating account of Stalin's crimes, particularly those against party members. These revelations shocked many of the party faithful, for Stalin had been viewed as the "genius of all time." Now he was presented as a criminal.

■ **Description**
What were the strengths and weaknesses of the communist world by the 1970s?

In the Soviet Union, the superpower of the communist world, the cold war justified a continuing emphasis on military and defense industries after World War II and gave rise to a Soviet version of the military-industrial complex. Soviet citizens, even more than Americans, were subject to incessant government propaganda that glorified their system and vilified that of their American opponents.

As the communist world expanded, so too did divisions and conflicts among its various countries. Many in the West had initially viewed world communism as a monolithic force whose disciplined members meekly followed Soviet dictates in cold war solidarity against the West. And Marxists everywhere contended that revolutionary socialism would erode national loyalties as the "workers of the world" united in common opposition to global capitalism. Nonetheless, the communist world experienced far more bitter and divisive conflict than did the Western alliance, which was composed of supposedly warlike, greedy, and highly competitive nations.

Czechoslovakia, 1968
In August 1968, Soviet forces invaded Czechoslovakia, where a popular reform movement proclaiming "socialism with a human face" threatened to erode established communist control. The Soviet troops that crushed this so-called Prague Spring were greeted by thousands of peaceful street demonstrators begging them to go home. (Libor Hajsky/CTK/AP Photo)

In Eastern Europe, Yugoslav leaders early on had rejected Soviet domination of their internal affairs and charted their own independent road to socialism. Fearing that reform might lead to contagious defections from the communist bloc, Soviet forces actually invaded their supposed allies in Hungary (1956–1957) and Czechoslovakia (1968) to crush such movements. In the early 1980s, Poland was seriously threatened with a similar action. The brutal suppression of these reform movements gave credibility to Western perceptions of the cold war as a struggle between tyranny and freedom and badly tarnished the image of Soviet communism as a reasonable alternative to capitalism.

Even more startling, the two communist giants, the Soviet Union and China, found themselves sharply opposed, owing to territorial disputes, ideological differences, and rivalry for communist leadership. The Chinese bitterly criticized Khrushchev for backing down in the Cuban missile crisis, while to the Soviet leadership, Mao was insanely indifferent to the possible consequences of a nuclear war. In 1960, the Soviet Union backed away from an earlier promise to provide China with the prototype of an atomic bomb and abruptly withdrew all Soviet advisers and technicians, who had been assisting Chinese development. By the late 1960s, China on its own had developed a modest nuclear capability, and the two countries were at the brink of war, with the Soviet Union hinting at a possible nuclear strike on Chinese military targets. Their enmity certainly benefited the United States, which in the 1970s was able to pursue a "triangular diplomacy," easing tensions and simultaneously signing arms control agreements with the USSR and opening a formal relationship with China. Beyond this central conflict, a communist China in fact went to war against a communist Vietnam in 1979, while Vietnam invaded a communist Cambodia in the late 1970s. Nationalism, in short, proved more powerful than communist solidarity, even in the face of cold war hostilities with the West.

Despite its many internal conflicts, world communism remained a powerful global presence during the 1970s, achieving its greatest territorial reach. China was emerging from the chaos of the Cultural Revolution. The Soviet Union had matched U.S. military might; in response, the Americans launched a major buildup of their own military forces in the early 1980s. Despite American hostility, Cuba remained a communist outpost in the Western Hemisphere, with impressive achievements in education and health care for its people. Communism triumphed in Vietnam, dealing a major setback to the United States. A number of African countries affirmed their commitment to Marxism. Few people anywhere expected that within two decades most of the twentieth century's experiment with communism would be over.

Paths to the End of Communism

More rapidly than its beginning, and far more peacefully, the communist era came to an end during the last twenty years of the twentieth century. It was a drama in three acts. Act One began in China during the late 1970s, following the death of its towering revolutionary leader Mao Zedong in 1976. Over the next several decades, the CCP gradually abandoned almost everything that had been associated with Maoist communism, even as the party retained its political control of the country. Act Two took place in Eastern Europe in the "miracle year" of 1989, when popular movements toppled despised communist governments one after another all across the region. The climactic Act Three in this "end of communism" drama occurred in 1991 in the Soviet Union, where the entire "play" had opened seventy-four years earlier. There the reformist leader Mikhail Gorbachev (GORE-beh-CHOF) had come to power in 1985 intending to revive and save Soviet socialism from its accumulated dysfunctions. Those efforts, however, only exacerbated the country's many difficulties and led to the political disintegration of the Soviet Union on December 25, 1991. The curtain had fallen on the communist era and on the cold war as well.

■ **Change**
What explains the rapid end of the communist era?

Behind these separate stories lay two general failures of the communist experiment, measured both by their own standards and by those of the larger world. The first was economic. Despite their early successes, communist economies by the late 1970s showed no signs of catching up to the more advanced capitalist countries.

The highly regimented Soviet economy in particular was largely stagnant; its citizens were forced to stand in long lines for consumer goods and complained endlessly about their poor quality and declining availability. This was enormously embarrassing, for it had been the proud boast of communist leaders everywhere that they had found a better route to modern prosperity than their capitalist rivals had. Furthermore, these comparisons were increasingly well known, thanks to the global information revolution. This failure had security implications as well, for economic growth, even more than military capacity, was the measure of state power as the twentieth century approached its end.

The second failure was moral. The horrors of Stalin's Terror and the gulag, of Mao's Cultural Revolution, of something approaching genocide in communist Cambodia—all of this wore away at communist claims to moral superiority over capitalism. Moreover, this erosion occurred as global political culture more widely embraced democracy and human rights as the universal legacy of humankind, rather than the exclusive possession of the capitalist West. In both economic and moral terms, the communist path to the modern world was increasingly seen as a road to nowhere.

Communist leaders were not ignorant of these problems, and they moved aggressively to address them, particularly in China and the Soviet Union. But their approach to doing so varied greatly, as did the outcomes of those efforts. Thus, much as the Russian and Chinese revolutions differed and their approaches to building socialism diverged, so too did these communist giants chart distinct paths during the final years of the communist experiment.

China: Abandoning Communism and Maintaining the Party

As the dust settled from the political shakeout following Mao's death in 1976, Deng Xiaoping (dung shee-yao-ping) emerged as China's "paramount leader," committed to ending the periodic upheavals of the Maoist era while fostering political stability and economic growth. Soon previously banned plays, operas, films, and translations of Western classics reappeared, and a "literature of the wounded" exposed the sufferings of the Cultural Revolution. Some 100,000 political prisoners, many of them high-ranking communists, were released and restored to important positions. A party evaluation of Mao severely criticized his mistakes during the Great Leap Forward and the Cultural Revolution, while praising his role as a revolutionary leader.

Even more dramatic were Deng's economic reforms. In the rural areas, these reforms included a rapid dismantling of the country's system of collectivized farming and a return to something close to small-scale private agriculture. Impoverished Chinese peasants eagerly embraced these new opportunities and pushed them even further than the government had intended. Industrial reform proceeded more gradually. Managers of state enterprises were given greater authority and encouraged to act like private owners, making many of their own decisions and seeking profits.

China opened itself to the world economy and welcomed foreign investment in special enterprise zones along the coast, where foreign capitalists received tax breaks and other inducements. Local governments and private entrepreneurs joined forces in thousands of flourishing "township and village enterprises" that produced food, clothing, building materials, and much more.

The outcome of these reforms was stunning economic growth and a new prosperity for millions. Better diets, lower mortality rates, declining poverty, massive urban construction, and surging exports—all of this accompanied China's rejoining of the world economy and contributed to a much-improved material life for millions of its citizens. To many observers, China was the emerging economic giant of the twenty-first century. On the other hand, the country's burgeoning economy also generated massive corruption among Chinese officials, sharp inequalities between the coast and the interior, a huge problem of urban overcrowding, terrible pollution in major cities, and periodic inflation as the state loosened its controls over the economy. Urban vices such as street crime, prostitution, gambling, drug addiction, and a criminal underworld, which had been largely eliminated after 1949, surfaced again in China's booming cities. Nonetheless, something remarkable had occurred in China: an essentially capitalist economy had been restored, and by none other than the Communist Party itself. Mao's worst fears had been realized, as China "took the capitalist road."

Although the party was willing to largely abandon communist economic policies, it was adamantly unwilling to relinquish its political monopoly or to promote democracy at the national level. "Talk about democracy in the abstract," Deng Xiaoping declared, "will inevitably lead to the unchecked spread of ultra-democracy and anarchism, to the complete disruption of political stability, and to the total failure of our modernization program. . . . China will once again be plunged into chaos, division, retrogression, and darkness."[16] Such attitudes associated democracy with the chaos and uncontrolled mass action of the Cultural Revolution. Thus, when a democracy movement spearheaded by university and secondary school students surfaced in the late 1980s, Deng ordered the brutal crushing of its brazen demonstration in Beijing's Tiananmen Square before the television cameras of the world.

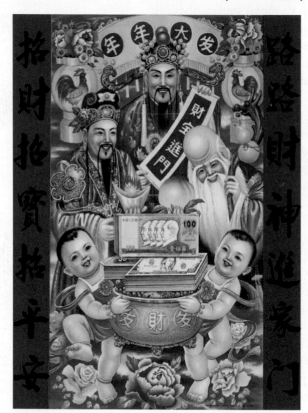

After Communism in China
Although the Communist Party still governed China in the early twenty-first century, communist values of selflessness, community, and simplicity had been substantially replaced for many by Western-style consumerism. This New Year's Good Luck poster from 1993 illustrates the new interest in material wealth in the form of American dollars and the return of older Chinese cultural patterns represented by the traditional gods of wealth, happiness, and longevity. The caption reads: "The gods of wealth enter the home from everywhere." (Zhejiang People's Art Publishing House/Stefan R. Landsberger Collections/International Institute of Social History, Amsterdam/www.chineseposters.net)

China entered the new millennium as a rapidly growing economic power with an essentially capitalist economy presided over by an intact and powerful Communist Party. Culturally, some combination of nationalism, consumerism, and a renewed respect for ancient traditions had replaced the collectivist and socialist values of the Maoist era. It was a strange and troubled hybrid.

The Soviet Union: The Collapse of Communism and Country

By the mid-1980s, the reformist wing of the Soviet Communist Party, long squelched by an aging conservative establishment, had won the top position in the party as Mikhail Gorbachev assumed the role of general secretary. Like Deng Xiaoping in China, Gorbachev was committed to aggressively tackling the country's many problems — economic stagnation, a flourishing black market, public apathy, and cynicism about the party. His economic program, launched in 1987 and known as *perestroika* (per-uh-STROI-kuh) (restructuring), paralleled aspects of the Chinese approach by freeing state enterprises from the heavy hand of government regulation, permitting small-scale private businesses called cooperatives, offering opportunities for private farming, and cautiously welcoming foreign investment in joint enterprises.

But in cultural and political affairs, Gorbachev moved far beyond Chinese reforms. His policy of *glasnost* (GLAHS-nohst) (openness) now permitted an unprecedented range of cultural and intellectual freedoms. In the late 1980s, glasnost hit the Soviet Union like a bomb. Newspapers and TV exposed social pathologies — crime, prostitution, child abuse, suicide, corruption, and homelessness — that previously had been presented solely as the product of capitalism. Films broke the ban on nudity and explicit sex. TV reporters climbed the wall of a secluded villa to film the luxurious homes of the party elite. Soviet history was also reexamined as revelations of Stalin's crimes poured out of the media. The Bible and the Quran became more widely available, atheistic propaganda largely ceased, and thousands of churches and mosques were returned to believers and opened for worship. Plays, poems, films, and novels that had long been buried "in the drawer" were now released to a public that virtually devoured them. "Like an excited boy reads a note from his girl," wrote one poet, "that's how we read the papers today."[17] And beyond glasnost lay democratization and a new parliament with real powers, chosen in competitive elections. When those elections occurred in 1989, dozens of leading communists were rejected at the polls. In foreign affairs, Gorbachev moved to end the cold war by making unilateral cuts in Soviet military forces, engaging in arms control negotiations with the United States, and refusing to intervene as communist governments in Eastern Europe were overthrown.

But almost nothing worked out as Gorbachev had anticipated. Far from strengthening socialism and reviving a stagnant Soviet Union, the reforms led to its further weakening and collapse. In a dramatic contrast with China's booming economy,

■ **Comparison**

How did the end of communism in the Soviet Union differ from communism's demise in China?

the Soviet Union's planned economy spun into a sharp decline as it was dismantled before a functioning market-based system could emerge. Inflation mounted; consumer goods were in short supply, and ration coupons reappeared; many feared the loss of their jobs. Unlike Chinese peasants, few Soviet farmers were willing to risk the jump into private farming, and few foreign investors found the Soviet Union a tempting place to do business.

Furthermore, the new freedoms provoked demands that went far beyond what Gorbachev had intended. A democracy movement of unofficial groups and parties now sprang to life, many of them seeking a full multiparty democracy and a market-based economy. They were joined by independent labor unions, which actually went on strike, something unheard of in the "workers' state." Most corrosively, a multitude of nationalist movements used the new freedoms to insist on greater autonomy, or even independence, from the Soviet Union. Environmental issues were prominent in many of these movements. Their leaders argued that centralized decision making in Moscow treated the non-Russian areas as colonies to be exploited and was responsible for numerous environmental outrages. Activists in the Baltic region, for example, protested phosphorite mining in Estonia, a proposed nuclear reactor in Lithuania, and the construction of a massive hydroelectric station in Latvia. The Chernobyl explosion and the government's initial reluctance to fully disclose what happened only added fuel to these growing anti-Soviet movements. In the face of these mounting demands, Gorbachev resolutely refused to use force to crush the protesters, another sharp contrast with the Chinese experience.

Events in Eastern Europe now intersected with those in the Soviet Union. Gorbachev's reforms had lit a fuse in these Soviet satellites, where communism had been imposed and maintained from outside. If the USSR could practice glasnost and hold competitive elections, why couldn't Eastern Europe do so as well? This was the background for the "miracle year" of 1989. Massive demonstrations, last-minute efforts at reforms, the breaching of the Berlin Wall, the surfacing of new political groups—all of this and more quickly overwhelmed the highly unpopular communist regimes of Poland, Hungary, East Germany, Bulgaria, Czechoslovakia, and Romania, which were quickly swept away. This success then emboldened nationalists and democrats in the Soviet Union. If communism had been overthrown in Eastern Europe, perhaps it could be overthrown in the USSR as well. Soviet conservatives and patriots, however, were outraged. To them, Gorbachev had stood idly by while the political gains of World War II, for which the Soviet Union had paid in rivers of blood, vanished before their eyes. It was nothing less than treason.

A brief and unsuccessful attempt to restore the old order through a military coup in August 1991 triggered the end of the Soviet Union and its communist regime. From the wreckage emerged fifteen new and independent states, following the internal political divisions of the USSR (see Map 21.4). Arguably, the collapse of the Soviet Union was due less to its multiple problems and more to the unexpected consequences of Gorbachev's efforts to address them.

The Soviet collapse represented a unique phenomenon in the world of the late twentieth century. Simultaneously, the world's largest state and its last territorial

Map 21.4 The Collapse of the Soviet Empire

Soviet control over its Eastern European dependencies vanished as those countries threw off their communist governments in 1989. Then, in 1991, the Soviet Union itself disintegrated into fifteen separate states, none of them governed by communist parties.

empire vanished; the world's first Communist Party disintegrated; a powerful command economy broke down; an official socialist ideology was repudiated; and a forty-five-year global struggle between the East and the West ended. In Europe, Germany was reunited, and a number of former communist states joined NATO and the European Union, ending the division of the continent. At least for the moment, capitalism and democracy seemed to triumph over socialism and authoritarian governments. In many places, the end of communism allowed simmering ethnic tensions to explode into open conflict. Beyond the disintegration of the Soviet Union, both Yugoslavia and Czechoslovakia fragmented, the former amid terrible violence and the latter peacefully. Chechens in Russia, Abkhazians in Georgia, Russians in the Baltic states and Ukraine, Tibetans and Uighurs in China—all of these minorities found themselves in opposition to the states in which they lived.

As the twenty-first century dawned, the communist world had shrunk considerably from its high point just three decades earlier. In the Soviet Union and Eastern Europe, communism had disappeared entirely as the governing authority and dominant ideology. In the immediate aftermath of the Soviet collapse, Russia quickly and haphazardly privatized many of its state-owned firms, vastly enriching their new and well-connected owners, who came to be called the "oligarchs." The result was cata-strophic as the country experienced a sharply contracting economy, widespread pov-erty and inequality, and declining life expectancy. Not until 2006 did its economy recover to the level of 1991. Even then, much of Russia's subsequent economic growth depended substantially on the export of oil and gas, rather than on competi-tive manufacturing. Russia's military intervention in Ukraine in 2014 prompted Western economic sanctions, which, together with the sharply declining price of oil on the world market, resulted in a major downturn in Russian economic life, at least temporarily. Some twenty-five years after the collapse of the Soviet Union, the continuing weakness and vulnerability of the Russian economy were evident.

Elsewhere, China had largely abandoned its communist economic policies as a market economy took shape, spurring remarkable economic growth. Like China, Vietnam and Laos remained officially communist, even while they pursued Chinese-style reforms, though more cautiously. Even Cuba, which was beset by economic crisis in the 1990s following the end of massive Soviet subsidies, began after 2008 to allow small businesses, private food markets, the buying and selling of cars, the sale of computers and cell phones, and luxury hotels for tourists, while still harshly suppressing opposition political groups. A growing cultural openness allowed films highly critical of Cuban society to be produced and shown publicly, including one, *Juan of the Dead*, that portrayed Cuba in 2010 as a country of dazed zombies. And in late 2014, after more than five decades of efforts to isolate a communist-ruled Cuba from the larger international arena, the United States finally began to reopen diplomatic relations with this Caribbean nation.

An impoverished North Korea remained the most unreformed and repressive of the remaining communist countries and the only major flashpoint of cold war–era conflicts. Its small nuclear arsenal controlled by an unpredictable leadership made it a cause of great concern in the region and beyond. And its alleged ability to hack into Sony Pictures computers in late 2014 to protest an unflattering film portrayal of the North Korean leader illustrated the intersection of popular culture, a world linked by the Internet, and global political conflicts.

But as a primary source of international tensions or as a compelling path to modernity and social justice, communism was effectively dead. The brief commu-nist era in world history had ended. However, the rivalries of the Great Powers had certainly not ended, as Russia and China alike continued to challenge American global dominance. Russian president Vladimir Putin deeply resented the loss of his country's international stature after the breakup of the Soviet Union and what he regarded as U.S. efforts to intrude upon Russia's legitimate interests. By 2014 issues involving the eastward expansion of NATO and the Russian intervention in Ukraine had brought the relationship between Russia and the West to something resembling cold war–era hostility. And the rising economic and military power of China gen-erated many tensions in its relationship with the United States in East Asia and the Pacific world. The demise of communism, in short, did not bring about a golden age of international harmony, as the geopolitical and economic competition of major nation-states persisted.

To Judge or Not to Judge

Should historians or students of history make moral judgments about the people and events they study? On the one hand, some would argue, scholars do well to act as detached and objective observers of the human experience. The task is to describe what happened and to explain why things turned out as they did. Whether we approve or condemn the outcomes of the historical process is, in this view, beside the point. On the other hand, all of us, scholars and students alike, stand somewhere. We are members of particular cultures; we have values and outlooks on the world that inevitably affect the way we think about the past. Perhaps it is better to recognize and acknowledge these realities than to pretend to some unattainable objectivity that places us above it all. Furthermore, making judgments is a way of caring about the past, of affirming our continuing relationship with those who have gone before us.

The question of making judgments arises strongly in any examination of the communist phenomenon. In a United States lacking a major socialist tradition, sometimes saying anything positive about communism or even noting its appeal to millions of people has brought charges of whitewashing its crimes. Within the communist world, even modest criticism was usually regarded as counterrevolutionary and was largely forbidden and harshly punished. Certainly, few observers were neutral in their assessment of the communist experiment.

Were the Russian and Chinese revolutions a blow for human freedom and a cry for justice on the part of oppressed people, or did they simply replace one tyranny with another? Was Stalinism a successful effort to industrialize a backward country or a ferocious assault on its moral and social fabric? Did Chinese reforms of the late twentieth century represent a return to sensible policies of modernization, a continued denial of basic democratic rights, or an opening to capitalist inequalities, corruption, and acquisitiveness? Passionate debate continues on all of these questions.

Communism, like many human projects, has been an ambiguous enterprise. On the one hand, communism brought hope to millions by addressing the manifest injustices of the past; by providing new opportunities for women, workers, and peasants; by promoting rapid industrial development; and by ending Western domination. On the other hand, communism was responsible for mountains of crimes — millions killed and wrongly imprisoned; massive famines partly caused by radical policies; human rights violated on an enormous scale; lives uprooted and distorted by efforts to achieve the impossible.

Studying communism challenges our inclination to want definitive answers and clear moral judgments. Can we hold contradictory elements in some kind of tension? Can we affirm our own values while acknowledging the ambiguities of life, both past and present? Doing so is arguably among the essential tasks of growing up and achieving a measure of intellectual maturity. In that undertaking, history can be helpful.

Second Thoughts

What's the Significance?

Russian Revolution (1917), 933–36
Bolsheviks/Lenin, 935
Guomindang, 937–38
Mao Zedong, 937–38
Chinese Revolution, 938
Stalin, 938; 941–44
building socialism, 938–40
Zhenotdel, 941
collectivization, 942–43

Cultural Revolution, 945–46
Great Purges/Terror, 946–47
Anna Dubova, 948–49
Cuban Revolution / missile crisis, 952
Nikita Khrushchev, 952–56
Deng Xiaoping, 959–60
perestroika/glasnost, 961
Mikhail Gorbachev, 961–62

Big Picture Questions

1. Why did the communist experiment, which was committed to equality, abundance, and a humane socialism, generate failed economies and oppressive, brutal, and totalitarian regimes?
2. In what ways did communism have a global impact beyond those countries that were governed by communist parties?
3. What was the global significance of the cold war?
4. "The end of communism was as revolutionary as its beginning." Do you agree with this statement?
5. **Looking Back:** What was distinctive about twentieth-century communist industrialization and modernization compared to the same processes in the West a century earlier?

Next Steps: For Further Study

Archie Brown, *The Rise and Fall of Communism* (2009). A global overview of the communist phenomenon in the twentieth century by a respected scholar.

Jung Chang, *Wild Swans* (2004). A compelling view of twentieth-century Chinese history through the eyes of three generations of women in a single family.

Timothy Check, *Mao Zedong and China's Revolutions* (2002). A collection of documents about the Chinese Revolution and a fine introduction to the life of Mao.

John L. Gaddis, *The Cold War: A New History* (2005). An overview by one of the most highly regarded historians of the cold war.

Peter Kenez, *A History of the Soviet Union from the Beginning to the End* (1999). A thoughtful overview of the entire Soviet experience.

Robert Strayer, *The Communist Experiment* (2007). A comparative study of Soviet and Chinese communism.

"Mao Zedong Internet Archive," http://www.marxists.org/reference/archive/mao. A Web site offering the translated writings of Mao, including poetry and some images.

"Soviet Archives Exhibit," http://www.ibiblio.org/expo/soviet.exhibit/entrance.html. A rich Web site from the Library of Congress, focusing on the operation of the Soviet system and relations with the United States.

WORKING WITH EVIDENCE

Poster Art in Mao's China

"I wanted to be the girl in the poster when I was growing up. Every day I dressed up like that girl in a white cotton shirt with a red scarf around my neck, and I braided my hair in the same way. I liked the fact that she was surrounded by revolutionary martyrs whom I was taught to worship since kindergarten."[18] As things turned out, this young girl, Anchee Min, did become the subject of one of the many thousands of propaganda posters with which the Chinese communist government flooded the country during the thirty years or so following the Chinese Revolution of 1949.

In China, as in other communist countries, art served the state and the Communist Party. Nowhere was this more apparent than in these propaganda posters, which were found in homes, schools, workplaces, railway stations, and elsewhere. The artists who created these images were under the strict control of Communist Party officials and were expected to use their skills to depict the party's leaders and achievements favorably, even grandly. They were among the "engineers of the human soul" who were reshaping the consciousness of individuals and remaking their entire society. One young man, born in 1951, testified to the effectiveness of these posters: "They . . . were my signposts through life. They made sure we did not make mistakes. . . . My life is reflected in them."[19]

The posters that follow illustrate the kind of society and people that the communist leadership sought to create during the years that Mao Zedong ruled the country (1949–1976). The realities behind these images, of course, were often far different.

Coming to power in 1949, Chinese Communist Party leaders recognized that their enemies were by no means totally defeated. A persistent theme throughout the years of Mao's rule was an effort to eliminate those enemies or convert them to the communist cause. Spies, imperialist sympathizers, those infected with "bourgeois values" such as materialism and individualism, landowners or capitalists yearning for the old life—all of these had to be identified and confronted. So too were many "enemies" within the Communist Party itself, people who were suspected of opposition to the radical policies of Mao. Some of these alleged enemies were killed, others imprisoned, and still others—millions of them—were subjected to endless self-criticism sessions or sent down to remote rural areas to "learn from the peasants." This need to demolish the old society and old values is reflected in Source 21.1, a poster from 1967, the height of the Cultural Revolution (see pages 945–47). Its caption reads: "Destroy the Old World; Establish the New World."

■ Notice the various items beneath this young revolutionary's feet. What do they represent to the ardent revolutionaries seeking to "destroy the old world"? What groups of people were most likely to be affected by such efforts?

■ What elements of a new order are being constructed in this image?

■ How does the artist distinguish visually between the old and the new? Note the use of colors and the size of various figures and objects in the poster.

Courtesy, University of Westminster Poster Collection, London

Source 21.1 Smashing the Old Society

The centerpiece of Mao's plans for the vast Chinese countryside lay in the "people's communes." Established during the Great Leap Forward in the late 1950s, these were huge political and economic units intended to work the land more efficiently and collectively, to undertake large-scale projects such as building dams and irrigation systems, to create small-scale industries in rural areas, and to promote local self-reliance. The leaders who created the communes also sought to move China more rapidly toward genuine communism by eliminating virtually every form of private property and emphasizing social equality and shared living. Commune members ate together in large dining halls, and children were cared for during the day in collective nurseries rather than by their own families. Source 21.2, a poster created in 1958 under the title "The People's Communes Are Good," shows a highly idealized image of one such commune. See also the celebratory poster on page 945.

The actual outcomes of the commune movement departed radically from its idealistic goals. Economic disruption occasioned by the creation of

Source 21.2 Building the New Society: The People's Commune

Shanghai Educational Publishing House/Stefan R. Landsberger Collections/International Institute of Social History, Amsterdam/www.chineseposters.net

communes contributed a great deal to the enormous famines of the late 1950s and early 1960s, in which many millions perished. Furthermore, efforts to involve the peasants in iron and steel production through the creation of much-heralded "backyard furnaces," illustrated in Source 21.2, proved a failure. Most of the metal produced in these primitive facilities was of poor quality and essentially unusable. Such efforts further impoverished the rural areas as peasants were encouraged to contribute their pots, pans, and anything made of iron to the smelting furnaces.

■ What appealing features of commune life and a communist future are illustrated in this poster and the poster on page 945? Notice the communal facilities for eating and washing clothes as well as the drill practice of a "people's militia" unit at the bottom of Source 21.2.

■ One of Mao's chief goals was to overcome the sharp division between industrial cities and the agricultural countryside. How is this effort illustrated in these posters?

Among the core values of Maoist communism were human mastery over the natural order, rapid industrialization, and the liberation of women from ancient limitations and oppressions in order to mobilize them for the task of building socialism. Source 21.3, a 1975 poster, illustrates these values. Its caption reads: "Women Can Hold Up Half the Sky; Surely the Face of Nature Can Be Transformed."

■ In what ways does this poster reflect Chinese communism's core values?

■ How is the young woman in this image portrayed? What does the expression on her face convey? Notice her clothing and the shape of her forearms, and the general absence of a feminine figure. Why do you think she is portrayed in this largely sexless fashion? What does this suggest about the communist attitude toward sexuality?

■ What does this image suggest about how the party sought to realize gender equality? What is the significance of the work the young woman is doing?

■ Notice the lights that illuminate a nighttime work scene. What does this suggest about attitudes toward work and production?

A central feature of Chinese communism, especially during the Cultural Revolution of 1966–1976, was the growing veneration, even adoration, of Chairman Mao. Portraits, statues, busts, and Mao badges proliferated. Everyone was expected to read repeatedly the "Red Treasured Book," which offered a selection of quotations from Mao's writings, believed to facilitate solutions to almost all problems, both public and private. Many families erected "tablets of loyalty" to Mao, much like those previously devoted to ancestors.

Source 21.3 Women, Nature, and Industrialization

我們心中最紅最紅的紅太陽毛主席和我們在一起

Source 21.4 The Cult of Mao

People made pilgrimages to "sacred shrines" associated with key events in his life. Schoolchildren began the day by chanting, "May Chairman Mao live ten thousand times ten thousand years."

And Mao was the centerpiece of endless posters. Source 21.4, a poster created in 1968, portrays a familiar scene from the Cultural Revolution. Millions of young people, organized as Red Guards and committed to revolutionary action, flocked to Beijing, where enormous and ecstatic rallies allowed them to catch a glimpse of their beloved leader and to unite with him in the grand task of creating communism in China. The poster's caption reads: "The reddest, reddest, red sun in our heart, Chairman Mao, and us together."

■ What relationship between Mao and his young followers does the poster suggest? Why might some scholars have seen a quasi-religious dimension to that relationship?

■ How do you understand the significance of the "Red Treasured Book" of quotations from Mao, which the young people are waving?

■ How might you account for the unbridled enthusiasm expressed by the Red Guards? In this case, the poster portrays the realities of these rallies with considerable accuracy. Can you think of other comparable cases of such mass enthusiasm?

DOING HISTORY

Poster Art in Mao's China

1. **Reading communist intentions:** Based on these visual sources, how would you describe the kind of society that the Chinese Communist Party sought to create in China during Mao's lifetime?

2. **Distinguishing image and reality:** Based on the narrative of this chapter and especially on what happened after Mao's death, assess the realities that lay behind these visual sources. To what extent do the posters accurately represent the successes of Maoist communism? What insights do they shed on its failures?

3. **Defining audience and appeal:** To whom do you think these posters were directed? What appeal might they have for the intended audience?

4. **Noticing change:** How could you use these posters to define the dramatic changes that transformed China since 1949? How might a traditional Chinese official from the nineteenth century respond to them?

5. **Assessing posters as evidence:** What are the strengths and limitations of poster art for understanding Chinese communism under Mao?

CHAPTER 22

The End of Empire

The Global South on the Global Stage
1914–present

"During my lifetime I have dedicated myself to this struggle of the African people. I have fought against white domination, and I have fought against black domination. I have cherished the ideal of a democratic and free society in which all persons live together in harmony and with equal opportunity. It is an ideal which I hope to live for and to achieve. But, if need be, it is an ideal for which I am prepared to die."[1]

Nelson Mandela, South Africa's nationalist leader, first uttered these words in 1964 at his trial for treason, sabotage, and conspiracy to overthrow the apartheid government of his country. Convicted of those charges, he spent the next twenty-seven years in prison, sometimes working at hard labor in a stone quarry. Often the floor was his bed, and a bucket was his toilet. For many years, he was allowed one visitor a year for thirty minutes and permitted to write and receive one letter every six months. When he was finally released from prison in 1990 under growing domestic and international pressure, he concluded his first speech as a free person with the words originally spoken at his trial. Four years later, in 1994, South Africa held its first election in which blacks and whites alike were able to vote. The outcome of that election made Mandela the country's first black African president, and it linked South Africa to dozens of other countries all across Africa, Asia, and Oceania that had thrown off European rule or the control of white settlers during the second half of the twentieth century.

Variously called decolonization or the struggle for independence, that process carried an immense significance for the history of the twentieth century. It marked a dramatic change in

Independence and Development   In the eyes of most Asians and Africans, the struggle for national independence from European colonial rule was but a prelude to and prerequisite for the even greater struggle for modern development, symbolized here by a photo from 2012 showing South African high school students in a computer-education classroom.

the world's political architecture, as nation-states triumphed over the empires that had structured much of the world's political life in the nineteenth and early twentieth centuries. It mobilized millions of people, thrusting them into political activity and sometimes into violence and warfare. Decolonization signaled the declining legitimacy of both empire and race as a credible basis for political or social life. It promised not only national freedom but also personal dignity, abundance, and opportunity.

What followed in the decades after independence was equally significant. Political, economic, and cultural experiments proliferated across these newly independent nations, which faced enormous challenges: the legacies of empire; their own deep divisions of language, ethnicity, religion, and class; their rapidly growing numbers; the competing demands of the capitalist West and the communist East; and the difficult tasks of simultaneously building modern economies, stable politics, and coherent nations. And they confronted all of these in a world still shaped by the powerful economies and armies of the wealthy, already-industrialized nations. The emergence of these new nations onto the world stage as independent and assertive actors has been a distinguishing feature of world history in this most recent century.

> **SEEKING THE MAIN POINT**
>
> In what ways did the experience of the "Global South" during the past century register on the larger stage of world history?

Toward Freedom: Struggles for Independence

In 1900, European colonial empires in Africa, Asia, the Caribbean region, and Pacific Oceania appeared as enduring features of the world's political landscape. Well before the end of the twentieth century, they were gone. The first major breakthroughs occurred in Asia and the Middle East in the late 1940s, when the Philippines, India, Pakistan, Burma, Indonesia, Syria, Iraq, Jordan, and Israel achieved independence. The period from the mid-1950s through the mid-1970s was an age of African independence as colony after colony, more than fifty in total, emerged into what was then seen as the bright light of freedom. During the 1970s, many of the island societies of Pacific Oceania—Samoa, Fiji, Tonga, the Solomon Islands, Kiribati—joined the ranks of independent states, almost entirely peacefully and without much struggle as the various colonial powers willingly abandoned their right to rule. Hawaiians, however, sought incorporation as a state within the United States, rather than independence, attracting opposition from some American conservatives who were not easily persuaded that this multiethnic society was genuinely American. Finally, a number of Caribbean societies—the Bahamas, Barbados, Belize, Jamaica, Trinidad, and Tobago—achieved independence during the 1960s and 70s, informed by a growing awareness of a distinctive Caribbean culture. Cuba, although formally independent since 1902, dramatically declared its rejection of American control in its revolutionary upheaval in 1959. Efforts to join a number of former British colonies into a Federation of the West Indies failed, and by 1983 the Caribbean region hosted sixteen separate independent states.

A MAP OF TIME

1915	Gandhi returns to India from South Africa
1923–1938	Turkey's secular modernization initiated under Kemal Atatürk
1928	Muslim Brotherhood established in Egypt
1947	Independence of India/Pakistan
1948	Establishment of state of Israel; apartheid formally established in South Africa
1949	Independence of Indonesia; communist victory in China
1955	Bandung Conference of nonaligned nations
1957–1975	Independence of African countries
1959	Cuban Revolution
1960–1970s	Wave of military coups in Africa and Latin America
1973	OPEC oil embargo
1979	Revolution in Iran
1980s–1990s	Growth of democratic movements and governments in Africa and Latin America
1988–1989	Founding of al-Qaeda
1994	End of apartheid in South Africa; genocide in Rwanda
2011	Arab Spring in the Middle East
2013	Turkish young people in Istanbul protest the Islamist and authoritarian trends of the government
2013	Iran elects a moderate president, raising hopes of agreement with the West on its nuclear program
2014	Radical Islamist organization Boko Haram captures over 200 schoolgirls in northern Nigeria
2015	Radical French Muslims in Paris attack a satirical magazine that had lampooned the Prophet Muhammad

The End of Empire in World History

At one level, this vast process was but the latest case of imperial dissolution, a fate that had overtaken earlier empires, including those of the Assyrians, Romans, Arabs, and Mongols. But never before had the end of empire been so associated with the mobilization of the masses around a nationalist ideology. Nor had these earlier cases generated a plethora of nation-states, each claiming an equal place in a world of nation-states. More comparable perhaps was that first decolonization, in which the European colonies in the Americas threw off British, French, Spanish, or Portuguese rule during the late eighteenth and early nineteenth centuries (see Chapter 16). Like their earlier counterparts, the new nations of the twentieth century claimed an international status equivalent to that of their former rulers. In the Americas, however, many of the colonized people were themselves of European origin, sharing much of their culture with their colonial rulers. In that respect, the freedom struggles of the twentieth century were very different, for they not only asserted political independence but also affirmed the vitality of their cultures, which had been submerged and denigrated during the colonial era. In Oceania, for example, the idea of a "Pacific Way" sought to articulate a style of political action in keeping with what were held to be "traditional" principles—decision making by consensus and resolving differences in a fashion that left no one feeling defeated.

■ **Comparison**

What was distinctive about the end of Europe's African and Asian empires compared to other cases of imperial disintegration?

The twentieth century witnessed the demise of many empires. The Austrian and Ottoman empires collapsed following World War I, giving rise to a number of new states in Europe and the Middle East. The Russian Empire also unraveled, although it was soon reassembled under the auspices of the Soviet Union. World War II ended the German and Japanese empires. African and Asian movements for independence shared with these other end-of-empire stories the ideal of national self-determination. This novel idea—that humankind was naturally divided into distinct peoples or nations, each of which deserved an independent state of its own—was loudly proclaimed by the winning side of both world wars. It gained a global acceptance, particularly in the colonial world, during the twentieth century and rendered empire illegitimate in the eyes of growing numbers of people.

Empires without territory, such as the powerful influence that the United States exercised in Latin America, likewise came under attack from highly nationalist governments. An intrusive U.S. presence was certainly one factor stimulating the Mexican Revolution, which began in 1910. One of the outcomes of that upheaval was the nationalization in 1937 of Mexico's oil industry, much of which was owned by American and British investors. Similar actions accompanied Cuba's revolution of 1959 and also occurred in other places throughout Latin America and elsewhere. National self-determination and freedom from Soviet control likewise lay behind the Eastern European revolutions of 1989. The disintegration of the Soviet Union itself in 1991 brought to an inglorious end the last of the major territorial empires of the twentieth century and led to the birth of fifteen new national states. Although the winning of political independence for Europe's African and Asian colonies was perhaps the most spectacular challenge to empire in the twentieth century, that process was part of a larger pattern in modern world history (see Map 22.1).

Explaining African and Asian Independence

As the twentieth century closed, the end of European empires seemed an almost inevitable phenomenon, for colonial rule had lost any credibility as a form of political order. What could be more natural than for people to seek to rule themselves?

Yet at the beginning of the century, few observers were predicting the collapse of these empires, and the idea that "the only legitimate government is national self-government" was not nearly so widespread as it subsequently became. This situation has presented historians with a problem of explanation—how to account for the fall of European colonial empires and the emergence of dozens of new nation-states.

One approach to explaining the end of colonial empires focuses attention on fundamental contradictions in the entire colonial enterprise. The rhetoric of Christianity, Enlightenment thought, and material progress sat awkwardly with the realities of colonial racism, exploitation, and poverty. The increasingly democratic values of European states ran counter to the essential dictatorship of colonial rule. The ideal of national self-determination was profoundly at odds with the possession of colonies that were denied any opportunity to express their own national character. The enormously powerful force of nationalism, having earlier driven the process of European empire building, now played a major role in its disintegration. Colonial rule, in this argument, dug its own grave because its practice ran counter to established European values.

But why did this "fatal flaw" of European colonial rule lead to independence in the post–World War II decades rather than earlier or later? In explaining the timing of the end of empire, historians frequently use the notion of "conjuncture," the coming together of several separate developments at a particular time. At the international level, the world wars had weakened Europe, while discrediting any sense of European moral superiority. Both the United States and the Soviet Union, the new global superpowers, generally opposed the older European colonial empires, even as they created empire-like international relationships of their own. Meanwhile, the United Nations provided a prestigious platform from which to conduct anticolonial agitation. All of this contributed to the global illegitimacy of empire, a novel and stunning transformation of social values that was enormously encouraging to anticolonial movements everywhere.

At the same time, social and economic circumstances within the colonies themselves generated the human raw material for anticolonial movements. By the early twentieth century in Asia and the mid-twentieth century in Africa, a second or third generation of Western-educated elites, largely male, had arisen throughout the colonial world. These young men were thoroughly familiar with European culture; they were deeply aware of the gap between its values and its practices; they no longer viewed colonial rule as a vehicle for their peoples' progress as their fathers had; and they increasingly insisted on immediate independence. Moreover, growing numbers of ordinary people—women and men alike—were receptive to this message. Veterans of the world wars; young people with some education but no jobs commensurate with their expectations; a small class of urban workers who were increasingly aware of their exploitation; small-scale female traders resentful of European privileges; rural dwellers who had lost land or suffered from forced labor; impoverished and insecure newcomers to the cities—all of these groups had reason to believe that independence held great promise.

■ Change
What international circumstances and social changes contributed to the end of colonial empires?

**Map 22.1
The End of Empire
in Africa and Asia**

In the second half of the twentieth century, under pressure from nationalist movements, Europe's Asian and African empires dissolved into dozens of new independent states.

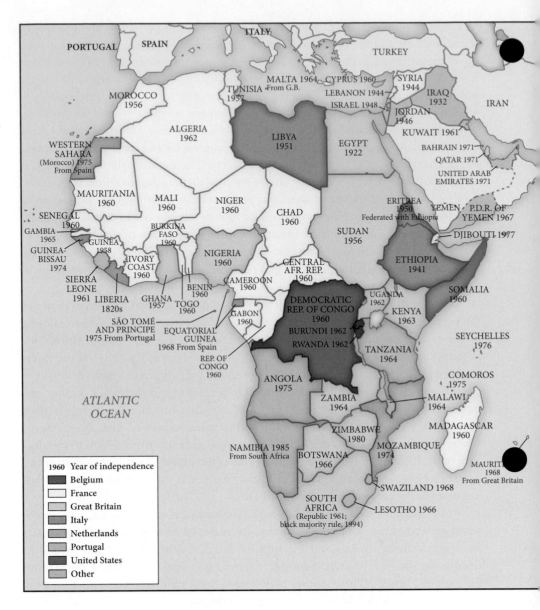

PORTUGAL   SPAIN   ITALY
TURKEY

MALTA 1964 CYPRUS 1960   SYRIA
From G.B.   1944
TUNISIA   LEBANON 1944   IRAQ
1957   ISRAEL 1948 JORDAN 1932   IRAN
MOROCCO   1946
1956
ALGERIA   LIBYA   EGYPT   KUWAIT 1961
1962   1951   1922   BAHRAIN 1971
WESTERN   QATAR 1971
SAHARA   UNITED ARAB
(Morocco) 1975   EMIRATES 1971
From Spain
MAURITANIA MALI   NIGER   ERITREA   YEMEN P.D.R. OF
1960   1960   1960   1950   YEMEN 1967
                          CHAD   Federated with Ethiopia
SENEGAL   1960   SUDAN   DJIBOUTI 1977
1960   1956
GAMBIA   BURKINA
1965   FASO
GUINEA- 1960   NIGERIA   ETHIOPIA
BISSAU GUINEA   1960   1941
1974   1958   IVORY   CENTRAL
        COAST   AFR. REP.   SOMALIA
SIERRA 1960   1960   UGANDA   1960
LEONE   BENIN CAMEROON 1962
1961   LIBERIA 1960 1960 KENYA
       1820s GHANA TOGO DEMOCRATIC 1963
             1957 1960 REP. OF CONGO
SÃO TOMÉ   GABON 1960   SEYCHELLES
AND PRINCIPE   1960 BURUNDI 1962 1976
1975 From Portugal EQUATORIAL RWANDA 1962
        GUINEA   REP. OF TANZANIA
        1968 From Spain CONGO 1964
                  1960   COMOROS
ATLANTIC   ANGOLA   1975
OCEAN   1975 ZAMBIA MALAWI
                          1964   1964
                     ZIMBABWE   MADAGASCAR
                     1980   1960
                  NAMIBIA 1985 MOZAMBIQUE
                  From South Africa BOTSWANA 1974 MAURIT
                          1966   1968
                                       SWAZILAND 1968 From Great Britain
                     SOUTH
                     AFRICA LESOTHO 1966
                  (Republic 1961;
                  black majority rule, 1994)

1960	Year of independence
	Belgium
	France
	Great Britain
	Italy
	Netherlands
	Portugal
	United States
	Other

Such pressures increasingly placed colonial rulers on the defensive. As the twentieth century wore on, these colonial rulers began to plan—tentatively at first—for a new political relationship with their Asian and African subjects. The colonies had been integrated into a global economic network, and local elites were largely committed to maintaining those links. In these circumstances, Europeans could imagine retaining profitable economic interests in Asia, Africa, and Oceania without the expense and trouble of formal colonial governments. Deliberate planning for decolonization included gradual political reforms; investments in railroads, ports, and

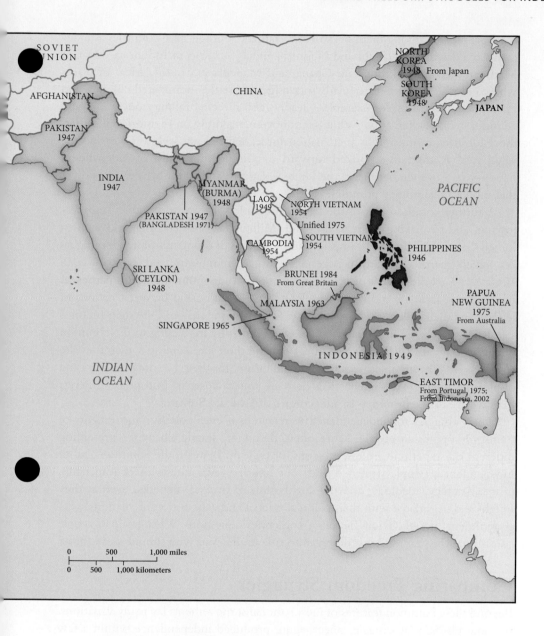

telegraph lines; the holding of elections; and the writing of constitutions. To some observers, it seemed as if independence was granted by colonial rulers rather than gained or seized by nationalist movements.

But these reforms, and independence itself, occurred only under considerable pressure from mounting nationalist movements. Creating such movements was no easy task. Leaders, drawn everywhere from the ranks of the educated few and almost always male, organized political parties, recruited members, plotted strategy, developed an ideology, and negotiated with one another and with the colonial state. The most prominent among them became the "fathers" of their new countries as independence dawned—Gandhi and Nehru in India, Sukarno in Indonesia, Ho Chi Minh in Vietnam, Nkrumah in Ghana, and Mandela in South Africa. In places where colonial rule was particularly intransigent—settler-dominated colonies and Portuguese territories, for example—leaders also directed military operations and administered liberated areas. While such movements drew on memories of earlier, more localized forms of resistance, nationalist leaders did not seek to restore a vanished past. Rather, they looked forward to joining the world of independent nation-states, to membership in the United Nations, and to the wealth and power that modern technology promised.

■ Description
What obstacles confronted the leaders of movements for independence?

A further common task of the nationalist leadership was to recruit a mass following, and to varying degrees, they did. Millions of ordinary men and women joined Gandhi's nonviolent campaigns in India; tens of thousands of freedom fighters waged guerrilla warfare in Algeria, Kenya, Mozambique, and Zimbabwe; in West Africa workers went on strike and market women joined political parties, as did students, farmers, and the unemployed. The relationship between nationalist leaders and their followers was frequently fraught with tension. One such Indonesian leader, educated in Holland, spoke of his difficulty in relating to the common people: "Why am I vexed by the things that fill their lives, and to which they are so attached? Why are the things that contain beauty for them . . . only senseless and displeasing for me? We intellectuals here are much closer to Europe or America than we are to the primitive Islamic culture of Java and Sumatra."[2]

Thus struggles for independence were rarely if ever cohesive movements of uniformly oppressed people. More often, they were fragile alliances representing different classes, ethnic groups, religions, or regions. Beneath the common goal of independence, people struggled with one another over questions of leadership, power, strategy, ideology, and the distribution of material benefits, even as they fought and negotiated with their colonial rulers. The very notion of "national self-government" posed obvious but often-contentious questions: What group of people constituted the "nation" that deserved to rule itself? And who should speak for it?

Comparing Freedom Struggles

Beyond these common features of most nationalist movements lay many variations. In some places, that struggle, once begun, produced independence within a few years, four in the case of the Belgian Congo. Elsewhere it was measured in many decades. Nationalism surfaced in Vietnam in the early 1900s, but the country achieved full political independence only in the mid-1970s, having fought French colonial rulers, Japanese invaders during World War II, and U.S. military forces in the 1960s and 1970s, as well as Chinese forces during a brief war in 1979. Tactics too varied considerably. In many places, West Africa for example, nationalists relied on peaceful political pressure—demonstrations, strikes, mass mobilization, and negotiations—to achieve independence. Elsewhere armed struggle was required.

Eight years of bitter guerrilla warfare preceded Algerian independence from France in 1962.

While all nationalist movements sought political independence for modern states, their ideologies and outlooks also differed. Many in India and the Islamic world viewed their new nations through the prism of religion, while elsewhere more secular outlooks prevailed. In Indonesia, an early nationalist organization, the Islamic Union, appealed on the basis of religion, while later groups espoused Marxism. Indonesia's primary nationalist leader, Sukarno, sought to embrace and reconcile these various outlooks. "What is Sukarno?" he asked. "A nationalist? An Islamist? A Marxist? . . . Sukarno is a mixture of all these isms."[3] Nationalist movements led by communist parties, such as those in Vietnam and China, sought major social transformations as well as freedom from foreign rule, while those in most of Africa focused on ending racial discrimination and achieving political independence with little concern about emerging patterns of domestic class inequality.

Two of the most extended freedom struggles—in India and South Africa— illustrate both the variations and the complexity of this process, which was so central to twentieth-century world history. India was among the first colonies to achieve independence and provided both a model and an inspiration to others, whereas South Africa, though not formally a colony, was among the last to throw off political domination by whites.

The Case of India: Ending British Rule

Surrounded by the Himalayas and the Indian Ocean, the South Asian peninsula, commonly known as India, enjoyed a certain geographic unity. But before the twentieth century, few of its people thought of themselves as "Indians." Cultural identities were primarily local and infinitely varied, rooted in differences of family, caste, village, language, region, tribe, and religious practice. In earlier centuries— during the Mauryan, Gupta, and Mughal empires, for example—large areas of the subcontinent had been temporarily enclosed within a single political system, but always these were imperial overlays, constructed on top of enormously diverse Indian societies.

So too was British colonial rule, but the British differed from earlier invaders in ways that promoted a growing sense of Indian identity. Unlike previous foreign rulers, the British never assimilated into Indian society because their acute sense of racial and cultural distinctiveness kept them apart. This served to intensify Indians' awareness of their collective difference from their alien rulers. Furthermore, British railroads, telegraph lines, postal services, administrative networks, newspapers, and schools as well as the English language bound India's many regions and peoples together more firmly than ever before and facilitated communication, especially among those with a modern education. Early nineteenth-century cultural nationalists, seeking to renew and reform Hinduism, registered this sense of India as a cultural unit.

■ **Change**
How did India's nationalist movement change over time?

The most important political expression of an all-Indian identity took shape in the Indian National Congress (INC), often called the Congress Party, which was established in 1885. This was an association of English-educated Indians—lawyers, journalists, teachers, businessmen—drawn overwhelmingly from regionally prominent high-caste Hindu families. It represented the beginning of a new kind of political protest, quite different from the rebellions, banditry, and refusal to pay taxes that had periodically erupted in the rural areas of colonial India. The INC was largely an urban phenomenon and quite moderate in its demands. Initially, its well-educated members did not seek to overthrow British rule; rather they hoped to gain greater inclusion within the political, military, and business life of British India. From such positions of influence, they argued, they could better protect the interests of India than could their foreign-born rulers. The British mocked their claim to speak for ordinary Indians, referring to them as "babus," a derogatory term that implied a semi-literate "native" with only a thin veneer of modern culture.

As an elite organization, the INC had difficulty gaining a mass following among India's vast peasant population. That began to change in the aftermath of World War I. To attract Indian support for the war effort, the British in 1917 had promised "the gradual development of self-governing institutions," a commitment that energized nationalist politicians to demand more rapid political change. Furthermore, British attacks on the Islamic Ottoman Empire antagonized India's Muslims. The end of the war was followed by a massive influenza epidemic, which cost the lives of millions of Indians. Finally, a series of violent repressive British actions antagonized many. This was the context in which Mohandas Gandhi (1869–1948) arrived on the Indian political scene and soon transformed it.

Gandhi was born in the province of Gujarat in western India to a pious Hindu family of the Vaisya, or business, caste. He was married at the age of thirteen, had only a mediocre record as a student, and eagerly embraced an opportunity to study law in England when he was eighteen. He returned as a shy and not very successful lawyer, and in 1893 he accepted a job with an Indian firm in South Africa, where a substantial number of Indians had migrated as indentured laborers during the nineteenth century. While in South Africa, Gandhi personally experienced overt racism for the first time and soon became involved in organizing Indians, mostly Muslims, to protest that country's policies of racial segregation. He also developed a concept of India that included Hindus and Muslims alike and pioneered strategies

Mahatma Gandhi
The most widely recognized and admired figure in the global struggle against colonial rule was India's Mahatma Gandhi. In this famous photograph, he is sitting cross-legged on the floor, clothed in a traditional Indian garment called a dhoti, while nearby stands a spinning wheel, symbolizing the independent and nonindustrial India that Gandhi sought. (Margaret Bourke-White/Time Life Pictures/Getty Images)

of resistance that he would later apply in India itself. His emerging political philoso-phy, known as *satyagraha* (truth force), was a confrontational, though nonviolent, approach to political action. Gandhi argued:

> Non-violence means conscious suffering. It does not mean meek submission to the will of the evil-doer, but it means the pitting of one's whole soul against the will of the tyrant. . . . It is possible for a single individual to defy the whole might of an unjust empire to save his honour, his religion, his soul.[4]

Returning to India in 1915, Gandhi quickly rose within the leadership ranks of the INC. During the 1920s and 1930s, he applied his approach in periodic mass campaigns that drew support from an extraordinarily wide spectrum of Indians — peasants and the urban poor, intellectuals and artisans, capitalists and socialists, Hindus and Muslims. The British responded with periodic repression as well as concessions that allowed a greater Indian role in political life. Gandhi's conduct and actions — his simple and unpretentious lifestyle, his support of Muslims, his frequent reference to Hindu religious themes — appealed widely in India and transformed the INC into a mass organization. To many ordinary people, Gandhi possessed magical powers and produced miraculous events. He was the Mahatma, the Great Soul.

His was a radicalism of a different kind. He did not call for social revolution but sought the moral transformation of individuals. He worked to raise the status of India's untouchables, the lowest and most ritually polluting groups within the caste hierarchy, but he launched no attack on caste in general and accepted support from businessmen and their socialist critics alike. His critique of India's situation went far beyond colonial rule. "India is being ground down," he wrote in 1909, "not under the English heel, but under that of modern civilization" — its competitiveness, its materialism, its warlike tendencies, its abandonment of religion.[5] Almost alone among nationalist leaders in India or elsewhere, Gandhi opposed a modern industrial future for his country, seeking instead a society of harmonious self-sufficient villages drawing on ancient Indian principles of duty and morality.

Gandhi also embraced efforts to mobilize women for the struggle against Britain and to elevate their standing in marriage and society. While asserting the spiritual and mental equality of women and men, he regarded women as uniquely endowed with a capacity for virtue, self-sacrifice, and endurance and thus particularly well suited for nonviolent protest. They could also contribute by spinning and weaving their families' clothing, while boycotting British textiles. But Gandhi never completely broke with older Indian conceptions of gender roles. He wrote, "The duty of motherhood . . . requires qualities which man need not possess. She is passive; he is active. She is essentially mistress of the house. He is the bread-winner."[6] Hundreds of thousands of women responded to Gandhi's call for participation in the independence struggle, marching, demonstrating, boycotting, and spinning. The moral and religious context in which he cast his appeal allowed them to do so without directly challenging traditional gender roles.

■ **Change**

What was the role of Gandhi in India's struggle for independence?

Gandhi and the INC leadership had to contend with a wide range of movements, parties, and approaches whose very diversity tore at the national unity that they so ardently sought. Whereas Gandhi rejected modern industrialization, his own chief lieutenant, Jawaharlal Nehru, thoroughly embraced science, technology, and industry as essential to India's future. And not everyone accepted Gandhi's nonviolence and his inclusive definition of India. A militant Hindu organization preached hatred of Muslims and viewed India as an essentially Hindu nation. Some in the Congress Party believed that efforts to improve the position of women or untouchables were a distraction from the chief task of gaining independence. Whether to participate in British-sponsored legislative bodies without complete independence also became a divisive issue. Furthermore, a number of smaller parties advocated on behalf of particular regions or castes. India's nationalist movement, in short, was beset by division and controversy.

■ **Description**
What conflicts and differences divided India's nationalist movement?

By far the most serious threat to a unified movement derived from the growing divide between the country's Hindu and Muslim populations. As early as 1906, the formation of an All-India Muslim League contradicted the Congress Party's claim to speak for all Indians. As the British allowed more elected Indian representatives on local councils, the League demanded separate electorates, with a fixed number of seats for Muslims. As Muslims were a distinct minority within India, some of them feared that their voice could be swamped by a numerically dominant Hindu population, despite Gandhi's inclusive sensibility. Some Hindu politicians confirmed those fears when they cast the nationalist struggle in Hindu religious terms, hailing their country, for example, as a goddess, Bande Mataram (Mother India). When the 1937 elections gave the Congress Party control of many provincial governments, some of those governments began to enforce the teaching of Hindi in schools, rather than Urdu, which is written in a Persian script and favored by Muslims. This policy, as well as Hindu efforts to protect cows from slaughter, antagonized Muslims.

As the movement for independence gained ground, the Muslim League and its leader, Muhammad Ali Jinnah (JIN-uh), argued that those parts of India that had a Muslim majority should have a separate political status. They called it Pakistan, meaning "land of the pure." In this view, India was not a single nation, as Gandhi had long argued. Jinnah put his case succinctly:

> The Muslims and Hindus belong to two different religious philosophies, social customs, and literatures. They neither intermarry nor interdine [eat] together and, indeed, they belong to two different civilizations.[7]

With great reluctance and amid mounting violence, Gandhi and the Congress Party finally agreed to partition as the British declared their intention to leave India after World War II (see Map 22.2).

Thus colonial India became independent in 1947 as two countries—a Muslim Pakistan, itself divided into two wings 1,000 miles apart, and a mostly Hindu India governed by a secular state. Dividing colonial India in this fashion was horrendously

Map 22.2 The Partition of British South Asia

The independence of British India witnessed the violent partition of the subcontinent into a largely Hindu India and a Muslim Pakistan. Later, in 1971, East Pakistan established itself as the separate state of Bangladesh.

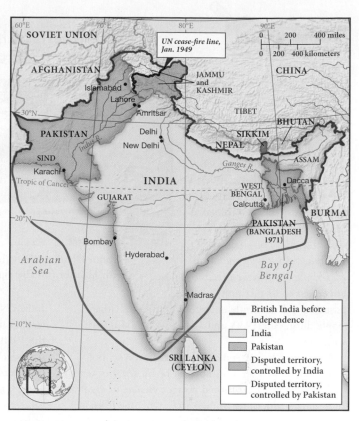

painful. A million people or more died in the communal violence that accompanied partition, and some 12 million refugees moved from one country to the other to join their religious compatriots. Gandhi himself, desperately trying to stem the mounting tide of violence in India's villages, refused to attend the independence celebrations. Only a year after independence, he was assassinated by a Hindu extremist. The great triumph of independence, secured from the powerful British Empire, was overshadowed by the great tragedy of the violence of partition. (See Zooming In: Abdul Ghaffar Khan, page 988.)

The Case of South Africa: Ending Apartheid

The setting for South Africa's freedom struggle was very different from that of India. In the twentieth century, that struggle was not waged against an occupying European colonial power, for South Africa had in fact been independent of Great Britain since 1910. Independence, however, had been granted to a government wholly controlled by a white settler minority, which represented less than 20 percent of the total population. The country's black African majority had no political rights whatsoever within the central state. Black South Africans' struggle therefore was against this internal opponent rather than against a distant colonial authority, as in India. Economically, the most prominent whites were of British descent. They or their forebears had come to South Africa during the nineteenth century, when Great Britain was the ruling colonial power. But the politically dominant section of the white community, known as Boers or Afrikaners, was descended from the early Dutch settlers, who had arrived in the mid-seventeenth century. The term "Afrikaner" reflected their image of themselves as "white Africans," permanent residents of the continent rather than colonial intruders. They had unsuccessfully sought independence from a British-ruled South Africa in a bitter struggle (the Boer War, 1899–1902), and a sense of difference and antagonism lingered. Despite continuing

Abdul Ghaffar Khan, Muslim Pacifist

Born in 1890 in the Northwest Frontier Province of colonial India, Abdul Ghaffar Khan hailed from a well-to-do landowning family among the Muslim Pathan people, widely known for their tribal conflicts. Abdul Khan himself described his people as "inclined to be violent, . . . always ready to inflict harm and injury on their own brethren."[8] So it is all the more remarkable that a widespread movement of Islamic nonviolent resistance to British rule emerged among the Pathan people during the 1930s and 1940s, with Abdul Khan as its leader.

As a boy, Khan attended a British mission school, which he credited with instilling in him a sense of service to his people. He later turned down a chance to enter an elite military unit of the Indian army when he learned that he would be required to defer to British officers junior to him in rank. His mother opposed his own plan to study in an English university, and so he turned instead to the "service of God and humanity." In practice, this initially meant social reform and educational advancement within Pathan villages, but in the increasingly nationalist environment of early twentieth-century

Abdul Ghaffar Khan (left) with Gandhi (on the right).

photo: © Hulton-Deutsch Collection/Corbis

India, it soon meant anti-colonial politics as well.

Deeply impressed with Gandhi's message of nonviolent protest, in 1929 Abdul Khan established the Khudai Khidmatgar, or "Servants of God," movement in his home region. Committed to nonviolence, social reform, the unity of the Pathan people, and the independence of India, the Khudai Khidmatgar soon became affiliated with the Indian National Congress, led by Gandhi, which was the leading nationalist organization in the country. During the 1930s and early 1940s, Abdul Khan's movement gained a substantial following in the Frontier Province, becoming the dominant political force in the area. Moreover, it largely adhered to its nonviolent creed in the face of severe British oppression and even massacres. In the process, Abdul Khan acquired a prominent place beside Gandhi in the Congress Party and an almost legendary status in his own Frontier region. His imposing six-foot-three stature, his constant touring of Pathan villages, his obvious commitment to Islam, his frequent imprison-

hostility between white South Africans of British and Afrikaner background, both felt that their way of life and standard of living were jeopardized by any move toward black African majority rule. The intransigence of this sizable and threatened settler community helps explain why African rule was delayed until 1994, while India, lacking any such community, had achieved independence almost a half century earlier.

■ **Comparison**
Why was African rule in South Africa delayed until 1994, when it had occurred decades earlier elsewhere in the colonial world?

Unlike a predominantly agrarian India, South Africa by the early twentieth century had developed a mature industrial economy, based initially in gold and diamond mining, but by midcentury including secondary industries such as steel, chemicals, automobile manufacturing, rubber processing, and heavy engineering.

ment by the British—all of this fostered a saintly image of the Pathan leader. The wells he drank from were thought to cure diseases. He became Badshah Khan (the king of khans) or the Frontier Gandhi.

It was a remarkable achievement. Gandhi's close associate Jawaharlal Nehru later wrote that both he and Gandhi were astonished that "Abdul Gaffar Khan made his turbulent and quarrelsome people accept peaceful methods of political action, involving enormous suffering."[9] In large measure, this had happened because Abdul Khan was able to root nonviolence in both Islam and Pathan culture. In fact, he had come to nonviolence well before meeting Gandhi, seeing it as necessary for overcoming the incessant feuding of his Pathan people. The Prophet Muhammad's mission, he declared, was "to free the oppressed, to feed the poor, and to clothe the naked."[10] Nonviolent struggle was a form of jihad, or Islamic holy war, and the suffering it generated was a kind of martyrdom. Furthermore, he linked nonviolent struggle to Pathan male virtues of honor, bravery, and strength.

By the mid-1940s, however, Pathan Muslims increasingly favored a separate state (Pakistan) rather than an alliance with Hindus in a unified India, as Gandhi and Abdul Khan so fervently hoped for. Abdul Khan's political critics stigmatized him as "Hindu," while many orthodox Islamic scholars viewed his more inclusive and nonviolent view of Islam as a challenge to their authority and their understanding of the faith. When the Congress finally and reluctantly accepted the partition of India into two states, Abdul Khan felt betrayed. "You have thrown us to the wolves," he said.

Despite his deep disappointment about partition and the immense violence that accompanied it, Abdul Khan declared his allegiance to Pakistan. But neither he nor his Servants of God followers could gain the trust of the new Pakistani authorities, who refused to recognize their role as freedom fighters in the struggle against colonial rule. His long opposition to the creation of Pakistan made his patriotism suspect; his advocacy of Pathan unity raised fears that he was fostering the secession of that region; and his political liberalism and criticism of Pakistani military governments generated suspicions that he was a communist. Thus he was repeatedly imprisoned in Pakistan and in conditions far worse than he had experienced in British jails. He viewed Pakistan as a British effort at divide and rule, "so that the Hindus and the Muslims might forever be at war and forget that they were brothers."[11]

Until his death in 1988 at the age of ninety-eight, he held firmly to his Islam-based nonviolent beliefs. But like Gandhi, he was far more widely admired than he was imitated.

Questions: Why do you think Abdul Khan is generally unknown? Where does he fit in the larger history of the twentieth century?

Particularly since the 1960s, the economy benefited from extensive foreign investment and loans. Almost all black Africans were involved in this complex modern economy, working in urban industries or mines, providing labor for white-owned farms, or receiving payments from relatives who did. The extreme dependence of most Africans on the white-controlled economy rendered individuals highly vulnerable to repressive action, but collectively the threat to withdraw their essential labor also gave them a powerful weapon.

A further unique feature of the South African situation was the overwhelming prominence of race, expressed since 1948 in the official policy of apartheid, which attempted to separate blacks from whites in every conceivable way while retaining

Africans' labor power in the white-controlled economy. An enormous apparatus of repression enforced that system. Rigid "pass laws" monitored and tried to control the movement of Africans into the cities, where they were subjected to extreme forms of social segregation. In the rural areas, a series of impoverished and over-crowded "native reserves," or Bantustans, served as ethnic homelands that kept Africans divided along tribal lines. Even though racism was present in colonial India, nothing of this magnitude developed there.

As in India, various forms of opposition—resistance to conquest, rural rebellions, urban strikes, and independent churches—arose to contest the manifest injustices of South African life. There too an elite-led political party provided an organizational umbrella for many of the South African resistance efforts in the twentieth century. Established in 1912, the African National Congress (ANC), like its Indian predecessor, was led by male, educated, professional, and middle-class Africans who sought not to overthrow the existing order, but to be accepted as "civilized men" within it. They appealed to the liberal, humane, and Christian values that white society claimed. For four decades, its leaders pursued peaceful and moderate protest—petitions, multiracial conferences, delegations appealing to the authorities—even as racially based segregationist policies were implemented one after another.

Change
How did South Africa's struggle against white domination change over time?

Women were denied full membership in the ANC until 1943 and were restricted to providing catering and entertainment services for the men. But they took action in other arenas. In 1913, they organized a successful protest against carrying passes, an issue that endured through much of the twentieth century. Rural women in the 1920s used church-based networks to organize boycotts of local shops and schools. Women were likewise prominent in trade union protests, including wage demands for domestic servants and washerwomen. By 1948, when the Afrikaner-led National Party came to power on a platform of apartheid, it was clear that peaceful protest, whether organized by men or by women, had produced no meaningful movement toward racial equality.

During the 1950s, a new and younger generation of the ANC leadership, which now included Nelson Mandela, broadened its base of support and launched non-violent civil disobedience—boycotts, strikes, demonstrations, and the burning of the hated passes that all Africans were required to carry. All of these actions were similar to and inspired by the tactics that Gandhi had pioneered in South Africa and used in India twenty to thirty years earlier. The government of South Africa responded with tremendous repression, including the shooting of sixty-nine unarmed demonstrators at Sharpville in 1960, the banning of the ANC, and the imprisonment of its leadership, including Nelson Mandela.

At this point, the freedom struggle in South Africa took a different direction than it had in India. Its major political parties were now illegal. Underground nationalist leaders turned to armed struggle, authorizing selected acts of sabotage and assassination, while preparing for guerrilla warfare in camps outside the country. Active opposition within South Africa was now primarily expressed by student groups that were part of the Black Consciousness movement, an effort to foster pride, unity, and political awareness among the country's African majority, with a particular emphasis on mobilizing women for the struggle. Such young people were at the center of an explosion of protest in 1976 in a sprawling, segregated, impoverished black neighborhood called Soweto, outside Johannesburg, in which hundreds were killed. The initial trigger for the uprising was the government's decision to enforce education for Africans in the hated language of the white Afrikaners rather than English. However, the momentum of the Soweto rebellion persisted, and by the mid-1980s spreading urban violence and the radicalization of urban young people had forced the government to declare a state of emergency. Furthermore, South Africa's black labor movement, legalized only in 1979, became increasingly active and political. In June 1986, to commemorate the tenth anniversary of the Soweto uprising, the Congress of South African Trade Unions orchestrated a general strike involving some 2 million workers.

Beyond this growing internal pressure, South Africa faced mounting international

Nelson Mandela
In April 1994, the long struggle against apartheid and white domination in South Africa came to an end in the country's first democratic and nonracial election. The symbol of that triumph was Nelson Mandela, long a political prisoner, head of the African National Congress, and the country's first black African president. He is shown here voting in that historic election. (© Peter Turnley/Corbis)

demands to end apartheid as well. Exclusion from most international sporting events, including the Olympics; the refusal of many artists and entertainers to perform in South Africa; economic boycotts; the withdrawal of private investment funds—all of this isolated South Africa from a Western world in which its white rulers claimed membership. None of this had any parallel in India.

The combination of these internal and external pressures persuaded many white South Africans by the late 1980s that discussion with African nationalist leaders was the only alternative to a massive, bloody, and futile struggle to preserve white privileges. The outcome was the abandonment of key apartheid policies, the release of Nelson Mandela from prison, the legalization of the ANC, and a prolonged process of negotiations that in 1994 resulted in national elections, which brought the ANC

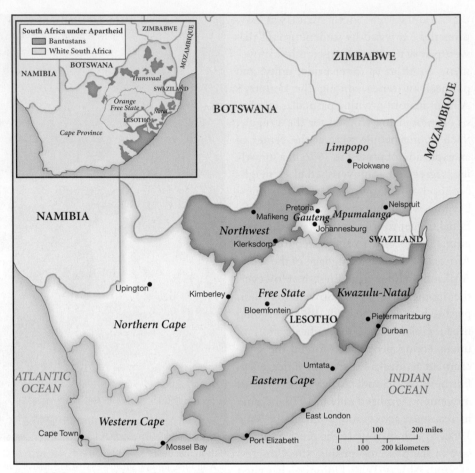

Map 22.3   South Africa after Apartheid

Under apartheid, all black Africans were officially designated as residents of small, scattered, impoverished Bantustans, shown on the inset map. Many of these people, of course, actually lived in white South Africa, where they worked. The main map shows the new internal organization of the country as it emerged after 1994, with the Bantustans abolished and the country divided into nine provinces. Lesotho and Swaziland had been British protectorates during the colonial era and subsequently became separate independent countries, although surrounded by South African territory.

to power. To the surprise of almost everyone, the long nightmare of South African apartheid came to an end without a racial bloodbath (see Map 22.3).

As in India, the South African nationalist movement was divided and conflicted. Unlike in India, though, these divisions did not occur along religious lines. Rather, it was race, ethnicity, and ideology that generated dissension and sometimes violence. Whereas the ANC generally favored a broad alliance of everyone opposed to apartheid (black Africans, Indians, "coloreds" or mixed-race people, and sympathetic whites), a smaller group known as the Pan Africanist Congress rejected cooperation with other racial groups and limited its membership to black Africans. During the urban uprisings of the 1970s and 1980s, young people supporting the Black Consciousness movements and those following Mandela and the ANC waged war against each other in the townships of South African cities. Perhaps most threatening to the unity of the nationalist struggle were the separatist tendencies of the Zulu-based Inkatha Freedom Party. Its leader, Gatsha Buthelezi, had cooperated with the apartheid state and even received funding from it. As negotiations for a transition to African rule unfolded in the early 1990s, considerable violence between Inkatha followers, mostly Zulu migrant workers, and ANC supporters broke out in a number of cities. None of this, however, approached the massive killing of Hindus and Muslims that accompanied the partition of India. South Africa, unlike India, acquired its political freedom as an intact and unified state.

SUMMING UP SO FAR

How and why did the anticolonial struggles in India and South Africa differ?

Experiments with Freedom

Africa's first modern nationalist hero, Kwame Nkrumah (KWAH-may ehn-KROO-mah) of Ghana, paraphrased a biblical quotation when he urged his followers, "Seek ye first the political kingdom and all these other things will be added unto you." But would winning the political kingdom of independence or freedom from European rule really produce "all these other things"—release from state oppression, industrial growth, economic development, reasonably unified nations, and a better life for all? That was the central question confronting the new nations emerging from colonial rule. They were joined in that quest by already independent but nonindustrialized countries and regions such as China, Thailand, Ethiopia, Iran, Turkey, and Central and South America. Together they formed the bloc of nations known variously as the third world, the developing countries, or the Global South. Those countries accounted for about 90 percent of the fourfold increase in human numbers that the world experienced during the twentieth century. Between 1950 and 2000, the populations of Asia and Africa alone grew from 64 percent of the world's total to 70 percent, with an estimated increase to 79 percent by 2050. (See Snapshot: World Population Growth, page 994.) That immense surge in global population, at one level a great triumph for the human species, also underlay many of the difficulties these nations faced as they conducted their various experiments with freedom.

Almost everywhere, the moment of independence generated something close to euphoria. Having emerged from the long night of colonial rule, free peoples had the opportunity to build anew. The developing countries would be laboratories for fresh approaches to creating modern states, nations, cultures, and economies. In the decades that followed, experiments with freedom multiplied, but the early optimism was soon tempered by the difficulties and disappointments of those tasks.

SNAPSHOT   World Population Growth, 1950–2011

The great bulk of the world's population growth in the second half of the twentieth century occurred in the developing countries of Asia, Africa, the Middle East, and Latin America.[12]

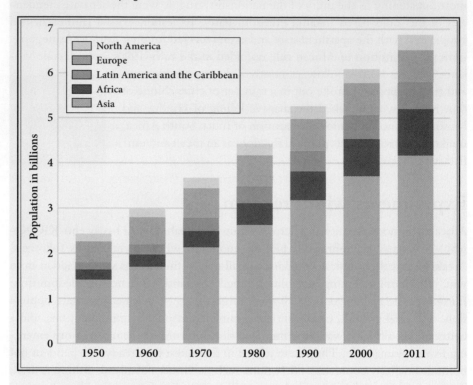

Experiments in Political Order: Party, Army, and the Fate of Democracy

All across the developing world, efforts to create political order had to contend with a set of common conditions. Populations were exploding, and expectations for independence ran very high, often exceeding the available resources. Many developing countries were culturally very diverse, with little loyalty to a central state. Nonetheless, public employment mushroomed as the state assumed greater responsibility for economic development. In conditions of widespread poverty and weak private economies, groups and individuals sought to capture the state, or parts of it, both for the salaries and status it offered and for the opportunities for private enrichment that public office provided.

This was the formidable setting in which developing countries had to hammer out new political systems. The range of that effort was immense: Communist Party control in China, Vietnam, and Cuba; multiparty democracy in India and South

Africa; one-party democracy in Mexico, Tanzania, and Senegal; military regimes for a time in much of Latin America, Africa, and the Middle East; personal dictatorships in Uganda and the Philippines. In many places, one kind of political system followed another in kaleidoscopic succession.

As colonial rule drew to a close, European authorities in many places attempted to transplant democratic institutions to colonies they had long governed with such a heavy and authoritarian hand. They established legislatures, permitted elections, allowed political parties to operate, and in general anticipated the development of constitutional, parliamentary, multiparty democracies similar to their own.

It was in India that such a political system established its deepest roots. There Western-style democracy, including regular elections, multiple parties, civil liberties, and peaceful changes in government, has been practiced almost continuously since independence. What made this remarkable democratic continuity possible?

The struggle for independence in India had been a prolonged affair, thus providing time for an Indian political leadership to sort itself out. Furthermore, the British began to hand over power in a gradual way well before complete independence was granted in 1947. Thus a far larger number of Indians had useful administrative or technical skills than was the case elsewhere. In sharp contrast to most African countries, for example, the nationalist movement in India was embodied in a single national party (the Congress Party), which encompassed a wide variety of other parties and interest groups. Its leaders, Gandhi and Nehru in particular, were genuinely committed to democratic practice, which, some have argued, allowed elites from the many and varied groups of Indian society to find a place in the political system. Even the tragic and painful partition of colonial India into two countries minimized a major source of internal discord as independent India was born. Moreover, Indian statehood could be built on common cultural and political traditions that were far more deeply rooted than in many former colonies.

Elsewhere in the colonial world, democracy proved a far more fragile transplant. Among the new states of Africa, for example, few retained their democratic institutions beyond the initial post-independence decade. Many of the apparently popular political parties that had led the struggle for independence lost mass support and were swept away by military coups. When the army took power in Ghana in 1966, no one lifted a finger to defend the party that had led the country to independence only nine years earlier. Other states evolved into one-party systems, and still others degenerated into personal tyrannies or dictatorships. Freedom from colonial rule certainly did not automatically generate the internal political freedoms associated with democracy.

Africans sometimes suggested that their traditional cultures, based on communal rather than individualistic values and concerned with achieving consensus rather than majority rule, were not compatible with the competitiveness of party politics. Others argued that Western-style democracy was simply inadequate for the tasks of development confronting the new states. Creating national unity was surely more difficult when competing political parties identified primarily with particular ethnic

■ **Change**
What led to the erosion of democracy and the establishment of military government in much of Africa and Latin America?

or "tribal" groups, as was frequently the case in Africa. Certainly Europe did not begin its modernizing process with such a system. Why, many Africans asked, should they be expected to do so?

The economic disappointments of independence also contributed to the erosion of support for democracy. By almost any measure, African economic performance since independence has been the poorest in the developing world. As a result, college and high school graduates were unable to find the white-collar careers they expected; urban migrants had little opportunity for work; farmers received low prices for their cash crops; consumers resented shortages and inflation; and millions of impoverished and malnourished peasants lived on the brink of starvation. These were people for whom independence was unable to fulfill even the most minimal of expectations, let alone the grandiose visions of a better life that so many had embraced in the early 1960s. Since modern governments everywhere staked their legitimacy on economic performance, it is little wonder that many Africans became disaffected and withdrew their support from governments they had enthusiastically endorsed only a few years earlier. Further resentments arose from the privileges of the relatively well-educated elite who had found high-paying jobs in the growing bureaucracies of the newly independent states. Such grievances often found expression in ethnic conflict, as Africa's immense cultural diversity became intensely politicized. An ethnically based civil war in Nigeria during the late 1960s cost the lives of millions, while in the mid-1990s ethnic hatred led Rwanda into the realm of genocide. (See Zooming In: Mozambique, page 998.)

These economic disappointments, class resentments, and ethnic conflicts provided the context for numerous military takeovers. By the early 1980s, the military had intervened in at least thirty of Africa's forty-six independent states and actively governed more than half of them. In doing so, they swept aside the old political parties and constitutions and vowed to begin anew, while promising to return power to civilians and restore democracy at some point in the future.

A similar wave of military interventions swept over Latin America during the 1960s and 1970s, leaving Brazil, Argentina, Peru, Chile, Uruguay, Bolivia, the Dominican Republic, and other countries governed at times by their armed forces. However, the circumstances in Latin America were quite different from those in Africa. While military rule was something new and unexpected in Africa, Latin American armed forces had long intervened in political life. The region had also largely escaped the bitter ethnic conflicts that afflicted so many African states, though its class antagonisms were more clearly defined and expressed. Furthermore, Latin American societies in general were far more modernized and urbanized than those of Africa. And while newly independent African states remained linked to their former European rulers, long-independent Latin American states lived in the shadow of a dominant United States. "Poor Mexico," bemoaned Porfirio Díaz, that country's dictator before the Mexican Revolution, "so far from God and so close to the United States."

But beneath the changes in political regimes in Latin America lay the more deeply rooted transformations of the twentieth century: population growth and large-scale migration from rural areas to the urban slums of big cities; industrial development and trade union activism; rural poverty and sharp divisions between rich and poor; resentment against American economic and political power; and the influence of ideas deriving from European socialism, the American New Deal, the Mexican Revolution, and Christian "liberation theology." All of this pushed Latin American politics away from the elitist orientation that had largely prevailed since independence toward concerns with economic development, social reform, mass participation, nationalism, and anti-imperialism.

These issues found expression in a wide range of political movements and government programs. Early in the century, the revolution in Mexico and a peaceful program of radical state-directed social reforms in Uruguay were early examples of the new politics. During the 1930s, the Aprista movement in Peru blended ideas of Latin American uniqueness, democratic socialism, the full integration of indigenous peoples into society, and anti-imperialism into a political outlook that had appeal in many parts of the continent. The "social justice" program of Juan Perón in Argentina between 1945 and 1955 enacted a large body of social and labor legislation, aimed largely at the mass of long-ignored and marginalized urban workers. A broadly similar program took shape in Brazil under the leadership of Getúlio Vargas. The Cuban Revolution of 1959 likewise gave expression to these ideas

Slums and Skyscrapers
The enormous disparities that have accompanied modern economic development in Latin America and elsewhere are illustrated in this photograph from São Paulo, Brazil. (© Florian Kopp/Image BROKER/age fotostock)

and sought to export them to the rest of Latin America. The 1960s and later years witnessed guerrilla warfare in Peru, Bolivia, and Colombia and short-lived left-wing governments in Guatemala, Brazil, and Nicaragua.

Chile illustrated both these new political directions and the fears they generated. In 1970, Chileans narrowly elected to the presidency a Marxist politician, Salvador Allende, who soon launched an ambitious program to achieve a peaceful transition to socialism. In an effort to redistribute wealth, he ordered prices frozen and wages raised. Nationalization of major industries followed—including copper, coal, steel, and many banks—without compensation to their former owners, many of whom were foreign corporations. In rural areas, land reform programs soon seized large estates, redistributing them to small farmers. And Allende warmly welcomed Fidel Castro for a month-long visit in 1971. It was an audacious effort to achieve genuinely revolutionary change by legal and peaceful means.

Mozambique: Civil War and Reconciliation

In the decades after independence, many Asian and African countries experienced bitter civil wars—Nigeria, Rwanda, Somalia, Sri Lanka, Cambodia, and Burma among others. As their conflicts ended, these countries have faced the issue of reconciliation among former enemies who often hated, despised, and feared one another. Such has been the case in Mozambique, a

The *Tree of Life* in Mozambique in 2005.

Portuguese colony in southeastern Africa, which achieved its independence in 1975, after a ten-year armed struggle led by a party called the Front for the Liberation of Mozambique (FRELIMO).

Mozambique's newly independent government, controlled by FRELIMO, came to power in a single-party Marxist-oriented state with strong support from the communist world. Some of its policies—a socialist agenda, dismissal of many traditional chiefs, imprisonment of opponents in "reeducation" camps, forced resettlement of scattered farmers in communal villages—soon antagonized many people. Opposition came together as the Mozambique National Resistance (RENAMO) and found support from the threatened white-ruled regimes in neighboring Rhodesia and South Africa. As weapons from many sources flowed into the country, a terrible civil war erupted in 1977, lasting fifteen years. Alto-

gether, 1 million or more people were killed and another 5 million were displaced, accounting for nearly half the country's population. On both sides, it was a brutal conflict, with RENAMO especially employing systematic mass killings, rape, and mutilation as a tactic of war. By the end of the 1980s, the military stalemate in Mozambique, coupled with the collapse of white rule in southern Africa and the abandonment of communism in the Soviet Union and China, provided conditions for negotiations, an end to the fighting, and finally a new constitution. In the early 1990s, Mozambique emerged as a democratic, multiparty, market-oriented democracy, and since then the nation has held regular elections every five years.

RENAMO supporters have participated in those elections, and some of their fighters have been integrated into Mozambique's military forces. But the Mozambican government has not initiated any large-scale process to deal with the enormous abuse and trauma that so many people experienced. State authorities authorized a general amnesty for all crimes committed during the civil war, but they expressed no official recognition of the suffering

photo: David Rose/Panos Pictures

But internal opposition mounted—from the bureaucracy, military officers, church hierarchy, and wealthy business and landlord elites as well as various small-business and middle-class elements, climaxing in a huge strike in late 1972. Furthermore, the U.S. government, which had long armed, funded, and trained military forces throughout Latin America, actively opposed the Allende regime, as did U.S. corporations. A CIA document declared, "It is firm and continuing policy that Allende be overthrown by a coup."[13] And in September 1973, he was. What followed was an extraordinarily repressive military regime, headed by General Augusto Pinochet, which lasted until the restoration of democracy in 1988.

involved or compassion for the victims. Nothing similar to South Africa's Truth and Reconciliation Commission emerged in Mozambique. The government, Christian churches, and local chiefs alike urged forgiveness without revenge, but offered little to deal with the emotional scars and social conflicts that the civil war had generated. It was, critics charged, "reconciliation without truth." Indirectly, however, by acknowledging the legitimacy of customary institutions and practices, which FRELIMO had earlier tried to destroy, the government made it possible for local initiatives to operate within a traditional setting.

One of these initiatives involved the spirits of dead soldiers, known as *gamba*, who returned to possess particular individuals. Traditional healers created rituals designed to appease these spirits. Such ceremonies brought alienated people together, reminded them of the violence of the civil war, elicited confessions of wrongdoing, and set appropriate compensations. In these encounters, local people, whose families and communities were often torn apart by the war, found a way to confront the past and to experience some reconciliation within a culturally familiar setting.

Yet another remarkable private initiative of reconciliation with the past involved young people, many of whom had been forced to participate in the civil war as teenagers. In partnership with the Christian Council of Mozambique, they created a "transforming weapons into tools" project, which sought to collect and destroy some of the millions of weapons left over from the civil war. Animated by the biblical "swords into plowshares" notion, this project invited people to exchange their weapons for tools, such as sewing machines, hoes, plows, bicycles, and construction material. Hundreds of thousands of weapons, perhaps millions, were turned in. One village that recovered a very large number of weapons received a tractor in return. The weapons were then taken apart and turned over to Mozambican artists, who fashioned them into remarkable sculptures—chairs, trees, animals, musical instruments, bicycles, human figures, and more.

Among the most memorable of those sculptures was a *Tree of Life*, some ten feet tall and weighing 1,000 pounds, accompanied by birds and animals, all made from pieces of dismantled weapons. The symbolism of weapons transformed into objects of comfort or inspiration allowed people to confront the past, while evoking some sense of hope and possibility from the tragedy of the civil war. There was irony too in this project. The *Tree of Life* was commissioned by and displayed in the British Museum, thus returning to Europe some of the weapons that originated in Europe to fuel the civil war in Mozambique.

Questions: What common features do these various reconciliation efforts share, and how do they differ? What possible responses to them can you imagine?

Chile's return to democratic practice was a small part of a remarkable late twentieth-century political reversal, a globalization of democracy that brought popular movements, multiparty elections, and new constitutions to many countries all around the world. This included the end of military and autocratic rule in Spain, Portugal, and Greece as well as the stunning rise of democratic movements, parties, and institutions amid the collapse of communism in the Soviet Union and Eastern Europe. But the most extensive expression of this global reemergence of democracy lay in the developing countries. By 2000, almost all Latin American countries had abandoned their military-controlled regimes and returned to some form of democratic governance. So too did most African states previously ruled by soldiers, dictators, or single parties. In Asia, authoritarian regimes, some long established, gave way to more pluralistic and participatory political systems in South Korea, Taiwan, Thailand, the Philippines, Iraq, and Indonesia. And in 2011, mass movements in various Arab countries—Tunisia, Egypt, Libya, Syria, Bahrain, Yemen—had challenged or ended the hold of entrenched, corrupt, and autocratic rulers, while proclaiming their commitment to democracy, human dignity, and honest government. What might explain this global pattern and its expression in the Global South in particular?

One factor surely was the untethering of the ideas of democracy and human rights from their Western origins. By the final quarter of the twentieth century, democracy was increasingly viewed as a universal political principle to which all could aspire rather than an alien and imposed system deriving from the West. Democracy, like communism, feminism, modern science, and Christianity, was a Western import that took root and substantially lost its association with the West. It was therefore increasingly available as a vehicle for social protest in the rest of the world.

Perhaps the most important internal factor favoring a revival of democracy lay in the apparent failure of authoritarian governments to remedy disastrous economic situations, to raise standards of living, to provide jobs for the young, and to curb pervasive corruption. The oppressive and sometimes-brutal behavior of repressive governments humiliated and outraged many. Furthermore, the growth of civil society with its numerous voluntary groups provided a social foundation, independent of the state, for demanding change. Disaffected students, professionals, urban workers, religious organizations, women's groups, and more joined in a variety of grassroots movements, some of them mobilized through social media, to insist on democratic change as a means to a better life. Such movements found encouragement in the demands for democracy that accompanied the South African struggle against apartheid and the collapse of Soviet and Eastern European communism. And the end of the cold war reduced the willingness of the major industrial powers to underwrite their authoritarian client states.

But the consolidation of democratic practice was an uncertain and highly variable process. Some elected leaders, such as Hugo Chávez in Venezuela and Vladimir Putin in Russia, turned authoritarian once in office. Even where parliaments existed, they were often quite circumscribed in their powers. Outright electoral fraud tainted democratic institutions in many places, while established elites and oligarchies found it possible to exercise considerable influence even in formal democracies, and not only in the Global South. Chinese authorities brutally crushed a democratic movement in 1989. The Algerian military sponsored elections in 1992 and then abruptly canceled them when an Islamic party seemed poised to win. And the political future of the Arab Spring remained highly uncertain, as a military strongman became a civilian politician and returned to power in Egypt in 2014. Nonetheless, this worldwide revival of democracy represented the globalization of what had been a Western idea and the continuation of the political experiments that had begun with independence.

Experiments in Economic Development: Changing Priorities, Varying Outcomes

At the top of the agenda everywhere in the Global South was economic development, a process that meant growth or increasing production as well as distributing the fruits of that growth to raise living standards. This quest for development, now operating all across the planet, represented the universal acceptance of beliefs unheard of not many centuries earlier—that poverty was no longer inevitable and that it was possible to deliberately improve the material conditions of life for everyone. Economic development was a central promise of all independence struggles, and it was increasingly the standard by which people measured and granted legitimacy to their governments.

Achieving economic development, however, was no easy or automatic task. It took place in societies sharply divided by class, religion, ethnic group, and gender and in the face of explosive population growth. In many places, colonial rule had provided only the most slender foundations for modern development, as new nations often came to independence with low rates of literacy, few people with managerial experience, a weak private economy, and transportation systems oriented to export rather than national integration. Furthermore, the entire effort occurred in a world split by rival superpowers and economically dominated by the powerful capitalist economies of the West. Despite their political independence, most developing countries had little leverage in negotiations with the wealthy nations of the Global North and their immense transnational corporations. It was hardly an auspicious environment in which to seek a fundamental economic transformation.

Beyond these difficulties lay the question of what strategies to pursue. The academic field of "development economics" was new; its experts disagreed and often changed their minds; and conflicting political pressures, both internal and international, only added to the confusion. All of this resulted in considerable controversy, changing policies, and much experimentation.

One fundamental issue lay in the role of the state. All across the developing world and particularly in newly independent nations, most people expected that state authorities would take major responsibility for spurring the economic development of their countries. After all, the private economy was weakly developed; few entrepreneurs had substantial funds to invest; the example of rapid Soviet industrialization under state direction was hopeful; and state control held the promise of protecting vulnerable economies from the ravages of international capitalism. Some state-directed economies had real successes. China launched a major industrialization effort and massive land reform under the leadership of the Communist Party. A communist Cuba, even while remaining dependent on its sugar production, wiped out illiteracy and provided basic health care to its entire population, raising life expectancy to seventy-six years by 1992, equivalent to that of the United States. Elsewhere as well—in Turkey, India, South Korea, and much of Africa—the state provided tariffs, licenses, loans, subsidies, and overall planning, while most productive property was owned privately.

■ **Change**
What obstacles impeded the economic development of third-world countries?

■ **Change**
How and why did thinking about strategies for economic development change over time?

Yet in the last three decades of the twentieth century, an earlier consensus in favor of state direction largely collapsed, replaced by a growing dependence on the market to generate economic development. This was most apparent in the abandonment of much communist planning in China and the return to private farming (see Chapter 21, pages 959–60). India and many Latin American and African states privatized their state-run industries and substantially reduced the role of the state in economic affairs. In part, this sharp change in economic policies reflected the failure, mismanagement, and corruption of many state-run enterprises, but it was also influenced by the collapse in the Soviet Union of the world's first state-dominated economy. Western pressures, exercised through international organizations such as the World Bank, likewise pushed developing countries in a capitalist direction. In China and India, the new approach generated rapid economic growth, but also growing inequalities and social conflict. But as the new millennium dawned, a number of developing countries once again asserted a more prominent role for the state in their quests for economic development and social justice. In China, Russia, Brazil, Saudi Arabia, Mexico, India, and elsewhere, state-owned companies currently buy and sell shares on the stock market, seeking profits in an economic system that has been called "state capitalism." Thus the search for an appropriate balance between state action and market forces in the management of modern economies continues.

A related issue involved the most appropriate posture for developing countries to adopt toward the world market as they sought to industrialize. Should they try to shield themselves from the influences of international capitalism, or were they better off vigorously engaging with the global economy? In the aftermath of the Great Depression of the 1930s, many Latin American countries followed the first path. Their traditional reliance on exporting agricultural products and raw materials had largely collapsed as the world economy sharply contracted (see Chapter 20, page 893). So they chose an alternative approach, known as import substitution industrialization, intended to reduce their dependence on the uncertain global marketplace by processing their own raw materials and manufacturing their own consumer goods behind high tariff barriers if necessary.

Brazil, for example, largely followed such policies from the 1930s through the late 1970s with some success. Between 1968 and 1974, the country experienced rapid industrial growth, dubbed the "Brazilian miracle." By the early 1980s, the country produced about 90 percent of its own consumer goods. But Brazil's industrialization was also accompanied by massive investment by foreign corporations, by the accumulation of a huge national debt to foreign lenders, by periodic bouts of inflation, and by very high levels of social inequality and poverty. Brazil's military president famously remarked in 1971: "The economy is doing fine but the people are doing badly."

The classic contrast to Latin American approaches to industrial development lay in East Asia, where South Korea, Taiwan, Hong Kong, and Singapore chose a different strategy. Rather than focusing on industrial production for domestic consumption, they chose to specialize in particular products for an export market—textiles, electronic goods, and automobiles, for example. Many of these industries were labor-intensive, drawing large numbers of women into the workforce, though at very low wages. Initiated in the 1960s, this export-led industrialization strategy generated rapid economic growth, propelling these countries into the ranks of the industrialized world by the end of the century. In the 1980s and 1990s, Brazil too entered the world market more vigorously, developing export industries in automobiles, steel, aircraft, computers, and more.

Other issues as well inspired debate. In many places, an early emphasis on city-based industrial development, stirred by visions of a rapid transition to modernity, led to a neglect or exploitation of rural areas and agriculture. This "urban bias" subsequently came in for much criticism and some adjustment in spending priorities. (See Snapshot: Global Urbanization, page 1004.) A growing recognition of the role of women in agriculture led to charges of "male bias" in development planning and to mounting efforts to assist women farmers directly. Women were also central to many governments' increased interest in curtailing population growth. Women's access to birth control, education, and employment, it turned out, provided powerful incentives to limit family size. Another debate pitted the advocates of capital- and technology-driven projects (dams and factories, for example) against those who favored investment in "human capital," such as education, technical training, health care, and nutrition. The benefits and drawbacks of foreign aid, investment, and trade have likewise been contentious issues.

Economic development was never simply a matter of technical expertise or deciding among competing theories. Every decision was political, involving winners and losers in terms of power, advantage, and wealth. Where to locate schools, roads, factories, and clinics, for example, provoked endless controversies, some of them expressed in terms of regional or ethnic rivalries. It was an experimental process, and the stakes were high.

The results of those experiments have varied considerably. (See Snapshot, Chapter 23, page 1031, for global variations in economic development.) East Asian countries in general have had the strongest record of economic growth. South Korea, Taiwan, Singapore, and Hong Kong were dubbed "newly industrialized countries," and China boasted the most rapid economic growth in the world by the end of the twentieth century, replacing Japan as the world's second-largest economy. In the 1990s, Asia's other giant, India, opened itself more fully to the world market and launched rapid economic growth with a powerful high-tech sector and an expanding middle class. Oil-producing countries reaped a bonanza when they were able to demand much higher prices for that essential commodity in the 1970s and later. By 2008, Brazil ranked as the eighth-largest economy in the world with a rapidly growing industrial sector, while Turkey and Indonesia numbered in the top twenty. Limited principally to Europe, North America, and Japan in the nineteenth century, industrialization had become a global phenomenon by the early twenty-first.

SNAPSHOT   Global Urbanization, 1950–2014

In 1950, 29.6 percent of the world's population lived in urban areas, while by 2014 that figure had risen to 54 percent. This chart highlights the top twenty cities in terms of their population in those two years.[14] What changes can you identify in the size of those cities and in their geographic distribution?

		1950			2014	
Rank	City	Country	Population in millions	City	Country	Population in millions
1	New York City	USA	12.3	Tokyo	Japan	37.8
2	Tokyo	Japan	11.3	Delhi	India	24.9
3	London	UK	8.4	Shanghai	China	23.0
4	Paris	France	6.5	Mexico City	Mexico	20.84
5	Moscow	USSR	5.6	São Paulo	Brazil	20.83
6	Buenos Aires	Argentina	5.1	Mumbai	India	20.7
7	Chicago	USA	5.0	Osaka	Japan	20.1
8	Calcutta	India	4.5	Beijing	China	19.5
9	Shanghai	China	4.3	New York/Newark	USA	18.6
10	Osaka	Japan	4.2	Cairo	Egypt	18.4
11	Los Angeles	USA	4.0	Dhaka	Bangladesh	17.0
12	Berlin	Germany	3.3	Karachi	Pakistan	16.1
13	Philadelphia	USA	3.1	Buenos Aires	Argentina	15.0
14	Rio de Janeiro	Brazil	2.95	Calcutta	India	14.8
15	Leningrad/St. Petersburg	USSR	2.9	Istanbul	Turkey	14.0
16	Mexico City	Mexico	2.88	Chongqing	China	12.9
17	Bombay/Mumbai	India	2.86	Rio de Janeiro	Brazil	12.8
18	Detroit	USA	2.77	Manila	Philippines	12.76
19	Boston	USA	2.55	Lagos	Nigeria	12.6
20	Cairo	Egypt	2.5	Los Angeles area	USA	12.3

Elsewhere, the story was very different. In most of Africa, much of the Arab world, and parts of Asia—regions representing about one-third of the world's population—there was little sign of catching up, and there had been frequent examples of declining standards of living since the end of the 1960s. Between 1980 and 2000, the average income in forty-three of Africa's poorest countries dropped by 25 percent, pushing living standards for many below what they had been at independence.

But in the early twenty-first century, a number of African countries began to experience encouraging economic growth, an expanding middle class with some money to spend, and more international investment. Some observers began to speak about "Africa rising."

Scholars and politicians alike argue about the reasons for such sharp differences in economic performance. Variations in factors such as geography and natural resources, colonial experiences, regional cultures, the degree of political stability and social equality, state economic policies, population growth rates, and forms of involvement with the world economy—all of these have been invoked to explain the widely diverging trajectories among developing countries.

Microloans
Bangladesh's Grameen Bank pioneered an innovative approach to economic development by offering modest loans to poor people, enabling them to start small businesses. Here a group of women who received such loans meet in early 2004 to make an installment payment to an officer of the bank. (Rafiqur Rahman/Reuters/Landov)

Experiments with Culture: The Role of Islam in Turkey and Iran

The quest for economic development represented the embrace of an emerging global culture of modernity with its scientific outlook, its technological achievements, and its focus on material values. Developing countries were also exposed to the changing culture of the West, including feminism, rock and rap, sexual permissiveness, consumerism, and democracy. But the peoples of the Global South had inherited cultural patterns from the more distant past as well. A common issue all across the developing world involved the uneasy relationship between these older traditions and the more recent outlooks associated with modernity and the West. How should traditional African "medicine men" relate to modern hospitals? What happens to Confucian-based family values when confronted with the urban and commercial growth of recent Chinese history? Such tensions provided the raw material for a series of cultural experiments in the twentieth century, and nowhere were they more consequential than in the Islamic world. No single answer emerged to the question of how Islam and modernity should relate to each other, but the experiences of Turkey and Iran illustrate two quite different approaches to this fundamental issue (see Map 22.4). (See Working with Evidence: Contending for Islam, page 1012, for more on this topic.)

In the aftermath of World War I, modern Turkey emerged from the ashes of the Ottoman Empire, led by an energetic general, Mustafa Kemal Atatürk

■ **Comparison**
In what ways did cultural revolutions in Turkey and Iran reflect different understandings of the role of Islam in modern societies?

Map 22.4   Iran, Turkey, and the Middle East
Among the great contrasts of a very diverse Middle East has been between Turkey, the most secular and Western-oriented country of the region, and Iran, home to the most sustained Islamic revolution in the area.

(ATT-a-turk) (1881–1938), who fought off British, French, Italian, and Greek efforts to dismember what was left of the old empire. Often compared to Peter the Great in Russia (see Chapter 13, page 576), Atatürk then sought to transform his country into a modern, secular, and national state. Such ambitions were not entirely new, for they built upon the efforts of nineteenth-century Ottoman reformers, who, like Atatürk, greatly admired European Enlightenment thinking and sought to bring its benefits to their country.

To Atatürk and his followers, to become modern meant "to enter European civilization completely." They believed that this required totally removing Islam from public life and relegating it to the personal and private realm. Atatürk argued, "Islam will be elevated, if it will cease to be a political instrument." In fact, he sought to broaden access to the religion by translating the Quran into Turkish and issuing the call to prayer in Turkish rather than Arabic.

Atatürk largely ended, however, the direct political role of Islam. The old sultan, or ruler, of the Ottoman Empire, whose position had long been sanctified by Islamic tradition, was deposed as Turkey became a republic. Furthermore, the caliphate, by which Ottoman sultans had claimed leadership of the entire Islamic world, was abolished, although in fact it had atrophied to the point of having almost no real authority outside of Turkey. All Sufi organizations, sacred tombs, and religious schools were closed and outlawed, and a number of religious titles abolished. Islamic courts were likewise dissolved, while secular law codes, modeled on those of Europe, replaced the *sharia*. In history textbooks, pre-Islamic Turkish culture was celebrated as the foundation for all ancient civilizations. The Arabic script in which the Turkish language had long been written was exchanged for a new Western-style alphabet that made literacy much easier but rendered centuries of Ottoman culture inaccessible to these newly literate people. (See Working with Evidence, Source 22.1, page 1012, for an example of Atatürk's thinking.)

The most visible symbols of Atatürk's revolutionary program occurred in the realm of dress. Turkish men were ordered to abandon the traditional headdress known as the fez and to wear brimmed hats. Atatürk proclaimed:

A civilized, international dress is worthy and appropriate for our nation, and we will wear it. Boots or shoes on our feet, trousers on our legs, shirt and tie, jacket and waistcoat—and of course, to complete these, a cover with a brim on our heads.[15]

Although women were not forbidden to wear the veil, many elite women abandoned it and set the tone for feminine fashion in Turkey.

In Atatürk's view, the emancipation of women was a cornerstone of the new Turkey. In a much-quoted speech, he declared:

> If henceforward the women do not share in the social life of the nation, we shall never attain to our full development. We shall remain irremediably backward, incapable of treating on equal terms with the civilizations of the West.[16]

Thus polygamy was abolished; women were granted equal rights in divorce, inheritance, and child custody; and in 1934 Turkish women gained the right to vote and hold public office, a full decade before French women gained that right. Public beaches were now opened to women as well. As in the early Soviet Union, this was a state-directed feminism, responsive to Atatürk's views, rather than reflecting popular demands from women themselves.

These reforms represented a "cultural revolution" unique in the Islamic world of the time, and they were imposed against considerable opposition. After Atatürk's death in 1938, some of them were diluted or rescinded. The call to prayer returned to the traditional Arabic in 1950, and various political groups urged a greater role for Islam in the public arena. Since 2002, a moderate Islamic party has governed the country, while the political role of the military, long the chief defender of Turkish secularism, has diminished. By 2010, an earlier prohibition on women wearing headscarves in universities had largely ended. Nevertheless, the secularism of Atatürk persisted for many Turks and provided a major element in large-scale protests against the government in 2013. But elsewhere in the Islamic world, other solutions to the question of Islam and modernity took shape.

Westernization in Turkey
Mustafa Kemal Atatürk, the founder of modern Turkey, often appeared in public in elegant European dress, symbolizing for his people a sharp break with traditional Islamic ways of living. Here he is dancing with his adopted daughter at her high-society wedding in 1929. (Hulton Archive/Getty Images)

A very different answer emerged in Iran in the final quarter of the twentieth century. That country seemed an unlikely place for an Islamic revolution. Under the government of Shah Mohammad Reza Pahlavi (r. 1941–1979), Iran had undertaken what many saw as a quite successful and largely secular modernization effort. The country had great wealth in oil, a powerful military, a well-educated elite, and a solid alliance with the United States. Furthermore, the shah's so-called White Revolution, intended to promote the country's modernization, had redistributed land to many of Iran's impoverished peasants, granted women the right to vote, invested substantially in rural health care and education, initiated a number of industrial projects, and offered workers a share in the profits of those industries. But beneath the surface of apparent success, discontent and resentment were brewing. Traditional small-scale merchants felt threatened by an explosion of imported Western goods and by competition from large businesses. Religious leaders, the *ulama*, were offended by state control of religious institutions and by secular education programs that bypassed Islamic schools. Educated professionals found Iran's reliance on the West disturbing. Rural migrants to the country's growing cities, especially Tehran, faced rising costs and uncertain employment.

A repressive and often-brutal government allowed little outlet for such grievances. Thus opposition to the shah's regime came to center on the country's many mosques, where Iran's Shia religious leaders invoked memories of earlier persecution and martyrdom as they mobilized that opposition and called for the shah's removal. The emerging leader of that movement was the high-ranking Shia cleric Ayatollah Ruhollah Khomeini (ko-MAY-nee) (1902–1989), who in 1979 returned from long exile in Paris to great acclaim. By then, massive urban demonstrations, strikes, and defections from the military had eroded support for the shah, who abdicated the throne and left the country.

What followed was also a cultural revolution, but one that moved in precisely the opposite direction from that of Atatürk's Turkey—toward, rather than away from, the Islamization of public life. The new government defined itself as an Islamic republic, with an elected parliament and a constitution, but in practice conservative Islamic clerics, headed by Khomeini, exercised dominant power. A Council of Guardians, composed of leading legal scholars, was empowered to interpret the constitution, to supervise elections, and to review legislation—all designed to ensure compatibility with a particular vision of Islam. Opposition to the new regime was harshly crushed, with some 1,800 executions in 1981 alone for those regarded as "waging war against God."[17]

Khomeini believed that the purpose of government was to apply the law of Allah as expressed in the sharia. Thus all judges now had to be competent in Islamic law, and those lacking that qualification were dismissed. The secular law codes under which the shah's government had operated were discarded in favor of those based solely on Islamic precedents. Islamization likewise profoundly affected the domain of education and culture. In June 1980, the new government closed some 200 universities and colleges for two years while textbooks, curricula, and faculty were "purified" of un-Islamic influences. Elementary and secondary schools, largely secular under the shah, now gave priority to religious instruction and the teaching of Arabic, even as about 40,000 teachers lost their jobs for lack of sufficient Islamic piety. Pre-Islamic Persian literature and history were now out of favor, while the history of Islam and Iran's revolution predominated in schools and the mass media. Western loan words were purged from the Farsi language and replaced by their Arabic equivalents.

As in Turkey, the role of women became a touchstone of this Islamic cultural revolution. By 1983, all women were required to wear the modest head-to-toe cov-

Women and the Iranian Revolution
One of the goals of Iran's Islamic revolution was to enforce a more modest and traditional dress code for the country's women. In this photo from 2004, a woman clad in a *chador* and talking on her cell phone walks past a poster of Ayatollah Khomeini, who led that revolution in 1979. (AP Images)

ering known as hijab, a regulation enforced by roving groups of militants, or "revolutionary guards." Those found with "bad hijab" were subject to harassment and sometimes lashings or imprisonment. Sexual segregation was imposed in schools, parks, beaches, and public transportation. The legal age of marriage for girls, set at eighteen under the shah, was reduced to nine with parental consent and thirteen, later raised to fifteen, without it. Married women could no longer file for divorce or attend school. Yet, despite such restrictions, many women supported the revolution and over the next several decades found far greater opportunities for employment and higher education than before. By the early twenty-first century, almost 60 percent of university students were women. And women's right to vote remained intact.

While Atatürk's cultural revolution of westernization and secularism was largely an internal affair with little interest in extending the Turkish model abroad, Khomeini clearly sought to export Iran's Islamic revolution. He openly called for the replacement of insufficiently Islamic regimes in the Middle East and offered training and support for their opponents. In Lebanon, Syria, Bahrain, Saudi Arabia, Iraq, and elsewhere, Khomeini appealed to Shia minorities and other disaffected people, and Iran became a model to which many Islamic radicals looked. An eight-year war with Saddam Hussein's highly secularized Iraq (1980–1988) was one of the outcomes and generated enormous casualties. That conflict reflected the differences between Arabs and Persians, between Sunni and Shia versions of Islam, and between a secular Iraqi regime and Khomeini's revolutionary Islamic government.

After Khomeini's death in 1989, some elements of this revolution eased a bit. For a time, enforcement of women's dress code was not so stringent, and a more moderate government came to power in 1997, raising hopes for a loosening of strict

Islamic regulations. By 2005, however, more conservative elements were back in control and a new crackdown on women's clothing soon surfaced. A heavily disputed election in 2009 revealed substantial opposition to the country's rigid Islamic regime, and a more moderate leadership returned to power in 2013. Iran's ongoing Islamic revolution, however, did not mean the abandonment of economic modernity. The country's oil revenues continued to fund its development, and by the early twenty-first century Iran was actively pursuing nuclear power and perhaps nuclear weapons, in defiance of Western opposition to these policies.

REFLECTIONS

History in the Middle of the Stream

Historians are usually more at ease telling stories that have clear endings, such as those that describe ancient Egyptian civilization, Chinese maritime voyages, the collapse of the Aztec Empire, or the French Revolution. There is a finality to these stories and a distance from them that makes it easier for historians to assume the posture of detached observers, even if their understandings of those events change over time. Finality, distance, and detachment are harder to come by when historians are describing the events of the past century, for many of its processes are clearly not over. The United States' role as a global superpower and its wars in Iraq and Afghanistan, the fate of democracy in Latin America and the Arab world, the rise of China and India as economic giants, the position of Islam in Turkey and Iran— all of these are unfinished stories, their outcomes unknown and unknowable. In dealing with such matters, historians write from the middle of the stream, often uncomfortably, rather than from the banks, where they might feel more at ease.

In part, that discomfort arises from questions about the future that such issues inevitably raise. Can the spread of nuclear weapons be halted? Will democracy flourish globally? Are Islamic and Christian civilizations headed for a global clash? Can African countries replicate the economic growth experience of India and China? Historians in particular are uneasy about responding to such questions because they are so aware of the unexpectedness and surprising quality of the historical process. Yet those questions about the future are legitimate and important, for as the nineteenth-century Danish philosopher Søren Kierkegaard remarked, "Life can only be understood backward, but it is lived forward." History, after all, is the only guide we have to the possible shape of that future. So, like everyone before us, we stumble on, both individually and collectively, largely in the dark, using analogies from the past as we make our way ahead.

These vast uncertainties about the future provide a useful reminder that although we know the outcomes of earlier human stories—the Asian and African struggles for independence, for example—those who lived that history did not. Such awareness can perhaps engender in us a measure of humility and greater sympathy with those whose lives we study. However we may differ from our ancestors across time and place, we share with them an immense ignorance about what the future holds.

Second Thoughts

What's the Significance?

decolonization, 975–82
Indian National Congress, 984
Mahatma Gandhi / *satyagraha*, 984–87
Muslim League, 986
Muhammad Ali Jinnah, 986
Abdul Ghaffar Khan, 988–89
African National Congress, 990–93
Nelson Mandela, 990–93

Black Consciousness / Soweto, 991
military government, 995–98
Mozambique's civil war, 998–99
globalization of democracy, 999–1000
import substitution industrialization /
    export-led industrialization, 1002–3
Mustafa Kemal Atatürk, 1005–7
Ayatollah Ruhollah Khomeini, 1008–9

Big Picture Questions

1. In what ways did the colonial experience and the struggle for independence shape the agenda of developing countries in the second half of the twentieth century?
2. How would you compare the historical experiences of India and China in the twentieth century?
3. From the viewpoint of the early twenty-first century (2000–2015), to what extent had the goals of nationalist or independence movements been achieved?
4. **Looking Back:** To what extent did the struggle for independence and the postcolonial experience of African and Asian peoples in the twentieth century parallel or diverge from that of the earlier "new nations" in the Americas in the eighteenth and nineteenth centuries?

Next Steps: For Further Study

Chinua Achebe, *Anthills of the Savannah* (1989). A brilliant fictional account of post-independence Nigeria by that country's foremost novelist.

Frederick Cooper, *Africa since 1940* (2002). A readable overview of the coming of independence and efforts at development by a leading historian of Africa.

Ramachandra Guha, *India after Gandhi: The History of the World's Largest Democracy* (2007). A thoughtful account of India's first six decades of independence.

John Isbister, *Promises Not Kept* (2006). A well-regarded consideration of the obstacles to and struggles for development in the Global South.

Nelson Mandela, *Long Walk to Freedom: The Autobiography of Nelson Mandela* (1995). Mandela's account of his own amazing life as nationalist leader and South African statesman.

W. David McIntyre, *British Decolonization, 1946–1997* (1998). A global history of the demise of the British Empire.

Complete Site on Mahatma Gandhi, http://www.mkgandhi.org. A wealth of resources for exploring the life of Gandhi.

"Stunning Economic Growth in China," http://abcnews.go.com/WNT/video/stunning-economic-growth-china-12155618. A brief video from ABC News that explores the reasons for China's rapid economic growth in recent decades.

WORKING WITH EVIDENCE

Contending for Islam

Over the past century, the growing intrusion of the West and of modern secular culture into the Islamic world has prompted acute and highly visible debate among Muslims. Which ideas and influences flowing from the West could Muslims safely utilize, and which should they decisively reject? Are women's rights and democracy compatible with Islam? To what extent should Islam find expression in public life as well as in private religious practice? The documents that follow show something of these controversies while illustrating sharp variations in the understanding of Islam.

Source 22.1

A Secular State for an Islamic Society

Modern Turkey emerged from the ashes of the Ottoman Empire after World War I and adopted a distinctive path of modernization, westernization, and secularism under the leadership of Mustafa Kemal Atatürk (see pages 1005–7). Such policies sought to remove Islam from any significant role in public life, restricting it to the realm of personal devotion, and included abolition of the caliphate, by which Ottoman rulers had claimed leadership of the entire Islamic world. In a speech delivered in 1927, Atatürk explained and justified these policies, which went against the grain of much Islamic thinking.

- On what grounds did Atatürk justify the abolition of the caliphate?

- What additional actions did he take to remove Islam from a public or political role in the new Turkish state?

- What can you infer about Atatürk's view of Islam?

- How did Atatürk's conception of a Turkish state differ from that of Ottoman authorities? In what ways did he build upon Ottoman reforms of the nineteenth century? (See Chapter 19, pages 846–49.)

Mustafa Kemal Atatürk
Speech to the General Congress of the Republican Party
1927

[Our Ottoman rulers] hoped to unite the entire Islamic world in one body, to lead it and to govern it. For this purpose, [they] assumed the title of Caliph [successor to the Prophet Muhammad]. . . . It is an unrealizable aim to attempt to unite in one tribe the various races existing on the earth, thereby abolishing all boundaries. . . .

If the Caliph and the Caliphate were to be invested with a dignity embracing the whole of Islam . . . , a crushing burden would be imposed on Turkey. . . . [Furthermore], will Persia or Afghanistan, which are [Muslim] states, recognize the authority of the Caliph in a single matter? No, and this is quite justifiable, because it would be in contradiction to the independence of the state, to the sovereignty of the people.

[The current constitution] laid down as the first duty of the Grand National Assembly that "the prescriptions of the Shari'a [Islamic law] should be put into force. . . ." [But] if a state, having among its subjects elements professing different religions and being compelled to act justly and impartially toward all of them . . . , it is obliged to respect freedom of opinion and conscience. . . . The Muslim religion includes freedom of religious opinion. . . . Will not every grown-up person in the new Turkish state be free to select his own religion? . . . When the first favorable opportunity arises, the nation must act to eliminate these superfluities [the enforcement of sharia] from our Constitution. . . .

Under the mask of respect for religious ideas and dogmas, the new Party [in opposition to Atatürk's reformist plans] addressed itself to the people in the following words: "We want the re-establishment of the Caliphate; we are satisfied with the religious law; we shall protect the Medressas [Islamic schools], the Tekkes [places for Sufi worship], the pious institutions, the Softahs [students in religious schools], the Sheikhs [Sufi masters], and their disciples. . . . The party of Mustapha Kemal, having abolished the Caliphate, is breaking Islam into ruins; they will make you into unbelievers . . . they will make you wear hats." Can anyone pretend that the style of propaganda used by the Party was not full of these reactionary appeals? . . .

Gentlemen, it was necessary to abolish the fez [a distinctive Turkish hat with no brim], which sat on our heads as a sign of ignorance, of fanaticism, of hatred to progress and civilization, and to adopt in its place the hat, the customary headdress of the whole civilized world, thus showing that no difference existed in the manner of thought between the Turkish nation and the whole family of civilized mankind. . . . [Thus] there took place the closing of the Tekkes, of the convents, and of the mausoleums, as well as the abolition of all sects and all kinds of [religious] titles. . . .

Could a civilized nation tolerate a mass of people who let themselves be led by the nose by a herd of Sheikhs, Dedes, Seids, Tschelebis, Babas, and Emirs [various religious titles]? . . . Would not one therewith have committed the greatest, most irreparable error to the cause of progress and awakening?

Source: *A Speech Delivered by Ghazi Mustapha Kemal, October 1927* (Leipzig: K. F. Koehler, 1929), 377–79, 591–93, 595–98, 717, 721–22.

Source 22.2
Toward an Islamic Society

Even as Kemal Atatürk was seeking to remove Islam from the public life of Turkey, a newly formed Muslim organization in Egypt was strongly advocating precisely the opposite course of action. Founded in 1928 by impoverished schoolteacher Hassan al-Banna (1906–1949), the Muslim Brotherhood argued in favor of "government that will act in conformity to the law and Islamic principles." As the earliest mass movement in the Islamic world advocating such ideas, the Brotherhood soon attracted a substantial following, including many poor urban residents recently arrived from the countryside. Long a major presence in Egyptian political life, the Brotherhood has frequently come into conflict with state authorities. In 1936, it published a pamphlet, addressed to Egyptian and other Arab political leaders, which spelled out its views about the direction toward which a proper Islamic society should move.

- How does this document define the purposes of government?
- How does the Muslim Brotherhood understand the role of Islam in public life?
- To what extent was this document anti-Western in its orientation?
- How might Kemal Atatürk respond to these views?

THE MUSLIM BROTHERHOOD
Toward the Light
1936

After having studied the ideals which ought to inspire a renascent nation on the spiritual level, we wish to offer, in conclusion, some practical suggestions. . . . The following are the chapter headings for a reform based upon the true spirit of Islam:

I. In the political, judicial, and administrative fields:

1st. To prohibit political parties and to direct the forces of the nation toward the formation of a united front;

2nd. To reform the law in such a way that it will be entirely in accordance with Islamic legal practice;

3rd. To build up the army, to increase the number of youth groups; to instill in youth the spirit of holy struggle, faith, and self-sacrifice;

4th. To strengthen the ties among Islamic countries and more particularly among Arab countries which is a necessary step toward serious examination of the question of the defunct Caliphate;

5th. To propagate an Islamic spirit within the civil administration so that all officials will understand the need for applying the teachings of Islam;

6th. To supervise the personal conduct of officials because the private life and the administrative life of these officials forms an indivisible whole; . . .

9th. Government will act in conformity to the law and to Islamic principles; . . . The scheduling of government services ought to take account of the hours set aside for prayer. . . .

II. In the fields of social and everyday practical life:

1st. . . . [T]o strongly condemn attacks upon public mores and morality;

2nd. To find a solution for the problems of women, a solution that will allow her to progress and which will protect her while conforming to Islamic principles. This very important social question should not be ignored because it has become the subject of polemics and of more or less unsupported and exaggerated opinion;

3rd. To root out clandestine or public prostitution and to consider fornication as a reprehensible crime the authors of which should be punished;

4th. To prohibit all games of chance (gaming, lotteries, races, golf);

5th. To stop the use of alcohol and intoxicants—these obliterate the painful consequences of people's evil deeds;

6th. To . . . educate women, to provide quality education for female teachers, school pupils, students, and doctors;

7th. To prepare instructional programs for girls; to develop an educational program for girls different than the one for boys;

8th. Male students should not be mixed with female students—any relationship between unmarried men and women is considered to be wrong until it is approved;

9th. To encourage marriage and procreation—to develop legislation to safeguard the family and to solve marriage problems;

10th. To close dance halls; to forbid dancing;

11th. To censor theater productions and films; to be severe in approving films;

12th. To supervise and approve music;

13th. To approve programs, songs, and subjects before they are released, to use radio to encourage national education;

14th. To confiscate malicious articles and books as well as magazines displaying a grotesque character or spreading frivolity;

15th. To carefully organize vacation centers;

16th. To change the hours when public cafes are opened or closed, to watch the activities of those who habituate them—to direct these people towards wholesome pursuits, to prevent people from spending too much time in these cafes;

17th. To use the cafes as centers to teach reading and writing to illiterates, to seek help in this task from primary school teachers and students;

18th. To combat the bad practices which are prejudicial to the economy and to the morale of the nation, to direct the people toward good customs and praiseworthy projects such as marriage, orphanages, births, and festivals.

19th. To bring to trial those who break the laws of Islam, who do not fast, who do not pray, and who insult religion;

20th. To transfer village primary schools to the mosque. . . .

21st. Religious teaching should constitute the essential subject matter to be taught in all educational establishments and faculties;

22nd. To memorize the Quran in state schools . . . in every school students should learn part of the Quran;

24th. . . . Support for teaching the Arabic language in all grades—absolute priority to be given to Arabic over foreign languages;

25th. To study the history of Islam, the nation, and Muslim civilization;

26th. To study the best way to allow people to dress . . . in an identical manner;

27th. To combat foreign customs (in the realm of vocabulary, customs, dress, nursing) and to Egyptianize all of these (one finds these customs among the well-to-do members of society);

28th. To orient journalism toward wholesome things, to encourage writers and authors, who should study specifically Muslim and Oriental subjects;

29th. To safeguard public health through every kind of publicity—increasing the number of hospitals, doctors, and out-patient clinics;

30th. To call particular attention to the problems of village life (administration, hygiene, water supply, education, recreation, morality).

III. The economic field:

1st. Organization of the zakat tax [an obligatory payment to support the poor] according to Islamic precepts, using zakat proceeds for welfare projects such as aiding the indigent, the poor, orphans; the zakat should also be used to strengthen the army;

2nd. To prevent the practice of usury, to direct banks to implement this policy; the government should provide an example by giving up the interest fixed by banks for servicing a personal loan or an industrial loan, etc.;

3rd. To facilitate and to increase the number of economic enterprises and to employ the jobless, to employ for the nation's benefit the skills possessed by the foreigners in these enterprises;

4th. To protect workers against monopoly companies, to require these companies to obey the law, the public should share in all profits;

5th. Aid for low-ranking employees and enlargement of their pay, lowering the income of high-ranking employees; . . .

7th. To encourage agricultural and industrial works, to improve the situation of the peasants and industrial workers;

8th. To give special attention to the technical and social needs of the workers, to raise their level of life and aid their class;

9th. Utilization of certain natural resources (unworked land, neglected mines, etc.). . . .

Source: Hasan al-Banna, "Towards the Light," in Robert Langdon, *The Emergence of the Middle East* (Van Nostrand, 1970).

Source 22.3
Progressive Islam

By the late twentieth century, the most widely publicized face of Islam, at least in the West, derived from groups sympathetic to the views of the Muslim Brotherhood, though these groups often expressed themselves in a more militant and aggressive fashion than the Brotherhood did. The Iranian revolution of 1979, for example, brought to power an Islamist government able to infuse public life with "the spirit of Islam," as they understood it, purging those who disagreed with their interpretation of the faith. In Saudi Arabia, Afghanistan, and elsewhere in the Islamic world, governments sought to implement various aspects of the Muslim Brotherhood's Islamist agenda, sometimes brutally. And social movements in other places, such as al-Qaeda, the Islamic State in Iraq and Syria, and Boko Haram in northern Nigeria, looked forward to the creation of societies governed by the sharia, or Islamic law, and were willing to undertake violent action to achieve those goals.

But these were not the only voices speaking in the name of Islam. All across the Islamic world, others argued that Muslims could retain their distinctive religious sensibility while embracing democracy, women's rights, technological progress, freedom of thought, and religious pluralism. Such thinkers were following in the tradition of nineteenth-century Islamic modernism (see Chapter 19, pages 847–49), even as they recalled earlier centuries of Islamic intellectual and scientific achievement and religious tolerance. That viewpoint was expressed in a pamphlet composed by a leading American Muslim scholar, translator, and Sufi teacher, Sheikh Kabir Helminski, in 2009.

- Against what charges does Sheikh Kabir seek to defend Islam? How does this document reflect the experience of 9/11?

- In what ways are Sheikh Kabir's views critical of radical, or "fundamentalist," ideas and practices?

- How does this document articulate the major features of a more progressive or liberal Islam? What kinds of arguments does Sheikh Kabir employ to make his case?

- To whom might these arguments appeal? What obstacles do they face in being heard within the Islamic world?

- How might Hassan al-Banna or Kemal Atatürk respond to these views?

Kabir Helminski
Islam and Human Values
2009

If the word "Islam" gives rise to fear or mistrust today, it is urgent that American Muslims clarify what we believe Islam stands for in order to dispel the idea that there is a fundamental conflict between the best values of Western civilization and the essential values of Islam. . . .

Islamic civilization, which developed out of the revelation of the Qur'an in the seventh century, affirms the truth of previous revelations, affirms religious pluralism, cultural diversity, and human rights, and recognizes the value of reason and individual conscience. . . .

[One issue] is the problem of violence. . . . Thousands of Muslim institutions and leaders, the great majority of the world's billion or more Muslims, have unequivocally condemned the hateful and violent ideologies that kill innocents and violate the dignity of all humanity. . . .

Islamic civilizations have a long history of encouraging religious tolerance and guaranteeing the rights of religious minorities. The reason for this is that the Qur'an explicitly acknowledges that the diversity of religions is part of the Divine Plan and no religion has a monopoly on truth or virtue. . . .

Jerusalem, under almost continuous Islamic rule for nearly fourteen centuries, has been a place

where Christians and Jews have lived side by side with Muslims, their holy sites and religious freedom preserved. Medieval Spain also created a high level of civilization as a multi-cultural society under Islamic rule for several centuries. The Ottoman Empire, the longest lived in history, for the more than six centuries of its existence encouraged ethnic and religious minorities to participate in and contribute to society. It was the Ottoman sultan who gave sanctuary to the Jews expelled from Catholic Spain. India was governed for centuries by Muslims, even while the majority of its people practiced Hinduism. . . .

[T]he acceptance of Islam must be an act of free will. Conversion by any kind of coercion was universally condemned by Islamic scholars. . . .

There are many verses in the Qur'an that affirm the actuality and even the necessity of diversity in ways of life and religious belief: [For example,] *O mankind, truly We [God] have created you male and female, and have made you nations and tribes that ye may know one another* [Surah 49:13]. . . .

In general, war is forbidden in Islam, except in cases of self-defense in response to explicit aggression. If there is a situation where injustice is being perpetrated or if the community is being invaded, then on a temporary basis permission is given to defend oneself. This principle is explained in the following verses: *And fight in God's cause against those who war against you, but do not commit aggression— for, verily, God does not love aggressors* [Surah 2:190].

[I]n recent decades . . . an intolerant ideology has been unleashed. A small minority of the world's one and a half billion Muslims has misconstrued the teachings of Islam to justify their misguided and immoral actions. It is most critical at this time for Muslims to condemn such extreme ideologies and their manifestations. It is equally important that non-Muslims understand that this ideology violates the fundamental moral principles of Islam and is repugnant to the vast majority of Muslims in the world. . . . So-called "suicide-bombers" did not appear until the mid-1990s. Such strategies have no precedent in Islamic history. The Qur'an says quite explicitly: *Do not kill yourselves* [4:29]. . . .

Muslims living in pluralistic societies have no religious reasons to oppose the laws of their own societies as long as they are just, but rather are encouraged to uphold the duly constituted laws of their own societies. . . . Islam and democracy are compatible and can coexist because Islam organizes humanity on the basis of the rule of law and human dignity.

The first four successors to the Prophet Muhammad were chosen by the community through consultation, i.e., a representative democracy. The only principle of political governance expressed in the Qur'an is the principle of Consultation (Shura), which holds that communities will "*rule themselves by means of mutual consultation*" [Surah 42:38].

Following the principles of the Qur'an, Muslims are encouraged to cooperate for the well-being of all. The Qur'an emphasizes three qualities above all others: peace, compassion, and mercy. The standard greeting in Islam is "As-Salam alaykum (Peace be with you)."

An American Muslim scholar, Abdul Aziz Sachedina, expresses it this way: "Islam does not encourage turning God into a political statement since humans cannot possess God. . . ."

[T]here is nothing in the Qur'an that essentially contradicts reason or science. . . . Repeatedly the Qur'an urges human beings to "reflect" and "use their intelligence."

Islam is not an alien religion. It does not claim a monopoly on virtue or truth. It follows in the way of previous spiritual traditions that recognized One Spirit operating within nature and human life. It continues on the Way of the great Prophets and Messengers of all sacred traditions.

Source: Selections from Kabir Helminski, *Islam and Human Values*, unpublished pamphlet, 2009.

Source 22.4
Islam and Women's Dress

Among the contested issues in the Islamic world, none have been more prominent than those involving the lives—and the bodies—of women. Within this controversy, matters of dress have loomed large. The Iranian revolution sought to impose hijab on its women (see pages 1008–10), while the French government sought to prevent its Muslim women from covering up. In early 2014, billboard advertisements showing women's bodies in Istanbul, Turkey, were sprayed with black paint, and next to one of them was scrawled, "Do not commit indecency." In response, a prominent and outspoken writer and scholar, Elif Shafak, declared that "uncovered Turkish women are feeling uncomfortable and unwanted in their own country."[18] The sources that follow present two diverging views on the question of women's dress, the first from a young Afghan woman named Emaan, who is a writer and poet, and the second from a British Muslim woman of Pakistani background, Saira Khan, who is a TV personality in Britain.

- How might you summarize the debate between these points of view? Are there areas of agreement as well as those of difference?

- What kinds of evidence or arguments do Emaan and Saira Khan use to make their cases? How do they use the Quran to support both sides of the debate?

- What larger issues or principles are at stake in this controversy?

EMAAN

Hijab: The Beauty of Muslim Women
2010

Hijab means "being covered." Islam requires Muslim women to cover themselves in public and in the presence of a person who is not *mahram* (people or family who are allowed to see women without cover). . . .

Proper *hijab* (concealment for the Muslim woman) dictates that the entire body must be covered, although the face and hands should be exposed. As Prophet Muhammad . . . said, "If the woman reaches the age of puberty, no part of her body should be seen but this, and he pointed to his face and hand."

Hijab has three roles that should be considered by Muslim women: it should be not form fitted, it should not be transparent, and it should not be attractive.

Hijab has many benefits for Muslim women as well as for the society that they live in. A Muslim woman is allowed to show her beauty only to her husband, to her family and to her women friends. It's considered a way of preventing attraction. Because when a woman shows her beauty in public it attracts the attention of men and it can lead men to act inappropriately.

The *hijab* also promotes more respect from a husband to a Muslim woman, as he sees his wife being faithful only to him and he is then convinced to be faithful only to his wife.

The *Qur'an* also emphasizes that the *hijab* is a way of keeping society . . . from abusing women. It's mentioned in the *Qur'an*: "Tell believing women to avert their glances and guard their private parts and not to display their charms except what (normally) appears of them. They should draw their coverings over their bosoms and not show their charms except to their husbands" (24:30–31).

In the western world, Muslim women are seen as oppressed and passive. Most think that Muslim women's rights are violated according to Islamic law. Wearing a *hijab* doesn't make a woman passive because scarves cover the heads, not the minds, of Muslim women. . . .

Islam respects women and does not allow them to be used as objects in public or through the media. Most people are concerned about women being used as sex objects, as in the western world today. But *hijab* saves Muslim women from this contemporary concern. *Hijab* equalizes all women and avoids concerns of artifice among women.

In contrast, it lets women focus on their spiritual, intellectual, and professional development and work comfortably in public spaces without being worried about their looks or concerned about the men around them.

Hijab has given the Muslim women freedom from constant attention to their physical parts, because their appearance is not subjected to public scrutiny. Their beauty, or perhaps lack of it, has been removed from the realm of what can legitimately be discussed.

Islam did not introduce wearing the burqa, veiling, and covering the face; it existed in previous cultures in India and the Arab world. . . . Islam does not oblige women to wear a burqa or veil. The wearing of the burqa or veil is a cultural custom, not an Islamic mandate. . . . Most of the restrictions are not from Islam, but rather from cultural customs sometimes wrongly justified under an Islamic banner.

I, as a Muslim woman, feel very comfortable wearing the *hijab*. For me the *hijab* means religious

devotion, discipline, reflection, respect, freedom, and modernity. I am pro-democracy because for me democracy means having choices in how to live our lives. I also support and promote mutual respect between Muslim and non-Muslim women. I want the world to treat Muslim women with the same respect they treat other women, from other religions and cultures who wear headscarves such as Hindu women, Jewish women, Greek women, and Catholic nuns. The assumption that wearing a *hijab* is oppressive should change from an oppressive idea to a liberating one.

Source: Emaan, "Hijab: The Beauty of Muslim Women," Afghan Women's Writing Project, June 29, 2010, http://awwproject.org/2010/06/hijab-the-beauty-of-muslim-women/.

Saira Khan

Why I, as a British Muslim Woman, Want the Burkha Banned from Our Streets
2009

Shopping in Harrods last week, I came across a group of women wearing black burkhas, browsing the latest designs in the fashion department. The irony of the situation was almost laughable. Here was a group of affluent women window shopping for designs that they would never once be able to wear in public. Yet it's a sight that's becoming more and more commonplace. In hardline Muslim communities right across Britain, the burkha and hijab—the Muslim headscarf—are becoming the norm. . . .

And yet, as a British Muslim woman, I abhor the practice and am calling on the Government to follow the lead of French President Nicolas Sarkozy and ban the burkha in our country.

The veil is simply a tool of oppression which is being used to alienate and control women under the guise of religious freedom.

My parents moved here from Kashmir in the 1960s. They brought with them their faith and their traditions, but they also understood that they were starting a new life in a country where Islam

was not the main religion. My mother has always worn traditional Kashmiri clothes. . . . When she found work in England, she adapted her dress without making a fuss. She is still very much a traditional Muslim woman, but she swims in a normal swimming costume and jogs in a tracksuit. . . .

I have read the Koran. Nowhere in the Koran does it state that a woman's face and body must be covered in a layer of heavy black cloth. Instead, Muslim women should dress modestly, covering their arms and legs. Many of my adult British Muslim friends cover their heads with a headscarf—and I have no problem with that. The burkha is an entirely different matter. It is an imported Saudi Arabian tradition, and the growing number of women veiling their faces in Britain is a sign of creeping radicalisation, which is not just regressive, it is oppressive and downright dangerous. . . . It sends out a clear message: "I do not want to be part of your society."

Every time the burkha is debated, Muslim fundamentalists bring out all these women who say:

"It's my choice to wear this." Perhaps so—but what pressures have been brought to bear on them? The reality, surely, is that a lot of women are not free to choose.

And behind the closed doors of some Muslim houses, countless young women are told to wear the *hijab* and the veil. These are the girls who are hidden away, they are not allowed to go to university or choose who they marry. In many cases, they are kept down by the threat of violence.

The burkha is the ultimate visual symbol of female oppression. It is the weapon of radical Muslim men who want to see Sharia law on Britain's streets, and would love women to be hidden, unseen and unheard. It is totally out of place in a civilised country.

[French] President Sarkozy is absolutely right to say: "If you want to live here, live like us."

It is time for ministers and ordinary British Muslims to say, "Enough is enough." For the sake of women and children, the Government must ban the wearing of the hijab in school and the burkha in public places.

Two years ago, I wore a burkha for the first time for a television programme. It was the most horrid experience. It restricted the way I walked, what I saw, and how I interacted with the world. It took away my personality. I felt alienated and like a freak. It was hot and uncomfortable, and I was unable to see behind me, exchange a smile with people, or shake hands.

If I had been forced to wear a veil, I would certainly not be free to write this article. Nor would I have run a marathon, become an aerobics teacher or set up a business.

Source: Saira Khan, "Why I, as a British Muslim Woman, Want the Burkha Banned from Our Streets," *Daily Mail*, June 24, 2009, http://www.dailymail.co.uk/debate/article-1195052/Why-I-British-Muslim-woman-want-burkha-banned-streets.html.

DOING HISTORY

Contending for Islam

1. **Understanding the issues:** What are the core concerns that divide the writers of these documents?

2. **Comparing Islamic modernists:** How do you think Kemal Atatürk would have responded to later Islamic modernists such as Sheikh Kabir and perhaps Saira Khan?

3. **Imagining a conversation:** What issues might arise in a conversation among the five authors represented here? Can you identify any areas of agreement? On which points would they probably never agree?

4. **Explaining variations:** What personal or historical circumstances might help to account for the very different understandings of Islam that are reflected in these documents?

Image created by Reto Stockli, Nazmi El Saleous, and Marit Jentoft-Nilsen, NASA GSFC

CHAPTER 23

Capitalism and Culture

The Acceleration of Globalization
since 1945

Memey, a young uneducated woman from Java in Indonesia, was in a very difficult situation early in the twenty-first century. Her husband had died, leaving her in poverty with a young child. When she heard from a neighbor about waitressing opportunities in Malaysia, she saw a way of providing for her son. So she entered Malaysia illegally and was met by a contact person, who took her shopping for clothes and makeup. "After dinner," she later recalled, "a man came for me and took me to a hotel room nearby to start work. That was when it finally dawned on me that it was not a waitressing job. I was being made to work as a sex worker." Witnessing other women severely beaten or threatened, Memey was afraid to run away. After about four months in this situation, she was able to escape with the help of a sympathetic client, returning to Indonesia with bitter memories and an HIV infection. Subsequently she found work with an organization devoted to helping other women in her position.[1]

Memey was but one of millions of women victimized by international networks of sex trafficking. Those networks represented one dark and tragic thread in a vast web of political relationships, economic transactions, cultural influences, and the movement of people across international borders that linked the world's separate countries and regions, binding them together more tightly, but also more contentiously. By the 1990s, this process of accelerating engagement among distant peoples was widely known as globalization. Debating the pros and cons of this encompassing pattern of interaction and exchange has been central to global discourse over the past half century or more. More importantly, it has

One World This NASA photograph, showing both the earth and the moon, reveals none of the national, ethnic, religious, or linguistic boundaries that have long divided humankind. Such pictures have both reflected and helped create a new planetary consciousness among growing numbers of people.

been central to the lives of billions of individuals, like Memey, and to the societies they inhabit.

Although the term was relatively new, the process was not. From the viewpoint of world history, the genealogy of globalization reached far into the past. The Arab, Mongol, Russian, Chinese, and Ottoman empires; the Silk Road, Indian Ocean, and trans-Saharan trade routes; the spread of Buddhism, Christianity, and especially Islam—all of these connections had long linked the societies of the Eastern Hemisphere, bringing new rulers, religions, products, diseases, and technologies to many of its peoples. Later, in the centuries after 1500, European maritime voyages and colonizing efforts launched the Columbian exchange, incorporating the Western Hemisphere and inner Africa firmly and permanently into a genuinely global network of communication, exchange, and often exploitation. During the nineteenth century, as the Industrial Revolution took hold and Western nations began a new round of empire building in Asia and Africa, that global network tightened further, and its role as generator of social and cultural change only increased.

These were the foundations on which twentieth-century globalization was built. A number of prominent developments of the past century, explored in the previous three chapters, operated on a global scale: the world wars, the Great Depression, communism, the cold war, the end of empire, and the growing prominence of developing countries. But global interaction quickened its pace and deepened its impact after World War II. From the immense range of interactions that make up modern globalization, this chapter focuses on four major processes: the transformation of the world economy, the emergence of global feminism, the response of world religions to modernity, and the growing awareness of humankind's enormous impact on the environment.

SEEKING THE MAIN POINT

To what extent has globalization fostered converging values and common interests among the world's peoples? In what ways has it generated new conflicts among them?

The Transformation of the World Economy

When most people speak of globalization, they are referring to the immense acceleration in international economic transactions that took place in the second half of the twentieth century and continued into the twenty-first. Many have come to see this process as almost natural, certainly inevitable, and practically unstoppable. Yet the first half of the twentieth century, particularly the decades between the two world wars, witnessed a deep contraction of global economic linkages as the aftermath of World War I and then the Great Depression wreaked havoc on the world economy. International trade, investment, and labor migration dropped sharply as major states turned inward, favoring high tariffs and economic autonomy in the face of a global economic collapse.

■ **Change**
What factors contributed to economic globalization in the second half of the twentieth century?

The aftermath of World War II was very different. The capitalist victors in that conflict, led by the United States, were determined to avoid any return to such Depression-era conditions. At a conference in Bretton Woods, New Hampshire, in

A MAP OF TIME

1919–1946	League of Nations
1945	United Nations, World Bank, and International Monetary Fund established
1960	Organization of Petroleum Exporting Countries founded
1962	Rachel Carson publishes *Silent Spring*
1963	Betty Friedan publishes *The Feminine Mystique*
1967	Six-day Arab-Israeli war
1970	Greenpeace established
1973–1974	Arab members of OPEC place an embargo on oil exports to the West
1979	Convention on the Elimination of All Forms of Discrimination against Women adopted by UN; Iranian revolution
1982	Law of the Sea Convention establishes international agreement about the uses of the world's oceans
1994	North American Free Trade Agreement (NAFTA) enacted
1995	World Trade Organization created
1997	Kyoto protocol on global warming introduced
2001	September 11 attacks on World Trade Center and Pentagon
2008	Global economic crisis begins
2011	Osama bin Laden killed
2013–2014	The Islamic State, a radical jihadist organization, proclaims a new caliphate in parts of Syria and Iraq
2014	Tunisia's new constitution enshrines many rights of women; World Bank declares China the world's largest economy; People's Climate March in conjunction with the UN-sponsored Leaders Climate Summit

1944, they forged a set of agreements and institutions (the World Bank and the International Monetary Fund [IMF]) that laid the foundation for postwar globalization. This "Bretton Woods system" negotiated the rules for commercial and financial dealings among the major capitalist countries, while promoting relatively free trade, stable currency values linked to the U.S. dollar, and high levels of capital investment.

Technology also contributed to the acceleration of economic globalization. Containerized shipping, huge oil tankers, and air express services dramatically lowered transportation costs, while fiber-optic cables and later the Internet provided the communication infrastructure for global economic interaction. In the developing countries, population growth, especially when tied to growing economies and modernizing societies, further fueled globalization as dozens of new nations entered the world economy.

The kind of economic globalization taking shape in the 1970s and later was widely known as neoliberalism. Major capitalist countries such as the United States and Great Britain abandoned many earlier political controls on economic activity as their leaders and businesspeople increasingly viewed the entire world as a single market. This approach to the world economy favored the reduction of tariffs, the free global movement of capital, a mobile and temporary workforce, the privatization of many state-run enterprises, the curtailing of government efforts to regulate the economy, and both tax and spending cuts. Powerful international lending agencies such as the World Bank and the IMF imposed such free market and pro-business conditions on many poor countries if they were to qualify for much-needed loans. The collapse of the state-controlled economies of the communist world only furthered such unrestricted global capitalism. In this view, the market, operating both globally and within nations, was the most effective means of generating the holy grail of economic growth. As communism collapsed by the end of the twentieth century, "capitalism was global and the globe was capitalist."[2]

Reglobalization

These conditions provided the foundations for a dramatic quickening of global economic transactions after World War II, a "reglobalization" of the world economy following the contractions of the 1930s. This immensely significant process was expressed in the accelerating circulation of goods, capital, and people.

■ **Connection**
In what ways has economic globalization more closely linked the world's peoples?

World trade, for example, skyrocketed from a value of some $57 billion in 1947 to about $18.3 trillion in 2012. Department stores and supermarkets around the world stocked their shelves with goods from every part of the globe. Twinings of London marketed its 120 blends of tea in more than 100 countries, and the Australian-based Kiwi shoe polish was sold in 180 countries. In 2005, about 70 percent of Walmart products reportedly included components from China. And the following year, Toyota replaced General Motors as the world's largest automaker, with manufacturing facilities in at least eighteen countries.

Money as well as goods achieved an amazing global mobility in three ways. The first was "foreign direct investment," whereby a firm in, say, the United States opens a factory in China or Mexico (see Map 23.1). Such investment exploded after 1960 as companies in rich countries sought to take advantage of cheap labor, tax breaks, and looser environmental regulations in developing countries. A second form of money in motion has been the short-term movement of capital, in which investors annually spent trillions of dollars purchasing foreign currencies or stocks likely to increase in value and often sold them quickly thereafter, with unsettling conse-

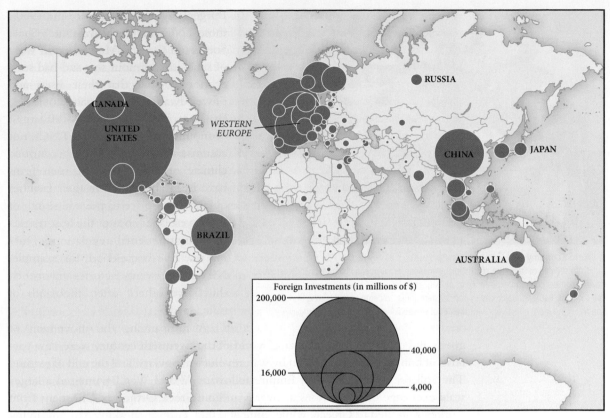

Map 23.1   Globalization in Action: Foreign Direct Investment in the Late Twentieth Century

Investment across national borders has been a major expression of globalization. This map shows the global distribution of investment inflows as of 1998. Notice which countries or regions were receiving the most investment from abroad and which received the least. How might you account for this pattern? Keep in mind that some regions, such as the United States, Western Europe, and Japan, were major sources of such investment as well as recipients of it.

quences. A third form of money movement involved the personal funds of individuals. By the end of the twentieth century, international credit cards had taken hold almost everywhere, allowing for easy transfer of money across national borders. In 2012, MasterCard was accepted at some 33 million businesses in 220 countries or territories.

Central to the acceleration of economic globalization have been huge global businesses known as transnational corporations (TNCs), which produce goods or deliver services simultaneously in many countries. For example, Mattel Corporation produced Barbie, that quintessentially American doll, in factories located in Indonesia, Malaysia, and China, using molds from the United States, plastic and hair from Taiwan and Japan, and cotton cloth from China. From distribution centers in Hong Kong, more than a billion Barbies were sold in 150 countries by 1999.

A World Economy
Indian-based call centers that serve North American or European companies and customers have become a common experience of globalization for many. Here employees in one such call center in Patna, a major city in northeastern India, undergo voice training in order to communicate more effectively with their English-speaking callers. (Indiapicture/Alamy)

Burgeoning in number since the 1960s, those TNCs, such as Royal Dutch Shell, Sony, and General Motors, often were of such an enormous size and had such economic clout that their assets and power dwarfed that of many countries. By 2000, 51 of the world's 100 largest economic units were in fact TNCs, not countries. In the permissive economic climate of recent decades, such firms have been able to move their facilities quickly from place to place in search of the lowest labor costs or the least restrictive environmental regulations. During one five-year period, for example, Nike closed twenty factories and opened thirty-five others, often thousands of miles apart.

Accompanying the movement of goods and capital in the globalizing world of the twentieth century were new patterns of human migration, driven by war, revolution, poverty, and the end of empire. The collapse of the Ottoman Empire following World War I witnessed a large-scale exchange of populations as over a million Greek Orthodox Christians from Turkey relocated to Greece, while some 400,000 Turkish-speaking Muslims living in Greece moved in the other direction. Fleeing anti-Semitism, fascism, and the Holocaust, Jews emigrated to what is now Israel in large numbers, generating in the process a flow of Palestinian refugees to settlements in neighboring countries. Political repression and forced labor in the Soviet Union pushed millions into the camps of the gulag, primarily in Siberia. In South Africa, an industrializing economy and apartheid policies drew millions of male workers from the countryside into mines and factories, often under horrific conditions. In the early twenty-first century, over a million Chinese have migrated to Africa, where Chinese trade and investment have mounted.

But perhaps the most significant pattern of global migration since the 1960s has featured a vast movement of people from the developing countries of Asia, Africa, and Latin America to the industrialized world of Europe and North America. Pakistanis, Indians, and West Indians moved to Great Britain; Algerians and West Africans to France; Turks and Kurds to Germany; Filipinos, Koreans, Cubans, Mexicans, and Haitians to the United States. A considerable majority of these people have been dubbed "labor migrants." Most moved, often illegally and with few skills, to escape poverty in their own lands, drawn by an awareness of Western prosperity and a belief that a better future awaited them in the developed countries. By 2003, some 4 million Filipino domestic workers were employed in 130 countries. Young women by the hundreds of thousands from poor countries have been recruited as sex workers in wealthier nations, sometimes in conditions approaching slavery. Smaller numbers of highly skilled and university-trained people, such as doctors and computer scientists, came in search of professional opportunities less available in their own countries. All of this represented a kind of reverse "development aid"—as either cheap labor or intellectual resources—from poor countries to rich. Still other peoples moved as refugees, fleeing violence or political oppression in places such as Vietnam, Cambodia, Sudan, Uganda, Cuba, and Haiti.

Many of those people in motion were headed for the United States, drawn by its reputation for wealth and opportunity. In the forty years between 1971 and 2010, almost 20 million immigrants arrived in the United States legally, and millions more entered illegally, the vast majority of both from the Latin American/ Caribbean region and from Asia. Mexicans have been by far the largest group of immigrants to the United States, and many have arrived without legal documentation, an estimated 6.65 million during the first decade of the twenty-first century alone. Often their journeys north have been dangerous as they confronted long treks through burning deserts, sought to evade American immigration authorities, and depended on the expensive and sometimes unreliable "coyotes" who facilitated the smuggling of people across the border. Once in the United States, many of these immigrants provided inexpensive manual labor in fields, factories, and homes of the well-to-do, even as the money they sent back to their families in Mexico represented that nation's largest source of foreign exchange. The presence of migrants from the Global South has prompted considerable cultural and political conflict in both the United States and Europe, illustrated by a prolonged controversy about the wearing of headscarves by Muslim girls in French public schools.

Growth, Instability, and Inequality

The impact of these tightening economic links has provoked enormous debate and controversy. Amid the swirl of contending opinion, one thing seemed reasonably clear: economic globalization accompanied, and arguably helped generate, the most remarkable spurt of economic growth in world history. On a global level, total world output grew from a value of $7 trillion in 1950 to $73 trillion in 2009 and on a per capita basis from $2,652 to $10,728.[3] This represents an immense, rapid, and unprecedented creation of wealth with a demonstrable impact on human welfare. Life expectancies expanded almost everywhere, infant mortality declined, and literacy increased. The UN Human Development Report in 1997 concluded that "in the past 50 years, poverty has fallen more than in the previous 500."[4]

Far more problematic have been the instability of this emerging world economy and the distribution of the wealth it has generated. Amid overall economic growth, periodic crises and setbacks have shaped recent world history. Soaring oil prices contributed to a severe stock market crash in 1973–1974 and great hardship for many developing countries. Inability to repay mounting debts triggered a major

■ Connection
What new or sharper divisions has economic globalization generated?

financial crisis in Latin America during the 1980s and resulted in a "lost decade" in terms of economic development. Another financial crisis in Asia during the late 1990s resulted in the collapse of many businesses, widespread unemployment, and political upheaval in Indonesia and Thailand.

But nothing since the Great Depression more clearly illustrated the unsettling consequences of global connectedness in the absence of global regulation than the worldwide economic contraction that began in 2008. An inflated housing market—or "bubble"—in the United States collapsed, triggering millions of home foreclosures, growing unemployment, the tightening of credit, and declining consumer spending. Soon this crisis rippled around the world. Iceland's rapidly growing economy collapsed almost overnight as three major banks failed, the country's stock market dropped by 80 percent, and its currency lost more than 70 percent of its value—all in a single week. In Africa, reduced demand for exports threatened to halt a promising decade of economic progress. In Sierra Leone, for example, some 90 percent of the country's diamond-mine workers lost their jobs. The slowing of China's booming economy led to unemployment for one in seven of the country's urban migrants, forcing them to return to already-overcrowded rural areas. Impoverished Central American and Caribbean families, dependent on money sent home by family members working abroad, suffered further as those remittances dropped sharply. Contracting economies contributed to debt crises in Greece, Italy, and Spain and threatened to unravel European economic integration. Calls for both protectionism and greater regulation suggested that the wide-open capitalist world economy of recent decades was perhaps not as inevitable as some had thought. Whatever the overall benefits of the modern global system, economic stability and steady progress were not among them.

Nor was equality. As Europe's Industrial Revolution began to take hold in the early nineteenth century, a wholly new division appeared within the human community—between the rich industrialized countries, primarily in Europe and North America, and everyone else. In 1820, the ratio between the income of the top and bottom 20 percent of the world's population was three to one. By 1991, it was eighty-six to one.[5] The accelerated economic globalization of the twentieth century did not create this global rift, but it arguably has worsened the North/South gap and certainly has not greatly diminished it. Even the well-known capitalist financier and investor George Soros, a billionaire many times over, acknowledged this reality in 2000: "The global capitalist system has produced a very uneven playing field. The gap between the rich and the poor is getting wider."[6] That gap has been evident, often tragically, in great disparities in incomes, medical care, availability of clean drinking water, educational and employment opportunities, access to the Internet, and dozens of other ways. It has shaped the life chances of practically everyone. (See Snapshot, opposite.)

These disparities were the foundations for a new kind of global conflict. As the East/West division of capitalism and communism faded, differences between the rich nations of the Global North and the developing countries of the Global South

SNAPSHOT   Global Development and Inequality, 2011

This table shows thirteen commonly used indicators of "development" and their variations in 2011 across four major groups of countries defined by average level of per capita income.[7] In which areas has the Global South most nearly caught up with the Global North?

Gross National Income per Capita with Sample Countries	Low Income: $995 or Less (Congo, Kenya, Ethiopia, Afghanistan, Myanmar)	Lower Middle Income: $996–$3,945 (India, China, Egypt, Algeria, Indonesia, Nigeria)	Upper Middle Income: $3,946–$12,195 (Mexico, Brazil, Turkey, Russia, Iran)	Upper Income: $12,196 or More (USA, Western Europe, Japan, South Korea, Australia)
Life expectancy M/F in years	58/60	66/70	68/75	77/83
Deaths under age 5 per 1,000 live births	120	60	24	7
Deaths from infectious disease: %	36	14	11	7
Access to toilets: %	35	50	84	99
Years of education	7.9	10.3	13.8	14.5
Literacy rate: %	66	80	93	99
Population growth: % annual	2.27	1.27	.96	.39
Urban population: %	27	41	74	78
Cell phones per 100 people	22	47	92	106
Internet users per 100 people	2.3	13.7	29.9	68.3
Personal computers per 100 people	1.2	4.3	11.9	60.4
Cars per 1,000 people	5.8	20.3	125.2	435.1
Carbon dioxide emissions: metric tons per capita	1	3	5	13

assumed greater prominence in world affairs. Highly contentious issues have included the rules for world trade, availability of and terms for foreign aid, representation in international economic organizations, the mounting problem of indebtedness, and environmental and labor standards. Such matters surfaced repeatedly in international negotiations during the second half of the twentieth century and into the twenty-first. In the 1970s, for example, a large group of developing countries joined together to demand a "new international economic order" that was more favorable to the poor countries. Not much success attended this effort. More recently, developing countries have contested protectionist restrictions on their agricultural exports imposed by rich countries seeking to protect their own politically powerful farmers.

Beyond active resistance by the rich nations, a further obstacle to reforming the world economy in favor of the poor lay in growing disparities among the developing countries themselves. The oil-rich economies of the Middle East had little in common with the banana-producing countries of Central America. The rapidly industrializing states of China, India, and South Korea had quite different economic agendas than impoverished African countries. Such disparities made common action difficult to achieve.

Economic globalization has contributed to inequalities not only at the global level and among developing countries but also within individual nations, rich and poor alike. In the United States, for example, a shifting global division of labor required the American economy to shed millions of manufacturing jobs. With recent U.S. factory wages far higher than those of China, many companies moved their manufacturing operations offshore to Asia or Latin America. This left many relatively unskilled American workers in the lurch, forcing them to work in the low-wage service sector, even as other Americans were growing prosperous in emerging high-tech industries. Even some highly skilled work, such as computer programming, was outsourced to lower-wage sites in India, Ireland, Russia, and elsewhere. Mounting income inequality and the erosion of the country's middle class became major issues in American political debate.

Globalization divided Mexico as well. The northern part of the country, with close business and manufacturing ties to the United States, grew much more prosperous than the south, which was a largely rural agricultural area and had a far more slowly growing economy. Beginning in 1994, southern resentment boiled over in the Chiapas rebellion, which featured a strong anti-globalization platform. Its leader, known as Subcomandante Marcos, referred to globalization as a "process to eliminate that multitude of people who are not useful to the powerful."[8] China's rapid economic growth likewise fostered mounting inequality between its rural households and those in its burgeoning cities, where income by 2000 was three times that of the countryside. Economic globalization may have brought people together as never before, but it also divided them sharply.

The hardships and grievances of those left behind or threatened by the march toward economic integration have fueled a growing popular movement aimed at criticizing and counteracting globalization. Known variously as an anti-globalization, alternative globalization, or global justice movement, it emerged in the 1990s as an international coalition of political activists, concerned scholars and students, trade unions, women's and religious organizations, environmental groups, and others, hailing from rich and poor countries alike. Thus opposition to neoliberal globalization was itself global in scope. Though reflecting a variety of viewpoints, that opposition largely agreed that free trade and market-driven corporate globalization had lowered labor standards, fostered ecological degradation, prevented poor countries from protecting themselves against financial speculators, ignored local cultures, disregarded human rights, and enhanced global inequality, while favoring the interests of large corporations and the rich countries.

This movement appeared dramatically on the world's radar screen in late 1999 in Seattle at a meeting of the World Trade Organization (WTO). An international body representing 149 nations and charged with negotiating the rules for global commerce and promoting free trade, the WTO had become a major target of globalization critics. "The central idea of the WTO," argued one such critic, "is that *free trade*—actually the values and interests of global corporations—should supersede all other values."[9] Tens of thousands of protesters—academics, activists, farmers, labor union leaders from all over the world—descended on Seattle in what became a violent, chaotic, and much-publicized protest. At the city's harbor, protest organizers created a Seattle Tea Party around the slogan "No globalization without representation," echoing the Boston Tea Party of 1773. Subsequent meetings of the WTO and other high-level international economic gatherings were likewise greeted with large-scale protests and a heavy police presence. In 2001, alternative globalization activists created the World Social Forum, an annual gathering to coordinate strategy, exchange ideas, and share experiences, under the slogan "Another world is possible." It was an effort to demonstrate that neoliberal globalization was not inevitable and that the processes of a globalized economy could and should be regulated and subjected to public accountability. (See Working with Evidence, Source 23.3, page 1068.)

Globalization and an American Empire

For many people, opposition to this kind of globalization also expressed resistance to mounting American power and influence in the world. An "American Empire," some have argued, is the face of globalization (see Map 23.2), but scholars, commentators, and politicians have disagreed about how best to describe the United States' role in the postwar world. Certainly it has not been a colonial territorial empire such as that of the British or the French in the nineteenth century. Seeking to distinguish themselves from Europeans, Americans generally have vigorously denied that they have an empire at all.

In some ways, the U.S. global presence might be seen as an "informal empire," similar to the ones that Europeans exercised in China and the Middle East during the nineteenth century. In both cases, dominant powers sought to use economic penetration, political pressure, and periodic military action to create societies and governments compatible with their values and interests, but without directly governing large populations for long periods. In its economic dimension, American dominance has been termed an "empire of production," which uses its immense wealth to entice or intimidate potential collaborators.[10] Some scholars have emphasized the

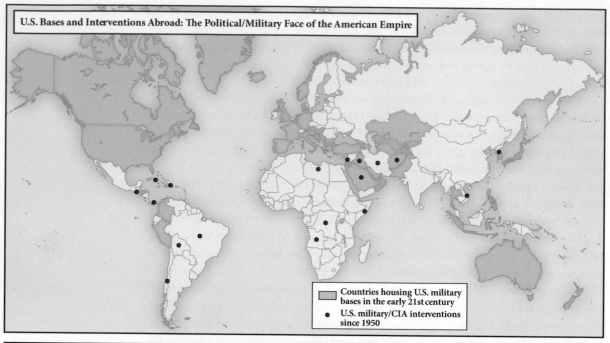

U.S. Bases and Interventions Abroad: The Political/Military Face of the American Empire

Countries housing U.S. military
bases in the early 21st century

• U.S. military/CIA interventions
since 1950

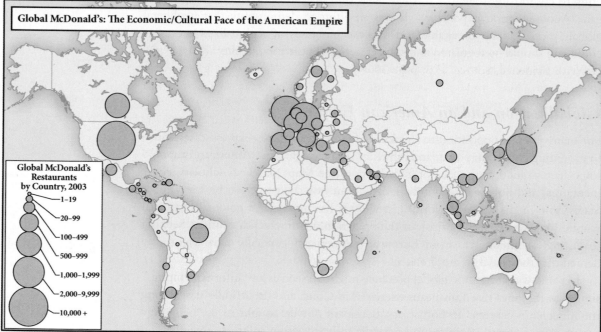

Global McDonald's: The Economic/Cultural Face of the American Empire

Global McDonald's
Restaurants
by Country, 2003

1–19

20–99

100–499

500–999

1,000–1,999

2,000–9,999

10,000 +

Map 23.2 Two Faces of an "American Empire"

Those who argue that the United States constructed an empire in the second half of the twentieth century point both to its political/military alliances and interventions around the world and to U.S. economic and cultural penetration of many countries. The distribution of U.S. military bases, a partial indication of its open and covert interventions, and the location of McDonald's restaurants indicate something of the scope of America's global presence in the early twenty-first century.

United States' frequent use of force around the world, while others have focused attention on the "soft power" of its cultural attractiveness, its political and cultural freedoms, the economic benefits of cooperation, and the general willingness of many to follow the American lead voluntarily.

With the collapse of the Soviet Union and the end of the cold war by the early 1990s, U.S. military dominance was unchecked by any equivalent power. When the United States was attacked by Islamic militants on September 11, 2001, that power was unleashed first against Afghanistan (2001), which had sheltered the al-Qaeda instigators of that attack, and then against Iraq (2003), where Saddam Hussein allegedly had been developing weapons of mass destruction. In the absence of the Soviet Union, the United States could act unilaterally without fear of triggering a conflict with another major power. Although the Afghan and Iraqi regimes were quickly defeated, establishing a lasting peace and rebuilding badly damaged Muslim countries have proved difficult tasks. Thus, within a decade of the Soviet collapse, the United States found itself in yet another global struggle, an effort to contain or eliminate Islamic "terrorism."

Since the 1980s, as its relative military strength has peaked, the United States has faced growing international economic competition. The recovery of Europe and Japan and the emergent industrialization of South Korea, Taiwan, China, and India substantially reduced the United States' share of overall world production from about 50 percent in 1945 to 20 percent in the 1980s. By 2008 the United States accounted for just 8.1 percent of world merchandise exports. Accompanying this relative decline was a sharp reversal of the country's trade balance as U.S. imports greatly exceeded its exports. In 2014 the World Bank reported that China had overtaken the United States as the world's largest economy, even as it held much of the mounting American national debt.

However it might be defined, the exercise of American power, like that of many empires, was resisted abroad and contested at home. In Korea, Vietnam, Cuba, Iraq, Afghanistan, and elsewhere, armed struggle against U.S. intervention was both costly and painful. During the cold war, the governments of India, Egypt, and Ethiopia sought to diminish American influence in their affairs by turning to the Soviet Union or playing off the two superpowers against each other. Even France, resenting U.S. domination, withdrew from the military structure of NATO in 1967 and expelled all foreign-controlled troops from the country. In 2014, Russia strongly expressed its opposition to Western efforts to incorporate former Soviet territories or dependencies into NATO or the European Union by seizing Crimea and pressuring Ukraine to remain within the Russian sphere of influence. Many intellectuals, fearing the erosion of their own cultures in the face of well-financed American media around the world, have decried American "cultural imperialism." By the early twenty-first century, the United States' international policies—such as its refusal to accept the jurisdiction of the International Criminal Court; its refusal to ratify the Kyoto protocol on global warming; its doctrine of preemptive war, which was exercised in Iraq; and its apparent use of torture—had generated widespread opposition.

Within the United States as well, the global exercise of American power generated controversy. The Vietnam War, for example, divided the United States more sharply than at any time since the Civil War. It split families and friendships, churches and political parties. The war provided a platform for a growing number of critics, both at home and abroad, who had come to resent American cultural and economic dominance in the post-1945 world. It stimulated a new sense of activism among students in the nation's colleges and universities. Many of them came to see America itself as an imperialist power. A similar set of issues, protests, and controversies followed the American invasion of Iraq in 2003.

The Globalization of Liberation: Focus on Feminism

More than goods, money, and people traversed the planet during the most recent century. So too did ideas, and none was more powerful than that of liberation. Communism promised workers and peasants liberation from capitalist oppression. Nationalism offered subject peoples liberation from imperialism. Advocates of democracy sought liberation from authoritarian governments.

The 1960s in particular witnessed an unusual convergence of protest movements around the world, suggesting the emergence of a global culture of liberation. Within the United States, several such movements—the civil rights demands of African Americans and Hispanic Americans; the youthful counterculture of rock music, sex, and drugs; the prolonged and highly divisive protests against the war in Vietnam—gave the 1960s a distinctive place in the country's recent history. Across the Atlantic, swelling protests against unresponsive bureaucracy, consumerism, and middle-class values likewise erupted, most notably in France in 1968. There a student-led movement protesting conditions in universities attracted the support of many middle-class people, who were horrified at the brutality of the police, and stimulated an enormous strike among some 9 million workers. France seemed on the edge of another revolution. Related but smaller-scale movements took place in Germany, Italy, Japan, Mexico, Argentina, and elsewhere.

The communist world too was rocked by protest. In 1968, a new Communist Party leadership in Czechoslovakia, led by Alexander Dubcek, initiated a sweeping series of reforms aimed at creating "socialism with a human face." Censorship ended, generating an explosion of free expression in what had been a highly repressive regime; unofficial political clubs emerged publicly; victims of earlier repression were rehabilitated; secret ballots for party elections were put in place. To the conservative leaders of the Soviet Union, this "Prague Spring" seemed to challenge communist rule itself, and they sent troops and tanks to crush it. Across the world in communist China, another kind of protest was taking shape in that country's Cultural Revolution (see Chapter 21, page 945).

In the developing countries, a substantial number of political leaders, activists, scholars, and students developed the notion of a "third world." Their countries, many only recently free from colonial rule, would offer an alternative to both a decrepit Western capitalism and a repressive Soviet communism. They claimed to pioneer new forms of economic development, of grassroots democracy, and of cultural renewal. By the late 1960s, the icon of this third-world ideology was Che Guevara, the Argentine-born revolutionary who had embraced the Cuban Revolution and subsequently attempted to replicate its experience of liberation through guerrilla warfare in parts of Africa and Latin America. Various aspects of his life story—his fervent anti-imperialism, cast as a global struggle; his self-sacrificing lifestyle; his death in 1967 at the hands of the Bolivian military, trained and backed by the American CIA—made him a heroic figure to third-world revolutionaries. He was popular as well among Western radicals, who were disgusted with the complacency and materialism of their own societies.

Che Guevara

In life, Che was an uncompromising but failed revolutionary, while in death he became an inspiration to third-world liberation movements and a symbol of radicalism to many in the West. His image appeared widely on T-shirts and posters, and in Cuba itself a government-sponsored cult featured schoolchildren chanting each morning "We will be like Che." This billboard image of Che was erected in Havana in 1988. (© Tim Page/Corbis)

No expression of this global culture of liberation held a more profound potential for change than feminism, for it represented a rethinking of the most fundamental and personal of all human relationships—that between women and men. Feminism had begun in the West in the nineteenth century with a primary focus on suffrage and in several countries had achieved the status of a mass movement by the outbreak of World War I (see Chapter 16, pages 723–27). The twentieth century, however, witnessed the globalization of feminism as organized efforts to address the concerns of women took shape across the world. Communist governments—in the Soviet Union, China, and Cuba, for example—mounted vigorous efforts to gain the support of women and to bring them into the workforce by attacking major elements of older patriarchies (see Chapter 21, pages 940–42). But feminism took hold in many cultural and political settings, where women confronted different issues, adopted different strategies, and experienced a range of outcomes.

Feminism in the West

In the West, organized feminism had lost momentum by the end of the 1920s, when many countries in Western Europe and North America had achieved women's suffrage. When it revived in the 1960s in both Western Europe and the United States, it did so with a quite different agenda. In France, for example, the writer and philosopher Simone de Beauvoir in 1949 had published *The Second Sex*, a book arguing that women had historically been defined as "other," or deviant from the "normal" male sex. The book soon became a central statement of a reviving women's movement. French feminists staged a counter–Mother's Day parade under the slogan "Celebrated one day; exploited all year." To highlight their demand to control their own bodies, some 343 women signed a published manifesto stating that they had undergone an abortion, which was then illegal in France.

Across the Atlantic, millions of American women responded to Betty Friedan's book *The Feminine Mystique* (1963), which disclosed the identity crisis of educated women, unfulfilled by marriage and motherhood. Some adherents of this second-wave feminism took up the equal rights agenda of their nineteenth-century predecessors, but with an emphasis now on employment and education rather than voting rights. A more radical expression of American feminism, widely known as "women's liberation," took broader aim at patriarchy as a system of domination, similar to those of race and class. One manifesto from 1969 declared:

■ Comparison

What distinguished feminism in the industrialized countries from that in the Global South?

> We are exploited as sex objects, breeders, domestic servants, and cheap labor. We are considered inferior beings, whose only purpose is to enhance men's lives. . . . Because we live so intimately with our oppressors, we have been kept from seeing our personal suffering as a political condition.[11]

Thus liberation for women meant becoming aware of their own oppression, a process that took place in thousands of consciousness-raising groups across the country. Many such women advocated direct action rather than the political lobbying favored by equal rights feminists. They challenged the Miss America contest of 1968 by tossing stink bombs in the hall, crowning a live sheep as their Miss America, and disposing of girdles, bras, high-heeled shoes, tweezers, and other "instruments of oppression" in a Freedom Trashcan. They also brought into open discussion issues involving sexuality, insisting that free love, lesbianism, and celibacy should be accorded the same respect as heterosexual marriage.

Yet another strand of Western feminism emerged from women of color. For many of them, the concerns of white, usually middle-class, feminists were hardly relevant to their oppression. Black women had always worked outside the home and so felt little need to be liberated from the chains of homemaking. Whereas white women might find the family oppressive, African American women viewed it as a secure base from which to resist racism. Solidarity with black men, rather than separation from them, was essential in confronting a racist America. Viewing mainstream feminism as "a family quarrel between White women and White men," many women of African descent in the United States and Britain established their own organizations, with a focus on racism and poverty.[12]

Feminism in the Global South

As women mobilized outside of the Western world during the twentieth century, they faced very different situations than did white women in the United States and Europe. For much of Asia, Africa, and Latin America, the predominant issues—

colonialism, racism, national independence, poverty, development, political oppression, and sometimes revolution—were not directly related to gender. Women were affected by and engaged with all of these efforts and were welcomed by nationalist and communist leaders, mostly men, who needed their support. But once independence or the revolution was achieved, the women who had joined those movements often were relegated to marginal positions.

The different conditions within developing countries sometimes generated sharp criticism of Western feminism. To many African feminists in the 1970s and later, the concerns of their American or European sisters were too individualistic, too focused on sexuality, and insufficiently concerned with issues of motherhood, marriage, and poverty to be of much use. Furthermore, they resented Western feminists' insistent interest in cultural matters such as female genital mutilation and polygamy, which sometimes echoed the concerns of colonial-era missionaries and administrators. Western feminism could easily be seen as a new form of cultural imperialism. Moreover, many African governments and many African men defined feminism of any kind as "un-African" and associated with a hated colonialism.

Women's movements in the Global South took shape around a wide range of issues, not all of which were explicitly gender based. In the East African country of Kenya, a major form of mobilization was the women's group movement. Some 27,000 small associations of women, an outgrowth of traditional self-help groups, had a combined membership of more than a million by the late 1980s. Members provided support for one another during times of need, such as weddings, births, and funerals, and took on community projects, such as building water cisterns, schools, and dispensaries. In one province, for example, women's groups focused on providing permanent iron roofing for homes. Some groups became revolving loan societies or bought land or businesses. One woman testified to the sense of empowerment she derived from membership in her group:

> I am a free woman. I bought this piece of land through my group. I can lie on
> it, work on it, keep goats or cows. What more do I want? My husband cannot
> sell it. It is mine.[13]

Elsewhere, other issues and approaches predominated. In the North African Islamic kingdom of Morocco, a more centrally directed and nationally focused feminist movement targeted the country's Family Law Code, which still defined women as minors. In 2004, a long campaign by Morocco's feminist movement, often with the help of supportive men and a liberal king, resulted in a new Family Law Code, which recognized women as equals to their husbands and allowed them to initiate divorce and to claim child custody, all of which had previously been denied.

In Chile, a women's movement emerged as part of a national struggle against the military dictatorship of General Augusto Pinochet, who ruled the country from 1973 to 1990. Because they were largely regarded as "invisible" in the public sphere, women were able to organize extensively, despite the repression of the Pinochet regime. From this explosion of organizing activity emerged a women's movement that crossed class lines and party affiliations. Human rights activists, most of them women, called attention to the widespread use of torture and to the "disappearance" of thousands of opponents of the regime, while demanding the restoration of democracy. Poor urban women by the tens of thousands organized soup kitchens, craft workshops, and shopping collectives, all aimed at the economic survival of their families. Smaller numbers of middle-class women brought more distinctly feminist perspectives to the movement and argued pointedly for "democracy in the country and in the home." This diverse women's movement was an important part of the larger national protest that returned Chile to democratic government in 1990.

International Feminism

Perhaps the most impressive achievement of feminism in the twentieth century was its ability to project the "woman question" as a global issue and to gain international recognition for the view that "women's rights are human rights." Like slavery and empire before it, patriarchy lost at least some of its legitimacy during this most recent century, although clearly it has not been vanquished.

Feminism registered as a global issue when the United Nations (UN), under pressure from women activists, declared 1975 as International Women's Year and the next ten years as the Decade for Women. The UN also sponsored a series of World Conferences on Women over the next twenty years. By 2006, 183 nations, though not the United States, had ratified a UN Convention on the Elimination of All Forms of Discrimination against Women, which committed them to promote women's legal equality, to end discrimination, to actively encourage women's development, and to protect women's human rights. Clearly, this international attention to women's issues was encouraging to feminists operating in their own countries and in many places stimulated both research and action.

This growing international spotlight on women's issues also revealed sharp divisions within global feminism. One issue was determining who had the right to speak on behalf of women at international gatherings—the official delegates of male-dominated governments or the often more radical unofficial participants representing various nongovernmental organizations. North/South conflicts also surfaced at these international conferences. In preparing for the Mexico City gathering in 1975, the United States attempted to limit the agenda to matters of political and civil rights for women, whereas delegates from third-world and communist countries wanted to include issues of economic justice, decolonization, and disarmament. Feminists from the South resented the dominance and contested the ideas of their Northern sisters. One African group highlighted the differences:

> While patriarchal views and structures oppress women all over the world, women are also members of classes and countries that dominate others and enjoy privileges in terms of access to resources. Hence, contrary to the best intentions of "sisterhood," not all women share identical interests.[14]

An Aspect of Brazilian Feminism
Protesting macho culture and violence against women, demonstrations in São Paulo, Brazil, began in 2011, challenging the assumption that female victims of rape were responsible for those attacks because of how they dressed. Participants marched as "sluts," wearing sexually provocative clothing, while urging the "transformation of the world by feminism." The "slutwalk" shown here took place in São Paulo in mid-2014. (© Aaron Cadena Ovalle/epa/Corbis)

Nor did all third-world groups have identical views. Some Muslim delegates at the Beijing Conference in 1995 opposed a call for equal inheritance for women because Islamic law required that sons receive twice the amount that daughters inherit. In contrast, Africans, especially in non-Muslim countries, were aware of how many children had been orphaned by AIDS and felt that girls' chances for survival depended on equal inheritance.

Finally, beyond such divisions within international feminism lay a global backlash among those who felt that its radical agenda had undermined family life, the proper relationship of men and women, and civilization generally. To Phyllis Schlafly, a prominent American opponent of the Equal Rights Amendment, feminism was a "disease" that brought in its wake "fear, sickness, pain, anger, hatred, danger, violence, and all manner of ugliness."[15] In the Islamic world, Western-style feminism, with its claims of gender equality and open sexuality, was highly offensive to many and fueled movements of religious revivalism that invited or compelled women to wear the veil and sometimes to lead highly restricted lives. The Vatican, some Catholic and Muslim countries, and at times the U.S. government took strong exception to aspects of global feminism, particularly its emphasis on reproductive rights, including access to abortion and birth control. Thus feminism was global as the twenty-first century dawned, but it was very diverse and much contested.

Religion and Global Modernity

Beyond liberation and feminism, a further dimension of cultural globalization took shape in the challenge that modernity presented to the world's religions. To the most "advanced" thinkers of the past several hundred years—Enlightenment writers in the eighteenth century, Karl Marx in the nineteenth, and many academics and secular-minded intellectuals in the twentieth—religion was headed for extinction in the face of modernity, science, communism, or globalization. In some places—Britain, France, the Netherlands, and the Soviet Union, for example—religious belief and practice had declined sharply. Moreover, the spread of a scientific culture around the world persuaded small minorities everywhere, often among the most highly educated, that the only realities worth considering were those that could be measured with the techniques of science. To such people, all else was superstition, born of ignorance. Nevertheless, the far more prominent trends of the last century have been those that involved the further spread of major world religions, their resurgence in new forms, their opposition to elements of a secular and global modernity, and their political role as a source of community identity and conflict. Contrary to earlier expectations, religion has played an unexpectedly powerful role in this most recent century.

Buddhism, Christianity, and Islam had long functioned as transregional cultures, spreading far beyond their places of origin. That process continued in the twentieth century. Buddhist ideas and practices such as meditation found a warm reception in the West, as did yoga, originally a mind-body practice of Indian origin. Christianity of various kinds spread widely in non-Muslim Africa and South Korea and less extensively in parts of India. By the end of the twentieth century, it was growing even in China, where perhaps 7 to 8 percent of China's population—some 84 to 96 million people—claimed allegiance to the faith. No longer a primarily European or North American religion, Christianity by the early twenty-first century found some 62 percent of its adherents in Asia, Africa, Oceania, and Latin America. In some instances, missionaries from those regions have set about the "re-evangelization" of Europe and North America. Moreover, millions of migrants from the Islamic world have planted their religion solidly in the West. In the United States, for example, a substantial number of African Americans and smaller numbers of European Americans engage in Islamic practice. For several decades, the writings of the thirteenth-century Islamic Sufi poet Rumi have been best sellers in the United States. Religious exchange, in short, has been a two-way street, not simply a transmission of Western ideas to the rest of the world. More than ever before, religious pluralism characterizes many of the world's societies, confronting people with the need to make choices in a domain of life previously regarded as given and fixed.

Fundamentalism on a Global Scale

Religious vitality in the twentieth century was expressed not only in the spread of particular traditions to new areas but also in the vigorous response of those traditions to the modernizing and globalizing world in which they found themselves. One such response has been widely called "fundamentalism," a militant piety—defensive, assertive, and exclusive—that took shape to some extent in every major religious tradition. Many features of the modern world, after all, appeared threatening to established religion. The scientific and secular focus of global modernity challenged the core beliefs of religion, with its focus on an unseen realm of reality. Furthermore, the social upheavals connected with capitalism, industrialization, and globalization thoroughly upset customary class, family, and gender relationships that had long been sanctified by religious tradition. Nation-states, often associated with particular religions, were likewise undermined by the operation of a global economy and challenged by the spread of alien cultures. In much of the world, these disruptions came at the hands of foreigners, usually Westerners, in the form of military defeat, colonial rule, economic dependency, and cultural intrusion.

To such threats, fundamentalism represented a religious response, characterized by one scholar as "embattled forms of spirituality . . . experienced as a cosmic war between the forces of good and evil."[16] Although fundamentalisms everywhere looked to the past for ideals and models, their rejection of modernity was selective, not wholesale. What they sought was an alternative modernity, infused with particular religious values. Most, in fact, made active use of modern technology to communicate their message and certainly sought the potential prosperity associated with modern life. Extensive educational and propaganda efforts, political mobilization of their followers, social welfare programs, and sometimes violence ("terrorism" to their opponents) were among the means that fundamentalists employed.

The term "fundamentalism" derived from the United States, where religious conservatives in the early twentieth century were outraged by critical and "scientific" approaches to the Bible, by Darwinian evolution, and by liberal versions of Christianity that accommodated these heresies. They called for a return to the "fundamentals" of the faith, which included a belief in the literal truthfulness of the scriptures, in the virgin birth and physical resurrection of Jesus, and in miracles. After World War II, American Protestant fundamentalism came to oppose political liberalism and "big government," the sexual revolution of the 1960s, homosexuality and abortion rights, and secular humanism generally. Many fundamentalists saw the United States on the edge of an abyss. For one major spokesman, Francis Schaeffer (1912–1984), the West was about to enter "an electronic dark age, in which the new pagan hordes, with all the power of technology at their command, are on the verge of obliterating the last strongholds of civilized humanity." He declared, "A vision of darkness lies before us. As we leave the shores of Christian Western man behind, only a dark and turbulent sea of despair stretches endlessly ahead . . . unless we fight."[17]

■ **Change**
In what respect did the various religious fundamentalisms of the twentieth century express hostility to global modernity?

And fight they did! At first, fundamentalists sought to separate themselves from the secular world in their own churches and schools, but from the 1970s on, they entered the political arena as the "religious right," determined to return America to a "godly path." "We have enough votes to run this country," declared Pat Robertson, a major fundamentalist evangelist and broadcaster who ran for president in 1988. Conservative Christians, no longer willing to restrict their attention to personal salvation, had emerged as a significant force in American political life well before the end of the century.

In the very different setting of independent India, another fundamentalist movement—known as Hindutva (Hindu nationalism)—took shape during the 1980s, although the concept had appeared as early as 1923 and Gandhi's assassination in 1948 had occurred at the hands of men in that movement. Like American fundamentalism, it represented a politicization of religion within a democratic context. To its advocates, India was, and always had been, an essentially Hindu land, even though it had been overwhelmed in recent centuries by Muslim invaders, then by the Christian British, and most recently by the secular state of the post-independence decades. The leaders of modern India, they argued, and particularly its first prime minister, Jawaharlal Nehru, were "the self-proclaimed secularists who . . . seek to remake India in the Western image," while repudiating its basically Hindu religious character. The Hindutva movement took political shape in an increasingly popular party called the Bharatiya Janata Party (BJP), with much of its support coming from urban middle-class or upper-caste people who resented the state's efforts to cater to the interests of Muslims, Sikhs, and the lower castes. Muslims in particular were defined as outsiders, potentially more loyal to a Muslim Pakistan than to India. The BJP became a major political force in India during the 1980s, winning a number of elections and promoting a distinctly Hindu identity in education, culture, and religion. Its sweeping victory in national elections in 2014 raised questions about how its Hindu nationalism would fare in twenty-first-century India.

Creating Islamic Societies: Resistance and Renewal in the World of Islam

The most prominent of the late twentieth-century fundamentalisms was surely that of Islam. Expressed in many and various ways, it was an effort among growing numbers of Muslims to renew and reform the practice of Islam and to create a new religious/political order centered on a particular understanding of their faith. Earlier renewal movements, such as the eighteenth-century Wahhabis (see pages 660–61) focused largely on the internal problems of Muslim societies, while those of the twentieth century responded as well to the external pressures of colonial rule, Western imperialism, and secular modernity.

■ **Change**
From what sources did Islamic renewal movements derive?

Emerging strongly in the last quarter of the twentieth century, Islamic renewal movements gained strength from the enormous disappointments that had accumulated in the Muslim world by the 1970s. Conquest and colonial rule; awareness of the huge technological and economic gap between Islamic and European civilizations; the disappearance of the Ottoman Empire, long the chief Islamic state; elite enchantment with Western culture; the retreat of Islam for many to the realm of private life—all of this had sapped the cultural self-confidence of many Muslims by the mid-twentieth century. Political independence for former colonies certainly represented a victory for Islamic societies, but it had given rise to major states—Egypt, Pakistan, Indonesia, Iraq, Algeria, and others—that pursued essentially Western and secular policies of nationalism, socialism, and economic development, often with only lip service to an Islamic identity.

Even worse, these policies were not very successful. A number of endemic problems—vastly overcrowded cities with few services, widespread unemployment, pervasive corruption, slow economic growth, a mounting gap between the rich and poor—flew in the face of the great expectations that had accompanied the struggle against European domination. Despite formal independence, foreign intrusion still persisted. Israel, widely regarded as an outpost of the West, had been reestablished as a Jewish state in the very center of the Islamic world in 1948. In 1967, Israel inflicted a devastating defeat on Arab forces in the Six-Day War and seized various Arab territories, including the holy city of Jerusalem. Furthermore, broader signs of Western cultural penetration persisted—secular schools, alcohol, Barbie dolls, European and American movies, scantily clad women. (For more on Muslim views on Barbie dolls, see Zooming In: Barbie and Her Competitors in the Muslim World, page 1046.) The largely secular leader of independent Tunisia, Habib Bourguiba, argued against the veil for women as well as polygamy for men and discouraged his people from fasting during Ramadan. In 1960, he was shown on television drinking orange juice during the sacred month to the outrage of many traditional Muslims.

This was the context in which the idea of an Islamic alternative to Western models of modernity began to take hold more broadly, although its origins go back to the Young Ottomans of the 1860s. The intellectual and political foundations of this Islamic renewal had been established earlier in the century. Its leading figures, such as the Indian Mawlana Mawdudi and the Egyptian Sayyid Qutb, insisted that the Quran and the sharia (Islamic law) provided a guide for all of life—political, economic, and spiritual—and a blueprint for a distinctly Islamic modernity not dependent on Western ideas. It was the departure from Islamic principles, they argued, that had led the Islamic world into decline and subordination to the West, and only a return to the "straight path of Islam" would ensure a revival of Muslim societies. That effort to return to Islamic principles was labeled *jihad*, an ancient and evocative religious term that refers to "struggle" or "striving" to please God. In its twentieth-century political expression, jihad included the defense of an authentic Islam against Western aggression and vigorous efforts to achieve the Islamization of social and political life within Muslim countries. It was a posture that would enable Muslims to resist the seductive but poisonous culture of the West. Sayyid Qutb had

Barbie and Her Competitors in the Muslim World

"I think every Barbie doll is more harmful than an American missile," declared Iranian toy seller Masoumeh Rahimi in 2002. To Rahimi, Barbie's revealing clothing, her shapely appearance, and her close association with Ken, her longtime unmarried companion, were "foreign to Iran's culture." Thus Rahimi warmly welcomed the arrival in 2002 of Sara and Dara, Iranian Muslim dolls meant to counteract the negative influence of Barbie, who had long dominated Iran's toy market. Created by the Iranian government, Sara and her brother, Dara, represented eight-year-old twins and were intended to replace Barbie and Ken, the sale of which the authorities had officially banned in the mid-1990s because they represented a "Trojan horse" for Western values. Sara came complete with a headscarf to cover her hair in modest Muslim fashion and a full-length white chador enveloping her from head to toe. She and her brother were described as helping each other solve problems,

A Syrian girl examining Fulla dolls at a toy store in Damascus in 2005.

photo: © Khaled Al-Hariri/Reuters/Landov

while looking to their loving parents for guidance, hardly the message that Barbie and Ken conveyed.[18]

In 2003, a toy company based in Syria introduced Fulla, a doll depicting a young Muslim woman about the same age as Barbie, perhaps a grown-up version of Sara. Dressed modestly in a manner that reflected the norms of each national market, Fulla was described by her creator as representing "Muslim values." Unlike Barbie, with her boyfriend and a remarkable range of careers, including astronaut and president of the United States, Fulla was modeled on the ideal traditional Arab woman. She interacted with male family members rather than a boyfriend and was depicted only as a teacher or a doctor, both respected professions for women in the Islamic world. But she did share an eye for fashion with Barbie. Underneath her

witnessed that culture during a visit to the United States in the late 1940s and was appalled by what he saw:

> Look at this capitalism with its monopolies, its usury . . . at this individual freedom, devoid of human sympathy and responsibility for relatives except under force of law; at this materialistic attitude which deadens the spirit; at this behavior like animals which you call "free mixing of the sexes"; at this vulgarity which you call "emancipation of women"; at this evil and fanatical racial discrimination.[19]

■ **Comparison**
In what different ways did Islamic renewal express itself?

By the 1970s, ideas and organizations favoring the Islamization of public life echoed widely across the Islamic world and found expression in many ways. At the level of personal practice, many people became more religiously observant, attending mosque, praying regularly, and fasting. Substantial numbers of women, many

modest outer dress, Fulla wore stylish clothing, although it was less revealing than that of her American counterpart, and, like Barbie, she chose from an extensive wardrobe, sold separately of course. "This isn't just about putting the hijab [a headscarf covering a woman's hair and chest] on a Barbie doll," Fawaz Abidin, the Fulla brand manager, noted. "You have to create a character that parents and children want to relate to."[20]

Fulla proved far more popular than Sara among Muslim girls, becoming one of the best-selling dolls in the Muslim world. In part, the adoption by Fulla's creators of Western marketing techniques, similar to those that had been used to promote Barbie for decades, lay behind the doll's remarkable success. Fulla-themed magazines appeared on newsstands, and commercials advertising Fulla dolls and their accessories permeated children's television stations in the Muslim world. "When you take Fulla out of the house, don't forget her new spring abaya [a long, robe-like full-body covering]!" admonished one advertisement. Fulla's image was used to market an endless number of other licensed products, including branded stationery, backpacks, prayer rugs, bikes, and breakfast cereals, all in trademark "Fulla pink." In this respect, Fulla and Barbie shared a great deal. Despite Fulla's success, Barbie has continued to enjoy a loyal following in the region, in part because of her exotic qualities. "All my friends have Fulla now, but I still like Barbie the best," one ten-year-old Saudi girl stated. "She has blonde hair and cool clothes. Every single girl in Saudi looks like Fulla. . . . What's so special about that?"

The widespread availability of Barbie in the Muslim world provides one small example of the power of global commerce in the world of the early twenty-first century. But Sara and Fulla illustrate resistance to the cultural values associated with this American product. Still, Sara, Fulla, and Barbie had something in common: nearly all were manufactured in East Asian factories. Indeed, the same factories frequently manufactured the rival dolls. This triangular relationship of the United States, the Muslim world, and East Asia symbolized the growing integration of world economies and cultures as well as the divergences and conflicts that this process has generated. These linked but contrasting patterns involve much more than dolls in the early twenty-first century, for they define major features of the world we all share.

Questions: What can Barbie, Sara, and Fulla tell us about the globalized world of the twenty-first century? What different values and sensibilities do they convey?

of them young, urban, and well educated, adopted modest Islamic dress and the veil quite voluntarily. Participation in Sufi mystical practices increased in some places. Furthermore, many governments sought to anchor themselves in Islamic rhetoric and practice. During the 1970s, President Anwar Sadat of Egypt claimed the title of "Believer-President," referred frequently to the Quran, and proudly displayed his "prayer mark," a callus on his forehead caused by touching his head to the ground in prayer. Under pressure from Islamic activists, the government of Sudan in the 1980s adopted Quranic punishments for various crimes (such as amputating the hand of a thief) and announced a total ban on alcohol, dramatically dumping thousands of bottles of beer and wine into the Nile.

All over the Muslim world, from North Africa to Indonesia (see Map 23.3), Islamic renewal movements spawned organizations that operated legally to provide social services—schools, clinics, youth centers, legal-aid societies, financial

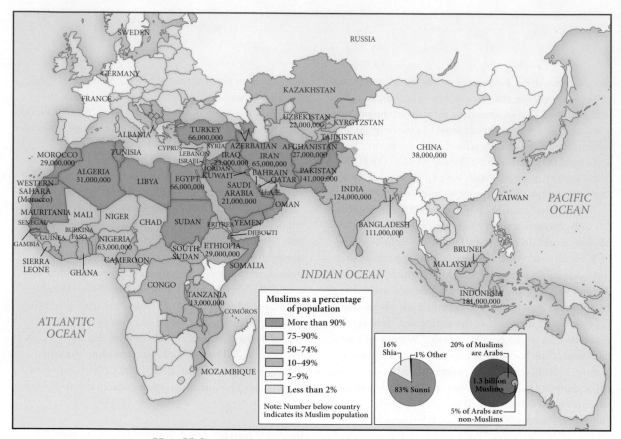

Map 23.3   The Islamic World in the Early Twenty-First Century

An Islamic world of well over a billion people incorporated much of the Afro-Asian landmass but was divided among many nations and along linguistic and ethnic lines as well. The long-term split between the majority Sunnis and the minority Shias also sharpened in the new millennium.

institutions, publishing houses—that the state offered inadequately or not at all. Islamic activists took leadership roles in unions and professional organizations of teachers, journalists, engineers, doctors, and lawyers. Such people embraced modern science and technology but sought to embed these elements of modernity within a distinctly Islamic culture. Some served in official government positions or entered political life and contested elections where it was possible to do so. The Algerian Islamic Salvation Front was poised to win elections in 1992, when a frightened military government intervened to cancel the elections, an action that plunged the country into a decade of bitter civil war. Egypt's Muslim Brotherhood did come to power peacefully in 2012, but was removed by the military a year later amid widespread protests against its policies.

Movements embracing another face of religious renewal, however, sought the forcible overthrow of what they saw as compromised regimes in the Islamic world, most successfully in Iran in 1979 (see Chapter 22, pages 1007–10), but also in Afghanistan (1996), northern Nigeria (2009–2015), and parts of Syria and Iraq (2013–2015). Here Islamic movements succeeded in seizing state power or controlling certain territories and began to implement, sometimes brutally, a program of Islamization based on the sharia. Elsewhere military governments in Pakistan and Sudan likewise introduced elements of sharia-based law. Hoping to spark an Islamic revolution, the Egyptian Islamic Jihad organization assassinated President Sadat in 1981, following Sadat's brutal crackdown on both Islamic and secular opposition groups. One of the leaders of Islamic Jihad explained:

> We have to establish the Rule of God's Religion in our own country first, and to make the Word of God supreme. . . . There is no doubt that the first battlefield for jihad is the extermination of these infidel leaders and to replace them by a complete Islamic Order.[21]

Islamic revolutionaries also took aim at hostile foreign powers. Hamas in Palestine and Hezbollah in Lebanon, supported by the Islamic regime in Iran, targeted Israel with popular uprisings, suicide bombings, and rocket attacks in response to the Israeli occupation of Arab lands. For some, Israel's very existence was illegitimate. The Soviet invasion of Afghanistan in 1979 prompted widespread opposition aimed at liberating that country from atheistic communism and creating an Islamic state. Sympathetic Arabs from the Middle East and other Muslims flocked to the aid of their Afghan compatriots.

Among them was the young Osama bin Laden, a wealthy Saudi Arab, who created an organization, al-Qaeda (meaning "the base" in Arabic), to funnel fighters and funds to the Afghan resistance. At the time, bin Laden and the Americans were on the same side, both opposing Soviet expansion into Afghanistan, but they soon parted ways. Returning to his home in Saudi Arabia, bin Laden became disillusioned and radicalized when the government of his country allowed the stationing of "infidel" U.S. troops in Islam's holy land, where the faith had begun, during and after the first American war against Iraq in 1991. By the mid-1990s, he had found a safe haven in Taliban-ruled Afghanistan, from which he and other leaders of al-Qaeda planned their attack on the World Trade Center and other targets in the United States on September 11, 2001. Although they had no standing as Muslim clerics, in 1998 they had issued a *fatwa* (religious edict) declaring war on America:

> For over seven years the United States has been occupying the lands of Islam in the holiest of places, the Arabian Peninsula, plundering its riches, dictating to its rulers, humiliating its people, terrorizing its neighbors, and turning its bases in the Peninsula into a spearhead through which to fight the neighboring Muslim peoples. . . . The ruling to kill the Americans and their allies — civilians and military — is an individual duty for every Muslim who can do it in any country in which it is possible to do it, in order to liberate the al-Aqsa Mosque in Jerusalem and the holy mosque [in Mecca] from their grip, and in order for their armies to move out of all the lands of Islam, defeated and unable to threaten any Muslim.[22]

Hamas in Action

The Palestinian militant organization Hamas, founded in 1987 as an offshoot of Egypt's Muslim Brotherhood, illustrates two dimensions of Islamic radicalism. On the one hand, Hamas repeatedly sent suicide bombers to target Israeli civilians and sought the elimination of the Israeli state. A group of would-be suicide bombers are shown here in white robes during the funeral of colleagues killed by Israeli security forces in late 2003. On the other hand, Hamas ran a network of social services, providing schools, clinics, orphanages, summer camps, soup kitchens, and libraries for Palestinians. The classroom pictured here from 2006 was part of a school founded by Hamas. (left: Andrea Comas/Reuters/Landov; right: Abid Katib/Getty Images)

Elsewhere as well—in East Africa, Indonesia, Great Britain, Spain, France, Saudi Arabia, and Yemen—al-Qaeda or groups associated with it launched scattered attacks on Western interests. At the international level, the great enemy was not Christianity itself or even Western civilization, but irreligious Western-style modernity, U.S. imperialism, and the American-led economic globalization so aptly symbolized by the World Trade Center. Ironically, al-Qaeda itself was a modern and global organization, many of whose members were highly educated professionals from a variety of countries.

Despite this focus on the West, the violent struggles undertaken by politicized Islamic activists were directed as much against elements within the Islamic world as they were against the external enemy. Broadly known as Salafis, these activists and their supporters sought to follow what they understood to be the example of the *salaf*, or "ancestors," men of Muhammad's time and shortly thereafter. Their understanding of Islam, heavily influenced by Wahhabi ideas (see pages 660–61), was in various ways quite novel and at odds with classical Islamic practice. It was highly literal and dogmatic in its understanding of the Quran, legalistic in its effort to regulate the minute details of daily life, deeply opposed to any "innovation" in religious practice, inclined to define those who disagreed with them as "non-Muslims," and drawn to violent jihad as a legitimate part of Islamic life. It was also deeply skeptical about the interior spiritual emphasis of Sufism, which had informed so much of earlier Islamic culture. The spread of Salafi Islam owed much to massive financial backing from oil-rich Saudi Arabia, which funded Wahhabi/Salafi mosques and schools across the Islamic world and in the West as well.

Religious Alternatives to Fundamentalism

Militant revolutionary fundamentalism has certainly not been the only religious response to modernity and globalization within the Islamic world. Many who shared a desire to embed Islamic values more centrally in their societies have acted peacefully and within established political structures. In Turkey, Egypt, Jordan, Iraq, Palestine, Morocco, Tunisia, and Lebanon, Islamic parties with various agendas made impressive electoral showings in the 1990s and the early twenty-first century. Considerable debate among Muslims has raised questions about the proper role of the state, the difference between the eternal law of God (sharia) and the human interpretations of it, the rights of women, the possibility of democracy, and many other issues. (See Working with Evidence: Contending for Islam, Chapter 22, page 1012.) Some Muslim intellectuals and political leaders have called for a dialogue between civilizations; others have argued that traditions can change in the face of modern realities without losing their distinctive Islamic character. In 1996, Anwar Ibrahim, a major political and intellectual figure in Malaysia, insisted:

> [Southeast Asian Muslims] would rather strive to improve the welfare of the women and children in their midst than spend their days elaborately defining the nature and institutions of the ideal Islamic state. They do not believe it makes one less of a Muslim to promote economic growth, to master the information revolution, and to demand justice for women.[23]

In Turkey, a movement inspired by the teachings of Fethullah Gulen, a Turkish Muslim scholar and preacher, has sought to apply the principles of Islamic spirituality and Sufi piety to the problems of modern society. Gaining a mass following in the 1990s and later, the Gulen movement has advocated interfaith and cross-cultural dialogue, multiparty democracy, nonviolence, and modern scientifically based education for girls and boys alike. Operating through schools, universities, conferences, newspapers, radio and TV stations, and various charities, it has a presence in more than 100 countries around the world. Claiming to be "faith-based but not faith limited," the movement rejects the "fundamentalist" label even as it has challenged a wholly secular outlook on public life. And in 2004–2005, a gathering in Jordan of scholars from all major schools of Islamic thought issued the "Amman Message," which called for Islamic unity, condemned terrorism, forbade Muslims from declaring one another as "apostate" or nonbelievers, and emphasized the commonalities shared by Muslims, Christians, and Jews.

Within other religious traditions as well, believers found various ways of responding to global modernity. A number of liberal and mainstream Christian groups spoke to the ethical issues arising from economic globalization. Many Christian organizations, for example, were active in agitating for debt relief for poor countries. Pope John Paul II (r. 1978–2005) voiced his concern about "the growing distance between rich and poor, [and] unfair competition which puts the poor nations in a situation of ever-increasing inferiority." Pope Francis (r. 2013–), the first pontiff from Latin America, sought even more emphatically to direct the attention of

Catholics toward the poor, the marginalized, and the suffering people of the world. Adherents of "liberation theology," particularly in Latin America, sought a Christian basis for action in the areas of social justice, poverty, and human rights, while viewing Jesus as liberator as well as savior.

In Asia, a growing movement known as "socially engaged Buddhism" addressed the needs of the poor through social reform, educational programs, health services, and peacemaking action during times of conflict and war. A leading proponent of this approach was the Buddhist monk Maha Ghosananda. In the late 1970s, when Cambodia had been ravaged by the "killing fields" of the Khmer Rouge communist regime, he repeatedly visited the squalid refugee camps to which so many Cambodians had fled. There he led religious services, and later peace marches, endlessly reciting an ancient Buddhist chant: "Hatred never ceases by hatred, but by love alone is healed. This is an ancient and eternal law." In short, religious responses to global modernity were articulated in many voices.

SUMMING UP SO FAR

How might you compare feminism and fundamentalism as global movements? In what ways did they challenge earlier values and expectations? To what extent were they in conflict with one another?

Experiencing the Anthropocene Era: Environment and Environmentalism

Even as world religions, fundamentalist and otherwise, challenged global modernity on cultural or spiritual grounds, burgeoning environmental movements in the 1960s and later also did so with an eye to the human impact on the earth and its many living creatures, including ourselves. Among the distinctive features of the twentieth century, none has been more pronounced than humankind's growing ability to alter the natural order and the mounting awareness of this phenomenon. When the wars, revolutions, and empires of this most recent century have faded from memory, environmental transformation and environmental consciousness may well seem to future generations the decisive feature of that century. Already, many scientists and other scholars have begun to refer to the current era, since at least the advent of the Industrial Revolution, as the Anthropocene, or the "age of man." That informal term has called attention to the lasting impact of human activity on the planet.[24] Species extinctions, increases of carbon dioxide in the atmosphere, the depletion of groundwater reserves, the enlargement of deserts, dead zones in the oceans, transformation of the landscape as wetlands shrink and urban centers grow—these and other environmental changes, all of them generated by human actions, will be apparent to our descendants thousands of years in the future, should they be around to reflect on them.

The Global Environment Transformed

Underlying the environmental changes of the twentieth century were three factors that vastly magnified the human impact on earth's ecological systems far beyond anything previously known.[25] One was the explosion of human numbers, an unprecedented quadrupling of the world's population in a single century, leaving the world of 2014 with about 7.2 billion people compared to about 1.6 billion in 1900. It was a demographic revolution born of medical and sanitation advances that dramatically lowered death rates and Green Revolution technologies such as genetically modified seeds and fertilizers that substantially increased world food supplies.

This vast enlargement of the human population meant more consumption and thus more demands on the earth's resources. It also fostered massive urbanization and global migration, even as it contributed to many political and social upheavals, especially in the second half of the century. By the end of the century, the rate of global population growth had begun to slow. From a peak of over 2 percent per year in the 1960s, it had dropped to 1.14 percent by 2014. This transition had occurred first in the more developed countries, where birth control measures were widely available, women were educated and pursuing careers, and large families were economically burdensome. This pattern began to take hold in developing countries as well, assisted by vigorous family-planning programs in many places, the most dramatic of which was China's famous "one-child family" policy. Experts predict that the modern population explosion will level off by the mid–twenty-first century at some 9 to 12 billion people, although whether the world economy and its resource base can support these enormously enhanced numbers remains an open question.

A second cause of environmental stress lay in the amazing new ability of humankind to tap the energy potential of fossil fuels—coal in the nineteenth century and oil in the twentieth. These fuels drove the industrialization process everywhere, with coal providing the major source for electricity generation and oil giving rise to the immense automobile industry. Hydroelectricity, natural gas, solar power, and nuclear power added to the energy resources available to our species.

These new sources of energy made possible a third contribution to environmental transformation—phenomenal economic growth—as modern science and technology immensely increased the production of goods and services. Between the 1890s and the 1990s, global industrial output grew by a factor of forty, although very unevenly across the planet. But almost everywhere—in capitalist, communist, and developing countries alike—the idea of economic growth or "development" as something possible and desirable took hold as a novel element of global culture.

These three factors were the foundations for the immense environmental transformations of this most recent century. Human activity had always altered the natural order, usually on a local basis, but now the scale of that impact assumed global and perhaps even geological proportions. The growing numbers of the poor and the growing consumption of the rich led to the doubling of cropland; a corresponding contraction of the world's forests, wetlands, and grasslands; and dramatic increases in the rate of erosion. Huge urban complexes have transformed the landscape in many places. With diminished habitats, numerous species of plants and animals either disappeared or were threatened with extinction at a rate many times greater than the background level. Certainly, massive species extinctions have occurred much earlier in the history of the planet (the dinosaurs, for example), but this wave of extinctions is happening at the hands of humankind. The human

■ **Change**
How can we explain the dramatic increase in the human impact on the environment in the twentieth century?

remaking of the ecosystem has also greatly increased the presence of plants and animals that have benefited from human activity—cattle, pigs, chickens, rats, wheat, corn, and dandelions. By some estimates, 90 percent of all plant activity now occurs in environments shaped by human action.

The global spread of modern industry, heavily dependent on fossil fuels, generated dramatic changes in the air, water, soil, and atmosphere with profound impacts on human life. China's spectacular economic growth since the 1980s, fueled largely by coal, has resulted in the equally spectacular pall of air pollution in its major cities. In 2004, the World Bank reported that twelve of the world's twenty most polluted cities were in China. Degradation of the world's rivers, seas, and oceans has also mounted as pesticides, herbicides, chemical fertilizers, detergents, oil, sewage, industrial waste, and plastics have made their way from land to water. By the 1960s, Lake Erie in the United States was widely reported as "dead." The Great Pacific Garbage Patch, an area of about 7 million square miles in the North Pacific, has trapped an enormous quantity of marine debris, mostly plastics, endangering oceanic food webs and proving deadly to creatures of the sea, which ingest or become entangled in this human garbage. Industrial pollution in the Soviet Union rendered about half of the country's rivers severely polluted by the late 1980s, while fully 20 percent of its population lived in regions defined as "ecological disasters." In addition, the release of chemicals known as chlorofluorocarbons thinned the ozone layer, which protects the earth from excessive ultraviolet radiation.

The most critical and intractable environmental challenge of recent decades has been global warming. Scientists became concerned about this phenomenon in the 1970s, although their research drew on earlier studies dating to the nineteenth century. By the end of the twentieth century, a worldwide scientific consensus had emerged that a dangerously warming climate was well under way, driven by human actions. Particularly responsible for this global warming has been the vastly increased burning of fossil fuels, which release heat-trapping greenhouse gases such as carbon dioxide into the atmosphere, as well as by the loss of trees that would otherwise remove the carbon dioxide from the air. By 2014, carbon dioxide concentration in the atmosphere, which had been roughly 275 ppm (parts per million) before the Industrial Revolution, had risen to 400 ppm, well above the level of 350 ppm that is generally considered "safe." Scientists have associated this global warming with all manner of environmental changes, both current and projected: the melting of glaciers and the rising of sea levels; extreme weather events such as floods, droughts, hurricanes, and typhoons; increased acidification of the oceans; decreased crop yields; disruptions of ecosystems and the extinction of many species. All of this has varied and will continue to vary substantially from region to region, but serious observers have begun to speak about the possibility of "a crisis that threatens our survival as a species."[26]

Beyond these weather- and climate-related changes, global warming has interacted with a variety of social conditions—poverty, inequality, oppression—to generate or exacerbate conflict and upheaval. Syria's bitter civil war, which has killed over 200,000 people and displaced or made refugees of many millions more since 2011, followed on the heels of a severe and prolonged drought and related crop failures. More broadly, in 2010 and 2011 extreme weather conditions characteristic of global warming—droughts, dust storms, fires, heavy rainfall—afflicted many grain-producing regions of the world, including Canada, Russia, China, Argentina, and Australia, causing a sharp spike in grain prices on the world market. The Middle East and North Africa, heavily dependent on grain imports, experienced sharply rising food prices, arguably aggravating social unrest and contributing to the political protests of the Arab Spring. Even the American military has taken climate change seriously. A 2007 report by a number of senior retired officers concluded that "climate change poses a serious threat to America's national security . . . [and] acts as a threat multiplier for instability in some of the most volatile regions of the world."[27]

Green and Global

Modern environmentalism, with its awareness of ecological damage and a desire to counteract it, dates to the late eighteenth or early nineteenth century.[28] One strand in this "first-wave environmentalism" lay in a direct response to early industrialization. Romantic poets such as William Blake and William Wordsworth denounced the industrial era's "dark satanic mills," which threatened the "green and pleasant land" of an earlier England. In opposing the extension of railroads, the British writer John Ruskin in 1876 declared, "The frenzy of avarice is daily drowning our sailors, suffocating our miners, poisoning our children and blasting the cultivable surface of England into a treeless waste of ashes."[29] Mahatma Gandhi came into contact with this strand of thinking during his time in England during the late 1880s. "God forbid," he later wrote, "that India should ever take to industrialism after the manner of the West." Another element in early environmentalism, especially prominent in the United States and Germany, derived from a concern with deforestation, drought, and desertification as pioneering settlers, lumbermen, miners, and the owners of colonial plantations inflicted terrible damage on the woodlands and pasturelands of the world. Articulated primarily by men of science, often those working in the colonial world, this approach sought to mobilize scientific expertise and state control to manage, contain, and tame modern assaults on the environment.

Protecting remaining wilderness areas was yet another aspect of early environmentalism. The first international environmental conference, held in London in 1900, aimed at preserving African wildlife from voracious European hunters. In the United States, it was the opening of the west to European settlers that threatened the natural order. "With no eye to the future," wrote naturalist John Muir in 1897, "these pious destroyers waged interminable forest wars . . . , spreading ruthless devastation ever wider and further." Muir understood the economic rationale for preserving the wilderness, but for him it also held spiritual significance. "Wilderness is a necessity . . . not only as fountains of timber and irrigating rivers, but as fountains of life."[30] This kind of sensibility found expression in the American national parks, the first of which, Yellowstone, was established in 1872.

These early examples of environmental awareness were distinctly limited, largely a product of literary figures, scientists, and some government officials. None of them attracted a mass following or provoked a global response. But "second-wave environmentalism," beginning in the 1960s, did both of these things, even as it found expression in many quite different ways.

This new phase of environmentalism is most often associated with the publication in 1962 of Rachel Carson's *Silent Spring*, exposing the chemical contamination of the environment with a particular emphasis on the use of pesticides. The book struck a chord with millions, triggering environmental movements on both sides of the Atlantic. (See Zooming In: Rachel Carson, page 1058.) Ten years later, the Club of Rome, a global think tank, issued a report called *Limits to Growth*, which warned of resource exhaustion and the collapse of industrial society in the face of unrelenting economic and population growth. Soon a mounting wave of environmental books, articles, treatises, and conferences emerged in Europe and North America, pushing back in various ways against the postwar emphasis on "development" and unending economic growth. That sensibility was aptly captured in the title of a best-selling book by British economist E. F. Schumacher in 1973: *Small Is Beautiful*.

■ **Comparison**

What differences emerged between environmentalism in the Global North and that in the Global South?

But what most clearly distinguished second-wave environmentalism was widespread grassroots involvement and activism. By the late 1990s, millions of people in North America, Europe, Japan, Australia, and New Zealand had joined one of the rapidly proliferating environmental organizations, many of them local. The issues addressed in these burgeoning movements were many and various: pollution, resource depletion, toxic waste, protecting wildlife habitats, nuclear power and nuclear testing, limiting development, and, increasingly at the top of the agenda in the twenty-first century, climate change. Beyond particular issues, proponents of "deep ecology" put forward an understanding of the world in which human beings were no longer at the center but occupied a place of equivalence with other species. Those supporting an "environmental justice" outlook were more concerned with the unequal impact of environmental problems on the poor, minorities, and developing countries.

The tactics of these movements were as varied as the issues they addressed. Much attention was given to public education and lobbying governments and corporations, often through highly organized and professionally run organizations. In Germany, New Zealand, and Australia, environmentalists created Green parties, which contested elections and on occasion shared power. Teach-ins, demonstrations, street protests, and various local actions also played a role in the strategies of environmental activists.

In the communist world, environmentalism was constrained by highly authoritarian states, which were committed to large-scale development. In the late 1980s, the Chinese government, for example, sharply repressed groups critical of the enormous Three Gorges Dam project across the Yangzi River. By the early twenty-first century, however, a grassroots environmental movement had taken root in China, expressed in hundreds of private groups and state-sponsored organizations. Many of these sought to ground their activism in Buddhist or Daoist traditions that stressed the harmony of humankind and the natural order. The Chinese state itself has enacted a large body of environmental laws and regulations.[31] In the Soviet Union during the 1970s and later, environmentalists were able to voice their concerns about the shrinking of the Aral Sea, pollution threats to Lake Baikal in Siberia, and poor air quality in many cities. After the nuclear disaster at Chernobyl in 1986, Gorbachev's policy of *glasnost* allowed greater freedom of expression as environmentalist concerns became part of a broader challenge to communism and Russian domination (see Chapter 21, pages 961–62).

Quite quickly, during the 1970s and 1980s, environmentalism also took root in the Global South, where it frequently assumed a distinctive character compared to the more industrialized countries. It was more locally based and had fewer large national organizations than in the West; it involved more poor people in direct actions; it was less engaged in political lobbying and corporate strategies; it was more concerned with issues of food security, health, and basic survival than with the rights of nature or wilderness protection; and it was more closely connected to movements for social justice.[32] Thus, whereas Western environmentalists defended forests where few people lived, the Chikpo, or "tree-hugging," movement in India sought to protect the livelihood of farmers, artisans, and herders living in areas subject to extensive deforestation. A massive movement to prevent or limit the damming of India's Narmada River derived from the displacement of local people; similar anti-dam protests in the American Northwest were more concerned with protecting salmon runs.

In the Global South, this "environmentalism of the poor" took shape in various ways, often in opposition to the gigantic development projects of national governments. Residents of the Brazilian Amazon basin, facing the loss of their livelihood to lumbering interests, ranchers, and government road-building projects, joined hands and directly confronted workers sent to cut down trees with their chainsaws. When the Thai government sought to create huge eucalyptus plantations, largely to supply Japanese-owned paper mills, Buddhist teachers, known as "ecology monks," mobilized peasants to put their case to public officials. In the Philippines, coalitions of numerous local groups—representing various religious, women's, human rights, indigenous peoples', peasant, and political organizations—mobilized large-scale grassroots movements against foreign-owned mining companies. And in Kenya, the Green Belt Movement organized groups of village women to plant millions of trees intended to forestall the growth of deserts and protect the soil.

By the early twenty-first century, environmentalism had become a matter of global concern and had prompted change at many levels. National governments acted to curtail pollution and to foster the use of renewable energy sources. By

Rachel Carson, Pioneer of Environmentalism

"Over increasingly large areas of the United States, spring now comes unheralded by the return of the birds, and the early mornings are strangely silent."[33] This was the appalling vision that inspired *Silent Spring*, a book that effectively launched the American environmental movement in 1962 with its devastating critique of unregulated pesticide use. Its author, Rachel Carson, was born in 1907 on a farm near Pittsburgh. Her childhood interest in nature led to college and graduate studies in biology and then a career as a marine biologist with the U.S. Department of Fisheries, where she was only the second woman hired for such a position. She was also finding her voice as a writer, penning three well-received books on the ecology of the sea.

Rachel Carson.

Through this work, Carson gained an acute awareness of the intricate and interdependent web of life, but she assumed that "much of nature was forever beyond the tampering hand of man." However, the advent of the atomic age, with the dramatic bombings of Hiroshima and Nagasaki in 1945, shook her confidence that nature was immune to human action, and she began to question the widely held assumption that science always held positive outcomes for human welfare. That skepticism gradually took shape around the issue of pesticides and other toxins deliberately introduced into the environment in the name of progress. In 1958, a letter from a friend describing the death of birds in her yard following aerial spraying for mosquito control prompted Carson to take on a project that became *Silent Spring*. Initially she called it "Man against the Earth."

From government agencies, independent scientists, public health specialists, and her own network of contacts, Carson began to assemble data about the impact of pesticides on natural ecosystems and human health. While she never called for their complete elimination, she argued for much greater care and sensitivity to the environment in employing chemical pesticides. She further urged natural biotic agents as a preferable alternative for pest control. The book also criticized the government regulatory agencies for their negligent oversight and scientific specialists for their "fanatical zeal" to create "a chemically sterile insect-free world." Chemical

photo: Erich Hartmann/Magnum Photos

2014, Germany was edging up on getting 30 percent of its energy from such sources, most of it from solar and wind, while Brazil and Canada received 82 percent and 62 percent respectively from renewables, primarily hydropower. Furthermore, some 6,000 national parks in over 100 countries served to protect wildlife and natural beauty. In addition to governments, many businesses found it useful to become more clearly "green." Reforestation programs were accordingly under way in China, Honduras, Kenya, and elsewhere. In recent years, international agreements have come close to eliminating the introduction of ozone-depleting substances into the atmosphere. And millions of individuals have altered their way

companies, she wrote, gave out only "little tranquilizing pills of half-truth" when confronted with evidence of their products' harmful results. While she worked hard to ensure the book's scientific credentials, it was a passionate work, fueled by Carson's "anger at the senseless brutish things that were being done." It was also a book written under growing personal difficulties. Her mother, for whom she had long been a caretaker, died in 1958, while Carson's own health too deteriorated as cancer and other ailments took their toll.

When *Silent Spring* was finally published in 1962, the book provoked a firestorm of criticism. Velsicol, a major chemical company, threatened a lawsuit to prevent its publication. Critics declared that following her prescriptions would mean "the end of all human progress," even a "return to the Dark Ages [when] insects and diseases and vermin would once again inherit the earth." Some of the attacks were more personal. Rachel Carson had never married, and Ezra Taft Benson, a former secretary of agriculture, wondered "why a spinster with no children was so concerned about genetics," while opining that she was "probably a communist." It was the height of the cold war era, and challenges to government agencies and corporate capitalism were often deemed "un-American" and "sinister."

Carson evoked such a backlash because she had called into question the whole idea of science as progress, so central to Western culture since the Enlightenment. Humankind had acquired the power to "alter the very nature of the [earth's] life," she declared. The book ended with a dire warning: "It is our alarming misfortune that so primitive a science has armed itself with the most modern and terrible weapons, and that in turning them against the insects, it has also turned them against the earth."

But Carson also had a growing number of enthusiastic supporters. Before she died in 1964, she witnessed the vindication of much of her work. Honors and awards poured in; she more than held her own against her critics in a CBS News program devoted to her book; and a presidential Science Advisory Committee cited Carson's work while recommending the "orderly reduction of persistent pesticides." Following her death, a range of policy changes reflected her work, including the creation of the Environmental Protection Agency in 1970 and the banning of the insecticide DDT in 1973. *Silent Spring* also motivated many to join the growing array of environmentalist groups.

Approaching her death, Carson applied her ecological understanding of the world to herself as well. In a letter to her best friend not long before she died, she recalled seeing some monarch butterflies leaving on a journey from which they would not return. And then she added: "When the intangible cycle has run its course, it is a natural and not unhappy thing that a life comes to an end."

Question: In what larger contexts might we understand Rachel Carson and the book that gained her such attention?

of life, agreeing to recycle, to install solar panels, to buy fuel-efficient cars, to shop in local markets, and to forgo the use of plastic bags.

But will these piecemeal efforts be enough to avoid the catastrophes that scientists predict will occur if global warming continues unchecked? Effective action on climate change, surely the most critical issue of the twenty-first century, has been difficult, partly because it would require some adjustment for citizens and corporations in the Global North and for elites everywhere. Furthermore, large-scale international agreement on global warming has come up against sharp conflicts between the Global North and South. Both activists and governments in the developing

Environmentalism in Action
These South Korean environmental activists are wearing death masks and holding crosses representing various coun-tries during an antinuclear protest in Seoul in 1996, exactly ten years after a large-scale nuclear accident at Chernobyl in the Soviet Union. The lead protester holds a placard reading "Don't forget Chernobyl!" (Yun Jai-hyoung/AP Photo)

countries have often felt that Northern initiatives to address atmospheric pollution and global warming would curtail their industrial development, leaving the North/South gap intact. "The threat to the atmospheric commons has been building over centuries," argued Indian environmentalist Vandana Shiva, "mainly because of industrial activity in the North. Yet . . . the North refuses to assume extra respon-sibility for cleaning up the atmosphere. No wonder the Third World cries foul when it is asked to share the costs." A Malaysian official put the dispute succinctly: "The developed countries don't want to give up their extravagant lifestyles, but plan to curtail our development."[34] Western governments argued that newly indus-trializing countries such as China and India must also agree to specific limits on their growing emissions if further global warming is to be prevented. Such deep disagreements between industrialized and developing countries have contributed to the failure of global efforts to reduce greenhouse gas emissions. But negotiations continue regarding a climate change treaty that would be legally binding on all par-ties or at least voluntarily accepted by them. Beyond such efforts to limit greenhouse gas emissions, more exotic solutions have also surfaced such as capturing and burying carbon emissions or injecting light-reflecting sulfur particles into the atmosphere.

More than any other widespread movement, global environmentalism came to symbolize "one world" thinking, a focus on the common plight of humankind across the artificial boundaries of nation-states. It also marked a challenge to modernity itself, particularly its consuming commitment to endless growth. The ideas of sustainability and restraint, certainly not prominent in any list of modern values, entered global discourse and marked the beginnings of a new environmental ethic. This change in thinking, although limited, was perhaps the most significant achievement of global environmentalism.

REFLECTIONS

Pondering the Past: Limitations and Possibilities

All of us engaged in the study of world history describe global changes, make global comparisons, assess connections among distant peoples, and explain, as best we can, and sometimes amid intense controversy, why things turned out as they did. But to put it mildly, these are not easy tasks, and the entire enterprise is subject to various challenges and to some outright limitations. One challenge derives from the limitations of our sources. We simply lack information about much that we would like to uncover. Who wouldn't like to know more about the thinking of our distant ancestors, the life of the Buddha or Jesus, or what was in the mind of Stalin during the upheavals of the 1930s? When written records are not available, scholars depend largely on material remains as they seek to reconstruct the past. Even when written sources are more plentiful, these materials often reflect the narrow experience of elites, leaving few sources available to assist in understanding the lives of women, peasants, slaves, and other marginalized groups.

Another challenge for students of world history lies in the particularities of time and place. In seeking to understand the past, we all start from somewhere specific—our own time and our own culture. Whether we are insiders or outsiders to the societies we explore, all of us operate within a set of assumptions and values that shape our understanding of the past. Views of Columbus in 1992, the 500th anniversary of his arrival in the Americas, differed greatly from what they had been a century earlier. Many in his Italian homeland no doubt view him differently than do Native Americans. The absence of women, until quite recently, from many historical accounts owes something to the fact that most writers of history were men. In these differences of time, place, gender, and position in society lies the source of much of the controversy that attends the study of history. It makes finality and objectivity difficult to achieve.

A further limitation derives from the unalterable "otherness" of every person. This is not so much a matter of ignorance as of mystery. Most of us have some difficulty understanding ourselves and those with whom we are on intimate terms in any full and final fashion. It is not so much that we lack information, but that we run up against what Elizabeth Cady Stanton famously called the "solitude of the self," which "no eye nor touch of man or angel has ever pierced." This profound individuality, this essential singularity, of every person makes it difficult to penetrate the inner recesses of human motivation, which are among the major drivers of the historical process.

Despite the challenges and limitations, as historians and students of history, we persist in the task, seeking what knowledge we can achieve, what insights we can gain, what perspective on our own lives we can generate. In doing so, historians have pioneered creative techniques for obtaining data—from DNA analysis to critical reading of ancient texts. We also make concerted efforts to identify our own assumptions and outlooks and, so far as is humanly possible, to set them aside as we seek to grasp the worlds of other times and places. We have at our disposal the marvelous human capacity of informed imagination: the ability to empathize with others based on our common humanity and our knowledge of their particular circumstances.

But historical understanding is always incomplete, relative, and subject to change. Nonetheless, the achievements of the historical enterprise are impressive and enormously enriching. Our subject—world history—makes us witnesses to the broad contours of the human journey and provides a context in which our individual lives can find a place and, perhaps, a measure of meaning. It serves to open us to and inform us about the wider world that shapes our daily experience. If we base our understanding of life only on what we personally experience in our own lives, we render ourselves both impoverished and ineffective.

World history opens a marvelous window into the unfamiliar. It confronts us with the "ways of the world," the whole panorama of human achievement, tragedy, and sensibility. It allows us some modest entry into the lives of people far removed from us in time and place. And it offers us company for the journey of our own lives. Pondering the global past with a receptive heart and an open mind can assist us in enlarging and deepening our sense of self. In exposing us to the wider experience of "all under Heaven," as the Chinese put it, world history can aid us in becoming wiser and more mature persons. That is among the many gifts that the study of the global past, despite its various challenges and limitations, offers to us all.

Second Thoughts

What's the Significance?

neoliberalism, 1026

reglobalization, 1026–29

transnational corporations, 1027–28

North/South gap, 1030–32

anti-globalization, 1032–33

Prague Spring, 1036

Big Picture Questions

1. In what ways did the Global North/South divide find expression in the past century?
2. What have been the benefits and drawbacks of globalization since 1945?
3. Do the years since 1914 confirm or undermine Enlightenment predictions about the future of humankind?
4. "The most recent century marks the end of the era of Western dominance in world history." What evidence might support this statement? What evidence might contradict it?
5. To what extent did the various liberation movements of the past century—communism, nationalism, democracy, feminism, internationalism—achieve their goals?
6. **Looking Back:** To what extent did the processes discussed in this chapter (globalization, feminism, fundamentalism, environmentalism) have roots in the more distant past? In what respects did they represent something new in the past century?

Next Steps: For Further Study

Karen Armstrong, *The Battle for God* (2000). A comparison of Christian, Jewish, and Islamic fundamentalism in historical perspective.

Nayan Chanda, *Bound Together: How Traders, Preachers, Adventurers, and Warriors Shaped Globalization* (2007). An engaging, sometimes humorous, long-term view of the globalization process.

Jeffry A. Frieden, *Global Capitalism: Its Fall and Rise in the Twentieth Century* (2006). A thorough, thoughtful, and balanced history of economic globalization.

Michael Hunt, *The World Transformed* (2004). A thoughtful global history of the second half of the twentieth century.

J. R. McNeill, *Something New under the Sun: An Environmental History of the Twentieth-Century World* (2001). A much-acclaimed global account of the rapidly mounting human impact on the environment during the most recent century.

Bonnie G. Smith, ed., *Global Feminisms since 1945* (2000). A series of essays about feminist movements around the world.

"Globalization," https://www.youtube.com/watch?v=3oTLyPPrZE4. A brief eight-minute animated primer on the causes and consequences of globalization.

"No Job for a Woman," http://www.iwm.org.uk/upload/package/30/women/index.htm. A Web site illustrating the impact of war on the lives of women in the twentieth century.

Faces of Globalization

Not many people in the world of the early twenty-first century remain untouched by globalization. For most of humankind, the pervasive processes of interaction among distant peoples has shaped the clothing we wear, the foods we eat, the products we consume, the ways we work, the music we listen to, the religions we practice, and the identities we assume. Such interactions are, in fact, difficult to avoid. The images that follow offer just a few reminders of the many dimensions of this immense process and provide grist for the mill of our reflection upon them.

Among the common experiences of globalization for some people living in Asia, Africa, or Latin America has been that of working in foreign-owned production facilities. Companies in wealthier countries have often found it advantageous to build such facilities in places where labor is less expensive or environmental regulations are less restrictive. China, Vietnam, Indonesia, Bangladesh, the Philippines, Mexico, Brazil, and various African states are among the countries that have hosted foreign-owned manufacturing operations. The worst of them—in terms of child labor, low pay, few benefits, and dangerous working conditions—have been called "sweatshops." Such abuses have generated an international movement challenging those conditions. Source 23.1 illustrates an interesting twist on this common feature of a globalized world economy—a Chinese-owned company producing Western-style blue jeans in Lesotho, a small country in southern Africa. The photo on page 1028 shows a parallel phenomenon—the outsourcing of services such as call centers as well as manufacturing.

- Why might China, itself the site of many foreign-owned factories, place such a factory in Africa? What does this suggest about the changing position of China in the world economy? What is the significance of the blue jeans for an understanding of contemporary globalization?

- Does this photograph conform to your image of a sweatshop? Why might many developing countries accept foreign-owned production facilities, despite the criticisms of the working conditions in them?

- Why do you think most of the workers in this photo are women? How might you imagine their motivations for seeking this kind of work? Keep in mind that the unemployment rate in Lesotho in the early twenty-first century was 45 percent.

brianafrica/Alamy

Source 23.1 Globalization and Work

■ What differences can you observe between the workers in this assembly factory and those in the Indian call center shown on page 1028? Do you imagine that workers in either setting consider themselves fortunate or exploited?

If globalization offered employment opportunities—albeit in often-wretched conditions—to some people in the developing countries, it also promoted a worldwide culture of consumerism. That culture placed the accumulation of material goods, many of them of Western origin, above older values of spiritual attainment or social responsibility. Nowhere has this culture of consumerism been more prominent than in China, where the fading of Maoist communism, the country's massive economic growth, and its new openness to the wider world combined to generate an unabashed materialism in the late twentieth and early twenty-first centuries. A popular slogan suggested that life in modern China required the "eight bigs": color TV, refrigerator, stereo, camera, motorcycle, a suite of furniture, washing machine, and an electric fan. Source 23.2 illustrates this culture of consumerism as well as one of the "eight bigs" in a poster from the post-Mao era. The poster on page 960 in Chapter 21 provides further illustration of Chinese consumerism.

Source 23.2 Globalization and Consumerism

- In what ways might these images be used to illustrate westernization, modernization, globalization, and consumerism?

- How might the young people on the motorcycle understand their own behavior? Do you think they are conscious of behaving in Western ways, or have these ways become Chinese?

- What is the significance of a Chinese couple riding a Suzuki motorcycle, a Japanese product probably manufactured in China under a license agreement?

- Beyond consumerism, how does this poster reflect changes in relationships between men and women in China after Mao? Is this yet another face of globalization, or does it remain a distinctly Western phenomenon?

- How might these images be read as a celebration of Chinese success? How might they be used to criticize contemporary Chinese society?

During the last several decades of the twentieth century, the process of economic globalization spawned various movements of resistance and criticism (see pages 1032–33). In dozens of developing countries, protesters demonstrated or rioted against government policies that removed subsidies, raised prices on essential products, froze salaries, or cut back on social services. Because such policies were often required by the World Bank or the International Monetary Fund as a condition for receiving much-needed loans, protesters often directed their anger at these international financial institutions. Activists in developed and developing countries alike have mounted large-scale protests against what they see as the abuses of unregulated corporate power operating in the world economy.

Source 23.3 shows one such activist in São Paulo, Brazil, during a demonstration in 2013, part of a series of marches and protests against the biotech giant Monsanto that were held in many countries around the world. The sign reads: "A better world according to Monsanto is a world with more cancer." A major producer of herbicides and genetically modified foods, Monsanto had also earlier in its history manufactured a number of highly controversial chemicals such as DDT, PCBs, Agent Orange, and bovine growth hormones. Its insistence on patent rights to some of its products has also generated contentious debate.

- What do the slogans and symbolism of this image reveal about the criticisms of corporate globalization? What political message does it convey?

- To what groups of people might such images be most compelling? How might Monsanto respond to such protesters?

Nelson Antoine/Associated Press

Source 23.3 Globalization and Protest

Among the many faces of globalization, none has grown more rapidly than Internet usage. In 1995, there were about 16 million users of the Internet, representing 0.4 percent of the world's population. By 2014, that number had swelled to almost 3 billion people, or 41 percent of the world's population. That kind of connectivity had profound implications for business, education, religion, social relationships, and politics. Source 23.4 shows a scene from the Arab Spring uprising in Cairo, Egypt, in early 2011 and illustrates the role of Internet-based social media such as Facebook and Twitter in mobilizing support during such protests. The sign around the young man's neck reads: "The age of fear has come to an end." It referred to the regime of longtime dictatorial ruler Hosni Mubarak, which was eventually overthrown in the uprising.

■ How do you think this young man would describe Facebook? How might he see it in relationship to the injustice and fear to which his signs refer?

■ How does his understanding and use of Facebook compare to yours?

Khaled Desouki/AFL/Getty Images

Source 23.4 Globalization and Social Media

- What capacities of the Internet and social media have made them such powerful political tools?

- In what other ways has the Internet transformed life on the planet and your own life?

Beyond politics and economics, globalization has had cultural dimensions as well. Various linguistic, religious, culinary, and artistic traditions have spread globally. Among them is yoga, a mind/body practice from India that has become a part of global culture. Source 23.5 shows a yoga class in a treatment program for teenagers facing homicide and robbery charges in a Mexico City prison in 2013. The instructor is a thirty-eight-year-old former drug dealer.

- Why might yoga be a helpful tool in dealing with young people charged with serious crimes?

- What does the use of yoga in a Mexican prison tell us about the globalization process and the assimilation of foreign practices?

Omar Torres/AFP/Getty Images

Source 23.5 Globalization and Culture

- The physical postures of yoga were long associated with and often a preparation for spiritual practices such as meditation, leading to a sense of union with the Divine. In what respects has yoga lost its original spiritual function as it has become assimilated into the cultures of many countries?

- What other cultural patterns from beyond the West have found a place in European and North American life as globalization has unfolded?

Source 23.6, a composite satellite photograph of the world at night taken in late 2000, reflects three aspects of the globalization process. The first is the growing consciousness of the earth as a single place, the common home of humankind. Such thinking has been fostered by and expressed in those many remarkable images of the earth taken from space or from the moon (see the photo on page 1022). In such photographs, no artificial boundaries of state or nation are visible, just a solitary planet cast against the immeasurable vastness of space. Second, this photograph shows the globalization of electricity, a central feature of modern life, which has taken place since the late nineteenth century. Third, and finally, the relative levels of electrification depicted in this image reflect the sharp variations in modern development across the planet as the twenty-first century dawned.

■ To what extent has your thinking about the earth and its inhabitants been shaped by images such as this?

■ Based on the electrification evident in this photo, what does this image show about the economic divisions of the world in the early twenty-first century?

■ Does this image support or contradict the Snapshot on page 1031? What features of this image might you find surprising?

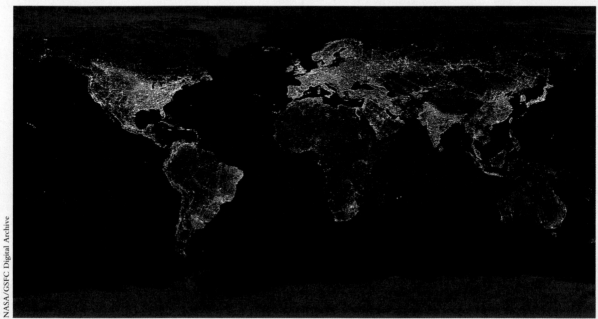

NASA/GSFC Digital Archive

Source 23.6 Globalization: One World or Many?

Faces of Globalization

1. **Defining differences:** Based on these images and the text of Chapter 23, in what different ways have various groups of people experienced globalization since the end of World War II?

2. **Noticing change:** Based on these images as well as those in the text of Chapter 23, in what respects does contemporary globalization differ from that of earlier times? What continuities might you observe? Consider in particular the question of who is influencing whom. Does recent globalization represent largely the impact of the West on the rest of the world, or is it more of a two-way street?

3. **Making assessments:** Opinions about contemporary globalization depend heavily on the position of observers—their class, gender, or national locations. How might you illustrate this statement using the images in this chapter?

4. **Seeking further evidence:** What images might you choose to illustrate visually the various faces of contemporary globalization? What images can you imagine that might be relevant fifty or a hundred years from now?

Notes

Chapter 12

1. Winona LaDuke, "We Are Still Here: The 500 Year Celebration," *Sojourners*, October 1991.
2. Brian Fagan, *Ancient North America* (London: Thames and Hudson, 2005), 503.
3. Quoted in Charles C. Mann, *1491: New Revelations of the Americas before Columbus* (New York: Alfred A. Knopf, 2005), 334.
4. Edward Dreyer, *Zheng He* (New York: Pearson Longman, 2007).
5. Louise Levanthes, *When China Ruled the Seas* (New York: Simon and Schuster, 1994), 175.
6. Niccolò Machiavelli, *The Prince* (New York: New American Library, 1952), 90, 94.
7. Christine de Pisan, *The Book of the City of Ladies*, translated by Rosalind Brown-Grant (New York: Penguin Books, 1999), pt. 1, p. 1.
8. Frank Viviano, "China's Great Armada," *National Geographic*, July 2005, 34.
9. Quoted in John J. Saunders, ed., *The Muslim World on the Eve of Europe's Expansion* (Englewood Cliffs, NJ: Prentice Hall, 1966), 41–43.
10. Quoted in C. R. N. Routh, *They Saw It Happen in Europe, 1450–1650* (Blackwell, 1965), 386.
11. Leo Africanus, *History and Description of Africa* (London: Hakluyt Society, 1896), 824–25.
12. Quoted in Craig A. Lockhard, *Southeast Asia in World History* (Oxford: Oxford University Press, 2009), 67.
13. Quoted in Patricia Risso, *Merchants and Faith* (Boulder, CO: Westview Press, 1995), 49.
14. Quoted in Stuart B. Schwartz, ed., *Victors and Vanquished* (Boston: Bedford/St. Martin's, 2000), 8.
15. Quoted in Michael E. Smith, *The Aztecs* (London: Blackwell, 2003), 108.
16. Smith, *Aztecs*, 220.
17. Quoted in Miguel Leon-Portilla, *Aztec Thought and Culture*, translated from the Spanish by Jack Emory Davis (Norman: University of Oklahoma Press, 1963), 7.
18. For a summary of this practice among the Aztecs and Incas, see Karen Vieira Powers, *Women in the Crucible of Conquest* (Albuquerque: University of New Mexico Press, 2005), chap. 1.
19. Ibid., 25.
20. Louise Burkhart, "Mexica Women on the Home Front," in *Indian Women of Early Mexico*, edited by Susan Schroeder et al. (Norman: University of Oklahoma Press, 1997), 25–54.
21. The "web" metaphor is derived from J. R. McNeill and William H. McNeill, *The Human Web* (New York: W. W. Norton, 2003).
22. Graph from David Christian, *Map of Time* (Berkeley: University of California Press, 2004), 343.
23. Quoted in Rosamund E. Mack, *Bazaar to Piazza* (Berkeley: University of California Press, 2002), 1.
24. This and all subsequent quotes come from Jerry Brotton, *The Renaissance Bazaar* (Oxford: Oxford University Press, 2002).

Part Four

1. Victor Lieberman, *Strange Parallels*, vol. 2 (Cambridge: Cambridge University Press, 2009).

Chapter 13

1. See Kevin Meerschaert, "U.S. Sen. Nelson Says Putin Wants to Rebuild Russian Empire," WJCT News, March 17, 2014, http://news.wjct.org/post/us-sen-nelson-says-putin-wants-rebuild-russian-empire; and Asli Aydintasbas, "Rebuilding the Turkish Empire: Fantasy or Reality?" *Advancing a Free Society*, April 17, 2013, http://www.hoover.org/research/rebuilding-turkish-empire-fantasy-or-reality.
2. Quoted in Thomas E. Skidmore and Peter H. Smith, *Modern Latin America* (New York: Oxford University Press, 2001), 15.
3. George Raudzens, ed., *Technology, Disease, and Colonial Conquest* (Boston: Brill Academic, 2003), xiv.
4. A major source for the life of Doña Marina is Bernal Díaz, *The Conquest of New Spain*, translated by J. M. Cohen (Baltimore: Penguin Books, 1963).
5. Charles C. Mann, *1493: Uncovering the New World Columbus Created* (New York: Alfred A. Knopf, 2011), 12.
6. Quoted in Noble David Cook, *Born to Die: Disease and the New World Conquest* (Cambridge: Cambridge University Press, 1998), 202.
7. Quoted ibid., 206.
8. Quoted in Charles C. Mann, *1491: New Revelations of the Americas before Columbus* (New York: Alfred A. Knopf, 2005), 56.
9. Geoffrey Parker, *Global Crisis* (New Haven, CT: Yale University Press, 2013), chap. 15.
10. Quoted in Mann, *1493*, 165.
11. Felipe Fernandez-Armesto, "Empires in Their Global Context," in *The Atlantic in Global History*, edited by Jorge Canizares-Esguerra and Erik R. Seeman (Upper Saddle River, NJ: Prentice Hall, 2007), 105.
12. Quoted in Alejandro Lugo, *Fragmented Lives; Assembled Parts* (Austin: University of Texas Press, 2008), 53.
13. Quoted in Anthony Padgen, "Identity Formation in Spanish America," in *Colonial Identity in the Atlantic World, 1500–1800*, edited by Nicholas Canny and Anthony Padgen (Princeton, NJ: Princeton University Press, 1987), 56.
14. Colin M. MacLachlan and Jaime E. Rodriguez, *The Forging of the Cosmic Race* (Berkeley: University of California Press, 1990), 244–45.
15. Ann Twinam, "Women and Gender in Colonial Latin America," in *Women's History in Global Perspective*, edited by Bonnie G. Smith (Urbana: University of Illinois Press, 2005), 2:195.
16. Quoted in James Lockhart and Stuart B. Schwartz, *Early Latin America* (Cambridge: Cambridge University Press, 1983), 206.
17. Mary Prince, *The History of Mary Prince* (1831; Project Gutenberg, 2006), http://www.gutenberg.org/ebooks/17851.
18. Derived from Skidmore and Smith, *Modern Latin America*, 25.
19. Kevin Reilly et al., eds., *Racism: A Global Reader* (Armonk, NY: M. E. Sharpe, 2003), 136–37.

20. Felipe Fernandez-Armesto, *The Americas: A Hemispheric History* (New York: Modern Library, 2003), 58–59.

21. Benjamin Wadsworth, *The Well-Ordered Family* (1712), 39.

22. Willard Sutherland, *Taming the Wild Fields: Colonization and Empire on the Russian Steppe* (Ithaca, NY: Cornell University Press, 2004), 223–24.

23. Quoted in Michael Khodarkovsky, *Russia's Steppe Frontier* (Bloomington: Indiana University Press, 2002), 216.

24. Andreas Kappeler, *The Russian Empire* (New York: Longman, 2001), 115–17, 397–99.

25. Khodarkovsky, *Russia's Steppe Frontier*, 222.

26. Geoffrey Hosking, "The Freudian Frontier," *Times Literary Supplement*, March 10, 1995, 27.

27. Peter Perdue, *China Marches West: The Qing Conquest of Central Eurasia* (Cambridge, MA: Harvard University Press, 2005), 10–11.

28. Quoted in Stephen F. Dale, "The Islamic World in the Age of European Expansion," in *The Cambridge Illustrated History of the Islamic World*, edited by Francis Robinson (Cambridge: Cambridge University Press, 1996), 80.

29. Quoted in P. Lewis, *Pirs, Shrines, and Pakistani Islam* (Rawalpindi, Pakistan: Christian Study Centre, 1985), 84.

30. Quoted in Stanley Wolpert, *A New History of India* (New York: Oxford University Press, 1993), 160.

31. Lewis Melville, *Lady Mary Wortley Montagu: Her Life and Letters* (Whitefish, MT: Kessinger, 2004), 88.

32. Jane I. Smith, "Islam and Christendom," in *The Oxford History of Islam*, edited by John Esposito (Oxford: Oxford University Press, 1999), 342.

33. Charles Thornton Forester and F. H. Blackburne Daniell, *The Life and Letters of Ogier Ghiselin de Busbecq* (London: C. Kegan Paul, 1881), 1:405–6.

34. Caroline Finkel, *Osman's Dream: The History of the Ottoman Empire* (New York: Basic Books, 2007), 231–33.

35. Jean Bodin, "The Rise and Fall of Commonwealths," chap. 7, Constitution Society, accessed February 21, 2012, http://www .constitution.org/bodin/bodin_4.htm.

36. Speros Vryonis, "Isidore Glabas and the Turkish Devshirme," *Speculum* 31, no. 3 (1956): 436–37.

37. Kathryn Hain, "Devshirme Is a Contested Practice," *Utah Historical Review* 2 (2012): 175.

Chapter 14

1. Jacob Wheeler, "From Slave Post to Museum," *Christian Science Monitor*, December 31, 2002.

2. M. N. Pearson, ed., *Spices in the Indian Ocean World* (Aldershot: Valorium, 1996), xv.

3. Quoted in Paul Lunde, "The Coming of the Portuguese," *Saudi Aramco World*, July/August 2005, 56.

4. Quoted in Patricio N. Abinales and Donna J. Amoroso, *State and Society in the Philippines* (Lanham, MD: Rowman and Littlefield, 2005), 50.

5. Quoted in Craig A. Lockard, *Southeast Asia in World History* (Oxford: Oxford University Press, 2009), 85.

6. Anthony Reid, *Southeast Asia in the Age of Commerce, 1450–1680* (New Haven, CT: Yale University Press, 1993), 2:274, 290.

7. Tonio Andrade, *How Taiwan Became Chinese* (New York: Columbia University Press, 2008).

8. Anthony Reid, *Charting the Shape of Early Modern Southeast Asia* (Chiang Mai: Silkworm Books, 1999), 227.

9. Quoted in Adam Clulow, "Like Lambs in Japan and Devils outside Their Land: Diplomacy, Violence, and Japanese Merchants in Southeast Asia," *Journal of World History* 24, no. 2 (2013): 343.

10. Kenneth Pomeranz and Steven Topic, *The World That Trade Created* (Armonk, NY: M. E. Sharpe, 2006), 28.

11. Makrand Mehta, *Indian Merchants and Entrepreneurs in Historical Perspective* (Delhi: Academic Foundation, 1991), chap. 4.

12. Andre Gunder Frank, *ReOrient: Global Economy in the Asian Age* (Berkeley: University of California Press, 1998), 131.

13. Quoted in Richard von Glahn, "Myth and Reality of China's Seventeenth Century Monetary Crisis," *Journal of Economic History* 56, no. 2 (1996): 132.

14. Dennis O. Flynn and Arturo Giraldez, "Born with a 'Silver Spoon,'" *Journal of World History* 6, no. 2 (1995): 210.

15. Quoted in John Hemming, *The Conquest of the Incas* (New York: Harcourt, 1970), 372.

16. Quoted in Mark Elvin, *The Retreat of the Elephant* (New Haven, CT: Yale University Press, 2004), 37.

17. Quoted in Robert Marks, *The Origins of the Modern World* (Lanham, MD: Rowman and Littlefield, 2002), 81.

18. See John Richards, *The Endless Frontier* (Berkeley: University of California Press, 2003), pt. 4. Much of this section is drawn from this source.

19. Quoted in Elspeth M. Veale, *The English Fur Trade in the Later Middle Ages* (Oxford: Clarendon Press, 1966), 141.

20. Quoted in Herbert Milton Sylvester, *Indian Wars of New England* (Cleveland, 1910), 1:386.

21. Quoted in Richards, *Endless Frontier*, 499.

22. Richards, *Endless Frontier*, 504.

23. Quoted in "Fur Trader," The Iroquois Confederacy, Portland State University Graduate School of Education, October 1, 2001, http:// www.iroquoisdemocracy.pdx.edu/html/furtrader.htm.

24. Pamela McVay, *Envisioning Women in World History* (New York: McGraw-Hill, 2009), 86.

25. These figures derive from the Trans-Atlantic Slave Trade Database, accessed December 11, 2014, http://www.slavevoyages.org/tast /assessment/estimates.faces.

26. Quoted in Charles E. Curran, *Change in Official Catholic Moral Teaching* (Mahwah, NJ: Paulist Press, 2003), 67.

27. David Brion Davis, *Challenging the Boundaries of Slavery* (Cambridge, MA: Harvard University Press, 2003), 13.

28. Quoted in Bernard Lewis, *Race and Slavery in the Middle East* (New York: Oxford University Press, 1990), 52–53.

29. Audrey Smedley, *Race in North America* (Boulder, CO: Westview Press, 1993), 57.

30. Kevin Reilly et al., eds., *Racism: A Global Reader* (Armonk, NY: M. E. Sharpe, 2003), 131.

31. Quoted in Donald R. Wright, *The World and a Very Small Place in Africa* (Armonk, NY: M. E. Sharpe, 1997), 109–10.

32. John Thornton, *Africa and Africans in the Making of the Atlantic World* (Cambridge: Cambridge University Press, 1998), 72.

33. Thomas Phillips, "A Journal of a Voyage Made in the Hannibal of London in 1694," in *Documents Illustrative of the History of the Slave Trade to America*, edited by Elizabeth Donnan (Washington, DC: Carnegie Institute, 1930), 399–410.

34. Erik Gilbert and Jonathan T. Reynolds, *Africa in World History* (Upper Saddle River, NJ: Pearson Educational, 2004), 160.

35. Trans-Atlantic Slave Trade Database, accessed December 11, 2014, http://www.slavevoyages.org/tast/assessment/estimates.faces.

36. Paul Adams et al., *Experiencing World History* (New York: New York University Press, 2000), 334.
37. Anne Bailey, *African Voices in the Atlantic Slave Trade* (Boston: Beacon Press, 2005), 153–54.
38. This account is based largely on Thomas Bluett, *Some Memoirs of the Life of Job . . .* (London, 1734), http://docsouth.unc.edu/neh/bluett /bluett.html/; and James T. Campbell, *Middle Passages* (New York: Penguin Books, 2007), 1–14.
39. Francis Moore, *Travels into the Inland Parts of Africa* (London, 1755), 146–47.
40. Erik Gilbert and Jonathan Reynolds, *Trading Tastes: Commodity and Cultural Exchange to 1750* (Upper Saddle River, NJ: Pearson/ Prentice Hall, 2006), 9.
41. Quoted in Alex Szogyi, ed., *Chocolate: Food of the Gods* (Santa Barbara, CA: Greenwood Press, 1997), 166.
42. James Grehan, "Smoking and 'Early Modern' Sociability: The Great Tobacco Debate in the Ottoman Middle East (Seventeenth to Eighteenth Centuries)," *American Historical Review* 111, no. 5 (2006): 1352–77.

Chapter 15

1. Andrew Rice, "Mission from Africa," *New York Times Magazine*, April 8, 2009; "African Missionaries Take Religion to the West," *Church Shift*, August 7, 2006, http://www.churchshift.org/in-the -press/70-african-missionaries-take-religion-to-the-west.
2. Quoted in http://frontline-org-za.win03.glodns.net/articles /thereformation_lectures.htm (accessed December 18, 2014).
3. Glenn J. Ames, *Vasco da Gama: Renaissance Crusader* (New York: Pearson/Longman, 2005), 50.
4. Cecil Jane, ed. and trans., *Selected Documents Illustrating the Four Voyages of Columbus* (London: Hakluyt Society, 1930–1933), 2:2–18.
5 Nancy E. van Deusen, "Úrsula de Jesús," in *The Human Tradition in Colonial Latin America*, edited by Kenneth J. Andrien (Wilmington, DE: Scholarly Resources, 2002), 88–103; Úrsula de Jesús, *The Souls of Purgatory: The Spiritual Diary of a Seventeenth-Century Afro-Peruvian Mystic*, edited and with a scholarly introduction by Nancy E. van Deusen (Albuquerque: University of New Mexico Press, 2004).
6. Quoted in Marysa Navarro et al., *Women in Latin America and the Caribbean* (Bloomington: Indiana University Press, 1999), 37.
7. Quoted in James Rinehart, *Apocalyptic Faith and Political Violence* (New York: Palgrave Macmillan, 2006), 42.
8. Quoted in Nicolas Griffiths, *The Cross and the Serpent* (Norman: University of Oklahoma Press, 1996), 263.
9. Quoted in Joanna Waley-Cohen, *The Sextants of Beijing* (New York: W. W. Norton, 1999), 76–77.
10. Richard M. Eaton, "Islamic History as Global History," in *Islamic and European Expansion*, edited by Michael Adas (Philadelphia: Temple University Press, 1993), 25.
11. Patricia Buckley Ebrey, ed. and trans., *Chinese Civilization: A Sourcebook* (New York: Free Press, 1993), 257.
12. Robert Bly and Jane Hirshfield, trans., *Mirabai: Ecstatic Poems* (Boston: Beacon Press, 2004), ix–xi.
13. Quoted in Steven Shapin, *The Scientific Revolution* (Chicago: University of Chicago Press, 1996), 66.
14. This section draws heavily on Toby E. Huff, *The Rise of Early Modern Science* (Cambridge: Cambridge University Press, 2003), 48, 52, 76.
15. Ibid., 87, 288.

16. Jerome Cardano, *The Book of My Life*, translated by Jean Stoner (London: J. M. Dent, 1931), 189.
17. Quoted in Shapin, *Scientific Revolution*, 28.
18. Quoted ibid., 61.
19. Quoted in Andrew Lossky, *The Seventeenth Century: Sources in Western Civilization* (New York: Free Press, 1967), 72.
20. Quoted in Shapin, *Scientific Revolution*, 33.
21. For this observation, see Clifford R. Backman, *The Cultures of the West: A History* (Oxford: Oxford University Press, 2013), 473.
22. Pope John Paul II, "Faith Can Never Conflict with Reason," *L'Osservatore Romano*, November 4, 1992.
23. Quoted in Lossky, *Seventeenth Century*, 88.
24. Quoted in Shapin, *Scientific Revolution*, 68.
25. David C. Lindberg and Ronald L. Numbers, "Beyond War and Peace: A Reappraisal of the Encounter between Christianity and Science," *Perspectives on Science and Christian Faith* 39, no. 3 (1987): 140–49.
26. H. S. Thayer, ed., *Newton's Philosophy of Nature: Selections from His Writings* (New York: Hafner Library of Classics, 1953), 42.
27. Immanuel Kant, "What Is Enlightenment?" translated by Peter Gay, in *Introduction to Contemporary Civilization in the West* (New York: Columbia University Press, 1954), 1071.
28. Voltaire, *A Treatise on Toleration* (1763), chap. 22, http://www .constitution.org/volt/tolerance.htm.
29. Quoted in Margaret C. Jacob, *The Enlightenment* (Boston: Bedford/ St. Martin's, 2001), 103.
30. Quoted in Karen Offen, *European Feminisms, 1700–1950* (Stanford, CA: Stanford University Press, 2000), 39.
31. Quoted in Toby E. Huff, *Intellectual Curiosity and the Scientific Revolution* (Cambridge: Cambridge University Press, 2010), 48.
32. Quoted in Jonathan Spence, *The Search for Modern China* (New York: W. W. Norton, 1999), 104.
33. Waley-Cohen, *Sextants of Beijing*, 105–14.
34. Benjamin A. Elman, *On Their Own Terms: Science in China, 1550–1900* (Cambridge, MA: Harvard University Press, 2005).
35. Quoted in David R. Ringrose, *Expansion and Global Interaction, 1200–1700* (New York: Longman, 2001), 188.
36. Quoted in Sergiusz Michalski, *The Reformation and the Visual Arts* (New York: Routledge, 1993), 7.
37. Quoted in Angela Vanhaelen, "Iconoclasm and the Creation of Images in Emanuel de Witte's *Old Church in Amsterdam*," *Art Bulletin*, June 2005, 5.
38. David Brett, *The Plain Style* (Cambridge: Letterworth Press, 2004), 61–62.
39. Gauvin Alexander Bailey, *Art on the Jesuit Missions in Asia and Latin America* (Toronto: University of Toronto Press, 1999), 102–4.
40. John W. O'Malley et al., *The Jesuits* (Toronto: University of Toronto Press, 1999), 381.

Part Five

1. Quoted in Ross Dunn, *The New World History* (Boston: Bedford/ St. Martin's, 2000), 17.
2. William H. McNeill, "*The Rise of the West* after 25 Years," *Journal of World History* 1, no. 1 (1990): 7.

Chapter 16

1. Quoted in Keith M. Baker, "A World Transformed," *Wilson Quarterly* (Summer 1989): 37.
2. Quoted in Thomas Benjamin et al., *The Atlantic World in the Age of Empire* (Boston: Houghton Mifflin, 2001), 205.

3. Jack P. Greene, "The American Revolution," *American Historical Review* 105, no. 1 (2000): 96–97.

4. Quoted ibid., 102.

5. Quoted in Susan Dunn, *Sister Revolutions* (New York: Faber and Faber, 1999), 11, 12.

6. Quoted ibid., 9.

7. Quoted in Lynn Hunt et al., *The Making of the West* (Boston: Bedford/St. Martin's, 2003), 625.

8. Lynn Hunt, ed., *The French Revolution and Human Rights* (Boston: Bedford, 1996), 123.

9. Bonnie S. Anderson and Judith P. Zinsser, *A History of Their Own* (New York: Harper and Row, 1988), 283.

10. Hunt, *French Revolution*, 29.

11. From James Leith, "Music for Mass Persuasion during the Terror," copyright James A. Leith, Queen's University Kingston.

12. Franklin W. Knight, "The Haitian Revolution," *American Historical Review* 105, no. 1 (2000): 103.

13. Quoted in David P. Geggus, *Haitian Revolutionary Studies* (Bloomington: Indiana University Press, 2002), 27.

14. John C. Chasteen, *Born in Blood and Fire* (New York: W. W. Norton, 2006), 103.

15. Peter Winn, *Americas: The Changing Face of Latin America and the Caribbean* (Berkeley: University of California Press, 2006), 83.

16. Quoted in Thomas E. Skidmore and Peter H. Smith, *Modern Latin America* (New York: Oxford University Press, 2001), 33.

17. Quoted in David Armitage and Sanjay Subrahmanyam, eds., *The Age of Revolutions in Global Context, c. 1760–1840* (New York: Palgrave Macmillan, 2010), xxiii.

18. James Walvin, "The Public Campaign in England against Slavery," in *The Abolition of the Atlantic Slave Trade*, edited by David Eltis and James Walvin (Madison: University of Wisconsin Press, 1981), 76.

19. Michael Craton, "Slave Revolts and the End of Slavery," in *The Atlantic Slave Trade*, edited by David Northrup (Boston: Houghton Mifflin, 2002), 200.

20. Ludmilla A. Trigos, *The Decembrist Myth in Russian Culture* (New York: Palgrave Macmillan, 2009), xv–xxiii.

21. Joseph Dupuis, *Journal of a Residence in Ashantee* (London: Henry Colburn, 1824), 162–64.

22. Eric Foner, *Nothing but Freedom* (Baton Rouge: Louisiana State University Press, 1983).

23. Quoted in Daniel Moran and Arthur Waldron, eds., *The People in Arms: Military Myth and National Mobilization since the French Revolution* (Cambridge: Cambridge University Press, 2003), 14.

24. Barbara Winslow, "Feminist Movements: Gender and Sexual Equality," in *A Companion to Gender History*, edited by Teresa A. Meade and Merry E. Wiesner-Hanks (London: Blackwell, 2004), 186.

25. Quoted in Claire G. Moses, *French Feminism in the Nineteenth Century* (Albany: SUNY Press, 1984), 135.

26. Raden Adjeng Kartini, *Letters of a Javanese Princess* (New York: W. W. Norton, 1964). Unless otherwise noted, all quotes come from this source.

27. Quoted in Jooste Cote, "Raden Ajeng Kartini," in *Gender, Colonialism and Education*, edited by Joyce Goodman and Jayne Martin (London: Woburn Press, 2002), 204.

Chapter 17

1. R. K. Prabhu and U. R. Rao, eds., *The Mind of Mahatma Gandhi* (Ahmedabad, India: Navjeevan Trust, 1960; Mahatma Gandhi's Writings, Philosophy, Audio, Video & Photographs), under "The Curse of Industrialization," http://www.mkgandhi.org/momgandhi/chap49.htm.

2. Edmund Burke III and Kenneth Pomeranz, eds., *The Environment and World History* (Berkeley: University of California Press, 2009), 41.

3. Gregory T. Cushman, *Guano and the Opening of the Pacific World* (Cambridge: Cambridge University Press, 2013), chaps. 1–3.

4. Ricardo Duchesne, *The Uniqueness of Western Civilization* (Leiden: Brill, 2011).

5. Joel Mokyr, *The Lever of Riches* (New York: Oxford University Press, 1990), 40–44.

6. Lynda Shaffer, "Southernization," *Journal of World History* 5, no. 1 (1994): 1–21.

7. Kenneth Pomeranz, *The Great Divergence* (Princeton, NJ: Princeton University Press, 2000). See also Jack Goldstone, *Why Europe? The Rise of the West in World History, 1500–1850* (Boston: McGraw-Hill, 2009).

8. Pier Vries, "Are Coal and Colonies Really Crucial?" *Journal of World History* 12, no. 2 (2001): 411.

9. E. L. Jones, *The European Miracle* (Cambridge: Cambridge University Press, 1981), 119.

10. David Christian, *Maps of Time* (Berkeley: University of California Press, 2004), 390.

11. Quoted in Mokyr, *Lever of Riches*, 188.

12. Quoted in Prasannan Parthansaranthi, "Rethinking Wages and Competitiveness in the Eighteenth Century," *Past and Present* 158 (February 1998): 79.

13. Maxine Berg, *Luxury and Pleasure in Eighteenth-Century Britain* (Oxford: Oxford University Press, 2005), 79–84.

14. Peter Stearns, *The Industrial Revolution in World History* (Boulder, CO: Westview Press, 1998), 36.

15. Goldstone, *Why Europe?* chap. 8.

16. Eric Hopkins, *Industrialization and Society* (London: Routledge, 2000), 2.

17. Mokyr, *Lever of Riches*, 81.

18. Eric Hobsbawm, *Industry and Empire* (New York: New Press, 1999), 58. This section draws heavily on Hobsbawm's celebrated account of British industrialization.

19. Samuel Smiles, *Thrift* (London: John Murray, 1875), 30–40.

20. Quoted in Bonnie S. Anderson and Judith P. Zinsser, *A History of Their Own* (New York: Harper and Row, 1988), 2:131.

21. Hobsbawm, *Industry and Empire*, 65.

22. Peter Stearns and John H. Hinshaw, *Companion to the Industrial Revolution* (Santa Barbara, CA: ABC-CLIO, 1996), 150.

23. Quoted in Herbert Vere Evatt, *The Tolpuddle Martyrs* (Sydney: Sydney University Press, 2009), 49.

24. Ellen Johnston, *Autobiography, Poems, and Songs* (Glasgow: William Love, 1867; Google Books, 2006), http://books.google.com/books/about/Autobiography_poems_and_songs.html?id=QUwCAAAAQAAJ.

25. Hobsbawm, *Industry and Empire*, 171.

26. Dirk Hoeder, *Cultures in Contact* (Durham, NC: Duke University Press, 2002), 331–32.

27. Carl Guarneri, *America in the World* (Boston: McGraw-Hill, 2007), 180.

28. Much of this feature draws from E. P. Thompson, *The Making of the English Working Class* (New York: Vintage Books, 1966).

29. Quoted in Hoeder, *Cultures in Contact*, 318.

30. Derived from Paul Kennedy, *The Rise and Fall of the Great Powers* (New York: Random House, 1987), 149.

31. John Charles Chasteen, *Born in Blood and Fire* (New York: W. W. Norton, 2006), 181.

32. Peter Bakewell, *A History of Latin America* (Oxford: Blackwell, 1997), 425.

33. Michael Adas, *Machines as the Measure of Men* (Ithaca, NY: Cornell University Press, 1990).

Chapter 18

1. Quoted in Robert Strayer, *The Making of Mission Communities in East Africa* (London: Heinemann, 1978), 89.

2. Quoted in Heinz Gollwitzer, *Europe in the Age of Imperialism* (London: Thames and Hudson, 1969), 136.

3. Quoted in Steven Roger Fischer, *A History of the Pacific Islands* (New York: Palgrave Macmillan, 2013), 112.

4. Charles Griffith, *The Present State and Prospects of the Port Phillips District . . .* (Dublin: William Curry and Company, 1845), 169.

5. Robert Knox, *Races of Man* (Philadelphia: Lea and Blanchard, 1850), v.

6. Quoted in Ralph Austen, ed., *Modern Imperialism* (Lexington, MA: D. C. Heath, 1969), 70–73.

7. Quoted in Julian Burger, "Echoes of History," *New Internationalist*, August 1988, http://www.newint.org/issue186/echoes.htm.

8. Quoted in John Iliffe, *Africans: The History of a Continent* (Cambridge: Cambridge University Press, 1995), 191.

9. Quoted in Nicholas Tarling, "The Establishment of Colonial Regimes," in *The Cambridge History of Southeast Asia*, edited by Nicholas Tarling (Cambridge: Cambridge University Press, 1992), 2:76.

10. R. Meinertzhagen, *Kenya Diary* (London: Oliver and Boyd, 1957), 51–52.

11. Quoted in Neil Jamieson, *Understanding Vietnam* (Berkeley: University of California Press, 1993), 49–57.

12. Mrinalini Sinha, *Colonial Masculinity* (Manchester: Manchester University Press, 1995), 35; Jane Burbank and Frederick Cooper, *Empires in World History* (Princeton, NJ: Princeton University Press, 2010), 308–9.

13. Nupur Chaudhuri, "Clash of Cultures," in *A Companion to Gender History*, edited by Teresa A. Meade and Merry E. Wiesner-Hanks (London: Blackwell, 2004), 437.

14. Quoted in Donald R. Wright, *The World and a Very Small Place in Africa* (Armonk, NY: M. E. Sharpe, 2004), 170.

15. Quoted in Scott B. Cook, *Colonial Encounters in the Age of High Imperialism* (New York: HarperCollins, 1996), 53.

16. Craig Timberg and Daniel Halperin, *Tinderbox* (New York: Penguin Press, 2012), 52.

17. D. R. SarDesai, *Southeast Asia: Past and Present* (Boulder, CO: Westview Press, 1997), 95–98.

18. Quoted in G. C. K. Gwassa and John Iliffe, *Records of the Maji Maji Rising* (Nairobi: East African, 1967), 1:4–5.

19. Iliffe, *Africans*, 216.

20. Derived from Adam McKeown, "Global Migration, 1846–1940," *Journal of World History* 15, no. 2 (2004): 156.

21. Quoted in Basil Davidson, *Modern Africa* (London: Longman, 1983), 79, 81.

22. This section draws heavily on Margaret Jean Hay and Sharon Stichter, eds., *African Women South of the Sahara* (London: Longman, 1984), especially chaps. 1–5.

23. Jean Davison, *Voices from Mutira* (Boulder, CO: Lynne Reinner, 1996), 51–74.

24. Quoted in Robert A. Levine, "Sex Roles and Economic Change in Africa," in *Black Africa*, edited by John Middleton (London: Macmillan, 1970), 178.

25. Quoted in Mike Davis, *Late Victorian Holocausts* (London: Verso, 2001), 37.

26. Josiah Kariuki, *Mau Mau Detainee* (London: Oxford University Press, 1963), 5.

27. Quoted in Harry Benda and John Larkin, *The World of Southeast Asia* (New York: Harper and Row, 1967), 182–85.

28. Quoted in William Theodore de Bary, *Sources of Indian Tradition* (New York: Columbia University Press, 1958), 619.

29. Quoted in Edward W. Smith, *Aggrey of Africa* (London: SCM Press, 1929).

30. Strayer, *Making of Mission Communities*, 78–82, 136–39.

31. Unless otherwise noted, this essay and all the quotes derive from Philip Goldberg, *American Vedas* (New York: Harmony Books, 2010), 47–66; and Diana L. Eck, *A New Religious America* (New York: HarperCollins, 2001), 94–104.

32. Quoted in William Theodore de Bary, *Sources of Indian Tradition* (New York: Columbia University Press, 1958), 652.

33. C. A. Bayly, *The Birth of the Modern World* (Oxford: Blackwell, 2004), 343.

34. Nirad Chaudhuri, *Autobiography of an Unknown Indian* (London: John Farquharson, 1968), 229.

35. Edward Blyden, *Christianity, Islam, and the Negro Race* (Edinburgh: Edinburgh University Press, 1967), 124.

36. John Iliffe, *A Modern History of Tanganyika* (Cambridge: Cambridge University Press, 1979), 324.

Chapter 19

1. "Full Text of Hu Jintao's Speech," July 1, 2011, http://cpcchina.chinadaily.com.cn/news/2011-07/01/content_12819337.htm. Accessed December 31, 2014.

2. Dun J. Li, ed., *China in Transition, 1517–1911* (New York: Van Nostrand Reinhold, 1969), 112.

3. Quoted in Jonathan D. Spence, *The Search for Modern China* (New York: W. W. Norton, 1999), 169.

4. Quoted in Vincent Shih, *The Taiping Ideology: Its Sources, Interpretations, and Influences* (Seattle: University of Washington Press, 1967), 73.

5. Barbara Hodgson, *Opium: A Portrait of the Heavenly Demon* (San Francisco: Chronicle Books, 1999), 32.

6. Hsin-Pao Chang, ed., *Commissioner Lin and the Opium War* (New York: W. W. Norton, 1970), 226–27.

7. This account of Lin Zexu draws from Spence, *Search for Modern China*; and Arthur Waley, *The Opium War through Chinese Eyes* (London: George Allen and Unwin, 1968).

8. Quoted in Teng Ssu and John K. Fairbanks, eds. and trans., *China's Response to the West* (New York: Atheneum, 1963), 69.

9. Quoted in Magali Morsy, *North Africa: 1800–1900* (London: Longman, 1984), 79.

10. Quoted in M. Sukru Hanioglu, *The Young Turks in Opposition* (New York: Oxford University Press, 1995), 17.

11. Marius B. Jansen, *The Making of Modern Japan* (Cambridge, MA: Harvard University Press, 2002), 33.

12. Quoted in Carol Gluck, "Themes in Japanese History," in *Asia in Western and World History*, edited by Ainslie T. Embree and Carol Gluck (Armonk, NY: M. E. Sharpe, 1997), 754.

13. Quoted in S. Hanley and K. Yamamura, *Economic and Demographic Change in Pre-Industrial Japan* (Princeton, NJ: Princeton University Press, 1977), 88–90.

14. Quoted in Harold Bolitho, "The Tempo Crisis," in *The Cambridge History of Japan*, vol. 5, *The Nineteenth Century*, edited by Marius B. Jansen (Cambridge: Cambridge University Press, 1989), 230.

15. Kenneth Henshall, *A History of Japan* (New York: Palgrave, 2004), 67.

16. Quoted in James L. McClain, *Japan: A Modern History* (New York: W. W. Norton, 2002), 177.

17. Quoted in Renée Worringer, *Ottomans Imagining Japan* (New York: Palgrave Macmillan, 2014), 59.

18. Quoted in Ono Kazuko, *Chinese Women in a Century of Revolution* (Stanford: Stanford University Press, 1989), 60.

19. Quoted in Jonathan D. Spence, *The Gate of Heavenly Peace* (New York: Penguin Books, 1981), 85.

20. Quoted in Charlotte Beahan, "Feminism and Nationalism in the Chinese Women's Press, 1902–1911," *Modern China* 1, no. 4 (1975): 384.

21. Quoted in J. A. Mangan and Fan Hong, eds., *Freeing the Female Body: Inspirational Icons* (London: Frank Cass Publishers, 2001), 45.

Part Six

1. J. R. McNeill, *Something New under the Sun* (New York: W. W. Norton, 2000), 3–4.

Chapter 20

1. John Innes, "Scotland's Oldest Man Turns 107," *Scotsman*, June 25, 2003, http://www.aftermathww1.com/oldestscot.asp; Associated Press, "One of Last British WWI Veterans Dies at 109," NBC News .com, November 21, 2005, http://www.nbcnews.com/id/10138446/.

2. Quoted in John Keegan, *The First World War* (New York: Vintage Books, 1998), 3.

3. Adapted from Lynn Hunt et al., *The Making of the West: Peoples and Cultures* (Boston: Bedford/St. Martin's, 2001), 1024.

4. Benito Mussolini, *The Political and Social Doctrine of Fascism*, translated by Jane Soames (London: Leonard and Virginia Woolf at the Hogarth Press, 1933).

5. Stanley Payne, *History of Fascism, 1914–1945* (Madison: University of Wisconsin Press, 1995), 208.

6. Quoted in Laurence Rees, *The Nazis: A Warning from History* (New York: New Press, 1997), 62.

7. Quoted in Claudia Koonz, *Mothers in the Fatherland* (New York: St. Martin's Press, 1987), 75.

8. Klaas A. D. Smelik, ed., *Etty: The Letters and Diaries of Etty Hillesum* (Grand Rapids: Erdmans, 2002).

9. Quoted in James L. McClain, *Japan: A Modern History* (New York: W. W. Norton, 2002), 378.

10. Quoted ibid., 414.

11. Quoted in Marius B. Jansen, *The Making of Modern Japan* (Cambridge, MA: Harvard University Press, 2000), 607.

12. Quoted ibid., 639.

13. Robert Jungk, *Brighter Than a Thousand Suns: A Personal History of the Atomic Scientists* (New York: Harcourt Brace, 1958), 201.

14. Quoted in John Keegan, *The Second World War* (New York: Viking Penguin, 1989), 186.

15. Merry E. Wiesner et al., *Discovering the Global Past*, 3rd ed. (Boston: Houghton Mifflin, 2007), 422.

16. Quoted in Kyosuke Yamamoto, "Drafts Show A-Bomb Survivor Bridged Differences in Anti-nuke Speech at U.N.," *Asahi Shimbun*, December 21, 2013, http://ajw.asahi.com/article/behind_news /social_affairs/AJ201312310065.

17. Quoted in Ralph F. Keeling, *Gruesome Harvest* (Chicago: Institute of American Economics, 1947), 60.

18. John Lewis Gaddis, *We Now Know: Rethinking Cold War History* (Oxford: Oxford University Press, 1997), 52.

19. Adam Gopnik, "The Big One: Historians Rethink the War to End All Wars," *New Yorker*, August 23, 2004, 78.

Chapter 21

1. Quoted in Ronald Suny, *The Soviet Experiment* (Oxford: Oxford University Press, 1998), 357.

2. Quoted in Bonnie S. Anderson and Judith P. Zinsser, *A History of Their Own* (New York: Harper and Row, 1988), 2:299.

3. Quoted in William M. Mandel, *Soviet Women* (Garden City, NJ: Doubleday, 1975), 44.

4. Yuan-tsung Chen, *The Dragon's Village* (New York: Penguin Books, 1980), 85.

5. Such figures are often highly controversial. See Maurice Meisner, *Mao's China and After* (New York: Free Press, 1999), 413–25; and Roderick MacFarquhar, ed., *The Politics of China* (Cambridge: Cambridge University Press, 1997), 243–45.

6. Douglas Weiner, "The Predatory Tribute-Taking State," in *The Environment and World History*, edited by Edmund Burke III and Kenneth Pomeranz (Berkeley: University of California Press, 2009), 284–90.

7. Richard F. Kaufman and John P. Hardt, eds., *The Former Soviet Union in Transition* (Armonk, NY: M. E. Sharpe, 1993), 580–83.

8. Barbara Engel and Anastasia Posadskaya-Vanderbeck, eds., *A Revolution of Their Own* (Boulder, CO: Westview Press, 1998), 17–46.

9. Quoted in John L. Gaddis, *The Cold War: A New History* (New York: Penguin Press, 2005), 57.

10. Quoted in Dean Rusk, *As I Saw It* (New York: Norton, 1990), 245.

11. Quoted in Frank Mankiewicz and Kirby Jones, *With Fidel: A Portrait of Castro and Cuba* (New York: Ballantine Books, 1976), 83.

12. Quoted in Paul Mason, *Cuba* (New York: Marshall Cavendish, 2010), 14.

13. Quoted in Peter Roman, *People's Power: Cuba's Experience with Representative Government* (Lanham, MD: Rowman and Littlefield, 2003), 63.

14. Ronald Steel, *Pax Americana* (New York: Viking Press, 1970), 254.

15. Quoted in Donald W. White, *The American Century* (New Haven, CT: Yale University Press, 1996), 164.

16. Deng Xiaoping, "The Necessity of Upholding the Four Cardinal Principles in the Drive for the Four Modernizations," in *Major Documents of the People's Republic of China* (Beijing: Foreign Language Press, 1991), 54.

17. Quoted in Abraham Brumberg, *Chronicle of a Revolution* (New York: Pantheon Books, 1990), 225–26.

18. Anchee Min et al., *Chinese Propaganda Posters* (Köln: Taschen, 2003), 5.

19. Quoted ibid., 10.

Chapter 22

1. Nelson Mandela, "Statement from the Dock . . . in the Rivonia Trial," African National Congress, April 20, 1964, http://www.anc.org.za /show.php?id=3430&t=Famous Speeches.

2. Quoted in Craig A. Lockard, *Southeast Asia in World History* (Oxford: Oxford University Press, 2009), 138–39.

3. Quoted in J. D. Legge, *Sukarno: A Political Biography* (New York: Praeger, 1972), 341.

4. Quoted in Jim Masselos, *Nationalism on the Indian Subcontinent* (Melbourne: Nelson, 1972), 122.

5. Mahatma Gandhi, *Indian Home Rule* (Auckland, New Zealand: The Floating Press, 2014), 35.

6. Quoted in Bidyut Chakrabarty, *Social and Political Thought of Mahatma Gandhi* (New York: Routledge, 2006), 139.

7. Quoted in Stanley Wolpert, *A New History of India* (Oxford: Oxford University Press, 1993), 331.

8. Badshah Khan, *My Life and Struggle* (Delhi: Hind Pocket Books, 1969), 96–97.

9. Jawaharlal Nehru, *The Discovery of India* (New York: John Day Co., 1946), 486.

10. Quoted in M. S. Korejo, *The Frontier Gandhi* (New York: Oxford University Press, 1993), 25.

11. Khan, *My Life*, 209–10.

12. Adapted and updated from Lynn Hunt et al., *The Making of the West: Peoples and Cultures* (Boston: Bedford/St. Martin's, 2009), 968; and Population Reference Bureau, *World Population Data Sheet, 2011,* http://www.prb.org/pdf11/2011population-data-sheet_eng.pdf.

13. Quoted in Paul E. Sigmund, *The Overthrow of Allende and the Politics of Chile* (Pittsburgh: University of Pittsburgh Press, 1977), 122.

14. 1950 data from United Nations, "World Urbanization Prospects, the 2011 Revision," Figure 11a; 2014 data from United Nations, Department of Economic and Social Affairs, Population Division (2014), *World Urbanization Prospects: The 2014 Revision, Highlights*, Table II, p. 26, http://esa.un.org/unpd/wup/Highlights/WUP2014 -Highlights.pdf.

15. Quoted in Bernard Lewis, *The Emergence of Modern Turkey* (London: Oxford University Press, 1968), 268–69.

16. Quoted in Patrick B. Kinross, *Ataturk: A Biography of Mustafa Kemal* (New York: Morrow, 1965), 390.

17. Sandra Mackey, *The Iranians* (New York: Penguin, 1998), 306.

18. Elif Shafak, "Turkey's Culture Wars," *New York Times*, July 23, 2014.

Chapter 23

1. "Put Yourself in My Shoes: A Human Trafficking Victim Speaks Out," United Nations Office on Drugs and Crime, November 28, 2012, http://www.unodc.org/unodc/en/frontpage/2012/November /put-yourself-in-my-in-my-shoes-a-human-trafficking-victim -speaks-out.html.

2. Jeffry A. Frieden, *Global Capitalism: Its Fall and Rise in the Twentieth Century* (New York: W. W. Norton, 2006), 476.

3. Lester R. Brown, "Gross World Product, 1950–2009," in *World on the Edge* (New York: W. W. Norton, 2011; Earth Policy Institute), http://www.earth-policy.org/books/wote/wote_data.

4. United Nations, *Human Development Report 1997*, 2, http://hdr .undp.org/en/content/human-development-report-1997.

5. Michael Hunt, *The World Transformed* (Boston: Bedford/St. Martin's, 2004), 442.

6. Quoted in Frieden, *Global Capitalism*, 408.

7. "Map Supplement," *National Geographic* (Washington, DC: National Geographic Society, March 2011).

8. Quoted in Manfred B. Steger, *Globalization: A Very Short Introduction* (Oxford: Oxford University Press, 2003), 122.

9. Quoted in Frieden, *Global Capitalism*, 459.

10. Charles S. Maier, *Among Empires: American Ascendancy and Its Predecessors* (Cambridge, MA: Harvard University Press, 2006), chap. 5.

11. Quoted in Sarah Shaver Hughes and Brady Hughes, *Women in World History* (Armonk, NY: M. E. Sharpe, 1997), 2:268.

12. Susan Kent, "Worlds of Feminism," in *Women's History in Global Perspective*, edited by Bonnie G. Smith (Urbana: University of Illinois Press, 2004), 1:305–6.

13. Quoted in Wilhelmina Oduol and Wanjiku Mukabi Kabira, "The Mother of Warriors and Her Daughters: The Women's Movement in Kenya," in *Global Feminisms since 1945*, edited by Bonnie G. Smith (London: Routledge, 2000), 111.

14. Quoted in Mary E. Hawkesworth, *Globalization and Feminist Activism* (New York: Rowman and Littlefield, 2006), 124.

15. Phyllis Schlafly, *The Power of the Christian Woman* (Cincinnati: Standard, 1981), 117.

16. Karen Armstrong, *The Battle for God* (New York: Alfred A. Knopf, 2000), xi.

17. Quoted ibid., 273.

18. "Muslim Dolls Tackle 'Wanton Barbie,'" BBC News, March 5, 2002, http://news.bbc.co.uk/2/hi/middle_east/1856558.stm.

19. Quoted in John Esposito, *Unholy War* (Oxford: Oxford University Press, 2002), 57.

20. Quoted in Katherine Zoepf, "Barbie Pushed Aside in Mideast Cultural Shift. Little Girls Obsessed with Fulla in Scarf," *International Herald Tribune*, September 22, 2005, 2. The passages concerning Fulla are largely drawn from this article.

21. Quoted in Esposito, *Holy War*, 63.

22. "Al Qaeda's Second Fatwah," PBS News Hour, February 23, 1998, http://www.pbs.org/newshour/updates/military-jan-june98 -fatwa_1998/.

23. Anwar Ibrahim, "The Ardent Moderates," *Time*, September 23, 1996, 24.

24. Jan Zalasiewicz et al., "The New World of the Anthropocene," *Environmental Science and Technology* 44, no. 7 (2010): 2228–31.

25. See J. R. McNeill, *Something New under the Sun: An Environmental History of the Twentieth-Century World* (New York: W. W. Norton, 2001).

26. Naomi Klein, *This Changes Everything* (New York: Simon and Schuster, 2014), 2.

27. Center for Naval Analysis, *National Security and the Threat of Climate Change*, 2007, 6, http://www.cna.org/reports /climate.

28. This section on environmentalism draws heavily on Ramachandra Guha, *Environmentalism: A Global History* (New York: Longman, 2000).

29. Quoted ibid., 14.

30. Quoted ibid., 50, 53.

31. Guobin Yang, "Global Environmentalism Hits China," *Yale Global Online*, February 4, 2004, http://yaleglobal.yale.edu/content /global-environmentalism-hits-china.

32. Timothy Doyle, *Environmental Movements in Minority and Majority Worlds: A Global Perspective* (New Brunswick, NJ: Rutgers University Press, 2005).

33. Rachel Carson, *Silent Spring* (Boston: Houghton Mifflin, 1962), 103. In addition to Carson's book, this account of her life draws on Mark Hamilton Lytle, *The Gentle Subversive: Rachel Carson, "Silent Spring," and the Rise of the Environmental Movement* (New York: Oxford University Press, 2007), and Arlene R. Quaratiello, *Rachel Carson: A Biography* (Westport, CT: Greenwood Press, 2004).

34. Quoted in Shiraz Sidhva, "Saving the Planet: Imperialism in a Green Garb," *UNESCO Courier*, April 2001, 41–43.

Acknowledgments

Chapter 12

"Truly do we live on earth" from AZTEC THOUGHT AND CULTURE: A STUDY OF THE ANCIENT NAHUATL MIND by MIGUEL LEON PORTILLA. Reproduced with permission of UNIVERSITY OF OKLAHOMA PRESS in the format Republish in a book via Copyright Clearance Center.

Chapter 13

Document 13.3: *Memoirs,* from *Louis XIV* by Robert Campbell, Pearson Education Limited. © Longman Group UK Limited 1993. Used by permission of Taylor & Francis Books UK.

Document 13.4: *The Incas of Pedro de Cieza de León* by PEDRO DE CIEZA DE LEÓN. Reproduced with permission of UNIVERSITY OF OKLAHOMA PRESS in the format Republish in a book via Copyright Clearance Center.

Chapter 15

"What I was paid" from *Mirabai*, translated by Robert Bly and Jane Hirschfield. Copyright © by Robert Bly and Jane Hirschfield. Reprinted by permission of Beacon Press, Boston.

Chapter 18

"Fine wine but no good friends" from Neil L. Jamieson, *Understanding Vietnam*, © 1995 by the Regents of the University of California. Published by the University of California Press. Used by permission of the University of California Press.

Chapter 19

Document 19.1: From *Sources of Chinese Tradition: From 1600 Through the Twentieth Century*, compiled by Wm. Theodore de Bary and Richard Lufrano. Copyright © 2000 by Columbia University Press. Reprinted with the permission of the publisher.

Chapter 20

Etty Hillesum material from Collection Jewish Historical Museum, Amsterdam. Used by permission of the Etty Hillesum Research Centre.

Document 20.1: Adolf Hitler, *Mein Kampf*, translated by Ralph Manheim (Boston: Houghton Mifflin, 1943). Published also by Hutchinson. Used by permission of Houghton Mifflin Harcourt and Random House Group Limited.

Document 20.2: Reprinted by permission of the publisher from *Kokutai No Hongi: Cardinal Principles of the National Entity of Japan*, translated by John Owen Gauntlett, and edited with an introduction by Robert King Hall, pp. 52, 79, 80, 81, 82, 83, 87, 89–90, 93, 94, 144–145, 178, 181–182, Cambridge, Mass.: Harvard University Press. Copyright © 1949 by the President and Fellows of Harvard College. Copyright © renewed 1977 by Robert King Hall.

Chapter 22

Document 22.4a: From Afghan Women's Writing Project: http://awwproject.org/2010/06/hijab-the-beauty-of-muslim-women/. Used by permission.

Document 22.4b: From *Daily Mail*, June 24, 2009. Online: http://www.dailymail.co.uk/debate/article-1195052/Why-I-British-Muslim-woman-want-burkha-banned-streets.html. Used by permission.

Index

China *(continued)*
 Opium Wars and, 714, 838, 839
 Ottoman Empire and, 846, 849–851
 partition of, 833*(i)*
 peasants in, 692–693, 863
 Philippines and, 607–608
 popular culture in, 662–663
 Portugal and, 605
 prosperity in, 960
 rebellions against, 698
 reforestation in, 1058
 reforms in, 837, 843–844, 859, 863, 865, 866
 religion and culture in, 661–663
 Russia and, 840
 science in, 665
 self-strengthening in, 842–844
 silk in, 838*(t)*, 841
 silver and, 612–614, 839
 socialism in, 938–947
 society in, 836
 Soviet Union and, 957–958
 spheres of influence in, 840, 842*(m)*
 Taiwan and, 609, 840
 trade in, 507, 611
 Turkic peoples and, 504
 Vietnam and, 840
 women in, 726–727, 837, 843, 867, 868–869*(d)*, 941–942, 971*(v)*
 as world's largest economy, 1035
 World War I and, 887
 after World War I, 890–891
 World War II and, 912
 Zheng He voyages and, 507–509, 508*(i)*, 513–514, 515
Chinese Communist Party (CCP), 915, 936, 937, 942, 958
Chinese Empire, under Qing dynasty, 577–580, 578*(i)*, 579*(m)*
Chinese revolution, 936–938
Chinookan peoples, 502
chlorofluorocarbons, 1054
chocolate, from Mesoamerica, 636, 637*(v)*
Christendom
 Islam and, 516, 536
 Spanish colonialism and, 607
Christianity. *See also* specific groups
 in Africa, 816–818
 Byzantine, 584
 in China, 548, 657–659, 683–685, 684*(v)*, 836, 839
 conversion to, 567, 816, 817–819

cultural impact of, 643–644
 in early modern era, 679–686
 economic globalization and, 1051–1052
 in European colonies, 815, 816–817, 817–818, 817*(i)*
 European exploration and, 513, 651
 globalization of, 644–659, 650–651*(m)*, 679–686
 growth of, 547
 "heathens" and, 792
 in India, 663, 685–686, 686*(v)*, 818–819
 Islam and, 584, 1017*(d)*
 in Japan, 548, 610, 854
 in Latin America, 567, 682–683, 683*(v)*
 in Mexico, 656
 Ottoman Empire and, 584–585, 586–587
 religious culture of, 529
 Roman Catholicism vs. Eastern Orthodoxy, 644
 science and, 664–665
 in Spain, 1017*(d)*
 in Spanish America, 567
 as transregional culture, 1042
 in Western Hemisphere, 677
Christine de Pizan (Venetian writer), 512–513
Chulalongkorn (Siam), 815*(i)*
churches
 Catholic, 679–681
 Protestant, 649, 679–681
Churchill, Winston (British prime minister), 915
CIA (Central Intelligence Agency, U.S.), 1037
Cieza de León, Pedro de (Spanish chronicler), 596–597, 597–598*(d)*
cities and towns. *See also* state (nation); urbanization
 of colonial world, 808
 crowding in, 750, 803, 808
 in England, 750
 in Europe, 602–603
 in Latin America, 996–997, 997*(i)*
 populations of, 1004*(t)*
 after World War II, 915
City of Ladies (Christine de Pizan), 512
city-states
 in Africa, 514*(m)*
 in Italy, 510

civilization(s). *See also* culture; empire(s); First Civilizations; society
 in Americas, 522–529
 in China, 505–509
 European, 509–510
 European perceptions of, 792
 Islam as, 515–522
 second wave of, 793
"civilizing mission," 792, 813
civil rights movement (U.S.), 1036
civil service system. *See also* bureaucracy; examination system
 in China, 837, 871*(d)*
 colonial, 506, 800
civil wars
 in Japan, 855
 in Russia, 935
classes. *See also* caste system
 in France, 697
 gender and, 725
 industrialization and, 757, 761
 Marx on, 674
class struggle, 777–779*(d)*. *See also* Marx, Karl
Clavius, Christoph (astronomer), 668–669
clergy
 Catholicism, Protestantism, and, 647
 as first estate, 686*(i)*, 704, 731, 731*(v)*, 732, 732*(v)*
 Luther and, 645–646
climate. *See also* environment; global warming
 changes in, 1054–1055
 environmental damage and, 1054, 1059
 treaty for, 1060–1061
clitorectomy, in Gikuyu culture, 810, 816–817
cloth and clothing. *See also* cotton and cotton industry; silk and silk industry
 for Iranian women, 1008–1009
 in Turkey, 1006–1007, 1018–1019, 1019–1020*(d)*
Club of Rome, *Limits to Growth* by, 1056
coal, 743*(m)*, 746
co-colonization, in Taiwan, 609
codes of law. *See* law codes
coffee
 from Ethiopia, 636
 in Haiti, 709

Erie, Lake, "death" of, 1054
Eritrea, 850, 980(m)
estates (classes), in France, 696(i), 704, 731–732, 731(v), 732(v)
estates (land), Spanish, in Philippines, 607
Estonia, 962
ethics, of globalization, 1051–1052
Ethiopia
  coffee from, 636
  colonization and, 980(m)
  Italian invasion of, 797, 850–851, 851(i), 898
  Japan compared to, 851
ethnicity
  in Africa, 821–822, 995–996
  in Eastern Europe, 963
  in Russian Empire, 573
EU. See European Union
eunuchs, in China, 506–507, 508–509
Eurasia. See also Asia; Europe and Europeans
  China and, 579
  spice trade and, 521
  trade in, 529
Eurocentrism, 689–690
  countering, 588, 690–693
European Coal and Steel Community, 917
Europe and Europeans. See also empire(s); Eurasia; specific locations
  in 1500, 511(m)
  in 16th century, 531
  Asia and, 602–611, 604(m), 609(i)
  China and, 530, 743–744, 832(i), 838
  Christianity in, 1042
  Common Market in, 917
  competition in, 742
  culture and, 510–513
  disease exchange and, 618
  in early modern era, 547–548
  economy in, 1035
  Enlightenment in, 671–675
  fascism in, 896–898
  fur trade and, 616
  government in, 514–515
  in Great Depression, 893
  Holocaust and, 914
  Industrial Revolution and, 741–744, 743(m), 767(t), 773
  Latin America and, 770
  Little Ice Age in, 560–561
  manufactured goods from, 846

maritime voyages by, 513–515
  Marshall Plan aid to, 917
  migration from, 755–757, 756(m), 762, 770
  nations of (ca. 1880), 721(m)
  Native Americans and, 618
  Ottomans and, 585, 846
  perceptions of "other" by, 790–791
  prominence in modern age, 533
  racial views of, 791–792, 791(i)
  racism and, 791–792, 791(i)
  Reformation in, 648(m)
  Renaissance in, 500
  Scientific Revolution in, 665–670
  scramble for Africa by, 794, 825–827, 826(v), 828(v), 829(v), 830(v)
  silver and, 562, 563, 564
  silver trade and, 615
  slaves in, 626
  state building and, 510
  tea and porcelain in, 635(v)
  women in, 914
  before World War I, 886(m)
  World War I and, 891
  after World War I, 889(m)
  World War II and, 909–910, 911(m)
  after World War II, 882, 916–919
European Economic Community (EEC), 917
European Parliament, 917
European Union (EU), 882, 917, 918(m)
  Germany in, 963
  Russia and, 1035
euro zone, 917
evangelicals, antislavery sentiments and, 715
evolution (human), Darwin and, 674, 791(i)
Ewe people (Ghana), 809
examination system, in China, 506, 666, 842–843, 865, 866
exchange. See also trade
  African-European, 561
  global webs of, 531
  silver for, 613
  and status in early modern world, 634–640
expansion. See also imperialism; migration
  in Islamic world, 659–661
  of Ottoman Empire, 516
  of Russia, 620

exploration. See also navigation
  Chinese, 500, 507–508, 513
  Christianity and, 651–652
  by Columbus, 498(i)
  European, 513–515
export-led industrialization, 1003
exports. See trade
extinction, 674, 1053–1054
  environment and, 1052

Facebook, 1068
factories
  in England, 750
  women in, 914
faith. See religion(s)
Family Law Code (Morocco), 1039
family planning, population growth and, 1053
famines
  in China, 945(i)
  in India, 812
  in Soviet Union, 943
farms and farming. See also agriculture
  in Africa, 809
  collective, 942–943
  fertilizers and, 738–739
  among Iroquois-speaking peoples, 503
  subsistence, 802
  women in, 809
fascism. See also Nazi Germany
  in Europe, 896
  in Germany, 898
  in Italy, 896–898
fatwa (religious edict), 1049
Federalist Papers, 704
Federation of the West Indies, 976
Feminine Mystique, The (Friedan), 1038
feminism, 532, 875
  beginnings of, 706, 723–727
  in Brazil, 1041(i)
  in China, 945–946
  communist, 940–942
  divisions in, 1040–1041
  globalization of, 1036–1041
  in Global South, 1038–1040
  international, 1040–1041
  in Japan, 857
  in Java, 726–727, 726(i)
  maternal, 725
  opposition to, 725
  protests and, 724, 725(i)

Fulbe peoples and, 505
Hindus and, 521
India and, 521, 580, 663–664, 799,
  820, 984, 986, 988–989, 1044
intellectual thought from, 536–537
Judaism and, 1017(d)
laws of, 1007
in Malacca, 522
Muslim Brotherhood and, 1014, 1014–
  1016(d)
Muslim societies and, 1044–1050
in Philippines, 607
progressive, 1016, 1017–1018(d)
reforms in, 660–661
Renaissance Europe and, 536–544
renewal movements in, 1044–1050,
  1048(m)
Salafi, 1050
science in, 665
"second flowering of," 521
in Songhay, 518–520
in Southeast Asia, 521
Spain and, 1017(d)
spread of, 1042
terrorism against U.S. and, 1035
trade and, 531, 605
as transregional culture, 1042
Turkey and, 848, 850
values in, 1017–1018(d)
women in, 726–727, 1008–1009,
  1018–1019, 1019–1020(d), 1020–
  1021(d), 1041, 1046–1047
Islamic empire. *See* Arabs and Arab
  world; Islam; Muslims
Islamic jihad, 1049
Islamic law. *See* sharia
Islamic modernism, 848
Islamic renewal, 1044–1050, 1048(m)
Islamization, in Iran, 1008–1009
island hopping, in World War II, 908(m)
islands, of Southeast Asia, 660
Israel
  Islam and, 1045, 1049
  state of, 976, 980(m)
  after World War II, 914
Istanbul. *See* Constantinople
Italy. *See also* Roman Empire
  anti-Semitism in, 899
  as Axis power, 895, 909
  communism in, 932
  debt crisis in, 1030
  emigration from, 756, 770

Ethiopia and, 850–851, 851(i), 980(m)
fascism in, 896–898
government in, 510
imperialism of, 793
Libya and, 829
unification of, 720, 721(m), 790
women in, 900
World War I and, 883, 886(m)
after World War II, 917
Ivory Coast, women in, 809

Jahan (Shah), 553
Jahangir (Mughal Empire), 685–686
  memoirs of, 580–581, 590–591, 591–
    592(d)
Jamaica
  Haitian Revolution and, 710, 715
  after slavery, 718
Janissaries, in Ottoman Empire, 520(i),
  587, 846, 847
Japan. *See also* Pearl Harbor attack;
    samurai warriors
  atomic bombings of, 908(m), 909,
    912–913, 912(i)
  authoritarianism in, 901–906
  as Axis power, 895, 909
  *Cardinal Principles of the National Entity
    of Japan,* 925–927(d)
  China and, 832(i), 840, 842(m), 843,
    859, 860(m), 907, 938
  Christianity in, 548, 854
  civil wars in, 855
  comfort women and, 913
  Confucianism in, 853, 856
  constitution in, 856, 857
  Dutch and, 676, 854
  education in, 856, 857
  environmentalists in, 1057
  Ethiopia compared to, 851
  Europe and, 610, 676
  government in, 905
  Great Depression in, 904
  imperialism of, 793, 797, 859, 860(m),
    907
  industrialization in, 613, 692, 740, 857,
    858
  Korea and, 797, 859–860, 860(m), 931
  labor in, 906
  League of Nations and, 859, 907
  Manchuria and, 907
  Meiji restoration in, 855
  merchants in, 742, 852, 853

migration from, 805, 807(t)
military in, 906
modernization in, 855–858, 858(i)
nationalism in, 722–723
opening of, 854–855, 854(i)
parliament in, 856
Pearl Harbor attack by, 909
peasants in, 852
Philippines and, 607
population growth in, 613
Portugal and, 610
Rape of Nanjing and, 912
religion in, 856
Russia and, 859, 860(m)
samurai in, 852–853, 855, 856
silver in, 611, 612, 613
suffrage in, 901
Taiwan and, 797, 859–860, 860(m)
Tokugawa shogunate in, 852–854, 855
trade in, 854
United States and, 852, 854–855,
  854(i)
West and, 856, 859
women in, 726, 857, 858, 902, 903,
  904(i)
in World War I, 887
after World War I, 890
after World War II, 918–919
Japanese Empire, 795(m)
Java, 521, 610, 660
  cultivation system in, 803–804
  feminism in, 726–727, 726(i)
  Muslims in, 660
jazz, 888, 956
Jefferson, Thomas (U.S. revolutionary
    leader and president), 698–699
Jehovah's Witnesses, 914
Jerusalem
  Arab world and, 1045
  Islam and, 1017(d)
  Ottoman Empire and, 584
Jesuits, 649, 652
  in China, 657–659, 658(i), 684
  European sciences and, 675
  in India, 685–686
Jews and Judaism. *See also* Arabs and
    Arab world; Israel; Palestine;
    Zionism
  Holocaust and, 902–903, 902(i), 914
  Islam and, 1017(d)
  Nazi Germany and, 899–900, 900(i)
  in Ottoman Empire, 584

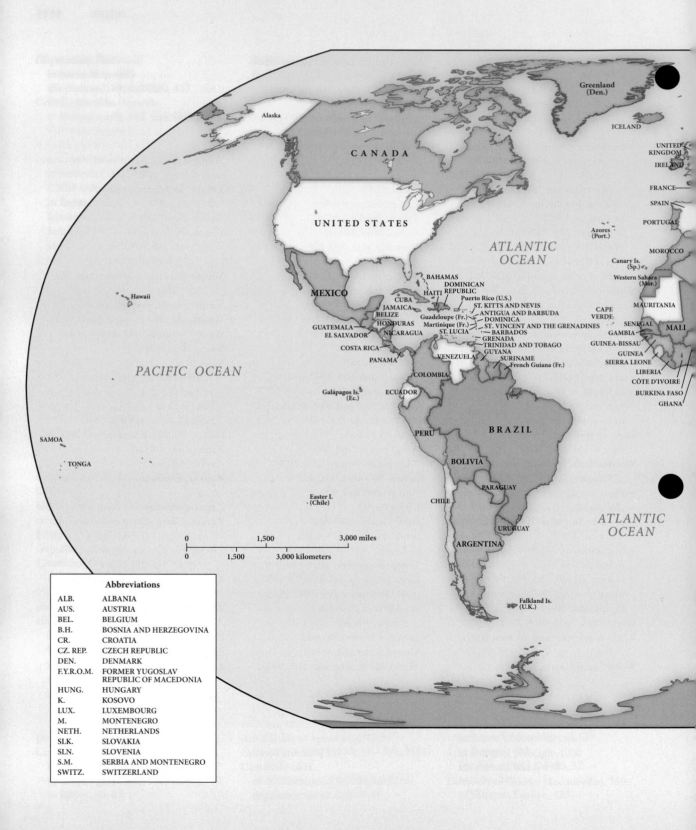

Greenland
(Den.)

ICELAND

Alaska

UNITED
KINGDOM

IRELAND

C A N A D A

FRANCE

SPAIN

PORTUGAL

ATLANTIC
OCEAN

Azores
(Port.)

MOROCCO

UNITED STATES

Canary Is.
(Sp.)

Western Sahara
(Mor.)

Hawaii

MEXICO

BAHAMAS

DOMINICAN
REPUBLIC

HAITI

Puerto Rico (U.S.)

CUBA

JAMAICA

BELIZE

HONDURAS

Guadeloupe (Fr.)

Martinique (Fr.)

ST. LUCIA

ST. KITTS AND NEVIS

ANTIGUA AND BARBUDA

DOMINICA

ST. VINCENT AND THE GRENADINES

BARBADOS

GRENADA

TRINIDAD AND TOBAGO

CAPE
VERDE

MAURITANIA

SENEGAL

GAMBIA

GUINEA-BISSAU

MALI

GUATEMALA

EL SALVADOR

NICARAGUA

COSTA RICA

PANAMA

VENEZUELA

GUYANA

SURINAME

French Guiana (Fr.)

GUINEA

SIERRA LEONE

LIBERIA

CÔTE D'IVOIRE

BURKINA FASO

GHANA

COLOMBIA

PACIFIC OCEAN

Galápagos Is.
(Ec.)

ECUADOR

PERU

B R A Z I L

BOLIVIA

SAMOA

TONGA

Easter I.
·(Chile)

PARAGUAY

CHILE

URUGUAY

ATLANTIC
OCEAN

ARGENTINA

0   1,500   3,000 miles

0   1,500   3,000 kilometers

Falkland Is.
(U.K.)

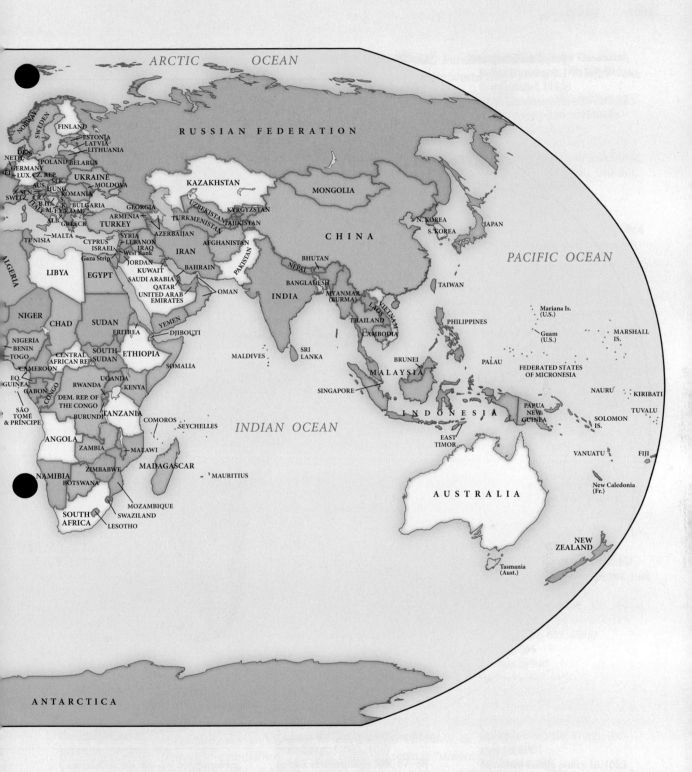

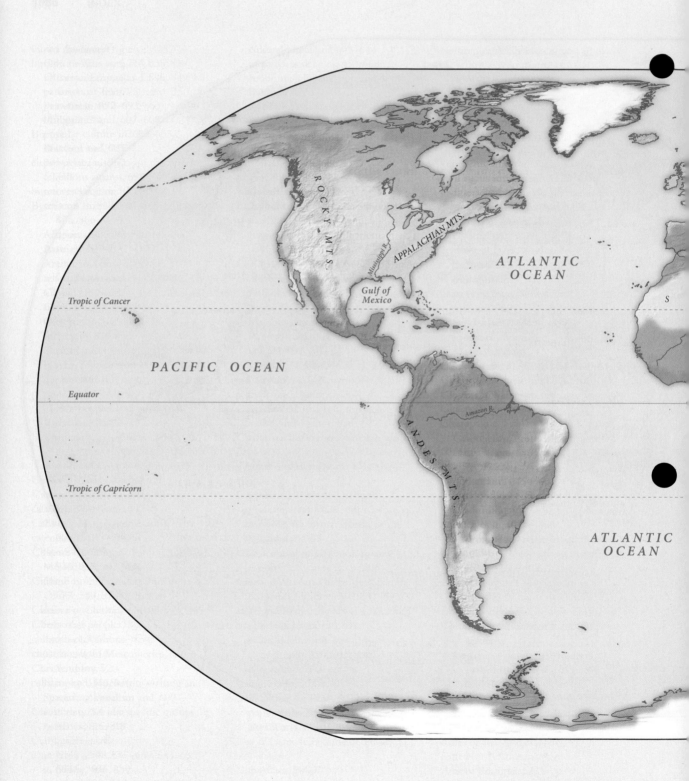

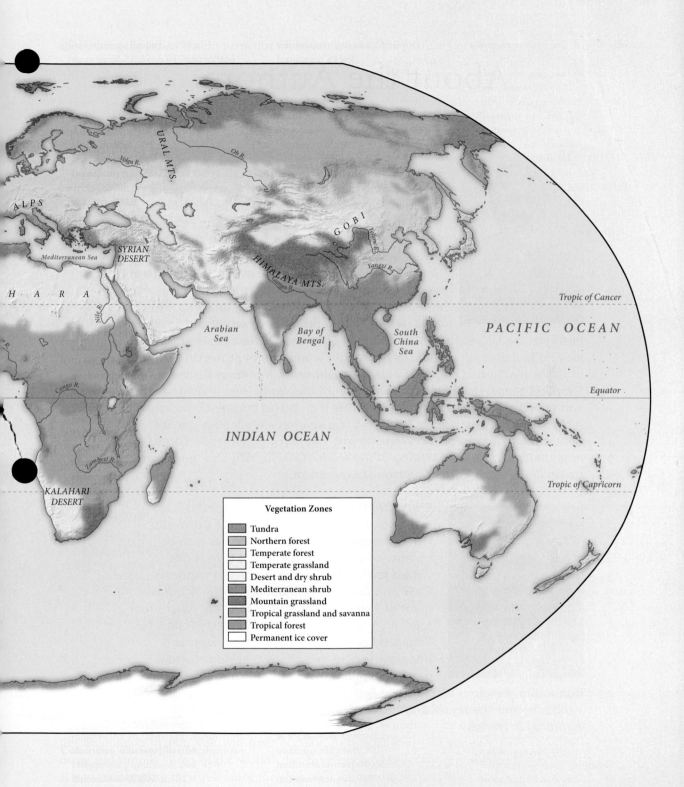

URAL MTS.

Volga R.

Ob R.

ALPS

Mediterranean Sea

SYRIAN DESERT

GOBI

HIMALAYA MTS.

Yellow R.

Yangzi R.

Ganges R.

H A R A

Nile R.

Arabian
Sea

Bay of
Bengal

South
China
Sea

Tropic of Cancer

PACIFIC OCEAN

Congo R.

Equator

INDIAN OCEAN

Zambezi R.

Tropic of Capricorn

KALAHARI
DESERT

Vegetation Zones

- Tundra
- Northern forest
- Temperate forest
- Temperate grassland
- Desert and dry shrub
- Mediterranean shrub
- Mountain grassland
- Tropical grassland and savanna
- Tropical forest
- Permanent ice cover

About the Authors

Robert W. Strayer (Ph.D., University of Wisconsin) brings wide experience in world history to the writing of *Ways of the World*. His teaching career began in Ethiopia, where he taught high school world history for two years as part of the Peace Corps. At the university level, he taught African, Soviet, and world history for many years at the State University of New York–College at Brockport, where he received the Chancellor's Awards for Excellence in Teaching and for Excellence in Scholarship. In 1998 he was visiting professor of world and Soviet history at the University of Canterbury in Christchurch, New Zealand. Since moving to California in 2002, he has taught world history at the University of California, Santa Cruz; California State University, Monterey Bay; and Cabrillo College. He is a longtime member of the World History Association and served on its Executive Committee. He has also participated in various AP World History gatherings, including two years as a reader. His publications include *Kenya: Focus on Nationalism, The Making of Mission Communities in East Africa, The Making of the Modern World, Why Did the Soviet Union Collapse?,* and *The Communist Experiment.*

Eric W. Nelson (D.Phil., Oxford University) is a professor of history at Missouri State University. He is an experienced teacher who has won a number of awards, including the Governor's Award for Teaching Excellence in 2011 and the CASE and Carnegie Foundation for the Advancement of Teaching Professor of the Year Award for Missouri in 2012. He is currently Faculty Fellow for Engaged Learning, developing new ways to integrate in-class and online teaching environments. His publications include *The Legacy of Iconoclasm: Religious War and the Relic Landscape of Tours, Blois and Vendôme,* and *The Jesuits and the Monarchy: Catholic Reform and Political Authority in France.*